DISCERNMENT

Learn to discern between false light and true light —
by becoming skilled in the word of righteousness!

Hebrews 5:13-14

CHARLES PRETLOW

Discernment
*Learn to discern between false light and true light —
by becoming skilled in the word of righteousness!*

First printing May 2013
Copyright © 2013 Charles Pretlow

All rights reserved. Printed in the United States of America. No part of this publication may be reproduced, stored in a retrieval system, or transmitted, in any form or by any means electronic, mechanical, physical, audio, or otherwise, without the prior written permission of the author.

Unless otherwise indicated, all Scripture quotations are from the Holy Bible, English Standard Version ® (ESV®), copyright © 2001 by Crossway, a publishing ministry of Good Publishers. Used by permission. All rights reserved.

ISBN 978-0-9801768-4-1

Published by -
Wilderness Voice Publishing, LLC
Canon City, Colorado USA
www.wildernesspublishing.com

About the Cover

Aurora borealis: The cover is a photo of the aurora borealis (Northern Lights) glowing above a church. The Northern Lights phenomenon acquired the name "aurora" for the Roman goddess of the dawn and "borealis" (*boreas* in Latin) for the god of the north wind.

In simple terms, the aurora borealis is electrical current flowing through the atmosphere generated under certain conditions, and giving off a beautiful and mesmerizing light that flows in the atmosphere as if it were a wind. Scientists estimate that the power of the aurora borealis, if harnessed, would surpass the electrical kilowatts generated in all of North America.

Angel of light ministries: Using the aurora borealis for the cover is a metaphor for the work of Satan, who appears as an angel of light with a demonic wind that counterfeits the wind of the Holy Spirit.

Many ministries, denominations, and movements throughout the body of Christ have built a foundation upon false doctrine originated by Satan who sends his workers as perceived servants of righteousness. These false teachers and false shepherds walk in *false light* and have learned to harness a *demonic counterfeit power*; this power is supernaturally real but it is not of God.

The false light and demonic power appears like the aurora borealis; beautiful, mesmerizing, misleading and, if harnessed, very powerful in performing signs and wonders, just as Christ warned: *"For false christs and false prophets will arise and perform great signs and wonders, so as to lead astray, if possible, even the elect"* (Matthew 24:24).

Those who lack discernment and those who buy into Satan's angel-of-light schemes tap into a demonic, counterfeit spiritual power; this power is like a borealis wind that causes the Northern Lights to mysteriously glow and flow.

Angel-of-light ministries have a power accompanied with a twisted light that appears to affect a person's life; however, the changes are superficial, never truly affecting the heart or character of the deceived.

The message of the cross: Jesus said to his disciples, *"It is the Spirit who gives life; the flesh is of no avail"* (John 6:63). A true disciple will learn to enter into a death like Christ's, by embracing the cross and crucifying the works of the flesh. Through the discipline of the Lord in life's challenges, a true disciple becomes Christ-like in character. They are not followers who work for Christ; rather, they are disciples who have Christ working through them and who have learned to distinguish between good and evil.

The cross is the avenue for God's power to flow through the true saint who has died to the using Christ's name in the flesh. It is for those who have learned to discern the difference between the power of the Holy Spirit and the spiritual power of the human spirit harnessed by Satan and his minions; for many are deceived by the spiritual powers of the flesh that is acclaimed to be the power of God. False teachings obscure the work of the cross, minimizing the need to suffer in the process of entering into a death like Christ's and be raised into the fullness of life in Christ.

The message of the cross must be worked into the life of every true servant of Christ so that the true power of God may flow unrestrained in purity and glory—the glory that belongs to our Lord and Savior Jesus Christ.

"For the word of the cross is folly to those who are perishing, but to us who are being saved it is the power of God."

1 Corinthians 1:18

Contents

Introduction	7
Acknowledgements, and Disclaimer	9
Chapter 1: The Saint's Darkest Hour is Coming	11
Chapter 2: Last Days EVIL—Defined and Discerned	31
Chapter 3: False Leaders and the Gates of Hell	77
Chapter 4: Doctrines of Demons and Implanted Weeds	131
Chapter 5: The Pseudo-Christian and Churchianity	153
Chapter 6: Discerning the Spiritual Powers of the Flesh	195
Chapter 7: True Leadership, Growth in Christ and Safe Fellowship	239
Chapter 8: Developing Our Powers of Discernment	269
Chapter 9: The Midnight Cry Final Awakening!	341
Index	363
About the Author and Ministry Information	367

Introduction

Christians should be realizing that things in the world and within the body of Christ are not going as advertised according to most pulpits. Unfortunately, those seeking truth are experiencing a hard time getting help in the form of sound teachings that brings deeper understanding of God's words and insight to the harder teachings of Christ.

This book introduces the sincere Christian to the solid food of the Word, challenging each reader to examine teachings often held dear but not supported by sound doctrine found in Scripture. Give yourself opportunity to learn what Christ and the Apostles taught—what they forewarned concerning this very hour.

The sincere believer in Christ must become skilled in properly understanding the written Word of God, that each may walk in true righteousness while maintaining a deep communion with the Holy Spirit. Abiding in Christ is obtainable by embracing and suffering the difficult discipline and training in everyday experiences of life guided by the Lord.

One cannot magically download the gift of discernment—only diligent study of the Word of God with his training will allow our powers of discernment to increase. In these dark times that are now upon us, as the end of this age unfolds, there is no other way to navigate safely and stand at his appearance.

Christ clearly warned about the time that is upon us now, when many would come in his name and lead astray many. The writers of the New Testament, especially the Apostles Peter and Paul, describe in detail how insidious, pervasive and persuasive the end-of-this-age deception for Christians will be.

Many want the ability to distinguish between spirits, seeking this gift of the Holy Spirit; however, few Christians learn how to allow their powers of discernment to grow. True discernment can only increase when we become skilled in properly handling the Word of Righteousness, which requires embracing the harder, more difficult teachings of Christ and the Apostles.

The deeper things of God have become hard to explain to Christians who receive the elementary teachings of Christ repeatedly, missing the meat of the Word—it is the deeper and more difficult Scriptures when embraced that facilitate growing up into salvation. Only by learning and applying these difficult teachings will the saint gain an edge in the war against the end-of-the-age powers of darkness.

Satanic principalities have succeeded in implanting within the church imposters, impersonators, and deceitful workers who operate as gates of hell and oppose the true body of Christ, deceive naïve Christians and attack the true saint.

As the end of this age closes, darkness and evil will be almost impossible to detect as Satan carries out his last-days deception. The devil appears as an angel of light, using false teachers and false prophets who espouse destructive heresies.

This resource will introduce the sincere disciple of Christ to the meat of the Word, expounding biblical principles often ignored or overlooked.

This introductory work is meant to challenge and encourage the sincere disciple to diligently study and take courage to enter Christ's school of ministry. May every sincere believer learn to navigate in these dark times—for this present darkness will only get darker and more dangerous.

Most Scripture passages are not merely cited, but written out to help explain the biblical principles without causing you to lose your place in the book when looking up a passage in your Bible. Unless indicated, Scriptures are presented in the English Standard Version, a fairly recent and credible word-for-word English translation. Take time to read the passages and ask the Holy Spirit for insight. Though you may be familiar with a cited passage, deeper insights often come when reading a familiar verse in conjunction with an exhortation or insight that we have garnered in these many years of ministry and study. Quoted passages may have portions <u>underlined</u> to aid in stressing the scriptural principle or meaning.

Dear reader, if you are serious about becoming a mature servant of Christ, then you will certainly benefit from using this book as a resource to carefully study, apply, and share with others as a ministry tool. In addition, my associate in ministry, Carly Poe has published a study guide and workbook to help in personal study, workshops and group study, *Discernment Study Guide, Workbook and Discernment Journal* ISBN 978-0-9801768-2-7.

These publications are an excellent start in becoming skilled in applying the Word of Righteousness and having the Holy Spirit train you in distinguishing good from evil and increasing your powers of discernment.

> To that end, may God strengthen you with the ever-increasing knowledge of our Lord Jesus Christ that you may become mature in him, no longer tossed to and fro by every wind of doctrine by the cunning of deceitful men.

Charles Pretlow
May 2013

Acknowledgments and Disclaimer

This work is dedicated to Christ and his commission given to each of his bondservants; that is to make disciples who embrace all that Christ taught and commands. This book also represents the Lords work and grace upon earthen vessels—me and other team members—and is aimed at glorifying the true Christ, so that he may become preeminent in you, the reader, and your life.

Acknowledgment of others who helped directly in the writing are Rachel, for her editorial and proofreading expertise, and to Carly who volunteered long hours for initial proofing and for content review in lesson development for her study guide, workbook and journal that complements this publication. Not least, my family, fellowship brethren, friends, and counselees through the many years—whose battles, sufferings, and victories have proved invaluable as references and examples. In addition, we acknowledge the saints before us, who helped in our discipleship growth and training, as they testified to their transformed lives as they sought the high call of God in Christ Jesus.

Disclaimer: We share this work in hope that the information, exhortation, testimony and commentary herein will benefit the reader, to help each draw closer to the true Christ, learning to walk in his fullness and in perfect obedience.

There is no guarantee for success by simply reading or applying the principles we share. As stated by the Apostle Paul, it is up to each and every Christian to: *"work out your own salvation with fear and trembling, for it is God who works in you, both to will and to work for his good pleasure"* (Philippians 2:12-13). It is not our responsibility to do this work for you, to make you understand the Gospel of Christ or try to convince you to embrace what we have learned and have applied for ourselves and now share.

None of us can blame our pastor, favorite teacher or author, minister, or upbringing for our not growing up into salvation in Christ. For once we hear the truth of the Gospel and receive the witness of the Holy Spirit to that truth it is up to each of us to exercise our faith in obedience to allow God to conform us to the image of his son.

Hungering after the true Christ, embracing his discipline, learning obedience and obtaining the grace of God will allow Christ to guide and empower you and cause you to safely arrive into eternity.

"Now to him who is able to keep you from stumbling and to present you blameless before the presence of his glory with great joy, to the only God, our Savior, through Jesus Christ our Lord, be glory, majesty, dominion, and authority, before all time and now and forever. Amen" (Jude 1:24-25).

Chapter One

The Saint's Darkest Hour is Coming

End-of-this-Age Darkness

Few Christians know exactly how the end of this age will unfold; all manner of interpretations, variations and some out right myths claim to be the "right" scenario of the next coming of Christ.

Most Christians believe they will escape any trouble since they believe the rapture will occur before the Great Tribulation begins. The belief that Christians are exempt from suffering and are not required to endure the Great Tribulation is lulling millions to take their ease. Thus, many avoid becoming mature in Christ and preparing for the coming terribly dark and evil days. Jesus clearly said that his appearance would happen at the end of that trouble-filled time:

"*<u>Immediately after the tribulation of those days</u> the sun will be darkened, and the moon will not give its light, and the stars will fall from heaven, and the powers of the heavens will be shaken. Then will appear in heaven the sign of the Son of Man, and then all the tribes of the earth will mourn, and they will see the Son of Man coming on the clouds of heaven with power and great glory. And he will <u>send out his angels with a loud trumpet call, and they will gather his elect</u> from the four winds, from one end of heaven to the other*" (Matthew 24:29-31: see also Mark 13:24-27).

No one knows the hour or the day that Christ will appear; however, Jesus expects us to be ready: "*You also must be ready, for the Son of Man is coming at an hour you do not expect*" (Luke 12:40).

Through the years false leaders who predicted the exact day that Christ would appear have duped many; these false predictions and the many false doctrines about how the end of this age will unfold have seduced many into a deep sleep with few realizing that his coming is very near.

The doctrine of pre-tribulation rapture (where Christ catches Christians up into the air and rescues all before the Great Tribulation begins) is just one example of the many false teachings that cause millions to stay immature, weak, and carnal, in love with this world, playing church, and living in false peace and false joy. Peter referred to these last-days false teachings as *destructive* and warned they will lead many away from following the true Christ. Millions of deceived Christians believe they walk in true light, but in reality, they walk in gross darkness.

As trouble increases and the days become even more evil and dark, those walking in false light are at great risk of stumbling and falling away. Jesus warned, "*If then the light in you is darkness, how great is the darkness!*" (Matthew 6:23).

This is fact—you can count on this to happen because Jesus said it! *"For many will come in my name, saying, 'I am the Christ,' and they will lead many astray... Then there will be great tribulation, such as has not been from the beginning of the world until now, no, and never will be. And if those days had not been shortened, no human being would be saved; but for the sake of the elect those days will be shortened. Then if any one says to you, 'Lo, here is the Christ!' or 'There he is!' do not believe it. <u>For false Christs and false prophets will arise and show great signs and wonders, so as to lead astray, if possible, even the elect</u>"* (Matthew 24:5, 21-24).

The indicators of the coming trouble that God allows Satan to inflict upon the world (including Christians) appear in the news daily, yet few take heed.

One major sign that Jesus foretold is how the world would become immoral and degenerate, reaching the same level of wickedness that caused God to bring forth the flood during the days of Noah and then later to cause fire and brimstone to fall upon on the cities of Sodom and Gomorrah. The same kind of immoral perversion is now widespread and ever growing all through America and around the world.

This sign and many other notable signs that Jesus described are now abounding, growing in frequency with ever-increasing intensity. Yet most Christians are spell bound and taking their ease.

The Lure and Deceit of the World and False Christianity

Jesus warned specifically about the cares of this life and false leaders coming in his name trapping and leading astray followers of Christ. The affection for worldly things and concerns of this life have enticed millions of good hearted Christians into believing that the world will sooner or later become a place of safety and peace.

False doctrine proclaiming that God's people are destined to prosper and live in peaceful coexistence with the world has seized the mind and heart of otherwise reasonable believers. Trying to present the truth to most Christians about the coming persecution and trouble that will crest into the Great Tribulation—all before the rapture occurs—often becomes combative.

Denial of the truth has become so intense that a belligerent hardness of heart resists the Holy Spirit's confirming nudges. This stubborn denial has indeed become a snare or trap, just as Jesus warned:

"But watch yourselves lest your hearts be weighed down with dissipation and drunkenness and cares of this life, and that day come upon you suddenly like a trap. For it will come upon all who dwell on the face of the whole earth. But stay awake at all times, praying that you may have strength to escape all these things that are going to take place, and to stand before the Son of Man" (Luke 21:34-36).

Discerning the hour, avoiding the lure of the world and steering clear of false Christianity are the rudimentary principles found in Scripture that allows the Holy Spirit to train us in discernment. Few are truly skilled at distinguishing good from evil, false light from sound doctrine or at recognizing the schemes of the devil through deceitful workers.

The Last-Days Evils Are upon Us
A Gradual Flood of Evils has Desensitized Millions of Christians

America is adrift on a boiling sea of immorality, corruption, cultural decay, political upheaval, and social factions of discontent—and it is even in the process of committing national security suicide by extreme debt, drastic reduction in its armed forces and out-of-control immigration! Every institution in America has an evil or immoral taint upon it.

The populace of America is witnessing discontent and immorality erupting in a continuous stream of troubles and evils in the news—daily. People are begging for something positive, uplifting, and hopeful. Yet the level of wickedness surpasses America's desire for good.

Americans spend millions on prescription drugs to numb fears, anxieties, and other stress-related symptoms. (Annually, over $800 million dollars is spent on "anti-anxiety pills". The U.S. accounts for 5% of the world's population and consumes 33% of these types of pills. *Neurogen Pharmaceutical Business Review*, July 2006)

America is weighed down with affliction upon affliction, perplexities, and a maze of calamities, (the roaring of the waves of the sea), and America is constantly on the verge of economic meltdown—yet for most the *party-hardy* and *just-have-fun* lifestyle plays on.

Forty-five years ago, who could have imagined the level of wickedness, national and international perplexities, robberies, murders, sexual immorality, perversion, extreme differences in political ideology, lawless idolatry, drunkenness, orgies, and sinful passions that are now common-place?

Through the last four social generations, Americans as a people (including most Christians) gradually absorbed these drastic changes and most continue to live as if nothing is amiss. *"As were the days of Noah, so will be the coming of the Son of Man. For as in those days before the flood they were eating and drinking, marrying and giving in marriage, until the day when Noah entered the ark, and they were <u>unaware until the flood came and swept them all away, so will be the coming of the Son of Man</u>"* (Matthew 24:37-39). Yes, America and millions of Christians are unaware of what is coming upon this country and the world.

The moral majority, first led by the Reverend Jerry Falwell, Pat Robertson, and then Focus on the Family's James Dobson, made great strides in influencing public sentiment against the many immoral evils overtaking this country; but now the cry for national repentance is just a faint whisper.

The homosexual element in society has emerged as a powerful voice pressuring politics and much of liberal Christianity to accept whatever darkness people choose to surround themselves with, and this pressure is mounting.

The fight by the righteous had its power drained by the many church scandals that the moral majority leaders became embroiled in, causing much of the Christian populace of America to recoil from the moral conservative agenda. Many witnessing the continuous string of leadership scandals in the news now look upon Christians as hucksters and hypocrites. Peter prophesied about these false leaders: *"And many will follow their licentiousness, and <u>because of them the way of truth will be reviled</u>. And in their greed they will exploit you with false words"* (2 Peter 2:2-3 RSV).

A definite blow came to the moral conservatives when Ted Haggard, then president of the National Association of Evangelicals resigned after admitting he had solicited a male prostitute for homosexual sex and methamphetamines. The national elections of 2006 and 2008 and the shocking loss of the presidential race of 2012 reflect a continuous revulsion by voters toward the morality champions—a revulsion that directly reflects upon evangelical, Pentecostal, and charismatic hypocrisy. Thus, those opposed to the moral conservatives have gained control of the senate and continue to keep in place a president who has anti-American ideology and is determined to destroy the constitutional foundations of this country.

What remains now is a whimpering moral *minority*, with evangelical Christians across America having less and less influence politically. James Dobson, during his retirement speech on April 12, 2009, stated, "We are awash in evil and the battle is still to be waged. We are right now in the most discouraging period of that long conflict. Humanly speaking, we can say we have lost all those battles."

Few realize that not only are the battles lost, but also the *entire war* is lost in the attempt to save America. The righteous are now powerless politically in stopping the ever-growing flood of evil. America has morally gone past the point of no return and final judgment is looming.

America—Past the Point of No Return

I am convinced that the prayers of the righteous will not turn the tide of immorality and spare this nation from judgment.

Jesus described how at the end of this age perverted elements in society would adversely influence much of the culture to act out wickedness as it was in the days of Noah and Lot. The mounting wickedness is *not* another cycle where a prayer-ignited revival will sweep this nation back to righteousness. Proof of this position is the failure to win back the White House to a more conservative leader.

In spite of clear deception, failed promises and outright lies, the populace and many blocks of voting Christians voted to keep a clearly deceitful person in power. This is the beginning of what the Apostle Paul foresaw concerning the anti-Christ: *"The coming of the lawless one is by the activity of Satan with all power and false signs and wonders, and with all wicked deception for those who are perishing, because they refused to love the truth and so be saved. Therefore God sends them a strong delusion, so that they may believe what is false, in order that all may be condemned who did not believe the truth but had pleasure in unrighteousness"* (2 Thessalonians 2:9-12).

Jesus clearly warned that there would be no nation exempt from the last-day's judgments, and that God's people would be forced to come away from trying to fight to maintain any sort of national-religious conclave of peace, security, and religious freedom.

Rather, Christ stressed that we are to be living in such closeness to him that these days will be exhilarating in spite of the gloom and doom—living unattached to this world, trusting in his protection and perfect guidance.

Abraham attempted to intercede for those of Sodom and Gomorrah, that the inhabitants would be spared—only to hear from God that there were not enough righteous to hold back the impending judgment. However, God saved Lot and his family and this is still the plan of God in these last days; to save the righteous from judgment and wrath about to pour out upon the world.

Sodomite Intimidation and Vexation

It is now like the days of Lot in Sodom when lawlessness and homosexual wickedness took control of the whole city. When a mob of homosexuals attempted to assault Lot's angelic visitors, Lot tried to reason with them and stop their attack. They turned against Lot and threatened him with harm.

"'I beg you, my brothers, do not act so wickedly. Behold, I have two daughters who have not known any man. Let me bring them out to you, and do to them as you please. Only do nothing to these men, for they have come under the shelter of my roof.' But they said, 'Stand back!' And they said, 'This fellow came to sojourn, and he has become the judge! Now we will deal worse with you than with them.' Then they pressed hard against the man Lot, and drew near to break the door down. But the men reached out their hands and brought Lot into the house with them and shut the door. And they struck with blindness the men who were at the entrance of the house, both small and great, so that they wore themselves out groping for the door" (Genesis 19:7-11).

Lot's attempt to reason with obsessed homosexuals, even sinfully offering his daughters as an alternative for their madness, enraged the lawless crowd all the more.

Now America is leading the way to a global lawlessness concerning this same kind of wickedness. Jesus and the Apostles warned about all of this as signs of the end, but few discern the hour!

The fight for morality and purity must begin in the saint's own life; we must wake up and come away from a world that is about to receive the wrath of God. Give up trying to take back America; the wicked are gaining complete control and any attempt to restore morality, freedom, and civility will just bring abuse.

"And if he rescued righteous Lot, greatly distressed by the sensual conduct of the wicked (for as that righteous man lived among them day after day, he was tormenting his righteous soul over their lawless deeds that he saw and heard); then the Lord knows how to rescue the godly from trials, and to keep the unrighteous under punishment until the day of judgment, and especially those who indulge in the lust of defiling passion and despise authority" (2 Peter 2:7-10).

The angels finally convinced Lot to leave, but then when it was time to go, Lot and his family hesitated as if spellbound.

"As morning dawned, the angels urged Lot, saying, 'Up! Take your wife and your two daughters who are here, lest you be swept away in the punishment of the city.' But he lingered. So the men seized him and his wife and his two daughters by the hand, the Lord being merciful to him, and they brought him out and

set him outside the city. And as they brought them out, one said, 'Escape for your life. Do not look back or stop anywhere in the valley. Escape to the hills, lest you be swept away.'" (Genesis 19:15-17).

Lot and his family were vexed and tormented in their souls because of the lawlessness and the sensuality of the people. Then when it came time to leave, Lot lingered. He and his whole family had to be dragged out of Sodom.

The same vexation that Lot experienced in Sodom is now everywhere, throughout America's sensuous and lawless culture. Every day Christians and their families are exposed to defiling scenes.

Unfortunately, millions of Christians linger over the filth and perversion pouring through television commercials, in the super market line, the news, music, movies, and the sensuous and deviling images from the people they see every day in shopping malls, schools, and even while driving—there is no place to hide from the continuous bombardment of defiling sensuality.

What is even more disheartening is the thousands upon thousands of Christians hooked on pornography—through the Internet, their cable TV, and in motel rooms while traveling.

Gradually, the masses of God's people have absorbed defiling images, slowly desensitized as they linger over the milder forms of perversion. The spell binding power of this last-days sensuous culture has drugged most of God's people to accept what was once an abomination.

In this condition, a great portion of otherwise godly people would have a very hard time leaving if the rapture occurred now. Many are at risk of being left behind as they linger over the sensuous love of this world and would likely look back or even hide from Christ's appearance in shame because of the defilements within them.

This is a major reason why the rapture will occur at the end of the Great Tribulation, when a multitude that no one can count will become cleansed and prepared for Christ's appearance: *"These are the ones coming out of the great tribulation. They have washed their robes and made them white in the blood of the Lamb"* (Revelation 7:14).

The future of America is in God's hands (or rather, taken out of God's protection due to rebellion), and according to the end-of-this-age truth taught by Christ, from here on out it will not be pretty. The wicked will gain power and eventually have complete control until the wrath of God falls, then when Christ returns to set up his millennial one-thousand-year reign the righteous get America *and* the whole world back.

Do not be as Lot, lingering, put in a trance by this culture's spellbinding sensuality; do not be like Lot's wife clinging to the American dream and embracing an Americanized Gospel.

Rather, give up the world and do not look back. Learn to hear and obey Christ's voice—that he may keep you safe during the Great Tribulation and then rescue you from the coming wrath of God.

Stop fighting with the wicked over control of America. It is time to look to the coming Kingdom of God where the righteousness of Christ and those in Christ will soon reign.

However, you may wonder, will there be anything good come from this nation again? Look for the answer to this question as you read chapter nine, "The Midnight Cry Final Awakening!"

From Swaggart to Haggard — in Between and Since

There are many milestone departures from our founding ancestors' biblically moral constructs in our modern era, but the most damning has been the failure of the Christian church to righteously influence society. The moral majority's ability to influence the conscience of the American culture gradually fell to disgrace; during the time from Jimmy Swaggart's fall to the Ted Haggard exposé in 2006 (including all the Christian scandals and extravagant madness in the public's eye in between and since). This has made the populace in America sickened of the moral majority and any so-called return to righteousness.

Peter warned that when Christians were no longer a salt-and-light influence they would be hated by the world. *"There will be false teachers among you, who will secretly bring in destructive heresies, even denying the Master who bought them, bringing upon themselves swift destruction. And many will follow their sensuality, and <u>because of them the way of truth will be blasphemed</u>. And in their greed they will exploit you with false words. Their condemnation from long ago is not idle, and their destruction is not asleep"* (2 Peter 2:1-3).

The destructive heresies (false teachings) that we discuss in the ensuing chapters are the main reason why so many sincere leaders succumb to the lust of the flesh, the lust of the eyes and the pride of life. I believe Jimmy Swaggart and Ted Haggard would not have become poster boys for the moral decline within the last-days church if they had not first been victims of the many popular yet destructive heresies.

The way of truth is now cursed and hated by the populace of America and the wicked people now exercising national influence have been given over to a debased mind. God has given up the many to the lust of their hearts and to impurity.

"Since they did not see fit to acknowledge God, God gave them up to a debased mind to do what ought not to be done. They were filled with all manner of unrighteousness, evil, covetousness, malice. They are full of envy, murder, strife, deceit, maliciousness. They are gossips, slanderers, haters of God, insolent, haughty, boastful, inventors of evil, disobedient to parents, foolish, faithless, heartless, ruthless. Though they know God's decree that those who practice such things deserve to die, they not only do them but give approval to those who practice them" (Romans 1:28-32).

You will see the far left, the immoral, and the perverse gain more control, change the laws of the land and act out rage towards anyone who holds them to account.

Given Over to a Debased Mind and an Evil Heart
Wickedness no longer restrained by righteousness and the Gospel message

Darkness and evil have finally engulfed society, yet so very few of God's people realize that America has passed the point of no return. The floodgates of hell have injected lawlessness, deceit, and perversion at every level of society and tainted every sacred institution. The very pillars of our culture have become rotten.

The influence of the righteous and the message of repentance and judgment along with salvation have become laughable to the wicked. Most influential thinkers and policy implementers in politics, finance, education, psychology, philosophy, and the judicial system venomously maintain a bias against God, righteousness, and justice. The foundations of American culture and society are being transformed to a new world order described in Scripture as corrupt, wicked, and opposed to Christ.

Grade school children are instructed to accept perverted sexual lifestyles and taught the "how too" in sexual intercourse. In June 2012, two weeks before the end of the school year, the parents of an Onalaska Washington fifth-grade class became livid when their children described what oral and anal sex was. The explanation came from their grade school principal who conducted the class as part of Washington State's required sex education curriculum. James Gilliland, a father of one of the fifth graders explained that this kind of descriptive sex education is far too explicit and made this statement: "Basically it's the same as raping the kid's mind and taking their innocence." ("Raping Their Innocence: Parents Outraged," June 19, 2012, theblaze.com).

This is just a small part of the homosexual agenda that has become blatant, belligerent, and intimidating. This is an example of the growing political power and incessant determination to reach right into the family and proselytize children into changing their sexuality.

The homosexual lobby is aggressively pressing for legal reforms that forbid parents and therapists to correct any propensity towards perversion within their child. In 2012, California Governor Jerry Brown signed a bill into law that requires schools throughout the state to teach students about the accomplishments of homosexuals throughout history.

The moral majority and other movements and organizations such as Focus on the Family have sputtered to a halt in stopping the flood of filth and perversion. God's people are powerless just as Lot and his angelic visitors were unable to stop the incensed homosexual deviants determined to assault these visitors sent to rescue Lot and his family.

The Apostle Paul warns, *"For although they knew God, they did not honor him as God or give thanks to him, but they <u>became futile in their thinking</u>, and their foolish hearts were darkened. Claiming to be wise, they became fools, and exchanged the glory of the immortal God for images resembling mortal man and birds and animals and reptiles. <u>Therefore God gave them up in the lusts of their hearts to impurity, to the dishonoring of their bodies among themselves, because they exchanged the truth about God for a lie and worshiped and served the creature rather than the Creator</u>, who is blessed forever! Amen"* (Romans 1:21-24).

God's people need to understand that many now are beyond correction, beyond help, beyond repentance—God has given them over to a base mind because they refused to love the truth and had pleasure in unrighteousness. We must learn to discern those whom God has abandoned and learn to work with those whom God desires to bring into the fold.

An Enraged Violence-Filled Culture
No safe place other than in the center of God's perfect will, abiding in the true Christ!

Many Americans have become prone to violence with hearts impacted by dormant rage—many are one disturbance away from getting even with the world. There are many reasons for all this pent-up anger and rage, which when ignited makes logic vanish.

Common-sense reasoning and civility is quickly disappearing in large sections of the populace. Many easily become incensed with others over the slightest differences. This is especially true of the poor who can develop bitter hatred towards people who have more than they do. With anarchist overtones, the deep discontent of the poor towards the rich hit the nation's attention during the recent Occupy Wall Street protests.

The United States, once a melting pot of peace-loving immigrants looking for opportunity and freedom, is transforming into a smelting pot of angry, disgruntled, disenchanted, and belligerent working-class people expecting a life-style of the rich and famous. The American dream is dissipating before our eyes and there is brewing a gigantic division throughout the country.

High unemployment and poor working conditions for the bottom end of the working class along with poverty, ignorance, and lack of moral stability is creating a tinderbox for anarchy, lawlessness, and disorder—fueled by a constant stream of violence in the news that is flooding television and the cinema.

Masses of parents leave children to their own devices influenced by a violence-filled culture through Hollywood's incessant theme of blood, gore, and mayhem coupled with violent video games, which drill rapid images deep into the psyche of millions of frustrated, dysfunctional families and their children.

What we have witnessed repeatedly in violent and perverse entertainment is now frequent headline news. Massacres, murders, road rage, lawless chaos, and mayhem are almost every day tragic events for America—and Hollywood and other violent entertainment venues continue to outdo the previous in explicit horror and graphic realism.

One of the most insidious portrayals of evil personified in cinema was the second-to-the last Batman movie, *The Dark Knight*, released in 2008, starring Christian Bale as Batman and Heath Ledger as the Joker.

The Joker character in this release of Batman demonstrated one of the best caricatures of Satan, capturing many of the devil's attributes of evil, ruthlessness, revenge, and senseless mayhem and anarchy. Worse, the movie's plot subtly shrouded the Joker's character in a sympathetic light towards his mania.

Many believe that Ledger's premature death related directly to his role as the Joker. The following is an excerpt from a Daily News online article concerning comments by Jack Nicholson about Heath Ledger's role in playing the Joker and his death.

Jack Nicholson, who played the Joker in 1989—and who was furious he wasn't consulted about the creepy role—offered a cryptic comment when told Ledger was dead.

> "Well," Nicholson told reporters in London early Wednesday, "I warned him."
> Though the remark was ambiguous, there's no question the role in the movie earmarked as this summer's blockbuster took a frightening toll.
> Ledger recently told reporters he "slept an average of two hours a night" while playing "a psychopathic, mass-murdering, schizophrenic clown with zero

empathy... I couldn't stop thinking. My body was exhausted, and my mind was still going."

Prescription drugs didn't help, he said.

(Joe Neumaier, "Jack Nicholson warned Heath Ledger on 'Joker' role" *New York Daily News*, January 24, 2008)

The lone shooter of the Century movie theatre in Aurora, Colorado, James Eagan Holmes, on July 20, 2012, dressed in tactical clothing, set off tear gas grenades, and shot into the audience with multiple firearms, killing 12 people and injuring 58 others. This massacre, specifically timed with the midnight screening of the latest Batman movie, entitled *The Dark Knight Rises* was part of Holmes' psychotic plan.

All the more ghastly is how the evidence found in Holmes' apartment and his method of operation followed the Joker's character portrayed by Ledger in the 2008 Batman movie.

This is a direct correlation between a culture of violence imposing terror upon the innocent through deranged individuals, brainwashed and infatuated with violence.

We live in a godless generation with no moral compass. Hate-centered and love-starved people are everywhere, suffering from numbed consciences. Our culture is producing thousands of narcissists who are divided and demonized, ready to explode in murderous rage if deprived of their selfish agenda. The demons are having a blast, as they trigger outbursts of rage within their hosts against random victims or upon those who displease these crazed and demonized human time bombs.

Indeed, this violent, godless culture with the devil's aid has created human time bombs and the situation is getting as bad as it was with IEDs and insurgent attacks in Iraq or Afghanistan. The safest place is to learn to dwell in the shadow of the wings of the Almighty, resting in the Lord, seeking and finding God's perfect will, and abiding in Christ.

Jesus warned that the coming trouble will only get worse and there will be no place to hide other than to follow his advice: *"For it will come upon all who dwell on the face of the whole earth. But stay awake at all times, praying that you may have strength to escape all these things that are going to take place, and to stand before the Son of Man"* (Luke 21:35-36).

Lawlessness and Cold Love
The World and America are on the Threshold of Persecution Madness!

Jesus warned that near the end of the birth pangs of the coming Kingdom lawlessness and persecution of Christians would escalate worldwide. Wickedness and lawlessness would become so hideous that the love of many would grow cold. (The Greek word for love in the following referenced passage is *agape*, primarily meaning God's kind of love towards each other and love towards God.)

"Then they will deliver you up to tribulation and put you to death, and you will be hated by all nations for my name's sake. And then many will fall away and betray one another and hate one another. And many

false prophets will arise and lead many astray. And because lawlessness will be increased, <u>the love of many will grow cold</u>. But the one who endures to the end will be saved" (Matthew 24:9-13).

Hatred toward Christians is increasing, and in the near future, certain events will cause intense persecution to come upon Christians who desire to follow Christ and obey his Gospel.

We must choose to embrace all that Christ taught; the problem is few Christians pay close enough attention to those more difficult words of Christ or the harder writings of the Apostles. Most ignore them or misunderstand them, leaving themselves unprepared for the coming trials and unable to walk in discernment.

The Apostle Paul wrote the following about the end times that we are now in: *"<u>But understand this, that in the last days</u> there will come times of stress. For men will be lovers of self, lovers of money, proud, arrogant, abusive, disobedient to their parents, ungrateful, unholy, inhuman, implacable, slanderers, profligates, fierce, haters of good, treacherous, reckless, swollen with conceit, lovers of pleasure rather than lovers of God, holding the form of religion but denying the power of it. <u>Avoid such people</u>."* (2 Timothy 3:1-5 RSV).

If we do not understand how vile most people will become, we will not learn how to stay clear of such people. During the coming days leading up to Christ's appearance, many who claim to be believers in Christ, who appear now to be religious, will fall away and not obey the Gospel of Jesus Christ. Paul describes some as imposters, some as deceivers, and others as wolves disguised as servants; and Peter describes these as accursed children and waterless springs. Others who are not ready run the risk of becoming apostate, destroying their faith by rejecting conscience—their love for God and godly love for others will grow cold.

The false will be great in number and they will learn to hate the true Christian. If we do not learn to avoid such people now, but continue to have improper relationships or continue to fellowship with such people, we will be giving them opportunity to betray us as they live in hate and sell out true believers during the coming persecution. Many already are insidious demonic avenues undermining harmony, purity, and maturity throughout the body of Christ.

If you discover your fellowship is lukewarm and denying the power of Christ to truly transform and make one a true disciple of Christ, flee that fellowship or congregation! It is much safer and healthier to fellowship with a few who are serious than to have your faith languish in a seemingly prosperous church that is wayward.

The Mystery of Lawlessness and the Power of Chaos

We see the Apostle Paul's prediction about lawlessness and the anti-Christ rising to leadership as the end of this age closes, in this passage: *"Let no one deceive you in any way. For that day will not come, unless the rebellion comes first, and the man of lawlessness is revealed... For the mystery of lawlessness is already at work... The coming of the lawless one is by the activity of Satan with all power and false signs and wonders, and with all wicked deception for those who are perishing, because they refused to love the truth and so be saved. Therefore God sends them a strong delusion, so that they may believe what is false, in order that all may be condemned who did not believe the truth but had pleasure in unrighteousness"* (2 Thessalonians 2:3-12).

Many pundits, theologians, political analysts, conservatives, and Christians wonder how President Obama achieved reelection. If we understand the above passage and what it conveys concerning the mystery lawlessness and its power to deceive, it is not hard to understand Obama's successful campaign and administration strategy.

The mystery of lawlessness is imprinted all over Obama's campaign including the opinions of his surrogates and supporters. Movements like Occupy Wall Street incites class warfare between the poor and the rich, enlisting the dark side of human nature by inciting jealousy, bitterness, greed, hatred, revenge, and racism—and promising security, freedom, and handouts to freeloaders and illegal immigrants in the form of government entitlements. America is becoming awash with the embittered and lazy as the far left continues to come up with new ways to buy their vote.

Couple these lies and promises at the expense of taxpayers and the demonization of righteousness with the character assassination of his opponents and the help of the media—it is no longer a mystery.

Whether or not Obama is the anti-Christ—time will tell—we should be able to see how the mystery of lawlessness is reaching its final thrust to bring in the lawless one.

The majority of the populace in America and much of the world now has pleasure in unrighteousness and refuses to love truth. Can you discern the delusional spell on people everywhere?

In addition to the church of America, Christianity as a whole is powerless, confused, divided, and in love with this age—a lukewarm people that is about to be spewed from the mouth of Christ and trampled upon by the world (unless God intervenes).

God's people are busy trying to save America and the world in order to continue to be materially blessed, causing most to accumulate for themselves *"teachers to suit their own passions"* and turn away *"from listening to the truth and wander off into myths"* (see 2 Timothy 4:3-5). The body of Christ is confused, divided, lukewarm, and shallow, idolizing false leaders. No wonder America has lost its way and is rushing towards anarchy and chaos. Christianity has lost the ability to guide, effectively influence, and demonstrate by example a moral foundation to the populace of America.

Civility, stability, and reason are being swallowed up by anarchist ideology (everyone doing what is right in their own eyes) and in some cases it incites deliberate chaos. Sacred institutions, valued principles, and our constitutional foundations—the glue that keeps the fabric of society civil—is all, one by one, weakening. We are witnessing the systematic dismantling of the very foundation of a civilized and righteous culture in preparation for its replacement by a new world order and control of an expanded United Nations agenda.

This is the power of purpose-driven chaos and is a pre-tribulation work of Satan to undermine all godly foundations that he might empower a human god that the world will rally unto and worship. We must discern the hour if we expect any hope of enduring to the end to stand before Christ when he appears. We must learn to walk in day-to-day discernment, for the saint's darkest hour is coming upon us.

Lethargic and Lukewarm Followers
A product of the love of money, prosperity and false leadership

The Apostle John prophesied on behalf of Christ concerning the seven churches in Asia. Five of these churches were, metaphorically speaking, in hot water with Christ. Only two churches, Smyrna and Philadelphia, received a clean bill of health.

Those five faulty churches listed in Revelation had various maladies, summed up as follows:

- **The church at *Ephesus*** -had abandoned the love they had at first towards Christ and were so far away from Christ that their lamp stand would be removed unless they repented.

- **Christians in *Pergamum*** -fellowshipped with believers who embraced the teachings of Balaam, which encouraged idol worship and sexual immorality, and some of the Pergamum Christians held to the teachings of the Nicolaitans (a Christian sect of the time) who practiced the same kind of immorality. Jesus said through the Apostle John's writings that if they did not repent, *"I will come to you soon and war against them with the sword of my mouth"* (Revelation 2:16).

- **Many Christians in *Thyatira*** -tolerated a woman named Jezebel who practiced sexual immorality, and in turn taught and seduced Christians to do the same, as well as sacrificing to idols. Unless she repented, Christ pronounced that judgment through the Apostle John on the woman Jezebel would be severe sickness, her children would be slain, and those who committed adultery with her would be thrown into great tribulation.

- **Christians in *Sardis*** -also received a bad grade from Christ because most Christians there were spiritually dead but pretended to be alive. These Christians were worshipping Christ by rote, just going through the motions, yet actually believing they were alive in Christ. Jesus said of them, *"You have a reputation of being alive, but you are dead."* Jesus then warns, *"If you will not wake up, I will come like a thief, and you will not know what hour I will come against you"* (Revelation 3:1-3).

- **The church in *Laodicea*** -is the last church listed in Revelation, and in my opinion these believers received the most severe rebuke from Christ and were at risk of rejection by Christ. These Christians were prosperous and content in life, saying to themselves *"I have prospered, and I need nothing"* —they were lethargic (sluggish, dull, lackluster) and Jesus declared to them, *"So, because you are lukewarm , and neither hot nor cold, I will spit you out of my mouth."* (Revelation 3:16-17).

False teachings over the last century have infected churches and fellowships across America with all the same issues of the five churches rebuked in Revelation, especially lethargy. Some denominations have passed the point of no return, becoming apostate by embracing abominable practices and immoral behavior.

Christians more than ever in love with this world and are at risk of judgment as most leaders continue to preach *all is okay* even as the afflictions of the birth pangs increase.

An extreme lack of the life, energy, and inspiration that is normally associated with on-fire Christians is the norm, just as it was with the Christians in Laodicea. Christians in America and most other industrialized nations wallow in a lukewarm condition.

Prosperity teachings have plagued millions upon millions of lukewarm Christians, causing them to seek to make life on earth a blissful journey, free of anxiety and cares, especially when it comes to money. Teachers of prosperity twist Christ's teachings on being "anxious for nothing" to mean that God will bend over backwards to make the faithful Christian prosperous and in need of nothing—and cause them to become rich with money.

Thus, a lukewarm condition has become predominant; with teachings' depicting the faithful Christian having a lifestyle like that of America's rich and famous: the prosperous Christian who needs nothing!

However, Jesus said, *"No servant can serve two masters, for either he will hate the one and love the other, or he will be devoted to the one and despise the other. You cannot serve God and money"* (Luke 16:13).

According to Christ and Scripture, "abundant life in Christ" actually means receiving the *spiritually rich* life (*zōē* life) that is found in a right relationship with Father God, rather than the carnal, worldly life (*psuchē* life) that Christ instructs his disciples to hate and have crucified.

The false doctrine of prosperity undermines true worship and servant hood, causing many to seek God in order to receive riches on earth. Fellowships that embrace prosperity doctrines find it necessary to serve up entertaining worship and worldly activities to soothe pangs of the heart that these false doctrines conceal but do not eradicate.

These teachings veil the love of money covering up bitterness, jealousy, envy, greed, and many other emotional and mental maladies and mixed motives. Many struggling Christians fall for this error partly due to wounds to their spirit and hidden defilements from their pre-Christian sinful lifestyle.

The Apostle Paul wrote about this destructive issue: *"But if we have food and clothing, with these we will be content. But those who desire to be rich fall into temptation, into a snare, into many senseless and harmful desires that plunge people into ruin and destruction. For the love of money is a root of all kinds of evils. It is through this craving that some have wandered away from the faith and <u>pierced themselves with many pangs</u>"* (1 Timothy 6:8-10).

If you are embracing these false doctrines concerning prosperity, doctrines that veil a love for money, you will never walk in true discernment. This idol—or any idol of heart—will cause great difficulty for Christians, and subvert efforts to become discerning and effective in ministry.

In the coming days many believers will not give up these lies and will wander from the true faith in Christ, plunging themselves into ruin.

Lack of Knowledge and Understanding—Lack of Discipline

Christians learn to work tirelessly for Christ by serving the church, missions, the nursery, Sunday school—the list is endless. However, much of this activity in working for Christ (via the church) is driven by carnal energy managed by carnal and false leaders who produce church workers, instead of making disciples of Christ. Few learn to embrace the discipline of the Lord and crucify the motives of the flesh in order that they might allow Christ's Spirit to work through them.

They learn to work for Christ, but never reach an understanding through the discipline of the Lord that will enable the power of Christ to *do the work through them.*

The author of the book of Hebrews expounds on how we must enter into the *rest of God* and allow him to work through us, rather than doing the work for him in the energy of wrong motives and selfish intentions.

We are to learn how to allow the Word of God to become a dynamic knife that cuts to the root of the thoughts and intentions of our hearts (see Hebrews 4:11-13).

Many are motivated to serve God (in the church) for mixed reasons. Furthering the Gospel is a legitimate reason, but often other reasons such as insecurities, jealousy, or selfish ambition are intermingled in the heart. These not-so-noble reasons, veiled from the exuberant servant, provide tremendous energy. This condition prevails throughout the body of Christ and can diminish and even block the true power of Christ. Thus, the spiritual power and energy of the flesh becomes a substitute for Christ's power. This false spiritual power grows and becomes the drive for worship, ministry, and most of life's activities. Jesus warned, *"Apart from me you can do nothing."* Christ also taught, *"It is the Spirit who gives life; the flesh is of no avail"* (John 15:5; 6:63).

Full Grown Evil Weeds amongst the Wheat
Waterless springs, accursed children and spiritual vampires invading fellowship

Doctrines inspired by demons tend to captivate people who are looking for an easy road in life. Like selling products to "make life easy," evangelists and pastors sell a message of *entitlement theology* where how the believer approaches God's throne of grace is similar to making a list for Santa Clause to fill. Christians have become passive, weak and dependent on leadership that prances about advertising a special anointing that they can bestow upon the faithful follower—provided they donate and vicariously participate in the faith of the so-called superlative leader.

It is difficult for true ministers of the Gospel to preach the harder teachings of Christ and to encourage believers to pick up their cross daily. They compete with celebrity Christians paraded constantly on TBN or other Christian broadcasting venues, touting how to become financially blessed, or how to glow in the anointing. The prosperity gospel message incites greed, lust and bitter jealousy amongst many who seek God for a free ride in life—free of suffering and free from the hard work of self-disclosure. Concealing bitterness and unbelief is a major work of Satan upon God's people. God is not against having material wealth, but against idolatry of wealth where the love of money consumes the heart.

Self-pity and self-indulgence are the major character deficiencies within those who become full-grown weeds[1] and follow entitlement Christianity. It is important to understand that many wounded Christians have a weak faith yet desire to become Christ-like in character. Sometimes it is hard to distinguish between a weak-faith, wounded Christian and embittered, false Christians who have an agenda of "God and God's people owe me" (my definition of entitlement Christianity).

The Apostle Peter warns about this type of person coming into fellowship, *"For, speaking loud boasts of folly, they entice by sensual passions of the flesh those who are barely escaping from those who live in error. They promise them freedom, but they themselves are slaves of corruption For whatever overcomes a person, to that he is enslaved"* (2 Peter 2:18-19).

It is no longer safe in most fellowships, as false brethren full of darkness come in as Peter explained, *"They are blots and blemishes, reveling in their deceptions, while they feast with you. They have eyes full of adultery, insatiable for sin. They entice unsteady souls. They have hearts trained in greed. Accursed children! Forsaking the right way, they have gone astray. They have followed the way of Balaam, the son of Beor, who loved gain from wrongdoing, but was rebuked for his own transgression; a speechless donkey spoke with human voice and restrained the prophet's madness"* (2 Peter 2:13-16).

Ministry Case: *A job here, a job there*

While filling the position of counseling pastor for a Foursquare church back in the late eighties, and early nineties I would hold services for prayer and ministry on Thursday nights during our support group meetings. Dozens of people would come, primarily to receive a word of wisdom, knowledge, discernment or prophecy, but a few would apply the work of the cross during the week to bring death to their carnal issues. A pattern began to develop, similar to the pattern we commonly see within the body of Christ today. They came to receive encouraging manifestations of the Spirit, but continued in their self-indulgent life styles.

Many received prophecies that immediately came to pass, while other prophecies took longer. One distraught woman, abused by her former husband and tricked into giving up custody of her children, came for ministry. The Lord told me to tell her: "You'll get custody!" And this happened miraculously and quickly.

Most of these ministry meetings would last way into the night. Struggling Christians who participated in our support work also received counsel and teachings on the work of the cross in dying to carnal issues and how to experience the comfort and healing work of the Holy Spirit.

Then the Holy Spirit increasingly prompted more tough-love words and these people slowly drifted away. One Christian man who came frequently was trying to push himself into

---

[1] Jesus explained that at the end of this age the devil would secretly plant evil people amongst the righteous. This diabolical plan is well underway as many fellowships, families, government, and institutions suffer evil people disguised as good people. This issue will be explained extensively in chapter four, "Doctrines of Demons and Implanted Weeds."

ministry; however, he would never request counsel. In fact when sharing any difficulties, he refused to receive sound counsel and work on his carnal issues.

He became unemployed and came to one of the prayer meetings requesting prayer for a job. He had an application at Boeing and expected that I would prophesy that job into reality. I prayed and received this from the Holy Spirit: "A job here, a job there—don't worry about it." He said, "I can't receive that, pray again." I told him I would not; that was what the Lord told me to tell him. As it turned out, this person did have temporary jobs here and there, however, he continually fretted.

Sometime later, he came to me privately and asked me to hear from the Lord for him about going into full-time ministry. The Lord told me that he was going to go through a real fiery trial. He did not want to hear that.

About six months later, his wife exposed him to the church for abusing her and her children and asked him to leave. She sued for divorce which caused bankruptcy; he also had run up their credit beyond their ability to repay.

A few years later, we ran into him. He was living in his car, acting as if nothing was wrong. This man refused to hear the harder corrective messages and the whole counsel of God. He only wanted things prophesied to him that were pleasant.

Many of these people came for personal ministry to receive a prophetic message that suited them. Much of the body of Christ struggles in this condition, and they stay in this weak narcissistic state because there are plenty of ministries, pastors, and false prophets hearing from their own spirit and prophesying out of their own minds—prophesying delusions and lies. The coming trouble is going to shut down these lying ministries and false prophets. Ω

End-of-the-Age Vortex of Trouble
The saint's darkest hour is coming—"watch, pray and obey" will be our only lifeline from God!

Jesus warned of the time that is now upon us in many ways. However, I want to repeat the following words of Christ because they give clear direction on surviving the coming whirlpool of trouble that will sweep the world into utter chaos:

"For it will come upon all who dwell on the face of the whole earth. But <u>stay awake at all times, praying that you may have strength to escape</u> all these things that are going to take place, and to stand before the Son of Man" (Luke 21:35-36).

There will be no safe place to hide; no stockpiles of food, guns, and ammunition will see you through this coming trouble; gold and silver will not be a haven of safety; and there will not be a pre-tribulation rapture.

Then what can the saint rely on, or rather *who*? The Lord will take us through the coming fires. The strategy to escape is abiding in the true Christ, led by the true Holy Spirit, with an unceasing determination in watchfulness, genuine prayer and walking in obedience under the fullness of his grace, trusting him every step of the way.

Do we really believe the accounts of God's deliverance? Noah and his family, Lot and his family, Daniel and the den of lions, Shadrach, Meshach and Abednego from the fiery furnace, the Apostles from prison, Peter from prison—the list could go on and on!

God is about to let Satan create chaos and for the lukewarm and false Christian, it will seem that God is not on the throne. However, the Great Tribulation is Satan's hour and God will use this time of trouble to purify his church and reap the end-of-the-age harvest of multitudes.

Discern the time that we are in and wake up now before the midnight cry, so you can see clearly in this dark time and discern who is of God, and who is of the world and of the evil one!

America Is on the Brink!
A nation continually afflicted before final judgment

America is not exempt from judgment as some theologians and preachers proclaim. Since the beginning of the 2008 financial crisis, the financial stability of this country has been on the brink. The "fiscal cliff" is now the catch phrase used by politicians and pundits for this ongoing economic and financial crisis. America and the world is about to go over the fiscal cliff and fall into Satan's dark abyss, resulting in the cry for a one world monetary system and a smart leader to lead the world into peace and prosperity.

Stepping back and looking at the big picture, we should realize that for some time, at least since 9/11, this nation has suffered one affliction upon another. In every way, from natural disasters to economic and financial chaos—along with unrest with unions, increased crime, and mass murders—this nation is on the brink of a complete collapse of the economy and the dollar.

Soon, God will be raising his voice with increased birth pangs of the coming Kingdom—increasing with intensity and frequency. Distresses will soon overshadow all the news.

"And there will be signs in sun and moon and stars, and on the earth distress of nations in perplexity because of the roaring of the sea and the waves, people fainting with fear and with foreboding of what is coming on the world" (Luke 21:25-26).

People will become terrified as the experts, scientists, the government, elected officials, and so-called theologians will not have any sound words to restore peace of mind. The president and his administration will run out of alibies and excuses—there will be no calming answers as God finally begins to act and raise his voice, one affliction upon the next, warning of the coming final judgment.

The prepared saints will have the reality of Christ's words ringing clearly in their hearts and minds: *"Now when these things begin to take place, straighten up and raise your heads, because your redemption is drawing near"* (Luke 21:28).

The Voices of the True Prophets Drowned Out

In 1973, David Wilkerson wrote a very disturbing message concerning things he saw coming to America and to the church. His book, *The Vision* received little support or acceptance by the body of Christ. Wilkerson and his family took a lot of rejection, criticism, and persecution for being obedient.

In this book, David introduces the vision, stating:

> "It is a vision of five tragic calamities coming upon the earth. I saw no blinding lights, I heard no audible voices, nor did I hear from an angel. While I was in prayer late one night, these visions of world calamities came over me with such impact that I could do nothing but kneel, transfixed, and take it all in.
>
> At first I did not want to believe what I saw and heard. The message of the vision was too frightening, too apocalyptic, too discomforting to my materialistic mind. But the vision came back to me, night after night. I couldn't shake it off. Deep in my heart I am convinced that this vision is from God, that it is true, and that it will come to pass." (David Wilkerson, *The Vision,* Old Tappan, NJ: Spire Books 1974, pp. 11-12).

I read David's book in 1974, and it played a key role in my decision to leave the Marine Corps to go into fulltime ministry. However, most of my Christians friends at the time outright downplayed the prophetic warnings in the book. Pick the book up for yourself today, if you are not familiar with Wilkerson's vision, and see how complete his vision was. Reading this prophetic warning should have the same chilling effect that it had on David: frightening, apocalyptic, and discomforting. However, I believe most who hear the true warnings of judgment now merely shrug it off due to being desensitized by all the false alarmists, end-of-the-age movies, and last-days literature. Few have any room left in their hearts to emotionally respond as they should. Since David's vision, published in 1974, the five tragic calamities have occurred over a forty-year span of time—leaving many with the attitude described by Peter:

"Knowing this first of all, that <u>scoffers will come in the last days with scoffing</u>, <u>following their own sinful desires</u>. They will say, '<u>Where is the promise of his coming</u>? For ever since the fathers fell asleep, all things are continuing as they were from the beginning of creation.' For they deliberately overlook this fact, that the heavens existed long ago, and the earth was formed out of water and through water by the Word of God, and that by means of these the world that then existed was deluged with water and perished. But by the same word the heavens and earth that now exist are stored up for fire, being kept until the day of judgment and destruction of the ungodly. But do not overlook this one fact, beloved, that with the Lord one day is as a thousand years, and a thousand years as one day. The <u>Lord is not slow to fulfill his promise as some count slowness, but is patient toward you, not wishing that any should perish, but that all should reach repentance</u>" (2 Peter 3:3-9).

Even with proof, most now—like most then—still say, "We do not want to hear anything bad—just preach and prophesy about good and pleasant things." Israel demanded the same things the church is demanding today—pleasant prophecies, peace, and prosperity; and most Christians desire to hear the magic thinking lies that fill hearts with false hope and false peace.

They accumulate for themselves teachers that suit their own liking. Not too many true prophets last long in the body of Christ; they refuse to soften the message even in the face of rejection. These men and women of God refuse to practice cunning or underhanded methods to keep financial support coming in. They resist the temptation to teach and preach, as do many of the false prophets and teachers today; running from coast to coast, spewing out deceit, and selling their wares like door-to-door vacuum sales representatives. Indeed, they sell their messages and compete with one another using flattery to gain advantage.

These imposters speak visions and soothing words that are lies from their own spirit. For ill gain, they have daubed the "crumbling wall of protection" with whitewash (pretty paint), selling God's people a bill of goods. What is so terrible is that far too many of God's people want it so and buy into it, whole-heartedly.

Paul prophesied, *"Indeed all who desire to live a godly life in Christ Jesus will be persecuted, while evil men and impostors will go on from bad to worse, deceivers and deceived"* (2 Timothy 3:12-13).

God's people are deceived into thinking their wall of protection is secure. In reality, it is like a homebuyer who bought a house full of dry rot. The seller lied and covered up the rotten condition of the foundation and main supporting timbers with paint. It looks good on the outside, but when the storm comes, it will crumble. (See Ezekiel 13:1-16).

This is a dark time for the naïve and deceived saint, and it will become even darker until denial is broken. The afflictions already upon this country are frightening, at least to the discerning saint. I wonder how much worse it must become before the majority of God's people wake up.

Chapter Two

Last Days EVIL—Defined and Discerned

Evil
A bad four-letter word avoided in our common vernacular

There are many definitions in cultures and religions throughout the world concerning the concept of evil; for our purpose as disciples of Christ, the Bible's explanation of evil must be our standard.

Evil is on the increase worldwide. Evil atrocities inflicted upon humans by humans throughout modern history are beyond measure. When I was an eighteen-year-old in high school in 1968, part of our required curriculum was viewing a documentary on the genocide carried out by Nazi Germany upon the Jews and other peoples Hitler deemed worthless. My father, at about the same age in 1942 as I was in 1968 was in the U.S. Navy fighting in the Pacific to oppose the Japanese Empire from invading countries such as Australia and New Zealand. There was a real urgency in the Pacific theater—to prevent rape and pillage as was inflicted by the invading forces of Japan in Indonesia and China, where they committed the worst of their atrocities, the Nanking Massacre in 1937. In 1942, Japan was on the verge of invading Australia.

Those who fought abroad and at home in factories, who withstood the Axis war machine (Germany, Italy, and Japan) were later to be known as the greatest generation. As they pass away rapidly, few in our current active generations appreciate and understand the evils of that recent era. Even in the seventies, with my generation, few of us truly comprehended the awful horror unleashed upon the world just thirty years prior. My father made sure his children knew what his generation endured in standing against worldwide evil unleashed. Etched in my mind and carried in my heart are the stories my father, mother, aunts, and uncles told of working and fighting for freedom against Japan, Italy, and Nazi Germany.

In 1975, during my first year at Bible college, Corrie ten Boom spoke at a student chapel. I was about five years older than most of the other freshman. Corrie received far less notice than other speakers such as NFL lineman Norman Evans did, speaking about his faith and about new Seattle Seahawks team—however; it was Corrie's words that moved me. Norm's talk electrified the students and was the buzz on campus. Corrie ten Boom, was a famed author, speaker, and survivor of several Nazi concentration camps—this woman had truly seen evil—yet the students' reactions and comments were not exactly enthusiastic. Yet to me and few other students she was the most profound of all speakers we had through my years attending.

I do not remember what Norm spoke of, other than in general terms as a celebrity Christian sharing the typical testimony of being born again and becoming so happy. However, Corrie's words penetrated my life; her testimony was sobering and inspiring and still rings in my spirit.

She gave a stern warning to the student body of Seattle Pacific College on that day. The essence was that—what happened in her country, Holland, and all of Europe can happen here. Evil will gain victory even in America, when God's people forget, fall asleep, and ignore Christ and his teachings. With the warning of the coming darkness, Corrie emphasized how important discernment would become for Christians. Fewer and fewer born-again Christians understand what is now at our doorsteps. Most lack the ability to detect evil lurking in every corner of society as well as in fellowship—we must learn hear from the Holy Spirit and recognize evil that is now randomly surfacing causing trouble, discord, mayhem, and death.[2]

Christ Defines Evil

In the following passage, Christ describes the very foundation of human evil by citing the work of the evil one. Christ pinpoints Satan's most insidious work: developing people who appear to be good, yet who intensely hate truth and live a lie. *"You are of your father the devil, and your will is to do your father's desires. He was a murderer from the beginning, and has nothing to do with the truth, because there is no truth in him. When he lies, he speaks out of his own character, for he is a liar and the father of lies"* (John 8:44).

Hypocrites—those who lie to themselves and believe the lie—develop what I term a *good evil nature*: looking good outwardly by lying to themselves, which easily allows them to convince others of their false goodness. Their very nature abhors truth and instinctively attacks the truth in others. The good evil become Satan's servants who murder truth, life, and liveliness in those they influence and attempt to convert to their own evil lie.

"Woe to you, scribes and Pharisees, hypocrites! For you shut the kingdom of heaven in people's faces. For you neither enter yourselves nor allow those who would enter to go in. Woe to you, scribes and Pharisees, hypocrites! For you travel across sea and land to make a single proselyte, and when he becomes a proselyte, you make him twice as much a child of hell as yourselves" (Matthew 23:13-15).

Philosophers, great thinkers and theologians throughout history have tried to understand and explain human evil, especially since the revelation of the horrors of Nazi Germany and Hitler's ability to mislead millions, taking them down the garden path to genocide. Even with all the documentation and education, the world and far too many Christians are still blind to the work of evil as it continues to prosper globally, nationally, in community, in family and fellowship.

---

[2] No one is safe, even while attending fellowship. Case in point: Mathew Murray, 24 on December 9, 2007 was deranged and demon driven and went on a rampage killing two and wounding two at the Youth With A Mission training center in Arvada Colorado. Then he traveled to Colorado Springs, killed two more people, and wounded three more at New Life Church during Sunday fellowship. There are other notable attacks on places of worship recently with the prospect of more to come, as persecution, lawlessness, the demonized insane, and hatred grows within our culture.

An Evil World Getting Worse

Whether we want to accept the truth or not, the fact is we live in a very evil world. The end of World War II did not eradicate mass evils. Mass murders by one race or religion against another have become worse, beyond comprehension. Evil is on the verge of consuming the whole world once again. Jesus said of this coming evil, *"For then there will be great tribulation, such as has not been from the beginning of the world until now, no, and never will be. And if those days had not been cut short, no human being would be saved"* (Matthew 24:21-22).

This chapter will not tackle the whole subject of evil and the coming evils that will consume the whole world in war and mass brutality. We will focus on what Christ taught and how he defined evil in relation to Satan's character and his influences toward human evil as described in attitude and behavior in day-to-day living.

Evil is alive and thriving everywhere; the next-door neighbor who you thought you knew, a homeless street person acting strange, a pedophile running a local daycare, a beloved high school student who for no apparent reason goes on a killing spree.

Unexplained hatred of race towards race, hatred of the Jews, the various genocides in Africa, the list is virtually endless. Understanding evil is impossible apart from the Bible's explanation and Christ's teachings. Once we understand evil's true nature and its agenda, the only hope of overcoming evil and the final eradication of evil comes from Scripture and in the second coming of Christ.

Breaking Denial that Evil Exists and Defining Its Nature

Christians who maintain a "Pollyanna" denial concerning the existence of evil will soon have their imaginary world-view shattered. Those who continue to play the positive thinking "glad game" in life will not withstand the coming rise of evil.

We must embrace the true biblical world-view concerning evil and it's remedy in order to successfully navigate in the coming dark days—because the days are evil and evil will become over-the-top, touching everyone. For a short season, the devil and evil will have dominion over the whole world. Suffering and calamities will become unprecedented—for the devil and his angels are in the process of being kicked out of heaven and thrown down to the earth. *"Woe to you, O earth and sea, for the devil has come down to you in great wrath, because he knows that his time is short!"* (Revelation 12:12). A literal hell on earth will prevail until Christ returns.

Those who believe they are exempt from the coming unleashed powers of evil are sadly mistaken; soon the lost, the unprepared and self-righteous Christians alike will cry like Job due to the extreme evil about to befall them. Those who wake up, deal with their denial, and pay the price to stand in the coming flood of evils will glorify God, endure to the end, and overcome in Christ.

Theology that teaches a cure or healing for human evil is an outright lie—a satanic lie. Ministries and Christian workers who are naïve in these matters will be in for the shock of their lives. It is through evil people that the devil performs his most terrible work. If we bury our heads in the sand, look the other way, and pretend that we will be magically insulated from the powers of hell and the work of evil, then we can expect extra and unnecessary misery.

The Apostle Paul laid out a powerful guide on avoiding evil and overcoming the devil's works: *"Take note of those who create dissensions and difficulties, in opposition to the doctrine which you have been taught; avoid them. For such persons do not serve our Lord Christ, but their own appetites, and by fair and flattering words they deceive the hearts of the simple-minded* [naïve]. *For while your obedience is known to all, so that I rejoice over you, I would have you wise as to what is good and guileless* [no longer deceived] *as to what is evil; then the God of peace will soon crush Satan under your feet"* (Romans 16:17-20 RSV).

We must learn to be aware of evil, be alert, and abide in the true Christ—learn to allow the Spirit to lead in all things and learn what is pleasing to the Lord.

The days are becoming dark and evil because Satan has an army of servants who have sold out to evil. *"Look carefully then how you walk, not as unwise but as wise, making the best use of the time, because the days are evil. Therefore do not be foolish, but understand what the will of the Lord is"* (Ephesians 5:15-17).

The Hour of Evil and the Power of Darkness
A time in every disciple's life where discernment is perfected

The righteous in charge of the Temple worship system got away with murder—the murder of our Lord. Imagine the disciples' reaction and the emotions that filled their hearts when the Temple leaders came to arrest Jesus. They were prepared to fight; in fact, Peter drew his sword and cut off an ear of one of the arresting guards. Jesus stopped Peter and the others, healed the ear of the wounded servant, and then said to the chief priests and the others that came to arrest him, *"Have you come out as against a robber, with swords and clubs? When I was with you day after day in the temple, you did not lay hands on me. But this is your hour, and the power of darkness"* (Luke 22:52-53).

As we discuss evil and its reality, it is important to understand that Christ will allow his sincere servants to endure a time when evil will prevail in their life and in their ministry. When we are ready, Christ will lead us through a time of defeat, just as he allowed the apostles to suffer humiliation and asked them to submit to the powers of darkness and not to fight it.

Until we taste the power of evil and its treachery, and reel from evil's surreal and deadly force, we will always be under its shadow and threat. In addition, I must add, staying ignorant and hiding will not excuse us from the last-days evil invading our culture and the world—no one will be exempt. *"For it will come upon all who dwell on the face of the whole earth. But stay awake at all times, praying that you may have strength to escape all these things that are going to take place, and to stand before the Son of Man."* (Luke 21:35-36).

Reading and study is vital. We must learn and embrace all that Christ taught and we must understand that he will perform the same kind of training that he arranged for the Apostles.

When we break denial concerning evil (especially evil that appears good) and understand how easily evil can work in the power of darkness, then we must endure it personally. Suffering at the hands of evil after we have learned of it drives the lessons home and trains us to avoid or deal with evil God's way. Jesus taught the disciples about evil in detail, and repeatedly; however, not until they endured the powers of darkness did they know and understand.

Jesus still teaches his disciples, and then trains them in all aspects of living in a dark, evil, and dangerous world. Then and only then will our hearts no longer be deceived by evil's lies and flattery, and our naiveté will turn to wisdom. *"Behold, I am sending you out as sheep in the midst of wolves, so be wise as serpents and innocent as doves"* (Matthew 10:16).

The Apostle Paul sheds more light on those times when all seems lost and the powers of darkness prevail. He wrote, *"For we do not want you to be ignorant, brothers, of the affliction we experienced in Asia. For we were so utterly burdened beyond our strength that we despaired of life itself. Indeed, we felt that we had received the sentence of death. But that was to make us rely not on ourselves but on God who raises the dead. He delivered us from such a deadly peril, and he will deliver us. On him we have set our hope that he will deliver us again"* (2 Corinthians 1:8-10).

Quite candidly, most Christians learn to rely on their own strength and clouded wisdom and in their immaturity try to deal with evil and attempt to expose darkness. (If Jesus had allowed Peter and the other disciples fight against his arrest, all would have been lost.)

Dear friend, if you are serious about God using you mightily in the coming days, then brace for an hour of suffering when evil seems to win and the powers of darkness run roughshod over certain areas of your life and ministry. The disciples were not arrested with Christ, but they did hide from the wicked until that hour of evil passed.

Sinners who do Evil versus the Wicked who are Evil
We must learn to discern between the two—help the one as the Lord leads and avoid the other.

All have sinned and have done evil in the sight of God. As Scripture states *"All of us have become like one who is unclean, and all our righteous acts are like filthy rags; we all shrivel up like a leaf, and like the wind our sins sweep us away."* (Isaiah 64:6).

Make no mistake; God is in the business of redeeming sinners who have done evil in his sight. However, human evil instituted by the evil one—those who travel to the dark side and past a point of no return—these become the devil's own. The evil that they have become required a complete giving over to Satan, meaning they gave up their birthright including giving up their faith and rejecting their conscience.

Jesus was tempted in the wilderness to bow down to Satan and in return receive ruler-ship over all the kingdoms of the world. Of course Jesus answered from the heart, *"You shall worship the Lord God and him only shall you serve"* (Matthew 4:10). We must understand that down through the centuries many have taken the devil's offer, including many shallow believers. Moreover, in these days Satan will have many takers who give up their faith and salvation to receive comfort, material wealth, power and pleasure now. Many are in this condition and suffer a variety of afflictions, especially when they are of no further use to the devil or when the wrath of God catches up with them.

The Apostle Paul lamented this fact concerning the unredeemable of the world, writing, *"Pray for us, that the word of the Lord may speed ahead and be honored, as happened among you, and that we <u>may be delivered from wicked and evil men. For not all have faith</u>"* (2 Thessalonians 3:1-2).

Consider Judas the betrayer and ask—did Christ fail him? Of course not, for Jesus knew of Judas from the beginning, that he was the son of perdition: *"For Jesus knew from the beginning who those were who did not believe, and who it was who would betray him"* (John 6:64). Jesus continually warned his disciples of the evil wolves awaiting them and Christ allowed evil to live with them day after day right up to the betrayal. After Judas betrayed the Lord, the disciples were no longer naïve concerning the infiltration of evil amongst the brethren.

Discerning disciples of Christ must break out of denial and become trained in defining what evil is, based on Scripture. They must call evil what it is—*evil*—and most carefully discern between the sinner who has done evil and repents, and those who are evil and who want to be let off the hook and avoid the consequences for selling out to the devil.

A profound example of how the Lord distinguishes and responds to these two types of people is in the account of Christ's death on the cross. As you know, Christ died between two thieves who also hung on crosses The following narrative speaks to us on having the right attitude and approach in dealing with either.

"One of the criminals who were hanged <u>railed at him</u>, saying, 'Are you not the Christ? Save yourself and us!' But the other rebuked him, saying, 'Do you not fear God, since you are under the same sentence of condemnation? And we indeed justly, for we are receiving the due reward of our deeds; but this man has done nothing wrong.' And he said, 'Jesus, remember me when you come into your kingdom.' And he said to him, 'Truly, I say to you, today you will <u>be with me in Paradise</u>' (Luke 23:39-43).

Many who are evil rail at God for reaping what they have sown. They come to God's people begging for prayer and relief—only to exhaust church resources and tax the prayers of the undiscerning saints. Jesus said nothing to the ranting criminal who was receiving due punishment. However, the repentant and courageous sinner, who accepted his due reward with a contrite heart, heard these glorious words from Christ: *"Today you will be with me in Paradise."*

Evil people, including many so-called righteous Christians will end like Esau who sold his birthrights for a single meal, and then afterward, *"when he desired to inherit the blessing, he was rejected, for he found no chance to repent, though he sought it with tears"* (Hebrews 12:17).

Many of those who cross over into darkness have a unique way of making themselves look saintly by pointing out the sins, mistakes, and failures of others to maintain denial of their wickedness. These often become leaders in fellowship, and Jesus referred to them as wolves, which prey on the naïve saint.

Good Evil—the Most Insidious Evil of All

Judas appeared to be one of the good guys—he cast out devils and healed the sick in Christ's name as he worked, slept, ate, and fellowshipped with the other inner-circle disciples. As the hour of betrayal neared, Jesus exposed Judas to the other eleven during the last supper. Even then, the disciples had no clue what was going on, why or what was about to happen. (See John 13:21-30).

That is the way it is with so many sincere disciples in this hour; few understand how easily evil is cloaked in decency and beauty, yet become dumbfounded when evil's destruction takes its toll.

In 1982, Johanna Michaelsen wrote *The Beautiful Side of Evil*. In her work, she addressed the deceptive work of psychics and mediums infiltrating most cultures and entering into many churches; however, the work was weak on exposing the false teachings forming from within the church and the counterfeiting gifts that now are predominate in most denominations and independent fellowships.

Jesus pinpointed the evil on the inside of church as he confronted the most insidious evil of all. The most destructive were the false leaders who appeared spotless and perfect—those whom he equated to whitewashed tombs. These are the beautiful evil and the most deadly.

"Woe to you, scribes and Pharisees, hypocrites! For you are like whitewashed tombs, which <u>outwardly appear beautiful</u>, but within are full of dead people's bones and all uncleanness. So you also <u>outwardly appear righteous to others</u>, but <u>within you are full of hypocrisy and lawlessness</u>" (Matthew 23:27-28).

It was these religious leaders of the hour that Satan was able to enlist in getting Christ murdered. The Pharisees had developed a very lucrative racket in keeping God's people ignorant and in bondage by impressing the naive with their religious goodness.

Coupled with the scribes and Pharisees was one of Christ's own disciples that betrayed him for thirty pieces of silver as Scripture describes *"Then Satan entered into Judas called Iscariot, who was of the number of the twelve. He went away and conferred with the chief priests and officers how he might betray him to them. And they were glad, and agreed to give him money. So he consented and sought an opportunity to betray him to them in the absence of a crowd"* (Luke 22:3-6).

In my years of biblical studies, research, ministry, and counseling, plus taking into account my success in overcoming my own evil nature—I have come to understand that Satan's greatest success in developing and spreading evil is through the good evil in society, especially in church.

M. Scott Peck wrote one of the more insightful works that I discovered in my research. He was a noted author who wrote several new-age-oriented books, mixing psychology and theology, and unfortunately, those works helped contribute to the current new-age deception engulfing much of Christianity.

However, I must give credit where credit is due. Peck's work entitled *People of the Lie: The Hope for Healing Human Evil* published in 1983 was ground breaking. Due to Peck's influences from Catholicism and psychology, along with his new-age notions, most evangelical theologians, authors, and teachers ignored this insightful work. I found *People of the Lie* a good start in dealing with human evil and the devil's influences upon the world. However, Peck missed most of Christ's teachings and the more important New Testament principles that truly define and accurately identify evil at work.

In *People of the Lie*, the underlying theme was developing hope to heal human evil. Unfortunately, healing human evil at its core contradicts Scripture—human evil that passes the point of no return, along with Satan and his minions can only be dealt with by God and through God's plan. That plan calls for the permanent eradication of evil, sin, the devil, and those of like nature, which is the second death in the lake of fire. *"The devil who had deceived them was thrown into the lake of fire and sulfur where the beast and the false prophet were, and they will be tormented day and night forever and ever…. Death and Hades gave up the dead who were in them, and they were judged, each one of them, according to what they had done. Then Death and Hades were thrown into the lake of fire. This is the second death, the lake of fire. And if anyone's name was not found written in the book of life, he was thrown into the lake of fire"* (Revelation 20:10; 13-15).

Peck did illuminate three notable principles of Scripture I want to share:

1) <u>Sins are not the issue, but evil's self-righteous inner stance:</u> "It is not their sins per se that characterizes evil people; rather it is the subtlety and persistence and consistency of their sins. This is because the central defect of the evil is not the sin but the refusal to acknowledge it." (M. Scott Peck, *People of the Lie* Simon and Schuster, 1983 p. 69). [Christ's teaching on the importance of acknowledging sin is found in the story of the Pharisee and tax collector in Luke 18:9-14.]

2) <u>The truly evil are ordinary people:</u> "They are not designated criminals. More often than not they are 'solid citizens'—Sunday school teachers, policemen, or bankers, and active in the PTA. How can this be? How can they be evil and not designated as criminals. The key lies in the word 'designated.' They are criminals in that they commit 'crimes' against life and liveliness. But except in rare instances—such as the case of a Hitler—when they might achieve extraordinary degrees of political power that remove them from ordinary restraints, their 'crimes' are so subtle and covert that they cannot clearly be designated as crimes." (Peck, *People*, p. 69). [The main theme of Christ's teachings concerning evil is that they are wolves dressed as sheep. See Matthew 7:15-20].

3) <u>Evil people are defined by their absolute denial of sin</u>: "If evil people cannot be defined by the illegality of their deeds or the magnitude of their sins, then how are we to define them? The answer is by the consistency of their sins. While usually subtle, their destructiveness is remarkably consistent. This is because those who have 'crossed over the line' are characterized by their absolute refusal to tolerate the sense of their own sinfulness." (Peck, *People*, p. 71). [Scripture tells us that the rejection of one's pain of conscience is what takes us into darkness, passing the point of no return. See 1 Timothy 1:19-20. Disassociation is an aspect of denial and becomes evil's defense when people are confronted with the fact of their sin; they maintain their intolerance of ownership by minimizing, rationalizing, or justifying their evil deeds—in some cases completely forgetting the evil they do by using a form of self-induced amnesia.]

Over the years, we have composed a set of character and behavioral components that help define the good evil. To emphasize again, the good evil or beautiful evil are the most difficult to detect and it is from the many hard lessons of our own training and discipline in the Lord that we share.

Having a few issues in life from the following list of components does not determine that one is necessarily evil in nature, shrouded in a cloak of decency. However, understanding the following components and learning to hear from the Holy Spirit rightly will help determine if a person is wounded and redeemable or has gone beyond the point of no return. This is an axiom that has helped us and will help you: In ministry, learn to work where God is working. Jesus ignored the thief that railed, yet during his own agony, our Lord ministered to the other thief who called out.

The Apostle Paul wrote, *"I appeal to you, brothers, to <u>watch out for those</u> who cause divisions and create obstacles contrary to the doctrine that you have been taught; <u>avoid them</u>. For such persons do not serve our Lord Christ, but their own appetites, and by smooth talk and flattery they deceive the hearts of the naive. For your obedience is known to all, so that I rejoice over you, but I want you to be wise as to what is good and innocent as to what is evil. The God of peace will soon crush Satan under your feet"* (Romans 16:17-20).

We must become skilled in discernment, watching out for the good evil, which is the most deceitful. The following list will help identify the fruit that emanates from their core being, as Jesus taught, *"You will recognize them by their fruits. Are grapes gathered from thorn bushes, or figs from thistles? So, every healthy tree bears good fruit, but the diseased tree bears bad fruit. A healthy tree cannot bear bad fruit, nor can a diseased tree bear good fruit. Every tree that does not bear good fruit is cut down and thrown into the fire. Thus you will recognize them by their fruits.* (Matthew 7:16-20).

- Lack of empathy towards others (empathy is defined as the ability to identify somebody else's feelings or difficulties with compassion, mercy, and understanding).
- A narcissistic approach in relationships—controlling and manipulative.
- Easily falls into stints of self-pity when things do not go the way they should.
- Often emanate a self-righteous air and arrogance towards those of a lesser social stature in life, or are racist.
- Builds self up at the expense of others, often pointing out the failures of others. Has an extreme, insecure drive to constantly appear good and be correct or right, especially during arguments or disagreements.
- Often maintains a cowardly approach to life and is frequently overcome with hysteria in crisis—lacks faith and character for healthy risk taking. Lives in terror of discovery and fear of failure.
- Anxious about money and finances, often stingy— or the opposite—overly giving to gain the advantage in relationships.
- Extreme hatred and rage bottled up within but not exhibited. Usually a flat affect or expressionless look with frozen body language appears when rubbed the wrong way.
- Changes accounts of situations or events; own version is usually slanted and perceptions of what actually took place are distorted. Self-deception can fabricate lying to the point of believing own lies.
- Callous and often lacks conscience; unwilling to admit wrongdoing.
- Revengeful, spiteful, and mean-spirited—will conspire with others to get even.

- Easily maintains a relationship double standard in confession. Often uses forgiveness to own advantage. Minimizes the seriousness of own faults and over emphasizes the faults and failures of others. Expects complete forgiveness for own mistakes because they believe it was not really their fault. In contrast, their forgiveness has strings attached.
- Often energy in life, work, sports, church work, and ministry is driven by bitter jealousy with selfish-ambition that is very hard to detect. Flattery becomes a powerful tool to gain personal advantages in relationships.
- Often weird physical, emotional and mental symptoms occur when confronting the good evil. Many experience confusion, loss of pep-energy, or overwhelming oppression when working with the good evil, and some experience a revulsion in the presence of the good evil, which can be confusing if one is not trained in discernment. Our personal spirit often will act as an early warning radar as we spiritually sense the presence of evil. Many who are evil in nature cohabitate with an evil spirit, and the resident demonic evil defiles many within its proximity.
- Becomes a tireless martyr, bringing upon selves undue suffering and in turn enlist people to feel sorry for their plight; then will use pity on others as a flattering tool to gain an advantage. (Self-pity is one of Satan's favorite human traps).
- In contrast to the martyr-personality variation, opposes the message of the cross, death to self, and personal suffering.
- Dislikes and attacks those who are weak. Perfectionist; has a hard time comprehending compassion or true mercy. Uses pity on others to manipulate, keeping others dependent. Unconsciously does not want others walking in faith dependent on Christ and can become disappointed if someone becomes independent of their approval.
- Often imputes own hidden (unconscious), sinful motives to the behavior and actions of others; falsely accuses others.
- Gossips, slanders, and points out flaws until the victim's reputation is ruined. Will pick at or deride victims until they act out wickedness. Enlists others to aid in attacks.
- Tends to conceal true feelings and intentions of the heart; is superficial in relationships, having little or no true humility, self-disclosure, or repentance. Has a hard time admitting failures, and mistakes or errors are minimized, rationalized and/or justified if caught red-handed.
- Cannot respect others and allow them to work out their own problems. In self-centeredness, becomes a meddler, trying to fix everything and everybody—many self-centered attempts in helping others stem from delusional thinking and conceited sense of self-importance.

Understanding that the good evil is the most sinister of evils is paramount. This is how evil gains entrance to fellowships, relationships, and leadership, so Satan can easily deceive naïve Christians, taking them down the garden path to trouble and even destruction.

Jesus said of the good evil of his day, *"But woe to you, scribes and Pharisees, hypocrites! For <u>you shut the kingdom of heaven in people's faces</u>. For you neither <u>enter yourselves nor allow those who would enter to go in</u>. Woe to you, scribes and Pharisees, hypocrites! For you travel across sea and land to make a single proselyte, and when <u>he becomes a proselyte, you make him twice as much a child of hell as yourselves</u>"* (Matthew 23:13-15).

Evil Perpetrated Against Children
Resentful parents who reject God's attitude concerning children

Jesus delineated evil against children as the most heinous. He addressed those who perpetrated evil against a child, causing them to sin, saying the punishment will be so great that *"it would be better for him* [or her] *to have a great millstone fastened around his neck and to be drowned in the depth of the sea"* (Matthew 18:6). In our vernacular, it would better that such a person be summarily, instantly executed on the spot.

Child abuse is at epidemic proportions throughout the world and in America. We see headlines routinely exposing crimes by adults and parents against children. However, the headlines do not tell the true extent of child abuse. In her book, *Let the Children Come,* Jeanette Harder discusses how child abuse also includes child neglect:

> "Abuse is an overt act by a parent or a caregiver that brings harm to a child; neglect is the failure of a parent or caregiver to meet the needs of a child. Of the abuse and neglect reported to CPS [Child Protective Services] in the United States in 2008 and substantiated, nearly three-fourths (71 percent) was for some type of neglect… If we were to judge the prevalence of abuse and neglect from the headlines of our local newspapers, we would believe that sexual abuse and horrific cases of physical abuse occur the most often. Unless they are deemed especially heinous or malicious, cases of child neglect and physical abuse do not make the headlines." (Jeanette Harder, *Let the Children Come: Preparing Faith Communities to End Child Abuse and Neglect,* Scottdale, PA: Herald Press, 2010, p. 20)

Yes, neglecting children is a more prominent abuse than physical, sexual or emotional—and there is no excuse for any form of abuse. However, there is a form of child abuse impossible to track, and far more widespread. As a pastor and counselor, this abuse became apparent in ministering to parents who complained that their children were becoming unmanageable, unruly, and belligerent and in some cases delinquent.

These were Christian parents following, as best they could, biblical principles in child rearing. Yet, with most, I begin to pick up a common underlying thread of parental resentment. This is very strong root issue with Christian and non-Christian parents alike.

Unidentified parental resentment, in my assessment, is one of the main factors in the breakdown of wholesome and functional family living. Most adults do not set out to be abusers, neglectful, abandoning, or an absentee parent. Most couples, when building a family sooner than later, feel the weight of "frustrating responsibility" in rearing children, which usually stems from lack of finances and demand on their time.

The most common root cause for evil perpetrated against children is resentment towards the weight of responsibility in having and raising children. Few parents understand God's love and concern for children and his desire to have parents replicate that same love and care.

In counseling and teaching, parents were shown that the problems were not their children mysteriously turning unruly or belligerent, rather these were telltale symptoms showing the parents their lack of underlying joy toward having children.

For far too many, parenting is considered work and drudgery to be done dutifully. Moreover, most fulfill their parental role with an outward smile, yet internally they wish they were working on their career, or doing ministry, doing a hobby, or off somewhere saving the world.

Eventually, these internal frustrations grow into avoidance patterns where quality time for play, training, nurturing, and mentoring became a "one-minute encounter"[3] in child rearing. Short cuts, cancellations, excuses, and substitutions become ways out of the drudgery in raising children. Toys, gadgets, TV, and video games become the substitute for the fathering and mothering that God meant to grow children into mature and responsible adults.

In the church and in society we are reaping from our children the resentment we subtly demonstrated that has now provoked generation upon generation of children to seethe with anger. The Apostle Paul admonishes parents, especially fathers to be there for their children. *"Fathers, do not provoke your children to anger, but bring them up in the discipline and instruction of the Lord"* (Ephesians 6:4).

Poor parenting and resentful parents, as well as abusive parents are some of the major reasons for the increase in evil, where pent-up rage and anger is being unleashed throughout all levels of society; from the poor to the rich, from the illiterate to the educated, acts of evil are ever increasing.

Demonic Fracking of the Human Psyche
Malignant splitting of the human soul and fragmentation of the human spirit

Evil progresses through a specific plan implemented by the devil—and that plan is insidious and effective. Satan and his angels and demons are not ignorant, but rather quite intelligent in their work to understand God's creation—human beings who are created in his likeness.

Satan's goal is to murder and destroy God's work and pervert the human creation into the devil's nature—that of being a liar and murderer. The devil's work is to program people to be selfish and heartless creations—to destroy any vestige of goodness, and to crush the desire to be good. Evil's work is to eradicate faith in God, and the devil's most effective method is to

---

[3] The term *one-minute encounter* in child rearing is my attempt to encapsulate the trend towards easing the conscience and maintaining denial that child rearing is drudgery and all too often resented by frustrated parents. Many parents have taken the cue to minimize parenting time from the popular book *The One Minute Manager*, by Ken Blanchard and Spencer Johnson, published in 1982.

penetrate the soul of humankind and hijack the human spirit or, if not, then crush it beyond redemption.

Fracking of the earth: I have chosen a physical activity in oil and natural gas production to illustrate evil's main agenda in penetrating into the soul (psyche) of God's human creation. (When I refer to evil as an entity, it is in the context of Satan and his minions—both demonic and human).

Oil and natural gas fracking is defined as hydraulic injection of water and chemicals below the surface of the earth to force the extraction of petroleum, natural gas or other substances. This process creates fissures or fractures in the shale and other rock formations that contain these resources. This technique forces these resources to the surface through these enlarged fractures for recovery and refinement.

Recently, satellite surveillance revealed a mysterious patch of lights in the North Dakota night, where no major cities exist. Research revealed that the source of these lights were from new oil and gas fields developed by fracking. The lights are from hundreds of oil rigs lit at night and the fiery flares of natural gas burning. Oil and gas wells often require that excess vapor be lit on fire to handle the unusable by-product of drilling.

(Robert Krulwich, "A Mysterious Patch of Lights up in the North Dakota Dark" *On Science* Robert January 16, 2013).

Environmentalists have become distraught with the newly discovered oil and natural gas fields in North Dakota and contend that the fracking process and burning of the excess gasses are damaging to the environment.

Demonic fracking of the soul: Now let me explain this modern oil and gas exploration and extraction process in relation to evil's work in fracking the human soul and breaking the human spirit.

Abuse, Hypocrisy, Provoking to Anger and the Power of the Tongue: In the book of James, you find the explanation as to how hell penetrates the innocent, wounding and crushing soul and spirit and then creating its own evil human nature, expanding evil's work from generation to generation:

"*The tongue is a fire, a world of unrighteousness. The tongue is set among our members, <u>staining the whole body</u>, <u>setting on fire the entire course of life</u>* [or wheel of birth], *and <u>set on fire by hell</u>*" (James 3:6).

The above passage sums up the devils work of contaminating God's creation by capitalizing on evil and destructive words spoken into the lives of others, especially children. Not just words but also actions—abusive, neglectful actions and parental resentment create mental images that resonate destructive thoughts within the psyche of each victim and these thoughts can be set on fire by demons as they look to find permanent residence in the mind, the spirit, and then the heart.

Example: In the case of abusive parents who withhold appropriate affection and affirmation towards their child, one or both in a fit of anger may tell the child *they should have never been born*. This can drive evil images and thoughts deep into the heart and mind of that child easily shattering the child's spirit.

The child becomes emotionally, mentally, and spiritually stained from this type of evil and falls prey to the early development of mental illness. Their course of life or inner nature is set in a destructive direction (*set on fire*) and develops inner character filled with untruths, lies, and misbeliefs to include associated painful negative emotions.

The demonic now can fuel and inflame these wounds (*set on fire by hell*) and inject demonic harmonizing negative thoughts into the psyche and drill even deeper, looking to create or enlarge fissures or cracks in character and expand damage to inner self-worth and self-image. This explains the portion of our passage: *"setting on fire the entire course of life and set on fire by hell."*

Under these conditions, children and naive adults are defenseless to fend off a fiery barrage of painful lies that create internal beliefs about self, others, and God. In order to survive the points of impact from those abusive words and actions, we as humans have the ability to make the painful thoughts and beliefs disappear from the conscious mind.

For most victims, instantaneous amnesia makes the flood of evil thoughts and painful feelings become walled off from the core person, almost instantly repressed deep into the corridors of the mind via imagination, pretending, and denial. Each person has varied abilities in disassociating[4] away what happened and hiding the painful residue. The most prevalent is some form of forgetfulness, which protects the core conscious person, but does not make the defiling residue from the abuse go away—it just buries the painful memories and emotional side effects deeper into the psyche and spirit of the victim.

James G. Friesen, Ph.D., in 1991 wrote a ground-breaking book tying child abuse, survival through disassociation, and demonic infestation directly to mental illness, in particular to Multiple Personality Disorders (now termed *dissociative identity disorder*). He explains dissociation as follows:

> "Dissociation is the most wonderful protection against pain that any child could ever develop. There could be no more effective defense—the child pretends the traumatic event happened to someone else, and then… Poof!... COMPLETLEY forgets about it. It is gone…." (James G. Friesen, *Uncovering the Mystery of MPD,* San Bernardino, CA: Here's Life Publishers, 1991, p. 114.)

Through dissociation, depending the survivor's dissociative abilities, one can forget the abuse and the pain, but hell and the demonic have not forgotten. The demons will attempt to inspire evil thoughts as soon as possible and incite further abusive encounters. Hell will methodically reignite the painful fiery lies to enlarge the cracks and fissures within the victim's psyche and spirit. Eventually symptoms of mental illness and instability begin to appear.

"A gentle tongue is a tree of life, but <u>perverseness in it breaks the spirit</u>" (Proverbs 15:4).

---

[4] Dr. Friesen in his book, Uncovering the Mystery of MPD states the following concerning dissociative abilities: "Every child has a certain amount of dissociative ability (DA). Some can use dissociation if they undergo a relatively small amount of abuse, others can dissociate for a moderate amount of abuse, still others are able to dissociate only for extreme abuse, and a few can hardly dissociate for even the most serious abuse imaginable… Probably about 25 percent of children have a DA high enough to use dissociation for relief from chronic sexual or physical abuse. When these children grow up they develop MPD if they have been abused." (pp. 116-117).

"A glad heart makes a cheerful face, but <u>by sorrow of heart the spirit is crushed</u>" (Proverbs 15:13).
"A joyful heart is good medicine, but <u>a crushed spirit dries up the bones</u>" (Proverbs 17:22).
"A man's spirit will endure sickness, but <u>a crushed spirit who can bear?</u>" (Proverbs 18:14).

These passages denote how one's personal spirit can become broken, wounded, and crushed to the point of physical and mental illness. Knowing this, the goal of the demonic is to set on fire the inner life of those who are hapless and defenseless, who have no power or help to escape from the clutches of evil. Satan wants access to the person's spirit, like those fracking (hydrocracking) to push up oil or natural gas from its protective rock formations, to destroy elements of a healthy nurtured spirit—to destroy grace, life, liveliness, hope, faith and a sense of being wanted and loved by God.

In the book of James, the term *double minded* describes a person who is unstable in all their ways. In the original Greek language the term double-minded means "twice a soul" or "two souled." In my studies, the psychological condition labeled MPD or DID directly corresponds to the biblical double-minded or twice-a-soul condition—the condition of many who were abused, neglected, and resented in childhood. The Bible refers to these mental disorders as being "crushed in spirit" and "divided of soul" (the soul consists of the heart and mind, where the heart is the seat of emotions and the mind is the seat of thoughts and reason).

With the moral decline of the American culture, hidden abuses, resentful and absentee parents, and a weak Gospel message emanating from Christianity, many are losing the battle for their souls. Drugs, crime, sexual perversion, alcoholism and mental instability are the telltale indicators of a lost generation. The symptoms of mental illness, emotional instability, pent-up rage, and hopelessness (having a crushed spirit) are everywhere and must be discerned for one's own healing and for work in ministry. Thousands are being demonically fractured and are exploding onto society, taking their own lives and the lives of others.

The goal of the devil is to turn the wounded and divided soul and those who are crushed in spirit to the dark side—either creating unstable maniacal time bombs or taking them captive to become the beautiful evil.

When wounded early on, the beautiful evil learned to use the dissociative elements of lying and pretending to create the beautiful evil that looks outwardly good, while completely believing their own lie and denying their evil intent in all of their living.

Millions are losing their souls to darkness in the internal battle of maintaining faith with good conscience, or they are giving into the lies and temptations of the evil one.

Life's Ultimate Battle Is Within
Choosing between light and darkness—God and the devil

The American culture as a whole and much of Christianity has lost sight of the real battle in life. Remember the old cartoons depicting the temptation of life, where good versus evil is presented with the little popup caricatures, the devil on one side of the person's head and an angel on the other, presenting the temptation and the warning respectively?

This example of the battle between good and evil used to be a universal message in just about all parts of our culture—but not anymore.

The lines between right and wrong are blurred. Now the popular moral message in our culture is learning how to get away with wrong, doing what is right in one's own eyes is the common theme for morality. This has created a rich environment for the devil in his effort to birth, develop, and implant evil all through society and within Christianity.

Regardless of the lack of moral direction for our culture and for much of Christianity, the ultimate battle for everyone still boils down to choosing between light and darkness, good and evil, right and wrong—between God and the devil.

"For all who have sinned without the law will also perish without the law, and all who have sinned under the law will be judged by the law. For it is not the hearers of the law who are righteous before God, but the doers of the law who will be justified. <u>For when Gentiles, who do not have the law, by nature do what the law requires, they are a law to themselves, even though they do not have the law. They show that the work of the law is written on their hearts, while their conscience also bears witness, and their conflicting thoughts accuse or even excuse them on that day</u> when, according to my gospel, God judges the secrets of men by Christ Jesus" (Romans 2:12-16).

Regardless, everyone, with no exception will give account for their decisions, and as the end of this age draws near, more and more people will be making a deal with the devil and taking up with darkness to survive in Satan's world that is going mad.

Those who become evil do so as cowards; they refuse to enter the internal battle and fight to keep a clear conscience. They believe the devil's lie in spite of the many warnings from God through the conscience and what little moral code of conduct remains in society—they end up choosing the devil's lie.

Many make a covenant with death, as they believe they should have never been born. Self-hatred turns into revenge—exacting retribution on self and others for being born. They become pawns in Satan army of darkness. Some may find repentance; however, most that make concessions with evil gradually sell themselves to the devil and seal their destiny.

The Erosion of Parenthood in America
Much of the blame falls on terrible parenting and poor societal role models

My parents were dysfunctional and abusive and our family was chaotic. Dad was a logger and construction worker and we were continually on the move from town to town in the greater Northwest, (Washington, Oregon, and Idaho). I attended eighteen different schools before I graduated from high school and since I was the oldest, Dad had me working in the woods during summers starting at the age of twelve, and then for two more summers after that.

The work was equivalent to a man's job: running heavy equipment, a power chainsaw, and setting chokers (attaching cable to haul logs into the loading area). Several times, I came close to being severely injured and the situations could have possibly killed me.

As a WWII vet, my father survived several intense naval battles in the Pacific and suffered post-traumatic stress disorder (PTSD), not just from war but also from being orphaned, fostered, and then adopted as a youngster, which included varied forms of child abuse. Dad was a walking time bomb with a lit fuse, a rage-oholic as well as an alcoholic.

My expertise in explaining these sobering conditions, the biblical solutions, and the work of evil upon a stained society comes from my own victory through Christ in overcoming the pull of darkness and the lie of Satan. In looking back at the culture of America in my formative years, it was godly examples that God used to help keep my faith and receive Christ when he called. I attended church about six times before I came to Christ at the age of twenty-three in 1973.

Even though there was abuse and turmoil, one of the major positive influences in my life growing up was the father-images and male role models that my parents looked up to, as we all did in the family. The Gospel of Christ flowed into society freely, through all institutions, grade school Christmas plays—even TV ended the broadcast day with a Scripture reading, a hymn, and our national anthem in recognition of God.

The culture during the fifties and sixties was much more wholesome than today—it was family orientated and "G-rated" across the board: theatre, movies, TV, radio, and Hollywood were all censored and screened to protect the public from perversion and defiling graphic images and filthy discourse.

Sports figures were stand-up men and women who played down their success humbly and shunned any arrogance or egotistical antics. Heroes on the silver screen for the most part were upright and bad guys were distinct from the good guys; going bad was portrayed as not worth it—"crime doesn't pay" was the overall message.

Now the American culture in its unbridled wickedness is driving the wounded and crushed into the arms of the devil, creating and forging evil out of unstable souls.

Fatherhood: the Fatality of the Gender War

Family TV portrayed husband and fathers as sensitive and wise; wives and mothers were caring, nurturing, and supportive. In spite of evil lurking in society—though covered up and hidden—at least the fostering, packaging, and glorification of evil did not flow into our culture like a flood through all entertainment and media channels, as it now does. Now it is all out of the closet, as it states in Romans: *"Though they know God's decree that those who practice such things deserve to die, they not only do them but give approval to those who practice them"* (Romans 1:32).

In that era, portrayal of fatherhood was wholesome, full of character traits that young men desired to emulate, not only in marriage but also in all male endeavors; as a teacher, coach, politician, police officer, minister, and so on.

Culture flipped from appreciating and emulating a solid father-figure role model to a weak and bubbling caricature of male inferiority. Women began to perceive their role as a strong woman taking care of a weak man, and men began to perceive themselves as boys never having to grow up or constantly having to prove themselves. Fatherhood as a whole has developed the need to have a woman in the background propping them up.

Parents in America have sacrificed their children to strange gods and idols of entertainment, sexuality, toys, video games, and TV. Resentment towards parenting children has taken its toll in the abortion of millions upon millions of unwanted infants—a culture that says no to life because of the responsibilities of parenting.

The iniquity of resentful and absentee parenting has become the major source of evil producing character throughout our culture.

Poor parenting and lack of responsible fatherhood and motherhood must take the major blame for increased mental and emotional instability among the young adults, teens, and children in our nation. Like a snowball rolling downhill, turning into an avalanche, we as a nation have parented a lost generation. We are reaping what we have sown as a people who abandoned the ways of righteousness and turned to what is evil in the eyes of God. We are guilty of abandoning our children to the devil, eradicating even the name of God from our children's minds.

"The LORD, the LORD, a God merciful and gracious, slow to anger, and abounding in steadfast love and faithfulness, keeping steadfast love for thousands, forgiving iniquity and transgression and sin, but who will <u>by no means clear the guilty</u>, <u>visiting the iniquity of the fathers on the children and the children's children, to the third and the fourth generation</u>" (Exodus 34:6-7).

Most reputable counselors, psychiatrists and therapists will agree that the majority of children brought to them for mental and emotional issues suffer from dysfunctional, neglectful, resentful, and often abusive parenting.

Payday Is Coming to Absentee and Divorced Parents
Parents reaping the whirlwind for provoking their children to rage—including Christians

In David Wilkerson's vision, he saw rebellion of teens coming towards hypocritical parents who secretly resented and avoided the responsibility of rearing children. This is a major tragedy spreading like wildfire, growing out of control across this nation.

Hatred towards authority and parents is turning into white-hot rage as we witness teens and young adults massacring their parents. Christians and ministers of the Gospel were not exempt and in his vision, as Wilkerson saw preachers' kids included in the now full-rolling rebellion and rage of America's youth. In his book *The Vision*, written in 1973, part of Wilkerson's vision of the end days included the repercussions of hypocrisy from ministers and their children:

"Along with those who rise up in rebellion will be the sons and daughters of ministers, who one day will stand before dad or mother and say with hatred:

"You are a phony. You've preached one thing and live another. You said your marriage was impossible to work out, and yet you expected me to handle impossible problems without giving in. Get lost now, old man! And don't do any more preaching to me. You couldn't handle the problems of life, so you have nothing at all to say to me."

The Bible says that godly mothers will live to hear their daughters rise up and call them blessed. But in this next decade, many, many, mothers are going to live to see their daughters rise up and curse them. A generation of teen-age girls will rise up and curse a generation of mothers who were caught up in a sensuous world of drinking, carousing, smoking, cheating, and divorcing." (Wilkerson, *The Vision*, pp. 70-71.)

When I was a young Christian while still in the Marines in 74, one of the senior staff sergeants came to me asking for help for his young teenage son. I was leading the youth group for the base's protestant chaplain; this inspired others to acknowledge that God was working in my life, especially when my orders for early discharge came through that I might pursue college in preparation for fulltime ministry.

This master sergeant knew how to lead and manage Marines in his charge, but using a "do as I say, not as I do', approach in child rearing was not working. I suggested that his son join the youth group, but my orders for discharge came through before I could establish a meaningful rapport with this troubled teen.

Years later, I learned that this teen eventually took matters into his own hands concerning the dictatorial approach he was receiving from his father. The son in frustration became enraged by the continual provoking, retrieved his father's shotgun, and killed his dad. It was over borrowing the family car, which his dad told him he could not borrow!

An associate in ministry shared the following, after hearing of the recent carnage in New Mexico (January 20, 2013). If you recall, a fifteen-year-old killed his mother and siblings, patiently waited for his father to come home, and then murdered him too. His father was in the ministry, and extended family, friends, and their church community could not imagine why this tragedy occurred. The investigation's only clues so far is that this young man's murderous outrage was ignited because he was perturbed with his mother and he was heavily into violent video games.

> "What I think of when I read these news articles of 'churched' people going through this hell, is my past experiences in the churches that I attended, especially when I was an usher.
>
> I noticed when people came to church they would drop their kids off and did not want to be bothered. I am sure you know that part of the job of an usher is also to keep a look out, keep order, and help maintain security.
>
> How many times I'd watch the parents get lost in the worship, jump up and down, and allow their kids to run rampant, play video games (right next to them), be on the phone—pay zero attention to the child nor do anything about it. How many times we as ushers had to play the parent in these situations—with the actual parents looking on. How many elders and people dedicated to multiple ministries

in the church were consumed with "ministry" and especially youth ministry, yet their kids—their family lives—and their marriages were absolute disasters; they had no relationship or home life—and these kids felt abandoned and saw the church as a sham. These were the children of the leadership, those who had the persona of being the most spiritual. I am not saying this was the case with this tragedy in New Mexico, but it would not surprise me." (Walter, associate in ministry, citing his personal experience in a former fellowship ministering as an usher).

Christian Marriages Made in the Flesh

Many pastors actually push singles or the divorced into a relationship prematurely. Leaders in general believe a Christian marriage will solve problems of loneliness, insecurities, and financial constraints, and keep Christian singles from burning up with passion and falling into sexual intimacy outside of the marriage bed.

A large number of potentially destructive relationships are put together within the church because of these false reasons. Many Christians suffering in a state of self-indulgence suffer and struggle because of past defilements or an evil unbelieving heart. The Apostle Paul declares those allowed to stay in this self-indulgent state, to be dead while they live and some actually stray after Satan, (see 1 Timothy 5:3-16).

Much of the Christian dating scene develops into unhealthy relationships and sexual intimacy driven by demonically heightened passions of the flesh. Demons of lust infest and oppress millions of defiled Christians and most pastors try to help by developing a singles ministry that pushes couples into marriage, doing little to help in becoming cleansed of past sexual defilements.

Teachings are presented to make the sexual side of marriage no different from how the pagans approach the marriage bed. Lust, perversion, and idolatry of the human body have become the standard in demonstrating physical intimacy within Christian marriages. In an attempt to keep partners from wandering or straying into pornography—teaching on godly love within the Christian marriage is often ignored.

The Apostle Paul warned specifically about allowing paganism to enter into the Christian marriage. *"For this is the will of God, your sanctification: that you abstain from unchastity; that each one of you know how to take a wife for himself in holiness and honor, <u>not in the passion of lust like heathen who do not know God</u>; that no man transgress, and wrong his brother in this matter, because the Lord is an avenger in all these things, as we solemnly forewarned you. <u>For God has not called us for uncleanness, but in holiness</u>. Therefore whoever disregards this, disregards not man but God, who gives his Holy Spirit to you"* (1 Thessalonians 4:3-8 RSV).

Physical intimacy within the Christian marriage is meant to be special and experienced in holiness and honor where the Holy Spirit is not grieved. However, milder forms of defilements and perversion practiced in society are openly invited as a way to enhance the marriage.

Self-indulgence, sensuality, relationship idolatry, and material possessions have made far too many Christian marriages weak and ineffective in ministering to their family, friends, and neighbors. Scripture directs Christian marriages to seek God's perfect will for the marriage and warns of developing a divided devotion between serving Christ and living for each other (a form of relationship idolatry).

The Apostle Paul explains the remedy for this now widespread problem in Christian marriage today, *"I want you to be free from anxieties. The unmarried man is anxious about the things of the Lord, how to please the Lord. <u>But the married man is anxious about worldly things, how to please his wife, and his interests are divided.</u> And the unmarried or betrothed woman is anxious about the things of the Lord, how to be holy in body and spirit. <u>But the married woman is anxious about worldly things, how to please her husband.</u> I say this for your own benefit, not to lay any restraint upon you, but to <u>promote good order and to secure your undivided devotion to the Lord</u>"* (1 Corinthians 7:32-35).

Perhaps harder for many to accept is the fact that false leadership and a lack of sound teaching led many deceived Christians to marry an evil person disguised as a Christian.

Jesus taught, *"What therefore God has joined together, let not man separate"* (Matthew 19:6); however, because of the infiltration of self-indulgent, irreligious, and immoral people within Christianity, many naïve and wounded yet sincere Christians are married to wolves within the church. Far too many sincere Christians have become spiritually joined together with devils disguised as Christians—by the powers of hell.

Escaping such a destructive, evil marriage (put together by the devil) becomes nearly impossible especially when many decry any kind of Christian divorce as an outright sin. What is even more devilish and disturbing is that the true believer usually is made to look like the villain when conflicts arise or when accountability to change is counseled by leadership.

Few in pastoral marriage counseling discern the self-righteous evil, as so often the spouse who has true faith, yet suffers from defilements, will act out sin—while the evil person looks like a saint. Divinely inspired and Christ-disciplined discernment and wisdom for those in leadership and for Christian workers will be paramount in sorting out and helping this kind of marriage. We need divinely instilled and inspired wisdom concerning human nature, like Solomon in 1 Kings 3:16-28. Remember how Christ discerned the situation with the woman caught in adultery who was about to be stoned?

Saints Married to Evil Christians
Implanted weeds used to blackmail God's people, draining life and liveliness

Drunken stupor is a good description of the state of Christians enslaved to unhealthy and even destructive relationships with non-believers as well as false believers.

Sincere Christians maintain improper relations with old friends and sinful family members, and often make friends with false Christians who are unsavory, yet profess to know God. Undiscerning Christians and wayward fellowships attract these types of people like a magnet dragged in dirt collects iron filing debris. Through flattery and deceit, they secretly infiltrate the family of God. These types of people are often strewn throughout one's families of origin, yet most pulpits, for church growth's sake, encourage true believers to get these reprobate people in the family saved and integrated into fellowship.

Jesus described the situation concerning evil amongst Christians at the end of this age in the parable of the weeds. (See Matthew 13:24-30, 36-43). An important key principle found in this parable is how the weeds are so intertwined with the wheat that removing the weeds prematurely will damage the wheat. This is a form of demonic blackmail and requires maturity and leadership by the Holy Spirit to deal with evil people married to or in relationship with true Christians.

The devil's work is to interweave or bond spiritually, emotionally, and psychologically with naïve, immature, and wounded true believers. The evil (weeds) are poisonous (noxious) and suck life and liveliness from the fellowship and individuals in relationship; they have no knowledge of God, yet claim to know God. Foolishly, the unsuspecting saint falls head over heels in relationship, friendship, fellowship, and marriage with evil.

Dealing with evil in a marriage and within family can become a nightmare because of the bonding. The deceit becomes so enthralling, even when the victim acknowledges the trap, that escaping becomes nearly impossible, because the evil person takes advantage of an unclean and naïve condition within their victim. Wounded and weak Christians become so entangled that any attempt to confront evil is dropped for fear of irreparable harm to the victim and to others involved who are also enthralled by the evil person's lie.

"To the pure, all things are pure, but to the defiled and unbelieving, nothing is pure; but both their minds and their consciences are defiled. They profess to know God, but they deny him by their works. They are detestable, disobedient, unfit for any good work" (Titus 1:15-16).

In the book of Jude, the New Testament author brings a poignant description of how these evil people work and how they will become a real problem in the last days: *"These are grumblers, malcontents, following their own sinful desires; they are loud-mouthed boasters, showing favoritism [flattery] to gain advantage. But you must remember, beloved, the predictions of the apostles of our Lord Jesus Christ. They said to you, 'In the last time there will be scoffers, following their own ungodly passions. It is these who cause divisions, worldly people, devoid of the Spirit'"* (Jude 1:16-19 RSV).

These people act like stellar Christians and walk in many deceptions, deceiving the naïve, gullible, sin-laden and untrained believer; Peter also describes these as follows: *"They count it pleasure to revel in the daytime. They are blots and blemishes, reveling in their deceptions, while they feast with you. They have eyes full of adultery, insatiable for sin. They entice unsteady souls. They have hearts trained in greed. Accursed children!"* (2 Peter 2:13, 14).

"Accursed children" is a harsh description by the Apostle Peter, but most are just that—people who have become evil in nature through and through and made shipwreck their faith. However, not all who act as such have crossed over to the dark side permanently to the point of becoming reprobate—or having neglected so great a salvation (Hebrews 2:1-3).

Discerning the difference between a Judas-type false Christian and a carnal, wounded Christian is very difficult and requires the hard knocks of life's experiences in the discipline of the Lord.

If you understand that this type of person is a real threat, then study, and become trained in the word of Righteousness consistently, then you will succeed in having your mental and spiritual perceptivity improved. Count the cost, because it will take constant practice—and often-painful trial and error—but in the end, you will be able to distinguish good from evil.

Most fellowships are inundated with "accursed children" who deceitfully worm their way into the life of the fellowship and latch onto weaker but sincere Christians (unsteady souls), especially those who need validation through relationships.

These unhealthy relationships eventually become a network of the *intermingled*: a mixing of the naïve and weak but true believers with busybodies and meddlers who grow to be a powerful influence on others and poison much of fellowship life—they are noxious weeds planted by Satan.

This type of fellowship network, laced with such people, creates an intoxicating hold on the weak and the untrained, where relationship activities filled with fun and pleasure take the place of healthy and mature body-life growth.

Problems arise when the unstable or naïve Christian wakes up from their *drugged state* that is fostered by lack of sound doctrine and unhealthy relationships within the church, their family of origin, extended family system, and even with their spouse. Breaking away can become a real troublesome battle.

Few ministries and few pastors understand how to help Christians stuck in a destructive relationship and cannot teach how to biblically break off a relationship, especially an evil marriage.

The Typical Dynamics of a Destructive Relationship
True believers married to an evil false Christian who acts religious but spiritually destroys

Wounded people tend to marry up in their thinking, looking to find their "better half" to bring stability into their life. The partner they find who has the sense of goodness takes on the "better half" role, which often fits their inner perception of self, that of a strong moral person taking care of the wayward. Most marriages starting out on this kind of foundation have relationship dynamics that impinge upon the other, where they both counterbalance the others inner agenda.

The moral, more stable spouse becomes more righteous (sometimes inciting abuse if they perceive themselves as a victim or a martyr) in order to keep the original bonding dynamics in place, while the other acts out instability and often becomes more destructive to self and the relationship. Both eventually resent the marriage and each other's role, however, neither understands why. Instead of bonding, these counterbalancing dynamics polarize the relationship, driving the marriage apart.

Many times the wounded and unstable in the relationship becomes a Christian (they are the one that needs help from God) and find that their "better half" does not need Christ, since they think of themselves as already religious and good. Often the "better half" self-righteously becomes a religious Christian to keep up their self-image of being the moral and stable partner.

At this point in this type of a relationship, when one becomes born again, while the other becomes religious, the religious one runs the risk of becoming a "good evil" person. The newly born-again partner saw their own evil and repented, though the hidden agenda for each is still in place. This type of marriage is more frequent in the body of Christ since little is taught on the perils of self-righteousness, religiosity, and being in denial of one's sin nature and the works of the flesh as a Christian.

This type of so-called Christian marriage can be compared to the relationship between two men going to the Temple:

"He also told this parable to some who trusted in themselves that they were righteous, and treated others with contempt: 'Two men went up into the temple to pray, one a Pharisee and the other a tax collector. The Pharisee, standing by himself, prayed thus: 'God, I thank you that I am not like other men, extortioners, unjust, adulterers, or even like this tax collector. I fast twice a week; I give tithes of all that I get.' But the tax collector, standing far off, would not even lift up his eyes to heaven, but beat his breast, saying, 'God, be merciful to me, a sinner!' I tell you, this man went down to his house justified, rather than the other. For everyone who exalts himself will be humbled, but the one who humbles himself will be exalted" (Luke 18:9-14).

If the truly born-again believer in the marriage continues to mature there will come a show down, because the other will naturally become more contemptuous and spiritually destructive—unless the self-righteous partner is confronted and deals with their self-righteous inner stance. If not, the pharisaical partner will most likely grow into an implanted weed used by Satan. Separating from such a relationship in any form, whether it be separating from a sibling, a friend or a spouse, is vital and must be done God's way. This separation process will be difficult and the biblical principles to embrace are covered in chapter eight. A more detailed method for separating from an "evil weed spouse" disguised as a Christian will be covered in a forthcoming publication dealing with devils planted amongst the wheat.

Learning to Not Trust Yourself to False Christians

Great care must be taken to learn how <u>not to be</u> open hearted and vulnerable to these types of people, whether they call themselves Christians, are a family member, an old friend or a new acquaintance. Saying no to the narcissistic false Christian, family member, or old friend who preys on others will be difficult but vital in maintaining a healthy life in Christ.

Again, few pastors receive solid training to help on this all-important aspect of maturing in Christ; it is very difficult for new Christians to break from sick and unhealthy relations with family and old friends. Most will be on their own in attempting to establish proper boundaries, primarily due to the sad fact that most pastors and other Christians oppose such work. Often, when the sincere Christian attempts to avoid the false, a battle for life and freedom can easily turn into a living nightmare.

Many who attempt to avoid such in fellowship become persecuted, maligned, and ridiculed for not being a loving Christian or a true servant to others. Learning to be wise as a serpent and innocent as a dove is part of becoming mature as a disciple of Christ. We must understand there are wolves strewn throughout our culture, but the most deceiving and destructive are found in fellowship. Few pastors and elders dare confront the wolf (often running in packs) as they intuitively sense the wolf's power to destroy and so cowardly make concessions with evil and look the other way. (See Matthew 10:16-25).

Another descriptive term used by the Apostle Peter for these troublemakers carousing in fellowship is that of a "waterless spring." These present themselves as believers who have life in Christ to share with others, but in reality they are like vampires and drain faith and life from the weak and the undiscerning; invariably they instigate trouble and defile others, yet stay undetected.

The following case is a sad example of a wife who gave up her first pledge to Christ and lusted after a wealthy husband—choosing to stay with an evil so-called Christian because he was very industrious and smart and owned a business that brought in a large income.

Ministry Case: *A beautiful mind*

Please bear with me as I take time to explain the relationship background concerning this couple who came to us for counseling and expressed a strong interest in our ministry. They indicated that they had gone to several different churches looking for sound fellowship that helped Christians prepare for the coming dark times. The husband was very into the end-times survival mentality, actively stockpiling supplies, firearms and ammunition.

They seemed to be open to the harder teachings of Christ and the need to become ready for very difficult times. He was in business with his father, where they jointly owned a small manufacturing firm that had several lucrative contracts. There seemed to be no problem financially and their generosity was a real blessing.

Some red flags began to pop up during normal conversations and eventually, the wife shared that their relationship was rocky and that they had a major fight and temporarily separated just prior to their first contact with our ministry. We developed a mentoring relationship with the couple and began to counsel long distance by phone, primarily with her.

She explained that he had an explosive temper, was abusive in disciplining their children and at times physically abused her. Some of the relationship stress came from his inability to stand up to his former wife who he would often allow to stay in their home when she visited the child they had together, of whom he had custody. Eventually, they paid me to fly out, spend a weekend at their home, and do some counseling.

During my stay, I became more concerned. Their lifestyle was chaotic and they exercised very little control on purchasing material things—exhibited by compulsive buying and tons of toys for the children. The house was messy with stacks of laundry, and cluttered with unfinished projects, both inside and outside in the yard. Though he was part owner in the family business with his parents, she also worked part time in fulfilling large orders.

He had a very expensive gun collection and was an ardent survivalist convinced that the government was all too intrusive and he feared losing constitutional freedoms. During my visit, I tried to get each to share their backgrounds and learn of their childhood upbringing. My other goal was to explain in depth how wounds and defilements to the spirit were causing trouble for themselves and their relationship with each other. I extensively explained the troubling symptoms of double-mindedness as outlined in the book of James.

At the end of my stay, I had hoped that they had reached a level of understanding that allowed them to start working on their specific issues (taking ownership of their carnal issues and problems as listed by Paul in his letter to the Christians in Galatia).

His parents were Christian, and as stated earlier, he (not his wife) was part owner of the family business. Both had a background of sexual perversion, as well as destructive and unhealthy relationships. Sex and jealousy appeared to be a very influential and disabling aspect in their relationship. She had a very abusive childhood and she eventually revealed a history of seizures for which she was on prescribed medication. Her seizures came during times of intense stress within the relationship.

He sported a long beard that fit perfectly with his outlook on life as a pioneer, patriot, and survivalists. They both were realizing how chaotic society might become during the end-of-the-age birth pangs. Both had new vehicles and he maintained supplies and a heavy arsenal of weapons in case, as he put it "all hell broke loose." He was proud that he had obtained five functional fully automatic (machine) guns used in WWII. He led me to believe he had a federal firearms license and that these normally illegal weapons were legal for him to own in his case.

The challenge was helping both learn to trust Scripture and to become comfortable with me as a pastor and counselor—that they might begin confessing their hang-ups and secret sins. After my weekend stay, their relationship appeared to be calmer for some time. Based on her reports by phone both were making progress. However, his parents proved to be intrusive and controlling and this would often incite stress and tension within their relationship.

Gathering accurate history, discerning issues of heart not disclosed and determining the severity of their double-minded condition were the main goals in counsel. They seemed genuine but very unstable and weak on understanding the deeper things of God and faith in Christ.

I sought the Lord for direction concerning how involved our ministry should become with this couple, since she was susceptible to hysteria and he was obviously carrying pent up rage and suffered from extreme fears (paranoia).

With my short counseling visit and continued periodic mentoring by phone, they indicated they were getting direction and hope for their relationship. At this point, they decided to come to Colorado for a week, enjoy local sights, and become more familiar with our ministry, looking for opportunities to become more involved.

Their one-week stay consisted of resting and sightseeing, with time spent in fellowship to increase trust in the counseling aspects of our ministry.

It was about four months later that they decided to come back for a two-week stay and receive intensive counseling. The first week of counseling would focus on his issues, then he would fly back home and be with the children while she spent the next week counseling exclusively on her issues. Both would enter joint counseling in another trip in the near future.

The first week counseling revealed that his family of origin had all the characteristics of what we term an evil cult family system (will explain this term later in chapter eight, in the section titled

Dealing with Carnal and Evil Cult Family Systems). Both parents were Christian hypocrites where the treatment of children followed the axiom: "children are to be seen and not heard" — extreme lack of nurturing prevailed and any required parental involvement was resented. His childhood consisted of harsh discipline, strict outer religiosity, and little interaction.

During his week, the most significant breakthrough session occurred when the Holy Spirit brought to his remembrance the day his father did one of the most grievous acts that helped crush his spirit. (*"A gentle tongue is a tree of life, but perverseness in it breaks the spirit"* Proverbs 15:4).

He had remembered many incidents where his father promised things and did not follow through, however in prayer the Holy Spirit led me to tell him that there was a terrific wound that was central to his troubled life and struggle in truly knowing God's love — the love of God as our heavenly Father. *"Behold, you delight in truth in the inward being, and you teach me wisdom in the secret heart"* (Psalm 51:6). In agreement, I led in prayer that the memory of this incident would surface.

In his secret heart, the hidden truth was about to be revealed. Within a minute of that prayer a memory surfaced which he could actually visualize in his mind's eye and see the incident unfold.

He began to describe what he saw happen to him as a young boy. The memory was like looking at a video tape where he saw himself continually asking his father to come outside and play catch. His father kept pushing him away, but finally in a resentful way his father got up, went outside with him, took the baseball and threw it so hard and fast that there was no time to bring up his glove to catch the ball, thus it sped past his glove hitting him in the chest painfully. Then his dad just walked back into the house.

As he described the memory, intense rage emerged and then deep sobbing. I instructed him that he needed to embrace a season of prayer for healing this deep wound to his spirit, along with his willingness to forgive, yet hold his father accountable for the continued evil he practiced towards him and his wife and his children.

There was much more discovered, and explanation of the biblical principles of cleansing, healing, and restoration to a wounded spirit and damaged emotions took up much of the time in each session. For him, the hardest principles to grasp were those used by the Holy Spirit to heal a double-minded condition.

Toward the end of the week of his counseling time, I had his wife participate in a session — she wanted to bring up an issue they had between the two of them. She felt uncomfortable with sexual activities he often insisted upon and wanted to clarify in counsel and Scripture how inappropriate that activity was within their marriage.

When I pointed out his wife's concerns, he became very defensive and somewhat belligerent and obstinate and his behavior made it obvious he lacked empathy and consideration towards his wife. He was still agitated after the session but within five minutes, he seemed happy (later I realized that he switched into a different personality).

His week of counseling ended and Saturday he returned home while his wife continued to start her week of counseling on Monday. The children had been staying with his parents and now he would return home, go back to work, and pick up the children from daycare as usual.

(Discussions with his wife concerning the negative influence his father and brother had upon him became an important issue. He worked with his father and brother in the business and he was heavily involved in pornography with them and exchanging perverse jokes that were usually demeaning towards women.)

Monday evening he called his wife to see how her counseling was proceeding. Each evening he would call and on the Wednesday evening call he starting pressing her to agree to engage in unhealthy sex, about which she continued to hold her ground and not cave into his demands.

The next day, after her morning counseling session, he again called to see if she had changed her mind, and again,—she said no. Immediately he wanted to talk to me on the phone. The conversation became stressful due to his lack of reason and selfish demands.

It was at this point I realized he had worked himself up into a panic state and become very disagreeable and unreasonable. I calmed him down and assured him that everything would work out fine and we then hung up from the telephone call.

She was listening to my half of the conversation and when I was finished, we had a lengthy discussion, reviewing his history of violence, outbursts of rage, threats to the family, and frequent contemplation of suicide when boxed into a corner. We recommended that she hold him accountable and require him to submit to professional medical help. To accomplish this she would have to separate herself and the children and actually hide from him in a safe place.

The next three days he would be traveling to pick up his son, while their two younger daughters stayed with his parents. This was her window of opportunity to get back home to the children and get to a safe place. That next morning she was on a flight back home.

All went well in getting this accomplished, and when he returned home her letter to him explained her course of action—that he needed to contact a psychiatrist for help and if not she would file a domestic violence complaint.

He immediately contacted me and I instructed him to find appropriate professional help, that I could not help him any further. (The goal was to have him submit himself and have prescribed, appropriate medication, making sure he would not be able to harm himself or anyone else. Success for this plan would be predicated on contacting a properly trained professional who could see through his lies.)

Unfortunately, he involved his parents and used them to contact his wife to notify her of his intentions. He threatened that if she would not come back or if she called the sheriff, he would barricade himself in the house and take as many of the SWAT team out as possible before they killed him.

Under pressure from the family, she relented and agreed to go back to him if he promised to see a psychiatrist. This he did, and then he called me after a few sessions with his therapist and informed me that he was getting better and was on anti-psychotic medication. (This is what I had hoped for and what I refer to as a "chemical straightjacket" since he had great potential of doing harm to his family or himself.)

This person had a powerful charm and great ability to deceive. His therapist fell for the act and actually blamed my counsel for his problems.

Eventually, this woman submitted to the demands of his perverted sex to keep a comfortable lifestyle.

As for him, his psychiatrist diagnosed him as being a *paranoid schizophrenic genius* akin to John Forbes Nash, Jr., whom the actor Russell Crowe portrayed in the Ron Howard movie *A Beautiful Mind*. Thus, with proper medication he would be harmless and continue with life as a very smart entrepreneur.

The last contact from this so-called believer was a text message sent to me that contained a filthy joke about a women abused sexually. In this way, he boldly let me know he got his own way. Ω

Biblical Diagnosis –versus– Secular Psychology

What is God's diagnosis concerning this kind of so-called Christian? The following is an abbreviated paraphrase of 2 Peter 2:4-22 describing this man very accurately:

Bold and willful, reviling others without fear, an irrational creature of instinct that needed to be permanently restrained, who defiled his wife, family, and friends. He became a blot on society, carousing with others in pleasure-seeking activities and indulged in the lust of defiling passions. He refused correction and despised authority of Scripture applied in counsel. He was into pornography (adulterous in his heart) and insatiable for sin, having a heart trained in greed and living out a cursed life, as he had forsaken the right way.

Peter describes this type of person as being like a waterless spring with no true substance to contribute to others, and driven like a mist in a storm. Enslaved to his pet sins he enticed others with his licentious (immoral) passions of the flesh. He became so entangled in his defiling lifestyle that his last state is far worse than when he first heard about Christ.

His secular psychological diagnosis of having a sick, yet beautiful mind is an absolute contradiction to Peter's description and God's diagnosis concerning this type of person: *"What the true proverb says has happened to them: 'The dog returns to its own vomit, and the sow, after washing herself, returns to wallow in the mire"* (2 Peter 2:22).

There are many such people planted throughout society, growing up in sick family systems and coming to the household of God, professing to know God. Yet as the Apostle Paul instructs, *"Their minds and their consciences are defiled. They profess to know God, but they deny him by their works. They are <u>detestable, disobedient, unfit for any good work</u>"* (Titus 1:15-16). Discerning weeds planted and growing amongst the fellowship of the saints will become one of the most valued abilities in the coming dark days—the ability to distinguish good from evil.

We must comprehend that we are in the last days and Scripture's description and warnings are to be taken seriously and applied appropriately. These times are now perilous and will only get worse, *"Evil people and impostors will go on from bad to worse, deceiving and being deceived"*

(2 Timothy 3:13). You will be unable to avoid such people if you continue to live on the milk of the Word and be content just attending church.

It is never too late to give God permission to do whatever it takes and to start to become disciplined by his hand and become skilled in the word of Righteousness—to become willing to be trained by the practice of distinguishing good from evil. Allow God to put you in his daily school of discernment.

Criminally Evil—Prisons Overflowing into Society
The mystery of lawlessness creating anarchy and chaos—the bad evil growing exponentially

Our culture is becoming more and more sympathetic to what I call the Bonnie and Clyde mentality; rob from the rich and give to ourselves. We see this form of evil on the rise throughout society—the criminally evil.

These people know they are at war with God and society, and pride themselves as sociopaths taking revenge out on anybody who stands in their way. They see themselves as victims of the so-called good people of the world and make no bones about their lawlessness and crimes against humanity. They are drug dealers, drug cartel members, robbers, rapists, gang member criminals, anarchists and hate filled swindlers—all lawlessly making a living.

Some of these may repent as many over the years have done. However, as Jesus warned, *"because lawlessness will be increased, the love of many will grow cold."* Society will see less bad evil repent, and prisons overflowing becoming maxed out—criminals will be let back into the streets without reform.

Society is now being flooded with hardened criminals who have learned to skirt the law and avoid detection. Robberies, home invasions, white-collar crimes, fraud, identity theft, smuggling, bribes, black mail, homicides, kidnapping, and rape will increase.

Parts of urban America will look like a war zone, with police avoiding patrolling certain parts of criminalized neighborhoods. This bad evil or criminal evil is part of the end-of-the-age lawlessness inspired by Satan to saturate society with fear. It is all part of the plan for society to beg for world peace and a government-controlled society—soon the majority of Americans will gladly give up liberty and freedom for an anti-Christ rule and order that promises peace and security.

As lawlessness grows, so will the instability of the mentally deranged living within communities throughout the nation. Hundreds of thousands are functional time bombs on the verge of explosion.

Hordes of Malignantly Evil Spirits Cohabitating in the Schizophrenic
Homicidal, suicidal, vicious, maliciously hateful, revengeful and resentful human time bombs

We are witnessing last-days horrors in the news weekly, sometimes daily with reports of mass murders, suicide-murders, and crime sprees throughout society. No one is safe in going to the store, to the bank, the movies, or their children when sent to school or college.

The community mental health systems and associated resources are overtaxed and the mentally ill who break the law are funneled into overcrowded prisons. Society, the government and mental health experts are at a loss for explanations and solutions. Blaming management, knee-jerk reaction, and procrastination are politics as usual concerning the mentally ill.

Sara Kliff, in a Washington Post online article cited Jeneen Interlandi's comments and other statistics to help bring some clarity to the results of the Community Mental Health Centers Act of 1963. That law pushed for the deinstitutionalization of the mentally ill, and pushed the very unstable out into the community away from psychiatric institutions:

> By treating the rest [mentally ill] in the least-restrictive settings possible, the thinking went, we would protect the civil liberties of the mentally ill and hasten their recoveries. Surely community life was better for mental health than a cold, unfeeling institution.
>
> But in the decades since, the sickest patients have begun turning up in jails and homeless shelters with a frequency that mirrors that of the late 1800s. "We're protecting civil liberties at the expense of health and safety," says Doris A. Fuller, the executive director of the Treatment Advocacy Center, a nonprofit group that lobbies for broader involuntary commitment standards. "Deinstitutionalization has gone way too far."
>
> Access to mental health care is worse than other types of medical services. The Bureau of Labor Statistics estimated in 2010 that the country had 156,300 mental health counselors. Access to mental health professionals is worse than for other types of doctors: 89.3 million Americans live in federally-designated Mental Health Professional Shortage Areas, compared to 55.3 million Americans living in similarly-designated primary-care shortage areas and 44.6 million in dental health shortage areas." ("Seven facts about America's mental health-care system" Washington Post Online, December 17, 2012)

Crazy Evil—Walking Time Bombs
America's mental health crisis is exploding right before our eyes

The truth behind all the irrational chaos and mayhem is simple—the world, especially America, is witnessing the results of Satan's last-days plan to terrorize society so that we yearn for a world order that will again bring peace and security. The mentally ill, in particular those who have become severely divided, are walking and living hosts for hordes of evil spirits whose agenda is to destroy, murder, steal, rape, and take out as many humans as they can for they know their time is short.

Hundreds of thousands of mentally ill, borderline, and emotionally disturbed people (especially the younger generation of adults and teens), are exploding right before our eyes, one after another. They become irrational and crazed, driven by white-hot rage, yet show no remorse, empathy, or pity concerning their crimes or for their victims.

In their mentally and emotionally sick inner-world, these people have unintentionally invited hell to cohabitate within (although some have deliberately turned to the devil). These human time bombs are now ripe for demonic use—to either make them explode in rage upon the world, or if they are still functional, send them into family, church, business, and the world to become agents of hell to poison and spiritually attack life and liveliness. (These are Satan's implanted terrorists, likened unto the Jihadist driven by a perverted and distorted view of Islam).

Many become criminals with no remorse, taking from society what they believe is rightfully theirs and in the process stealing and destroying property and life while feeling completely justification—and without remorse.

Through the ages, these human evils have always been with us, but never to the extent that we see now. The reasons for this landslide of evils befalling humanity are in the Scriptures:

- False Christianity, increased wickedness and the godly love gone cold, Matthew 24:9-12
- False teachers with destructive heresies, licentious practices, and greedy exploitation that has made the Gospel reviled and even hated by many, 2 Peter 2:1-3
- Satanic activity instituting lawlessness using counterfeit signs and wonders in preparation for the anti-Christ rule along with the hatred of truth, lust for instant gratification and pleasure, causing God to give many over to a strong delusion, 2 Thessalonians 2:9 12
- Great stress from lawlessness, narcissism, the love of money, arrogance and abuse gone viral, hatred of what is right and good, love of pleasure, and many who claim to be religious yet practice these wicked activities and hold a counterfeit faith, 2 Timothy 3:1-9

Last-days evil is surging upon society from all directions, and leading the way are unbalanced people turning into monsters without notice. Unfortunately, many who suffer wounds to the spirit and double-mindedness will have symptoms and behavioral characteristics similar to those who are demon possessed and deranged, yet somewhat functional. As end-of-the-age trouble mounts and the economic crisis continues, more and more hurting people will turn to the visible body of Christ (churches and fellowships) for help. These will include the dispossessed, the professional street person, and the mentally ill—along with the unemployed and people in various personal emergencies and crises.

The mentally deranged, (those who have turned to evil) will increasingly pose greater threats to fellowships, Christian workers, and social relief ministries. Discerning between the wounded and the mentally-ill-evil will soon be of utmost importance. Many who are mentally disturbed and wounded have turned to evil inviting the demonic to live within.

These have believed lies and lied to themselves, and in some form or another made a pact with the devil. Most suppress extreme rage and like a pressure cooker are ready to explode. With the evil beliefs that they embrace, along with demonic infestation, they reap mental illness and the inability to think rationally.

Crazy evil is one of Satan's last-days works to terrorize people and manipulate a lawless approach to take away everyday freedoms that most have taken for granted.

During the sixties, most state-run mental health institutions were exposed as ghastly centers of abuse and experimentation. Soon legislation of laws and regulations gave the mentally ill sweeping civil rights and dramatically deinstitutionalized the mentally ill who were a danger to themselves and others.

The population of the public mental hospitals shrank from an average population of over 500,000 during the mid-fifties to only tens of thousands today. The process of deinstitutionalizing the mentally ill over the last forty years has forced society to absorb the mentally ill, including dangerous psychotics suffering from paranoid schizophrenia, bipolar disorder and psychotic depression. (See E. Fuller Torrey, *The Insanity Offense*, London, UK: Castle House, 2012 pp. 1-7.)

The mentally ill, deranged, and demon possessed are systematically shoved by the hundreds of thousands into stressed families, understaffed outpatient clinics, poorly staffed halfway houses, prisons, jails, and the alleys, subways, abandoned buildings, and dark street corners all across the nation. Today, experts are at a loss to offer any solution in protecting society from the evil mentally ill time bombs lurking everywhere. Not only are the wicked and evil emboldened today, but also now, more than the ever, crazy evil people possessed by the devil and his demons are being ignited like time bombs. Like teens out on a nighttime prank tipping sleeping cows, Satan and his minions are "insanity tipping" the schizophrenically deranged and demonically possessed.

In his book *The Insanity Offense*, E. Fuller Torrey asserts that over the past five decades, hundreds of thousands of mentally ill with severe psychiatric disorders have been discharged from public mental hospitals with laws making it impossible to adequately treat, protect, and care for these people. They end up in the streets, in poorly staffed outpatient clinics, or living with relatives having virtually no supervision. The author attempts to warn us that thousands upon thousands of mentally ill are on the edge, and society is at great risk of more and more random deadly outbursts.

However insightfully Torrey or any other secular expert may assert their conclusions concerning these deadly offenses by the insane, this morally depreciated culture, with Satan's help has produced insanity time bombs to be used by the devil in his end-of-age war against mankind and God's people.

David Brooks of the *New York Times* endorses *The Insanity Offense* by stating: "Torrey's book describes a nation that has been unable to come up with a humane mental health policy—one that protects the ill from their own demons and society from their rare but deadly outbursts."

It is ironic that Brooks, as with so many, refer to the mentally unbalanced as suffering from their own demons, when in reality secular psychiatry ignores the existence of God, the devil, or his demons—let alone that they might have anything to do with the insane and insanity.

Children raised in dysfunctional and abusive family systems often turn to fantasy and delusional thinking to escape the pain of living. Passivity, irrational thinking, and illiterate become the foundation of relationship development and social interaction. Teens and young adults from these family systems lack social coping skills and often feel out of place and turn to various dissociative activities, such as gaming, fantasy movies made realistic, and other unsavory activities and behaviors. They lack reason, common sense, and wisdom and often become bored. The old proverb, "Idle hands are the Devil's workshop" might have been old-school thinking; however, this adage describes this generation of lost souls on the verge of anarchy. Like the Apostle Paul predicted, *"In the last days there will come times of difficulty. For people will be lovers of self, lovers of money, proud, arrogant, abusive, disobedient to their parents, ungrateful, unholy, heartless, unappeasable, slanderous, without self-control, brutal, not loving good, treacherous, reckless, swollen with conceit, lovers of pleasure rather than lovers of God"* (2 Timothy 3:1-4). A lost generation that is abusive, disobedient, heartless, brutal, treacherous, reckless—ready to explode at any moment.

The functionally insane and possessed roam society putting the whole population at risk. Of course, there are statistically safer places than the densely populated cities. However, suburbs and rural areas are now at much greater risk. The most recent mass killing in Newtown, Connecticut, underscores Torrey's claim.

Judgment in every manner is coming upon a violent, perverted, self-centered and pleasure-filled culture that has become a breeding ground for these demonically driven human time bombs.

Few in ministry understand the dangers of the mentally ill people who are also evil. The Apostle Paul wrote this about evil people: *"Pray for us, that the word of the Lord may speed ahead and be honored, as happened among you, and that we may be delivered from wicked and evil men. For not all have faith"* (2 Thessalonians 3:1-2). We must understand that evil men and women exist and that they do not have faith and thus are reprobate (unredeemable).

As we discussed, there are the good evil, (like Pharisees) and the bad evil (the criminally wicked who know they are evil and do not care). There is the borderline evil (those who are in a battle to go all the way to the dark side), and then there is the crazy evil (those who threw away their faith and suffer from a debased mind—and want back into the fold of God on their own terms).

Discerning Between the Wounded and the Demon Possessed-Mentally Ill

Pastors, Christian workers and professional counselors must learn how to discern the difference between people suffering from a wounded spirit, damaged emotions and mild personality disorders from those who have become enraged at life and live on the edge, hiding intense hate towards God. The crazy evil have become severely split in the core, with an outer persona that seems stable at a distance, but hides an evil inner core where the demonic resides.

The crazy evil struggle with their internal contradictions, but the good evil jumped entirely over to the dark side without splitting or becoming unstable. Demons do not have to invade and fight to stay in control as they do with the crazy evil, the good evil buy completely into their own lie and develop an evil character that requires minimal maintenance by the demonic. The devil or a demon can fill the good evil's heart at will, as Satan did with Judas.

All categories of evil people develop an evil core (heart) by rejecting their conscience repeatedly until any sense of guilt is vanquished and empathy towards others is no longer felt. When one's conscience no longer stings when doing wrong or thinking evil, then faith in God and the fear of God disappears, leaving God no alternative but to give an evil-prone person up to a debased mind (mental illness) and demonic aggravation, possession, and co-habitation.

The criminally wicked in prison know their own condition and what they are about, however the criminally insane and mentally ill evil live in extreme delusion, believing their own lies. These people are able to pretend that they are not inwardly evil as they portray an outer goodness, albeit living a troubled and unstable life.

Through years of study and observation, I have found that most secular psychologist and therapists consider the belief in God to be the cause of most mental anguish. Sin, guilt, self-condemnation, the thought of hell and religion in general are considered the major reasons for mental anguish, which is like throwing an iron life ring to a drowning person.

Biblical solutions found in the proper understanding of Christ and his teachings are virtually ignored by most that practice psychiatry or work as psychologists. Instead of turning to Scripture to help people overcome mental and emotional disturbances, most prescribe psychotropic medication that eventually aggravates the patients destructive urges. Research and studies are starting to surface that indicate some of the prescribed drugs are directly related to mass shootings, suicide, and other psychotic behaviors—while the pharmaceutical lobby aggressively opposes any government studies and investigations.

> "Psychiatrists can't predict what adverse side affects you might experience because not one of them knows how their drugs work.
>
> Psychotropic drugs are increasingly being exposed as chemical toxins with the power to kill. Psychiatrists claim their drugs save lives, but according to their own studies, psychotropic drugs can double the risk of suicide. And long-term use has been proven to create a lifetime of physical and mental damage, a fact ignored by psychiatrists.
>
> Common and well-documented side effects of psychiatric drugs include mania, psychosis, hallucinations, depersonalization, suicidal ideation, heart attack, stroke and sudden death.
>
> Not only that, but the US Food and Drug Administration admits that probably one to ten percent of all the adverse drug effects are actually reported by patients or physicians." (Citizens Commission on Human Rights, "Psychiatric Drugs—Side Effects" www.cchr.org)

Thus, laws and regulations endorsed by blinded and overly sympathetic advocates for the mentally ill and enforced by liberal courts have emptied the state mental hospital of patients, many of whom are evil in their core. Society and the mentally ill are no longer protected by institutionalized care and physical restraint. The mentally ill have more protection under the law to do harm to others than the law-abiding citizen walking down the street or an innocent child in grade school.

Satan is spewing evil upon the innocent without notice, as a system of hodgepodge psychiatric theories flush the mentally ill (crazy evil) like refuse into society with prescribed medication as restraint, without supervision or authority to assure compliance.

The local community mental health system, for profit halfway houses, family, friends, or missions becomes the caregivers and supervisors who have no authority to legally commit or physically restrain the obviously crazy evil. Those who are on the verge of committing a felony, at risk of harming self or others, lurk within society with immunity to proactive restraint.

If they are caught doing a crime, most are funneled into local jails and the penal system, and many bounce back into the streets free to harass and threaten again. Only when they murder or really rack up enough felonies are they committed to long-term confinement in the few state mental health hospitals for the criminally insane.

All this, coupled with states reducing mental health budgets, has allowed the mentally insane to roam freely and randomly do evil. No more padded cells and strait jackets or supervision by qualified clinicians and full-time psychiatrists to protect society (and self) from harm.

Rather, now therapy and maintenance is attempted with psychotropic drugs administered by relatives or clinicians who have no authority to enforce compliance, nor any legal recourse to have these mentally ill time bombs committed—until they murder or do great harm.

As morality and the existence of God have been removed from government and public view, for some time now psychology and psychiatry also have removed the idea of God, the devil, and consequences for doing evil. America has issued the crazy evil a permanent "get out of jail free card"—declaring the insane exempt from responsibility and accountability.

The fear of God and hell, along with legal consequences for doing evil has evaporated and has been replaced by the insanity immunity legal clause—meaning: In criminal trials, the insanity defense is where the defendant claims they are not responsible for their actions due to mental health problems.

Those heading towards becoming criminally insane or falling into evil mental illness know they are immune to the same punishment deserved by the ordinary criminal. In their rage, rebellion, and narcissistic entitlement mentality they disregard any mental illness stigma.

This nation has created the insanity immunity option for those who decide to go over to the dark side. Yes, there are exceptions and yes, there are reasons that can be traced down in their history—abuse, parental neglect and hypocrisy, dabbling and playing with evil and eventually inviting hell to live within. Most pretend away or lie to cover the facts that drove them into darkness and caused them to reap mental illness and demon possession. Nevertheless, accountably and the real threat of long term or permanent restraint help some to choose light instead of darkness.

Of course, many are mentally slow or retarded, suffering from various physiological diseases and illnesses that create symptoms of mental illness. However, we are examining the characteristics that Scripture describes as evil people who have gone to the dark side and suffer mental illness as a result.

The New Testament writers Peter, Paul and Jude list the following characteristics and attributes of evil people referred to as accursed children and waterless springs (crazy evil):

- They indulge in the lust of defiling passions.
- They despise authority.
- They act like irrational animals—creatures of instinct.
- They revile matters of which they are ignorant.
- They suffer wrong for wrongdoing (lead a troubled life).
- They party in the daytime and are unafraid and selfish (narcissistic).
- These are adulterous, greedy, and insatiable for sin.
- These forsake right living and entice others into sinning.
- They are enslaved to corruption.
- They defile their own flesh, reject authority, and walk in the way of Cain (murder).
- They look after themselves exclusively and are often loudmouthed, obnoxious, and detestable.
- They use flattery to gain advantage in relationships.
- Many are given over to a base mind (insanity).
- They are perverted and full of sin and eventually become self-condemned (lost in the futility of their minds).
- They refuse to acknowledge or fear God and thus reap the consequences by being given over to a base mind and improper conduct.

In summary, the Apostle Paul describes their condition as follows: *"Since they did not see fit to acknowledge God, God gave them up to a <u>debased mind</u> to do what ought not to be done. They were filled with all manner of unrighteousness, evil, covetousness, malice. They are full of envy, <u>murder, strife, deceit, maliciousness</u>. They are gossips, slanderers, haters of God, insolent, haughty, boastful, <u>inventors of evil</u>, disobedient to parents, foolish, faithless, <u>heartless, ruthless</u>. Though they know God's decree that those who practice such things deserve to die, they not only do them but give approval to those who practice them"* (Romans 1:28-32).

Such people develop an evil heart that Satan and the demons can live within, possess and incite to do great evil and harm to others.

The following are some basic indicators to take note of concerning the demon driven mentally ill evil, who are walking time bombs:

- Marked personality changes
- Inability to cope with problems and daily activities.
- Strange ideas or delusions
- Excessive anxiety

- Prolonged feelings of sadness
- Marked changes in eating or sleeping patterns
- Thinking or talking about suicide
- Extreme highs or lows
- Abuse of alcohol or drugs
- Excessive anger and hostility—violent behavior and outbursts of rage
- Irrational fears and lack of reason
- Obsessions, obnoxious behavior, lack of empathy, and jealousy
- Self-pity and lack of ambition in doing hard work
- Compulsive behavior coupled with grandiose dreams or plans

Many in ministry try to cast out the demons from those suffering from a depraved mind, who are the so-called mentally ill. They think these people are demon possessed and if they cast out the demons, they would return to being normal. Unfortunately, few know the Word of God sufficiently or understand how Satan works through an evil human heart.

In addition, many Christians choose to be medicated rather than dealing with embedded defilements, wounds and impurities of heart. Most that came to us for counseling who were on medication chose to maintain the status quo, and stay on "meds" rather than do the painful hard work of becoming cleansed and healed mentally and emotionally.

One Christian woman whom our ministry helped told of a childhood spiritual wound she received from her father. As a young child, she witnessed her father beat to death their family pet dog with a baseball bat. He flew into a rage because the dog supposedly got too rough with her.

That and other vague memories came out in counseling. When we met her, she had been under the care of a local psychiatrist for over ten years. Her doctor had her on high doses of lithium. She had been involved in abusive relationships and had been dependent on alcohol and drugs from the time she was in college.

In the book of James, there are specific guidelines for recovering from such wounds to the spirit and dividedness of soul. We worked with her, but could only get so far. The painful truth about past bitterness and unresolved trauma was too hard for her to take in her drugged condition. After ten years of prescribed chemicals, she had become so passive and spiritually dead that she chose to stay medicated and leave her inner bitterness, jealousy, rage, fear and hatred alone. In her divided and drugged condition, she was content to stumble through life, pleading for prayer from others to help her succeed in just holding down a job.

Our training in discerning the severely mentally ill who were evil in nature was not easy. We became involved in counseling believers who struggled with emotional instability by holding a Bible study at a nearby recovery halfway house. Ten to fifteen people would attend our weekly meeting at the dorm, but over an eighteen month period only five showed interest and began to come to Sunday fellowship and counseling. Three of the five decided to leave things as they were and stay on SSI and live in the halfway house dorm, stumbling through life in a semi-zombie state of mind with dead emotions.

Of the two that stuck it out, only one made progress. This person is still working towards wholeness. This sister is off SSI and no longer on medication. It has not been easy for her and we have had to hold her accountable in love and firmness many times, yet she continues to move forward with Christ, as she successfully stays gainfully employed and contributing to the ministry work.

When we first met her at the halfway house, she would often sit in her room, bang her head against the wall, and pull out her hair. Her progress is directly related to her faith, courage, and hard work in piecing together memories of abuse and parental neglect and abandonment.

The other who desired to work things out became a prime lesson for our training, which we share with those in ministry to the homeless or to those falling through the cracks of America's failing mental health system. The following case describes briefly the nightmarish ordeal we as a ministry team endured in learning many valuable lessons.

Ministry Case: *The irrational ninja*

"John" received our help on and off for about three years. He left the halfway house, removed himself from SSI, and quit his medication when he received an inheritance after his father passed away. He moved in with his brother after they purchased their own home together. During this time he legally amassed a sizable firearms collection.

About two years later, he desired to relocate to Colorado to become more involved with the ministry and receive counseling and mentoring to overcome lingering issues. We had already established our own recovery house in Colorado where he would be staying when he moved to Colorado. Our ministry provided two live-in mentors who supervised his activities and we began a counseling schedule along with helping him find gainful employment. However, we soon discovered that he preferred spending time in his room playing on his computer and purchasing special TV gimmicks than finding gainful employment.

Our mentoring incorporated small job activities assigned to him, which proved to be futile in his case. He developed excuses for not finishing his assigned jobs and he continued spending his inheritance on strange projects.

His supervising mentors began to hold him accountable to various assigned chores in the house. We noticed more dramatic mood swings when applying pressure to hold him accountable to perform any kind of chore. Then he began lying and doing malicious and seemingly harmless pranks, such as shutting off the hot water to the upstairs rooms while other residents were showering.

Then other residents and our live-in mentors began to suspect him of rummaging through their personal effects. When confronted he became belligerent. In one incident, he obtained a gas mask, snuck a propane tank down into his room, and opened up the valve to test his new gadget. Fortunately, propane has a distinct odor and the team immediately found the source and dealt with his foolishness. He pleaded ignorance and pledged never to play around with such things again.

He was in his late twenties and had a history of just floating along while he was in the mental health system. He was classified as bi-polar and had been on various medications for his mood swings and bouts of mild depression. In counseling, he revealed that other boys had molested him in childhood and he began to remember vaguely being abused by his father.

His desires to work on his issues and continue to follow Christ were mostly positive which encouraged us to continue to work with him. However, we began to recognize that he was not sincere and began to consider asking him to move out on his own or to re-enter the community mental health system for evaluation. We observed more strange behavior that finally resulted in his slipping completely over to the dark side.

On one typical morning, he came up from his room dressed as if he was going out for a walk. It was beginning to get cold, especially at night and through the mornings as fall was quickly turning to winter in Colorado. He was observed wearing a ski mask and camouflage clothing when he came up the stairs to the kitchen area.

Our house supervisor saw him approach the kitchen counter behind her as she was eating her breakfast at the kitchen table. She concluded that he was going to prepare something to eat before he went outside for his walk. After the incident, she recalled that he acted more strangely than normal walking around closing curtains.

Then suddenly she felt a terrific shock to the back of her neck. She stood up screaming and turned to face her attacker. Her screams stunned him and he froze. Fortunately, he had misjudged his attack and missed connecting with a solid zap to the back of her neck with a Taser stun gun. (He had this stun gun by permission for self-protection during walks; his gun collection was secure in locked storage unit accessible only with a supervisor.)

He fled back down stairs to his room as our house supervisor called 911. When I arrived, the police and fire department were on the scene, tending to both. Our house supervisor was just shaken up. We explained our relationship with John and we insisted that he be taken in for observation and evaluation. We chose not to press charges; however, we did hope that the community mental health authorities would require some kind of confinement to protect the community.

We removed all of his possessions, put them in secure storage with his firearms collection, and notified the police of all his weapons. The only questionably illegal weapons were his set of ninja throwing stars, which the police confiscated. As we analyzed the whole episode, the ski mask and clothing that he wore on the morning of the attack, along with his strange stalking/stealth behavior, we realized—his behavior resembled the popularized martial art assassins,—the Japanese Ninjas. (Martial arts and ninja fighting were his favorite type of movies.)

John was released after a three-day stint for observation and I met him at the police station about two days later to give him the keys to the storage unit. He said nothing, but held a guilty, sheepish expression while I explained to him where his possessions were and that he could not return to the recovery house. He knew what he done was wrong, yet there was no remorse or apology.

When we were packing his possessions, we discovered that he had made audio recordings where he stated that the authorities were spying on him and that the FBI had a high-powered scanner capable of reading his mind. In addition, he thought his food was poisoned and decided to take a sample of his stool. He put the sample in a clear plastic bag and, positioned the bag under a heat lamp to see if any growth would appear—looking for evidence of being poisoned. Cleaning up his hidden projects was shocking and repulsive. He had successfully hidden these deeper paranoid symptoms as he presented an outwardly nice but wounded persona.

About ten days after the Taser episode John came knocking on the door demanding to come back and live in the home. (In his mind, it was still his house in spite of being informed otherwise). One of the residents spoke to him without unlocking the door and told him clearly he was not to be allowed back, and if he did not leave she would call 911.

He continued to make phone calls to us and hang up, sometimes ten times in a row. Finally, we never heard from again; however, we did see him a few months later about five miles from the recovery house. He was on the side of the road, sitting on grass and fumbling with a floor mat to his pickup truck. As I recall, when we saw John sitting in the grass, the scene reminded us of how king Nebuchadnezzar might have appeared when he was driven out of office and mentally stricken by the Lord, living with the beasts of the field and eating grass like an ox. (See Daniel 4:32.)

The community mental health system released him into the community where various soup kitchens, rescue missions and others living on the streets helped him get by. This lifestyle was the consequences of his choices and his rejecting accountability to change. John's unwillingness to repent and confess his sinfulness was directly related to having pleasure in unrighteousness. His rejection of conscience and lack of empathy towards others that he caused to suffer were strong indicators that he was evil. In extreme selfishness and self-pity, he gave up self-respect and cowardly avoided true self-disclosure. In the end, he was completely given over to a debased mind and an evil heart. Ω

This case and others that were similar proved to be valuable lessons for us in our discernment training. Our zeal to help wounded Christians was soon tempered by wisdom, caution, and resolve to hold each accountable. Feeling sorry for the emotionally broken who are falling through the cracks of a broken mental health system evaporated along with our naiveté.

As we recovered from our own childhood abuses (because we wanted wholeness and were willing to do the work), we learned that many preferred the self-pity trap. Most preferred to stay medicated, yet did not want to be held accountable to their sinful reactions to their own abuses and had pleasure in evil and chose to stay angry with God. When they heard our testimony, they wanted us to help them become free—magically.

We learned to work where God is working and learned to avoid helping evil people recover from the consequences of their wickedness. We learned the importance of detecting true repentance, learning to take note of any demonstration or fruit of repentance. Many become full of self-pity and shallow remorse for being held accountable—while the good-hearted, though messed up and wounded, will demonstrate godly grief over their self-centered sinfulness. *"For godly grief produces a repentance that leads to salvation without regret, whereas worldly grief produces death"* (2 Corinthians 7:10).

Further, we learned how to be very careful while working with a wounded Christian who may be evil in the core and not yet fully demonstrating the fruit thereof. This is vital, because there is a flood of hurting people coming into the church. Those Christian workers and pastors who have been sheltered from these people, who lack knowledge and training in dealing with the wounded and hurting will be poorly equipped to discern between the wounded and the crazy evil or to know how to help the sincere recover and how to avoid the game players and waterless springs who easily cause harm.

Some who are on their way to becoming crazy evil people might become spared judgment and become born again and turn to Christ, if they hear the truth and are held accountable in firmness and compassion—and not pitied for their instability.

Discernment concerning the various evil people in our culture who come to God's people for help will soon be a top priority for all saints learning to walk in ministry as God has ordained.

Understanding the Insanity Immunity Mentality

Like secular psychology and far too many ministries, we fell into the *insanity immunity mentality*—trapped by false pity into helping people who suffer from a debased mind because of the evil they had become and the evil they practiced. What complicates the issue in helping the crazy evil is their belief of being mentally ill and thus immune and exempt to any form of discipline or accountability.

John's background, from what we could assess and glean from his infrequent truthfulness, was that of acting out wickedness in homosexual acts as an adult. John alluded to having a homosexual relationship during his early twenties with a neighbor who was in law enforcement. He only mentioned it once or twice but never elaborated, and became evasive when asked to explain what had happened or how the sinful lifestyle began or ended.

Somewhere during his abuse by his father, John threw away his faith, crossed over to the dark side, and acted out his own brand of evil. Then, given over to a base mind he suffered delusions, paranoia, sleep disturbances, compulsions, and strange voices. In this state, like so many, he wanted freedom from the consequences of an evil heart and a base mind.

A prime example of how people who turn to evil are given up to a base mind and tormenting demons is the biblical story of King Saul. The Lord turned Saul over to an evil spirit when he became disobedient, and he then became jealous and tried to murder David. *"Now the Spirit of the Lord departed from Saul, and an evil spirit from the Lord tormented him"* (1 Samuel 16:14).

Many come to church for help, but do not truly come back to God in truthfulness and true repentance. Part of the reason for lack of true repentance and sincere effort to change is the stigma society has placed on the so-called mentally ill—insanity is exempt from accountability.

On the other hand, there are many who suffer as such and repent and seek help. These do not want to be labeled insane, and fortunately, the science of psychology has finally determined that there are cases of symptomatic neurosis that are not mental illness, but rather mental and emotional disorders.

These suffer wounds to the spirit, have double-minded symptoms, and are often plagued by the demonic. Satan is after them, trying to push them over completely to the dark side—to give up on God, reject their conscience and become evil—and many do become crazy evil.

For those who have not gone to the dark side, they still desire to embrace truth; however, most receive lies and half-truths concerning their condition, making help from others and the comfort and love of God seem hopeless and too distant.

For those who become evil, truth becomes hated and avoided, leaving God no alternative: *"Therefore God sends them a strong delusion, so that they may believe what is false, in order that all may be condemned who did not believe the truth but had pleasure in unrighteousness"* (2 Thessalonians 2:11-12).

To be effective in ministering to the wounded, every sincere pastor and Christian worker must increase their ability to discern—to learn to work where God is working and to avoid the accursed children who come for relief from being abandoned by God.[5]

Unfortunately, most who are dangerously mentally ill primarily suffer from schizophrenia and internally wage war against God. For a myriad of reasons these people have been wounded, rejected and lied to or have suffered some form of abuse, and through a process that formulates internal unbelief or misbeliefs (with Satan's help) result in blaming God and/or others for having to endure a living hell. They reject conscience and decide to throw in the towel concerning right and wrong, self-respect, and empathy for others. Extreme fear and self-pity sets in due to wrong beliefs as well.

In their extreme selfishness, they cross over into darkness internally, lying to themselves as Lucifer did when he rebelled and fell from grace. In anger and rage toward God, they take revenge out on others or upon themselves for living a tormented life. They become evil on the inside and on the outside lie to themselves and to others concerning their true beliefs and feelings.

In denial, they try to live in society; however, eventually for many the inner evil (with all the demons residing) emerges and clashes with the outer person, shattering the pretense. Progressively, symptomatic insanity appears in differing types in differing degrees and the charade breaks down as acute symptoms appear in the form of mental illness.

Breakdown occurs when converging inner evils clash with the outer self, resulting in the loss of mental equilibrium and rational thought dissipates, overtaken by base thinking and emotional rage.

On the other end of the spectrum, the stable evil, who succumb to the devil's complete transformation are able to live the lie successfully and become completely evil in nature.

---

[5] In chapter seven we elaborate in some detail concerning true deliverance and accountability to cleansing, purification and biblical character transformation—leading to healing, restoration, holiness and the fullness of Christ. This topic deserves its own publication, so look for a forthcoming book dealing with biblical principles of healing and recovery from a wounded spirit and damaged emotions.

Wounds, Defilements, and Double-Mindedness

The current lack of sound doctrine has forced Christians who suffer from wounds to the spirit and damaged emotions to fend for themselves or fall prey to secular psychology. Christians often carry all manner of defilements in their personal spirit and impurities in their heart, and have differing degrees of double-mindedness and fragmentation from a crushed spirit.

Few ministries know how to minister or counsel the struggling believer who sincerely loves Christ. These wounded Christians are continually searching for true peace and joy in Christ, but often believe peace in the Lord is an elusive pot of gold at the rainbow's end. They are ever pursuing the next magic formula presented by wayward teachers who constantly entice the wounded to pursue a false gospel nirvana (a complete and euphoric sense of happiness).

The book of James describes the symptoms of the double-minded Christian. The Greek word translated as "double-minded" is *dipsuchos* and properly translated as "twice a soul" or "two souled," meaning a divided heart, mind, and spirit. Young's Literal Translation translates this very important word (and condition) in this way:

"Be subject, then, to God; stand up against the devil, and he will flee from you; draw nigh to God, and He will draw nigh to you; cleanse hands, ye sinners! And purify your hearts, ye <u>two-souled</u>!" (James 4:7-8).

Unstable Christians flounder in their walk with Christ because they suffer from a two-souled *dipsuchos* condition: carrying impurities within the heart and defilements and wounds in the spirit, and suffering from a divided mind. In some cases they also suffer from a divided heart or a *double heart* (see Psalm 12:2).

Secular psychology calls a double-minded or a two-souled condition DID (dissociative identity disorder), formerly labeled MPD (multiple personality disorder). For a double-hearted condition, *schizophrenia* is the psychological term used and it has a wide spectrum of symptoms and related terms.

Christians who are two souled developed this condition as a coping or survival mechanism from trauma, primarily during childhood abuses. The destructive evils they encountered along with unresolved pain caused wounds to their spirit and damaged their emotions—marring and splitting their inner character and creating multiple personalities. For most new Christians, this condition is *not* recognized as the root problem to their instability.

Most are convinced that the initial born-again experience is a cure-all, but in reality it is just the *beginning* of salvation. Scripture teaches that we must embrace the process of sanctification that brings full cleansing, healing and transformation in Christ; it is a process of growing up into salvation and obtaining the grace of God and eternal security.

Until this occurs, Christians who suffer from wounds to their spirit and walk in a two-souled condition are vulnerable to charlatans and often become victims of wolves in sheep's clothing. In the worst cases, the false often cause those wounded and weak in faith to fall away from Christ, possibly never returning, risking their eternal salvation. Many who are divided succumb to the dark side, yet stay active in fellowship—looking good on the outside but potentially treacherous if they do not get their own way.

Most struggling and wounded Christians learn to pretend that evil does not exist or that evil will never come close to them—and that they have a new nature that is complete. They are to ignore issues from the past. If you are born again, you automatically have eternal security with a complete bill of health simply by believing in Christ.

Yes, we are to believe completely in our hearts all that Christ taught and act on those beliefs in obedience. James writes, *"You believe that God is one; you do well. Even the demons believe—and shudder! Do you want to be shown, you foolish person, that faith apart from works is useless"* (James 2:19-20). Our faith in Christ must demonstrate genuineness by our walking in obedience and observing all that Christ taught and commanded.

False doctrine directs Christians away from obedience to Christ and redirects them to follow false leaders. Confusion, lack of conviction, hesitation in doing what is right, and even cowering back from being obedient are symptoms of false doctrine and an impure condition; thus many believers are deceived and actually end up believing in Christ only partially.

Just as the Apostle Paul warned, many will follow myths (—false doctrines)—and fall prey to the devil's schemes. They will be as children, *"tossed to and fro by the waves and carried about by every wind of doctrine, by human cunning, by craftiness in deceitful schemes"* (Ephesians 4:14).

False leaders and false brethren have infiltrated the body of Christ, making most fellowships a harbor for the last-days insurgency of satanic implants; Jesus spoke of these in the parable of the weeds:

"And his disciples came to him, saying, 'Explain to us the parable of the weeds of the field.' He answered, 'He who sows the good seed is the Son of Man; the field is the world, and the good seed means the sons of the kingdom; the weeds are the sons of the evil one, and the enemy who sowed them is the devil; the harvest is the close of the age, and the reapers are angels. Just as the weeds are gathered and burned with fire, so will it be at the close of the age'" (Matthew 13:36-40).

True discernment is vital in dealing with the false, and the Apostle Paul stresses the following about detecting such: *"I appeal to you, brothers, to watch out for those who cause divisions and create obstacles contrary to the doctrine that you have been taught; <u>avoid them</u>. For such persons do not serve our Lord Christ, but their own appetites, and <u>by smooth talk and flattery they deceive the hearts of the naive.</u> For your obedience is known to all, so that I rejoice over you, but I want you to be <u>wise as to what is good and innocent as to what is evil</u>. The God of peace will soon crush Satan under your feet. The grace of our Lord Jesus Christ be with you"* (Romans 16:17-20).

Again, I must stress—wounded and defiled Christians are extremely vulnerable to the game playing false brothers and sisters who are Christian in name only. Peter described them as *"blots and blemishes, reveling in their deceptions, while they feast with you. They have eyes full of adultery, insatiable for sin. They entice unsteady souls. They have hearts trained in greed. Accursed children!"* (2 Peter 2:13-14).

Peter continues to describe the false brethren as waterless springs who *"entice by sensual passions of the flesh those who are barely escaping from those who live in error"* (2 Peter 2:18), and by promising freedom to Christians who are unsteady—those who have never been cleansed and transformed as believers.

Often we learn true discernment through conflict with those who claim to be Christian but are not. Eventually the discerning saint will learn how important it is to detect and avoid such. Look again at the Apostle Paul's admonishment: *"Avoid them. For such persons do not serve our Lord Christ, but their own appetites, and by smooth talk and flattery they deceive the hearts of the naïve"* (Romans 16:17-18).

You cannot avoid these troublemakers if your powers of discernment are not up to par because of a two-souled condition—many still suffer from past-unhealed trauma and defilements.

There are also Christians who are sincere and have not suffered wounds to the spirit but who are naïve because of lack of training and they fall prey to the flatteries of false Christians. Moving from the milk of the Word to the deeper things of God in the meat of the Word will increase our powers of discernment and spare us great trouble and heartache.

The last-days evils are not going to go away by our pretending; it is time to define evil and learn to discern evil.

We must become protected in Christ by embracing all that he taught, walking in true holiness and learning what is pleasing to God—and then doing it.

Chapter Three

False Leaders and the Gates of Hell

Why are most Christians unmindful or dismissive concerning the increasing darkness engulfing America and the world? What has happened to God's people across this nation? Where is the sense of desperation and anguish in prayer over their own sins, the condition of their loved ones and the sins of this nation? Where has the fear of God gone? We all should have the deep realization of foreboding judgment.

The Apostle Paul gives some insight as to why and how most Christians are in the dark during these last days. False leaders who are of corrupt mind and counterfeit faith, who oppose the truth, have now become very popular (see 2 Timothy 3:1-9).

These self-deceived leaders are able to sway others to follow them instead of following Christ. Most Christians today have become *"lovers of pleasure rather than lovers of God, having the appearance of godliness, but denying its power"* (2 Timothy 3:4-5). They look to leadership to magically solve their problems and make life on earth easy.

The body of Christ is swollen with new converts and masses of spiritual seekers who have come to Christ based on false promises by these false leaders. Of the sincere leaders, far too many are weak in dealing with the gritty issues associated with false doctrine and prefer to stay ignorant of the deeper and harder teachings of Christ. Thus, they leave most sincere Christians lacking sound doctrine to help them learn how to detect and confront the false, both in the pulpit and those who they sit next to in the pew.

Very few sincere and devoted leaders today dare take on the enormous power of the false. Thousands upon thousands of confused and fearful shepherds throughout the body of Christ dare not decry and point out the false—the potential repercussions and backlash would cost dearly, so keeping mum and compliance become the confused, struggling or weak shepherd's shelter. This condition of conformity by so many shepherds in the pulpits across America is similar to the passivity of the clergy across Europe during the 1920s and 30s.

Even good shepherds are easily mesmerized and deceived by the popular national super-leader's charisma, the mega-church-growth phenomenon and the charismatic movement craze—paralyzing pastors and elders to speak out in protest and warn.

There are some strong leaders and shepherds hanging in there, refusing, if you will, to bow down to Baal. However, true ministers of the Gospel are often demonized, marginalized, ignored, and blacklisted.

Smooth Talkers Who Flatter to Deceive

Christians learn to believe the best of people, to forgive and to walk the extra mile with those who are disagreeable, who are contentious or contrary and even abusive. We learn to turn the other cheek and not resist those who spitefully use and abuse.

However, Jesus also taught Christians to confront and avoid those who call themselves Christians yet practice abuse, sin against the brethren, and lack any remorse or change of heart. Very few understand that forgiveness does not relieve one of the responsibilities of holding an abusive, game-playing, selfish, or jealous Christian accountable. The following passage in Titus instructs us how to deal with someone that continues sinful behavior by ignoring or shunning them: *"As for a person who stirs up division, after warning him once and then twice, have nothing more to do with him, knowing that such a person is warped and sinful; he is self-condemned"* (Titus 3:10-11).

Many a heartache and much trouble can be avoided if sound doctrine is taught concerning mischief makers who sneak into fellowships and congregations throughout the body of Christ. Jude describes these false Christians as *"grumblers, malcontents, following their own sinful desires; they are loud-mouthed boasters, showing favoritism to gain advantage. But you must remember, beloved, the predictions of the apostles of our Lord Jesus Christ. They said to you, 'In the last time there will be scoffers, following their own ungodly passions.'* <u>*It is these who cause divisions, worldly people, devoid of the Spirit*</u>*"* (Jude 16-19).

Over the last forty years, huge influxes of worldly people devoid of the Spirit have infiltrated the body of Christ and many have climbed their way into leadership. Many embarrassing revelations and scandals highlight this problem; unfortunately, these exposés are the tip of the iceberg concerning the number of wolves misleading God's people today.

Jesus warned time after time about wolves and false prophets, and the writers of the New Testament explain clearly how these mischief-makers act and what motivates them.

The author of Jude also gives us specific information about these false Christians. If we are careful to study the harder Scriptures like the following passage, we will be able to expand our powers of discernment:

"For <u>certain people have crept in unnoticed</u> who long ago were designated for this condemnation, ungodly people, who <u>pervert the grace of our God into sensuality</u> and deny our only Master and Lord, Jesus Christ… Yet in like manner these people also, relying on their dreams, defile the flesh, reject authority, and blaspheme the glorious ones… But these people blaspheme all that they do not understand, and they are destroyed by all that they, like unreasoning animals, understand instinctively. Woe to them! For they walked in the way of Cain and abandoned themselves for the sake of gain to Balaam's error and perished in Korah's rebellion. These are blemishes on your love feasts, as they feast with you without fear, looking after themselves; waterless clouds, swept along by winds; fruitless trees in late autumn, twice dead, uprooted; wild waves of the sea, casting up the foam of their own shame; wandering stars, for whom the gloom of utter darkness has been reserved forever" (Jude 4-13).

Now, as the end of this age wraps up, Satan has and will continue to infiltrate the body of Christ with imposters, false leaders, troublemakers, and loud-mouthed boasters who are void of the Spirit and have made shipwreck their faith, yet parade as Christians.

Again, Jesus predicted this when he said that the devil would sow weeds among the wheat at the end of this age (see Matthew 13:24-43).

In review, we must be willing to allow the Lord to train us that we may clearly see the implants of Satan and learn how to distinguish good from evil. Jesus said we would know them by their fruits.

Unfortunately, few learn to detect the fruit of bad character until it is too late and the damage has been done.

Ministries Capitalizing on Carnal Spiritualism
Dreams, Visions and Prophesy from one's own Heart and Spirit

Most of the Pentecostal and charismatic denominations, movements, and elite ministries work from a foundation of competition. Carnal spiritualism has consumed this arm of the body of Christ where false manifestations supplant the true gifts of the Holy Spirit in a reckless drive to gain popularity and more followers. They have learned to pronounce from their own spirit dreams and visions and prophesy only to mesmerize and captivate God's people who are ignorant of God's Word and lack discernment.

They do not instruct God's people on how to deal with their issues, but try to outdo one another in interpreting the Word of God, trying to make themselves indispensable and standout from the other ministries. The anointing each seeks is in competition with one another and must come in larger doses with more intensity to outdo the other. The challenge is to take the recipient to a higher more exotic altered state of reality—I liken these experiences to doses of spiritual Prozac that numb the senses and any mental or emotional anguish.

Often they use another's wayward interpretation of Scripture or take insight from another ministry and make for themselves a special anointing that they can become identified with, making themselves distinct, having their own anointed brand. They market themselves as if they were automobile manufactures attempting to gain a larger market share or a special market niche.

Repeatedly, the prophets of Israel fell into this same devilish trap. Jeremiah brought the following indictment to the prophets of his day: *"Is not my word like fire, declares the Lord, and like a hammer that breaks the rock in pieces? Therefore, behold, I am against the prophets, declares the Lord, who steal my words from one another. Behold, I am against the prophets, declares the Lord, who use their tongues and declare, 'declares the Lord.' Behold, I am against those who prophesy lying dreams, declares the Lord, and who tell them and lead my people astray by their lies and their recklessness, when I did not send them or charge them. So they do not profit this people at all, declares the Lord"* (Jeremiah 23:29-32).

In Ezekiel's day the Lord declares that the prophets also refused to guide God's people wisely, but rather foolishly, they followed their own spirits and pronounced prophecies out of their own hearts. The Lord declared them jackals among the people of Israel, expecting God to fulfill their words, though the Lord did not send them. These "servants of God" saw false visions and lying divinations, just as it is today, many ministries and so-called apostles and prophets in this dark hour see false visions and prophesy lies, empowered by the counterfeiting spirits roaming throughout these carnal ministries and fellowships. (See Ezekiel 13:1-7).

The dangerous aspect of the counterfeit prophetic is that a spirit of divination is in operation and counterfeits the works of the Holy Spirit's gift of prophecy. Good counterfeiting, whether a painting, currency, or a spiritual gift looks almost identical to the real. A good counterfeit prophetic work will contain information about the recipient that demons know. Thus, the counterfeit prophecy will seemingly bring forth a secret of the heart that supposedly God would only know.

However, the application of biblical principles that confronts the tainted issue(s) of the heart is avoided. This makes the recipient of the false prophesy, false vision or false interpretation of a dream become deceived and enslaved even more. They believe and follow a course of action that is contrary to God's will and end up missing the truth that they desperately need to hear and understand.

Peter prophesied specifically concerning Ananias and Sapphira about their plot to assert themselves as special believers, and they fell dead instantly because they lied to the Holy Spirit. In another account, again Peter perceived that Simon the magician was in the gall of bitterness and the bonds of iniquity as a new believer in Christ. Simon approached Peter and offered to buy the power of God. (Acts 5:1-16 and Acts 8:9-23).

Dare any of these so-called prophets tell a troubled believer what they need to hear—what God truly sees in their secret heart? Prophesy and interpretation mixed with the Word of God out of context will not address the real issue, rather it puts the recipient at ease. That is why God calls these counterfeit activities reckless.

Ministry Case: *Spirit of divination*

Case in point: John Paul Jackson and Streams Ministries International.

Some time ago, I listened in on a Christian talk radio show where John Paul Jackson of Streams Ministries International was a guest. They had Christians call in for dream interpretation and prophetic pronouncements.

A woman called and described a dream she recently had where she was flying in the air trying to get the attention of certain family members. She described how in the dream she tried to counsel them or tell them what they should be doing but she was having no effect.

Jackson gave a very upbeat interpretation, informing the caller that she had a prophetic call to speak into the lives of others and that though few so far have received her gifting, in the near future God would increase the power of her gifting and many would receive her counsel and help.

When I heard his interpretation, my heart sank. Though I had already suspected Jackson's ministry was empowered by a counterfeiting spirit of divination, the seriousness of this misinterpretation for this caller would have a potentially negative and even destructive outcome, unless God intervened.

The truth about this Christian woman from my years of counseling was that her call to help others turned into an obsession and a care taking influence filled with meddling and a busy body approach in helping others.

The flying through the air aspect of her dream was God warning this woman that she had strayed into the practice of Christian sorcery. (Flying-through-the-air dreams most often are warnings from the Lord that one's spirit is being used to go out of body to carnally-spiritually influence others and is one's of the foundational practices of Christian sorcery.) Somehow, the spirit of sorcery had gained a stronghold within her spiritual life and now was able to use her personal spirit to influence others by implanting thoughts and spiritually manipulating circumstances into the lives she was obsessing over. Ω

Many Christians fall into Christian sorcery, praying wrongly and trying to do the work of the Holy Spirit. The root motivation is insecurity and the need to draw attention to self. A powerful example found in Scripture is the account of the slave women who had a spirit of divination empowering her to accurately predict the future and pronounce secrets that the spirit of divination knew about others that no one else knew. Her spiritual (demonic) gift made her owners financial gain.

When Paul and Silas encountered this slave woman, she followed them and repeatedly cried out, *"These men are servants of the Most High God, who proclaim to you the way of salvation."* She kept up this annoyance for many days until Paul commanded the spirit of divination to leave her, which it did within the hour. The owners became incensed at the loss of their fortune-making trade (using the spiritually gifted slave girl), so the owners orchestrated the arrest of Paul and Silas. (For the complete account read Acts 16:16-40.)

Ask yourself why this slave woman became obsessed with Paul and Silas, and why she incessantly pronounced to everyone who they were. The spirit of divination had an agenda and used the slave girl's need to draw attention to herself, elevating herself by proclaiming that Paul and Silas were servants of the most high—flattering Paul and Silas in an attempt to gain recognition from these two servants of Christ.

Only the demonic knew who these men were. There are many aspects of this account to consider, but the most insidious aspect is that this spirit of divination was conveying flattery. Flattery is what characterizes ministries like Jackson's and so many others working with a counterfeit spirit (which is really a spirit of divination in operation).

That is the tactic of the counterfeit gifting: using flattery to elevate a person in ministry who is empowered by a spirit of divination—thought to be the gift of prophecy or word of knowledge—all to gain credence, recognition, popularity and relationship advantage.

The Devil and the Gates of Hell

Jesus said, *"And I tell you, you are Peter, and on this rock I will build my church, and the gates of hell shall not prevail against it"* (Matthew 16:18). This he said when Peter had heard from God the Father that Jesus was the Christ, the Son of the living God.

Many misunderstand what Christ meant when he referred to Peter's revelation, and this is especially evident in the false doctrine within Catholicism insisting that the pope is a mystical-spiritual descendant of Peter and that the pope (and the Catholic church) is mysteriously that rock Christ said he would build his church upon.

To the contrary, the rock that Christ refers to is the *principle of personal revelation* of who Christ is, and that revelation comes only from God at the right time for those who have a good heart and faith. Jesus explains this principle further, *"No one can come to me unless the Father who sent me draws him; and I will raise him up at the last day. It is written in the prophets, 'And they shall all be taught by God.' Everyone who has heard and learned from the Father comes to me"* (John 6:44, 45).

This principle eliminates any human go between, since Christ is our high priest by which we gain access into the presence of God. *"For there is one God, and there is one mediator between God and men, the man Christ Jesus"* (1 Timothy 2:5). Now everyone who has true faith can develop a direct relationship with God, if one responds to the call of God. If one does not seek the Lord directly once God calls, there is no excuse for not growing up into salvation and into the fullness of Christ. We cannot blame the pope, our priest, our pastor, our favorite teacher, our spouse or our favorite Christian author if we do not arrive at a personal relationship with God and learn to be led by the true Holy Spirit.

The other important principle to comprehend concerning Christ building his church is the *gates of hell*. What did Christ mean when he said, *"And the gates of hell shall not prevail against it?"*

The gates of hell are people: Judas was a gate for hell's agenda; the high priest and the Pharisees were also human gates of hell. Elymas the magician was a gate of hell opposing Paul as he tried to share the Gospel with the proconsul. Paul referred to Elymas thus: *"You son of the devil, you enemy of all righteousness, full of all deceit and villainy"* (Acts 13:10).

Historically, Satan has been most successful in opposing God's people through false leaders and false brethren, corrupt priests, and false prophets. These human gates channel hell's agenda against God's people (the church).

The principle of coming to God in faith directly through Christ when the Holy Spirit reveals who Christ is—this what Christ meant when he said, *"on this rock I will build my church"* not on the person of Peter or any supposed descendants of Peter. We can have a direct relationship with God the Father, facilitated by Christ the Son of God who is our only intermediary.

No longer are we to seek out a priest, prophet, special apostle or pope to address and submit unto as an oracle for God. These are often used by the devil to mislead God's people. God's people become lazy and allow someone else to hear from the Lord for them.

With Christ as head of each of us, as each learns to be led by the Holy Spirit, unscrupulous leaders will have a hard time posing as intermediaries and exclusive oracles for God! *"For all who are led by the Spirit of God are sons of God"* (Romans 8:14).

More specifically, Christ taught that the religious leaders of his day were manipulators who misled God's people: *"The scribes and the Pharisees sit on Moses' seat, so practice and observe whatever they tell you—but not what they do. For they preach, but do not practice. They tie up heavy burdens, hard to bear, and lay them on people's shoulders, but they themselves are not willing to move them with their finger. They do all their deeds to be seen by others. For they make their phylacteries* *broad and their fringes long, and they love the place of honor at feasts and the best seats in the synagogues and greetings in the marketplaces and being called rabbi by others. <u>But you are not to be called rabbi, for you have one teacher, and you are all brothers. And call no man your father on earth, for you have one Father, who is in heaven. Neither be called instructors, for you have one instructor, the Christ. The greatest among you shall be your servant</u>. Whoever exalts himself will be humbled, and whoever humbles himself will be exalted"* (Mathew 23:2-12).

Inherently, God's people tend to follow leaders who do not have God's interests at heart. An aspect of our fallen nature is the tendency to idolize other people, making them responsible for our wellbeing and happiness, and often making them or allowing them to be responsible for our salvation, even putting them in the place of God.

False leaders and evil people appear to be knowledgeable, helpful, and gifted in speech, and often have a charismatic or flamboyant personality. They learn to elevate themselves to places of importance, at least in the eyes of weak and deceived people, and to gain false authority religiously and lord it over others. Many religious and denominational systems become misguided gates of hell to maintain control over the follower of Christ to manage, manipulate, and suppress. Through these religious systems, with the use of false doctrine, the Gospel of Christ becomes tainted, as evil people are allowed to gain positions of leadership.

Evil people who come in the name of God often carry out the devil's bidding. Evil people, as well as carnal and misguided Christians, easily become the gates of hell that come against God's people—Christ's church (the true body of Christ).

The most poignant example and training tool used by Christ was Judas the betrayer. Christ knew from the beginning who would betray him (and the other disciples) for a handful of silver; but Christ did not chase out Judas in the beginning for several reasons.

One reason in particular was to train the disciples what a gate of hell would typically act like (the fruit the person's life) and to drive home the importance of not allowing such to take root amongst the brethren. *"Beware of false prophets, who come to you in sheep's clothing but inwardly are ravenous wolves. You will recognize them by their fruits"* (Matthew 7:15-16).

The other reasons were to fulfill prophecy and expose the powers of darkness working through false leaders. Peter stated, *"Brothers, the Scripture had to be fulfilled, which the Holy Spirit spoke beforehand by the mouth of David concerning Judas, who became a guide to those who arrested Jesus. For he was numbered among us and was allotted his share in this ministry"* (Acts 1:16, 17).

Jesus also explained this about the leaders who arrested him, *"Have you come out as against a robber, with swords and clubs? When I was with you day after day in the temple, you did not lay hands on me. But this is your hour, and the power of darkness"* (Luke 22:52, 53).

We discover in the book of Acts that Peter applied discernment and prophesied the death of two potential gates of hell: a husband-and-wife team trying to gain credence and popularity within the early church.

Ananias and Sapphira tried to lie their way to recognition and gain credibility using proceeds from the sale of some property. The ploy was to say they donated the full amount of the sale when actually they held back some for themselves.

Peter confronted the husband saying, *"Ananias, why has Satan filled your heart to lie to the Holy Spirit and to keep back for yourself part of the proceeds of the land?"* (Acts 5:3). This is a clear example of how a person can become a gate of hell, where Satan fills a person's heart so that he might work through that person and oppose the church of Christ.

In another account in the book of Acts, Peter stopped another potential gate of hell. If it were not for Peter's training, Simon the magician would have become implanted among the new believers in Samaria, as this man actually tried to buy the power of the Holy Spirit from Peter (Acts 8:9-23).

Imagine if Peter had caved to Simon's offer and taken the money, laying hands on Simon to anoint him with the power of the Holy Spirit. Then imagine that Peter and Simon went off to start a ministry together offering the power of God for thirty pieces of silver to any taker.

This may seem to be an extreme conjecture; however, the practice of selling the power and the gifts of God has become a popular approach to raise donations. Many ministries continue to follow in the footsteps of several flamboyant televangelists who became famous during the 80's and 90's. One of the most infamous was Robert Tilton who led the way in what I term *Simon the magician Christian leadership*.

Tilton developed and perfected an infomercial-style televised ministry program to sell his supposed anointed power of God, including various gifts of the Holy Spirit. The foundation for his commercial success was his *Success-N-Life* doctrine that encouraged struggling believers to make vows of financial commitment to his ministry in order to reap vast material blessings from God. Tilton's method of selling the power of God to the naïve and gullible brought in close to $80 million annually until IRS investigation eventually led to shutting down his swindling operation.

Ministry Cases: *Drowned Ducks—False Gift of Faith*

In the early 90's a young women came to our counseling ministry for help. She was distraught over the loss of her pet ducks and why her gift of faith hadn't worked to save them from drowning during a terrible storm. They had wandered out into the middle of large pond. She saw that they were in trouble and began to pray and command them to return to shore and safety. In bold confidence, she began to exercise the gift of faith that she had purchased from Robert Tilton's ministry. She had even received a certificate from Tilton that bestowed upon her the gift of faith for her donation.

Unfortunately, the ducks had perished and now her faith in Christ was devastated. It took some time in counsel to help her understand that she had been deceived. She eventually worked through her own issues of heart to determine why she was so blind to Tilton's sham. More importantly, she learned that her own greed snared her to fall for the popular false doctrine of donating to another ministry to obtain the power of God and to get material blessings in life. Ω

Robert Tilton is still in ministry promoting a variation of his Success-N-Life program and hauling in more than $24 million a year. Millions of Christians fall for false doctrines that promise blessings if they financially support greedy ministries. Peter warned, *"And in their greed they will exploit you with false words"* (2 Peter 2:3).

Today this is a common practice for errant ministries of so-called modern-day apostles and prophets—to offer the gifts and the power of God for varied amounts of money. Many ministries will use similar false teachings to keep donations rolling in. There are many destructive heresies in operation today; the use of seed planting, prosperity through giving (give-to-get-teachings) or such teachings as the Law of Reciprocity proclaimed by Pat Robertson—all devised to encourage financial giving.

Rod Parsley devised a debt-burning gimmick and encouraged struggling believers burdened with financial debt to send in their list of debts with their best seed-faith offering. He then televised a ceremony placing all these lists of debt upon a specially constructed platform he termed the *blazed altar.*

Proclaiming by faith that all these debts were to be resolved by the power of God, the altar was set on fire to symbolically direct miracles to come upon those who participated, to become debt free—miraculously. There was no exhortation on dealing with why or how these Christians were so heavily indebted or sound doctrine presented to facilitate character change to prevent indebtedness to return.

Peter was right-on when he warned of this kind of evil invading Christianity in his epistle, prophesying: *"But false prophets also arose among the people, just as there will be false teachers among you, who will secretly bring in destructive heresies, even denying the Master who bought them, bringing upon themselves swift destruction. And many will follow their sensuality, and because of them the way of truth will be blasphemed. And in their greed they will exploit you with false words"* (2 Peter 2:1-3).

Today the devil has millions of gates of hell that open wide throughout the body of Christ—in pulpits, on national TV and sitting in the pews. Many have impurities of heart that help develop within them an evil hidden agenda that allows Satan to enter their hearts just as he did with Judas Iscariot, Ananias and Sapphira, and Simon the magician.

Few understand the devil's schemes or are able to detect and stand against the gates of hell. Unfortunately, the days ahead will be all the more treacherous as the end of this age closes, for Jesus warned, *"False christs and false prophets will arise and perform great signs and wonders, so as to lead astray, if possible, even the elect"* (Matthew 24:24).

We must start at the top and discern what type of leader we are embracing and whether they are bringing forth all that Jesus taught or if they are leaving out the harder teachings of Christ and adding their own. Are they wolves in sheep's clothing or carnal leaders going along with the popular consensus teachings that tickle the ears of the masses?

Further, we must learn to discern the everyday Christian who attends the local church who really couldn't care less about serving Christ. Paul describes this type of false Christian thus: *"Such persons do not serve our Lord Christ, but their own appetites, and by smooth talk and flattery they deceive the hearts of the naïve"* (Romans 16:17).

False Leaders Demonstrating Great Signs and Wonders

Church-leadership covering, shoo-in salvation, abundant life on earth fixation, giving to get, and harnessing the spiritual powers of the flesh are the main destructive heresies keeping God's people lukewarm and blind to the hour. False leaders use these false teachings to erode the truth of the Gospel, keeping God's people passive.

These destructive teachings come in varied forms, making erroneous promises—all to paint a wonderful life on earth if one follows their made-up pseudo-Christ, attends the right fellowship, or aligns with their favorite anointed leader.

Church growth in numbers is the new leadership mantra, instead of making disciples of those whom God has added to the congregation. Church growth obsession has become the main reason that so many pastors and elders turn to these false teachings and false national leaders. These half-truths and false promises draw multitudes of sincere seekers of God, as well as the insincere and the curious. Many come seeking the true Christ while others are testing the waters, looking for a magic ride through life.

The Apostle Paul addressed these same issues in his letter to the Corinthian Christians: *"I am afraid that as the serpent deceived Eve by his cunning, your thoughts will be <u>led astray from a sincere and pure devotion to Christ</u>. For if someone comes and <u>proclaims another Jesus</u> than the one we proclaimed, or if you <u>receive a different spirit</u> from the one you received, or if you <u>accept a different gospel</u> from the one you accepted, you put up with it readily enough"* (2 Corinthians 11:3-4). Few learn to challenge false leaders by thoroughly examining their teachings. Many ignorantly follow, only to succumb to a diluted relationship with Christ—and in many cases believers stray after *another Jesus, a different spirit*, and embrace *a different gospel*!

Many follow these false teachers and false prophets because the false leaders operate in a counterfeit faith and dispense sensuous spiritual experiences just as Peter wrote, *"And many will follow their sensuality"* (2 Peter 2:2); ("sensuality" meaning *pleasing to the senses*).

Counterfeit faith has spiritual power like the power that the Apostle Paul described in 2 Timothy. In the last-days false Christian leaders will come on the scene to mislead Christians with demonic spiritual powers. *"As Jannes and Jambres opposed Moses, so these men also oppose the truth, men <u>of corrupt mind and counterfeit faith</u>; but they will not get very far, for their folly will be plain to all, as was that of those two men"* (2 Timothy 3:8-9 RSV).

Jannes and Jambres were two sorcerers who worked with satanic powers in Pharaoh's court; they had power to duplicate or match in power the first three plagues that Moses and Aaron brought forth in the power of God.

The Apostle Paul is warning us that in these last-days false leaders will walk in a counterfeit faith that will produce signs and wonders in a so-called anointed power like the power behind those two sorcerers in the Pharaoh's court.

Jesus also warned of false prophets exercising signs and wonder in great power in the last days: *"For false Christs and false prophets will arise and show <u>great signs and wonders</u>, so as to lead astray, if possible, even the elect"* (Matthew 24:24).

Jesus warns that these people are false; however, the signs and wonders are *not* false but are great and backed by a demonic supernatural power (they are false in claiming to be of God).

Many do not take this seriously. Since Christ called these leaders false, many jump to the erroneous conclusion that the signs and wonders must be false as well. This produces the belief that *if the sign or wonder is real the leaders must be real,* causing such believers to overlook the subtle (or often blatant) errors in the doctrine that false leaders convey.

In this passage, Jesus did not say that false prophets would produce false signs and wonders—on the contrary, the power of the counterfeit manifests *real* miracles, wonders, and signs, even lifting oppression, facilitating so-called deliverance and, in some cases, actual physical healing.

Ministry Cases: *Satan's bait and switch tactic*

Many came to counseling describing how miraculously their emotional, mental, and physical symptoms disappeared when they became involved with the power of the counterfeit. Unfortunately, when they woke up to the deception, sought the truth, and followed the true Christ, in most cases those symptoms returned.

Oppression, bad thoughts, depression, extreme mood swings, and various debilitating aches, pains, and illnesses often become acute by demonic activity. This is primarily due to defilements still imbedded within the soul and spirit of the believer.

Satan and the demonic will back off from aggravating these imbedded issues, resulting in a temporary relief of the symptoms, in order to lead the deceived into a false doctrine. When a naïve or deceived Christian falls for a false doctrine associated with counterfeit signs and wonders a false deliverance often takes place. This subtle work is what we call "oppress the victim then bait and switch"—where the victimized believer is pulled into a destructive and potentially damning heresy in exchange for temporary relief.

Many coming to counsel renounced the false doctrines then began to work on their carnal character issues and hidden defilements. Then true healing of the symptoms and restoration in the true power of God became a reality. The book of James lays out the biblical formula for true deliverance, healing and wholeness.

Specifically, the following passage summarizes this process: *"Submit yourselves therefore to God. Resist the devil, and he will flee from you. Draw near to God, and he will draw near to you. Cleanse your hands, you sinners, and purify your hearts, you double-minded. Be wretched and mourn and weep. Let your laughter be turned to mourning and your joy to gloom. Humble yourselves before the Lord, and he will exalt you"* (James 4:7-10). Ω

What is false about these signs and wonders is that God supposedly brings them forth in his power; however, counterfeit faith with counterfeit demonic power can produce actual signs and wonders, often channeled through the human spirit. What is false about these signs and wonders is the claim that they are of God. One of the rudimentary teachings on discernment in the Old Testament that is seldom touched upon is as follows:

"If a prophet arises among you, or a dreamer of dreams, and <u>gives you a sign or a wonder, and the sign or wonder which he tells you comes to pass</u>, and if he says, 'Let us go after other gods,' which you have not known, 'and let us serve them,' you shall not listen to the words of that prophet or to that dreamer of dreams; <u>for the LORD your God is testing you</u>, to know whether you love the LORD your God with all your heart and with all your soul. You shall walk after the LORD your God and fear him, and keep his commandments and obey his voice, and you shall serve him and cleave to him" (Deuteronomy 13:1-4).

When we allow God to increase our powers of discernment, what we thought to be true—what we once heralded as great by those around us—are often shown to be a satanic lie to deceive many.

What the masses exalt in unison as wonderful is often a treacherous trap of the enemy, for Jesus warned, *"What is exalted among men is an abomination in the sight of God"* (Luke 16:15).

Mega-Crowd Enthrallment and Groupthink
Anointing Obsession, Leadership Idolatry and Blind Conformity—opening up more gates of hell

Huge crowds follow personality leaders. Masses attend various venues looking to get high from the counterfeit faith "anointing." The crowds themselves generate a party-like atmosphere where all manner of exotic and sensuous touches are lusted after from a so-called leader with the anointing; however, the sensuous encounters are mostly demonic in nature or an activation of one's own spirit. Few can discern between a genuine manifestation of the Holy Spirit and these conjured spiritual encounters.

These mega-crowds generate a spiritual aura that feeds on itself, fueled by a groupthink mentality (unquestioning conformity) that embraces shortcut theology. Few in a mega crowd venue, movement, or in a mega-church question what is preached and taught, because few search the Scriptures for the truth; few really desire to embrace all that Christ taught.

The name of Jesus is used to draw the crowds; however, the real attention is given to the anointed speaker who can minister in "the power," amazing, enthralling, and mesmerizing the massive crowds with signs and wonders.

These leaders and those who follow them use the name of Christ in the flesh; however, Christ is not working through them. Remember, Jesus warned, *"On that day many will say to me, 'Lord, Lord, did we not prophesy in your name, and cast out demons in your name, and do many mighty works in your name?' And then will I declare to them, 'I never knew you; depart from me, you workers of lawlessness.'"* (Matthew 7:22-23).

True disciples—both then and now—will have signs follow them that glorify Christ; but most that are revered today operate in a power that glorifies the anointing and the anointed leader.

In the book of Acts this type of person tried to arise to leadership after he became a believer in Christ and attempted to buy the anointing (the power of God). His name was Simon the magician.

Simon the magician had practiced sorcery before his conversion to Christ and had walked in a power that amazed the whole nation of Samaria with signs and wonders. He even bragged about being someone great. Crowds formed and followed him because the demonic power he practiced was considered by everyone to be the power of God.

"They all gave heed to him, from the least to the greatest, saying, 'This man is that power of God which is called Great.' And they gave heed to him, because for a long time he had amazed them with his magic" (Acts 8:10-11).

The crowds that followed Simon were mesmerized by the signs and wonders he performed by practicing his *magic supernatural powers*. When the Apostle Peter laid hands on new believers in Christ to impart the Holy Spirit, Simon (who had just become a believer himself) wanted to have this same power.[6]

Peter, walking in discernment, instantly detected Simon's lust for power. Take note how Peter dealt with Simon: *"Now when Simon saw that the Spirit was given through the laying on of the apostles' hands, he offered them money, saying, 'Give me also this power, that any one on whom I lay my hands may receive the Holy Spirit.' But Peter said to him, 'Your silver perish with you, because you thought you could obtain the gift of God with money! You have neither part nor lot in this matter, <u>for your heart is not right before God. Repent therefore of this wickedness of yours</u>, and pray to the Lord that, if possible, the <u>intent of your heart</u> may be forgiven you. For I see that you are in the <u>gall of bitterness and in the bond of iniquity</u>'"* (Acts 8:18-23).

The Apostle Peter stopped a disaster from taking place by confronting Simon and pointing out the intentions of his heart; Simon was like many today *in the gall of bitterness and in the bond of iniquity* and hungering for the power of God to make a name for themselves!

Satan is very much into harnessing this last-day's magic-and-sorcery-spiked generation. Many today are soaked in these abominable portrayals of supernatural magic. Then they become believers in Christ, like Simon, yet they are not confronted concerning their magic thinking like Peter confronted Simon. Few learn how to purify their hearts and become healed of their bitter jealousies, and be set free from the enthrallment of magic they ingested into their carnal nature (which is still defiled even after they believe in Christ) from living in a magic-laden culture. In chapter six we delve into the supernatural power of the human spirit harnessed by Satan through false doctrines and defilements from past involvement in the magic arts.

A Flood of Simon the Magician Christian Leaders
Working the crowds into a brain-dead mob who follow men

The gross darkness blinding the body of Christ over the last century has allowed the gates of hell to be opened wide by a flood of Simon the magician personality leaders. These become as Hollywood starlets with power to captivate, amaze, and mesmerize masses of naïve and deceived Christians.

---

[6] The true power of God will draw attention to those called to bring forth the Gospel of Christ. However, true servants do not hunger for power to promote themselves or their ministry.

In review, these false leaders have a power that draws attention to the leader using Christ's name. They draw large crowds and accumulate massive numbers of followers, gaining a strangle-hold upon the minds and hearts of millions.

Christ will say to these imposters, *"I never knew you; you workers of lawlessness."* These whom Christ warns about, those that he will reject on judgment day, had power to cast out demons, do mighty works, and even prophesy using the name of Christ.

Today's false leaders have demonic spiritual power to whip up crowds of followers into a mob-like frenzy, similar to the dynamic that took over the crowds following Christ, when a few in the crowd cried out and attempted to make Christ king.

When Christ miraculously multiplied the fish and loafs, those followers became a crowd determined to make Christ king because their stomachs were made full. Our Lord confronted their groupthink agenda and directed them to seek manna that comes from heaven.

Now these same desires to make life easy on earth and to fulfill physical needs in abundance become the false leaders' ticket to deceive. The number of Christians caught up in this deception is massive, emanating a consumer-like power that keeps the false leaders in business. That is, as long as they cater to the mob-mentality agenda—preaching and teaching gimmicks and myths that portray Christ to be a dispenser of earthly blessings.

Again, this devilish work spawns groupthink throughout Christianity, magnifying a mob mentality that transverses denominational lines, filling fellowships with believers only interested in hearing from the local pastor the same false doctrines. A form of blackmail double binds[7] local pastors and leaders to acquiesce to the strange theology that attempts to use Christ to make life on earth easy and to justify the congregation's *carnal desires*.

This mob mentality dynamic operates out of a *consensus theology* (what the masses like and agree on). The Apostle Paul warned, *"For the time is coming when people will not endure sound teaching, but having itching ears they will accumulate for themselves teachers to <u>suit their own passions</u>, and will turn away from listening to the truth and wander off into myths"* (2 Timothy 4:3, 4).

That time has come upon the body of Christ. The average evangelical-Pentecostal-charismatic Christian has learned to reject the harder teachings of Christ and the deeper doctrines of the New Testament writers, making these Simon-the-magician personality leaders into kings, queens, and idols.

Those neglected harder teachings of Christ are what help Christians grow up into salvation. The following principles and objectives are key indicators that produce maturity in Christ:

- The sanctification process nullifies the power of the sin nature by the power of Christ.
- The work of the believers' cross ends the works of the flesh.
- The fullness of life in Christ and the Kingdom of Heaven abide in the heart of the true saint.
- Maturity in Christ exposes hidden evil and falsehood.

Instead of growing into an understanding of these teachings, masses of Christians have accumulated *super-apostles* and *Simon-the-magician personality leaders*—teachers and pastors who

---

[7] See footnote 24 on page 245 for my use of the term double bind.

promote a consensus theology with a variety of teachings that tickle the ear and soothe the pain of conscience, relieving the conviction of the Holy Spirit.

A mob dynamic (noisy, excitable and often lacking rational wisdom) has taken over the masses of believers of all denominations participating in these false movements. Moved by flamboyant leaders, Christians gather in large numbers demonstrating unity and excitement for the activity of the meeting or the event, thinking they are serving Christ—however, most are deceived into just giving lip service to Christ's name.

The euphoria in these false movements acts like spiritual Prozac and will eventually saturate the wounded and hurting Christian, so that these activities will no longer be able to suppress the inner distressful symptoms. After a season, the false highs cannot outdo the previous level and many become burned out, drop out, or become overtaken by sin and fall back into their old nature life-style.

Another aspect of the group dynamics within these movements is the spiritual feeding frenzy that takes place, where many participants suck life from each other. An addictive spiritualism is developed that is really a lust for carnal fellowship, which is a form of group relationship idolatry.

The crowd and mob mentality has become a satanic stronghold where a form of carnal social networking or group-clique fellowshipping takes root. This is an addictive dynamic process that leads to a *church social networking idolatry*; where people network or hookup with each other in a supposed fellowshipping agenda bearing little or no fruit of mentoring, training in discipline, or Christ-like fellowship.

This *churchianity socializing and entertainment* diverts Christian fellowship and sincere heart-felt worship into idolatrous activities, just as Temple worship turned into worshipping the experience of going to Temple. An extreme danger exists in becoming lukewarm and a *social addict,* lusting for the mob energy generated by flamboyant leaders.

The true servant must avoid the euphoria generated by these false leaders and the resultant mob energy. The carnal enthusiasm used to promote the message of salvation in many cases amounts to leadership-generated hysteria. Often church members and Christian volunteers are stirred up in hysteria and enlisted to oppose any criticism toward their idolized leaders. The carnal prayer-power from this kind of group deception is destructive and can be deadly.

Learn to detect and avoid the popular event conferencing, group cliques, and church socializing idolatry that are counterproductive to true discipleship building and meaningful fellowship. Instead, seek the manna from above, learn to hear the true voice of Christ, and learn to walk in Kingdom life in holiness and embrace genuine fellowship with likeminded brethren.

Counterfeit Supernatural-Power Brokers
Idolatry of signs and wonders wrought by the superlative leader

The lust for supernatural power amongst much of the church has helped create a capitalistic approach in transferring the power of God to those who hunger after that power. A host of superlative supernatural power brokers have arisen demonstrating false signs and wonders that amaze the power-greedy believer. (These hunger not after Christ; rather they hunger after the power of God, using Christ's name).

Signs and wonders have become an idol of the heart for most, making it easy for Satan's counterfeit power swindles to work. These deceived followers of the counterfeit power brokers have little groundwork in sound doctrine to discern the spirit behind these signs and wonders.

The Apostle John instructed *"Beloved, do not believe every spirit, but test the spirits to see whether they are from God, for many false prophets have gone out into the world"* (1 John 4:1).

Foolishly, driven by wrong motives, many have fallen for Satan's counterfeit power scams due to the real supernatural power demonstrated by the devil's power brokers. To the undiscerning, these are real miracles, but they are signs and wonders manifested by Satan's counterfeit spiritual gifts he has groomed his power brokers to manifest.

As stated earlier, citing the Apostle Paul's prophesy again from 2 Timothy 3, in these last-days men will walk in a counterfeit faith that has power similar to the spiritual power conjured by the sorcerers in the Pharaoh's court. Jewish historians identified those two as Jannes and Jambres, and these two sorcerers demonstrated supernatural power to match tit-for-tat the plagues wrought by God through Moses and Aaron.

They worked as the Pharaoh's (and the devil's) supernatural power brokers who opposed the will of God. They were able to bring forth three plagues and help harden the Pharaoh's heart against Moses. However, on the fourth plague, they quit trying to match God's power, knowing that their powers could no longer match the power of God. (Satan and his demons have limited supernatural powers to affect the physical, compared to God, who is omnipotent!)

Unfortunately, God's people caught in the grip of these last-days charlatans assume this counterfeit spiritual power is of God, even though it is very limited. In simple comparison, a sincere study of Christ and his disciples' demonstrated power should raise a red flag! Becoming familiar with true servants of God in recent history, such as Smith Wigglesworth and his ministry would also help one illustrate the glaring difference between counterfeit supernatural power and the true power of God through Christ-like servants.

Stanley Frodsham, author, editor and teacher who ministered in the Pentecostal movement for over 60 years, in 1965 gave a profound prophecy addressing the dark hour we are in now. For 30 years, he was editor of the Pentecostal Evangel and wrote fifteen books, the best known being *With Signs Following* (1926, revised 1946,) a history of the Pentecostal movement, and a collection of Smith Wigglesworth's sermons *Ever Increasing Faith* (1924), along with a biography of Smith Wigglesworth, *Apostle of Faith* (1948).

The following is an excerpt of that prophecy given at the Elim Bible Institute USA, in 1965. The portion hones in on the many false leaders now active in the Pentecostal, charismatic and evangelical denominations and movements.

> "I warn you to search the Scriptures diligently these last days. For the things that are written shall indeed be made manifest. There shall come deceivers among my people in increasing numbers, who shall speak forth the truth and shall gain the favor of the

people. For the people shall examine the Scriptures and say, "What these men say is true." Then when they have gained the hearts of the people, then and then only shall they bring out these wrong doctrines. Therefore, I say that you should not give your hearts to men, nor hold people's persons in admiration. For by these very persons shall Satan enter into my people.

Watch for seducers. Do you think a seducer will brandish a new heresy and flaunt it before the people? He will speak the words of righteousness and truth, and will appear as a minister of light, declaring the Word. The people's hearts shall be won... For the deceiver will first work to gain the hearts of many, and then shall bring forth his insidious doctrines." (An excerpt of a prophecy given by Stanley Frodsham at the Elim Bible Institute USA, in 1965).

We must become skilled in the word of Righteousness and understand the biblical principles and characteristics of the power of God in action, and if possible witness true signs and wonders that are of God—wrought through true servants of Christ.

A test is coming as the end of this age closes: God is allowing Satan to manifest great power through false signs, wonders, and false gifting through spirits of divination. These false teachings, false leaders, and false signs and wonders will ferret out the true believer from the false. Jesus warned, *"For false christs and false prophets will arise and perform great signs and wonders, so as to lead astray, if possible, even the elect. See, I have told you beforehand"* (Matthew 24:24-25).

It is up to each Christian to become truly knowledgeable of Christ by knowing and comprehending all that he taught and by exerting faith into action. We must seek the true person of Christ that we *"grow up in every way into him who is the head, into Christ, from whom the whole body, joined and held together by every joint with which it is equipped, when each part is working properly, makes the body grow so that it builds itself up in love"* (Ephesians 4:15-16).

The following are two of many counterfeit supernatural-power brokers to highlight the seriousness of the devil's work in the midst of God's people.

Benny Hinn's Bolts of Supernatural Plasma

Many believe that the slain-in-the-Spirit phenomenon is just a massive hypnotic spell that Hinn and others like him cast upon those who attend their meetings. In Hinn's case, hundreds standing in the audience will fall back in their seats or fall on each other when Benny Hinn waves his arm and hand as if casting some kind of invisible ball of power.

Physical healings have been accredited to his ministry; however, there is much controversy because most cannot be substantiated. Again, we must remind ourselves that Christ and the Apostles warned that the signs and wonders would not determine the authenticity of a ministry, but rather the fruit of their character and the doctrine that they preach. Again, Apostle Paul warned back then: *"I know that after my departure fierce wolves will come in among you, not sparing the flock; and from among your own selves will arise men speaking twisted things, to draw away the disciples after them. Therefore be alert"* (Acts 20:29-31)—last-days wolves are fierce and very cunning.

Of course, God is in control; however, he does allow the power of the devil to be channeled through a false teacher or false prophet to test his people—again, see Deuteronomy 13:1-5. Many with itching ears and out-of-control passion, clamor after these sensuous manifestations, as the late David Wilkerson put it, they are committing spiritual fornication. The following is an excerpt from a message Wilkerson delivered around 2001 that addressed these counterfeit-sensuous manifestations and the over-the-top statements that Benny Hinn made in one of his meetings in Denver in 1999:

> "But when a man stands and tells the whole United States in one of his meetings "I curse a man or preacher who stands against my ministry, I curse him." That a man stands before the people on television and says, "Jesus Christ has told me, that one day he is personally going to attend and be in one of my meetings."
> That's blasphemy! That is the doctrine of demons. And yet you sit there and you say this sounds good, it looks good, looks like people are being healed, and you are being fornicated with. You're into fornication. Spiritual fornication because you don't have the discernment!"

The following is the exact quote from Benny Hinn during the meeting that Wilkerson decried:

> "I place a curse on every man and every woman that will stretch his hand against this anointing. I curse that man who dares to speak a word against this ministry."

This next quote from Benny Hinn was on a TBN televised interview where he proclaimed that Christ would physically be seen in one of his meetings:

> "I'm expecting to see, I'm telling you that, I feel it's going to happen. I know deep in my soul something supernatural is going to happen in Nairobi Kenya. I may very well come back; we may very well come back with footage of Jesus on the platform."

Source: (YouTube clip search "The late David Wilkerson exposes false prophet Benny Hinn")

Epilogue to this case with David Wilkerson exposing Benny Hinn: In April 2011, in an unexplainable tragedy, David Wilkerson died at the scene of a horrific head on collision with a semi-tractor trailer in Texas. Mysteriously, David, while driving his car wandered into the oncoming lane as he crossed a bridge. The truck driver had no way to avoid the collision. David was not wearing his seat belt and he died at the scene; however, his wife Gwen was wearing her restraint and she survived the accident.

I know firsthand that David was warned in 2004 concerning the deadly powers of the human spirit when boosted by the demonic, as is with Benny Hinn. Unfortunately, David did not understand the warning or ignored the teaching and warning.

Consequently, he was not prepared or trained by the Lord to become immune to such evil. As it states in Proverbs, *"Like a sparrow in its flitting, like a swallow in its flying, a curse that is causeless does not alight"* (Proverbs 26:2). Many Christians, even mature saints like David, are vulnerable to curses and witchcraft when one does not embrace the continued sanctifying work of the Holy Spirit, but rather leans on shortcut teachings that bypass the continued purifying work of God in their lives. *"Let us cleanse ourselves from every defilement of body and spirit, bringing holiness to completion in the fear of God"* (2 Corinthians 7:1).

In our discipline and training in the Lord concerning these matters, we soon realized that the curses and spiritual attacks by those who walk in counterfeit power are mitigated by our continued maturing and cleansing within our heart and personal spirit, as we learn to abide and continually walk in the fullness of Christ.

The power of God and his protection as part of the armor of God becomes stronger as we embrace the ongoing sanctifying work of the Holy Spirit and by embracing the work of the cross. Hard and sometimes exhausting in trials, this process exposes and allows the rooting out of inner hidden unbelief, defilements, carnal motives, self-dependency, and carnal character structures—those magnifying agents that cause a curse to take hold.

Rodney Howard Browne's Laughaholics; Strange and Unholy Fire

The Apostle Paul corrected the very charismatic Christians in Corinth in an attempt to get them to tone down the out-of-control speaking in an unknown tongue. In a polite manner, the apostle was trying to steer these carnal and over-exuberant believers back to reason and genuine fellowship in the Holy Spirit. *"But I, brothers, could not address you as spiritual people, but as people of the flesh, as infants in Christ"* (1 Corinthians 3:1). These believers were picking favorite self-glorifying leaders, edifying themselves through their personal spirit and leaving their minds unfruitful (passive). This carnal behavior was substituting sincere worship and growth in Christ. Collectively they practiced speaking in unknown tongues for self-edification, and their fellowship meetings appeared to be insane and confusing to outsiders or unbelievers.

He wrote, *"I thank God that I speak in tongues more than you all; nevertheless, in church I would rather speak five words with my mind, in order to instruct others, than ten thousand words in a tongue"* (1 Corinthians 14:18-19). Another important point he made in his letter is that all should seek the gift of prophecy, where the secret of the heart of an outsider or an unbeliever would be revealed. *"But if all prophesy, and an unbeliever or outsider enters, he is convicted by all, he is <u>called to account by all</u>, the secrets of his heart are disclosed, and so, falling on his face, he will worship God and declare that God is really among you"* (1 Corinthians 14:24-25). I recommend reading 1 Corinthians chapter 12 through chapter 14 in all sincerity, asking the Holy Spirit for insight to understand the Apostle's true intent in correcting these out-of-control, gift-obsessed believers. Then if possible, go online and do a YouTube search for *Rodney Howard Browne laughter* to view this so-called laughing ministry. (By the way, Rodney Howard Browne has referred to himself as "the Holy Ghost bar tender.")

How many wounded Christians struggle with secret sin and secret issues of the heart that need to be brought to the light for healing or repentance and cleansing—and instead witness insane babbling by self-edifying believers who bark like dogs, cackle like chickens, or stagger like drunken sailors on liberty? The following lengthy passage is the account concerning what happened to Aaron's sons when they became drunk and offered strange and unholy fire:

"And Nadab and Abihu, the sons of Aaron, each took his censer and put fire in it, and put incense on it, and <u>offered strange and unholy fire before the Lord</u>, as He had not commanded them. And there came forth fire from before the Lord and killed them, and they died before the Lord. Then Moses said to Aaron, This is what the Lord meant when He said,' I (and My will, not their own) will be acknowledged as hallowed by those who come near Me, and before all the people I will be honored.' And Aaron said nothing. Moses called Mishael and Elzaphan, sons of Uzziel uncle of Aaron, and said to them, 'Come near, carry your brethren from before the sanctuary out of the camp.' So they drew near and carried them in their under tunics [stripped of their priestly vestments] *out of the camp, as Moses had said. And Moses said to Aaron and Ithamar, his sons (the father and brothers of the two priests whom God had slain for offering false fire), 'Do not uncover your heads or let your hair go loose or tear your clothes, lest you die (also) and lest God's wrath should come upon all the congregation; but let your brethren, the whole house of Israel, bewail the burning which the Lord has kindled. And you shall not go out from the door of the Tent of Meeting, lest you die, for the Lord's anointing oil is upon you.' And they did according to Moses' word. And the Lord said to Aaron, '<u>Do not drink wine or strong drink, you or your sons, when you go into the Tent of Meeting, lest you die; it shall be a statute forever in all your generations. You shall make distinction and recognize a difference between the holy and the common or unholy, and between the unclean and the clean</u>; And you shall teach the Israelites all the statutes which the Lord has spoken to them by Moses.'"* (Leviticus 10 : 1-11; Amplified Bible)

These rules that God laid down for the priesthood were to deal with any irreverence toward God and the things of God. We can draw from the account that the reason the Lord killed Aaron's two sons was that they came before the Lord intoxicated, and in that state irreverently offered strange and unholy fire before the Lord. This act mocked God. It was, and still is an irreverent manner of worship. Here is how Jesus walked with God: *"In the days of his flesh, Jesus offered up prayers and supplications, with loud cries and tears, to him who was able to save him from death, and he was heard for his godly fear. Although he was a Son, he learned obedience through what he suffered; and being made perfect he became the source of eternal salvation to all who obey him, being designated by God a high priest after the order of Melchizedek"* (Hebrews 5:7-10).

Holy laughter or getting drunk in the Spirit is carnal spiritualism thought to be a sacrifice of praise and worship, but is no different from what Nadab and Abihu did before the Lord.

Exposing the Works of Darkness — Amongst the Brethren
House cleaning of the body of Christ — at every level

It is vital that we learn to perceive and rightly hear from the Holy Spirit concerning evil hidden in darkness in and among the fellowship of the saints. Increasing our understanding from the Scripture and dealing with our own hidden or ignored issues is vital, as is not shying away from the training and discipline of the Lord. We must embrace all that Christ taught and learn to work in unison with likeminded believers to build a sure foundation to successfully walk in the gifts of the Holy Spirit and ensure safe fellowship.

The time is upon us now when evil abounds. We are admonished in Scripture to, *"Take no part in the unfruitful works of darkness, <u>but instead expose them</u>. For it is shameful even to speak of the things that they do in secret. But when anything is exposed by the light, it becomes visible, for anything that becomes visible is light. Therefore it says, 'Awake, O sleeper, and arise from the dead, and Christ will shine on you.' Look carefully then how you walk, not as unwise <u>but as wise, making the best use of the time, because the days are evil</u>"* (Ephesians 5:11-16).

Those who desire to increase their powers of discernment will find a heavy burden with these new abilities. At times Christ will whisper in your ear secrets hidden in darkness and he will command that the hidden wickedness be exposed for all to see. Christ will command you to do spiritual battle until it is accomplished; and you can expect hell to come against you viciously when you obey Christ in exposing darkness!

Leaders in your fellowship should be actively teaching on learning how to expose hidden evils, and practicing exposing evil themselves, making sure the fellowship is bolstered by sincere and called intercessors, otherwise, exposing darkness in the flesh will be like trying to put out a fire with a can of gasoline.

The following ministry case may help you understand why the Apostle Paul's exhortation that all should prophesy should be taken seriously.

Ministry Case: *Church picnic darkness*

Early in our training and ministry, the gift of prophecy and the gift of discerning spirits proved powerful in exposing evil in fellowship. One case involved molestation, where a hidden pedophile was exposed and sent to jail. The following account will help in understanding the importance and effectiveness of these gifts in our call to expose darkness.

"Transgression speaks to the wicked deep in his heart; there is no fear of God before his eyes. For he flatters himself in his own eyes that his iniquity cannot be found out and hated. The words of his mouth are trouble and deceit; he has ceased to act wisely and do good. He plots trouble while on his bed; he sets himself in a way that is not good; he does not reject evil" (Psalm 36:1-4).

We had counseled a couple on and off for about a year. The husband resisted any true work in our sessions, but he still came occasionally at his wife's pressuring. When a charismatic evangelist came to his church, he went to a couple of these meetings. In his last counseling session with me, he reported that he was free of any problems because had been slain in the spirit and delivered, and that any further counseling was unnecessary.

I knew there was still a spirit of lust over him; that he was holding back in counseling concerning his secret sexual problems.

About six months later, this man called for prayer. He announced that two detectives had requested an interview with him. He was accused of molesting his four-year-old niece and he told me emphatically that he did not do it.

I asked the Holy Spirit what was the truth and I heard from the Lord right then and there, while on the phone, *"He is lying; he did it!"*

I told him that I would pray that "God's will be done" and that he should call me back and let me know what happened.

After the conversation on the phone, I prayed with another person for additional direction and confirmation and we both heard from the Lord that he had molested his niece. We continued to pray asking that God's will to be revealed in this matter. The Holy Spirit gave this answer: *"Pray that the lying spirit be broken over him and that he would go to jail for what he did."* We prayed accordingly.

The next day this person called me very distraught, saying that he took a lie detector test, failed it, and subsequently confessed to molesting his four-year-old niece. On the phone he confessed to me as well, giving details of when, where and how it happened—at a church picnic attended by hundreds of charismatic, tongues-speaking Christians, the same church that brought in false evangelists and false prophets practiced a counterfeit anointing.

At this particular church picnic, his sister had asked him to watch her daughter (his niece). While no one was looking, he molested her and later her parents suspected something was wrong and took to the doctor for an examination where it was confirmed that she had been violated.

The parents knew he was the only one alone with her during the time this could have happened.

I told him I would try to help him deal with this and support him as he faced up to his problems. (Note: Many pedophiles pass lie detector tests because they lie to themselves and believe the lie. Often a lying spirit will enable a pedophile to completely dissociate from the truth, sear or reject their conscience and lie without flinching.)

My gut reaction to his confession was disgust for his lack of empathy for hurting an innocent child, his own niece. He was wallowing in self-pity and had no concern for his victim. Typically, pedophiles sear their conscience completely and look upon their victims as objects, often blaming the victim for tempting them or for telling on them.

Child Protective Services stepped in and had this man removed from his home. He had two daughters who were now at risk. When he realized the full ramifications and consequences of his evil deed, he changed his story and denied he had done such a thing, accusing the police of coercing a confession.

As it was, he elicited pity from the same church that he attended, and soon there was a battle and division of fellowship over this situation. Few, including the pastor, were willing to hold this man accountable (as the Apostle Paul wrote, *"he is convicted by all, he is called to account by all, the secrets of his heart are disclosed"*). The attitude was one of forgiving the perpetrator and welcoming him into the fold with open arms, as if nothing ever happened. They believed his lie that he was tricked into confessing something he did not do, and put together a campaign to pressure his wife to take him back into the home while he was awaiting trial.

We counseled his wife to hold him accountable in spite of the overwhelming pressure from these so-called anointed and gifted Christians. I also told her that he had confessed to me as well. She held firm because it was determined their own daughters were at risk. (Later, it was revealed he previously had inappropriately touched his youngest daughter.)

The case went to trial and I submitted an affidavit stating that he had also confessed to me on the phone the day after he had failed the lie detector test and subsequently confessed to the police. The jury found him guilty beyond any doubt, and he received a five-year sentence for his crime.

This was God's will for such a liar and abuser of children. This so-called believer in Christ crossed the line into darkness. If we had not done what God wanted in prayer and had not been walking in the true gifts, Satan would have protected this man and most likely he would still be offending. This is an example of the true gifts of the Lord in action. Ω

Since this case back in the 1991, our powers of discernment have increased, allowing us to detect more readily abusers, liars, and human sharks swimming amongst the brethren seeking someone to devour. Through the years of counseling, one of the most difficult aspects was the burden bearing and support that needed to be conveyed to the many victims who recounted their abuse and pain during counseling. The Lord gave me and those assisting in counsel his love and grace many times. It was often very difficult to be able to keep composure and help bear their burdens as they shared their painful memories.

However, in the beginning of our counseling ministry there were times I became overwhelmed. At one point, during a counseling session, the counselee remembered a childhood trauma of horrific abuse perpetrated against her by her father. The burden of her pain was almost too much for me to bear. When I was alone after the session, and I asked God angrily, "Where were you?"

The answer I received from the Holy Spirit was almost instantaneous; "I had no one to send, or to intervene, but I am sending you now." That helped put the pain and suffering from my own childhood abuses, as well as hers, in a better light concerning God. The Lord showed me, for my own recovery from blaming God for my abuses and misfortunes, that Satan, through evil people did the harm. It is not God's will that people, especially children, suffer such things. Later, as I contemplated Scripture concerning Christ's passion and sacrifice, and how evil succeeded in abusing and murdering God's only son, I saw that Jesus was a man acquainted with grief and that he certainly understands and can heal us of our own deep wounds.

With this comfort, I have been able to help others overcome bitterness toward God. Unless we minister in the power and comfort of the Comforter, we fall short in ministering to the wounded, who desperately need to know another cares. We learn to weep with each with empathy for what they endured and in that, they can learn to believe, *"He heals the brokenhearted and binds up their wounds"* (Psalm 147:3), and *"The Lord is near to the brokenhearted and saves the crushed in spirit"* (Psalm 34:18).

However, the current state of the body of Christ lacks able soldiers who offer to stand in the gap, become burden bearers, and counsel God's wounded. Years ago, when I first entered the ministry I had the opportunity to hear a firebrand preacher call out to those who had an ear to hear that they enlist in God's army. The call was to offer one's self without reservation, to stand in the gap. He cited what God told Ezekiel concerning the detestable state Israel had fallen to: *"And I sought for a man among them who should build up the wall and stand in the breach before me for the land, that I should not destroy it, but I found none"* (Ezekiel 22:30).

The call of God upon a broken man or woman who offers themselves as a living sacrifice truly extends the love and comfort of God to the hopeless brokenhearted and crushed in spirit.

Discerning the False who Mislead God's People

The more difficult task since then has been discerning and understanding how these false leaders, false teachings, and false spirit manifestations have become a major avenue for hell to flow into the midst of fellowship after fellowship and mislead the many.

True leaders must take courage now and stand against the gates of hell. Shedding false doctrine and embracing all that Christ taught along with submitting to Christ's discipline in his school of ministry is how discernment starts to increase. Where are the true servants of Christ who are to be poured out as gifts to the body of Christ?

They are being prepared and are about to come upon the scene to equip the saints for the work of ministry in the coming final harvest. The true apostle, prophet, evangelist, pastor, and teacher are to present sound doctrine for the saint to grow by, that the church no longer be subjected to *"every wind of doctrine, by the cunning of men, by their craftiness in deceitful wiles."* (See Ephesians 4:11-16).

Peddlers of God's Word with a Twist

False leaders making converts to the wrong Jesus and making them children of hell!

Consensus theology affects fellowships and congregations across denominational lines. The demand to accommodate popular teachings forces appointment boards and elders to hire pastors who can *peddle God's Word,* instead of recognizing and appointing true shepherds commissioned by God—true servants who will faithfully make disciples of Christ.

Pastors are hired to go along with the pressure to propagate popular myths and consensus theology, with church growth measured solely by the number of attendees. "Bigger is better" becomes the local church mantra and working for the church supplants serving the true Christ and fostering true discipleship.

Masked by the pretense of unity in the mutual belief in Christ, these churches and ministries are actually in competition with one another—like competing businesses seeking market share and trying to create a niche to take in a larger piece of the pie (more believers).

In order to fulfill this greedy church growth mission a smorgasbord of carnal programs are available to market the church to lure and captivate converts.

Jesus confronted this same church growth travesty saying to the Temple leaders of his day, *"Woe to you, scribes and Pharisees, hypocrites! For you travel across sea and land to make a single proselyte, and when he becomes a proselyte, you make him twice as much a child of hell as yourselves"* (Matthew 23:15).

To keep both new converts and older believers happy, slogans and *hyper-counterfeit-faith mottos* keep the congregation pumped up with youthful energy. The local church is important, but not the answer as the end of the age unfolds. The answer is the true body of Christ grown into maturity, where the people of God are led by the Holy Spirit, bringing forth their testimony in power and exemplary living. The local church is overly focused upon, elevating leadership beyond Christ's purpose in leadership. The pastor, the facility, and building attendance and entertainment value have become a hiding place, where the saints learn to become passive. The work of the saints is the key; it is the ministry of the individual saint who is helped by leadership to be the temple of the Holy Spirit who is to do the work of ministry.

The following sampling of mottos reflects how the saints come to the local church to be entertained and not challenged to grow up into Christ. Leadership is to ensure that each saint matures and stands strong in ministry—to be able to minister in most cases, not just witness by dragging people to their "local church" to become passive and rely on the pastor and staff to do the work of ministry. (Seriously study Ephesians 4:11-16 to understand leadership role and the saints calling).

"The local church is the hope of the world, and its future rests primarily in the hands of its leaders" Bill Hybels, *Courageous Leadership* (Grand Rapids, MI: Zondervan, 2002), p. 27.

"Church should be like a dance club" Josh Reich, "Creating Worship for the Emerging Church," www.youthspecialties.com/articles October 2009.

Such mottos and slogans, laced with half-truths, keep emotional interest high and discernment dulled. Watered-down truths facilitate avoidance of the deeper teachings of Christ and eventually mottos, slogans and mantras pervert the basic tenants of Christianity.

"About this we have much to say which is hard to explain, since you have become <u>dull of hearing</u>. For though by this time you ought to be teachers, you need someone to <u>teach you again the first principles of God's word</u>. You need milk, not solid food; for everyone who lives on milk is unskilled in the word of Righteousness, for he is a child. But <u>solid food is for the mature, for those who have their faculties trained by practice to distinguish good from evil</u>" (Hebrews 5:11-14).

A new convert is touched by the Holy Spirit and responds in all sincerity; but then that new believer falls prey to one of these fellowships or embraces one of these national leaders and unknowingly has their new faith converted to a counterfeit faith. Many new converts rise to leadership and become even better at deception, becoming *twice as much a child of hell.*

This all leads to lukewarm relationships with Christ for most who call themselves Christians today. Even though many are practicing spiritual gifts with strange and exotic manifestations, very few are producing Christ-like character.

The empty manifestations of the counterfeit spirit within these spiritually exotic and "anointed" meetings often arouse the personal spirit of the believer, and offer temporary anesthetic effects. In the end, encounters of being slain in the spirit, barking like dogs, uncontrolled laughter and such other empty manifestations become a placebo, having no real power to purify and change the heart or cleanse and heal the personal spirit.

To add to the lies, magic incantations are championed, such as pleading the blood of Christ for protection when a struggling Christian has to wait for the next "fix" from a Holy Ghost bartender or a bolt of supernatural plasma from a Benny Hinn type of ministry.

Carnal Deliverance Ministries
Duped by Satan or beat up royally by the demonic

You may be familiar with the account in the book of Acts detailing how seven itinerant Jewish exorcists invoked the name of Christ in their attempt to cast out evil spirits from the possessed. One man, who was empowered by an evil spirit, overpowered all seven of these exorcists. They fled for their lives, naked and wounded. (See Acts 19:11-17).

This example of what not to do in taking on demonically possessed or oppressed people is often overlooked by people who follow Christ, yet operate in the flesh (on their own accord and in their own spiritual power). The Jewish exorcists received a rude awakening and severe punishment for invoking the name of Christ apart from Christ's delegated authority.

Their approach in addressing the evil spirit was as follows: *"I adjure you by the Jesus, whom Paul proclaims"* and the evil spirit answered them, *"Jesus I know, and Paul I recognize, but who are you?"* (Acts 19:13, 15). Today, many use Christ's name in attempting to cast out demons, but are not known by Christ and consequently get the runaround by the demonic.

Satan and the demonic have learned to play possum when carnal Christians attempt to cast them out of their hosts. The demonic pretends to leave or burrows deeper into the possessed inner recesses of these people's minds and spirits. Still, many in this type of ministry, in particular in Catholic exorcisms, often incur beatings by the demons and/or the possessed similar to that which was described in our story from the book of Acts.

In his book, *Hostage to the Devil*, Malachi Martin describes in detail five exorcisms and in each case those performing the rite of exorcism according to Catholic doctrine received a variety of abuses in the process. In our desire to understand biblical spiritual warfare and deliverance, Martin's work and research instructed us on what happens when one performs deliverance in the flesh using religious incantations and half-truths mixed with superstitious rituals.

What we discovered in our training was that our success increased and the physical and emotional torment along with other attacks were lessoned by our continual maturing in Christ and by submitting to the sanctifying work of the Holy Spirit and applying death to our own carnal motives.

As we submitted to the discipline of the Lord for cleansing of our own hidden defilements and unresolved carnal issues, Christ worked more and more through us. In turn, the demonic became less and less aggressive as we became more attuned to the voice of Christ and to his leadership in helping a troubled person fight off resident evil spirit(s).

In the days to come, ministries and Christian workers who pride themselves on carnal methods and superstitious rituals in casting out demons and evil spirits will begin to experience severe setbacks. In some cases, physical harm and even loss of life will be the results in their carnal efforts to cast out devils.

"Everything Demonic" Deliverance Ministries
A cat-and-mouse satanic deception about to burst into flames

What do we mean by calling false deliverance ministries a cat and mouse deception by Satan? "Cat and mouse" is the name of an old English idiom dating back to 1675, that means *a contrived action involving constant pursuit, near captures, and repeated escapes*—a never-ending contest leading to an impasse or stalemate.

Ceramic frogs, ceramic owls, crosses on church steeples, the spirit of Michael Jackson, tattoos, pierced ears, women who do not have their head's covered—this is a tiny part of a long diatribe list that Win Worley spouts off that are supposedly demonic in nature. His lengthy list is to be renounced and shunned in order to have the associated demons cast out. The list is comprised mostly of superstitious myths that are part of the false doctrines Worley and a few other deliverance ministries push in their self-deception in giving false hope to troubled and demonized believers.

Win Worley, and others that hold to this type of deliverance thinking and practice fall into Satan's cat-and-mouse wild goose chase in trying to help demonically oppressed Christians. These superstitious acts are harmful to the believer who seeks help yet is ignorant of sound doctrines that address true deliverance.

Adding insult to injury Worley commands angels to come and drag away the demons to wherever the Lord wills them to go. The Apostle Paul explains in his letter to the Christians in Colossae not to be disqualified through empty deceit according to human tradition and the elemental spirits of the world.

"Let no one disqualify you, insisting on <u>asceticism and worship of angels</u>, going on in detail about visions, <u>puffed up without reason by his sensuous mind</u>, and not holding fast to the Head, from whom the whole body, nourished and knit together through its joints and ligaments, grows with a growth that is from God. "If with Christ you died to the <u>elemental spirits of the world</u>, why, as if you were still alive in the world, do you <u>submit to regulations</u>—'Do not handle, Do not taste, Do not touch' (referring to things that all perish as they are used)—according to <u>human precepts and teachings</u>? These have indeed an <u>appearance of wisdom in promoting self-made religion and asceticism and severity to the body, but they are of no value in stopping the indulgence of the flesh</u>" (Colossians 2:18-23).

Worley frequently added stories to bolster his superstitious teaching that encompassed just about everything in life that was at one time related to curses, both in Scripture or used by the occult to help focus hexing and spell casting. Associated demons via one's ancestral linage, up to eight generations for both parents must be exorcised as well (according to Worley).

The most over-the-top superstitious spiritualism was Worley's claim that ceramic owls and frogs had to be removed from one's home and destroyed—again emphasizing that these creatures were used symbolically in occult practices, thus even without your knowledge these innate objects are actually channels to invite demons to run wild in your home.

His anecdotal tale for the ceramic owl and frog absurdity follows in my paraphrase:

> In this teaching, he gave an account of a woman who attended one of his prior meetings who had protested his claim about certain ceramic figurines being demonic in nature. She stated that this was just too much and that her ceramic owl in her kitchen was quite cute and benign. Worley said that he told this woman that the Lord would show her, that he was not trying to make her do anything.
>
> Then Worley finished his story saying that the woman came back later to another meeting stating that she got rid of her owl. She said, after hearing Worley's teachings, whenever she walked by that ceramic owl in her kitchen, she noticed the eyes of the owl followed her. This freaked her out and prompted her to get rid of it.

The truth of the matter is that Win Worley hexed this poor woman with a spirit of superstition (an elementary spirit of this world). The Apostle Paul challenged the Christians at Galatia who were falling back into religious rules by writing: *"O foolish Galatians! Who has bewitched you?"* (Galatians 3:1).

Worley and other so-called deliverance ministries using these superstitious teachings are bewitching many and putting many at risk of disqualification with their faith in Christ. Blaming issues of the flesh on demons and putting people back under religious regulations is actually the work of angel-of-light demonic principalities. Ministries like Worley's are deceived and in turn deceive others and most become puffed up without reason by their sensuous minds.

They have fallen into Satan's trick where the demons actually do manifest and play a cat-and-mouse-game with the leaders and those plagued by the demonic. The demons have their fun and then pretend to leave by burrowing deeper in the cracks and crevasses of the double-minded believer; or they leave, only to come back later in stronger force.

Typical wholesale group deliverance in these meeting leads to demons manifesting and in some cases violently. These teachings produce superstitious fanatics who rely on the false deliverances or temporary deliverances that may involve convulsions and other wrenching manifestations.

By *false deliverance*, we mean that the demons learn how to fake leaving and burrow deeper into the psyche and spirit of the tormented; and by *temporary deliverance* we mean these demons will leave but return later in strength, making the next infestation of the demonic even worse than before the initial deliverance work.

Another ploy by the demonic is what we call *abuse and switch*, where demons torment their victim, pushing them into seeking relief; however, the relief offered is all too often a false doctrine misleading the demonized Christian into an even darker snare. When the tormented is deceived and takes the bait, the tormenting demons relax their oppression and allow a stronger angel of light demon to take charge. The added demon has the assignment to mislead the deceived into a variety of bewitching carnal methods, superstitious rituals, and/or inviting counterfeiting spirits to captivate the deceived into a seemingly successful ministry that helps others, making them believe they have power over the demonic. Many start their own deliverance ministries characterized by a haughty and prideful spirit.

As the battles heat up, Satan will stop playing his cat-and-mouse game and bring the flames of hell deep within the mind and spirit of these foolish and disqualified believers, destroying the faith of a multitude of foolish Christians. Many will find themselves barred from the marriage feast. (See Mathew 7:21-23.)

Ministry Case: *Pleading Buckets*

Recently a sister from Georgia called and literally begged us for help. She complained that she was hearing from the Holy Spirit that God had abandoned her and that she was cut off from the vine to wither as an unfruitful branch.

As she told me her life's story and her symptoms it became apparent that she was very wounded and suffered from a twice a soul condition. I asked her if, as a child, had she been molested. Yes, she said, several times by an uncle.

I explained to her how these kinds of defilements, such as sexual abuse, and even verbal or physical abuse, will linger within Christians if we do not learn how to become cleansed and healed to recover from these past defilements. We must learn to submit to the biblical sanctification process that requires us to work out these hidden issues in faith, with the Lord's help so that we may experience Christ-like character transformation. (The symptoms and the demonic agitation all point to deeper issues within the heart, mind, and spirit.)

Further, I explained that being delivered from the demonic agitation is only the initial aspect of this process of complete deliverance. Many have the demonic chased off by another's prayer within a deliverance ministry; however, unresolved issues of heart and spirit give the demonic ground to come back later, and often the next round of torment becomes more aggravating.

The cycle goes on and on indefinitely until the victim loses sanity or gives up on God and falls away. I asked her what different prayers she employed for deliverance and protection, knowing that most likely I would get the classic superstitious prayer of pleading the blood of Christ over her for protection and deliverance.

Her answer, "I continually plead buckets of the blood of Christ, but it just does not work." After this admission, I began to explain sound doctrine from the book of James that laid out her condition and her road to recovery to receive true deliverance.

These hocus-pocus superstitious incantations are no different from those of Catholicism or voodoo-type superstitious rituals. James lays out the work for the demonically tormented Christian:

"Submit yourselves therefore to God. Resist the devil, and he will flee from you. Draw near to God, and he will draw near to you. Cleanse your hands, you sinners, and purify your hearts, you double-minded. Be wretched and mourn and weep. Let your laughter be turned to mourning and your joy to gloom. Humble yourselves before the Lord, and he will exalt you" (James 4:7-10). Ω

In this case, like so many, the demons may leave temporarily, but later return with other demons and gain and even stronger grip upon the soul and spirit of the beleaguered. This is what Jesus meant in the following explanation:

"When the unclean spirit has gone out of a person, it passes through waterless places seeking rest, but finds none. Then it says, 'I will return to my house from which I came.' And when it comes, it finds the house <u>empty, swept, and put in order</u>. Then it goes and brings with it seven other spirits more evil than itself, and they enter and dwell there, and the last state of that person is worse than the first" (Matthew 12:43-45).

Demonized Christians come to a deliverance ministry looking for relief and receive instructions to renounce their sinful ways, repent of past sins, and choose to follow Christ. They are prayed for, ministered to, slain in the spirit or experience some aspect of an exorcism and find relief—the demon or demons are chased out.

Turning over a new leaf is a fatal error: The demonized emptied their house of evil ways, swept it clean by renouncing, repenting, and choosing to live right before God. However—now comes the fatal error—these deceived souls were not instructed to bring to death the old carnal nature that gave place to their brand of wickedness. The carnal character structures that were the demonic strongholds are still in place and the demonic returns and finds the unsuspecting Christian wide open for infestation. The original demons return with other demons even more determined to take up permanent residence, and becoming more evil than before.

Many demonized Christians experience temporary deliverance and eventually find their condition becomes worse. In the end, most lose hope and believe that God has rejected them, and that they were never born again. Many who embrace false doctrines that promote a quick-fix approach in deliverance by just *turning over a new leaf* end up in deep darkness falling away, giving the demonic full reign.

Unfortunately, the "magic wand" deliverance ministries are very popular and many buy into the short cut teachings without applying any discernment. Lust for the anointing to cast out the devils and miraculously download bliss into one's spirit and soul is sweeping hundreds of thousands into Satan's end-of-the-age trap.

They do not understand the important work of the cross within their own lives that brings death to the works of the flesh with all its passions and desires. They do not receive instruction on how to put off the old nature that is like their former manner of life. The do not receive instruction on allowing hidden defilement exposed and healing of a double minded condition. Instead, they learn to avoid giving themselves to Christ and his character transformation discipline. Study Galatians 5:16-26; Ephesians 4:22-24; James 4:1-10; and Romans 8:9-17.

Many sincere pastors are too scared, confused, and/or ignorant to oppose these lies. Forced to go along with the consensus theology, they offer entertaining stories and positive-thinking messages in the place of sound explanation of Scripture. Even worse, many allow so-called deliverance ministries to traipse into their pulpit and have the whole congregation slain in the spirit and thus be "delivered."

There is an ever-growing cottage industry comprised of superlative apostles, ear-tickling prophets or motivational evangelists, where each learn to peddle their own versions of the

Gospel and practice goofy deliverance ministries. The common thread in each of these ministries is that they avoid holding Christians accountable to resist the devil by faith, to draw near to God, to humble themselves, and to allow the Holy Spirit to show them their deeply imbedded strongholds, where bitter jealousy, selfishness, and other issues of heart become bondage handles for the devil and his minions.

The exhortation of Scriptures that confronts wrong motives and teaches on working out these issues to become cleansed and healed is hard work and not very popular; thus it is virtually avoided.

The Apostle Paul addresses these same issues in his letters in order to counteract the spreading influence of false leaders within the first-century church; *"For we are not, like so many, peddlers of God's word; but as men of sincerity, <u>as commissioned by God</u>, in the sight of God we speak in Christ"* (2 Corinthians 2:17). We must learn to discern between the sincere who are commissioned by God and those who are hired to market God's Word.

Hounds of Glory

Another aspect in this nasty trap for the sincere Christian in training, is that these peddlers of God's Word claim to have the "anointing." Many men and women who seek glory for themselves claim they have the power of God. However, their claim is exaggerated and egotistical in order to compete for more followers. They keep prodding each other like the famous dueling banjo entertainers, seeking new heights of power to captivate and enchant more and more wayward, deceived, and naïve believers.

I call them *hounds of glory ministries,* run by leaders who have become expert in the craft of producing counterfeit signs and wonders. They do not glorify Christ; rather they exalt the power they wield.

A key to discerning those who use false power from those who walk in the true power of God is to understand the following words of Christ:

"When the Spirit of truth comes, he will guide you into all the truth, for he will not speak on his own authority, but whatever he hears he will speak, and he will declare to you the things that are to come. He will glorify me, for he will take what is mine and declare it to you. All that the Father has is mine; therefore I said that he will take what is mine and declare it to you" (John 16:13-15).

There are many glory hound ministers who do not abide in the Spirit of truth, for when the Spirit of truth is in operation Christ will genuinely receive the glory and those touched by the true anointing will seek after the true Christ. The true power of God will not cause believers to become zombies, giving up rational thought and discernment, and throw caution to the wind.

The Elijah List, one of these glory hound organizations, is a growing network of prophetic ministries promoting personal prophecies; however, these ministries on the Elijah List seldom prophesy the true condition of God's people, individually or as the body of Christ. Rather, the tendency is to tickle the ears of Christians who are looking for shortcuts, instant gratification and quick fix deliverance. These ministries have learned to prophesy out of their own spirit.

"Woe to the foolish prophets who follow their own spirit, and have seen nothing! Your prophets have been like jackals among ruins, O Israel. You have not gone up into the breaches, or built up a wall for the house of Israel, that it might stand in battle in the day of the Lord. They have seen false visions and lying divinations. They say, 'Declares the Lord,' when the Lord has not sent them, and yet they expect him to fulfill their word. Have you not seen a false vision and uttered a lying divination, whenever you have said, 'Declares the Lord,' although I have not spoken? ... They have misled my people, saying, 'Peace,' when there is no peace, and because... when the people build a wall, these prophets smear it with whitewash," (Ezekiel 13:3-10).

Watch out for ministries that tout the power of God over the lordship of Christ to gain credence and recognition with the masses. Most so-called prophets in this hour have learned to prophesy out of their own heart and personal spirit, but hear nothing from God.

Beware of false leaders and false ministries touting the ability to initiate revival—when in reality they takeover fellowships or meetings where a true work of God is in its initial stages. This is what has happened to most true moves of God that start in the hearts of hungry believers and the undiscerning, naïve pastor or leader.

Satan's most insidious work: Deceiving Christians with Scripture
The Word of Truth applied in the flesh becomes a deadly poison

In addition to the slanted discipleship curriculum, many popular personality leaders publish specially edited Bibles that I term *designer Bibles*[8] where exclusive insights and interpretation are laced throughout the footnotes and highlights. Today, few Christians study the Word of God in a desperate desire to know and learn to obey the true Christ and receive personal revelation of who he truly is through firsthand study of Scripture.

Satan knows Scripture and his servants have learned to apply the truth of the Scripture to fit their own perverted ideology and moneymaking agenda—making the Word of God a deadly poison. These wolves in sheep's clothing bypass the harder teachings of Christ because they are self-deceived; and many do so deliberately to exalt themselves.

The Apostle Paul warned, *"Evil people and impostors will go on from bad to worse, deceiving and being deceived"* (2 Timothy 3:13). Paul fought this insidious work of Satan in sending imposters amongst aspiring leaders of the brethren—writing, *"We have renounced disgraceful, underhanded ways; we refuse to <u>practice cunning or to tamper with God's word</u>, but by the open statement of the truth we would commend ourselves to every man's conscience in the sight of God"* (2 Corinthians 4:2).

Distorting Scripture by lifting verses out of context and using Christ's words or one of the Apostles' teachings in an underhanded manner has become easy to accomplish, since so few believers know the Word of God through intimate relationship with Christ and diligent study.

---

[8] Designer Bibles: In chapter 8, "Developing our Powers of Discernment," in the section titled Self-Discipline and Hard Work, (p 277), I explain at length the dangers of studying the Bible by embracing someone else's commentary interposed within Scripture.

The false learn cunning in tampering with God's Word as they portray the way of salvation and the Christian walk as easy and full of prosperity. Often false teachers attach special self-assigned credentials to their name to add credence to their claims, becoming experts in the art of manipulation to raise money, calling themselves bishops, apostles, and prophets. Others become so obsessed with academia and degrees in theology that they ignore the practical working of Scripture empowered by the Holy Spirit (Spirit of Truth). These become educated above their level of intelligence, unapproachable, aloof, and arrogant, as they miss knowing Christ personally. Just like the Pharisees and scribes as Christ proclaimed, *"You search the Scriptures because you think that in them you have eternal life; and it is they that bear witness about me, yet you refuse to come to me that you may have life"* (John 5:39-40).

Legalism and Christian Judaism is another deception that perverts the true message of the Gospel of Christ, where confusing Old Testament Scriptures (rules and regulations) are mixed with Christ's teachings, burdening the struggling Christian with carnal methods to appear holy—only to instill spiritual pride and self-righteousness. The Apostle Paul warned against making up rules, regulations, and special observances in Colossians, stating, *"These have indeed an appearance of wisdom in promoting self-made religion and asceticism and severity to the body, but they are of no value in stopping the indulgence of the flesh"* (Colossians 2:23).

Many sincere Christians take these shortcuts in applying the Word of God. In their hearts they desire to know Christ fully; however, they learn to apply Scripture incorrectly from teachings based on false presuppositions or concocted religious ideology that perverts the Gospel of Christ.

Making Followers of the Leader, Not Disciples of Christ

Christ commanded the original disciples to make disciples of all nationalities and to do so by *"teaching them to observe all that I have commanded you"* (Matthew 28:20).

He gives an ominous example of the outcome of not observing or obeying all his words:

"Why do you call me 'Lord, Lord,' and not do what I tell you? Everyone who comes to me and hears my words and does them, I will show you what he is like: he is like a man building a house, who dug deep, and laid the foundation upon rock; and when a flood arose, the stream broke against that house, and could not shake it, because it had been well built. But he who hears and does not do them is like a man who built a house on the ground without a foundation; against which the stream broke, and immediately it fell, and the ruin of that house was great" (Luke 6:46-49).

Here is a short list of popular teachers with their most notable published work, who twist Scripture to suit their false doctrine:
- **Rick Warren:** *Purpose-Driven Life*
- Teaches purpose-driven religious works in place of dying to selfish motives and learning to be led by the Holy Spirit, ministering in the power Christ.
- **Joyce Meyer:** *The Power of Being Positive*

Embraces self-power to overcome inner issues—teaches how to create a religious personality to overshadow negative carnal character; avoids discipline of the Lord and his transforming principles and work.

- **Joel Osteen:** *Your Best Life Now*
  Similar to Meyers and Warren, Osteen teaches positive thinking to develop a religious personality to serve God and also avoids the work of the cross in the believer's life where self-power is brought to death and Christ's power abiding leads and in fills with power to live *in* Christ (not *for* him in self-power).
- **Benny Hinn:** *The Anointing*
  Walks in promoting counterfeit spiritual manifestations, and embraces false doctrines that harness the spiritual powers of the flesh.
- **Kenneth Copeland:** *The Laws of Prosperity*
  Promotes a doctrine that financial blessings is the will of God for Christians, and that faith, positive speech, and donations to Christian ministries will always increase one's material wealth.
- **Pat Robertson:** *The Greatest Virtue: The Secret to Living in Happiness and Success*
  Like Hinn, and Copeland, Robertson embraces the prosperity doctrine—with a twist in his take on giving to God in order to get back more, (especially financially): The Law of Reciprocity.

These leaders and so many others like them bring forth doctrine that suits the passions of wayward and deceived Christians. They amass followers whose first loyalty is not to Christ, but to the leader and the deception that they disseminate.

One can tell by the titles of their books that they speak to believers who are looking for shortcuts and quick-fix teachings to overcome inner issues, unhappiness and lack of money. They twist Scriptures and make up formulas for Christians to follow in self-strength and they avoid teaching on the discipline of the Lord that exposes wrong motives of heart. As the Apostle Paul and Peter warned, people would not endure sound teachings and be led astray by false words. (2 Timothy 4:3-4; 2 Peter 2:2-3).

Typical Foundations for Popular False Teachings

Through years of study, observing results of false teachings, counseling others, and most importantly working out my own salvation as prescribed in Scripture, I have developed the following summary. The following are the most common faulty premises errant teachers employ, in developing a quick-fix or magical-thinking formula as a foundation for their teachings:

- You are a new creature in Christ and have been given a new and pure heart instantly—all things have become new—nothing should be bothering you.

- As a new Christian, you also have a new and pure spirit that is pristine and therefore you have all the promises of God in Christ at your disposal, it is just a matter of training your mind to claim them.
- To grow is merely matter of learning Scripture, becoming involved in fellowship and worship, and finding the right formula to change your old habits of thinking.
- True faith is defined as making things happen for God.
- In Christ, you can do all things. (However, these false leaders do not teach on growing up into Christ, abiding in Christ, and Christ dwelling within the believer, but merely teach that using Christ's name is equivalent to having Christ within.)
- You are now a child of God and you deserve a blessed life on earth.
- As anointed teachers, Christians need our insight and understanding, and they need to implement our unique interpretation of Scripture to become a successful Christian.
- The gifts of the Holy Spirit are opened to those who are baptized in the Spirit indicated by the gifts of tongues.
- Your special prayer language, when employed properly, will lead to a break through with miracles and inner peace.
- By naming the name of Christ, you are protected from being deceived and cannot lose your salvation. Demons must flee whenever you command them to leave.
- To become fulfilled and to do God's will you must become involved in a successful ministry, like the ministry God has given us (the false) — thus, you must become partners with an anointed work and then you will be shielded and blessed.
- God wants the world to be converted to Christianity and thus usher in the next millennium, and to accomplish this task God uses the local church, volunteer workers, and special leaders.
- Christians will be raptured or literally rescued by being caught up into the air before the Great Tribulation begins. (The truth is the rapture will occur at the end of the Great Tribulation just before the wrath of God is poured out upon a rebellious world.)

The following are the most common techniques applied in these carnal formulas that captivate the believer's mind. These popular self-help programs teach Christians to change character by will power, not by the transforming power of Christ working with the leadership of the Holy Spirit in his discipline.

- *Assert your faith by claiming,* appropriating, speaking forth, pronouncing, or thinking positively to change your attitude and receive what you want.
- *Enhance your faith by memorizing* and quoting Scripture, seed planting to receive, tithing, and practicing faithfully in prayer what you want into existence — then you will obtain your break-through and the abundant life God wants for you.
- *Overcome the enemy by changing* bad attitudes by thinking Scripture and right thoughts. Learn to command in Christ's name and claim the victory. Partner with

an anointed ministry that has power for deliverance that can miraculously break strongholds. Rebuke the devil when encountering bad thoughts.

Heartbreaking List of Fallen Personality Leaders

For years, the only high profile scandal with a national evangelist was Aimee Semple McPherson. She was in ministry from the 1920s into the 1940s. Her work ended with her death in 1944 from an accidental overdose of barbiturates.

Since then, with the advent of television, a wave of televangelists falling into public disgrace began in the 1970s, with Jim and Tammy Bakker along with Jimmy Swaggart in 1988, and Ted Haggard in 2006, being the most notable. From the 70s until now there have been *thirty-seven* high profile scandals making national and international headlines.

Sexual immorality and underhanded finances have been the main failures of these noted cases. Bringing more attention to possible greed was the 2007 probe by U.S. Senator Chuck Grassley. The senator became concerned with the financial extravagance within the prosperity Gospel movement, which prompted him to initiate a high-profile probe into the financial operations of the following six ministries: *Kenneth and Gloria Copeland, Creflo Dollar, Benny Hinn, Eddie L. Long, Joyce and David Meyer, and Randy and Paula White.*

Letters were sent to each ministry by Grassley's investigating committee asking the ministries to divulge specific financial information to determine whether ministry leaders inappropriately utilized funds collected.

Benny Hinn, Paula White, and Joyce Meyer responded to the committees' request; the other three ministries under investigation dug in their heels and refused to disclose to the committee any such information. Copeland, Dollar, and Long cited that the IRS is the only authority to request such information. They maintained that as such, the IRS was the government entity that could legally ask for such information or initiate an investigation. They concluded in their response that if the IRS asked for this information they would gladly comply. Eventually the senator's investigation ended without penalties for the pastors who refused to cooperate and without any definitive findings of wrongdoing. (Rachel Zole, "Televangelists Escape Penalty in Senate Inquiry," NBCNEWS.com, January 7, 2011.)

This list of scandals and the Senate investigation is comprised of famous Protestant evangelists. The outrageous and heartbreaking exposé of Catholic clergy molestation cases over the last 30 years and the Magdalene laundry asylums [9] is altogether another staggering statistic on how destructive heresies within Catholicism have claimed a massive number of victims.

---

[9] Magdalene laundry asylums: The Catholic Church ran asylums taking in sullied girls and women for penance and rehabilitation, but in fact, most were treated as inmates with some imprisoned for life. They were required to undertake hard physical labor, including laundry and needlework. They also endured a daily regime that included long periods of prayer and enforced silence. In Ireland, such asylums were known as Magdalene laundries. It has been estimated that up to 30,000 women passed through such laundries in Ireland. The last Magdalene asylum, in Waterford, Ireland, closed on September 25, 1996. (Frances Finnegan, *Do Penance or Perish: Magdalene Asylums in Ireland*, (New York, Oxford University Press, 2004).

The Apostle Paul describes the Catholic heresies almost perfectly in this passage:

"*Now the Spirit expressly says that in later times some will depart from the faith by devoting themselves to <u>deceitful spirits and teachings of demons</u>, through the insincerity of liars whose consciences are seared, who <u>forbid marriage and require abstinence from foods</u> that God created to be received with thanksgiving by those who believe and know the truth*" (1 Timothy 4:1-3).

The number of false doctrines found in Catholicism is vast and requires more time and pages then this volume on discernment can contain. Nonetheless, the discerning saint with a little additional self-study should arrive at the same deduction.

My real concern is addressing the insidious work of *deceitful spirits and teachings of demons* that is now widespread within the Protestant evangelical, charismatic, and Pentecostal expressions of the Christian faith. Those within the list of famously failed evangelical leaders did not start with a goal to have their life's work and ministries shamed or destroyed.

Destructive Heresies Reinforces Denial
Leaders and laymen alike are seeing their faith crumble and don't know why

Granted, some personality leaders are absolute impersonators where pretense and duplicity is deliberate; however, most are victims like those they victimize. Those leaders who fell from grace in the eyes of the world and the Christian community tried very hard to overcome their inner monsters and chase away the energizing demons.

Every attempt to gain victory and deliverance proved futile because of one main reason: Their own theology worked against every valiant effort.

They were convinced that they were born-again and instantly received a pure heart, a pure spirit, and the mind of Christ; so any perplexing inner character issues, habitual sins or overwhelming temptations were due to lack of faith, Satan, or missing the right self-help regimen or self-discipline routine.

Satan and faulty theology subverted the crucial point in their walk: seeking, finding and obeying the true Christ and dying to the works of the flesh. Each sincere Christian will sooner than later be led into a wilderness time (as Jesus was) to overcome the love of this world, the flesh, the sin nature, and the pride of life—taking away Satan's main strongholds in one's life.

Satan used Scripture out of context to tempt Jesus, tempting our Lord to take a shortcut. Each area of Christ's temptations in the wilderness will also be very real for every born-again Christian. Sooner than later, the devil will be allowed to bring forth a variation of Christ's wilderness temptations to each of us. As the end of this age comes to its climax, Scripture warns that Satan will be cast down to the earth and will make war against the saints in vicious wrath, for he knows his time is short.

Christians who have avoided the wilderness journey that forces the saint to deal with their carnal nature and hidden defilements are about to be thrust into a battle for their faith and their eternal salvation; many will fall away. Now is the time to discern between the false and the true—in doctrine and within leadership. Do not take one of the shortcuts that Satan offered these personality leaders.

As you research the testimony of each personality leader, a resounding pattern appears: as each hit bottom in their struggle to overcome, a quick-fix gimmick was inspired and embraced, and then a unique and intriguing map of God's Word became a marketed product to help others. Each packaged a formula for instant deliverance, prosperity, inner abundance of joy and peace, or some method to follow in one's self strength that would allow the achievement of Christian utopia on earth and Christian inner nirvana.

In short, Satan, impersonating the Holy Spirit, offered a plan and convinced each to either tempt God by taking a plunge off a cliff (metaphorically) because of unbelief, or use the spiritual powers of the flesh to turn rocks into bread, or indirectly serve the devil to receive glory and riches on earth.

Most importantly, the miserable oppression, depression, hopeless feelings, physical suffering, financial struggle, and spiritual anxiety—all fueled by the demonic—almost immediately disappeared. In the place of the devil's adversarial harassment comes false theology and false inner peace—and in the mind and heart of the deceived comes rejoicing and the euphoric thought, "At last, deliverance!"

Satan gladly backs off in exchange for a believer to advocate and promote false doctrine. Now that these various carnal plans seem to work, the denial of the true condition of heart becomes even more impacted. True humility of character was never obtained by overcoming the flesh, the world, and the devil by walking hand in hand with the true Christ all the way through the wilderness test.

These learn to abnegate or shun Christ's training as modeled by so many servants in the many biblical accounts. Christ proclaimed in Revelation to the church at Philadelphia, *"Because you have kept my word about patient endurance"* he promised an open door that no one could shut! (Revelation 3:10).

These successful personality leaders refused to keep Christ's word of patient endurance until Christ opened the door. Instead, they took a false door opened by the devil.

Arrogance, pride, and even haughtiness are the character attributes of most of these successful personality leaders, at least until they fall.

What is even more tragic are the following statistics (fruit of these destructive heresies) found among the everyday pastor or leader, with a devastating ripple effect upon their spouse, family and their flock—spreading waves of destruction to every corner of the body of Christ.

Reality Surveys Point to the Truth

The following is a distilled summation from surveys of pastors conducted from 1989 to 2006 by the Francis A. Schaeffer Institute of Church Leadership Development, Barna, Focus on the Family, and Fuller Seminary. The results of these surveys found posted on the following websites provide overwhelming statistics that point to the destructiveness of false doctrine for Christians and leadership: churchleadership.org; barna.org; barnabasministriesinc.org.

The following summations from these surveys reveal disturbing trends; these studies found that over 70% of pastors experience extreme stress and consider dropping out of the ministry. Approximately 35-40% do leave, with the majority doing so after five years in the pastorate.

In one survey, every participant indicated that they had a close associate in ministry or from seminary that had left the ministry due to trouble in their church, over stress and burnout, or a moral failure.

Approximately 90% of pastors in the same survey indicated that they are frequently fatigued on a weekly and daily basis. Almost 90% seriously considered at least one time leaving the ministry and 57% said they would quit if they had a better place to go.

Over 80% of those surveyed revealed that there was no regular discipleship or mentoring program for their congregation. An astounding 77% surveyed described their marriage as *not good*. In this same survey, 75% of the pastors felt they were unqualified or poorly trained by their seminaries to lead the congregation, to manage the church affairs, or to counsel others.

Seventy-two percent in ministry indicated that they studied the Bible in preparing for sermons or for lessons and did not adequately study Scripture for personal growth or personal devotion. A staggering 71% stated that they battle depression on a weekly and even daily basis and 38% said they were divorced or currently in the process of divorce.

Of those in this survey 30% indicated that they had been in an ongoing affair or had a one-time sexual encounter with a parishioner. In another revealing survey, it was estimated that fifteen hundred pastors leave the ministry each month due to spiritual burnout, trouble within the church or a moral failure. This study found 50% of pastors' marriages would end in divorce. Astoundingly, 80% felt unqualified and discouraged as a pastor with 50% saying they would leave if they had another way to make a living.

These studies go on to show even more disheartening statistics than summarized here. These findings listed above suffice in demonstrating the destructiveness of false teachings and false teachers upon those in ministry, let alone the body of Christ as a whole.

From Sunday school to seminary, Christians throughout all denominations, independent fellowships, and movements are not taught, warned, mentored, encouraged, or protected by solid leadership. There are few leaders now who have Christ-like character, who are truly called of God, and who know how to lead by example.

At the very root of this weak condition is this: Failure of leadership to fulfill Christ's great commission in building disciples of Christ. Few in leadership are trained by Christ in true discipleship and in turn fail to teach others to observe all of Christ's teachings. Most leaders lack a solid, unshakeable relationship with the person of Christ, which is paramount before entering into leadership!

The church age or the age of the Gentiles is turning out to be an era of misinterpreting the great commission—this grave error has taken a staggering toll upon God's people. Scripture predicts this condition will grow worse. The idolatry of the great evangelists preaching to the masses the salvation message with the intent to convert all nations (the whole world) to Christ was and is folly. The incessant drive for church growth—where numbers are the goal and leaders herd Christians into church like cattle—instead of making disciples of those called of God is about to end with a terrible falling away.

When the smoke of the coming trouble clears, true leaders will emerge with true Christ-like character. Last-day messengers of Christ who will bring forth sound doctrine in the true power of God will once more come to the forefront, similarly to the account in the book of Acts on the day of Pentecost. Many look for Pentecostal power, but few are prepared to walk in it.

True leaders are those who have stood the test and become transformed in character and have been taken captive by Christ as true servants of him and him only, who in turn will teach others how to allow Christ to transform them—God's way!

End-of-the-Age Fear Mongers and the Paranoid

"See that you are not led astray. For many will come in my name, saying, 'I am he!' and, 'The time is at hand!' Do not go after them. And when you hear of wars and tumults, do not be terrified, for these things must first take place, but the end will not be at once" (Luke 21:8-9).

Over the last 40 years, an increasing number of Christian seers have come out publicly warning of and prophesying disasters and calamities, and declaring dates on Christ's return. These have misled many, terrified many, and caused many to spin their wheels in preparing for disasters that never came. The result is many now just stop up their ears and ignore the true warnings of the end of this age—it is coming, but not all at once!

Ministry Case: *Pastor's hidden nukes*

In August of 2009, one pastor prophesied that terrorists had planted nuclear bombs throughout the Washington D.C., area and that by October 2009 they would be detonated. This warning spread like wildfire—through the Internet and by word of mouth—to the point of drawing the attention of Homeland Security and FBI investigators. This rumor turned out to be false and October 2009 passed without any terrorist attack. However, the impact on undiscerning Christians who fell for this false prophecy was very painful.

One Christian woman living in the D. C. area described the feelings of terror caused by this pastor's recklessness. Having no place to escape in advance, she became so distraught that she contemplated killing herself and her children rather than die by being incinerated in a terrorist nuclear attack.

More recently, Harold Camping and his followers put advertisements on billboards and signs across the country declaring that on May 21, 2011, Jesus Christ would return to earth. When Christ did not return on that date, he revised his prediction, stating that this was to happen on October 21, 2011. Of course, Camping's revised forecast failed and he had to apologize to all his flock and to the nation at large. One undiscerning Christian who followed this false alarmist invested his life's savings into the national billboard advertising campaign. Other followers became enraged, but most followers became bewildered and confused.

Now the pastor who warned of a terrorist nuke attack is back at it with the following lead to his next Internet radio show broadcast: "Is there an assassination plot in the works against the President of the United States? Will there be an Inauguration on January 20th and if so what will it mean? These thoughts and more will be discussed on tonight's broadcast." This kind of incendiary public discussion only leads to speculation and base suspicions, and this kind of obsessing may lead to another interview with the FBI. Ω

This type of recklessness has become common throughout the charismatic and Pentecostal movements, not just from unknown pastors but also such leaders such as Pat Robinson. The Apostle Paul in his first letter to Timothy describes these types of people as having a morbid craving for controversy; they create base suspicions, that they are puffed up, conceited, and know nothing. (See 1 Timothy 6:3-5.)

Jesus warned of this type of hapless nonsense becoming extreme during the birth pangs leading up to his appearance. These false alarmists use the birth-pang troubles as an opportunity to gain attention and amass followers. Fear-mongers in the pulpit get a popularity lift by sending out false alarms when God's people live in fear and are not ready for his coming. Remember, Jesus said, *"Do not be terrified."*

A true servant will see that the special time is approaching fast, and see how unprepared most are; thus, a true servant will warn with sound doctrine and sound the alarm for earnest prayer, beseeching God for more time to get ready.

Several ministries have risen to notoriety by preaching fear, predicting calamities, and drumming up speakers, prophets, and authors that promote the need to get ready in order to survive the impending doom. These ministries act much like the supermarket tabloids that take a hint of truth and weave lies and fabrication to sell copies.

The Prophesy Club, Messiah's Branch, Steve Quayle, Coast-to-Coast, and other similar ministries and radio talk shows promote conspiracy theories, propagate disaster scenarios, and sell survival kits, gold, and books that provide little help in addressing the true issues facing Christians.

These ministries prey on ignorant Christians who are waking up to the truth that this country is on the verge of judgment and that Christians will be required to endure the Great Tribulation.

Fear is a powerful motivator and most Christians panic when they first awake to this truth, not realizing their fear demonstrates they are not right with God. Instead of pursuing and embracing all that Christ taught in order to become prepared, protected, and led by the Holy Spirit, many become vulnerable to teachers who play on those fears.

This trend of false alarms and fear mongering will grow worse, with all manner of false teachers and false prophets spouting off and causing many to fall away or be led astray from the true Christ.

"For false christs and false prophets will arise and show great signs and wonders, <u>so as to lead astray, if possible, even the elect</u>. Lo, I have told you beforehand. So, if they say to you, 'Lo, he is in the wilderness,' do not go out; if they say, 'Lo, he is in the inner rooms,' <u>do not believe it</u>" (Matthew 24:24,-26).

If you do not allow Christ to discipline you and train you in true discernment, you will be at risk and prone to believe the lies that are about to be poured out—lies so powerful that the elect (true and mature Christians) will be at risk of being deceived.

How Satan Hijacks God's Work
The takeover of the Wales Revival that led to what we have now

True shepherds must learn how to avoid the pitfalls that befell the Wales revival and other true movements of God. Pastors and elders will have to give an account as to the care they exercised over God's vineyard.

Jessie Penn-Lewis and Evan Roberts began to preach and teach against these errors. They saw the root of the problem as being the lack of true available disciples to bring converts into the training and discipline of the Lord whereby they might learn to embrace the work of the cross. Their co-authored work entitled *War on the Saints* became a powerful assessment resource during the early years of our research concerning counterfeit movements.

Penn-Lewis wrote and preached extensively on the central importance of the work of the cross within the believer's life and how a move of the Holy Spirit upon a fellowship or community can be taken over by the counterfeiting work of the devil. One of her works, *The Awakening in Wales*, we quote here as she points out the perils of revival.

What we found in addition to Jessie's insights to be another central issue was and is the lack of trained and "crucified in the flesh" leaders and Christian workers to ensure that discipleship and mentoring took priority over meetings that used enthusiasm-producing hype instead of a stable, Spirit-filled life in Christ.

Penn-Lewis wrote:

> "Now as to the perils of revival: These again primarily may be briefly defined as, (1) the danger of acting or living by "feeling", or the sensuous life, instead of the spirit-life; and (2) the peril arising from the spirits of evil counterfeiting the workings of the Holy Spirit. Alongside of the danger of becoming dominated by "feelings" and emotions, the perils of Revival come mainly from the invisible world of spirits. The Counterfeiter is watching to counterfeit, and to insert his workings in the place of God's workings.... A very small inserted "stream", or "tincture" from the enemy causes mixture which may not be discerned at first, but which sooner or later produces fruit in confusion and trouble" (Jessie Penn-Lewis, *The Centrality of the Cross*, Fort Washington, PA: Christian Literature Crusade 1993, pp. 151-152.)

Jesus prepared the church for the day of Pentecost by making true disciples—first. These men were not obsessed with signs and wonders.

However, today, a true move of God is quickly pounced upon and taken over by wolves. The sincere but naïve believer is tricked into following the anointed power broker. Today, more than anytime in church history, mesmerizing counterfeit signs and wonders easily mislead God's people.

Jessie Penn-Lewis termed these exotic signs and wonders as *empty manifestations* which do nothing to transform character or instill true peace and the fruit of the Holy Spirit. Through a satanically contrived system of worship and exotic ministry, deceived believers are conditioned to crave the next exotic manifestation.

Recently, an associate in ministry informed me that her church is pushing to inspire and reignite the false Toronto Blessing revival in her local fellowship.

Impressed with growth and outer manifestations that supposedly bring Christians closer to God in divine ecstasy, a key leader started speaking about how the Wales Revival started this movement in 1904.

This teacher made a wild statement saying that Jessie Penn-Lewis was responsible for stopping the Wales revival from spreading to the whole world. This misinformed teacher asserted that Penn-Lewis pulled Evan Roberts aside and convinced him to back away from promoting this movement.

As I have shared earlier, Jessie Penn-Lewis and Evan Roberts worked together in denouncing the counterfeiting that overtook a true move of God and they attempted to correct and teach why and how the demonic counterfeited the real.

Unfortunately, there will be more assertions made by the proponents of these false movements as they spread lies about those who denounce this counterfeit activity. Judgment is coming to liars, and God will severely discipline the counterfeit servants and false teachers who practice carnal methods in getting God's people stirred up.

Cycle after cycle within movement after movement continues as these exotic and sensuous counterfeit experiences manifest in ever-increasing strange and irreverent forms.

The true ministers and shepherds who cry out to God for revival must understand how God prepares for revival and avoid the hijacking of what God desires.

A true move of God upon the lost, the backslidden, and the lukewarm Christian can only come when proper discipleship is established and maintained and a cadre of battle-hardened Christian workers are in the field doing the work of ministry.

This is the key for being able to experience true revival in any local fellowship or congregation. Understanding the necessity of true discipleship is absolutely imperative.

Ultra Control to Compensate for Lack of Mentoring and Discipleship

During the late sixties and seventies, a discipleship movement began in the church here in the U.S. referred to as the shepherding movement; this undertaking had good intentions and a goal to build disciples out of sincere believers.

Many Christians who submitted to this discipleship program were unstable and wayward (twice a soul or divided). To compensate for this, strict controls were put in place.

A hierarchy of shepherds was established from national leaders down to local shepherds, the local shepherds were placed in charge of small groups. Unfortunately, the leadership within this movement became overbearing and controlling. They themselves were never made to be a true disciple of Christ—it was a case of the blind leading the blind.

Again, this is another example of a movement's failure due to its carnal efforts in fulfilling Christ's commission—in review, let's read Christ's commission. *"Go therefore and make disciples of all nations, baptizing them in the name of the Father and of the Son and of the Holy Spirit, teaching them to observe all that I have commanded you; and lo, I am with you always, to the close of the age"* (Matthew 28:19-20).

We must discern that Christ was successful because he built a foundation for the church, initially, by making true disciples. These men had Christ-like nature and character burned into them as they were being taught and as they followed his example.

Jesus told the disciples to teach new disciples to observe all that he commanded. Few today teach others all that Jesus taught. The basic cause for this is many in leadership have never allowed Jesus to discipline them, intimately, in all that he commands.

In reality, true revival is founded on true discipleship teaching, where the training is done by the discipline of the Lord with like-minded believers supporting each other in what Jesus called *"entering the narrow gate, and walking the hard path that leads to life."*

Part of the solution to these problems will come when God's people no longer tolerate the false. When trouble comes, the false lose their power to deceive. Moreover, the sincere Christian will be outspoken and not tolerate the lies anymore because he or she has been burned-out long enough. Right now, far too many of God's sheep choose to stay ignorant and go along with anyone who promises a good time in the Lord. However, this trend will change as darkness and trouble touch the lives of all—sinners, the lukewarm, and the saints.

As the birth pangs increase and more trouble encroaches upon Christians, true revival, in many local fellowships will stay the course as God's people start to wake up and reject the false.

A great harvest is coming. Millions will awaken to the call of God for salvation and sanctification. A holy fear will sweep over these precious lost children of God.

In reading this, many may become disturbed as I challenge their rapture theories. Sorry to burst bubbles—the reality is Christ will not rapture his dear saints to safety until the great harvest is complete—during the Great Tribulation! The church may endure 10 months, 2 years, 5 years, or the entire Tribulation period. No one will know the exact duration or the exact day or hour, but we must be ready and able to endure until that great moment when we are called up at the sound of the last trumpet. We know that Jesus said, *"If those days had not been cut short, no human being would be saved. But for the sake of the elect those days will be cut short"* (Matthew 24:22).

The Lord expects his people to let their lights shine as a witness to millions who are lost and need to be drawn to the true Christ. There is coming a great harvest, and God is calling for his workers to be ready. He desires to purify and establish a people to stand as beacons of hope, and carry the pure message of Christ's Gospel and the good news of the coming Kingdom. (See Revelations 7:9-17.)

What Manner of Spirit?

Arrogant Christian leaders who sell their spiritual powers, driven by a spirit of destruction

"I have a few things against you: You have some there who hold the teaching of Balaam, who taught Balak to put a stumbling block before the sons of Israel, so that they might eat food sacrificed to idols and practice sexual immorality" (Revelation 2:14).

The story of Balaam is an Old Testament example of a leader who attempted to sell his spiritual gift to do evil against God's people. Balak, leader of the Moabites enlisted a well-known seer, Balaam, to curse God's people Israel. God stopped Balaam from this evil; however, Balaam skirted around God's constraint and told Balak how he could make the people of God stumble and create within the people of Israel a rebellion.

Balaam forsook the right way for money and misused his gifting, and this is the case for many in leadership today. As recounted in this chapter, many in leadership sell their spiritual gifting to God's people for donations or for popularity to maintain a steady stream of donations.

Many, like Benny Hinn (cursing those who challenge his anointing) become militant and arrogant in defending their error of following the way of Balaam. When confronted they fall into what the disciples almost fell into, which was attacking any opposition by cursing those who threatened them and their mission.

The account in Scripture concerning the disciple's desire to curse those who reject them or their doctrine is described as follows:

"When the days drew near for him to be taken up, he set his face to go to Jerusalem. And he sent messengers ahead of him, who went and entered a village of the Samaritans, to make preparations for him. But the people did not receive him, because his face was set toward Jerusalem. And when his disciples James and John saw it, they said, "Lord, do you want us to tell fire to come down from heaven and consume them?" But he turned and rebuked them, And they went on to another village" (Luke 9:51-56). In my ESV Bible and other translations there is a footnote to this passage: Some manuscripts add *and he said, "You do not know what manner of spirit you are of; for the Son of Man came not to destroy people's lives but to save them"*

These militant leaders like Benny Hinn and Kenneth Copeland, as well as their blinded followers do not know the spirit that drives them, or the kind of spirit that they have become. They become jealous and defensive toward anyone who may threaten their ministry and a spirit of destruction drives them.

The disciples learned to let the Lord defend their message and their mission, trusting the Lord to touch the hearts of those who might be in opposition. Recall how the high priest, the Pharisees, and Sadducees held counsel and had all the Apostles arrested, but fortunately by God's grace, Gamaliel, one of their own stood up to the counsel and brought reason to their spirit of destruction.

In the coming days, God will be releasing ministries and Christian workers who know the score and understand what is coming down. They will be new wine that will not be conformed to the old wineskins of the carnal ministries, or a watered down Gospel, or submit to the false.

If you are in a quandary concerning some of the insights and pronouncements presented in this resource, then embracing Gamaliel's wisdom will go a long way. It will give the Lord time to confirm what we share.

The counsel wanted to destroy the Gospel of Christ by killing all the Apostles, but Gamaliel said to the counsel:

"Men of Israel, take care what you are about to do with these men. For before these days Theudas rose up, claiming to be somebody, and a number of men, about four hundred, joined him. He was killed, and all who followed him were dispersed and came to nothing. After him Judas the Galilean rose up in the days of the census and drew away some of the people after him. He too perished, and all who followed him were scattered. So in the present case I tell you, keep away from these men and let them alone, for if this plan or this undertaking is of man, it will fail; but if it is of God, you will not be able to overthrow them. You might even be found opposing God!" (Acts 5:35-39).

Many in the coming days who have encased their faith in false doctrine and turned to a carnal self-powered Christianity will ignorantly, arrogantly, and pridefully be found opposing God and what he is about to do.

However, when the rug is pulled out from under prosperity and civility in society, as the birth pangs roar, many who opposed the truth of the coming Kingdom will wake up and find no opportunity to repent. *"Multitudes, multitudes in the valley of decision"* (Joel 3:14), where many ignorant, arrogant and pride driven Christians will find themselves unprepared and wander into the world looking for help and sustenance. (See the parable of the ten maidens in Matthew 25:1-13).

However, many who wandered off into false doctrine, and some who initially oppose this message, will turn back to the truth, submit to the Lord, and become prepared.

Spiritual Shrikes Incognito
Split personalities driven by bitter jealousy and selfish ambition, channeling for hell

As we complete this chapter on false leadership and the gates of hell, there is a category of people who become informal leaders and caretakers in the lives people who are weak and naïve, who struggle in life, and yet who desire to become good and successful. Many an immature saint and redeemable sinner have become victims of people who slowly and methodically destroy the faith and life in others, all in the guise of helping.

This type of person makes helping others to live right, their life's mission; however, in the process of helping they sabotage their efforts by emanating a spiritual aura of death. Unconsciously they demand perfection in others, yet continually point out failings in order to fulfill their bitter judgments towards others.

The term *shrike*[10] describes a person who lives to help others, yet in the process of helping will consistently belittle, humiliate, and berate ever so subtly, their person of interest, making

---

[10] The definition of *Shrike*: A small bird having a strong, hooked, and toothed bill that feeds on insects and on small birds and other animals. Members of certain species of this bird impales their prey on thorns or suspend it from the branches of trees to tear it apart more easily, and are said to kill more than is necessary for them to eat.

them consistently fail. Psychologists have used this term in the past in describing the destructiveness of a self-righteous embittered person. In my studies, this term became prominent in understanding the spiritual dynamics in harming others with snide remarks, correction, and criticisms.

In the context of our work, the spiritual shrike is a Christian do-gooder (or a self-righteous non-Christian) who tirelessly works to help others while simultaneously spiritually defiling those in their sphere of influence to fail.

They snare their victim with the promise to help and are Johnny-on-the-spot to give a hand and to give advice, and even to rescue the troubled when in crisis. This enhances a period of bonding where the shrike becomes freer to criticize and withhold empathy concerning mistakes made or during the sufferings in the trials of life. Genuine encouragement is withheld and discouraging criticism is freely dispensed. Even when success is achieved, what could have been done better is suggested frequently.

Like the shrike bird, these human shrikes emotionally and spiritually mutilate the others they try to help, and do so in an almost invisible manner. They make sure they maintain their hidden agenda as they approach each victim incognito. Their prey is the undiscerning and naïve who become dependent on the shrike's appearance of successful and holy living.

Many shrikes suffer from a split personality, where an evil spirit finds a comfortable place in the hidden dark side of the twice-a-soul spiritual shrike. Hatred, jealousy, bitterness, envy, revenge—any evil agenda is walled off through complete disassociation. The outer personality operates in absolute denial by putting on a pristine and caring mask.

This outer personality charade becomes believable to others who are ignorant, gullible, and undiscerning, due to the spiritual shrike's power to deceive—primarily because they believe their own lie!

The Apostle Paul referred to these types of people as false believers who are born of the flesh, not born of God. *"But just as at that time he who was born according to the flesh persecuted him who was born according to the Spirit, so also it is now"* (Galatians 4:29).

Those are the inner workings of a Christian spiritual shrike, being born out of religion and a carnal Gospel and instinctively hating those who are genuine and born of the Holy Spirit in true faith. The spiritual power to influence and defile others comes from an evil spirit within them, not much unlike Judas who betrayed Christ.

Other characteristics: These become pathological egotists, whose purpose is to run the lives of others, making sure every jot and tittle of religiosity is marked. Those who develop a desire for power usually solicit demonic help, where an evil spirit or spirits find ease to cohabitate since they permanently suppress all guilt of conscience. An attack can ensue when standing against their evil, confronting, or just saying no to their selfishness. (See Symptoms from a Demon-Boosted Human Spirit Attack in chapter six, "Discerning the Spiritual powers of the flesh")

Jesus said of them, *"You blind guides, straining out a gnat and swallowing a camel! ... You clean the outside of the cup and the plate, but inside they are full of greed and self-indulgence. ... You are like whitewashed tombs, which outwardly appear beautiful, but within are full of dead people's bones and all uncleanness. So you also outwardly appear righteous to others, but within you are full of hypocrisy and lawlessness"* (Matthew 23:25-28).

Evil Political Leaders with an Anti-Christ Agenda

Through the centuries historians have documented tyrannical leaders, giving theorists, psychologists, and social-political scientists ample data to explore the reasons why and how evil leaders rise to power.

From all the research and analysis, certain patterns, correlating background reasons, and influencing factors, there is more than enough information available to make a solid conjecture on how an evil leader comes into power. Writing on these findings may make good reading, however the discerning saints must understand why and how evil leaders come to power based on the truth found in Scripture.

Evil leaders in politics gain influence because God's people (who are to be salt and light to any nation) lose connection with God the Father, by not allowing Christ to be Lord of all. God's people in Germany during the years leading up to Nazism, fell into national pride, the love of this world, jealousy and bitterness, and hatred towards other peoples and in turn denied Christ as savior and Lord. Instead of holding Christ as the standard to measure the fruit and sincerity of any leader, they turned to their own understanding and fell headlong into darkness, giving power to a human (Hitler) to care for their well-being, to instill hope, and to secure prosperity.

Evil has always lurked in the dark corners of all cultures, and the Gospel of Christ shines into that darkness through a holy people after God's heart. When this kind of holy condition exists within the body of Christ, it will expose evil and will influence righteousness to rise in power instead of evil.

As the end of this age races to its finality, God's people in America, like God's people in pre-Nazi Germany, have lost sight of the lordship of Christ. They are no longer able to influence with righteousness, thus allowing evil to rise to power. As we look back over the last forty years or so, the trend towards evil politics and government is in direct correlation to the continuous string of sickening revelations of ministry leaders falling from grace and becoming national headline news. A nation will lose its moral compass in government when the people of God turn to wickedness.

The Apostle John in his epistle established for us a general understanding for the work of evil, in how the antichrist theme influences people and culture. *"Children, it is the last hour; and as you have heard that antichrist is coming, so now many antichrists have come; therefore we know that it is the last hour"* and who would be an antichrist or the final antichrist? *"This is the antichrist, he who denies the Father and the Son"* (1 John 2:18, 22).

Though written almost two thousand years ago, what the Apostle John understood from the Holy Spirit's inspiration still applies today, more than ever—antichrists have come and gone with the intent to denounce Jesus as the Christ (Savior and Lord). In succession through the centuries, each antichrist that has come, built for the next to be more perfected in deception. The final antichrist will succeed in deceiving the whole world, including Israel and America. (See 2 Thessalonians 2:9-12.)

The mystery of lawlessness and the rise of the final antichrist are coming to its full blossom. The people of America more than ever now look to a human for their wellbeing, source of hope, and surety for peace and prosperity. Like Nazi Germany, America as a people are turning to a human savior and denying that Jesus is the Christ. The majority of Americans have no qualms about erasing the influence of Christ upon this nation's history or its future.

In 1932 Hitler, in his second year as the chancellor of Germany, held a meeting with the top clergy of the nation. A courageous pastor at the meeting made the following statement: "Our concern, Herr Hitler, is not for the church. Jesus Christ will take care of His church. Our concern is for the soul of our nation." Hitler replied, "The soul of Germany—you can leave that to me." That brash pastor was ushered to the back of the group by the other clergy out of embarrassment, as the rest of God's leaders in the meeting said nothing.

Oscar-winning actor Jamie Foxx called Barack Obama "our lord and savior." Here is the exact quote from the November 2012 Soul Train awards in Vegas: "It's like church over here. It's like church in here. First of all, give an honor to God and our lord and savior Barack Obama. Barack Obama."

In November 2010, Newsweek declared Obama "god of all things" on its cover, and more recently, Florida A&M professor Barbara A. Taylor called Obama an "apostle' sent by God to create a political heaven on earth.

The end-of-the-age antichrist spirit is thriving as Satan continues to create mass deception, as he did in Nazi Germany with the rise of Hitler. I do not believe Obama is the antichrist; however, he is *an* antichrist, a cog in the linage, a linage of mesmerizing evil leaders promoting a mindset that rejects Jesus as the Christ and Lord and sets themselves up as the final and ultimate authority.

There are many accounts in Scripture concerning evil leadership that usurps God's will and commandments in favor of their own political base and selfish agenda.

Like Korah in the wilderness, evil leaders cause rifts in society by inciting people to reject godliness and godly leadership (Numbers 16). Like Hitler in his ideology outlined in his best seller *Mein Kampf* (My Struggle)—which helped him turn the populace of Germany away from civility towards revenge and scapegoat racism.

Take a quick survey of the Obama books, such as *The Audacity of Hope: Thoughts on Reclaiming the American Dream*, a subtle yet powerful literary work to enlist the disenchanted and the disgruntled, and to incite the embittered to make changes in the very foundation of society's structure, with the notion of taking from the so-called rich and handing it out to the downtrodden. This is the same evil principle Hitler used: enlisting the dark side of human nature to gain support and carry out a revengeful agenda. Granted, the rich in many cases used their wealth to oppress; however, this approach—to take from others to give to others who have not earned that wealth—is still stealing.

The principle employed is "lawlessness to correct wrongs" and to allow evil leadership to rise to power through deception. This is an aspect of what the Apostle Paul mentions as *"the mystery of lawlessness* [that] *is already at work"* (2 Thessalonians 2:7).

A good example in Scripture of lawlessness that correlates with the current political landscape of America and President Obama and his wife Michelle, is the evil perpetrated by Ahab and Jezebel, king and queen of Israel who reigned between 869 and 850 BC.

Scripture describes this evil duo: *"There was none who sold himself to do what was evil in the sight of the LORD like Ahab, whom Jezebel his wife incited. He acted very abominably in going after idols, as the Amorites had done, whom the LORD cast out before the people of Israel"* (1 Kings 21:25-26).

I refrain from describing the lengthy list of destructive laws and actions that no other predecessor has enacted, all undermining the very foundations of this nation. The main point to help discern a false leader, including this current president and his wife is the pattern of deception they use, including outright lies and the misuse of authority.

However, I will cite the most egregious acts conducted by these two last-days Ahab-and-Jezebel leaders who channel for hell—the present leaders that represent a nation that is rapidly turning into last-days Sodom culture.

The height of abomination from these two so-called believers in God is his and hers public support for homosexual marriage, and now the pressure President Obama is exerting upon the Boys Scouts of America—to openly accept homosexuals into their ranks and into leadership—to put young boys and young men into such vile influences—how outrageous![11]

No other president has sold himself to do what is evil in the sight of the Lord like President Obama. There is no comparison in American history; however, they both now rate in comparison to Ahab and Jezebel from Old Testament history.

Empowerment of last-days evil within politics is primarily accomplished through polarizing the masses by using deception and hidden lawlessness. A chaotic polarizing by creating extreme divisions between races, between the wealthy and the poor, between ideologies, between the religious and the non-religious, between unions and management, and so forth, are all similar to how Korah accomplished inciting division within the nation of Israel when they were all suffering in the wilderness.

Evil leaders throughout history and even more so today become prolific at projecting blame onto others for their failures. They become very capable of inciting bitter hatred and persecution towards designated scapegoats, and they develop a deceptive finesse in creating a straw man fallacy to refute valid criticism. In some cases evil leaders, like Ahab and Jezebel, abuse their leadership powers by murdering opponents (literally or through character assignation) by the use of threat and blackmail.

---

[11] As of May 24, 2013 the Boy Scouts of American finally succumbed to this evil pressure and voted to approve a plan to accept openly gay members; however, this organization is still under attack from the homosexual agenda with its pressing that openly gay adults can become scout leaders. Many conservatives within the Boy Scouts of America are now outraged over the outcome of the vote. They are threatening to leave and start a new organization for boys.

We see the same political oppression now in America, and there is no prospect of change for the better. Evil in leadership, in the church, in business, and in politics has taken America into the last-days darkness.

The Harbinger of the Harbinger
The resident, leaders of the nation and leaders of the church were procedurally warned!

The keynote speaker at the president's Inaugural Prayer Breakfast on January 21, 2013, was Rabbi Jonathan Cahn, a messianic Jew and author, minister, and teacher. His address to those attending the breakfast left no doubt that America is teetering on final judgment. The president and the leaders of this nation, as well as leaders of Christianity received warning and have no excuse for not heeding.

Jonathan's theme as keynote speaker was a summation of his New York Times bestselling book, *The Harbinger*. A harbinger, as defined in the context of Cahn's book, is the correlation between God's warnings and judgment upon ancient Israel and God's warning to America by way of the many afflictions of our time: 9/11, the financial crisis of 2007, the collapse of the global economy, and continued natural calamities.

The prophet Isaiah proclaimed to Israel the harbingers (omens and signs) that would solidify each turning point leading to Israel's total destruction. Thus, in his book *The Harbinger*, Rabbi Cahn explains the pattern of God's ways in warning a nation and his people of pending judgment.

The Harbingers prophetic message of looming judgment is God's faithfulness to call this nation and his people to true repentance. However, *The Harbinger's* warning for America, though precise, is missing God's ultimate purposes and warning in these last days. *The Harbinger's* warning is a harbinger within itself and was appointed by God to be given as a matter of procedure.

Cahn's book is still gaining vast readership and there was resounding applause at the inaugural breakfast by the sincere believer at each keynote that elevated the lordship of Christ—even as scoffers walked out at various junctures of Rabbi Cahn's speech.

The Harbinger, along with other prophetic warnings, has fallen on the deaf ears of the ungodly and has not awakened the faithful from their stupor. Yet *The Harbinger* is part of God's end-of-the-age procedural mercy warning—warning all concerning what is about to take place.

Rabbi Cahn, like most, wants to see America repent and return to Christ as Lord; however, these warnings, including *The Harbinger*, are too little, too late. These prophetic warnings are a matter of procedural steps that will leave God's people and a rebellious nation no excuse.

Just as Isaiah explained on behalf of God concerning Israel:, "The people <u>did not turn to him who struck them</u>, nor inquire of the Lord of hosts. So the Lord cut off from Israel head and tail, palm branch and reed <u>in one day</u>—<u>the elder and honored man is the head, and the prophet who teaches lies is the tail; for those who guide this people have been leading them astray, and those who are guided by them are swallowed up</u>. Therefore the Lord does not rejoice over their young men, and has no compassion on their fatherless and widows; for <u>everyone is godless and an evildoer, and every mouth speaks folly</u>. For all this his anger has not turned away, and his hand is stretched out still" (Isaiah 9:13-17).

The real prophetic message is found in the book of Revelation and it is the last-days message that every sincere saint must hear and heed, *"Come out of her, my people, lest you take part in her sins, lest you share in her plagues; for her sins are heaped high as heaven, and God has remembered her iniquities. Pay her back as she herself has paid back others, and repay her double for her deeds; mix a double portion for her in the cup she mixed. As she glorified herself and lived in luxury, so give her a like measure of torment and mourning, since in her heart she says, 'I sit as a queen, I am no widow, and mourning I shall never see.' <u>For this reason her plagues will come in a single day, death and mourning and famine,</u> and she will be burned up with fire; for mighty is the Lord God who has judged her"* (Revelation 18:4-8).

The true prophetic warning that all must embrace is the soon-to-come midnight cry. The true harbinger is the rejection of all omens and signs by God's people and this nation, including its leaders and its people. This leaves only the final call to wake up and come away from the love of America and the angst of losing America to the wicked. Chapter 9 will focus on the coming final proclamation.

There will not be another awakening in America to spare America from end-of-the-age judgments. From the president down to the common citizen, the whole populace is about to be overwhelmed by God speaking in the manner that Christ warned. *"And there will be signs in sun and moon and stars, and on the earth distress of nations in perplexity because of the roaring of the sea and the waves, people fainting with fear and with foreboding of what is coming on the world. For the powers of the heavens will be shaken"* (Luke 21:25-26).

The final proclamation is the midnight cry from a holy people—a people not of this world, rather those who abide in the Kingdom that is about to come—the true body of Christ beckoning God's people to come out and be ready to meet the bride groom. The birth pangs of the coming Kingdom are about to reach torturous final labor pains, where Christ the coming King of kings and Lord of lords appears.

The rise of the Antichrist is just around the Corner!
The ultimate evil leader promising good, but bringing the world to near total destruction!

Today Christians must take Christ's warning seriously. Politics and evil leaders will now directly affect everyone, especially the sincere disciple of Christ. The nastiest and most deceiving political leader is coming very soon. This warning is based on Christ's warnings and teaching concerning the end-of-the-age events to include the birth pangs and the Great Tribulation.

Jesus warns of false leaders coming soon, *"False christs and false prophets will arise and perform signs and wonders, to lead astray, if possible, the elect. But be on guard; I have told you all things beforehand"* (Mark 13:22-23). Yes, the antichrist is coming as an *activity of Satan with all power and false signs and wonders, and with all wicked deception*. The antichrist will promise world peace, prosperity and solutions for all the world's troubles; however, they will be lies covering up the intent to destroy Israel, and to marginalize and persecute out of existence all the true Christians.

Learning to discern people, including church leaders and political leaders will involve acquiring the ability to endure the trouble that is coming upon the world now. True discernment is vital to having a genuine faith in Christ that will lead to a sure salvation instead of deception leading to eternal damnation. (Seeing the activities that our Lord warns of will most likely bring waves of fear, hopelessness, and a sense of powerlessness. Take heart, Christ would not warn us to be on guard and to be awake if he did not have a plan to protect and deliver the sincere child of God all way through—to the end).

"Many false prophets will arise and lead many astray. And because lawlessness will be increased, the love of many will grow cold. But the <u>one who endures to the end will be saved</u>" (Jesus speaking of the end-of-this-age challenges in Matthew 24:11-13).

Chapter Four

Doctrines of Demons and Implanted Weeds

"Now <u>the Spirit expressly</u> says that in <u>later times</u> some will depart from the faith by <u>devoting themselves to deceitful spirits and teachings of demons</u>, through the insincerity of liars whose consciences are seared" (1 Timothy 4:1-2).

How can Christians embrace this warning from the Apostle Paul that they might stay alert to false doctrine? How does one know if he or she is following teachers who have an anointing fostered by deceitful spirits?

One must realize and confirm from the Lord that we are now in the last days, and with that revelation take the above passage seriously. When a sincere disciple awakens to this dark hour they will be amazed and alarmed as to how widespread false teachers have become and how devoted they are to counterfeiting spirits and false doctrine.

Deceived teachers, anointed by deceitful spirits have come to the forefront throughout Christianity with teachings that guide the sincere Christian as well as ignorant-naïve believers into a deeply veiled end-of-the-age plan of Satan.

Christ explains this insidious plan in the parable of the weeds found in Matthew 13:24-30 and 13:36-43, a plan to spring on God's people at the close of the age.

Satan's has successfully executed this plan through pretentious liars teaching doctrines of demons, resulting in the implantation of the devil's servants amongst the brethren. Most of these false teachers are self-deceived. The false have successfully promoted false doctrine, and due to that success have become seared in their conscience—unwilling to embrace the truth, refusing to consider Scripture that refutes their wayward doctrines.

Unfortunately, Christians who adhere to the many teachings of demons will not budge an inch in their stubborn insistence on following those who are deceivers. The Apostles Paul wrote of this dark time now, *"While evil people and impostors will go on from bad to worse, deceiving and being deceived"* (2 Timothy 3:13).

The goal of this chapter is to help those who are entrapped by these lying spirits to break denial of departing from faith in the true Christ, and break free from living under the spell of deceitful spirits. The goal is also to help those fighting these lies understand what they are facing concerning false believers who themselves have become devoted to the deceitful spirit and false teachings.

It may be easy to identify a false teaching by a leader and preach against it, or a Christian worker may explain a false doctrine to a deceived brother or sister; however, rooting out those in fellowship who embrace the false doctrine can easily mushroom into a major conflict. The unexpected collateral damage can be far-reaching and devastating. It is imperative that the leadership of the Holy Spirit be precisely followed, in all wisdom and discernment.

False Teachings Producing Gospel Hardened Carnal and False Believers
Many shipwreck their faith by rejecting conscience in religiosity

These teachings distort the truth of God's Word, drawing many sincere seekers of God as well as the reprobate to church, not by the Holy Spirit for true rebirth in Christ, but rather by activity of deceitful spirits. Many today have experienced a false conversion; however, God in his faithfulness will attempt to bring the deceived person back to a right relationship with Christ if they hear the truth in time.

A false conversion is experienced when the Holy Spirit has not called the person to salvation, but the person was drawn by the carnal persuasiveness of the preacher or evangelist. Many are tricked to try Jesus and then become snared in Christian religiosity. True salvation is to be initiated at the right time in a person's life by the power of the Holy Spirit. The curious who are not ready may come to the knowledge of salvation, but they must understand the cost of giving themselves to the lordship of Christ, then in true repentance call on God and his grace.

The prophet Hosea pronounced for God, *"My people are destroyed for lack of knowledge"* (Hosea 4:6). Satan's end-of-the-age plan will cause many to perish because they do not hear and learn the whole counsel of God and the Gospel of Christ in its entirety. They come to God on their terms, not on God's terms, not knowing the difference.

Further, many suffer from wounds to the spirit and damaged emotions, where they may become sincere, but later suffer from the symptoms of these wounds and impurities of heart. As it states in Jeremiah so it is today, *"For from the least to the greatest of them, everyone is greedy for unjust gain; and from prophet to priest, everyone deals falsely. They have healed the wound of my people lightly, saying, 'Peace, peace,' when there is no peace'"* (Jeremiah 6:13-14).

Many who experience a false conversion become what we term "Gospel hardened" and wreck their faith by continuing in false doctrine. They actually become like the wayward, but with a religious front. A Gospel-hardened believer can easily become like the wayward when they succeed in searing their conscience and harden their heart by rejecting truth that confronts them on their selfish motivation and intentions of the heart.

The Apostle Paul warned Timothy about this false doctrine trap: *"As I urged you when I was going to Macedonia, remain at Ephesus that you may charge certain persons <u>not to teach any different doctrine, nor to devote themselves to myths and endless genealogies, which promote speculations rather than the stewardship from God that is by faith</u>. The aim of our charge is love that issues from a pure heart and a <u>good conscience and a sincere faith</u>. Certain persons, by swerving from these, have wandered away into vain discussion, desiring to be teachers of the law, without understanding either what they are* *saying or the things about which they make confident assertions... <u>By rejecting this</u>,* [faith and conscience] *<u>some have made shipwreck of their faith</u>"* (1 Timothy 1:3-7; 19).

The wayward and the false believer responding to false doctrine in evangelism, and experiencing a false conversion, can both easily become the evil servants planted by the devil that are spoken of in Christ's end-of-the-age parables. Thus, we have Satan working very hard in planting and growing weeds amongst the saints, preparing for end-of-the-age conflict.

There is coming a great falling away, right around the corner, about which Jesus warned, *"Then they will deliver you up to tribulation and put you to death, and you will be hated by all nations for my name's sake. And then <u>many will fall away and betray one another and hate one another</u>"* (Matthew 24:9-10). Christ is speaking of the disaster that will soon hit all sincere Christians because of the falsely converted weeds that are massively implanted throughout the body of Christ.

We will discuss the parable of the weeds in detail later in this chapter. I want to point out the seriousness of the condition of the last-days church. We see that the priesthood and Temple leaders in Christ's days had fallen into the same spiritual state. We can focus on the condition of God's people today by using appropriate examples from the Word of God, those described in the Gospels who rejected Christ then: *"But woe to you, scribes and Pharisees, hypocrites! For you shut the kingdom of heaven in people's faces. For you neither enter yourselves nor allow those who would enter to go in. Woe to you, scribes and Pharisees, hypocrites! For you travel across sea and land to make a single proselyte, and when he becomes a proselyte, <u>you make him twice as much a child of hell</u> as yourselves"* (Matthew 23:13-15).

Today, just as Jesus said of the false in his day, false leaders and false doctrine inspired by demons are planting and growing sons and daughters of hell amongst the true believers and servants of Christ. Soon Satan will be cast down from heaven and make war on the saints using many tactics, with the most effective being the use of imposters and evil implants strewn throughout the body of Christ.

Now, few realize this could ever happen as we all witness the massive numbers of "on fire" Christians in all the various movements, with the rise of the mega-church and the ever-growing numbers of evangelical, Pentecostal, and charismatic believers. However, Christ is telling us in Matthew that many of these "on fire" Christians will fall away and betray the true believer due to the coming persecution and trouble.

Even being told in advance, the disciples still did not realize what was about to take place in less than a week—after Jesus rode into Jerusalem on a donkey when the massive crowds sang out, *"Hosanna to the Son of David! Blessed is he who comes in the name of the Lord! Hosanna in the highest!"* (Matthew 21:9). Within five days of Christ's triumphant entry, most of the people from that crowd turned on Christ at his trial yelled out *"Crucify him"* (Mark 15:13).

What is truly troubling about these implants and imposters is how the majority of Christians completely accept these false Christians as genuine. This plan by the evil one did not spring up overnight, but rather through a gradual exchange—replacing sound doctrine from the Gospel of Christ with the preaching of the doctrines of demons. Slowly and steadily, the true Gospel is replaced by a shadow Gospel (a compromised-empty Gospel that portrays a false Jesus) and few take note. The overwhelming majority of Christians across all denominations have learned to embrace another Jesus, a different Spirit, and a different Gospel.

This end-of-the-age sleight of hand and gradual exchange by the devil came about just as predicted: *"There will be false teachers among you, who will <u>secretly bring in destructive heresies</u>, even denying the Master who bought them, bringing upon themselves swift destruction. And <u>many will follow their sensuality</u>"* (2 Peter 2:1-2).

Mixed in any counterfeit work of Satan will be a large portion of truth, but truth implemented from wrong motives, or pushed into carnal methods within ministry, leads to grave error. Teachings founded in partial truth lead to counterfeit experiences, false conversions, and false maturity, resulting in many following a false Jesus.

Another Jesus, a Different Spirit, a Different Gospel, and Cheap Grace
Secretly perverting the grace of our God into sensuality

Preaching another Jesus is not new. The Apostle Paul warned the charismatic Christians in Corinth that they had readily submitted to a group of false apostles who came to them preaching another Jesus. Paul called them superlative apostles in that they elevated themselves above the original apostles, getting believers to accept a different Gospel and receive a different spirit—other than the true Gospel and the genuine Holy Spirit (see 2 Corinthians 11:3-15).

During the early seventies, a spiritual stir known as the Jesus People Movement drew many out of the hippie/flower-children movement into Christianity. Rock bands of this era depicted this movement in many songs. Perhaps the most popular song was "Spirit in the Sky." The lyrics portray a false concept of salvation and eternal security that far too many Christians embrace today: *"Never been a sinner, I've never sinned, I've got a friend in Jesus."* (Norman Greenbaum, "Spirit in the Sky," Reprise Records 1969). The main lyric quoted implies that sins and carnal issues are magically erased when we make Jesus our Savior and befriend him, disregarding the more important work of Christ upon our soul to bring us to eternal security, alive to God dead to the old self.

Thousands responded to the Jesus movement. Evangelical and Pentecostal denominations developed crusades and outreach ministries over the last thirty-five years to bring in more converts. Church growth campaigns presented the "get saved" message, turning it into the "become born again," message with evangelistic campaigns creating a variety of "instant salvation" and "guaranteed eternal security" promises.

Jesus had told Nicodemus that he must be born again, of the Spirit of God, and from that moment it would be like starting over and growing up again. Many are born anew of the Spirit but are never mentored to grow up into salvation. This is just as bad as a religious conversion (without the Holy Spirit's work of grace, inspired true repentance, and sense of being lost with no hope and the great need of a savior). Many taste the goodness of the Lord and the call of the Holy Spirit to salvation, only fall into false doctrine and back into sin, which results in the loss of salvation for many. *"For if, after they have escaped the defilements of the world through the knowledge of our Lord and Savior Jesus Christ, they are again entangled in them and overcome, the last state has become worse for them than the first. For it would have been better for them never to have known the way of righteousness than after knowing it to turn back from the holy commandment delivered to them"* (2 Peter 2:20-21).

Eternal security is a reality for the truly born of God who choose to grow up into salvation after God calls them to become born again. However, through the years many theologians have painted a skewed perception of salvation and eternal security. As we move through this chapter, you will understand the importance of working out our own salvation in the power of God, willingly. It is our free will, after God calls us, to confirm our call and election into eternal security, *"For if these things are yours and abound, they keep you from being ineffective or unfruitful in the knowledge of our Lord Jesus Christ. For whoever lacks these things is blind and shortsighted and has forgotten that he was cleansed from his old sins. Therefore, brethren, <u>be the more zealous to confirm your call and election, for if you do this you will never fall;</u> so <u>there will be richly provided for you an entrance into the eternal kingdom</u> of our Lord and Savior Jesus Christ"* (2 Peter 1:8-11).

Many converts struggled through lack of knowledge, as they fought temptations and lived in fear of backsliding, even fearing the loss of salvation. To bolster the faith of these struggling Christians, and not knowing the root problems, the false doctrine of eternal security spewed from pulpits everywhere. The preaching of the grace of God soothed the fears of many, but in reality, the result was that a false doctrine of cheap grace became the holding power from the pulpit to keep attendance up.

In Hebrews, the author warns of sinning deliberately after receiving the Gospel and ending up profaning the blood of the covenant and out raging the Spirit of grace. The doctrine of the grace of God through the last forty years has turned into a license to sin and not suffer any consequences. (See Hebrews 10:26-31). Jude writes specifically about how the false sneak in to undermine the true meaning of God's grace: *"For certain people have crept in unnoticed who long ago were designated for this condemnation, ungodly people, who <u>pervert the grace of our God into sensuality</u> and deny our only Master and Lord, Jesus Christ"* (Jude 1:4).

Dietrich Bonhoeffer, one of the Christians martyred by Hitler, wrote *The Cost of Discipleship*. He saw the carnal, weak, and lukewarm condition of the church in Germany leading up to the Nazi takeover. In this volume, Bonhoeffer penned the term "cheap grace."

> "*Cheap grace* is the preaching of forgiveness without requiring repentance, baptism without church discipline, communion without confession, absolution without personal confession. Cheap grace is grace without discipleship, grace without the cross, grace without Jesus Christ, living and incarnate.
>
> *Costly grace* is the treasure hidden in the field; for the sake of it a man will gladly go and sell all that he has. It is the pearl of great price to buy which the merchant will sell all his goods. It is the kingly rule of Christ, for whose sake a man will pluck out the eye which causes him to stumble, it is the call of Jesus Christ at

which the disciple leaves his nets and follows him." (Dietrich Bonhoeffer, *The Cost of Discipleship*, New York: Collier Books, 1961, p. 47).

Bonhoeffer challenged Christians in Germany, calling them lukewarm and apathetic, but few took heed. In Revelation, the Apostle John prophesying for Christ warned the church of Laodicea of being in a very dire condition, like the church of Germany. Christ warded, *"Because you are lukewarm, and neither hot nor cold, I will spit you out of my mouth"* (Revelation 3:16).

Indeed, Germany is a modern era example of what Christ warned the Christians at Laodicea concerning what would happen if they stayed lukewarm. We see that a whole nation, including Christians, was allowed to be thrown into terrible destruction. Christ did not, and will not, protect a people who speak his name, yet live apart from him and his lordship.

The majority of Christians in Germany were lukewarm, and over these many years, millions of Christians in America have now bought the lie that they are right with God and have eternal security even though they constantly give in to temptation, walk in carnal desires, practice secret sins, and live apart from his lordship. These people believe they are born of God; however, they follow another Jesus than that of the Bible, a different Spirit from Scripture, and a pathetically weak Gospel that has made the grace of God a licentious license to sin and love this world and its pleasures, believing they will not suffer any consequences.

Greed and the Abundant Life Syndrome

For most Christians, the abundant life in Christ has become misconstrued and confused with the American dream and good-times on earth—a doctrine inspired by hell that has many sincere believers struggling in a lukewarm faith, asleep during the darkest hour of the church age.

We must understand what Christ meant by the abundant life that he promises; if we do not, our powers of discernment will be skewed by a naturally carnal immaturity in life. The cares of this life will cause us to try to follow Christ, yet we will find ourselves stumbling in the dark with a few glimmering lights of hope here and there.

Jesus said of himself, *"I came that they may have <u>life</u> and have it abundantly"* (John 10:10).

However, Jesus also taught, *"Enter by the narrow gate. For the gate is wide and the way is easy that leads to destruction, and those who enter by it are many. For the gate is narrow and the way is hard that leads to <u>life</u>, and those who find it are few"* (Matthew 7:13, 14).

What kind of life is Christ talking about here? The word for *life* in these two passages in the original Greek is *zōē*, meaning the life we receive from Father God through Christ his son.

The other life that Jesus often spoke of is the *psuchē* life, where he states *"If anyone comes to me and does not hate his own father and mother and wife and children and brothers and sisters, yes, and even his own <u>life</u>, he cannot be my disciple. Whoever does not bear his own cross and come after me cannot be my disciple"* (Luke 14:26, 27).

Here in this passage, *psuchē* life denotes our natural life on earth or the seat of personality for our own life. This life is developed in the world, in family, and in significant relationships, and grows into dynamic dependencies—all based upon humanity's fallen-sin nature.

In this relationship-driven *psuchē* life, we derive our self-worth and our sense of wellbeing before we come to Christ and spiritually meet our heavenly Father. All too often, the *psuchē* life becomes controlling, demanding, self-centered, even idolatrous, and sometimes abusive. Thus, this natural life is the primary ingredient of the carnal life or life of the flesh that Scripture describes as being detrimental to the life of God within the believer's life.

The Apostle Paul describes the battle between God's Spirit and our carnal *psuchē* life as believers, where he states, *"But I say, walk by the Spirit, and you will not gratify the desires of the flesh. For the <u>desires of the flesh are against the Spirit, and the desires of the Spirit are against the flesh</u>, for these are opposed to each other, to keep you from doing the things you want to do"* (Galatians 5:16- 17).

Zōē life in Christ is often in opposition with our carnal or *psuchē* life. Therefore Christ commands that we hate this *psuchē* aspect of our life—within ourselves, and in its power within our relationships—not just our influence upon others but also its influence on us from others, including significant family members, extended family members, and our friends in the world. It is the carnal-*psuchē* life that most believers mistakenly want more of, which becomes easily confused with the life that Christ said he came to give, *"I came that they may have life and have it abundantly."*

Few are instructed on how to die to the carnal-*psuchē* life and have the Holy Spirit-filled *zōē* life in God become abundant, ever growing, and overflowing to others. This *zōē* life is not like the *psuchē* life that we have become so accustomed to and even addicted to.

The *psuchē* life dictates that we live for others and for ourselves, and often selfishly demands that others live for us—so that we humans become gods to each other and for each other.

The most harmful characteristics of this natural life are listed in Galatians: *"Now the works of the flesh are evident: sexual immorality, impurity, sensuality, idolatry, sorcery, enmity, strife, jealousy, fits of anger, rivalries, dissensions, divisions, envy, drunkenness, orgies, and things like these. I warn you, as I warned you before, that those who do such things will not inherit the kingdom of God"* (Galatians 5:19-21).

However, the characteristics of the *zōē* life in Christ are as follows: *"The fruit of the Spirit is love, joy, peace, patience, kindness, goodness, faithfulness, gentleness, self-control; against such things there is no law"* (Galatians 5:22-23).

This life in God is obtained by entering a journey where the carnal-*psuchē* life dies and it is replaced by the Holy Spirit filled *zōē* life, which is to become the believer's own life within.

Thus, the Apostle Paul finishes his explanation on the carnal-*psuchē* life by writing, *"And those who belong to Christ Jesus have crucified the flesh with its passions and desires"* (Galatians 5:24). Now review a harder teaching of Christ, *"For the gate is narrow and the way is hard that leads to life, and those who find it are few"* (Matthew 7:14).

The work of crucifying or dying to the carnal-*psuchē* life is not easy and often requires giving up or minimizing relationships that are based on the natural-worldly-carnal life.

Understanding the Difference in Christ's Meanings of Life

I have referred to Christians who embrace the prosperity message, and yet struggle to achieve a successful, materially blessed life, as suffering from the "abundant life syndrome."

Simply, few Christians are taught the difference between the meaning of the abundant life in Christ, and the carnal life of the world, a carnal-relationship life where the sense of wellbeing and self-identity stem from relationships, work, ministry, lifestyle preferences, hobbies, sports, education, material possessions (the car they drive), money, and all other manner of activities.

This lack of understanding, and lack of entering the right path that leads to abundant life in Christ, brings confusion, frustration, and relationship conflicts along with false peace and false joy. The idea of dying to the good feelings we receive from the carnal life is difficult to understand and often painful; however, when we put off the old nature, we learn to make way for the fullness of God to come; then our relationships and life in the world contain a wondrous peace and joy.

Rivers of living water (the Holy Spirit flowing freely) flow out from us into the lives of others. *"If anyone thirsts, let him come to me and drink. Whoever believes in me, as the Scripture has said, 'Out of his heart will flow rivers of living water'"* (John 7:37-38).

The abundant life syndrome affects millions of Christians as they lust after quick-fix doctrines, material possessions, money, and spiritually sensuous experiences that ease or attempt to deliver the deceived from the passions and desires of the flesh. These carnal desires stem from unresolved issues of the heart, such as bitterness, jealousy, unforgiveness, hidden defilements, insecurities, greed, judgments, and selfishness, these are some specific issues that Christians avoid dealing with properly which cause loss of peace, joy and contentment in the Lord—robbing them of the *zōē* life.

Therefore, the abundant life syndrome snares many who adhere to false theology and faulty thinking where the abundant life in Christ wrongly translates into a wonderful life on earth.

This major doctrine of demons perverts the beatitudes that Christ desires to instill into his lowly servant's heart. Instead, this demonic teaching instills pride of ownership, pride of success, pride of wealth and ease, pride of good looks, pride of knowledge, pride of the appearance of religion and self-righteousness, and pride of being a possessor of spiritual power. All these things and more erode true faith and swallow up the deceived with temporal happiness and false inner peace.

Pondering this should help you see that those stuck in this syndrome have very little power to discern the false from the true, good from evil, and to detect the powers of darkness that come as angels of light.

An Easy-Going Jesus and Shoo-In Salvation

So much of the Gospel of Christ is truncated and packaged to suit the wants and needs of the masses that follow Christ, who look to the Bible and to church leadership for a way to make life easy while on earth.

When Christ multiplied the five barley loaves and two fish and fed the masses, the people became so excited that they formed a plan to take Christ by force and make him king. When

Jesus perceived that the crowd was about to seize him, he left and went away—to be alone. When evening came, the disciples went down to the sea without Jesus, entered into a boat, and sailed across the sea to Capernaum.

The disciples ran into trouble when a strong wind arose and the sea became rough. As the disciples struggled with the night crossing, Christ came to them walking on water and entered the boat, and immediately the boat arrived at the far shore.

The next morning the crowds saw that Christ and the disciples had departed, so they got into boats also and crossed over to the far shore. When they found Christ on the other side of the sea at Capernaum, they said, *"Rabbi, when did you come here?"*

Jesus immediately said to the crowd, *"Truly, truly, I say to you, you are seeking me, not because you saw signs, but because you ate your fill of the loaves"* (see John 6:1-36).

Today many seek Christ to have their material-emotional-physical lives filled miraculously with contentment, happiness, and peace by so-called representatives of Christ who promise freedom and prosperity. Most carnal and false teachers equate having earthly needs and wants satisfied with Christ's promise of abundant life.

The false, as the Apostle Paul points out are, *"deprived of the truth, <u>imagining that godliness is a means of gain</u>. Now there is great gain in godliness with contentment, for we brought nothing into the world, and we cannot take anything out of the world. But if we have food and clothing, with these we will be content. But those who desire to be rich fall into temptation, into a snare, into many senseless and harmful desires that plunge people into ruin and destruction"* (1 Timothy 6:5-9).

The Lord saw that the masses wanted to make him a king, a form of manipulation to ensure Jesus would continue to fill their stomachs and make life easier in the world. Now we have many who present an *easy-going* Jesus with promises to make life easy on earth; a Santa Claus-Jesus who will cater to our every need and want, without offering any discipline or rebuke for having wrong motives and bad attitudes.

In the book of James, the author writes of the selfishness that now consumes so many believers: *"What causes quarrels and what causes fights among you? Is it not this, that your passions are at war within you? You desire and do not have, so you murder. You covet and cannot obtain, so you fight and quarrel. You do not have, because you do not ask. You ask and do not receive, because you ask wrongly, to spend it on your passions. You adulterous people! Do you not know that friendship with the world is enmity with God? Therefore whoever wishes to be a friend of the world makes himself an enemy of God"* (James 4:1-4).

This approach in coming to Christ and serving him is often accompanied with another faulty message: a different Gospel that allows for deliberate sinning with no repercussions, a message that fosters a lukewarm relationship with Christ, and a *come-one-come-all* invitation to salvation.

For years, preachers, teachers, and evangelists have proclaimed that all you have to do to be saved is to come forward publicly and confess Christ as Lord and your salvation will be a *shoo in*.

The old phrase *shoo in* came into use in the late 1920s with regard to horseracing. The phrase implied cheating: a horse was expected to win not on its abilities but by the race being fixed. In the original usage, the phrase carried the connotation that the horse was a winner even if it lackadaisically wandered up to the finish line and had to be "shooed in" by someone to cross the finish line.

Shoo-in theology is a term I use to describe the popular but erroneous teachings concerning salvation in Christ that so many profess today. Most Christians are ignorant of all that Christ and the Apostles taught concerning becoming born again and then working out one's salvation—in other words, growing up into salvation.

Growing up into Salvation

In 1 Corinthians Paul writes, *"Do you not know that in a race all the runners compete, but only one receives the prize? <u>So run that you may obtain it</u>. Every athlete exercises self-control in all things. They do it to receive a perishable wreath, but we an imperishable. Well, I do not run aimlessly, I do not box as one beating the air; but I pommel my body and subdue it, lest after preaching to others <u>I myself should be disqualified</u>"* (1 Corinthians 9:24-27 RSV).

Many follow Christ and yet do not know him or obey him, living a Christian lifestyle that is lukewarm at best. These believers are tricked and even self-deceived into cheating—taking shortcuts that put themselves in grave danger of disqualification.

The author of Hebrews wrote, *"Take care, brethren, lest <u>there be in any of you an evil, unbelieving heart, leading you to fall away from the living God</u>. But exhort one another every day, as long as it is called 'today,' that none of you may be hardened by the deceitfulness of sin. For we share in Christ, if only we hold our first confidence firm to the end…"* (Hebrews 3:12-14 RSV).

The Apostle Paul exhorts believers to *"work out your own salvation with fear and trembling; for God is at work in you, both to will and to work for his good pleasure"* (Philippians 2:12-13 RSV). Believers must work out their own salvation in humble contriteness of heart in all sincerity and singleness of mind—we are to grow up into a salvation that is real. In 1 Peter 2:2 it states, *"Like newborn babes, long for the pure spiritual milk, <u>that by it you may grow up to salvation</u>."*

This process cannot be done without the Spirit of Christ personally orchestrating challenging situations that force hidden issues of the heart and defilements of the spirit to surface; to train us to pay attention to these issues and deal with them God's way.

In other words, Christ brings divine pressure in life, encouraging us, challenging us and all too often humbling us due to our carnality that makes it hard for him to transform our character to be Christ-like. Changed by his power in lowliness and in true holiness; to be purified and transformed from the old carnal nature.

If our carnal nature is unresolved, it will usurp the fruit of the Holy Spirit and continue to undermine our relationship with Christ. Thus, the battle between the flesh and the Spirit will continue until we learn to cooperate and become dead to the carnal nature and alive to the Holy Spirit's presence.

For some, this is a mildly discomforting process, but for many Christians who suffer from wounds and defilements from their former manner of life, this process can be a long and excruciating journey (especially if we do not understand how to cooperate with God in his dealings).

The following Scriptures express the extreme importance of working out our own salvation—all the way—and growing up into eternal security in Christ. As a reminder, underlining certain words or phrases in a passage is used to highlight key points concerning the process of growing up into Christ, obtaining the grace of God and assuring eternal security when Christ-like character is formed within.

"Let us <u>cleanse ourselves from every defilement of body and spirit,</u> bringing holiness to completion in the <u>fear of God</u>" (2 Corinthians 7:1).

"So put away all malice and all deceit and hypocrisy and envy and all slander. Like newborn infants, long for the pure spiritual milk, that by it you may <u>grow up into salvation</u>" (1 Peter 2:1-2).

"See to it that no one fails to obtain the grace of God; <u>that no 'root of bitterness' springs up and causes trouble</u>, and by it many become defiled; <u>that no one is sexually immoral or unholy</u> like Esau, who sold his birthright for a single meal. For you know that afterward, when he desired to inherit the blessing, <u>he was rejected, for he found no chance to repent</u>, though he sought it with tears" (Hebrews 12:15-17).

"Take care, brothers, lest there be in <u>any of you an evil, unbelieving heart, leading you to fall away from the living God</u>. But exhort one another every day, as long as it is called 'today,' that none of you may be hardened by the deceitfulness of sin. For we share in Christ, if indeed we hold our original confidence firm to the end" (Hebrews 3:12-14).

"<u>Not everyone who says to me, 'Lord, Lord,' will enter the kingdom of heaven</u>, but the one who does the will of my Father who is in heaven. On that day many will say to me, '<u>Lord, Lord, did we not prophesy in your name, and cast out demons in your name, and do many mighty works in your name?</u>' And then will I declare to them, '<u>I never knew you; depart from me, you workers of lawlessness</u>'" (Matthew 7:21-23).

Many more passages could be quoted here to emphasize the importance of embracing all that Christ taught. It is disheartening that few Christians receive instruction on how to grow up into Christ and work out their own salvation. Instead, they are told that once you call on Jesus and become born again, you are a shoo-in and can never lose your salvation.

The final passage to help ourselves walk seriously in the fear of God and apply every word that Christ said is as follows: "And everyone <u>who hears these words of mine and does not do them</u> will be <u>like a foolish man</u> who built his house on the sand. And the rain fell, and the floods came, and the winds blew and beat against that house, and it fell, and great was the fall of it" (Matthew 7:26-27).

The sincere and humble Christian must learn to discern faulty teachings that proclaim Christ to be easy going, looking the other way concerning sin, disobedience, and carnal works.

Further, watch out for deceitful schemes from false teachers and false pastors who present the wide gate and easy path to salvation, where just claiming Jesus as our savior magically seals us into a state of eternal security. (Yes, there is eternal security for those who have worked out their own salvation in the fear of God and obtained the grace of God through the sanctifying discipline of the Lord.)

When we begin to see how deceitful these heresies are and renounce them, God will begin to work in our lives and train us to distinguish good from evil; our powers of discernment will begin to grow in leaps and bounds.

Oblivious to the Coming Judgments
Anguish over love of this world and over sin is unheard-of and the fear of God not needed

Jesus warned, *"But watch yourselves lest your hearts be weighed down with dissipation and drunkenness and cares of this life, and that day come upon you suddenly like a trap. For it will come upon all who dwell on the face of the whole earth. But stay awake at all times, praying that you may have strength to escape all these things that are going to take place, and to stand before the Son of Man"* (Luke 21:34-36).

Many on-fire Christians are at risk of becoming snared by the coming judgments because they did not embrace Christ's warnings and develop a humble healthy fear of God concerning sin and the cares of this life. Instead, the majority of God's people embrace concocted teachings and fables to stifle the fearful truth concerning judgments coming upon the world—(those warnings clearly recorded in Scripture).

The Apostle Paul wrote, *"People will not endure sound teaching ... wander off into myths"* (2 Timothy 4:3-4). The word *sound* (i.e., *sound teaching*) in this passage implies *healthy teaching* in the original language. God's people, for the most part, prefer myths that excuse them from becoming accountable to obtain true holiness and to cease and desist from wallowing in the love of this world, and hypocrisy—pretending to be in love with Jesus.

There is a lack of healthy fear of God and proper concern for what is coming upon the world. Developing a healthy fear of God comes by suffering while embracing the discipline of the Lord and listening to a steady diet of sound doctrine. This process of overcoming the power of the flesh requires suffering at the hands of Christ's in his loving discipline. *"Since therefore Christ suffered in the flesh, arm yourselves with the same way of thinking, for whoever has suffered in the flesh has ceased from sin, so as to live for the rest of the time in the flesh no longer for human passions but for the will of God"* (1 Peter 4:1-2).

A healthy fear of God produces a life of careful living (not carnal living), where obedience will produce a humble heart. Further, obedience will fashion our hearts to learn to be in touch with God's anguish over the condition of his people and the lost, creating a divine call to seek and live in the perfect will of God.

In his sermon entitled "A Call to Anguish" given in September 2002, the late David Wilkerson gave a startling message to help God's people wake up in time. You can view and listen to this message on YouTube by searching "A Call to Anguish." This message by David may help you catch how far away God's people as a whole have become—lukewarm and passive, not taking to heart the dire-condition America and God's people are in. We are at great risk of being spewed out of Christ's mouth (meaning a total loss of his intervening protection). *"So, because you are lukewarm, and neither hot nor cold, I will spit you out of my mouth"* (Revelation 3:16).

We must, as a people of God, shake off our stupor and unstop our ears to the coming judgments. Judgment is coming to God's people, then America and the world. A terrible time is coming as the end of this age closes. Jesus warned us not to be weighed down with anything, rather we are to stay awake at all times, praying for strength in order to escape the coming trouble!

Christ warns us passionately, so that each may escape the coming trouble that precedes his appearance and stand before him in confidence at the rapture. We must be watchful and obedient saints, living as emissaries of Christ whose citizenship is not of this world.

If you want to walk in true discernment—then wake up to the signs of his coming. Learn to walk in the true fear of God, and be in anguish over your own condition, the condition of God's people, and the condition of America. We are to learn to walk as Christ walked. *"In the days of his flesh, Jesus offered up prayers and supplications, with loud cries and tears, to him who was able to save him from death, and he was heard for his godly fear. Although he was a son, he learned obedience through what he suffered"* (Hebrews 5:7-8 RSV).

Affliction upon affliction is coming upon us and ever increasing. This is for the benefit of the sleeping saints—to wake up the body of Christ. Do not waste what little time is left. Jesus proclaimed, *"From the fig tree learn its lesson: as soon as its branch becomes tender and puts out its leaves, you know that summer is near. So also, when you see these things taking place, you know that he is near, at the very gates"* (Mark 13:28-29).

Kingdom Now Theology a Bust
The American dream is turning into the last-days Babylonian nightmare

Over the last 30 years, many false apostles and prophets have networked with each other, attempting to bring in the Kingdom of God now, that is, bring the Kingdom of Heaven down to earth through a powerfully influential church. Their theology and teachings are in direct contradiction to Christ's warnings about the end of the age, the Great Tribulation, the final harvest of souls and the rapture of the true Christian.

The truth is these people want to be in control and establish God's Kingdom on earth in the supposed power of God, which in reality is the spiritual power of their own flesh. These groups of false servants who appear to be righteous are just like those the Apostle Paul addressed in 2 Corinthians 11:14-15. These groups have numerous names that identify their insidious demonic agenda.

Terms that describe the Kingdom Now movement are Dominion Theology, Kingdom Now, and Reconstructionist, having a postmillennial eschatology foundation. [12] Other false movements similar in message are Latter-Rain, Toronto Blessing, Holy Laughter, Third Wave, Shepherding Movement, Promise Keepers, Brownsville Revival, and others around the world. *The Purpose-Driven Church* book outlines a similar agenda. Many ministries have sprung up preaching variations of this false doctrine where carnal motives drive church growth, contradicting the leadership of the Holy Spirit. (See Romans 8:14 and Galatians 5:18).

These misguided movements push for revival and restoration. Yes, hearts are burdened for the lost and the lukewarm Christian, but those in the movement suffer from the lust for power, an absolutely wrong motivation in serving Christ. They lust for a shortcut anointing or a

---

[12] Postmillennialists believe that they have a mandate from God to reconstruct society with biblical principles, which will usher in the Kingdom of God and the rule of Christ through the church—thus ushering in Christ's return.

baptism of fire by the Holy Spirit to magically-implant a Christ-like nature within each believer, in order to influence and transform the world—to present to Christ a Christian—controlled world—to facilitate Christ's return.

They have become militant warriors for God, trying to grasp the power of God and bring the Kingdom of Heaven down to earth. They hold the cross central to their teaching, but their message of the cross does not include the work of the cross in the believer's life that crucifies inner carnal motives and, personalities and exposes defilements of spirit.

Deceived, they take the easy way by trying to harness the power of their own spirit in the name of Christ. In truth, they serve a different Christ, work with a different spirit, and preach a perverted gospel.

Another aspect that blinds those embracing dominion theology and the purpose-driven message of converting the world to Christianity is a carnal love for this world and an obsession about happiness for this life—to perpetuate the American dream of prosperity—an unrelenting pursuit of life, liberty, and happiness. I hope that many who have been taken in by the Kingdom Now theology will wake up as they realize that their efforts have come to naught.

It is all a bust, because America and the world is racing in the opposite direction—moving quickly toward the end-of-the-age Babylon described in the book of Revelation. Moreover, America is leading the way with ever-expanding lawlessness, perverse filth, and debauchery—and leading the way on attacking virtue, goodness, righteousness, and godly love. These perverse changes in the American culture fly in the face of dominion theology as the birth pangs go viral and persecution increases—all about to sink all hope of Christianity saving America and the world and restoring peace and prosperity.

As we approach the midnight hour of peak darkness, the American dream will turn into a nightmare making the Great Depression seem like a cakewalk.

The Pre-tribulation Rapture Lie

The most influential doctrine spawned by hell, which keeps millions of believers lackadaisical and from properly growing up into salvation is the pre-tribulation rapture lie. Jesus was very clear concerning when he would send forth his angels to gather his elect—the true believers who are ready and watching. It is recorded in the Gospels of Matthew and Mark, and because it is paramount for us to understand and take heed, both passages are quoted:

"*<u>Immediately after the tribulation</u> of those days the sun will be darkened, and the moon will not give its light, and the stars will fall from heaven, and the powers of the heavens will be shaken; then will appear the sign of the Son of man in heaven, and then all the tribes of the earth will mourn, and they will see the Son of man coming on the clouds of heaven with power and great glory; <u>and he will send out his angels with a loud trumpet call, and they will gather his elect from the four winds, from one end of heaven to the other</u>*" (Matthew 24:29-31).

"*But in those days, <u>after that tribulation</u>, the sun will be darkened, and the moon will not give its light, and the stars will be falling from heaven, and the powers in the heavens will be shaken. And then they will* *see the Son of man coming in clouds with great power and glory. <u>And then he will send out the angels, and gather his elect from the four winds, from the ends of the earth to the ends of heaven</u>"* (Mark 13:24-27).

Christians are required to endure the terrible days leading up to Christ's appearance and it is at that point in time that the rapture of the saints will occur. The pre-tribulation rapture theory is conjecture and a convenient lie to soothe the fears of Christians who are not ready but believe they are. This lie, like most false doctrines, eases the painful conviction of the Holy Spirit for those in a self-deceived state.

Soon there will be great persecution directed at Christians that will cause many weak and false believers to fall away from the faith. Then, false prophets will deceive many Christians as the Great Tribulation takes place. Jesus put it this way: *"For then there will be great tribulation, such as has not been from the beginning of the world until now, no, and never will be. And if those days had not been shortened, no human being would be saved; but for the sake of the elect those days will be shortened. Then if any one says to you, 'Lo, here is the Christ!' or 'There he is!' do not believe it. For false christs and false prophets will arise and show great signs and wonders, so as to lead astray, if possible, even the elect. Lo, I have told you beforehand"* (Mathew 24:21-25 RSV).

The faithful Christian living now, as the end of this age unfolds, will be subjected to the Great Tribulation. This is Satan's trouble-making work, not the wrath of God. The rapture will occur at the end of Satan's time of trouble, just before the wrath of God is poured out upon the whole world. As true believers, we must be prepared to endure to the end of the Great Tribulation and be ready for Christ's appearance.

The ultimate test of discernment for the true saint will be during the coming Great Tribulation period when Satan will be allowed to deceive the whole world and if possible lead astray God's elect.

Christian Judaism: Another Bewitching, Enslaving Lie

God's call upon the Apostle Paul was to bring the Gospel to the Gentiles, as explained in the book Galatians; however, many overlook the fact that his commission also included opposing the Christian Jews who were determined to pervert the Gospel of Christ into some of the practices of Judaism, primarily circumcision.

Some of the Jewish Christian who Paul identified as false brothers began to coerce the new Gentile Christians into submitting to the Jewish tradition of circumcision. So troublesome were the Jewish Christian "Judaizers" that the Apostle Paul wrote to Titus insisting they be silenced. (See Titus 1:10-14).

Paul's background in Judaism was thorough and he zealously opposed Christianity before his conversion. Nevertheless, he gave up Judaism and its traditions after his personal encounter with Christ while traveling to Damascus on a mission to arrest Christians.

After he became a believer in Christ, he traveled to Arabia, where Christ's Spirit helped him understand the Gospel and learn how a relationship with Christ replaced the law (not the commandments), the traditions, the feasts and all the ancient ornate ceremonies and regulations. He explains in the book of Colossians how these religious activities are of no value in stopping the indulgences of the flesh; in fact he warned that by embracing Judaism one can suffer serious consequences, *"Look: I, Paul, say to you that if you accept circumcision, Christ will be of no advantage to you. I testify again to every man who accepts circumcision that he is obligated to keep the whole law. You are severed from Christ, you who would be justified by the law; you have fallen away from grace"* (Galatians 5:2-4).

With the last day's insurgency of false leaders and false prophets, there is also a large increase of Christian-Jewish sects insisting, persuading and coercing Christians to adhere to the laws and traditions of Judaism. This dangerous deception is growing rapidly and is very misleading for many.

Weak and deceived Christians become spellbound with the last-days Judaizers who are causing many to fall away from grace, putting their eternal salvation at risk. The Apostle Paul wrote, *"O foolish Galatians! Who has bewitched you?"* (Galatians 3:1), and indeed, today many are bewitched by the false preachers who mix Judaism into the Gospel of Christ.

These sects along with the deceitfulness of a widespread compromised Gospel are leading Christians to believe in the wrong Jesus. The Apostle Paul warned, *"See to it that no one takes you captive by philosophy and empty deceit, according to human tradition, according to the elemental spirits (principles) of the world, and not according to Christ."* (Colossians 2:8).

Ministry Case: *Your Jesus can't help you here*

In writing about Christian Judaism, I remembered a woman we helped back in the nineties; she was an acquaintance of one of our ministry team members. Unfortunately, this Christian woman chose to listen to false leaders who preach the wide-gate and easy-path gospel, her favorites being Joyce Meyer and Joel Osteen.

A few years ago, she shared a disturbing dream with our coworker. In the dream, she was in a house alone and suddenly all the windows and doors locked or became boarded up. She tried to leave to no avail, and in the dream, she realized that demons had locked her in this house.

Upon realizing this in the dream, she began to command the demons to open the door and let her leave. She commanded them in the name of Jesus; however, one of the demons in her dream laughed at her and said, "Your Jesus can't help you here."

She woke up very fearful and later in the week she told this dream to our coworker. In recounting her dream, she gave her own interpretation: that somehow it had something to do with her daughter who at the time was going through some difficulties.

Our coworker, knowing exactly what it meant informed her to the contrary; this dream was a warning for her, that she is following the wrong Jesus by embracing these false teachers and their heretical teachings.

She did not receive this interpretation and continued in self-deception, following false teachers. Later this woman put herself into a situation where demonic activity became acute in her life and she became depressed as a number of mounting difficulties became very stressful. At one point, she confessed that she was on the verge of losing her mind.

The outcome for her life is yet to unfold, as she still maintains that she is following the true Jesus, in spite of her debilitating symptoms. She never really found relief from her inner torment by applying the false doctrines of Meyer and Osteen. Therefore, she shifted to one of these Christian-Jewish sects, observing Saturday as the Sabbath and thinking about becoming involved in Christian Judaism; even worse, she obtained special clothing for praying, along with a book explaining how Judaism is for the Christian; all in hopes of finding happiness and bliss in life.

This woman's case is representative of many deceived Christians who sadly struggle in life and turn to false teachers and bewitching doctrines such as Christian Judaism. What is even sadder about this case, and many like hers, is the fact that the Lord warned her in a dream, yet did not perceive the warning. *"For God speaks in one way, and in two, though man does not perceive it. In a dream, in a vision of the night, when deep sleep falls on men, while they slumber on their beds, then he opens the ears of men and terrifies them with warnings, that he may turn man aside from his deed and conceal pride from a man; he keeps back his soul from the pit, his life from perishing by the sword"* (Job 33:14-18). Ω

This woman has hidden issues and defilements from the past that are painful to address, nevertheless, they must be cleansed in order that she may grow up into Christ and walk in his fullness. This person will listen to anyone, except those who teach the harder things of Christ. She is like so many who refuse to embrace those truths in Scripture that facilitate death to the flesh. *"Those who belong to Christ Jesus have crucified the flesh with its passions and desires"* (Galatians 5:24).

Many are following false teachers who operate in a counterfeit faith and capture Christians who are burdened with sins and easily led astray by the desires boiling up from unresolved issues from an impure heart. The Apostle Paul prophesied that the end of the age would bring times of stress. Many Christians are in a stressed-out condition and become trapped in an ever-learning cycle. They try every new teaching that promises freedom, but they never arrive at the knowledge of the truth just as the Apostle Paul described in 2 Timothy 3:1-9.

What is the truth that these people must arrive at? It is finding, abiding in, and obeying the true Christ. Christians, such as the person described in this case must understand how to be led by the true Holy Spirit in the discipline of Christ. Then they must take courage and allow the Holy Spirit to facilitate cleansing of impurities of heart and healing of damaged emotions and wounds to the spirit. This process is sanctification and produces Christ-like character. Each must become sanctified as Scripture admonishes: *"Let us cleanse ourselves from every defilement of body and spirit, bringing holiness to completion in the fear of God"* (2 Corinthians 7:1).

Confused and deceived Christians must understand how to grow up into Christ and avoid being led astray by those who preach a different Jesus, a Jesus that has no light to guide in the dark, a false Jesus whose name is powerless against the devil and his demons.

"You Will Be Like God"—Relationship Idolatry in the Church
Marriage and relationship idolatry prospering in the body of Christ

A basic overview of Scripture concerning relationships as Christians would clear up much confusion for troubled marriages, dysfunctional families and hot-and-bothered singles. Many in leadership push Christians into marriage long before they are ready—even if one was not called to marriage—making each in the marriage responsible for the other's wellbeing.

Most Christian women are convinced that life will become fulfilling only when and if they find the right man, and then, of course become married to their fantasized knight in shining armor. However, for many that picturesque wedding is the beginning of a destructive relationship.

The divorce rate for strong Christians who attend fellowship on a regular basis is fewer than the national divorce rate average, yet still high at 38%. (Bradley Wright, University of Connecticut professor, from his 2006 research of the 2004 Barna poll).

These divorce statistics do not reflect troubled Christian marriages that continue in their relationship, believing that divorce is not acceptable and resort to quietly living desperate and separate ways while living under the same roof. Marriage retreats, seminars, and couples encounter sessions, as well as Christian marriage counseling, are thriving ministries in huge demand throughout the body of Christ. Most of these ministries emphasize teaching and training each partner to learn how to be more and more caring and pleasing to each other. However, there are two radical ends of the spectrum within these types of teachings concerning how to please the opposite mate.

One end of the happy-Christian-marriage spectrum is teaching the wife to become a virtual doormat, totally submitting to the husband's wishes, barring physical abuse. The other far extreme is teaching the husband to treat his wife as an absolute queen, believing that if the wife is unhappy in any way, the husband has failed to be the head of the wife.

In general, these foundational marriage teachings take various New Testament passages and develop false doctrines that (in one-way or another) make a god out of the husband, or a god out of the wife, or both are taught to serve each other idolatrously.

Deceivingly, these approaches in patching up marriage relationships succumb to what Satan tricked Eve and then Adam with—becoming gods to each other, not needing to obey God as Lord: *"But the serpent said to the woman, 'You will not surely die. For God knows that when you eat of it your eyes will be opened, and <u>you will be like God</u>, knowing good and evil'"* (Genesis 3:4-5).

The Apostle Paul addresses this specifically in this passage, *"I want you to be free from anxieties. The unmarried man is anxious about the things of the Lord, how to please the Lord. But the <u>married man is anxious about worldly things, how to please his wife, and his interests are divided</u>. And the unmarried or betrothed woman is anxious about the things of the Lord, how to be holy in body and spirit. But the <u>married woman is anxious about worldly things, how to please her husband</u>. I say this for your own benefit, not to lay any restraint upon you, but to <u>promote good order and to secure your undivided devotion to the Lord</u>"* (1 Corinthians 7:32-35).

The Apostle is addressing the tendency for married Christians to become enthralled and anxious for each other, and eventually this will lead to relationship idolatry where Christ takes a backseat to the marriage. If one or the other in the marriage suffers from wounds to the spirit, this seemingly healthy approach in making each other happy will erode the marriage into chaos, where life falls from the leadership of the Holy Spirit into carnal lusts and worldly anxieties that guide and direct the relationship.

Of the two extremes, one suppresses the wife into an abused second-class-creation role, setting the selfish husband up to become a mini-dictator sanctioned by the church. With the other, the wife becomes a masterful manipulator who usually is never happy or satisfied with the husband's performance.

Even more insidious and potentially destructive is the importance placed by church leadership upon the single women in finding and marrying the perfect Christian man. This approach is a futile attempt to keep singles sexually safe and to keep the wandering eyes of the married from temptation; however, this only sweeps the dirt under the rug and creates a playground for Satan within fellowship. Again, the Apostle lays out sound instruction for leadership in his first letter to Timothy. Many struggle with this passage, and so did we until our studies proved what the Apostle was helping Timothy deal with culturally.

Timothy was in charge of the church in Ephesus, an affluent and very religious culture. The goddess Diana was worshipped, along with Artemis the moon goddess, goddess of hunting and patron (supporter and protector) of young girls.

Converts coming to the church in Ephesus carried these cultural defilements concerning the idolatry of women. When we read Paul's warning in his letter about the self-indulgent woman being "dead even while she lives" we now understand how serious this condition was, as widowed or young single women were coming to fellowship, not truly born again, but rather seeking a new religion and likely looking for a husband. (Read 1 Timothy 5:3-15.)

More than ever, looking for the perfect mate has become an American culture obsession; singles, widowed, and the divorced are flooding into churches and fellowships, seemingly to follow Christ, but really only to find a husband or wife. Most of these just play church and give lip service to the lordship of Christ.

Today, the Apostle Paul's exhortation applies to this increasing problem. In this letter, he addressed single women who were lusting for a husband and giving up their pledge of serving Christ, with many straying after Satan to find success in doing so. This warning applies to our idolatrous culture today, which is not much different from those in Ephesus who were thronging to a new religion in hopes of finding a mate; not serving Christ, but serving Satan indirectly through relationship idolatry.

Prepare for the End-of-the-Age Weed Uprising
Satan's implants—from obnoxious to noxious—distinguishing themselves from the righteous

Jesus foretold that at the end of this age there would be the removal of all causes of sin and all law-breakers from his Kingdom, the true body of Christ on earth.[13] Christ explains a multidimensional work by Satan that will come to full development towards the end of this age in what is termed the "parable of the weeds" found in Matthew 13:24-30 and 36-43.

---

[13] We must understand that the Kingdom of Christ is largely manifest in the world through the body of Christ and is not to be confused with the coming Kingdom of Heaven upon the earth when Christ physically returns to earth.

The problem and meaning that this allegory depicts is how the evil one, during the last days, will successfully plant evil people amongst the sons and daughters of Christ's Kingdom (the body of Christ is comprised of all true believers in Christ). These people (implanted weeds) will be of the same nature as that of the devil and are a major cause of sin and trouble throughout the world and within the body of Christ. Further, the toxic effects of these implanted weeds will grow drastically and peak when persecution against Christians becomes a worldwide rage.

A poignant example of an implanted satanic weed would be that of Judas whom Jesus referred to as the son of perdition and a devil. All should be acquainted with what Judas did and how Satan actually entered into Judas and used this implanted weed that lived and ministered with the disciples and then betrayed Christ. These end-of-the-age satanic weeds are troubling and dangerous as well as virtually undetectable, at least until they reach a certain threshold of maturity.

In Christ's explanation, he used the term for weed that is equivalent to the noxious weed commonly known as a tare or darnel. The darnel weed is a species of rye grass having a strong soporific (hypnotic, sleep-inducing poisonous effect) if ingested by an animal or human. The darnel resembles wheat until the ear appears, and then the difference is detectable.

Though very noxious, uprooting darnel like a common weed in one's garden is not a good idea, at least during its growth stage when growing amongst wheat, as its roots intertwine with that of the wheat. Therefore, we see in the parable, Christ explaining not to uproot the weeds until harvest, *"Lest in gathering the weeds you root up the wheat along with them"* (Matthew 13:29).

The grain of the darnel, if eaten can produce convulsions and even death. Other symptoms from consuming this poisonous weed are sleepiness or drowsiness, hypnotic episodes, unconsciousness, dilation of pupils, drunkenness or intoxication, trembling, inability to walk, hindered speech, labored breathing, nausea, vomiting, stomach pains, diarrhea, colic, stupefied actions or dimwittedness, and dimmed vision, as well as giddiness, apathy and abnormal sensations. (Australian Herb Guide: www.herbiguide.com.au)

As sincere disciples of Christ, we need to take note of why the Lord used the tare or darnel weed in this parable. Christ is clearly describing the insidious, troubling, and toxic characteristics of Satan's servants disguised as Christians (including many who appear good in society). The devil distributes these people throughout the world, in all parts of culture, especially in Christian fellowships and Christian sects that embrace false doctrine.

Few in leadership are trained to detect and properly deal with wounded Christians who struggle and cause trouble, let alone discern and chase out imposters and worldly people who are devoid of the Spirit (weeds).

End-of-the-Age Maturing of the Wheat and the Weeds
Distinguish between the wicked and the righteous

As the end of this age races towards us, the true body of Christ will wake up and become mature. At the same time, the implanted weeds will become mature to fulfill Satan's plans. This is crucial for every saint to understand: God's people must discern the weeds implanted in fellowship and within their lives, including work, marriage and even extended family.

Christ foretold that just prior to the Great Tribulation and the revealing of the anti-Christ there will a great falling away amongst Christians. *"Then they will deliver you up to tribulation and put you to death, and you will be hated by all nations for my name's sake. And then many will fall away and betray one another and hate one another"* (Matthew 24:9-10).

The implanted weeds that are now amongst the wheat will soon turn from being obnoxious (in their current semi-hidden state), and become very noxious to defile, attack, and undermine leadership, where many will walk in a spiritually toxic-deadly power. (We discuss the spiritually toxic power in chapter six, "Discerning the Spiritual powers of the flesh").

In the epistle of Jude, the author reminds us of the Apostles' forecast concerning the last days, *"'In the last time there will be scoffers, following their own ungodly passions.' It is these who cause divisions, worldly people, devoid of the Spirit"* (Jude 1:18-19). Jude explains how Enoch prophesied about the Lord coming with ten thousands of his holy ones to execute judgment upon the ungodly and the false, and describes evil weeds this way:

"But these people blaspheme all that they do not understand, and they are destroyed by all that they, like unreasoning animals, understand instinctively. Woe to them! For they walked in the way of Cain and abandoned themselves for the sake of gain to Balaam's error and perished in Korah's rebellion. <u>These are blemishes on your love feasts, as they feast with you without fear</u>, looking after themselves; waterless clouds, swept along by winds; fruitless trees in late autumn, twice dead, uprooted; wild waves of the sea, casting up the foam of their own shame; wandering stars, for whom the gloom of utter darkness has been reserved forever... These are <u>grumblers, malcontents, following their own sinful desires; they are loud-mouthed boasters, showing favoritism to gain advantage</u>" (Jude 1:10-13, 16).

Just as in Korah's rebellion, Satan, making the most of his implants in opposing God's people, is about to inspire a full-blown uprising. The Lord will allow this cataclysmic upheaval within the body of Christ so that the naïve saint, the lost yet redeemable, and the world will see the difference between the wicked and the righteous—just as it states in Malachi:

"Then once more you shall see the distinction between the righteous and the wicked, between one who serves God and one who does not serve him" (Malachi 3:18).

In reviewing Christ's explanation of the parable of the weeds, we now see why the mature saint must learn to discern a weed implanted by the devil and avoid such. It is the plan of Satan to take as many naïve, lukewarm, and undiscerning saints out by way entanglement and betrayal through his close of the age implanted weeds.

"The one who sows the good seed is the Son of Man. The field is the world, and the good seed is the children of the kingdom. The weeds are the sons of the evil one, and the enemy who sowed them is the devil. The harvest is the close of the age, and the reapers are angels. Just as the weeds are gathered and burned with fire, so will it be at the close of the age. The Son of Man will send his angels, and they will gather out of his kingdom all causes of sin and all law-breakers, and throw them into the fiery furnace. In that place there will be weeping and gnashing of teeth. Then the righteous will shine like the sun in the kingdom of their Father. He who has ears, let him hear" (Matthew 13:37-43).

There is a great and final awakening coming with the call to come out from amongst the wicked and the false. Many unprepared saints will find that they are in the valley of decision without understanding and discernment. The anti-Christ and the false church will have all the pat answers, and Satan's weeds will be there barking out lies and causing many to stumble and turn to the last-days deceptions of the evil one.

Give Christ permission to train you in proper discernment and to equip you with courage and wisdom to untangle yourselves from the weeds living in and around you.

Chapter Five

The Pseudo-Christian and Churchianity

Personality Leaders with an "I am the Christ" Message
Building followers of pseudo-christs

As the world spirals through what Jesus called the birth pangs of the coming Kingdom, we see the rise of the *personality leader* invading the body of Christ: *"For many will come in my name, saying, 'I am the Christ,' and they will lead many astray"* (Matthew 24:5).

In this passage Christ is warning us that deceivers will come as Christian believers (in his name), saying *"I am the Christ"* and Mark and Luke quote Christ as saying, *"I am He"* in place of *"I am the Christ"* (Mark 13:6, Luke 21:8).

Over the centuries, false leaders have appeared, literally saying that they are the Christ. Most recently, Jose Luis de Jesus Miranda, a pastor in Florida, declared himself to be Christ.

This may seem to be what Christ is warning us about; however, there is more to this passage than a few delusional Christians through the years declaring themselves to be the Christ in his second coming.

In Christ's statement, *"many will come in my name, saying 'I am the Christ,' and they will lead many astray."* I believe Christ is referring to the end-of-the-age influx of deceived leaders who have developed teachings that inadvertently cause nominal and naïve Christians to follow a different Christ than that of Scripture. It is not the demented person who believes they are second incarnation of Christ who is described in this passage; but rather, Christ is addressing the many confused and deceived leaders who do not truly know Christ but think they do. These leaders have learned to conform to a faulty caricature of a Christ they have made up.

We need to have discernment in the midst of the overwhelming rise of Christian leaders who, glowing with charisma and magnetic personality, entice many to follow their own version of Jesus Christ. It is much easier to follow an earthly version of Christ than by faith to seek, find and obey the real Lord Jesus Christ. That is why those who preach and teach their own version of Christ are very popular.

The Apostle Paul wrote to the Christians in Corinth confronting their carnality, *"I, brethren, could not address you as spiritual men, but as men of the flesh, as babes in Christ. I fed you with milk, not solid food; for you were not ready for it; and even yet you are not ready, for you are still of the flesh. For while there is jealousy and strife among you, are you not of the flesh, and behaving like ordinary men? For when one says, 'I belong to Paul,' and another, 'I belong to Apollos,' are you not merely men?* (1 Corinthians 3:1-4 RSV).

Already believers were beginning to accumulate favorite teachers and leaders; this was a subtle diversion creeping into certain fellowships within first-century Christianity—a diversion from following the true Christ—a diversion created by extolling various leaders, making them bigger than life and following them.

This issue clearly became even more destructive and sinister because the Apostle Paul had to address the Corinth Christians again, later in his second letter. They were now being led astray by a satanic inception—the personality leader. Paul addressed these personality leaders as impersonators of the real apostles, scornfully labeling this type of leader *super-apostles* who preached another Jesus—not the true Jesus.

These super-apostles elevated themselves above the original apostles and were causing Christians to follow a different Jesus—in reality, luring Christians to follow these super-apostles, who declared themselves to have the real Christ within them.

These super-apostles lacked true knowledge of the Lord Jesus Christ. As the Apostle Paul pointed out, *"I consider that I am not in the least inferior to these super-apostles. Even if I am unskilled in speaking, I am not so in knowledge; indeed, in every way we have made this plain to you in all things"* (2 Corinthians 11:5, 6). Paul declared them false apostles and boasting of operating in the same authority as the original Apostles. *"And what I do I will continue to do, in order to undermine the claim of those who would like to claim that in their boasted mission they work on the same terms as we do. For such men are <u>false apostles, deceitful workmen, disguising themselves as apostles of Christ</u>. And no wonder, for even Satan disguises himself as an angel of light. So it is no surprise if his servants, also, <u>disguise themselves as servants of righteousness</u>. Their end will correspond to their deeds"* (2 Corinthians 11:12-15).

Today, as then—and even more so—the body of Christ suffers from an astronomical rise of *super-apostles* who boast that they have within their lives the true Christ and preach a variant Gospel and emulate a self-styled Christ. They have developed a *pseudo-christ* for others to follow—a Christian personality, contrived in self-effort, created from a carnal interpretation of the Gospel—a figment out of their imagination.

These leaders do not allow the formation of true Christ-like character within their own person, nor do they abide in the true Spirit of Christ. This will be difficult for many to understand and discern because a personality leader *appears* to be a servant of righteousness. On the contrary, most are spiritually empowered by an angel of light principality. They use the Word of God out of context to devise and employ teachings that encourage the deceived to serve a different Christ (a pseudo-christ) in the flesh—these last-days super-apostles grossly lack understanding of the Word of God.

As the end of this age roars to its conclusion, discerning the *super-apostle* or *personality leader* who does not have the true Christ within will be paramount. The sincere saint must learn to detect pseudo-christ teachings and endure to the end without being led astray by the many that are now on the scene declaring, "I have the true Christ in me; embrace my teaching and follow me!"

The root of the problem is that these personality leaders have never endured the discipline of the Lord, have never worked out their own salvation in fear and trembling, and have never become true servants of Christ trained to lead by example, pointing to and glorifying the true Christ.

The Bible encourages us to allow God to build a Christ-like nature within us; however, these super-apostles develop their own version of Christ: a Christian personality that they believe to be Christ-like in character. They follow lying spirits, learning to lie and then in turn believing their own lie. The Holy Spirit warned of this through the Apostle Paul in 1 Timothy 4:1-2: *"Now the Spirit expressly says that in later times some will depart from the faith by devoting themselves to deceitful spirits and teachings of demons, through the <u>insincerity of liars whose consciences are seared</u>."* Because they believe their own lies and reject conscience and the conviction of the Holy Spirit, they can become very convincing!

Lacking the understanding of God's Word, they are unable to expound truthfully on Scripture or produce sound doctrinal resources to mentor and equip the sincere Christian. They are unable to assist others to grow up into the true Christ, who is to be the head (true leader of all) and to walk in maturity and stability. Instead, these leaders must rely on quick-fix gimmicks, slogans, and mottos mixed with some truth of Scripture. These false teachings contain conjecture and myths that teach Christians how to mimic a different Christ, learning to develop an outer Christian persona created in the image of the leader's version of Christ.

Satan's work through the personality leader is to keep Christians immature, gullible, and away from the lordship and leadership of Christ—the very opposite of what a true leader in Christ is called to do. The Apostle Paul explains the role of true leadership in Ephesians—that we as saints become equipped for the ministry by becoming mature in Christ, learning to be led and directed in life by him and walking in true discernment, avoiding the false. Further, we must all *"grow up in every way into him who is the head, into Christ, from whom the whole body, joined and held together by every joint with which it is equipped, when each part is working properly, makes the body grow so that it builds itself up in love"* (see Ephesians 4:11-16).

The true saint in this hour must learn to detect insincere leaders who have seared their own conscience, believe their own lies, and elevate themselves by claiming to be Christ-like in personality, coming in Christ's name, and in a roundabout way, saying, *"I am the Christ."*

The popular leaders that I call a "personality leader" do not overtly claim to be the Christ, but by their actions and teachings they lure people to follow them instead of the real Christ. Their charismatic personas imply that this is what a Christ-like Christian looks like, acts like and believes. The question you must ask yourself and allow God to answer for you is—are you following a manmade version of Christ, and if so, which personality leader are you idolizing and emulating?

Reprogramming the Mind in the Power of the Flesh
Creating and emulating a personality to cover carnal character flaws

Most consider Norman Vincent Peale, noted for *The Power of Positive Thinking*, to be the founder of the modern positive thinking and behavior modification ideology in Christianity.

Many since have built on Peale's work, expanding his theories on positive thinking to become the predominate basis of self-change ministries and literature that now fills the shelves of most Christian bookstores.

Now, the many works on positive thinking and its many derivatives, such as positive confession captivate millions to engage in various forms of mental gymnastics by thinking themselves into a Christ-like state of being. This is not any different from other religions, such as Buddhism or Hare Krishna, in making the mind create an inner personality and modified character structures.

The main damning results are that positive thinking—and positive confession circumvents Christ's work of transformation, personal spirit renewal and Christ-like character development. They teach emulation of a manmade image of Christ, instead of learning to be transformed in character by the real person of Christ.

We need to understand more specifically, how the "I am the Christ" personality leader gains such credibility and exercises such mesmerizing power over so many Christians.

These misguided teachers *do know* that God's people are crying out in desperate need to understand God's way of transforming his people within—within the core of their heart and mind—thoroughly. This is one reason why so many throng to and follow these wayward teachers. These teachers can empathize because they have struggled themselves, and in their own desperate search, they became led astray, misinformed or deceived, thinking that they discovered the true way because they achieved some success.

Thus, they can offer stories, testimonies, and anecdotes that resonate with the masses of confused, searching, and clamoring Christians who are hungry for answers. Thus, for many these answers seem to work. However, the success they achieve is through self-empowing methods that work on a temporal basis—that is, they work until a strong enough trial or test exposes the inner defilements and unchanged character flaws.

This prediction of the Apostle Paul rings out for today, *"evil people and impostors will go on from bad to worse, deceiving and being deceived"* (2 Timothy 3:13). Most errant teachings spring from teachers who tried very hard to change into a successful Christ-centered believer, but misunderstood God's way of inner transformation. Looking for an easy way to change, they became deceived by the devil and learned to mimic Christian character, using fabricated mind programming methods.

These methods are similar to the methods that Hollywood actors use to create an outer personality, making them seem successful at portraying a believable role. However, their core nature and character suffers little change, and when their role is over, they return to day-to-day living as the same old-self.

This is how well-meaning leaders end up becoming imposters, going from bad to worse— walking in self-concocted formulas created in self-deception, working a method that creates an outer persona that they believe to be real.

They are able to deceive effectively, becoming persuasive and believable because of their own self-deception *"deceiving and being deceived."* Most believe wholeheartedly that they have discovered the right way for godly inner transformation.

Perhaps one of the most prolific speakers, authors and teachers using the power of the flesh to reprogram the mind is Joyce Meyer. In 2005, Time magazine's "25 Most Influential evangelicals in America" ranked Meyer as 17th. (*Time*. February 7, 2005).

To demonstrate the typical carnal approach that many deceived teachers employ, I will use excerpts from a recent book published by Joyce Meyer in 2010: *Power Thoughts: 12 Strategies to Win the Battle of the Mind*.

Positive-Power Thoughts do not Change the Carnal Nature

Choosing Joyce Meyer's book as my prime example will help demonstrate how a popular and influential person in ministry does not make them error free. Every Christian will be held accountable to determine for themselves if the teachings of others are sound in doctrine and not misleading. Most persons entering into ministry do not set out to be deceived or deceive others, however, if one's core doctrines are faulty to begin with, as one attempts to address the many problems within the body of Christ, using teaching that harnesses self-power, then an error can become cataclysmic. Teachers, pastors, and those in ministry must take care to build upon the foundation of Christ, not adding to that foundation using false doctrine. (See 1 Corinthians 3:1-15.)

The following challenges the positive-thinking ministries, I use "Power Thoughts" as representative of most ministries who use the same or similar presumptions that are contrary to sound doctrine found in Scripture.

From the outset, Meyer states her faulty presupposition in her introduction:

> "I wholeheartedly believe our thoughts lead us, charting the course of our lives pointing us in certain directions that ultimately determine our destination in life. Our thoughts cause us to have certain attitudes and perspectives; they affect our relationships; they determine how productive we will be personally and professionally; and they greatly influence the overall quality of our lives. We absolutely must understand the power of our thoughts!" (*Power Thoughts*, New York,: Faith Works, 2010 p. 3)

Joyce Meyer's hypothesis concerning how negative thoughts control Christians in a negative way is contrary to solid doctrine from the Word of God. Her presupposition and foundation for her "Power Thoughts" teaching contradicts Christ's teaching where he states, "<u>Out of the heart come evil thoughts</u>, murder, adultery, sexual immorality, theft, false witness, slander" (Matthew 15:19).

In *Power Thoughts* Joyce states a very common error that many "positive thought" preachers make:

> "Indeed, very few people realize that we have the ability to choose our thoughts and decide what we want to think; most of us passively meditate on

whatever comes into our minds without ever realizing our enemy, Satan, uses our minds extensively to control us and keep us from fulfilling God's destiny for our lives. <u>Each person regenerated through receiving Jesus Christ as their Savior receives a new spirit and a new heart from God, but does not receive a new mind—the mind must be renewed. The intent of one's heart may be pure and yet the mind is still confused.</u> The Bible declares emphatically that we must be transformed by the entire renewal of the mind and attitude (see Romans 12:2). This is accomplished by a complete, diligent, and thorough study of God's word." (*Power Thoughts,* pages 5-6. Underlined added to highlight Meyer's faulty premise.)

Meyer's approach in changing one's life for the better is based on changing one's thought patterns. One's own thoughts mislead, and are the cause bad attitudes and faulty perspectives. Her assumption is that "thoughts" are the main source of problems for a born again Christian's, therefore unwanted and unhealthy thoughts must be replaced. Replacing bad thoughts, based on her method of transformation, is accomplished by deliberately thinking the right kind of thoughts. The work then is to learn to deliberately "think-the-right-thoughts" which will replace wrong thoughts. Meyers teaches a form of self-reprograming of the mind through repetitive right thought thinking.

This works to a point for some; however, this carnally manufactured doctrine attempts to change life patterns in the power of self and only covers or overshadows the real source of wrong thinking or bad thoughts. The transforming power to change our old nature (including impurities and bad attitudes of the heart that produce bad thoughts) must come from the Holy Spirit. *"And we all, with unveiled face, beholding the glory of the Lord, are being transformed into the same image from one degree of glory to another. For this comes from the Lord who is the Spirit"* (2 Corinthians 3:18).

Based on what Christ taught, negative thoughts are symptoms of a deeper problem within the heart. Evil and negative thoughts do not develop wrong attitudes, rather wrong thoughts stem from an impure heart and misbeliefs within the heart—for the unsaved as well as the believer. Christ as well as the Apostle Paul and James teach that the heart and intentions of the heart are what need to be changed by the Holy Spirit and through repentance and cleansing. Specifically, in the book of James the troubled Christian is admonished to follow a specific line in dealing with bad thoughts, bad behavior, and unwanted desires and feelings: *"Draw near to God, and he will draw near to you. Cleanse your hands, you sinners, and purify your hearts, you double-minded. Be wretched and mourn and weep. Let your laughter be turned to mourning and your joy to gloom. Humble yourselves before the Lord, and he will exalt you"* (James 4:8-10).

Therefore, bad thoughts (and sometimes even good thoughts) are indicators or symptoms pointing to issues of the heart. (We can have a seemingly good thought that produces wrong behavior because the motive driving the thought was selfish or unwise.)

Every sincere Christian should be very familiar with this passage: *"The heart is deceitful above all things, and desperately sick; who can understand it? 'I the Lord search the heart and test the mind, to give every man according to his ways, according to the fruit of his deeds"* (Jeremiah 17:9).

We must identify Meyer's faulty premise: her premise, like so many is that the newborn believer receives a new heart and a new spirit, but the mind is not renewed. "Each person regenerated through receiving Jesus Christ as their Savior receives a new spirit and a new heart from God, but does not receive a new mind—the mind must be renewed" (Meyers, *Power Thoughts,* page 6).

Carrying forward with her faulty doctrine: Bad thoughts come from wrong thinking and must be changed by thinking right or consciously making the effort to think positive thoughts. What is primarily missing in this approach to changing one's life scripturally is submitting to the Holy Spirit and understanding that the bad thoughts are symptoms, not the source. The real source of trouble is an impure heart and a defiled spirit, which is still part of the old nature and must be changed through admission, repentance, and regeneration by the Holy Spirit and by the renewing of the spirit of the mind.[14]

The transformation process is to be led by the Holy Spirit not by our self-determination to change ourselves by thinking positive thoughts. Wrong thoughts are symptoms of issues of the heart and character (internal beliefs) that we must observe and resist acting out. Then, as we acknowledge a bad thought, we must study and know Scripture, and pray to pursue God's help in getting to the root issue within the heart and spirit, for repentance, healing and then character change.

When the root issue within the heart or personal spirit is resolved, the bad thoughts stop in that particular area of one's life, because the impurities of the heart are cleansed and healed, and if necessary, a wound or defilement to our spirit is also cleansed and healed, changing the attitudes and transforming character. The Holy Spirit divinely orchestrates these moments of transformation, not by our self-initiated positive thinking rituals.

In this Holy Spirit-led process, often God tests the heart and the mind, wherein bad thoughts surface. Then we must take ownership of the bad thoughts and treat them as a symptom that points to an issue or issues of heart or a wrong attitude of heart; Scripture terms this process sanctification. A process that Christ and the Holy Spirit facilitates, where the heart, spirit and the spirit of the mind become truly cleansed and changed through the understanding of the following principles.

Principles of Holy Spirit-led Transformation

True faith in Christ is not trusting in our own goodness or abilities, but rather trusting in God's grace, love and guidance with the desire to be obedient. True faith grows as we continue

---

[14] The Apostle Paul in his letter to the Ephesians points out a deeper aspect of changing our old nature by what he termed "putting off the old nature" by the renewing of the spirit of our minds and then to "put on the new nature" that is created in the likeness of God. One can catch negative thoughts and attempt to replace them deliberately with good thoughts, however, in this passage Paul is teaching that there is a hidden aspect of the mind that need to change and lies below our deliberate thinking. This "spirit of the mind" appears to be directly connected to our former manner of life and our old nature. Paul does not describe how the spirit of our mind is to be renewed. However, other passages we have cited indicate this is a work is to be done in the power of the Holy Spirit in conjunction with our obedience in allowing the Word of God to be made alive in penetrating into the spirit of the mind, our personal spirit and our heart. (See Ephesians 4:17-24; 2 Corinthians 3:17-18; Hebrews 4:9-13.)

increasing our knowledge of Christ and as we learn to maintain humility and submit to the Holy Spirit's constant presence and the discipline of the Lord in life's everyday challenges.

The discipline of the Lord will include trials and strong demonic opposition. Incorporated in this process is the life changing power of the Holy Spirit, who is the one to instill true character change. (See 2 Corinthians 3:17-18).

The sanctification and transformation process is opposite to the believer learning to forcibly reprogram their mind in their own strength and volition. Rather, it is a work of faith in cooperation with the leadership of the Holy Spirit, as we seek, ask, and humbly receive revelation from the Holy Spirit, as he makes the written Word of God become living and active within our life. It is in this every day interaction with the living God as we go through life and the study of God's written Word where God works within us, *"discerning the thoughts and intentions of the heart"* (Hebrews 4:12)—this occurs by God's leading; most often when the believer is willing and ready to receive such disclosures from God.

The book of James proclaims sound doctrine based on Christ's teachings about the heart (and the aforementioned passage from Jeremiah).

James expounds more specifically about what it takes for a believer to travel down the wrong path in life: *"Each person is tempted when he is lured and enticed by his own desire"* (James 1:14), and in order to deal with the source of an unstable walk with Christ, James further clarifies, *"Submit yourselves therefore to God. Resist the devil, and he will flee from you. Draw near to God, and he will draw near to you. Cleanse your hands, you sinners, and purify you hearts, you double-minded. Be wretched and mourn and weep. Let your laughter be turned to mourning and your joy to gloom. Humble yourself before the Lord, and he will exalt you"* (James 4:7-10).

To continue with Joyce Meyer's teaching from *Power Thoughts*, she broke the book into two parts. In Part One, "It's All in Your Mind," Meyer lays out faulty premise after premise, taking selected passages of Scripture out of context to make her case that all the problems for the born again Christian are within the mind; that somehow the mind was left out when the heart and spirit was instantly made new, clean, and whole.

Methods that involve an "I mantra" as described in Joyce Meyer's book are self-sustained methods. This self-powered approach is actually disobedience and avoids trusting and resting in God's penetrating work as he sees fit in his timing. The Biblical principle of learning to obey and allow the Holy Spirit to lead in transforming our heart, spirit, and mind is explained with the following exhortation and command, *"So then, there remains a Sabbath rest for the people of God, for whoever has entered God's rest has also rested from his works as God did from his. Let us therefore strive to enter that rest, so that no one may fall by the same sort of disobedience"* (Hebrews 4:9-11).

In actuality, Meyers and others who teach various forms of self-powered transformation are teaching God's people to be self-trusting and disobedient, by not ceasing from their labors and resting in God's work of transformation.

God's way affords success to anyone who comes and submits to the leadership of the Holy Spirit for transformation. Meyer's way, as other such schemes relies on the abilities of the individual person to reconfigure their thought patterns. Some are highly apt in self-programming the mind, while others are not.

The right way is truly submitting to Christ and requires our turning our thoughts to him in prayer and working with the Holy Spirit, the gifts of the Spirit and knowledge of the Word of God to allow God to help us discern our, *"thoughts and intentions of the heart. And no creature is hidden from his sight, but all are naked and exposed to the eyes of him to whom we must give account"* (Hebrews 4:12-13).

This terrible mistake misleads Christians away from God as the source for true power to transform a person's nature and places the power to change in the hands of the believer. *"He is the source of your life in Christ Jesus, whom God made our wisdom and our righteousness and sanctification and redemption. Therefore, as it is written, 'Let the one who boasts, boast in the Lord'"* (1 Corinthians 1:30-31).

In Part Two, "Power Thoughts" Meyer focuses on her own special concoction or mix of Scripture and a set of manmade teachings designed to help Christians create a changed life—not a new life in Christ, but a life manufactured in the flesh religiously. Unfortunately, the results are the creation of the author's interpretation of a Christ-like persona. The following are her twelve power thoughts:

1. I can do whatever I need to do in life through Christ.
2. God loves me unconditionally!
3. I will not live in fear.
4. I am difficult to offend.
5. I love people and I enjoy helping them.
6. I trust God completely; there is no need to worry!
7. I am content and emotionally stable.
8. God meets all my needs abundantly.
9. I pursue peace with God, myself, and others.
10. I live in the present and enjoy each moment.
11. I am disciplined and self-controlled.
12. I put God first in my life.

Here is Satan's insidious work in Meyer's teachings: The power of "I" in positive thinking is real spiritual power—the spiritual power derived from the human spirit driven by self-programming. The power of the Holy Spirit and God's principles of transformation are ignored and completely sidestepped, and replaced by self-power, self-determination, and self-inner-drive. "I power" takes the place of God's power!

"I can do… I will not… I am… I love… I trust… I am content… I am emotionally stable… I, I, I…." This kind of mantra thinking is narcissistic and works by creating an outer persona that is a pseudo or caricature of man's interpretation of Christ-like personality by mimicking the false teacher.

These self-created personalities overshadow and suppress the source of bad thoughts—unwholesome attitudes and bad character that stem from an impure heart. The majority of believers have impurities in the heart and a defiled spirit that still holds bitter jealousy, unbelief, narcissism, and carnal ambitions—in many cases evil motives and unbelief. This is why James writes to unstable Christians, *"Submit yourselves therefore to God. Resist the devil, and he will flee from you. Draw near to God, and he will draw near to you. Cleanse your hands, you sinners, and purify your hearts you men of double mind"* (James 4:7-8 RSV).

Jesus distinctly warned, *"It is the Spirit who gives life; the flesh is of no avail"* (John 6:63 RSV). Christians who follow these teachers like Joyce Meyer have learned to build pseudo-Christian personalities stacked up, one upon another, like a house of cards—in the power of the flesh.

What is unsettling and yet somewhat encouraging concerning Joyce Meyer's work is that in an older publication, Joyce points out accurately and remarkably how the heart within the believer can become problematic. However, she holds that these problematic conditions come after one is born again (since God gave them a new heart and a new spirit at rebirth), thus afterward, by allowing wrong thoughts into the heart, the following conditions of heart can develop for a believer:

>   An Evil Heart   A Bitter, Unforgiving Heart
>   A Hard, Unbelieving Heart   A Faint Heart
>   A Proud Heart   A Reasoning Heart (Missing Faith)
>   A Hypocritical Heart   An Envious Heart

(Joyce Meyer, *The Power of Being Positive: Enjoying God Forever,* New York: Hachette Book Group, 2003, table of contents covering pages 51-65).

These listed conditions of the heart are described in Scripture and point to the new believer having these conditions before they were born again and not yet having been cleansed and transformed in the new believer. The issue is that the new believer does not understand how to deal with an impure heart or wounds to the spirit.[15] Simon, a former magician became a believer; however, Peter pointed out to this new believer that he was not right in his heart and clarified his condition by stating, *"For I see that you are in the gall of bitterness and in the bond of iniquity"* (Acts 8:23).

Warren, Meyer, Osteen, and so many other personality teachers help Christians use mind-power (the spiritual powers of the flesh) to create sickening-sweet, placating personalities to cover up the carnal nature and suppress the works of the flesh—resulting in a manmade caricature of the image of Christ. That is why so many pseudo Christians will say to Christ and then hear from Christ the following: *"'Lord, Lord, did we not prophesy in your name, and cast out demons in your name, and do many mighty works in your name?' And then will I declare to them, 'I never knew you; depart from me, you workers of lawlessness'"* (Matthew 7:22-23).

---

[15] The condition of a born-again Christian's heart and spirit prior to rebirth will determine how much deeper work must be allowed by the Holy Spirit during the sanctification process. Some people carry deep wounds to the spirit and severely damaged emotions. These can be in layers if the person suffers from a double-minded condition. If one renews the mind only, without dealing with impurities within the heart, the personal spirit, and the spirit of the mind—then for the most part working with the mind only amounts to creating an outer Christian personality that covers up wounds and defilement in the heart and spirit. See 2 Corinthians 7:1, James 4:8-10. Ephesians 4:22-24.

The test for teachers like those mentioned is their willingness to change their doctrinal errors concerning the transformation process. Most who teach the positive mind-set programming have a real heart for God's hurting. I believe most genuinely want to walk in the whole truth of the Gospel. However, when things begin to turn for the worst, as the birth pangs increase, these self-powered formulas will be seen for what they are. Which of these personality leaders will see their mistake and stand corrected—before it is too late?

The many that follow these teachers have learned to vicariously appropriate the leader's charisma, counterfeit faith, and emotional energy—inspiring and empowering followers to link up with the leader's approach in walking with Christ. The spiritual bond between the leader and the followers is facilitated by the demonic, thought to be the Holy Spirit bearing witness (this is a very powerful last-days counterfeit dynamic).

All this is why Peter explained that these false teachers would *"secretly bring in destructive heresies,"*—that we, as discerning saints must be careful; that we might detect their agenda and realize how serious, insidious, and widespread these viral faith-eating teachings[16] would be which are now very much upon us.

These teachings destroy true faith in Christ by subverting the work of the Holy Spirit and the power of Christ in transforming our inner character and personalities—putting this all-important work into the hands of the believer. These carnal methods bypass the narrow gate and hard path that Jesus commanded us to enter by—which is God's prescribed journey that leads to life.

"Enter by the narrow gate. For the gate is wide and the way is easy that leads to destruction, and those who enter by it are many. For the gate is narrow and the way is hard that leads to life, and those who find it are few" (Matthew 7:13-14).

These concocted carnal methods are simple and easily empowered by self-energy. The struggling believer is not offended by this approach; rather he is leered, coxed, babied, enticed, and promised success in order to feel good about buying into the specially designed carnal method.

Most of these teachings hinge around eliminating bad thoughts and unwanted feelings. The teachings are presented gingerly so as not to offend the hearer by admonishing and confronting an impure heart filled with bitterness, jealousy, selfishness, or greed. These self-serving teachers dare not impugn the carnal character of so many believers, followers that vote by donation to keep their favorite ear-tickling teachers in business.

Eventually, this personality house of cards created by self-power will crumble when the trials of life hit hard. For now, God has given those who desire these ear-tickling shortcuts over to these deceptions and has allowed Satan to back off from any forceful and truly humbling attacks.

Many have chosen to make shipwreck their faith and take Scripture out of context, nullifying or squelching the work of the Spirit in opposing the desires of the flesh. To continue

---

[16] *Faith-eating teachings* is another way of describing these destructive heresies. Instead of building up the faith of the new believer in Christ, with the understanding that the rebirth experience is just the beginning, these false teachings start to eat away at true faith in Christ. They redirect faith from Christ's working in them to self-help transformation schemes. Instead of helping the new believer brace for the next phase towards full salvation (sanctification), to expose hidden-unchanged issues of the heart and spirit by the hand of God, these teachers take Christ's position in transformation by way of their carnal teachings—saying in effect, "I am the Christ."

down this path will eventually sear the conscience and cause rejection of the conviction of the Holy Spirit.

A true child of God who desires to improve their powers of discernment will also desire His discipline. Remember, as the author of Hebrews points out, *"If you are left without discipline, in which all have participated, then you are <u>illegitimate children and not sons</u>"* (Hebrews 12:8).

The most insidious aspect that these "I am the Christ" personality leaders teach and incite in summary can be termed *self-induced mind control* (a form of self-deception), which leads a multitude of misguided Christians into the following condition:

Insidiously deceived condition defined: Masses of Christians live and work for the church or for the leader's agenda with a false sense of being *in Christ*. In reality, they have learned merely to use Christ's name to live a so-called purpose-driven life *for Christ*. This purpose-driven life is unwittingly driven or empowered by the spiritual powers of the flesh in a counterfeit faith, and enhanced by the demonic that counterfeits the Holy Spirit.

A deceived Christian in this condition lives and works for Christ, doing good works, walking in false gifts, and casting out devils using Christ's name—doing things for Christ. However, a true Christ-like nature is not formed within them and the Spirit of Christ is not dwelling within them, thus Christ is not working through them in his power. They are working *for* Christ but not allowing Christ to work through them.

Meyer's and so many like her are teaching Christians to avoid the discipline of God where the Christian learns to submit to the Holy Spirit and the Spirit of Christ concerning character transformation. These teachers are creating illegitimate Christians, not sons and daughters of the living God.

I repeat this warning by Christ about this deceived condition: *"Not everyone who says to me, 'Lord, Lord,' will enter the kingdom of heaven, but the one who does the will of my Father who is in heaven. On that day many will say to me, 'Lord, Lord, did we not prophesy in your name, and cast out demons in your name, and do many mighty works in your name?' And then will I declare to them, 'I never knew you; depart from me, you workers of lawlessness"* (Matthew 7:21-23).

I really do not know how to be more adamant and descriptive about this serious condition. If you have any suspicion that you may suffer from these destructive heresies or suspect that you are following a pseudo-Christ inspired by these personality leaders, then the section coming up, "Transforming our Carnal Nature—God's Way" will definitely help you get to know the true Christ.

The next few sections will help discern the many subtle self-transformation techniques or methods now marketed within society and within Christianity.

Worldly Motivational Leaders Using Principles that Work!
Stumbling on Christ's principles, teaching how to empower believers in the flesh and taking credit

In 1976, I was struggling to overcome my old carnal nature and did not have a clue concerning my issues related to a wounded and defiled spirit or damaged emotions and impurities of heart. My studies in Bible college were not helping; however, I worked part time in a Christian bookstore where I had access to a large selection of authors from past generations who wrote of a deeper work of grace after becoming born again and the work of the cross within the believer's life. These resources from the old-timers and a fading generation of hard-hitting preachers and authors, such as the following list gave great encouragement. These authors are still relevant, and go far beyond the pop Christian writings in the current morass of easy-read titles that fill the bookstores today.

David Wilkerson, Leonard Ravenhill, Corrie ten Boom, Jessie Penn-Lewis, John Bunyan, Jonathan Edwards, D. L. Moody, A. W. Tozer, Andrew Murray, Charles Spurgeon, John Wesley, Smith Wigglesworth, Charles Finney, Oswald Chambers, Dietrich Bonhoeffer, Watchman Nee, and others added to my resource library and helped me avoid most of the false teachings that mislead many today:

However, even with these resources I still struggled with issues of heart and spirit from my former manner of life and childhood abuses. The main conflict I had was the false teachings I embraced (as most Christians have through these many years); which were that God downloads and installs a complete new heart and new spirit at rebirth and therefore we can forget everything from the past and ignore all bad thoughts.

Back then, one of my Bible college professors addressed bad thoughts with the following cutesy adage, "Bad thoughts are like birds flying over your head, just don't let them land and build a nest." In an effort to climb out of the ruts of life and get into ministry prematurely (not knowing about trials and wilderness training), I tried several motivational authors that were starting to emerge. Og Mandino's book *The Greatest Salesman in the World* published in 1968 became a resource I discovered and attempted to employ so that I might jettison myself out of the doldrums into successful ministry and a fulfilled life as a Christian.

Read the following overview to help understand how "pick yourself up" carnal methods work for a while, or work for those who go all the way over to the devil's twisted lie that "you can do all things through Christ (in the flesh)." In *The Greatest Salesman in the World*, Mandino composed and prescribed "The Legend of the Ten Scrolls," with each scroll to be read and reread for at least three months, before moving to the next scroll.

Scroll I - *The Power of Good Habits*
Scroll II - *Greet Each Day with Love in Your Heart*
Scroll III - *Persist until You Succeed*
Scroll IV - *You Are Natures Greatest Miracle*
Scroll V - *Live Each Day as if it Were Your Last*
Scroll VI - *Master Your Emotions*
Scroll VII - *The Power of Laughter*
Scroll VIII - *Multiply Your Value Every Day*
Scroll IX - *All Is Worthless Without Action*
Scroll X - *Pray to God for Guidance*

(Og Mandino, *The Greatest Salesman in the World*, Bantam Books, 1968)

Mandino's primary theme was "do it now." In Scroll IX, "I will act now" is written 18 times. While his messages did have Christian connotations (referring to Paul as the greatest salesman in the world), it was still a message of repetitive actions to build good habits and overcome in life by tapping into your own carnal-spirit energy.

My attempt at applying Og Mandino's recipe for success to become *the greatest preacher in the world, the greatest husband in the world, and the greatest father and provider in the world* all fell desperately short. Part of the reason for failure was my own inability to drop my faith in Christ and no longer put my trust in him and obey him. I did not realize at the time that, Og's formula was in reality a work of the flesh that the Holy Spirit opposed, thus I could not apply his concoction of biblical principles and manmade mantras—unbeknownst to me the Holy Spirit was working within me and in conflict to these teachings.

The Next Generation of False Motivational Speakers
It is our responsibility to discern who they are and steer clear

Since then, the promotion of business and church motivational conferences has grown exponentially. Motivational speakers, such as the late Zig Ziglar, Steven Covey, and Og Mandino have passed away; however, because of speakers like them, a plethora of current motivational speakers carry on, leading the faith of many away from the person of Christ, into trusting their own self-energy and unique methods for success.

Meyer, Osteen, Warren, and so many others borrow these motivation concepts mixed with the positive thinking teachings from others like Norman Vincent Peal, then remix them into their own brand of manmade principles and wrap them up in a watered-down Gospel to promote their own teaching and ministry. I do not have the time to or space to list the new generation of motivational speakers; however, you have the foundation that I have learned to work from—Christ and all of his teachings and commands, such as the beatitudes. You must learn to discern for yourself!

Applying the beatitudes taught by Christ without knowing and following the person of Christ is foolish. These principles seem to work; however they lead to a damning shortcut, bypassing the work of the cross in the believer's life. This powerful deception puts the Christian in the driver's seat and says to live the Christian life without relying on the person of Christ, his discipline, and his grace and it will work most of the time, until real trouble comes.

Many proud and self-reliant Christians are in for a rude awaking, as many will soon need to truly understand the following passage: *"God chose what is low and despised in the world, even things that are not, to bring to nothing things that are, so that no human being might boast in the presence of God. He is the source of your life in Christ Jesus, whom God made our wisdom and our righteousness and sanctification and redemption. Therefore, as it is written, 'Let the one who boasts, boast in the Lord'"* (1 Corinthians 1:28-31 RSV). Many will wake up and find they foolishly did not have a right relationship with Christ and turn to the world for direction and substance in the dark days during the Great Tribulation.

Reprogramming the Mind Instead of Renewing the Spirit of the Mind
Manmade methods that create a religious personality to suppress the old nature.

These self-help methods are just another form of religious works that oppose God's grace. They hinder the Holy Spirit's work in searching into the depths of the believer's heart, mind, and spirit. Embracing one of these methods constitutes an act of disobedience in light of

Scripture and subverts faith in Christ. The believer learns to strive in their own strength to change their life in their own volition and energy.

Deceived believers learn to bend and shape their mind into a set of personalities within the framework of principles and mantras that seemingly produce appropriate thinking. The framework includes a mixture of wrongly interpreted biblical principles and Scripture applied in a prescribed manner, which, if followed rigorously, will produce desired results.

However, this type of approach to inner character change relegates the work of the person of the Holy Spirit into silence. Success is now in the hands of the believer's determination, not dependent on God's grace and the Word of God made active in the power of the Holy Spirit. Refer again to Hebrews 4:9-13, which affirms the serious consequences of going along with any type of self-change false teaching and not resting in God's work of character transformation.

David also wrote about hidden inner issues that cause sinful behavior and how the Lord desires to be in charge of illuminating and transforming our inner person, *"Behold, you delight in truth in the inward being, and you teach me wisdom in the secret heart"* (Psalm 51:6)

Psalm 51 deals extensively with the process that God uses in dealing with our secret issues that we ourselves do not want to acknowledge. Denial and a hardened heart and spirit are the real issues and if we will receive proper instruction concerning God's discipline and submit to him, then God can draw our attention to the issues we deny.

In the same psalm, David gives a picture of how to walk in God's grace that facilitates a close and intimate relationship, where revelation of our heart's thoughts and intentions come to us before they lead us into trouble and sin. David writes, *"For you will not delight in sacrifice, or I would give it; you will not be pleased with a burnt offering. The sacrifices of God are a broken spirit; a broken and contrite heart, O God, you will not despise"* (Psalm 51:16-17). In this hour, as the church wallows in a lukewarm condition, humbly walking in brokenness of spirit and contriteness of heart is avoided like a plague.

Once we realize this and submit to our loving and all-knowing Lord, he will work with us, daily guiding and revealing how our old nature is still active and negatively influencing us, usually in very deceitful ways.

The Apostle Paul expands on what David wrote in the Psalms with the following passage:

"Now this I say and testify in the Lord, that you must no longer walk as the Gentiles do, in the futility of their minds. They are darkened in their understanding, alienated from the life of God because of the ignorance that is in them, due to their hardness of heart. They have become callous and have given themselves up to sensuality, greedy to practice every kind of impurity. But that is not the way you learned Christ!—assuming that you have heard about him and were taught in him, as the truth is in Jesus, to put off your old self, which belongs to your former manner of life and is corrupt through deceitful desires, and to be renewed in the spirit of your minds, and to put on the new self, created after the likeness of God in true righteousness and holiness" (Ephesians 4:17-24).

In this directive from Scripture, we learn that we must no longer operate in the futility of our own mind and walk in hardness of heart, for we will certainly drift further and further away from the presence of God. Frustrated Christians who feel alienated from the life God throng to the mind reprogramming techniques offered so abundantly.

Many become trapped in one of these personality-developing schemes, only to learn how to suppress the old nature and the associated frustrating symptoms. They learn to battle bad thoughts and replace them with good thoughts, circumventing God's work in exposing the tip-of-the-iceberg issues of the heart, spirit, and the spirit of the mind.

It is God's plan to use our troubling symptoms as pointers and clues to the root issues of our old nature, which is yet to be changed. With the Holy Spirit working through the written Word of God, the thoughts and intentions of the heart, with the related spirit of the mind thought patterns, can now be changed by the power of God, provided we learn to cooperate.

The Holy Spirit through faith and the grace of God will personally renew and transform the spirit of our mind, purify our heart, and instill a new and right spirit within—gradually as we grow and seek him, encounter by encounter and trial by trial, until we have become transformed by his loving discipline, into his image or likeness.

He will break denial and remove the veil that blinds us to our inner wrongness if we humbly allow him to deal with us on his terms. *"But when one turns to the Lord, the veil is removed. Now the Lord is the Spirit, and where the Spirit of the Lord is, there is freedom. And we all, with unveiled face, beholding the glory of the Lord, are being transformed into the same image from one degree of glory to another. For this comes from the Lord who is the Spirit"* (2 Corinthians 3:16-18).

Systematic Dumbing Down of the Saints
Christians purposely driven from hearing Christ's voice

It is hard work to grow up into Christ and follow the leading of the Holy Spirit and the voice of the Good Shepherd. Leadership's main mission is to help Christians in their charge to hear the true voice of Christ and obey. The following passage clearly lays out the purpose for this all-important mission:

"And he gave the apostles, the prophets, the evangelists, the pastors and teachers, to equip the saints for the work of ministry, for building up the body of Christ, until we all attain to the unity of the faith and of the knowledge of the Son of God, to mature manhood, to the measure of the stature of the fullness of Christ, so that we may no longer be children, tossed to and fro by the waves and carried about by every wind of doctrine, by human cunning, by craftiness in deceitful schemes. Rather, speaking the truth in love, we are to grow up in every way into him who is the head, into Christ, from whom the whole body, joined and held together by every joint with which it is equipped, when each part is working properly, makes the body grow so that it builds itself up in love" (Ephesians 4:11-16).

Over the last thirty to forty years, the popular winds of doctrine have led God's people away from growing in maturity, learning to obey the voice of Christ who is to be head of all, and learning to practice true discernment.

These wayward teachings subtly elevate leadership to the point of replacing the individual Christian's responsibility in learning to hear and obey the voice of Christ. In their own self-deception false leaders devise cunning teachings that drive Christians (like cattle driven to market) to serve the leader's agenda. This type of dumbing down of the saints is what the Apostle Paul warned of: *"evil people and impostors will go on from bad to worse, deceiving and being deceived"* (2 Timothy 3:13).

Jesus is to be the head of all, where he has the freedom to lead and guide according to God's purposes. When the Holy Spirit has the reigns, there is harmony in fellowship and unity of faith, where the Holy Spirit has freedom to appoint, guide and manifest the gifts—as He wills. There will be respect for leadership and leadership will demonstrate the Gospel by example along with sound doctrine, authority and accountability. This kind of fellowship is rare, however that will change soon.

We must understand that the lack of knowledge and understanding hampers the work of Christ and the Holy Spirit in building sound body life. In the days of his flesh, Jesus confronted this type of dumbing down of God's people perpetrated by the scribes and Pharisees by pointing out: *"You shut the kingdom of heaven in people's faces. For you neither enter yourselves nor allow those who would enter to go in"* (Matthew 23:13). Today most in leadership contrive a purpose for the Christian layman that fulfills the dreams and schemes of leadership—contrary to God's will.

Satan's aim is to develop unwavering compliance to false leaders using false doctrines that systematically dumb down the followers of Christ. The devil does not want believers to search the Scriptures for themselves and earnestly seek for a dynamic relationship with Christ.

Using short-cut teachings that subvert the discipline and training of the Lord, Christians learn to become *mentally passive,* and *emotionally and spiritually dependent.* Millions become addicted to the false leader's gimmicks, flamboyant charisma and massive mesmerizing power. A blind allegiance turns into a spellbinding grip upon those who follow, since few challenge the teachings or question the source of any stirred up spiritual and emotional feelings.

Christians become programmed and scolded into passivity by leadership's deceitful schemes. Anyone who reads Scripture for themselves and realizes the deceit, then confronts or points out error, that person is taken aside to be shut up, pushed aside, or labeled as rebellious. Exposing a lie, a problem, or hidden darkness in these false movements will get abuse—the messenger is attacked and the problem or lie is covered up.

Masses of Christians across all evangelical, Pentecostal, and charismatic denominations and most movements are driven by what some call the emerging church agenda, where the hope and mission of Christianity is to convert the world to Christ through leadership and the local church, hoping to usher in the new millennium.

For many Christians, perhaps most, the emerging church ideology and goals appear biblical, but they ignore the truth of Christ concerning his second coming. This is an egregious doctrinal error devised by demons to snare ignorant Christians into financing a global effort to make the world a safer, peaceful place. The emerging church movement is a system of social beliefs with a Christian slant employed to usher in world order. This work is not of God, because it contradicts New Testament warnings and instruction on how believers should prepare and conduct themselves during the coming end-of-the-age events.

Every true saint desires peace upon the earth; however, to mislead Christians to think it can be facilitated in any other way than how Christ pronounced, is not helping the naïve and deceived become prepared for the coming difficult times, leading to Christ's return.

The emerging church movement is a deception that twists Scripture out of context, creating another false movement. It is turning Christianity into a church movement that merely competes with other religions for converts, social influence, and political posturing.

Participants of this modern emerging church movement dare not take what Jesus taught about his coming literally: that the end of this age becomes hell on earth, a time of terror for everyone—and that Christians must be prepared to endure this terrible time and minister the Gospel during the final harvest of souls for Christ.

The body of Christ is struggling to return to a true relationship with Christ. Reforming back to a true New Testament church as exemplified in Scripture is the Lord's top priority as the end of this age nears. He will accomplish this in the coming trials and present a spotless bride and restoration of sound doctrine, *"a chosen race, a royal priesthood, a holy nation, a people for his own possession"* (1 Peter 2:9), a church that influences culture by life example and demonstrates the true gifts of the Holy Spirit in purity.

Over the last 150 years, true demonstrations of the power of God in revival and of the gifts of the Spirit came and went; most were hi-jacked by false leadership and counterfeit spirit activity. Modern movements have turned deceptive such as the Azusa Street Revival, the Word of Faith movement, the Toronto Blessing, the Brownsville Revival and the Lakeland Revival.

Leadership in these movements lacked the character to lead by example to hold firm in preventing the subversion of the Holy Spirit's work. That is—to stay the course in fulfilling Christ's commission to make disciple who observe all that Christ taught and commanded.

Instead, most in leadership have fulfilled the Apostle Paul's fears: *"I know that after my departure fierce wolves will come in among you, not sparing the flock; and from among your own selves will arise men speaking twisted things, to draw away the disciples after them"* (Acts 20:29-30). This is the case now: Christians follow leadership, not Christ. The false easily subvert true faith in Christ by keeping God's people passive, lazy, ignorant, and spiritually doped up.

False leaders dare not teach the truth—the truth that Christ and the Apostles taught!—about Christ's personal leadership for each believer. Leadership must embrace discipline by his hand, in true discipleship, which will include trials and suffering. Leadership must pronounce the truth that Christians must be prepared to endure the Great Tribulation at the end of age.

In the coming days you will see God raise up true ministries and leaders who will glorify the true Christ, causing many to come away from the false leaders, false teachings, and false christs. A great shaking is coming to Christianity. Persecution and trouble will expose everything that is false, and the Holy Spirit will shine his light on the true servants of Christ!

When this happens, will you be able to discern the true servants of Christ from the false, those who serve their own agendas of self-glorification?

Saints Misled to be at War with God
Fighting against the Holy Spirit's work in opposing the desires of the flesh

There is a war that the Holy Spirit wages within every true born again believer. The Apostle Paul explains, *"For the desires of the flesh are against the Spirit, and the desires of the Spirit are against the flesh, for these are opposed to each other, <u>to keep you from doing the things you want to do</u>"* (Galatians 5:17). It is the responsibility of leadership to help the saints understand what these two opposing forces within their life feel like and how to work on the side of the Holy Spirit.

Few can detect their own unique desires of the flesh, which are still in operation, even though they have stopped living a sinful lifestyle. The carnal desire to draw attention to one's self was obvious while they lived in the world; however, for that same person as a new believer, the motives to volunteer for teaching Sunday school are most likely a desire of the flesh. In this case, (like so many), that exciting surge of energy for volunteering to teach often stems from unresolved jealousy and insecurity still smoldering within the new believer. That old carnal desire to draw attention to self is deceitfully at work.

The opportunity to prove one's self as someone special overrides any check of the Holy Spirit, since the call to volunteer came from the pulpit. Thousands of new yet immature Christians are misled to ignore the desires of the Spirit, especially when it comes to serving the church and becoming involved in ministry.

Few pastors warn those in their care of how the Holy Spirit works in putting checks within one's spirit concerning doing things out of God's will or in his timing. Few learn to wait upon the Lord for his timing or upon hearing from the Holy Spirit for confirmation—and few learn to discern the Lord's leading and his voice.

Christians must learn to stop fighting against the Holy Spirit's desires and learn to wage war on the side of God against the desires of the flesh. That requires discerning one's own desires of the flesh with the associated lustful energy in doing one's own thing, instead of seeking and doing God's perfect will.

Marketing Churchianity—Managing Instead of Maturing the Saints
Placement programs that subvert the Holy Spirit's direction and timing

The church-growth madness gripping most leaders has created a monstrous management nightmare. The massive influx of people—married couples, families, teens, youth, toddlers, infants, singles adults, seniors, and the elderly—has become staggering.

Many coming are not truly born of God and called by him, rather they are transient spiritual seekers looking for a magic carpet ride into happiness on earth.

When the crowds formed and followed Jesus, our Lord had compassion on the masses, *"because they were harassed and helpless, like sheep without a shepherd"* (Matthew 9:36). Jesus knew the vulnerability of crowds. He knew how crowds formed with the intent of following someone who might make life easier, but without discernment or defenses against the wolves. To exasperate the situation further, the "crowd mentality" helps keep individuals within the crowd helpless and hapless—everyone is doing it, so it must be the right thing to do.

The example given by Christ in managing the crowds that followed him was not taking advantage of their ignorance and misfortune in life. Instead, Christ established God's way of ministering and guiding the masses into a right relationship with their heavenly Father.

The real work that Christ commanded his disciples to do in ministering to the large crowds was to pray that God send trustworthy laborers or trained Christian workers to mentor individuals, to lead them from the *crowd mentality into individual maturity*.

To follow Christ's example and directive concerning the crowds, leaders of the masses of followers in fast-growing churches or movements must employ wisdom to raise up, train and deploy qualified workers. Many coming are mere transient spiritual seekers who are not necessarily sincere about Christ but are looking for an easy ride in life. Christ told the crowd who followed him what becoming his disciple would entail; that one must *"first sit down and count the cost"* (see Luke 14:15-33). Each new and potential follower of Christ must have access to mentoring, counseling, and sound doctrine—and be informed in no uncertain terms what is expected to be a true disciple and follower of Christ.

Jesus was not impressed with the crowds, for he knew the crowds had an agenda that was contrary to God's plans, and that agenda made the crowds open prey to charlatans.

Christ also knew that the crowds, as an aggregate, would not accept God's plan of redemption or God's way to become blessed. His message to the masses was meant to screen out the game players, the rainbow chasers, and the transient spiritualists who wanted God on their terms.

Unfortunately, today the majority of mega-church growth schemes do the very opposite of Christ's example and teach against sound teachings on convert/harvest management. Instead of warning and teaching the masses who throng to church about the costs of following Christ, they are managed like the crowds at rock concerts or at movie theatres.

The masses are funneled into church programs, events, and activities by the use of pre-calculated management methods developed from church management surveys. Surveys are often used to assess the so-called spiritual gifting of a potential volunteer; however, these surveys merely pigeon-hole individual volunteers into carnal talent pools.

Leadership hires professionals to manage massive pools of volunteers and handle large crowds at each service, event or conference. In order to place each volunteer into the right area of ministry, extensive questionnaires are administered to determine what kind of talent or ability God has given each volunteer.

These surveys categorize and recommend where each volunteer would most likely be best suited in the areas of church ministry. This helps the nightmarish problem of placing volunteers and utilizing their so-called gifting most effectively.

However, this approach amounts to manmade management of volunteer workers, where few are trained, nurtured and matured that they might be prepared to receive any true gifting from the Holy Spirit. Rather, these surveys analyze the carnal and natural talents, abilities, and passions of each person. This is a very dangerous approach because it negates the Holy Spirit's will and the all-important processes that cleanse, sanctify, discipline, call and then empower each convert for the work of the ministry—as the Holy Spirit wills. (See 1 Corinthians 12:1-11).

Mega-church management employs large-business management models with a twist of Scripture added to make participants believe they are serving God with their gifts and talents given to them from God. This generalizes or cuts God's will for each individual down to a very controlled framework that suits these manmade church growth agendas.

Let us face reality, this is a fantastic strategy to staff a non-profit, tax-exempt organization with free labor and grow it into a powerful people-collecting and money-making business. Many mega-churches and national ministries using these methods surge to a level of success comparable with a Fortune 500 business. They achieve success on the backs of deceived Christian workers who volunteer joyfully and ignorantly, thinking God is using them.

Joel Osteen's organization, his Lakewood Church in Houston, employs a large staff of professionals to manage over 5,000 volunteers who minister to over 40,000 church members, to the community and to the world. (Beliefnet.com, *Joel Osteen and the Littlest Big Church in the World*)

Ministry Case: *Just manage and funnel*

One of our associates in ministry gave the following account. Some ten years ago, he attended a church caught up in the Rick Warren Purpose-Driven program and its survey placement methods. He became actively involved in placement survey analysis and the placement interviewing process for new members. *The Purpose-Driven Church* was first published in 1995 and became very popular among pastors. In fact, George Barna in 2005 conducted a survey of American pastors and ministers, finding that Warren's book, *The Purpose-Driven Church*, was rated the second most influential book, second to its sequel, *The Purpose-Driven Life* also by Warren.

In this case our associate described how the church growth consultants instructed the pastor, leaders and placement volunteers *not* to pray with, counsel, or ask new members being processed any personal questions about their walk with Christ, how they came to know the Lord, or inquire about any struggles they may be encountering. He and the other volunteers helping to place new members in church ministry were to manage the process and not to offer any kind of ministry or advice.

In spite of these ultra-controlling rules, our associate saw that many of the new members he interviewed were too new in the Lord, or that they would clearly be out of their element if funneled into the ministry that the Purpose-Driven program and survey dictated.

Most disturbing to our associate was the lack of empathy or compassion by the church leaders and pastors demonstrated towards these new converts and Christians coming to the church looking for a new fellowship home. This and other glaring issues within the church's growth program convinced our associate to leave and find a fellowship that did not treat members with such a controlling and callous attitude. Ω

Purposely Driven by the Flesh

This type of callous, contrived, and controlling approach to church growth and ministry placement is now the standard—a short-cut gimmick to help manage the crowds who are stumbling, clawing, and floundering—who come to church looking for truth and the true Christ.

In some cases, local churches are experiencing what many consider a hostile takeover. Often, the Purpose-Driven plan is embraced by a few within the fellowship and they form a clique; and through a process defined by Rick Warren, this group pushes to invite the Purpose-Driven program affiliation to come in and help create church growth. Unwittingly, most pastors, elders, and the more stable members are clueless to the clandestine agenda to take control and install false doctrine and new leadership and chase out any that stand against the new church growth methods.

The following is a synopsis of the published plan produced by Church Transitions, an associate of Saddleback Church and a purveyor of Rick Warren's Purpose-Driven program. To squelch any resistance to the transition (takeover), Church Transitions trains the clique initiating the change how to take over the fellowship through eight published steps. Church members are not to be informed of the transition until the fourth step. After the sixth step in the process of change, if there are some in the church who voice concerns, the following is suggested:

1. Identify those who are resisting the changes;
2. Assess the effectiveness of their opposition;
3. Befriend those who are undecided about the changes;
4. Marginalize more persistent resisters;
5. Vilify those who stay and fight; and
6. Establish new rules that will silence all resistance.

Church members are not told until it is too late to make a difference. Basically, this is a well-planned approach to facilitating a hostile church takeover with underhanded, even ruthless tactics to oust all opposition. The members are forced to accept the changes or leave the church. (www.apprising.org, "Dan Southerland and Cult-like Hostile Takeover)

Rick Warren boasts:

"Be willing to let people leave the church. And I told you earlier the fact that people are gonna leave the church no matter what you do. But when you define the vision, you're choosing who leaves. You say, "But Rick, yes, they're the pillars of the church." Now, you know what pillars are. Pillars are people who hold things up.... And in your church, you may have to have some blessed subtractions before you have any real additions."   (Rick Warren, *Building a Purpose Driven Church* seminar Saddleback Church January 1998, quoted in "The Church Growth Movement: An Analysis of Rick Warren's "Purpose-Driven Church" *Foundation Magazine*, March-April 1998).

Billions of dollars pour into Rick Warren's Purpose-Driven Church movement and he has stated that he intends to send one billion Christians into the world to bring in the "Kingdom of Heaven," contrary to the teaching of Christ and the Apostles.

Another author and personality leader, Tim LaHaye, was instrumental in starting the false movement in reprogramming the Christian mind back in the mid-1960s, when he wrote, *Spirit-Controlled Temperament*. LaHaye used the ancient Greek theory for human temperament[17] and applied a variant of this theory as defined in modern psychology.

In the introduction to a new edition of the *Spirit-Controlled Temperament*, LaHaye's explains how he came to use an ancient concept for understanding human nature instead of the teachings of Christ and the Apostle's.

> "The theory of the four temperaments is not perfect; no theory on human behavior is. However, it is the oldest on record, going back more than three thousand years: In Proverbs 30:11-14 the wise man saw four kinds of people. About five hundred years later, the four were given names by Hippocrates, said to be the father of modern medicine. Galen, a Greek doctor, came up with a detailed list of the strengths and weaknesses of the four around A.D. 200. This has remained pretty much intact throughout history and is still the prevailing positions in Europe.
>
> Unfortunately, Sigmund Freud and his unscientific theories that based human behavior on environment and background rather than on inherited tendencies became the predominant view in America.
>
> Shortly after it was published in English, I read *Temperament and the Christian Faith* by the Norwegian theologian Ole Hallesby. This book about the four temperaments gave me new insight into why different people seemed beset by different sets of weaknesses. Hallesby suggested that we receive our natural tendencies for good and bad from our temperaments.
>
> *Spirit-Controlled Temperament* was the first book on the subject of temperament written in English for Christians. Since then I have written Transformed Temperaments, a biblical study of Peter the Sanguine, Paul the Choleric, Moses the Melancholy, and Abraham the Phlegmatic. My wife, Beverly, has written two books on the subject, *Spirit-Controlled Woman* and *How to Develop Your Child's Temperament*.

---

[17] Temperament: a prevailing or dominant quality of mind that characterizes somebody; excessive moodiness, irritability, or sensitivity; history in medieval physiology, the quality of mind resulting from various proportions of the four cardinal humors in somebody. Humor: (from Latin "liquid," or "fluid"), in early Western physiological theory, one of the four fluids of the body that were thought to determine a person's temperament and features. In the ancient physiological theory still current in the European Middle Ages and later, the four cardinal humors were blood, phlegm, choler (yellow bile), and melancholy (black bile); the variant mixtures of these humors in different persons determined their "complexions," or "temperaments," their physical and mental qualities, and their dispositions. The ideal person had the ideally proportioned mixture of the four; a predominance of one produced a person who was sanguine (Latin *sanguis*, "blood"), phlegmatic, choleric, or melancholic. Each complexion had specific characteristics, and the words carried much weight that they have since lost: *e.g.*, the choleric man was not only quick to anger but also yellow-faced, lean, hairy, proud, ambitious, revengeful, and shrewd. By extension, "humor" in the 16th century came to denote an unbalanced mental condition, a mood or unreasonable caprice, or a fixed folly or vice. (Encyclopedia Britannica Online, www.britanica.com).

Between us we have been privileged to popularize this ancient concept in the Christian community." (*Spirit-Controlled Temperament* Carol Stream, IL: Tyndale House 1994, pages 8-9)

LaHaye admittedly declares how he and his wife helped this ancient concept become popularized in the Christian community—unfortunately, this concept born in secularism, repudiates Christ's and the Apostles' teachings on Christ-like transformation by the work of the Holy Spirit. Many in the Christian community buy into these myths because these types of personality transforming methods are easy and fun.

This fabricated theory of human nature and its carnal patterns have become models in business management spilling over into church volunteer personality assessment. Such programs, (one in particular is the Keirsey Temperament Sorter) have become popular in individual, team, and organizational analysis. The Keirsey Sorter uses a variant of what LaHaye employed, pigeonholing people into four basic temperaments, but instead of using sanguine, choleric, melancholy, and phlegmatic as terms to categorize people (as LaHaye used), the Keirsey Temperament Sorter applies the following terms: *Guardings, Idealists, Rationals* and *Artisans*.

The following list defines what these terms mean in temperament categorization:

LaHaye's *Spirit-Controlled Temperament*:
- Sanguine: *pleasure-seeking and sociable*
- Choleric: *ambitious and leader-like*
- Melancholy: *introverted and thoughtful*
- Phlegmatic: *relaxed and quiet*

Keirsey Temperament Sorter:
- Guardians: *concrete and organized*
- Idealists: *abstract and compassionate*
- Rationals: *abstract and objective*
- Artisans: *concrete and adaptable*

In my training, study, and discipline, Christ changed my temperament, character, and attitudes from my former manner of life. These theories are just that, theories developed by people who do not know God's Word or principles in Christ-like character transformation. Notice the similarity of the above temperament categories as compared to the signs of the zodiac. The following is the example of Aries and the zodiac personality assessment:

Zodiac, Aries (March 21 - April 19):
- Life Pursuit: The thrill of the moment
- Vibration: Enthusiastic
- Secret Desire: To lead the way for others.

These assessments pigeonhole people in a similar way to reading a horoscope and are related to the practice of astrology and divination. However, this is my conclusion; you must learn to discern for yourself based on a solid relationship with Christ and a practical and complete working knowledge of Scripture.

To emphasize, Christian leaders are teaching Christians how to maximize their carnal nature to serve Christ, and bypass God's temperament changing process that transforms believer's nature—to become Christ-like. This may serve in well in a secular business environment; however, even in a managerial application it can easily stifle growth and temperament change through education, maturity, and promotion.

In a ministry application this approach truly hinders the Holy Spirit's work in calling, gifting, and transforming each individual saint to the work and gifting that God desires and appoints—for God has called Christ to live and be within us:

"For consider your calling, brothers: not many of you were wise according to worldly standards, not many were powerful, not many were of noble birth. But God chose what is foolish in the world to shame the wise; God chose what is weak in the world to shame the strong; God chose what is low and despised in the world, even things that are not, to bring to nothing things that are, so that no human being might boast in the presence of God. <u>He is the source of your life in Christ Jesus, whom God made our wisdom and our righteousness and sanctification and redemption</u>. Therefore, as it is written, 'Let the one who boasts, boast in the Lord'" (1 Corinthians 1:26-31).

It seems to me that this type of church personality sorting removes God and the transforming power of Christ from the mix and corrals Christians to stay in their carnal personalities and learn to maximize their fleshly strengths and minimize their fleshly weaknesses. In this, who gets the glory and what power is used in ministry?

Christians are duped more than ever. Unless the sincere disciple of Christ does not seek after true discernment and become skilled in the Word of Righteousness, he or she is at great risk.

Church Leadership as a Covering
Driving Christians instead of leading them by example

The doctrine of *covering* for Christians came to the forefront during the "Shepherding Movement" in the 1970s. It was instituted by well-meaning leaders within Christianity who saw how vulnerable most new converts were as they attempted to learn, grow, and mature as believers in Christ.

Many new believers fall away from the faith for lack of personal help and direction from more mature believers assisting in discipleship and mentoring. The problem had to be addressed and in so doing a movement to provide *individual shepherding* became popular; however, the teaching that was developed included unquestioning submission to the appointed shepherd.

A new believer was required to submit to a personal tutor or shepherd who often ruled as a mini-dictator. The movement became full of dictatorial shepherding where spiritual abuse became widespread.

Though this eventually was recognized as a tyrannical abuse of authority, the idea of a *church leadership covering* still permeates much of Christian thought, especially within the so-called anointed leadership movements and many other denominations' teachings.

Pastors and many heralded leaders use the covering doctrine—or, alternatively, the *don't touch God's anointed* teaching—to extend control and authority and to stifle any voice of dissent or correction, especially from the ordinary follower of Christ, whether within fellowships or within a special movement.

Having mature saints in the fold brings accountably; however, the insecure leader or one who is out for himself will tend to employ a *stifle-any-dissent* approach within fellowship.

Popular personality leaders and ministries that tout anointed leaders must keep their followers ignorant and passive. Otherwise, they will find themselves having to defend their error, spiritual abuse or exploitation. Unfortunately, many naïve and gullible Christians continue to support these false teachers as they passively follow along, feeling protected by the covering of their church or anointed leader.

Granted, many come to fellowship as troublemakers who stir up base suspicions and throw out theological speculations or wrangle about meaningless issues about words—all to challenge leadership's ability to deal biblically with such. This is another reason why weak, ignorant, or naïve leaders employ a heavy hand: to suppress potential fellowship squalls.

Few sincere leaders are trained to confront such in front of all with sound doctrine in an atmosphere that allows genuine questioning and comment to also come forth. Unfortunately, many pastors and leaders find themselves in over their heads, lacking administrative and management skills, confrontational skills, lacking training in mentoring and having little legal, practical understanding. All this amounts to weak leaders who are afraid of their own shadow.

This vacuum of leadership competency is a major reason why bold, brash, arrogant leaders rise to popularity and devise all manner of schemes that mislead and torment the saints throughout fellowships and congregations everywhere.

Again, I quote Peter in his warning about this wicked work of the devil through false shepherds and errant teachers, *"False prophets also arose among the people, just as there will be false teachers among you, who will <u>secretly bring in destructive heresies</u>, even denying the Master who bought them, bringing upon themselves swift destruction. And many will follow their sensuality, and because of them the way of truth will be blasphemed. And <u>in their greed they will exploit you with false words</u>"* (2 Peter 2:1-3). Millions are exploited today and have not a clue, as they happily sit in the pew playing church, not realizing that they are headed for terrible times.

The priests, Temple leaders and Pharisees did well in stifling dissent within the rank-and-file—they attacked Christ and the disciples for preaching, teaching, healing the sick and casting out demons without their approval and supervision.

Jesus and his disciples stood their ground and did not submit to their demands or waver under the pressure to submit to their authority.

Christ was not an anarchist teaching defiance towards all authority; however, by example our Lord demonstrated courage and proper personal authority to confront false authority.

False authority imposes control upon the lives of others by subverting true faith and obedience towards God.

When the Apostle Paul first came to Jerusalem after he had spent years in Arabia receiving revelation and understanding from Christ concerning the Gospel, he conferred with Peter and the other original disciples—those who were recognized as leaders in the new church.

The Apostle Paul in his letter to the Christians in Galatia explained how he had to stand against those walking in false authority attempting to impose error on other believers, while some of the original disciples kept silent. Paul described his attitude towards those who were reputed to be influential authorities in the church: *"From those who seemed to be influential (<u>what they were makes no difference to me; God shows no partiality</u>)—those, I say, who seemed influential added nothing to me"* (Galatians 2:6).

In context, Paul approached those in authority (the original disciples) to verify that he had not run in vain with the Gospel that Christ had revealed to him. Finding that they were in agreement, the original disciples realized that Paul had been entrusted to bring the Gospel to the Gentiles.

However, there were already Christian Jews attempting to force aspects of Judaism upon the new Gentile Christian converts, and Peter was reluctant to stop this heresy. Thus, when Paul saw Peter's actions he held Peter accountable: *"But when Cephas came to Antioch, I <u>opposed him to his face</u>, because he stood condemned. For before certain men came from James, he was eating with the Gentiles; but when they came he drew back and separated himself, fearing the circumcision party. And the rest of the Jews acted hypocritically along with him, so that even Barnabas was led astray by their hypocrisy. But when I saw that their conduct was not in step with the truth of the Gospel, I said to Cephas before them all, 'If you, though a Jew, live like a Gentile and not like a Jew, how can you force the Gentiles to live like Jews?'"* (Galatians 2:11-14).

Here we have an excellent example of true accountability within fellowship that demonstrates true submission to the lordship of Christ and the truth of the Gospel. The results of Paul confronting doctrinal error and opposing Peter's insincerity and fear convinced Peter and the rest of the original disciples that God had entrusted Paul to bring the Gospel to the Gentiles.

More importantly, Paul's courage to oppose Peter—an authority within the church along with the false brethren successfully stopped heresy from entering into the Gospel. As the Apostle Paul wrote, *"That the truth of the gospel might be preserved"* (Galatians 2:5).

To help those stuck in leadership idolatry, who are wrongly submitting to the error of the church covering doctrine, I cite the follow instructions from Christ:

"You know that those who are considered rulers of the Gentiles lord it over them, and their great ones exercise authority over them. But it shall not be so among you. But whoever would be great among you must be your servant, and whoever would be first among you must be slave of all. For even the Son of Man came not to be served but to serve, and to give his life as a ransom for many" (Mark 10:42-45).

Consider also this passage, *"The scribes and the Pharisees sit on Moses' seat, so practice and observe whatever they tell you—but not what they do. For they preach, but do not practice. They tie up heavy burdens, hard to bear, and lay them on people's shoulders, but they themselves are not willing to move them with their finger. They do all their deeds to be seen by others. For they make their phylacteries broad and their fringes long, and they love the place of honor at feasts and the best seats in the synagogues and greetings in the marketplaces and being called rabbi by others. But you are not to be called rabbi, for you have one teacher, and you are all brothers. And call no man your father on earth, for you have one Father, who is in heaven. Neither be called instructors, for you have one instructor, the Christ. The greatest among you shall be your servant. Whoever exalts himself will be humbled, and whoever humbles himself will be exalted"* (Matthew 23:2-12).

In 1 Peter the Apostle says that true leadership is demonstrated by being examples to the flock. *"I exhort the elders among you, as a fellow elder and a witness of the sufferings of Christ, as well as a partaker in the glory that is going to be revealed: shepherd the flock of God that is among you, exercising oversight, not under compulsion, but willingly, as God would have you; <u>not for shameful gain</u>, but eagerly; <u>not domineering over those in your charge</u>, but being examples to the flock. And when the chief Shepherd appears, you will receive the unfading crown of glory. Likewise, you who are younger, be subject to the elders. Clothe yourselves, all of you, with humility toward one another, for 'God opposes the proud but gives grace to the humble'"* (1 Peter 5:1-5).

It should be pointed out here that true leaders will listen to voices of dissent or correction and not put themselves above others, as we see the Apostle Peter stood humbly corrected by Paul.

On the other hand, true leadership will hold others accountable. True ministers of the Gospel lead by example and are courageous in opposing error and if necessary chase out those who persist in propagating error. A true and disciplined leader will deal with those who deliberately sin or who are habitual mischief-makers who resist correction. *"As for those who persist in sin, rebuke them in the presence of all, so that the rest may stand in fear"* (1 Timothy 5:20), *"As for a person who stirs up division, after warning him once and then twice, have nothing more to do with him, knowing that such a person is warped and sinful; he is self-condemned"* (Titus 3:10-11).

We are to respect true leadership and appreciate the difficulties associated with their position and their fearfully awesome accountability to God for their conduct and motives. For those who are fortunate to be part of a fellowship under true leadership, the following exhortation will also be helpful:

"Obey your leaders and submit to them, for they are keeping watch over your souls, as those who will have to give an account. Let them do this with joy and not with groaning, for that would be of no advantage to you." (Hebrews 13:17).

In dealing with a leader who strays, do not be afraid to point out error, and if such a leader is unwilling to be corrected, then move on and search for fellowship led by responsible leaders. There is responsibility in how to approach leadership when you believe there is false doctrine being taught.

1. Make sure you understand the error and know what the right teaching is. If it is disagreement over administrative preference or a petty inconsequential issue, then examine your own heart and see if you are a nit-picker who strains out a gnat and swallows a camel.

2. Do not gossip, undermine or gather others to build a consensus to help usurp and change the situation.
3. After prayer and confirmation from the Holy Spirit, approach key leadership or senior leadership with your concerns politely and respectfully.
4. Present your concern, asking for an explanation and allow for a thorough explanation. Then if you sense openness to receive you're expounding of what you believe to be the correct doctrine, present it. If not, then drop it and excuse yourself and don't bring it up again.
5. With this approach, you may help a leader see with the Holy Spirit bearing witness concerning your point. However, if there is a hardline taken and no room to consider your point, then let it go.
6. If the false teaching is significant and detrimental in the saint's growth and maturing to the fullness of Christ, then be prepared to leave.
7. Do not try to convince, change or undermine bad leadership. Rather, trust God to correct them, or if they are too far gone, trust God to bring them down in his timing.
8. It may be hard to find fellowship that is likeminded—finding a solid and safe fellowship is discussed in detail in chapter nine.

Small Group Indoctrination

Even in small group or cell work, true discipleship and mentoring is often replaced with indoctrinating teachings that support "working for God" by serving leadership's ideology and carnal church programs.

As previously mentioned, leading a host of popular group study programs is the, *The Purpose-Driven Life* and *The Purpose-Driven Church* literature by Rick Warren. This and similar programs are designed to make it easy for pastors to indoctrinate believers into conformity with the consensus theology and church growth ideology. These teaching systems blend destructive heresies with the elemental teachings of Christ to deceive the naïve or new convert to acquiesce or passively agree to living and working for the church and leadership's agenda.

This approach to discipleship subverts analytical study of Scripture and personal revelation from the Holy Spirit in applying the Word of God personally in life's experiences. This cloning process attempts to maintain conformity and passivity of mind—to eliminate genuine concern and dissent among group participants.

We have heard first-hand from participants how forceful, controlling and even scolding group leaders become in squashing any sincere questions. Any questioning regarding the "follow blindly" and "church growth" ideology that minimizes true Christ-like character transformation is virtually eliminated. Learning how to hear and obey the true voice of Christ within these curriculums is taboo.

These programs subtly contradict the Apostle Paul's directive on the personal growth and leadership objectives found in the book of Ephesians. *"To equip the saints for the work of ministry, for building up the body of Christ, until we all attain to the unity of the faith and of the knowledge of the Son of God, to mature manhood, to the measure of the stature of the fullness of Christ, so that we may no longer be children, tossed to and fro by the waves and carried about by every wind of doctrine, by human cunning, by craftiness in deceitful schemes"* (Ephesians 4:12-14).

Deceitful workers have learned to use Scripture out of context and distort God's intent, making the Word of God a commodity to be packaged, sold, and traded. The Gospel and the Holy Scriptures are now packaged and peddled like the infamous door-to-door encyclopedia salesperson.

Small groups are effective if there is a clear objective and a serious agenda aimed at building up each participant into a fuller relationship with Christ. A triage approach should be considered in determining what kind of small groups should be developed and provided. There are many specific ministries needed for the many types of troubled and wounded Christians that may come to fellowship. Small groups that support, mentor and train often need to be focused specifically on Christians who may be suffering and struggling to recover from certain things, such as divorce or an abusive childhood, while others may be called to evangelism or counseling and a small group class fits best. See chapter seven, the section entitled, "Five-fold Servant-leaders and the Saint's Work of Ministry."

Ushering in the Millennial Reign of the Church
Movements that usurp Christ's prophesy on eschatology.

Another movement that has its foundation built on false teachings is the New Apostolic Reformation (NAR) with such noted leaders as Chuck Pierce, C. Peter Wagner, and Cindy Jacobs. This movement includes prosperity teachings with the added heresy of dominionism—the belief that the influence of modern-day apostles and prophets will lead Christianity to institute righteousness on earth in all areas of life, through prayer and prophetically instilling godly leaders into politics, the legal system and all others important institutions in America and worldwide. The mission of the NAR is to usher in the millennial reign of Christ through Christianity—with NAR apostles and prophets steering Christianity and the world in the right direction.

The NAR movement takes the Apostle Paul's teaching about Christ providing leadership as gifts to the church to a new deceitful level. The NAR movement deliberately overlooks all the harder teachings of Christ, ignoring that the Kingdom of God will come upon the earth at the end of the Great Tribulation and after the wrath of God falls upon a rebellious world.

God never commissioned these self-appointed super-apostles and they undermine the true apostle, prophet, evangelist, pastor or teacher who has been called and trained by the hand of Christ for leadership.

These last-day's distracters and irresponsible Christian leaders misinterpret Scripture and recklessly deceive many. They twist the word of Righteousness to accommodate myths, manmade Christian ideology and hypothetical views on how the end of the age will come about. They cater to Christians who want the easy way in life; not at all taking into account what Jesus plainly taught concerning the end-of-this-age troubles and the difficulty of truly following Christ. The Apostle Paul instructed Timothy, *"Do your best to present yourself to God as one approved, a workman who has no need to be ashamed, rightly handling the word of truth"* (2 Timothy 2:15).

Pastors and teachers who refuse to carry out underhanded schemes and refuse to tamper with the word of truth, who preach and teach sound doctrine and all that Christ taught, find it hard to carry out the great commission because the truth of the Gospel is not easy to hear.

Currently, most Christians prefer to embrace a "wide-gate, easy-path Gospel," and will listen to anyone who can tickle their ears with false promises. Many will never arrive at the truth because they refuse to work out their own salvation, carry their end of the cross (working with Christ who carries the other end) and die to the works of the flesh.

What should a Christian do to avoid these dangers? Get your theology right—learn to understand the Word of God within context, taking into account the cultural issues of the time when the New Testament was written.

See that your doctrine agrees with what Christ taught. Christ's teachings are practical and deal with living in a corrupt world in his strength, in his love, and in God's grace and power—in true holiness. Base your theology on *all* that Jesus taught—not just the easy teachings but also the harder words of Christ.

Churchianity is Too Far Gone for Reform
Preparing for Christ's coming is about coming away from the false!

Many see churchianity within their fellowship and try to correct this last day apostasy. In most cases, attempting to reform the latent apostasy will be useless, costly, and even dangerous.

Make no mistake, the social dynamics of false fellowship and the spiritual power of wrongful prayers by false brethren and carnal Christians, when turned against a reformer, can be very destructive—even murderous. We have seen people who have stood up to a churchianity-plagued fellowship and witnessed their life end prematurely due to a heart attack, a strange accident, or the onslaught of a malignant illness.

As we garnered insights in our battles in helping others break free from false fellowships, often we would come in to the crosshairs of the carnal prayers from those opposing us in this part of our work. The list of incidents and maladies, such as near-fatal accidents, an onslaught of asthma-like attacks (see Charismatic church witches page 216), or overwhelming exhaustion were clearly related to the hellish spiritual power coming from these false or at best carnal believers.

Christian witchcraft prayer is defined as praying for one's own will and selfishness with malice in the heart—not seeking and praying for God's will to be done with pure motives. This becomes Satan's best practice to further his agenda, using a false or carnal Christian's own lawless-reckless spirit through praying wrongly.

Ministry Case: *Let my people go!*

Sally was heavily involved in church. For a while she was "gung-ho" to serve—volunteering as a Sunday school teacher, traveling on missions trips, and participating in cell groups. In her earnest endeavor to know the true Christ along with sincere Scripture study, she began to get warning twinges in her spirit about the popular doctrines and the character of leadership in her beloved charismatic/evangelical fellowship.

Then a mission's leader attending the fellowship took an interest in her and soon Sally found herself in awkward situations, where this leader (an older woman) began to be aggressive with sexual innuendos and bossy behavior, pushing Sally into more and more one-on-one encounters. The sexual comments from this leader became disturbing, causing Sally to back away from the relationship.

Finally, this leader's persistence to expand her relationship with Sally became a red flag. Sally took courage to talk to the fellowship's counselor and eventually lodged a complaint with the pastor. The pastor assured Sally that he would confront this leader for this kind of unbecoming behavior, and a few weeks later the woman approached Sally and apologized profusely but still pushed their relationship to continue.

Sally observed this women continue to make inappropriate comments and subtle sexual innuendos with other younger women in the fellowship. One was a comment on Facebook to a younger woman that said, "Hey sexy, let's get coffee."

Now Sally realized that most likely this woman was a sexual predator, looking for a vulnerable younger woman to groom into a clandestine lesbian relationship. Sally tried all the harder to stay clear of this woman, then once more Sally ran into her and this leader profusely apologized again, trying to make Sally feel guilty, even though she had forgiven her. Sally felt pressure from this woman to get back to a normal friendship.

The pastor had promised to follow-up, however, that never came about. It was about this time that Sally received one of our ministry tract-books entitled "Effective Spiritual Warfare" and after reading this book, the notion of changing fellowship become strong for Sally. She contacted me and after a couple of counseling visits, she was led by the Lord to attend our fellowship—she said she felt much safer and believed the Gospel we preached was not compromised.

Our counsel for her was to give ample notice to the fellowship she was leaving, so they could reassign her different duties and then she could quietly leave. The objective was to minimize any uproar, telling her friends minimum information, yet informing them that she was moving on and was safe.

Unfortunately, the pastor's wife and some of Sally's friends from the fellowship were not about to have a sheep in their care wander off. Their pursuit to find out why she was leaving became obsessive and over-the-top with subtle threats and accusing our ministry being a cult.

Fellowship acquaintances would approach Sally and corner her physically, or question her at her work at length or approach her while shopping. Finally, she warned several that if they continued to be intrusive, then she would be forced to obtain an anti-harassment order to restrain their obsessive efforts to control her life.

Then symptoms of headaches, overwhelming oppression, and even feelings of hopelessness would sweep over her, causing her to seek prayer support. Her fight to escape this fellowship's spiritual abuse and control turned into a major project of prayer and spiritual warfare for her and our fellowship.

Excessive emails, phone calls, and texting became another avenue of harassment. She finally wrote a letter to the pastor informing him that if this orchestrated campaign to drag her back into fellowship did not cease, she would take appropriate steps to stop it. She made it clear in the letter that she would be forced to tell everyone why she had to leave; she would be forced to inform them of how leadership looked the other way, knowing a leader with sexual defiling issues roamed freely in their fellowship. Ω

These people, like the Pharisees in Christ's day, employed character assassination tactics, implanted base suspicions, and sent out a barrage of carnal prayers (a form of sorcery) that carried murderous power. If it were not for our training and the gifts of the Holy Spirit, I believe illness, an accident or some serious mishap would have overtaken me or others in our ministry whom these people knew were helping Sally break free of their clutches.

The Temple leadership resisted Christ and his truth to the point of carrying out Christ's murder. Jesus did not come to reform Temple worship—it had gone beyond the point of no return and the destruction of the Temple by Rome reinforces the accuracy of our Lord's prophecies and the serious consequences of going beyond reform into apostasy.

Man's worship of religion and idolatry of leadership has plagued the body of Christ for centuries and now as the end of this age nears, Christian apostasy will reach the zenith of deception—no different from that of Israel in Christ's day.

Christ is not coming back a second time to reform the church, rather he will call the true body of Christ, his church, to come out and away from *churchianity*—another religious system gone bad.

We must embrace Christ's prophetic warnings for the last-days Christian; several are found in the Gospel of Matthew in chapter twenty-five that will help you with your studies. It is time to wake up, discern the darkness of the hour, and become prepared to respond to the midnight cry.

"But at midnight there was a cry, 'Behold, the bridegroom! <u>Come out to meet him</u>.' Then all those maidens rose and trimmed their lamps. And the foolish said to the wise, 'Give us some of your oil, for our lamps are going out.' But the wise replied, 'Perhaps there will not be enough for us and for you; go rather to the dealers and buy for yourselves.' And while they went to buy, the bridegroom came, and those who were ready went in with him to the marriage feast; and the door was shut. Afterward the other maidens came also, saying, 'Lord, lord, open to us.' But he replied, 'Truly, I say to you, I do not know you.' Watch therefore, for you know neither the day nor the hour" (Matthew 25:1-13 RSV).

Those stuck in churchianity are in the same condition as the foolish maidens in this prophetic parable. Many will fall away as persecution increases, and even more will do so when the anti-Christ comes as a world ruler during the Great Tribulation.

To emphasize again, Jesus was very clear on when the true Christian will be raptured to safety: *"But in those days, <u>after that tribulation</u>, ... then he will send out the angels, and <u>gather his elect from the four winds, from the ends of the earth to the ends of heaven</u>. From the fig tree learn its lesson: as soon as its branch becomes tender and puts forth its leaves, you know that summer is near. So also, when you see these things taking place, <u>you know that he is near, at the very gates</u>"* (Mark 13:24-29).

Time is running out and it is time to take heed and discern the hour; it is time to learn how to increase our powers of discernment for soon *"false christs and false prophets will arise and show signs and wonders, to lead astray, if possible, the elect. But take heed; I have told you all things beforehand"* (Mark 13:22-23).

The False Will Lead Many Astray
Do not let churchianity cause you to miss the final visitation.

False doctrines, false Temple leaders, a worship system turned to worshiping itself, and the love of this world caused Israel to miss the first advent of Christ. Now, just as then, most of God's people are in the same condition. It was a remnant within Israel that responded to Christ's first appearance and was used of God to start a new covenant church. Today, it is a remnant of sincere saints and obscure leaders who recognize the warning signs concerning America and churchianity.

Most churches, especially the high growth mega-churches have become a physical place to meet with each other socially. Meetings turn into a crowd-induced spiritual frenzy that feeds upon itself. This type of religious crowd spiritualism spawns a carnal dynamic relationship network—a carnal network that undermines sincere fellowship, derailing mentoring and genuine fellowship. Relationship interaction stays shallow with little to no accountability in regard to personal growth, burden bearing and mentoring. For most, Christian fellowship has become a physical place to get a buzz once or twice a week that perpetuates the false impression of growth in Christ.

Like the Pharisees' Temple worship system, mentioned previously, fellowship in this form has become a powerful blinding tool used by Satan to keep the majority of God's people alienated from the life God and asleep to the coming hour of visitation. Most Christians stuck in churchianity stay weak and dependent.

Jesus saw how the crowds were accosted, as individuals caught up in the crowd morass were constantly disheveled—*"harassed and helpless, like sheep without a shepherd"* (Matthew 9:36). Christ's remedy for the crowd chaos was to beseech God to send out laborers to work with those seeking God and help each on an individual basis—as he gave the example limiting his personal work to the group of twelve.

Now in these massive mega-church meetings, the spell of churchianity has made worshiping Christ, the Holy Spirit, and Father God into a perverted system where the act of worship itself becomes an idol and wolves roam freely undetected by leadership. The crowd dynamic easily turns into a gang mentality when challenged. (Most proponents of churchianity actually attack true Christians who see through the hype and preach the uncompromised Gospel of Christ.)

As stated previously, the physical and social church experience (fellowship networking) has developed into relationship addiction and leadership idolatry infected with carnal spiritualism and hypocrisy. Among other things, this fosters *clique dynamics* that inherently form within the mega-church culture, where a loosely formed sub-culture within the fellowship grows and gains a powerful controlling influence.

Carnal Christians and wolves in sheep's clothing, often having selfish ambitions to lead, learn how to gain powerful influence within these fellowship cliques. Clique leaders tend to undermine leadership by imposing an informal authority upon others and healthy body life becomes severely hampered.

In churchianity, gossip, meddling, backbiting, and under handed manipulation take the place of healthy discipleship and mentoring. Preferential attention is given to those who appear to have it together and a subtle indifference is aired towards those who appear to be messed up and in need of serious support.

The truly hurting are often avoided and even subtly shunned. Few dare to open up, those who desire healing and support get little attention by those (saints) who are supposed to be doing the work of ministry. Rather, they are ignored or pushed upon the pastor or other overworked staff.

Clique or gang dynamics can lead to informal prayer groups formed to oust those deemed out of step with the consensus theology or those who have begun to see the hypocrisy and confront the lies.

Rather than fighting this trend, mega-church fellowships—and even smaller congregations—give themselves over to churchianity. Churchianity uses social aspects of church fellowship to draw people in and is inherently chaotic, causing leadership to come up with crowd management techniques instead of training and disciplining Christian workers for the ministry.

Holidays such as Christmas and Easter become a powerful selling point for churchianity drawing new seekers or frustrated Christian into attendance replacing those leaving in disappointment or frustration. It all becomes a giant circus using carnal crowd management techniques.

Newcomers and God-seekers are now attracted by marketing slogans, not drawn by the Holy Spirit using solid Christian workers who know Christ intimately. Few receive help in the area of personal discipline that leads to maturity in Christ and support in obtaining the grace God. Church attendance, financial support, and volunteering become the standard to measure character and holiness.

Churchianity is a deception driven by a demonic power or principality of darkness. It causes leadership to become enthralled with church growth rather than growth in Christ-like character within those called by God. The outreach message of most churches accommodates and entices the curious seeker of God and gives the impression that following Christ will make life on earth easy.

"Come one, come all" is the message evangelists and pastors use to draw crowds; they are like carnival barkers, promising the blessings of God without warning of the cost of following Christ. Churchianity falsely promises freedom and a lifestyle that will magically meet every need.

The ranks of most fellowships, especially mega-church fellowships, contain pseudo-believers who never experienced the call of God unto salvation; most never experienced a true rebirth generated by the Holy Spirit, but they are told they have Christ within them. Most know of Christ and the elementary teachings of the Gospel, few are known by Christ and obey his voice.

Most are called by the will of man through manmade church growth marketing schemes with billboards, commercials, mailers, and cute bumper-sticker slogans like "Try Jesus." This causes an attachment to the ministry or church and not an attachment to the true Christ.

The pastor, amenities of the church building, and social dynamics of fellowship are touted, making churchianity compete with other churches. Churchianity concentrates on building up an organization and its facilities, not building the saints upon the foundation of Christ. Churchianity has reverted back to Temple worship and not building God's people into the Temple of the Holy Spirit

In churchianity, Christ and his discipline are seldom given proper place in worship and fellowship. There is no room for the work of the cross—allowing Christ to crucify the carnal desires and the works of the flesh—to be taught. Church events take the place of the lordship of Christ and true intimacy with the Holy Spirit. Churchianity easily becomes a delivery system for demonic spirits to present counterfeit spiritual experiences. Many become enthralled with these experiences and become addicted to fellowship, idolizing both.

The sincere Christian must be able to discern churchianity and flee its influences. If not, one will run the risk of missing the soon-to-come final move of God when the Holy Spirit, through true messengers of Christ, will impart a sense of urgency to wake up and come away from everything that is false.

Enlisting the "Gung-Ho" Faith of the Naïve
Churchianity—building upon another's work using wood, hay, straw

Like a giant vacuum, overly eager ministries enlist young, openhearted, naïve Christians to serve Christ in special manmade campaigns to convert the world, starting with the unsaved neighbor down the street. The naïve, carnal believers (new and old alike) unknowingly are having their immature faith hijacked from allowing Christ to be the foundation and perfecter of their faith. These ministries, in competition with each other, undermine proper maturing in Christ by building upon a true conversion with false doctrine and ministry gimmicks geared to make the new convert dependent upon leadership.

The Apostle Paul experienced firsthand how immature believers were captivated into following super-hero leaders. He warned the Christians at Corinth that they were of the flesh, since they were pursuing favorite teachers. *"For you are still of the flesh. For while there is jealousy and strife among you, are you not of the flesh, and behaving like ordinary men? For when one says, 'I belong to Paul,' and another, 'I belong to Apollos,' are you not merely men?"* (1 Corinthians 3:3-4 RSV).

Churchianity and its wayward leaders build upon the true work of the Holy Spirit through deceived Christian workers with *their* success in mind and not building up the new convert into Christ. Paul further explains, *"For no other foundation can anyone lay than that which is laid, which is Jesus Christ. Now if any one builds on the foundation with gold, silver, precious stones, wood, hay, straw—each man's work will become manifest; for the Day will disclose it, because it will be revealed with fire, and the fire will test what sort of work each one has done"* (1 Corinthians 3:11-13 RSV).

Unfortunately, churchianity does not build people into the body of Christ, with maturity in Christ as the objective. Rather, the initial foundation in Christ receives shabby construction from materials such as wood, hay and straw—false doctrine and short cut methods to expedite new workers into the work of churchianity. The idea of working together to build up the true body of Christ is unpopular; few leaders in churchianity take to heart the Apostles Paul's directive: *"For we are God's fellow workers; you are God's field, God's building."* (1 Corinthians 3:9 RSV).

The individual Christian becomes a cog in the ministry machinery where their young and impressionable minds and hearts are transformed into a "Gung-Ho" faith—faith in the group, the leaders, the agenda, and success measured by the number of conversions.

Part of the hijacking process is developing an indoctrinating system that takes what Christ taught about true faith and transfers faith in Christ to faith in the organization and its mission. Young converts are convinced they can move mountains, uproot trees, and do all things through Christ provided they wholeheartedly enlist in the church or organization's mission.

The term "gung-ho" means, "work together; work in harmony" and was taken from the name of a Chinese organization in the 1930s by Major Evans Carlson, USMC during WWII. Major Carlson saw a need to inspire his 2nd Marine Raider Battalion by instilling a special bond between these Marines who were being assembled as an elite force to perform amphibious landings in enemy held territory. As a former Marine, I can tell you that the term *gung ho* had become one of the Marine Corps' mottos that helped developed *esprit de corps* (a high level of morale) during basic training; however it took on a very different connotation held by seasoned veterans, higher ranking field officers, and senior staff non-commissioned officers.

That different meaning was disparaging and applied to young officers just out of Quantico or Annapolis who were over eager to prove themselves. An over eager 2nd or 1st lieutenant, especially in combat usually meant unnecessary casualties or a tactical blunder when that "gung ho" officer was left to his own devices.

The newly commissioned officers who had some common sense relied heavily on the seasoned veterans, especially the battalion's first sergeant or sergeant major, without portraying themselves as an inept officer. There was informal mentoring carried out by the higher-ranking enlisted veterans to ensure the newly commissioned officer, in his first command, became battle savvy in patience and wise leadership and seasoned warfare strategy.

However, in Vietnam there were occasional situations where a young, inept officer tried to make a name for himself and became gung-ho, often making risky, overzealous decisions. He would ignore sound advice from the seasoned vets that often caused unnecessary casualties.

If this kind of situation became acute, often and without a trace of evidence, that arrogant, gung ho newly commissioned officer met an untimely accident or even death from a stray fragmentation grenade ("frag") during incoming fire from the enemy (usually at night). The term "fragged" became an idiom in the Corps referring to irresponsible leaders who became casualties of friendly fire or "stray" explosions when under attack. I share this anecdote to illustrate how dangerous it is for these inept leaders in ministry to foolishly enlist carnal and naïve Christians to take on projects and engage in spiritual warfare out of God's timing or will, causing many casualties among so many immature believers.

When God raised up his army through his servant Gideon, God did the screening and commissioning of those who were ready to obey and approach the enemy's camp in quiet and stealth, not "gung ho," in an undisciplined manner, prone to clamor, complain, or be fearful or fumble prone.

Gideon raised an all-volunteer army for God, which numbered around 32,000 and prepared them to march against the Midianite army numbering around 135,000. On the route to the battlefield God commanded Gideon to dismiss those who were fearful and afraid, leaving behind about 10,000. Gideon's army now was outnumbered 13 to 1. Then God told Gideon, "There are still too many," and instructed Gideon to take the remaining 10,000 down to the water where they were to be tested. The test was simple, those who used their hands to lap up water while keeping alert, watching out for the enemy, were selected to continue in God's army, and those who got down on their hands and knees to lap water like a dog, sticking their face in the water and not staying alert were dismissed.

This left 300 to take on 135,000. The strategy that God gave Gideon, which would put to route 135,000 Midianites, did not require a sword drawn or arrow released. The weapons employed by each of the 300 were a trumpet, a pitcher, and a torch. (See Judges 7:1-25.)

Just as God commanded Gideon to go to war with only the committed and disciplined, even if they were few, the church would fare much better if we committed ourselves to minister only through mature and disciplined Christians. Those who prove themselves capable of relying on the power of God and the Holy Spirit's leading, and not rely on the power and wisdom of the flesh.

These wayward church growth plans enlisting gung-ho carnal and naïve workers will work for a season; however, the conversions produced are mostly born of the will of man in the power of the flesh, leaving very few born of the Spirit of God. When trouble and persecution come, and it soon will, these false converts will fall away. *"But to all who did receive him, who believed in his name, he gave the right to become children of God, who were born, not of blood nor of the will of the flesh nor of the will of man, but of God"* (John 1:12-13).

What is more troubling is the eventual burnout and instability that many of the gung-ho workers will eventually fall into, leaving a trail of confused and beleaguered Christians who backslide into secret sin, become hypocritical, or just become cynical and walk away from fellowship and turn their backs on God.

Denominationalism
Sectarian pride, elitism and disguised competition

We should all be thanking God for our freedom to worship according to what we believe, hopefully according to sound doctrine. With this freedom also comes the cult system of worship, subtle doctrinal error in denominations, carnal and new age practices in church liturgy, blatant error in statements of faith, and even apostate denominations practicing abominable worship. The ecumenical movement to align Protestant and Catholic is another gross error. Thus, the true seeker of God must be cautious!

However, many mainline Christian denominations agree on the basic tenets of the Gospel of Christ, but far too many carry sectarian pride and elitism. This "denominationalism" hampers the true body of Christ unity. Over the years, national evangelists such as Billy Graham helped break down the walls of pride and competition between mainline Protestant denominations to include non-denominational and independent fellowships.

Nevertheless, a true body of Christ unification is on the near horizon as God's people return to embrace all that Christ taught. In the coming trouble, during the increase in the birth pangs, more and more fellowships, congregations, and whole denominations will relinquish doctrinal error and give up carnal worship preferences. Many will wake up and begin to step away from denominationalism elitism, sectarian pride, and carnal religious methods.

Every true disciple of Christ must recognize that the church age is about to roar to its end. Staying loyal to a denomination or fellowship that keeps its stubborn ways and ignores the truth about the end-of-the-age coming of Christ will be foolish.

The coming midnight cry to all of Christendom, *"Here is the bridegroom! Come out to meet him"* (Matthew 25:6) will shock many awake. Not only must we give up the love of this world and the cares of this life, we must also walk away from the tethers of unbelief and wrongly placed loyalty that churchianity spawns within denominationalism.

The awake and discerning believer must relinquish bondage ties to fundamentalism, Mennonite-ism, Foursquare-ism, Vineyard-ism, Free Methodist-ism, and so on; and yes, Catholicism. Each true disciple of Christ must be willing to come out if necessary, if their fellowship or denomination still clings to carnal, religious, and worldly churchianity.

Continue to watch and pray for God's people from various denominations and sects, even non-denominational fellowships, to respond formally to the truth about Christ's coming and the trouble preceding his appearance and the rapture. Many will begin to work with each other, setting aside wrong interpretations of Scripture, and help prepare to endure to the end. The Holy Spirit has been hindered in drawing the sincere saint away from false and carnal doctrines; however, many of the barriers to body of Christ unity will begin to be removed as the birth pangs, persecution and the Great Tribulation brings pressure and discipline forcing the body of Christ to grow up quickly.

Denominations, fellowships and ministries who wake up will realize that it is more important to work in harmony to build up the body of Christ, than to each carv their own little sectarian niche. Many will work together fulfilling God's will for the end time church. That body of Christ attains *"the unity of the faith and of the knowledge of the Son of God, to mature manhood, to the measure of the stature of the fullness of Christ… Rather, <u>speaking the truth in love,</u> we are to grow up in every way into him who is the head, into Christ, from whom the whole body, joined and held together by every joint with which it is equipped, <u>when each part is working properly, makes</u>*

the body grow so that it builds itself up in love" (Ephesians 4:13-16). More on this in chapter nine, the section entitled "Birth Pangs, Persecution and the Great Tribulation."

Surrogate Bonding to the False Leader's Counterfeit Faith
Personality emulation/creation mistaken for Christ-like character development

Following a leader instead of Christ is dangerous and minimizes Christ's ability to transform the believer into character that is in the likeness of Christ, for he is the only one that can facilitate this all important transformation. Again, simply put by the Apostle Paul: *"And we all, with unveiled face, beholding the glory of the Lord, are being transformed into the same image from one degree of glory to another. For this comes from the Lord who is the Spirit"* (2 Corinthians 3:18).

Personality emulation of a personality leader is a diabolical side effect of following a leader versus following Christ. It slowly redirects faith in Christ to faith in self and a form of self-hypnotism, like going to hypnotist to stop smoking. Because self-programming is inadequate and at best only creates superficial character change to cover up the old nature and old carnal character structures, there develops an unhealthy dependency on the particular author or method embraced. In short, faith is directed towards the teaching and the teacher, not upon the living person of Jesus Christ, who is a life-giving Spirit, empowered to transform us at the very core (with our understanding and cooperation).

These teachings and teachers become surrogate mini-Christs to the follower. Faith in the counterfeit faith of the leader increases while faith in Christ slowly ebbs away, diverted to an unhealthy bond to another human being. The deceived Christian in reality learns to emulate the characteristics and personality traits of the teacher through the false teaching. Those deceived however, believe they are becoming Christ-like.

What is much more insidious is how counterfeiting angel of light principalities, using subordinate demons, are able to impart spiritual manifestations, producing temporal peace, contentment, and happiness.

Sometimes the demons reward the deceived with moments where the demonic affects the personal spirit, then in turn travels to the nervous system to affect nerve cell euphoria, producing high levels of serotonin, noradrenalin, and dopamine hormones.

Following false teachers that exclude the character-changing principles that Christ facilitates leads to great risk and merits review of Christ's warnings, this one in particular:

"Everyone then who hears these words of mine and does them will be like a wise man who built his house on the rock. And the rain fell, and the floods came, and the winds blew and beat on that house, but it did not fall, because it had been founded on the rock. And everyone who hears these words of mine and does not do them will be like a foolish man who built his house on the sand. And the rain fell, and the floods came, and the winds blew and beat against that house, and it fell, and great was the fall of it" (Matthew 7:24-27).

Many Christians will be able to with stand the coming storms from the increased birth pangs, lawless persecution towards Christians and the Great Tribulation because each took heed and applied all the commands and teachings of Christ.

However, multitudes of lukewarm and nominal Christians who embraced a shallow, watered-down Gospel presented by the many churchianity teachers and teachings will simply be washed away and become locked out of the coming marriage between Christ and the true Church.

Chapter Six

Discerning the Spiritual Powers of the Flesh
Satanic harnessing of this bewitched last-days generation

Satan has come to the last-days church convincing many that they must prove that they are children of God — by demonstrating great power, not only to the world but to each other, in the form of miracles, signs, and wonders.

Just as Satan tempted Christ, the devil challenges Christians to speak forth their heart's desires in Christ's name — regardless of God's will in the matter:

"Then Jesus was led up by the Spirit into the wilderness to be tempted by the devil. And after fasting forty days and forty nights, he was hungry. And the tempter came and said to him, 'If you are the Son of God, command these stones to become loaves of bread.' But he answered, 'It is written, Man shall not live by bread alone, but by every word that comes from the mouth of God.'" (Matthew 4:1-4).

Jesus did not fall for this deception, for he only did what he saw the Father doing and did only according to God's will, in the power of God. Jesus lived upon every word that proceeded from the mouth of God and taught his disciples to do the same.

The great commission is not to convert the world to Christianity, but to make disciples called by the Spirit of God, who learn to obey all that Christ taught. Few observe and embrace all of Christ's teachings, leaving many unknowledgeable of who the true Christ is and how to know if he truly abides within their hearts and spirit.

Far too many Christians learn to follow Christ, staying weak, confused, and insecure, and become all too willing to follow any teaching that promises spiritual power instantly. Those who do not receive sound doctrine and mentoring from another true disciple of Christ tend to fall for the false power promoters.

The last few generations of new Christians are predisposed to receive false power due to incessant indoctrination towards magic and miraculous signs and wonders; first by way of our culture with the constant barrage of witchcraft and fantasy, then by the many false teachers who walk in counterfeit spiritual power after they become Christians.

Many are taught to believe they can buy the power of God (in the form of offerings) willfully and receive it instantly without enduring Christ's discipline and preparations (as he did with the Apostles). Today, the motives for most Christians seeking spiritual power are to prove their self-worth, obtain recognition, and selfishly make life easy on earth.

Many learn to substitute life in the Holy Spirit and the power of the Holy Spirit with the spiritual powers of the flesh, which in the end produces nothing lasting or eternal.

Satan has come in powerful and deceitful ways that facilitate spiritual activities aimed at generating enthusiastic energy in serving God and in a counterfeit spiritual power.

There is an innate latent spiritual power in every human spirit, apart from the spiritual power of God by his Spirit, and apart from the supernatural power of Satan and the demonic. The difference between the human spirit and the Spirit of God should be obvious, for our personal spirit is breathed into man or woman at conception—from God himself. Further, we are made to be in his image, yet having our spiritual powers dormant and very limited until the rebirth experience by the Holy Spirit.

However, the dormant or latent spiritual power that lies within humanity is a highly prized target of Satan and his minions. The devil's end-of-the-age plan is to awaken the human spirit apart from God's plan found within the Gospel of Christ.

Satan's insidious work in awakening the human spirit on his terms will give the devil more evil power in opposing God's will, more agents with spiritual power to destroy faith in Christ, and make his end-of-the-age war against the saints more effective.

The harnessing of the human spirit is a significant part of the devil's work, which is now unfolding and will be arrayed against God's people on many fronts. It will become manifest within fellowships through carnal Christians deceived by false doctrine and practicing counterfeit gifts. Satan will use evil people in society such as new age practitioners, and cult and occult participants who hate God and hate Christians. Moreover, Christians will be attacked by any means, where the demonic can enlist and power boost the human spirit to oppose God's will and the work of the pure and true body of Christ.

Lust for Spiritual Power
Many believers still carry defilements from their former manner of life

Suppressed white-hot rage, a resentful heart, bitter jealousy and envy, selfish ambition and a contentious, revengeful spirit are popular satanic strongholds within the lives of far too many believers. Of course, Christians who suffer these issues do not go around displaying them, they learn to automatically suppress any revengeful or jealous reaction to life's disappointments or when others step on their toes.

James warned, "Who is wise and understanding among you? By his good conduct let him show his works in the meekness of wisdom. *But if you have bitter jealousy and selfish ambition in your hearts*, do not boast and be false to the truth. This is not the wisdom that comes down from above, but *is earthly, unspiritual, demonic. For where jealousy and selfish ambition exist, there will be disorder and every vile practice.* But the wisdom from above is first pure, then peaceable, gentle, open to reason, full of mercy and good fruits, impartial and sincere. And a harvest of righteousness is sown in peace by those who make peace" (James 3:13-18).

Few learn to deal with the past defilements that still reside within their heart and spirit. One of the major temptations offered by our culture to non-believers prior to a conversion is the acquisition of spiritual power to get one's own way. Hidden defilements and associated nasty motives of heart compound the carnal propensity to tap into spiritual power apart from God's plan found in the Gospel of Christ.

Sorcery, witchcraft, divination, necromancy, meditation, devil worship, vampirism, astral projection, and all manner of spiritual power delivery methods are now available and popularized in our magic-soaked culture. Movies, books, and television provide a steady stream of biblically forbidden practices, as our culture becomes all the more saturated with graphic images and instruction on how to practice these abominable activities, especially the practice of sorcery.

For years the introduction of seemingly mild and innocent forms of witchcraft, sorcery, divination, and necromancy have gradually seeped into the hearts and minds of children and adults, from generation to generation. Gradualism has now opened the flood-gates for our culture to roll in extreme wickedness with specific how-to instruction — like a dog rolling in rotting carrion.

With all this in mind, we can understand why false teachings and counterfeit spiritualism are in high demand by so many defiled Christians. Much of Christianity is obsessed with obtaining the power of God — allowing Satan's angel of light ministries (counterfeiting fallen angels) to grow exponentially in their diabolical work — all driven by the lust for spiritual power.

Deceived and misled believers run towards the false light ministries that promise the power of God — delivering counterfeit satanic power that loads up and activates the latent supernatural power of the human spirit. Multitudes of carnal Christians have received supernatural power flowing willy-nilly by the counterfeiting work of demons through their personal spirit. Now, almost universally throughout Christianity, that power is frequently turned loose on others, based (not on God's will) but according to their inner defilements and sick motives of heart.

Understanding the Latent Supernatural Power of the Human Spirit

You may have a nagging question by now concerning the supernatural power of the human spirit — is it real? Moreover, does Scripture give instructions on detecting and dealing with people who consciously or unconsciously activate the supernatural power of their own personal spirit? As you read on you will understand how the human spirit can affect others — to influence thought, cause trouble, injury, and even death.

In the book of Revelation, Scripture warns us concerning the end of the age and how a great Babylonian type empire will be able to deceive all the nations by its sorcery (Revelation 18:23). Even after the plagues fall upon a rebellious world, killing multitudes, those remaining alive, as Scripture foretells, will not *"repent of their murders or <u>their sorceries</u> or their sexual immorality or their thefts."* (Revelation 9:21).

In the book of Galatians, the Apostle Paul lists the works of the flesh, which every believer must deal with thoroughly and have the root passions and desires driving these forbidden behaviors dealt with permanently. *"Sexual immorality, impurity, sensuality, idolatry, <u>sorcery</u>, enmity, strife, jealousy, fits of anger, rivalries, dissensions, divisions, envy, drunkenness, orgies, and things like these. I warn you, as I warned* *you before, that those who do such things will not inherit the kingdom of God… And <u>those who belong to Christ Jesus have crucified the flesh with its passions and desires</u>"* (Galatians 5:19-24).

Many Christians balk at the notion that the human spirit has the potential of being harnessed by one's own willfulness and defilements, or by the devil and a demon. The thought of a person developing the ability to travel out of body and do evil should give concern; however, many relegate this idea to superstition or demonic fakery.

In order to comprehend this, we must first understand what functions the human spirit was meant to have—mainly the spirit is that part of a person created by God to allow communion with God and God only—as Scripture states: *"He yearns jealously over the spirit that he has made to dwell in us"* (James 4:5). In this age, we must further understand that Satan opposes God's desires and subverts God's intentions and plans—attempting to counterfeit the work of the Holy Spirit and other spiritual manifestation by God. Satan's ultimate goal in raising and grooming humans is to raise up the anti-Christ who will perform powerful signs and wonders.

The world has researched and studied, by way of science, the human body and the human soul; however, little scientific research or understanding concerning the human spirit has been attempted, other than paranormal research.

God created humans in his image having a spirit, with the life of our spirit breathed into us by God at conception. However, our spirit is not within itself independent or free. Our personal spirit imparted into us is held or restrained within our physical body for our own good. From conception on, we develop as a living soul until we die. In that process of living, the human spirit functions in a semi-dormant condition, and as the soul grows, and the human spirit can become defiled, wounded and awakened to become involved in forbidden spiritual activity (supernatural activities not explained by physical science or natural logic). Preferably, our spirit is to be kept pure and awakened by the Holy Spirit at the time of receiving the Gospel of Christ.

We can access our spirit with our mind through New Age, occult activity, or false Christian teachings. When these conditions occur, Satan and demonic spirits can influence the human spirit. Until the Holy Spirit regenerates the human spirit by way of being born again, the personal spirit is dead towards God—separated from the presence of God. However, the personal spirit can be awakened apart from God due to the influences of our soul, environment, and the spirit world (demonic).

Our spirit is God's way of communicating with us without literally or physically being in His presence. Due to our fallen nature, we cannot willfully enter into God's presence unless our intermediary, Jesus Christ, has regenerated our spirit. Through the born again experience, we come to Christ and our spirit is made alive to God.

Our soul interacts with the physical world but cannot communicate with God unless God reveals Himself to us through our spirit. When the Spirit of God touches us, we can now learn to hear through our spirit the voice of Christ and receive spiritual gifts from the Holy Spirit.

Our spirit is made to interact with God: *"The spirit of man is the lamp of the LORD, searching all his innermost parts"* (Proverbs 20:27). Jesus said of the human spirit, *"God is spirit, and those who worship him must worship in spirit and truth"* (John 4:24).

Our spirit has certain functions, apart from being born again. In spite of not being regenerated—and so being dead to God—our spirit can become awakened, influenced, damaged, and defiled before being made alive to God. The following passages will help shed light on how our spirit can be negatively affected by others and the spirit world:

"A gentle tongue is a tree of life, but perverseness in it breaks the spirit" (Proverbs 15:4).
"A glad heart makes a cheerful countenance, but by sorrow of heart the spirit is broken" (Proverbs 15:13).
"A cheerful heart is a good medicine, but a downcast spirit dries up the bones" (Proverbs 17:22).
"A man's spirit will endure sickness; but a broken spirit who can bear?" (Proverbs 18:14).

The human spirit helps sustain life, maintain hope, and enable humans to perceive spiritual and abstract concepts, intuition or perception and conscience, and gives the ability to sense evil. In addition, our personal spirit can sense spiritual entities—angels, the Spirit of God, Satan and demons. In these few passages, we are taught that the human spirit can become broken (shattered) with perverse words spoken in our hearing. Children are highly susceptible to receiving wounds to the spirit from abusive words and other negative influences.

Sorrow of heart can break one's spirit, and a downcast spirit can affect the immune system ("dries the bones"). Our bone marrow is a vital part of the body's immune system and blood cell production. The following is another passage to help develop a better understanding of the different functions of our spirit.

One important point before we look at this passage: our personal spirit is not necessarily purified and made right at our initial born-again experience. Depending on past defilements and wounds, our personal spirit can still suffer from defilements, wounds, and dividedness or fragmentation after we come to Christ. The following passage is a vital Scripture to confirm that our personal spirit can still carry defilements after we become a born again believer in Christ:

"Since we have these promises, beloved, let us cleanse ourselves from every <u>defilement of body and spirit</u>, bringing holiness to completion in the fear of God" (2 Corinthians 7:1). As a born-again Christian (meaning that the Holy Spirit drew us to Christ) we must learn to work with the Holy Spirit and the written Word of God in determining if our motives and intentions of the heart, are of God or if they originate from our carnal selfishness.

Separating the Spirit from the Soul
Bringing the human spirit back from the influence and control of the flesh and the devil

Part of the consequences for Adam and Eve's fall is that we all inherit a personal spirit intermingled within our soul and isolated from the presence of the Holy Spirit. Through the Gospel of Christ and the Word of God when empowered by the Holy Spirit, the human spirit can be redeemed from this intermeshed and fallen state, and be restored to have communion with God. We cannot do this on our own, even when we hear and believe in Jesus Christ and God's plan of salvation. However, if the Holy Spirit reveals himself and spiritually touches our spirit and ignites new spiritual life, in conjunction with hearing the Gospel we then are born again of God. (Many come to know of God, but were never born of God—these Christians suffer from false conversions.)

When the Holy Spirit does generate new life, a new spirit is created and implanted within our personal spirit—thus a person is born again—however, the old personal spirit is not completely transformed or made new in that born-again moment. The process of cleansing, purifying and character transformation initially begins, and this process is called sanctification.

We are sanctified and justified in God's eyes at the moment we believe in Christ and are born again (by the Holy Spirit), but we are not complete until we work out our salvation and grow up—grow from a newly born-again infant in Christ into a mature and eternally-secure disciple in Christ. An important aspect of the sanctification work on our part is to embrace the Word of God, to include all that Christ taught, and to allow the Holy Spirit, in conjunction with Scripture, to show us our true motives and intentions of our heart.

Growing up into Christ is a process to be led by God and it evolves out of our cooperation and effort in learning to know the person of Christ and his words. During this time of growth, we are under the umbrella or God's grace, yet at risk of falling away, sinning deliberately and backsliding, even losing our eternal life. When we become mature, having grown up into salvation, then we obtain the grace of God permanently, and have eternal security.

The author of Hebrews sheds more light on this growing up into maturity and its importance. *"Therefore let us leave the elementary doctrine of Christ and <u>go on to maturity</u>, not laying again a foundation of repentance from dead works and of faith toward God, and of instruction about washings, the laying on of hands, the resurrection of the dead, and eternal judgment. And this we will do if God permits. <u>For it is impossible to restore again to repentance those who have once been enlightened, who have tasted the heavenly gift, and have shared in the Holy Spirit, and have tasted the goodness of the Word of God and the powers of the age to come, if they then fall away,</u> since they are crucifying once again the Son of God to their own harm and holding him up to contempt. For land that has drunk the rain that often falls on it, and produces a crop useful to those for whose sake it is cultivated, receives a blessing from God. But if it bears thorns and thistles, it is worthless and near to being cursed, and its end is to be burned"* (Hebrews 6:1-8).

We must cease from our own motivational energy and learn how connected and defiled our spirit actually is, and how intermeshed our spirit is with our soul. We must die to our life's agenda and self-motivational energy and live by faith in the Son of God—it is a life exchange program between us and the person of Christ, where we learn to die to our will and learn and obey God's will for our life.

Our personal spirit must become separated from the ties to our soul (emotions, misbeliefs, bad attitudes, insecurities, jealousy, bitterness, etc.). When the Holy Spirit has a believer in a position to understand sanctification—they will give up trying to imitate Christ and learn to die to working for Christ religiously. Learn to stop assimilating holiness legalistically (hypocrisy) and allow Christ to transform your heart and create a new and right spirit so that living in righteousness becomes natural.

When we as believers allow the Holy Spirit to show us our true intentions of the heart and how our personal spirit easily follows those carnal agendas, we will begin to rest and abide in Christ. We will learn to allow his Spirit to lead and work through us, and we no longer energize ourselves to work for Christ, making our soul (emotions and willfulness) connect to our own spirit mistakenly, to witness to others, praise God, pray, or interact with others. Many learn to work for God, yet are not led by God; rather, they learn to tap into the power of their own spirit, thinking it is the Holy Spirit. In their determined self-energy, Satan's end-of-the-age angel of light false doctrines abound, deceiving many Christians and teaching them how to tap into the spiritual powers of the flesh.

"There remains a Sabbath rest for the people of God, <u>for whoever has entered God's rest has also rested from his works as God did from his</u>… For the Word of God is living and active, <u>sharper than any two-edged sword</u>, piercing to the division of soul and of spirit, of joints and of marrow, and <u>discerning the thoughts and intentions of the heart</u>. And no creature is hidden from his sight, but all are naked and exposed to the eyes of him to whom we must give account" (Hebrews 4:9-13).

When we learn to allow the Holy Spirit to show us our wrong motives and we work these issues out, our personal spirit is brought back to God (a process to be worked out). Our carnal self is then severed from our spirit, allowing the Holy Spirit to rest and abide in our spirit with minimal conflict.

How Satan's Works to Awaken the Human Spirit for His Purposes

Now the devil understands how our spirit can be harmfully entangled with our soul when we become a believer in Christ. Satan sets out to work in opposition to the Holy Spirit's work (in conjunction with God's Word) to separate the human spirit from the influence of our souls (as Christians). The devil does this work through false doctrine.

As for the heathen, they are led by the god of this world (the devil) to delve into the human spirit with all manner of forbidden practices—all related to harnessing the human spirit in an effort to bring inner peace, unity with nature, predict the future, communicate with invisible entities, and supernaturally influence self and others.

Over the centuries, and especially over the last 150 years, in underhanded ways Satan has inspired false doctrine that integrates mysticism and other forbidden practices to become mixed with the basic teachings of the Gospel. *"But false prophets also arose among the people, just as there will be false teachers among you, who will <u>secretly bring in destructive heresies</u>, even denying the Master who bought them, bringing upon themselves swift destruction"* (2 Peter 2:1).

These false teachers and their destructives heresies all relate to two basic objectives—to get disciples to follow the teacher and to obtain spiritual power by employing false teachings that awaken and control the human spirit by self-energy and will power.

The message of the cross, with its painful work in the believer's life, is avoided and believers are given a smorgasbord of shortcut methods to launch themselves into supernatural power, believing they have the power of God.

On the contrary, it is God's desire to bring our spirit back unto the Holy Spirit in purity, free of the passions and desires of the flesh. The power of his presence in its fullness can only be received through sanctification and by the piercing to the division of soul and spirit (allowing the Holy Spirit to show us our true intentions of the heart in all matters of life).

Many Christians think they have the power of God but only have a counterfeit power facilitated by the demonic.

A word of warning: When the true power of God begins to manifest through sanctified servants, many carnal and false believers will be inspired to become part of what God is doing or about to do and will want to participate. They will attempt to walk in the true power of God, and be at great risk of mentally and emotionally catching on fire and losing it. In some cases, those who attempt to infiltrate and hijack this coming move of God will literally die instantly similar to Ananias and Sapphira and burn up like stubble in a fire [spontaneous human combustion].

God's true power in the coming final awakening will not be sold, bought or counterfeited. The game players and unholy phonies will be put on notice as many will attempt to approach God's presence, and burst into flames (spontaneous human combustion). This burning of the wicked by a holy God will be similar to events such as Ananias and Sapphira dying at the feet of Peter (Acts 5:1-11), and Herod instantly eaten by worms by an angel of the Lord (Acts 12:20-24). Great fear will come upon the church and all who hear of these terrifying events.

An analogy to this is like trying to draw too much current through an impure conductor (wire) only to have the impurities in the wire heat up and actually melt the wire. A highly conductive element for electricity is gold highly refined—this element gives the least resistance to current or electron flow. Likewise the purer the human vessel (including the personal spirit), the more Christ is seen and the more power to glorify Christ can be applied by the Holy Spirit.

"I counsel you to <u>buy from me gold refined by fire</u>, so that you may be rich, and white garments so that you may clothe yourself and the shame of your nakedness may not be seen, and salve to anoint your eyes, so that you may see. Those whom I love, I reprove and discipline, so be zealous and repent. Behold, I stand at the door and knock. If anyone hears my voice and opens the door, I will come in to him and eat with him, and he with me. The one who conquers, I will grant him to sit with me on my throne, as I also conquered and sat down with my Father on his throne. He who has an ear, let him hear what the Spirit says to the churches'" (Revelation 3:18-22).

In the Power of the Lord or by the Power of the Flesh, Boosted by Demons
Astral projection of the human spirit—an evil end-of-the-age spiritual awakening

One of the basic teachings in the occult is learning how to astrally project one's own spirit to travel out of body. Astral projection, also known as out-of-body experience, is defined this way:

> Astral projection (or astral travel) is an interpretation of out-of-body experience (OBE) that assumes the existence of an "astral body" separate from the physical

body [personal spirit] and capable of traveling outside it. Astral projection or travel denotes the astral body leaving the physical body to travel in the astral plane.

The idea of astral travel is rooted in common worldwide religious accounts of the afterlife in which the consciousness' or soul's journey or "ascent" is described in such terms as "an... out-of body experience, wherein the spiritual traveler leaves the physical body and travels in his/her subtle body (or dream body or astral body) into 'higher' realms." It is therefore associated with near death experiences and is also frequently reported as spontaneously experienced in association with sleep and dreams, illness, surgical operations, drug experiences, sleep paralysis and forms of meditation.

It is sometimes attempted out of curiosity, or may be believed to be necessary to, or the result of, some forms of spiritual practice. It may involve "travel to higher realms" called astral planes but is commonly used to describe any sensation of being "out of the body" in the everyday world, even seeing one's body from outside or above. It may be reported in the form of an apparitional experience, or a supposed encounter with a doppelgänger, some living person also seen somewhere else at the same time." (Source: www.wikipedia.org/wiki/Astral_projection)

Throughout history, people have testified to seeing aberrations of known individuals appearing mystically in one location while that same person is known to be physically at a different physical location—at the same time. The term used to describe this phenomenon is *bilocation* and Wikipedia defines this as follows:

Bilocation, or sometimes multilocation, occurs when an individual or object is located (or appears to be located) in two distinct places at the same instant in time. The concept has been utilized in a wide range of historical and philosophical systems, including early Greek philosophy, shamanism, paganism, folklore, occultism and magic, the paranormal, Hinduism, Buddhism, spiritualism, Theosophy, the New Age and mysticism in general, as well as Christian [Catholic] mysticism and Jewish mysticism." (Source: www.wikipedia.org/wiki/Bilocation)

In definition there may be a difference between bilocation and astral projection; however, I believe bilocation is an out-of-body projection of the human spirit that becomes visible to others. In contrast, astral projection of a human spirit is invisible to others; however, others can experience spiritual, mental, or physical symptoms of an astrally projected human spirit upon their person.

New Testament Out-of-Body References

There are two passages in the New Testament that specifically address astral projection. However, you will not find in Scripture accounts that describe the "how to" of astral projection or bilocation since they are forbidden aspects of sorcery. I believe these aspects are some of the deeper things of Satan that Jezebel was teaching God's servants, as cited in Revelation 2:18-29.

The Apostle Paul wrote of a potential out of body experience: *"I know a man in Christ who fourteen years ago was caught up to the third heaven—<u>whether in the body or out of the body</u> I do not know, God knows. And I know that this man was caught up into paradise—whether <u>in the body or out of the body</u> I do not know, God knows—and he heard things that cannot be told, which man may not utter"* (2 Corinthians 12:2-4).

Paul knew this man and boasted of his testimony to others, however, he explains in the whole account that he refrains from boasting of such experiences, including revelations and visions of the Lord since there is nothing to be gained by bragging. The point to take note in this passage is that the man *may have been out of body*, as Paul mentioned.

Another description concerning the human spirit traveling out of body again comes from the Apostle Paul as he explains that his own personal spirit would be present when Christians in Corinth when they assembled to deal with a difficult situation:

"For though absent in body, I am present in spirit; and as if present, I have already pronounced judgment on the one who did such a thing. When you are assembled in the name of the Lord Jesus and <u>my spirit is present, with the power of our Lord Jesus</u>, you are to deliver this man to Satan for the destruction of the flesh, so that his spirit may be saved in the day of the Lord" (1 Corinthians 5:3-5).

Clearly, Paul is informing the Christians in Corinth that for some reason his spirit will be present when they were assembled to deal with the Christian doing evil. It must be understood that this future personal spirit out-of-body experience would be in the power of the Lord.

There are no other Scriptures relating to one's spirit being out of body apart from death. However, there are enough specifics in these passages to educate ourselves with the fact that this type of experience can happen. The only legitimate time for a Christian would be when the Lord deems it necessary and it is done in the power of the Lord.

There are teachings in various charismatic and Pentecostal circles that promote astral projection to be performed at will when wanting to visit others such as missionaries abroad. This teachings primarily uses Paul's letter to the Corinthian church citing the above passage. In 1990 this teaching was given to the congregation I ministered in as the counseling pastor. The guest speaker was a missionary who touted the ability to pray in tongues and experience spiritual out-of-body travel when he desired to visit his family in the U.S. while he was away as a missionary.

This is exactly what the Apostle Peter warned of: *"False teachers among you, who will secretly bring in destructive heresies."* (2 Peter 2:1). These teachings open up one's personal spirit to be harnessed by the will of that person in his or her selfishness, but also run great risk of being harnessed and power boosted by a counterfeiting demonic spirit.

The Spiritual powers of the flesh
Mistaken as manifestations of the Holy Spirit

These false doctrines taught by teachers manifesting false signs and wonders have gone viral through large parts of the body of Christ producing supernatural power. Unfortunately, the spiritual power that the flesh generates is often mistaken for the power of the Holy Spirit. False teachings create a tragic deception, where millions of Pentecostal, charismatic and evangelical Christians are tricked into conjuring up and embracing a spiritual power generated not by the Holy Spirit but by the human spirit.

This carnal spiritual power can pack a jolt—and if harnessed and directed the spiritual power generated can do great harm. When fully activated it can be likened to touching a low-amperage wire when grounded, which can be dangerous, even deadly—especially when the spiritual powers of the flesh is boosted by the demonic.

In reading the Hebrews reference in the previous chapter, take note of this part of that passage: *"For the Word of God is living and active, sharper than any two-edged sword, piercing to the division of soul and spirit"* (Hebrews 4:12).

Few learn to allow the Lord to show them how their own spirit and soul are still intertwined, which creates a mixed influence that can clog and even block the flow of the Holy Spirit.

Christ warns us concerning operating in our own spiritual power: *"On that day many will say to me, 'Lord, Lord, did we not prophesy in your name, and cast out demons in your name, and do many mighty works in your name?' And then will I declare to them, 'I never knew you; depart from me, you workers of lawlessness"* (Matthew 7:22-23). Many know of Christ just as many know of a famous movie star they have never met—and may even become swept up in the drama of the movie star's marriage, adoptions, and causes. So too, many hear about Christ, but never meet the true person of Christ. This is the condition of many—they experienced a false conversion or were never taught to grow up into salvation. (See Ephesians 4:15-16 and 1 Peter 2:1-3).

As you read on you will learn how carnal and false Christians, spiritualists, pagans, witchdoctors and New Age practitioners gain power to cast out demons, prophesy, and practice or perform supernatural works. Have you ever wondered by what power the sorcerers in the Pharaoh's court were able to keep up with the power of God for the first three plagues pronounced by Moses and Aaron?

The human spirit has spiritual power and the devil is working to unleash this dormant pent-up power against God's people.

Discerning the Power of the Lord and the Spiritual powers of the flesh

The true saint must learn to distinguish the spiritual power of the false from the true power of God released through his servants. The last days will contain powerful signs and wonders—so powerful that Christ warned they would, *"lead astray, if possible, even the elect."* (See Matthew 24:15-27.) Discerning the true from the counterfeit requires discipline and training.

Learning how to embrace the discipline of the Lord must be restored to the body of Christ. The sincere disciple of Christ must learn to grasp the words and principles of Christ that press out our carnal motives and brings to death the spiritual powers of the flesh. Those principles teach suffering and dying to self through trials and adversity—and if embraced with understanding and applying the Word of God—a separating between the soul and spirit takes place.

Unless this is accomplished, the carnal Christian will continue to struggle with their soul intertwined with their personal spirit, where emotions, ungodly attitudes, selfishness, and jealousies will continue to seep into their spirit and adversely affect others around them through their spirit. Satan's work is to take advantage of the soul and spirit enmeshment through false doctrine and counterfeit spiritual experiences and harness the spiritual powers of the flesh keeping the personal spirit tainted and controlled by self—not led by the indwelling Holy Spirit of God.

Love, grace, and holiness, as well as wisdom and discernment are brought together in the discipline of the Lord. *"It is for discipline that you have to endure. God is treating you as sons. For what son is there whom his father does not discipline? If you are left without discipline, in which all have participated, then you are illegitimate children and not sons. Besides this, we have had earthly fathers who disciplined us and we respected them. Shall we not much more be subject to the Father of spirits and live? For they disciplined us for a short time as it seemed best to them, but he disciplines us for our good, that we may share his holiness. For the moment all discipline seems painful rather than pleasant, but later it yields the peaceful fruit of righteousness to those who have been trained by it"* (Hebrews 12:7-11).

James 1:2-4 reads, *"Count it all joy, my brethren, when you meet various trials, for you know that the testing of your faith produces steadfastness. And let steadfastness have its full effect, that you may be perfect and complete, lacking in nothing."*

If you avoid the discipline of the Lord, you will lose your edge in increasing your powers of discernment. More than this, you run the risk of becoming an illegitimate child of God and hearing those terrifying words, *"I never knew you!"*

When we refuse to allow Christ to discipline us but attempt to serve him anyway, we end up using Christ's name but never coming to a place where the person of Christ is formed within us—where the Spirit works through us unfettered by our carnal issues. Thus, the power that is thought to be of God turns out to be the spiritual powers of the flesh, which often gets a power boost from the demonic, impersonating the Holy Spirit.

The Apostle Paul warned Christians at Galatia that they were being deceived in the way they were walking with Christ. If they continued in this condition, they would make Christ's sacrifice ineffective, which could actually make them severed from Christ. In frustration Paul wrote in the same letter, *"My little children … I am again in travail until Christ be formed in you!"* (See Galatians 4:8-20; 5:1-9).

The Apostle is saying that when Christ-like character is produced (formed within) the old carnal nature will be put off (a division of soul and spirit). Our soul (mind and heart) will not drive our own spirit, rather our spirit will become distinct and a home for the Holy Spirit: *"If a man loves me, he will keep my word, and my Father will love him, and we will come to him and make our home with him"* (John 14:23).

This must be accomplished in order for us to be led by the Spirit of God, that we would no longer be driven by our own spirit/flesh power, which can easily be awakened, conjured up, and enhanced by the deceitful wiles of men in their teaching of demon-inspired and demon empowered false doctrines.

Dark Human Spiritual Powers Growing—Exponentially

The spiritual power of human beings has the ability to influence or affect objects, animals, and the human body as well as affecting the spirit, emotions and thoughts of people. This spiritual power is somewhat weak when initially activated; however, the ability to influence or affect objects and people can grow in power, exponentially when a demon is solicited (directly or indirectly) to help increase these spiritual powers.

The Harry Potter books and movies are prime examples of how Satan wrongly awakens the spiritual power of the human spirit. This is just one of many examples of the practice of spiritualism and sorcery that is now ingrained within societies throughout the world. Once people are exposed to these evil practices, their personal spirit can easily become awakened to their own will (the flesh) and then as they grow deeper into these forbidden practices, their own spiritual powers can grow quickly.

These powers can be harnessed to influence the world around them. There is a reason that the practice of magic and sorcery is forbidden in Scripture—the power is real and dangerous! (See Deuteronomy 18:10-14.)

As the last days of this age careen to their end, Satan is finding more ways to unleash the powers of the human spirit. The devil is working to harness these powers through forbidden practices and in turn defile humans everywhere with forbidden spiritualism. The Harry Potter books and movies have exposed millions of susceptible children to these dark evils. Their little spirits are defiled and many become spiritually awakened, as they mimic what they see or read. Demons easily inspire many of those exposed to this darkness, and tempt and lure them into the deeper things of Satan.

The most insidious work of Satan is the widespread false gifts and false manifestations within many fellowships where the human spirit is harnessed by mistake and thought to be the work of the Holy Spirit. Millions of Christians have been deceived and defiled through false doctrines that teach Christians to delve into their personal spirit and learn to practice false gifts [18] (false tongues, false prophesy, and false manifestations).

---

[18] There is such a thing as a false tongue–and that is what many receive. The true gift of tongues (in a foreign language) is for today. However, the gift of an unknown tongue (or prayer language) is truly abused and has become a placebo for many and a wide-open path for the counterfeit to enter in by (a false tongue). Self-edification has become an obsession for a multitude, as many wander away from understanding the convicting work of the Holy Spirit that is often painful and confrontational. Instead, they chose to continue to get a "buzz" from speaking in an unknown language through their own spirit. Few who are into the gift of tongues can discern the Holy Spirit's presence and comfort from their own personal spirit that is energized by their own carnal selfishness, conjured willfully—this all to produce feelings of euphoria. *"For if I pray in a tongue, my spirit prays but my mind is unfruitful. What am I to do? I will pray with my spirit, but I will pray with my mind also; I will sing praise with my spirit, but I will sing with my mind also.... Nevertheless, in church I would rather speak five words with my mind in order to instruct others, than ten thousand words in a tongue. Brothers, do not be children in your thinking. Be infants in evil, but in your <u>thinking be mature</u>"* (1 Cor. 14:14-20). We suggest a thorough study of 1 Corinthians 14. Ask the Lord to help you understand why the Apostle Paul was putting on the breaks concerning this particular gift—encouraging these Christians to *grow up*. Another fallacy is the baptism of the Holy Spirit evidenced by speaking in tongues and only by speaking in a tongue. The disciples received the Holy Spirit when Christ first appeared to them after his resurrection, long before the day of Pentecost. (John 20:19-23). An excellent book on this controversial issue for additional study is *The Speaking in Tongues Controversy*, by Rick Walston ISBN-13: 978-1591607625.

Ministry Case: *The terrified wife*

A Christian woman came to counseling complaining about her abusive husband and seeking advice. In her first and only session, she listed the terrible threats, controlling behaviors, and verbal abuse that she had been continually subjected to over the past several years. I asked her why she had not turned to legal counsel to hold him accountable.

Her demeanor instantly changed to be defensive and stressed, her face turned ashen, as if the blood in her veins stopped flowing. She could not disguise the terror as her eyes showed pure panic. After a long uncomfortable pause, she finally said that seeking help from an attorney or filing a complaint to obtain a protection order was completely out of the question.

I had to ask why and the story she told me reminded me of some ghastly horror movie.

She explained that the reason she came to our ministry for counseling was that she thought that prayer might help. In her mind that was her last avenue for dealing with the monster that her husband had become. Amazingly, they both believed in Christ.

I explained that she must take courage and do her part by doing an intervention, along with prayer to stop his terrible behavior and that she should seek safe shelter while holding him accountable. It was at that point she broke down and explained in detail why she could not do this, as she gave an account of his spiritual powers of evil.

There was incident about a week prior to her coming for counsel and what took place had convinced her that any kind of intervention would cause her death or at the least cause her physical harm.

She explained: One evening, the week prior, her husband became inflamed in rage towards the next-door neighbor over a trivial matter. The next morning, as her husband went out the front door to work and was saying good-bye, he saw that same neighbor operating his tractor across the road in the neighbor's field.

She said her husband looked at the neighbor and spoke the word "die" in a very macabre-manner—and that very afternoon the neighbor was crushed to death in a rollover accident while operating his tractor. She said that similar things had happened over the years, particularly when he became angry, but never with this kind of destruction.

I tried to convince her that God would be her spiritual shelter and with our prayers and support as a fellowship, we would stand with her to help hold him accountable and get her to a safe place as she sought legal recourse.

Regrettably, she would have no part in any such course of action and chose to stay in the relationship hoping for the best. I never heard from her again. Ω

Christian Human Spirits Harnessed by Counterfeit Demonic Activity

Demonic principalities along with millions of "power demons" [19] have become co-habitants with people who have invited or sought supernatural powers to get their own way in life. This

---

[19] A "power demon" is assigned to mislead and nurture (through forbidden practices and false doctrine), a non-believer or a deceived Christian into seeking supernatural powers, apart from sound doctrine and the true gift, and gifts of the Holy Spirit.

may seem sensational—a concoction from an over-excited imagination inspired by a Vincent Price horror movie or Sissy Spacek's *Carrie* character.

However, the biblical accounts concerning sorcery and divination are real and evil can execute spiritual powers that affect a person's life, nervous system, thoughts, emotions, personal spirit, as well as the physical world and inanimate objects. The biblical account of Moses and Aaron standing up to the Pharaoh demonstrates such power as the Pharaoh's court magicians matched the power of God for the first three plagues.

"Aaron cast down his staff before Pharaoh and his servants, and it became a serpent. Then Pharaoh summoned the wise men and the sorcerers, and they, <u>the magicians of Egypt, also did the same by their secret arts</u>. For each man cast down his staff, and they became serpents... the fish in the Nile died, and the Nile stank, so that the Egyptians could not drink water from the Nile. There was blood throughout all the land of Egypt. <u>But the magicians of Egypt did the same by their secret arts</u>... Aaron stretched out his hand over the waters of Egypt, and the frogs came up and covered the land of Egypt. <u>But the magicians did the same by their secret arts</u> and made frogs come up on the land of Egypt" (Exodus 7:10 -8:7).

What is even more alarming is how sorcery (a listed work of the flesh that is forbidden in Galatians 5:16-26) has invaded fellowships, denominations, and charismatic movements everywhere as deceitful spirits seduce many Christians. *"The Spirit expressly says that in later times some will depart from the faith by <u>devoting themselves</u> to deceitful spirits and teachings of demons, through the insincerity of liars whose consciences are seared"* (1 Timothy 4:1-2).

This insidious work of the devil in modern Christianity began quietly back at the turn of the 1900s and has now become widespread. False movements believed to be outpourings of the Holy Spirit are now common and ever growing in wild and exotic manifestations affecting the human spirit, emotions, and the physical body.

The movement that started out as a desire to see the gifts of the Holy Spirit restored to the body of Christ quickly became hijacked by deceived leaders inspired by *deceitful spirits and teachings of demons*—a well-planned work of Satan to counterfeit the gifts of the Holy Spirit in these last days.

As you read on you will discover just how far reaching these teachings of demons have become. The most important aspect of discernment is detecting the counterfeiting activity of Satan and realizing how pervasive and powerful the counterfeiting spiritual manifestations have grown.

Jessie Penn-Lewis, Evan Roberts, Watchman Nee, and many other solid teachers warned during the first part of the 20th century about these devious works of Satan, teaching on and

---

Once a human candidate takes the bait and seeks after supernatural powers selfishly and apart from God's will, the power demon gains entrance into the human spirit. Power demons are akin to a spirit of sorcery and are a common evil spirit controlled, managed and dispensed by a fallen angel, (principality) that is in charge of growing false doctrine and promoting sorcery within society. A principality works to promote lies and false doctrine on a large scale, whereas power demons or spirits of divination are assigned to stay with an individual to work their craft. A comparison is that a principality is like a major in the military directing enlisted personal, where the principalities are higher in authority and power and direct the subordinate demons. The subordinate demons are assigned to do the individual detailed work through their human hosts.

warning how spiritualism from India, Asia, and Africa was beginning to infiltrate Christian doctrine.

Today, the teachers of these wayward movements have wholeheartedly *devoted themselves* to spreading, supporting and defending these false manifestations by rewriting history, distorting facts, and vilifying those past authors, preachers, and theologians who opposed these devilish activities. Anyone today who confronts these deceitful teachings can expect vicious attacks as well. Few Christians are exposed to the truth through sound doctrine and solid literature that explains and warns how these works of deceitful spirits have become so widespread.

The power of the human spirit is growing, and has become a substitute for many deceived believers, replacing the true cleansing and maturing work of the Holy Spirit. Today carnal Christians are taught to stir up their own personal spirit through false teachings and chant-like prayers and repetitive worship songs—they become convinced that this is God's way of bringing believers to maturity.

The Apostle Paul gave sensible guidelines about the gifts and speaking in an unknown tongue in his letter to the Christians at Corinth. Paul clearly states, *"He who speaks in a tongue edifies himself, but he who prophesies edifies the church"* (1 Corinthians 14:4 RSV). Most Pentecostal and charismatic Christians have become deceived through teachings that proclaim a personal prayer language will magically build up the individual Christian. The practice has become so out of hand, it is frequently used as a safety ejection seat to push when things seem to get too hot to handle. For any emotional pressure, trials, or demonic warfare that have disturbing side effects, the practice of speaking in a tongue becomes a panacea to edify and lift the believer into spiritual peace.

It works, for a season, since the personal spirit becomes active to numb the mind and heart to various symptoms—emotional, psychological, spiritual, and even physical. The demons back off from torment, giving the deceived temporary relief in a scheme to codify their seducing work, leading the deceived deeper into false doctrine and ritualistic practices—to go past the point of no return.

In truth, tongue-speaking believers who use their prayer language to escape these issues are opening themselves to demonic cohabitation. Those uncomfortable symptoms experienced are to be examined, rather than suppressed. The wide-spread practice of false tongues for self-edification has sucked millions of deceived Christians into extreme passivity of mind.

Thinking they are increasing their powers of discernment and growing in spiritual strength, they are actually becoming weaker and weaker—learning to avoid the discipline of the Lord and escape the emotional pain meant to show hidden impurities of the heart and spirit.

Speaking in tongues or other spiritual experiences such as being slain in the spirit, barking like a dog, or laughing uncontrollably becomes a carnal spiritual escape mechanism to help cope with the side effects of an impure heart and defiled spirit within the believer.

This type of escapism is often employed during a fiery trial that is allowed by God and meant to break denial, causing the believer to search their heart—to uncover hidden unbelief—with the help of the true Holy Spirit—and to expose, purge, cleanse, and heal issues of heart and defilements of spirit.

Christians caught up in this dark teaching learn to get a "buzz" or a "high" from their own personal spirit—grieving the Holy Spirit and hampering true growth in Christ. *This is a diabolical satanic plan using God's Word out of context against God's Word and sound doctrine.*

What is truly frightful about this unleashed wickedness amongst the masses of Pentecostal and charismatic Christians is how easy it is for Satan and the demonic to channel through a false tongue. The following case was a real revelation for us years ago and will demonstrate how serious speaking in a false tongue can be.

Ministry Case: *False tongues vacation wrecker*

Many Christians receive a false tongue and have no idea that they are in a carnal state spewing out demonic and carnal-spirit prayers that inflict mind control and other spiritual influences upon people. The so-called interpretations of these false tongues are false as well. When Christians do not pray according to God's specific will in a matter, but earnestly speak forth wrong prayers, then they are praying according to their own will and often Satan's. They become a channel for Satan, just as Peter channeled for Satan by rebuking Christ for the declaration of his coming death on the cross. Jesus responded to Peter's objections by saying, *"Get behind me, Satan! You are a hindrance to me; for you are not on the side of God, but of men"* (See Matthew 16:21-23 RSV; notice Jesus was looking at Peter but speaking to the devil).

Opposing the will of God in prayer, especially on behalf of others can have a serious effect and can cause great harm. If the Spirit leads us, we have peace and confidence in our prayers, for we pray according to God's will in true faith having no doubts. (See James 1:5-8 and 1 John 3:19-22.) Most who are deceived have a false peace, avoiding the Spirit's check, and pray amiss according to their own selfish will. Satan, as he did with Peter, loves to jump in and inspire Christians to pray according to their own will, which is invariably in opposition to God's will. (See Matthew 16:22-26, 1 John 3:18-24.)

When we first found out about this human psychic-spirit destructive power, it was through the disruption of a much-needed vacation. We had been working with a distraught Christian woman who was in a family crisis. Her problem was under control, so we had no qualms about going on our planned vacation, but she felt we were abandoning her.

This Christian was carnal and double-minded, but thought she was spiritual since she spoke in tongues, often for hours at a time. Remember, Paul addressed the Christians at Corinth as carnal though they practiced the gifts of the Holy Spirit. These Christians emphasized praying in unknown tongues, which became an overindulgent activity.

One problem after another occurred during preparation to leave on our vacation. Finally, the camper van we had borrowed to use broke down halfway to our destination. The alternator quit mysteriously and we had to limp back home by buying a new battery to keep the engine running. We realized this was a spiritual attack and started to seek the Lord concerning its source.

We were sure the spiritual attack came from this woman. Finally, a couple of nights after getting back home, I was praying and felt a strong spiritual oppression. The Lord gave a word of discernment and a word of knowledge that it was a spirit of witchcraft that was attacking me through this woman. I could not imagine how this woman could pray such evil until the Lord revealed that she was operating in a spirit of divination and sorcery in conjunction with her own personal spirit.

In her selfish and jealous heart, the spirit of sorcery was gaining access to us spiritually through her spirit. These evil counterfeit spirits were invited to set up residence within her spirit and became active by false gift manifestations in the many meetings she attended.

Her selfish motives of heart accessed her spirit and spewed out of body spirit attacks through her incessant speaking in a false tongue. She was oblivious to her own bitter resentment towards us, concealed deep in her secret heart. (God desires that we walk in truth within our inward being and in wisdom within our secret heart—see Psalm 51:6). Satan works feverishly to get carnal Christians to take on the world in the flesh and pray amiss—to pray according to man's will—aloof to God's purposes and to actually pray against God's specific will in a matter.

I rebuked her spirit and commanded the spirit of witchcraft to leave and the oppression lifted immediately.

This woman believed the false doctrine that gave her license to pray with her spirit in an unknown tongue, leaving her mind blanked out and unfruitful. In her passive condition, the demonic had the ability to use her spirit (now meshed with the demonic) to carry out her will through sorcery.

Many tongue-speaking Christians unwittingly become pawns of the devil, used to oppose others, thinking they are praying for what they think God would want. What is so very hard to understand is that carnal charismatic or Pentecostal Christians can become deeply encased in false manifestations through counterfeiting spirits—thinking they are walking in the Holy Spirit. This allows their personal spirit to become soaked in a form of cohabitation with the counterfeiting demonic, allowing their personal spirit to travel out of body and touch others, even objects, by the boosting power of the demonic. The false tongue or the so-called personal prayer language becomes a weapon in the hands of Satan to oppose God's will and cause mayhem, chaos, mental confusion, oppression, illness, and even death.

This is not an isolated case. We have experienced many attacks by errant believers who pray not according to God's will (speaking in a false tongue or praying amiss knowing what they are saying). Many become so spiritually obsessed they become accommodating hosts for a spirit of divination leading into the practice of sorcery to promote their will and unwittingly do Satan's bidding. This is widespread, where false doctrines succeed in promoting "Christian witchcraft." Ω

We have had many encounters with Christians who unwittingly practice sorcery through wrongful prayers or by speaking in a false prayer language. Millions have opened up their personal spirit to the demonic world in ignorance and selfishness. The primary reason why so many believers in Christ become recipients of counterfeiting demons and even allow demons to live as cohabitating guests is due to their outright rejection of the principle of the cross.

Christians are literally taught to live for Christ in the flesh, where false doctrine sanctions a carte blanche (unlimited power) theology in achieving one's goals in life by using Christ's name in prayer. As explained extensively in chapter five, the abundance of self-help "I can do all things in Christ" carnal methods give Christians license to practice living as a Christian in the flesh as long as they follow tailored religious mantras and formulas—to the "T."

The Apostle Paul in his epistle to the Philippians wrote this warning, "*Look out for the dogs, look out for the evildoers, look out for those who mutilate the flesh. For we are the real circumcision, who worship by the Spirit of God and glory in Christ Jesus and put no confidence in the flesh*" (Philippians 3:2-3).

Look out indeed. Discernment requires paying attention to doctrines taught and preached, and rightly understanding the teachings of the New Testament and Christ. Part of the Apostle Paul's battle was dealing with Christian Judaizers who were trying to impose the Jewish tradition of circumcision upon the Gentile believers. The above passage refers to this false doctrine as Paul calls us to look out for those who mutilate the flesh, meaning the circumcision party. However, this passage also implores the discerning Christian to lookout for evildoers and false workers who teach Christians to put confidence in their own self-abilities to follow Christ in fleshly spiritualism. True Christians learn to discern spirits and worship God by the Spirit of God, not in the power of their own spirit.

When we embrace the work of the cross daily, we learn to allow the Holy Spirit to point out our carnal-selfish motives, unresolved issues of heart, and learn to suffer death to our sinful passions and desires of the flesh. The following case exemplifies just how powerful an evil heart and demonically controlled spirit can become—within a Christian who refuses to pick up their cross daily and follow the true Christ.

Ministry Case: *The exploding glass of milk*

The Apostle Paul wrote to the Christians at Philippi, "*Brothers, join in imitating me, and keep your eyes on those who walk according to the example you have in us. For many, of whom I have often told you and now tell you even with tears, walk as enemies of the cross of Christ. Their end is destruction, their god is their belly, and they glory in their shame, with minds set on earthly things*" (Philippians 3:17-19).

This case was one of my first encounters with demonic power working through a deceived and rebellious Christian. The Lord was faithful in allowing an impromptu indoctrination to the enemy's power that I would soon face, working amongst Christians in the beginning of our counseling ministry.

It was June 1988 and the setting was a warm and sunny afternoon in the Puget Sound region of the Pacific Northwest. I was coming on board as the counseling pastor in a local Foursquare church (very charismatic in practice) and the senior pastor invited me for dinner with his wife and children.

Their home had a spacious back yard adjacent to a large open field that was really like a park with a well-manicured lawn. We were to dine outside on a family picnic table that was set with all the amenities to go with a steak and baked potato dinner.

My choice of refreshment was a large glass of milk to go with the main course. I remember taking note of the glass. It was very thick—molded to be childproof—one would have to drop it deliberately on concrete to break it, and then it may just chip or crack because of its thickness.

We enjoyed small talk as we began to have dinner and then the pastor's wife out of the clear blue said, "Tell me about this counseling ministry you're starting?"

I had just started to drink some milk as she asked her question, so I was looking at her, as I cut short my sip, and started to set the glass down in preparation to answer her question. Then with a burst, my glass of nearly full milk exploded.

Pieces of glass and milk sprayed everywhere, on my plate, on the tablecloth, on my hand and wrist, and onto the pastor's plate who sat across from me. We were all dumbfounded, except the pastor's wife—she had no expression and did not make eye contact with me, and like a robot got up to get a towel to start the cleanup.

The pastor and I both looked around the yard and across the field looking for someone who might have shot a BB gun, however, no one appeared and there was no evidence of that sort of mischief. It was as if the glass crumbled in my hand spontaneously.

Later, when we resumed eating our dinner, the pastor surmised that this was a personal attack directed at me by the devil himself, to harm me because of the ministry that I was about to start. The strange remote look upon the pastor's wife's face during the whole incident and her not entering into any discussion of what might have caused the glass to shatter became an indelible impression I shall never forget.

The truth of what happened finally surfaced months later, as the counseling ministry became effective, as well as controversial. The pastor and his wife had been struggling for some time in their relationship and because of word of mouth about the success of the counseling ministry; the pastor came for an appointment.

After I helped him understand in more detail the work of pastoral counseling, he convinced his wife to come in for a counseling session. Her session was a waste of time, as one of the false teachers convinced her that any troubling issues were merely demonic in nature. She expected me to pray a magical prayer to deliver the both of them of any oppression.

I explained to her the process of sanctification and the ongoing work of the cross within the believer's life where our carnal works become crucified—and how the Holy Spirit, working with competent counsel and the gift of prophecy would help her learn to deal with her hidden issues. I used one of our counseling diagrams in explaining this inner cleansing and healing work. I gave it to her to take with her. She ended the session stating that all these issues are in the past. This position was based on one of her favorite visiting evangelists and his teachings who came to preach occasionally, and often she would be slain in the spirit under his supposed anointing.

She folded the handout, stood up, walked over to the trash basket, smugly dropped the literature in the trash, and then walked out of my office. In counseling with the pastor, he shared that his wife had a difficult childhood, including molestation by her father.

This woman, as so many Christians who suffer from past defilements resulting in double mindedness and bitterness, had deeply embedded unresolved rage. This condition was active at our dinner and the exploding glass drama. Her issues, as well as her husband's, along with false doctrine over the prior years allowed her spirit to become a habitation for a spirit of murder and revenge.

The pastor's wife was the channel for the demonic flowing through her defiled spirit. This was the spiritual power source that attempted to harm me. Concerning her secret heart and spirit, and the resident evil demonic spirit within her, I was a threat (as a counselor) to expose the demonic stronghold and the truth of her unforgiving heart towards her father, her husband and any man that would threaten to expose her inner agenda.

Those teachings that the pastor and his wife chose to embrace led them to become enemies of the cross, and adversaries towards those who preach true sanctification and embracing one's cross daily. Ω

Brace for a Sorcery Mêlée between Carnal Christians and Evil-False Brethren

In days to come this type of demonic channeling through deceived carnal Christians will become acute, with the demonic assaulting fellowships by inciting Christians to turn on each other spiritually.

A Christian witchcraft mêlée will develop in many congregations that have embraced these false doctrines and fostered false manifestations. Any hidden bitter jealousy or selfish ambition within deceived and defiled Christians will boost the power of the human spirit through counterfeit power demons thought to be the Holy Spirit.

Illnesses, accidents, mishaps, even premature death, along with weird and chaotic circumstances will become out of hand, as many fellowships experience a satanically induced internal meltdown. Few pastors will understand what is happening and how this kind of spiritual attack on so many grew so quickly. Prayer against such will do little to stop this coming attack.

James addressed this very same situation in his epistle when he warned, *"But if you have bitter jealousy and selfish ambition in your hearts, do not boast and be false to the truth. This is not the wisdom that comes down from above, but is earthly, unspiritual, demonic. For where jealousy and selfish ambition exist, there will be disorder and every vile practice… What causes quarrels and what causes fights among you?* <u>*Is it not this, that your passions are at war within you? You desire and do not have, so you murder. You covet and cannot obtain, so you fight and quarrel. You do not have, because you do not ask. You ask and do not receive, because you ask wrongly, to spend it on your passions. You adulterous people!*</u> *Do you not know that friendship with the world is enmity with God? Therefore whoever wishes to be a friend of the world makes himself an enemy of God."* (James 3:14-16 and 4:1-4).

Another warning from the Apostle Paul describes the potential for real trouble when the flesh is not put to death within the fellowship: *"But if you bite and devour one another, watch out that you are not consumed by one another. But I say, walk by the Spirit, and you will not gratify the desires of the flesh. For the desires of the flesh are against the Spirit ... And those who belong to Christ Jesus have crucified the flesh with its passions and desires. If we live by the Spirit, let us also walk by the Spirit. Let us not become conceited, provoking one another, envying one another"* (Galatians 5:15-17, 24-26).

Many walk by a false spirit (often delving into their own spirit to conjure up a state of false bliss), which subtly suppresses the passions and desires of the flesh until a trial or relationship conflict arises. When that happens all hell can break lose in a fellowship, and within relationships, and even between spouses and family and between extended family members.

Someone who walks in a defiled spirit, who suffers from unresolved rage, bitter jealousy and selfishness, and who then opposes or disagrees with another can be deadly. Even worse is having several people like this together pray against your life or the ministry that God has assigned to you.

Three excellent resources that helped us years ago in determining the general characteristics of various abuses in fellowship and false leaders. The following titles that are still available:

- *The Subtle Power of Spiritual Abuse: Recognizing and Escaping Spiritual Manipulation and False Spiritual Authority Within the Church* by David Johnson and Jeffery VanVonderen, Bethany House, 1991
- *Predators in Our Pulpits: A Compelling Call to Follow Christ in These Perilous Times* by W. Phillip Keller, Harvest House, 1988
- *Charismatic Captivation: Authoritarian Abuse & Psychological Enslavement in Neo-Pentecostal Churches* by Steven Lambert, Th.D. Real Truth Publications, 2003

The following recent case will also help the sincere disciple of Christ realize the need for caution, wisdom, discernment, purity, and authority in defending against this kind of evil that is rapidly expanding throughout the body of Christ.

Ministry Case: *Charismatic church witches*

Our ministry became involved with a sister who was experiencing subtle spiritual abuse within a charismatic church nearby. One of our ministry team members became acquainted with her and was led to share a ministry publication entitled *Effective Spiritual Warfare*. She stated later that this resource on spiritual warfare confirmed what the Lord had been showing her over the past several years concerning the false teachings overtaking much of the church. Within a short period, this Christian sister sought our counsel and decided it was time to leave that charismatic-evangelical fellowship.

She tried to make the separation as simple and as quiet as possible; however, various friends in this fellowship along with the pastor's wife became upset about her leaving. A major stir over this grew into a spiritual battle that took on deadly symptoms.

What I will share here is just part of her and our battle concerning her decision and struggle to leave this controlling and abusive fellowship. A more detailed account of her escape is covered in the case entitled *Let my people go!* on page 183.

At the peak of the incident, I received a phone call from the charismatic pastor while I was in a discussion with another member of our fellowship. I answered the phone to let whoever was calling know that I would return their call later in the day.

The pastor introduced himself and immediately wanted to talk to me about the situation. I informed him that I was unable to talk at this time and took his number to call him back later. He seemed putout about not being able to discuss what was on his mind immediately.

Within a minute after the phone call, a sudden oppression swept over me with physical symptoms of weakness and shakiness, cold sweat and inability to focus. I had to cut short my meeting and lie down to fight off a spirit of sorcery coupled with a human spirit carrying out a murderous attack on me—the Holy Spirit revealed that this attack was because I said no to this pastor's demand for an immediate discussion at his convenience.

It took at least a half-hour in prayer and resting in a Holy Spirit-led fight to ward off this evil spiritual attack. It was later, after the next murderous attack on my person that I realized that the pastor's obsessive, hysterical wife had become embroiled in the belief that I was a cult leader ensnaring one of their sheep. It was she that put her husband up to make the call. Later, this assessment was confirmed by the comments of others whom the pastor and his wife enlisted to harass our new fellowship member as she began to be adamant in breaking off her ties to this so-called spirit filled charismatic fellowship.

God was faithful in warning me about the next attack from the pastor's wife. That warning came in the form of a bizarre dream I had about a week later. In this short but vivid dream, I was lying down with my mouth open and this woman stood over me pointing down my throat with her right index finger. I knew in the dream it was the pastor's wife. Then I immediately woke up puzzled.

A day later, I was near the end of a 4-mile run when suddenly I could not catch my breath. A sudden constriction at the top of my lungs caused me to stop and bend over resting my hands upon my knees while I gasped for air. I have never had an asthmatic attack in the past, (although I have had allergy flare ups). This constriction was strange and unrelenting and definitely not like an allergic reaction.

I was already breathing hard from just running up the hill portion of my work out, and the lack of oxygen became acute. In about twenty seconds of my gasping for air, I could feel myself begin to hyperventilate because my breathing was so rapid and shallow.

At this point, I began to pray under my breath and ask the Lord for help. Then I remembered the strange dream I had just had early in the morning the day before. The Holy Spirit called the dream to my remembrance to guide me in fighting off the person behind this attack. (It is vital to receive a word of knowledge as to who is doing the channeling for the demonic and whose human spirit is in the mix.)

Then in my thoughts, I commanded a spirit of murder and this woman's spirit to leave me in the name of Christ, since I was not able to speak. Within five seconds of that mental prayer in my spiritual battle, the symptoms stopped and I was able to breathe.

I walked for about ten yards while I continued to verbally command the demonic to leave and to say to this woman's out-of-body spirit, "The Lord rebuke you" I also prayed for the breaking of any prayers (curses) that were coming from this woman and others she had enlisted to pray for my demise. By then all the symptoms disappeared and I continued with my run.

About two months later, I had to stand in line at the post office next to another Christian woman who knew me and who was also upset with me over this situation. This encounter contained a brief mutual greeting while waiting in line (her greeting seemed friendly enough— showing no hostility or anger). However, within five minutes symptoms of nausea swept over me, a severe headache hit me, and I felt weakness in my legs and shortness of breath. During the ten-minute trip back home these symptoms persisted.

I knew this was a spiritual attack from this woman and when I arrived at home I laid down and began to pray, rest and fight this woman's out of-body-spirit off me along with the demons that were cohabitating within her spirit and heart.

These kinds of spiritual attacks from this group of charismatic Christians, (what we now term as Christian witchcraft) were very frequent for about a year but have slowed down in frequency and intensity. The Lord has been faithful in training us, strengthening us, and granting us gifts of the Holy Spirit to allow us to discern who is praying against us, opposing our message and projecting their personal spirit upon us to cause us harm. The next section explains the typical symptoms of human spirit attacks, backed by the demonic.

Actual principles of spiritual warfare, sanctification and other preparations and conditioning related to battling these types of attacks are covered in chapter eight, "Developing Our Powers of Discernment." Ω

Profile of Evil and the Carnally Wayward in Fellowship and Family

To begin, we must understand that many human spirits enlisted by the demonic to do evil are evil people by nature; however, many deceived Christians are carnally wayward and deceived into practicing human spirit sorcery. Demons are abundant with the evil as well as the carnal who have learned to practice their spirituality apart from the Holy Spirit.

A carnal or an evil person can have many demons residing within their being; however, the most dominate demonic force running the show behind the scene is an evil spirit. The following characteristics and symptoms of attack predominately come through the person who has turned to an evil agenda within their heart, and many who do so are satanically implanted weeds. The carnally driven can have many of the following characteristics and when they become angry or overly concerned towards others, those in their spiritual sights will have false prayers directed at them and often suffer some of these listed symptoms of attack.

Discerning and hearing rightly from the Holy Spirit concerning the source of attack, whether it is from a carnally deceived person or an evil weed is crucial. There is hope for the deceived carnal person; however, the evil requires great care in prayer and avoidance and greater caution in any open confrontation.

Before we list the profile characteristics and the symptoms of attack, the following excerpt from *Soul and Spirit* by Jessie Penn-Lewis will help illuminate the seriousness of this power now gaining great strength in Christianity through these last hundred plus years. Jessie describes how she learned of this evil and wicked power and how it came to her understanding:

"That same development of *psychic* power is taking place knowingly and *unknowingly*, all round us, bringing into action forces which are at the invisible powers of evil…

How this ignorant bringing into action of psychic force can affect spiritual believers has come to me in a recent letter. The writer says, 'I have just come through a terrible onslaught of the enemy. Hemorrhage, heart affection, panting and exhaustion. My whole body in a state of collapse. It suddenly burst upon me while at prayer to pray against all psychic power exercised upon me by (psychic) 'prayer'. By faith in the power of the Blood of Christ, I cut myself off from it, and the result was remarkable. Instantly my breathing became normal, the hemorrhage stopped, exhaustion vanished, all pain fled, and life came back to my body. I have been refreshed and invigorated ever since. God let me know in confirmation of this deliverance, that <u>my condition was the effect of a group of deceived souls who are in opposition to me 'praying' about me! God has used me to the deliverance of two of them, but the rest are in an awful pit</u>.'" (Jessie Penn-Lewis, *Soul and Spirit* Fort Washington, PA: Christian Literature Crusade 1989, 58.)

Profiling with Discernment
Taking note of their fruit — not prejudging with outward appearances

Jesus instructs Christians not to judge others wrongly by their race, mistakes, mannerisms, gender, station in life and so forth; however, in learning to practice true discernment, we must learn to judge rightly. *"Do not judge by appearances, but judge with right judgment"* (John 7:24). In addition, the Apostle Paul writes in 1 Corinthians, *"For what have I to do with judging outsiders? Is it not those inside the church whom you are to judge?"* (5:12). Jesus taught that we would recognize trouble-making Christians and evil wolves by their fruit, and the Apostle Paul implores us in the book of Romans to take note of those who cause dissension and difficulties. (Matthew 7:15-20; Romans 16:17-20.)

The general profile of characteristics of an evil person [20] hosting an evil spirit is as follows:

Mean, spiteful, jealous, and revengeful: When an evil person becomes offended, their inner unresolved rage and hatred of life finds a point of contact and release. Like a smoldering volcano,

---

[20] A carnal and deceived believer who suffers from defilements to the spirit and impurities of heart can have many of the same characteristics and can facilitate the same attack symptoms, although they are usually not as severe as in an evil person.

they can spew hateful curses and project mean and torturous spiritual oppression upon their victims. They will not quit until their revenge is satisfied or until they befall judgment for their own wickedness. However, their victims may find periodic relief when their opponent is distracted or enough time and distance removes them focus, (an "out-of-sight, out-of-mind" situation). The discerning saint who becomes strong and walks in the full armor of God can successfully ward off the evil attacks; however, the Lord may hold that discerning saint in the conflict until the evil they are fighting is exposed and judged through prayer and spiritual warfare.

Deceiving—hard to discern: Servants of evil learn to disguise themselves with a veneer of decency and often appear as servants of righteousness. Good works, tithes, and offerings become a way of rising to popularity amongst the naïve and gullible. In round about ways, they get recognition and credit as they subtly portray themselves as helpful, generous and outwardly loving. This outer chameleon camouflage disappears when in a crisis or conflict, or when forced to do the right thing that is unpopular. Under these conditions and certain life's stresses, their hidden narcissistic and cowardly nature can be seen more readily, especially by the discerning saint.

Beguiling and full of pretense: Developing an outer charming and appealing personality is another powerfully deceptive trait. Deliberate manipulation is accomplished through flattery and gushing compliments, all to gain a relationship advantage to control and manage others. This type of person learns to use subtlety or tidbits of knowledge, half-truths or lies to undermine their opponent in the eyes of others. Gossip, slander, and meddling are often a part of their profile. They learn to captivate followers who have difficulty in thinking logically and form informal fellowship or workplace cliques that can be used for their own agenda. They often present themselves as victims to others when challenged or confronted for their sly and underhanded ways. Another powerful tool is to lie if necessary. They learn to lie effectively by rewriting history according to their slant and force themselves to believe their own twisting of facts and truth. They become beguiling and persuasive.

Defiling through a cloak of decency: Another characteristic of an evil implant is that they develop an outer pristine demeanor that fools most people, including Christians. Like the darnel weed, their appearance is almost identical to wheat until full maturity. They learn the right mannerisms and enjoy the ability in learning to say the right thing at the right time; however, this whole outer cloak of decency conceals an evil heart and defiled spirit that seeps out and infects others. Others in their presence often are bombarded with evil thoughts. Unclean spirits residing with the resident evil spirit send out an aura of perversion. These self-righteous actors need others to slip up, act out sinfully, and in general become overwhelmed by sin. Unclean vibes emanating from an evil implant's defiling spirit magnify defilements in their victims. Taking ownership of one's own defilements within the heart and spirit is vital in discerning who may be heightening perverted or sinful urges.

Spiritually powerful: Disguised bitter jealousy and selfish ambition within the heart become the root issues allowing this type of person's spirit to become involved in out-of-body spirit attacks on others. If they do not like a person or lose an argument with an opponent, or if another person is blessed with talent or wealth and they are not, an evil or carnal Christian will direct their spirit force at the object of their jealousy or angst. People in their proximity often experience their health, finances, and relationships attacked for no apparent reason. Discerning if the source is one of the devil's implants or a carnal believer (who still has faith) can be very hard. In our research concerning the poisonous effects of the darnel weed we discovered many of the same symptoms from ingesting the darnel weed corresponded to symptoms of an attack by a carnal Christian praying wrongly as well as that of an evil person in an out-of-body attack.

Enlist others: Like the New Testament Jezebel operating as a satanic weed, evil implants seduce others to do evil and enlist others to undermine their opponent—often the opponent will be a true saint or a true leader. They have an uncanny ability to create informal groups and cliques in fellowships or in their extended family relations. Carnal Christians vulnerable to flattery become like lap dogs seeking the evil weed's approval and will defend and attack others who threaten the evil's veracity and credibility.

Indecisive, fearful and often hysterical: When an evil person or insecure carnal Christian is exposed, then usually hysteria and panic become major characteristics. Fear and hysteria become defense mechanisms. The adage – *fight or flight* also includes *freeze*, which is how this type of person reacts to serious confrontation with truth and the facts. Exposure of who they truly are induces terror, where emotions can run a wide spectrum—from numbness and expressionless response, to rage and combativeness to hysteria and withdrawal.

Most are Wounded and Weak Men and Women
Wounded adult children of dysfunctional families and abusive parents—who are in denial

Through our many years of ministry and counseling, we discovered that most of those who become vessels for evil used by the devil in human spirit attacks come from abusive, shame-based and perform-to-be-loved families. Some were survivors of what we term *evil cult family systems*, where hidden evil practices open large demonic doorways into the soul and spirit—causing severe fracking of the psyche and harm to the person's spirit. (Dealing with an evil cult family system will be covered in chapter eight, "Developing our Powers of Discernment," in the section entitled Cult Family Systems Hidden in the Church page 294).

Family pedophilia and abuse is far more of an epidemic than most want to admit. Through our years of study and training in pastoral counseling, literature, studies and through our own experiences, we can testify to the fact that our American culture fosters hidden abuse in all social levels. The following is an excellent summation of this by-product of hidden family abuse.

> The statistics on physical child abuse are alarming. It is estimated hundreds of thousands of children are physically abused each year by a parent or close relative. Thousands actually die as a result of the abuse. For those who survive, the emotional trauma remains long after the external bruises have healed. Communities and the

courts recognize that these emotional "hidden bruises" can be treated. Early recognition and treatment is important to minimize the long term effect of physical abuse. Whenever a child says he or she has been abused, it must be taken seriously and immediately evaluated.

Children who have been abused may display:
- a poor self-image
- sexual acting out
- inability to trust or love others
- aggressive, disruptive and sometimes illegal behavior
- anger and rage
- self-destructive or self-abusive behavior, suicidal thoughts
- passive, withdrawn or clingy behavior
- fear of entering into new relationships or activities
- anxiety and fears
- school problems or failure
- feelings of sadness or other symptoms of depression
- flashbacks, nightmares
- drug and alcohol abuse
- sleep problems

Often the severe emotional damage to abused children does not surface until adolescence or even later, when many abused children become abusing parents. An adult who was abused as a child often has trouble establishing lasting and stable personal relationships. These men and women may have trouble with physical closeness, touching, intimacy, and trust as adults. They are also at higher risk for anxiety, depression, substance abuse, medical illness, and problems at school or work. (American Academy of Child & Adolescent Psychiatry website, "Child Abuse: The Hidden Bruises," www.aacap.org)

Jesus dispensed some very difficult teachings and warnings. The following two describe the consequences for abusing children and the imperative command for adult Christians to break free from the spellbinding power of their family of origin and other significant relationships.

"Whoever causes one of these little ones who believe in me to sin, it would be better for him to have a great millstone fastened around his neck and to be drowned in the depth of the sea. Woe to the world for temptations to sin! For it is necessary that temptations come, but woe to the one by whom the temptation comes! And if your hand or your foot causes you to sin, cut it off and throw it away. It is better for you to enter life crippled or lame than with two hands or two feet to be thrown into the eternal fire. And if your eye causes you to sin, tear it out and throw it away. It is better for you to enter life with one eye than with two eyes to be thrown into the hell of fire" (Matthew 18:6-9).

Many who were abused become abusers themselves, while a great number of survivors do not continue the cycle, but still live in denial of their unresolved issues, wounds, and demonic strongholds. What is more difficult for the survivors, who become Christians, (as they resist doing evil themselves) is the struggle to break the unhealthy bonds with their abusive family system. These spiritual, emotional and psychological unhealthy attachments hinder their relationship with Christ, as they still live under the spell of their abusive or dysfunctional family of origin.

In the Gospel of Luke, Christ is firm about actually hating the carnal relationship life within family. Seemingly healthy families develop a love towards each other that is much stronger than our love for God, and this must be renounced and dealt with, lovingly but firmly, as a disciple of Christ. Christ is speaking of strong hatred, strong enough to discern and break the dysfunctional and selfish bonding that is innately characteristic of our carnal nature in significant relationships. (See Luke 14:25-33)

Symptoms from a Demon Boosted Human Spirit Attack

The following list of attack symptoms will help the discerning saint identify what is happening to them and discern the source of attack.

This is the typical sequence of emotional, spiritual, and physical symptoms of those under attack by an evil person or carnally wayward and deceived Christian practicing human spirit sorcery. These attacks can be murderous in nature. The subconscious inner hatred of these people can sometimes rise to the level of a conscious desire to murder their opponent.

Discouragement: The strong Christian will often lose confidence concerning their call and the promises of God. Christians under attack can also experience a severe shaking of their courage. Weaker Christians doubt their own salvation and feel overwhelmed by the walk of faith. Non-believers become more compulsive feeling nervous and insecure. Elijah experienced similar symptoms when Jezebel spiritually attacked him when Jezebel's courier gave Elijah her message. *"Then Jezebel sent a messenger to Elijah, saying, 'So may the gods do to me and more also, if I do not make your life as the life of one of them by this time tomorrow' Then he was afraid, and he arose and ran for his life..."* (Kings 19:2-3).

Spiritual heaviness and lethargy: Unexplainable heaviness. Lethargic or passivity towards prayer, the Word, or ministry with an inability to exercise basic spiritual authority in spiritual warfare. Feelings of revulsion, unexplained anxiety, or stress when in the presence of a defiling, evil, or unclean carnal believer.

Powerful negative emotions: Irritable and susceptible to emotional mood swings. Drugged feelings and lack of motivation to perform basic functions and activities. Frustration within relationships that can incite anger, arguments, or acting out sinfulness, even leading to domestic violence. Often impurities of heart and unresolved damaged emotions are incited in the presence of an evil or a defiling person.

Physical pain or illness: Spiritual oppression from a human spirit attack can cause nerve tension; the immune system becomes worn down because of spiritual and emotional stress.

Colds, flu, virus, and serious illnesses are symptomatic of a human spirit attack boosted by the demonic, even death can occur.

Frustrating circumstances and unexplainable accidents: This is where the more powerful demons or principalities may become enlisted to actually attack the victims. The spiritual oppression and out-of-body human-spirit attack brings on headaches, aching muscles, a tight pressure on and around the head. Often feelings of having a heart attack with chest pains and/or heart palpitations occurs accompanied with high blood pressure. The potency of the spiritual attacks can be powerful, causing immediate nausea, weakness, headaches, dizziness, malignant hypertension, extreme muscle spasms, and weird accidents or mishaps. In some cases severe physical injuries or death can occur.

The non-believer or weak Christian has the same oppressive symptoms but becomes angry, frustrated, and then deeply depressed, and through a prolonged attack can easily become clinically depressed. These symptoms often indicate that the victim needs deep healing of latent defilements within himself or herself.

Confusion: Feelings of disorientation, indecisiveness, loss of sense of direction if driving. Relationships become strained. Conversations can become scrambled with misunderstandings, mixed feelings, and disorder. Lies, twisting of the truth and misperceptions run rampant within relationships and the source (person) causing these problems is almost impossible to detect.

Hopelessness: A loss of vision for life, along with hopelessness and feelings of despondency including feelings of desperation and thoughts of suicide.

Withdrawal: A falling away from life, relationships and God. Irresponsible behavior and broken commitments.

Loss of will for living: For the strong Christian, strong desires to escape, quit or even ask God to take them home to heaven; for the weak-faith Christians or nonbelievers, suicidal feelings, sometimes to the point of attempted suicide.

Chapter eight covers additional aspects of resisting a demon-boosted human-spirit attack in the section entitled, Building up Immunity in the Inner Person.

Wounded and Deceived Christians Walking in Dark-Light
If the light in you is darkness, how great is that darkness—a warning to the arrogant Christian

Many Christians believe they are enlightened and walking on the cutting edge of what God is doing. They jump from movement to movement, from one new quick fix self-help book to the next—yet the work of the cross in the believer's life is relegated to obscurity. The foundation of the initial born-again experience may be genuine; however, what is built upon that foundation for many is wood, hay, and straw.

Almost in frantic search, Christians are looking for the next powerful book by their favorite author, the next movement to have the power of God downloaded, blasting their soul and spirit into Christian bliss. Many will one day see their work and effort was in vain, because they learned to rely on themselves to change rather than trusting God and his discipline to transform their character.

The Apostle Paul, in the following passage from 1 Corinthians, was correcting the obsession that was developing—an obsession of finding the magic leader to follow:

"But I, brothers, could not address you as spiritual people, but as people of the flesh, as infants in Christ. I fed you with milk, not solid food, for you were not ready for it. And even now you are not yet ready, for you are still of the flesh. For while there is jealousy and strife among you, are you not of the flesh and behaving only in a human way? For when one says, 'I follow Paul,' and another, 'I follow Apollos,' are you not being merely human?

What then is Apollos? What is Paul? Servants through whom you believed, as the Lord assigned to each. I planted, Apollos watered, but God gave the growth. <u>So neither he who plants nor he who waters is anything, but only God who gives the growth</u>. He who plants and he who waters are one, and each will receive his wages according to his labor. <u>For we are God's fellow workers. You are God's field, God's building</u>" (1 Corinthians 3:1-9).

Knowledge about God, Scripture, and the many angles of interpretation abounds, yet few truly know Christ and are known by him. Many are educating themselves beyond trusting faith, right into the arms of Satan's end-of-the-age trap: Christian carnal pride and puffed-up knowledge of false light.

"We know that 'all of us possess knowledge.' 'Knowledge' puffs up, but love builds up. If any one imagines that he knows something, he does not yet know as he ought to know. But if one loves God, one is known by him" (1 Corinthians 8:1-3).

Wounded and weak Christians clamor for more knowledge and more power, yet in the futility of their minds, they are still alienated from the life and love God. The sincere child of God must learn to walk in true light, abiding in Christ working with God, not working for him.

The practice of pretending the sin nature away, along with the performing works of the flesh, and redirecting the energy of the flesh to serve God is light that is truly dark. We must return to walking in the true light of Christ and his words, allowing any darkness to be revealed. As the Apostle John wrote:

"This is the message we have heard from him and proclaim to you, that God is light, and in him is no darkness at all. If we say we have fellowship with him while we walk in darkness, we lie and do not practice the truth. But if we walk in the light, as he is in the light, we have fellowship with one another, and the blood of Jesus his Son cleanses us from all sin. If we say we have no sin, we deceive ourselves, and the truth is not in us. If we confess our sins, he is faithful and just to forgive us our sins and to cleanse us from all unrighteousness. If we say we have not sinned, we make him a liar, and his word is not in us" (1 John 1:5-10).

Millions of Christians are convinced that they do not walk in sin or are driven by carnal desires. Self-deception by false doctrine and twisting the Word of God has led many away from a sincere devotion to Christ—and it has taken those same millions into gross darkness.

Most do not receive instruction on how to be careful that the light they have within is not darkness. Their heart's theological eye is fixed upon man's teachings and leaves the person of Christ out in the cold. Few in their wounded and weak state learn to walk in the light as he is in the light, that no darkness remains within. *"Your eye is the lamp of your body. When your eye is healthy, your whole body is full of light, but when it is bad, your body is full of darkness. Therefore be careful lest the light in you be darkness. If then your whole body is full of light, having no part dark, it will be wholly bright, as when a lamp with its rays gives you light"* (Luke 11:34-36).

Dark light is the spawning bed for false gifts and carnal works that allow wounded and insecure believers to have their faith hijacked and their personal spirit become harnessed by the counterfeit.

False Gifts
Words of knowledge and prophesies empowered by a counterfeiting spirit of divination

Christians today frequently hear that they need to have the baptism of the Holy Spirit as exhibited by speaking an unknown tongue, or sometimes, other supernatural manifestations. The argument is that this experience will bring fullness of life in Christ and power for ministry. Unfortunately, this approach bypasses the training and discipline of the Lord—the work of dying to self as a believer, and creates false confidence in an experience that does not affect character change (rather these experiences often create a superficial charismatic personality). In addition, believers become highly vulnerable to counterfeiting spirits and empty manifestations.

Remember, Christ pointed out that not everyone who walks in the gifts and casts out demons know him. Bypassing the work of the cross within the believer's life that crucifies passions and desires of the flesh, and then encouraging believers to think they have the true power of God is a very destructive heresy.

Christ's training program includes suffering to prepare his servants to walk in the power of the Holy Spirit and that same suffering with discipline is still required. However, modern Christians are led to believe that the baptism of the Holy Spirit is a way to jump into ministry and the full power of God. However, avoiding the suffering and discipline of Christ allows counterfeit demons and evil spirits to enter into the lives of these deceived Christians.

I urge every reader to seek the Lord in all honesty. Ask yourself if you have truly tested the spirits and are sure that your spiritual gifting is of God, or a facsimile carefully designed by false doctrine and false manifestations has opened your spirit to the counterfeit.

A Portion of My Personal Testimony
A new believer thrown to the wolves, nearly devoured—rescued by truth and the grace of God

When God called me to salvation in 1973, I was fulfilling a fast-track career in the Marines. He took hold of my heart so strongly, calling me to leave the military, and he paved the way for me to gain an unheard-of early discharge so that I could prepare for fulltime ministry by attending Bible college. It was very clear to me that God had his hand on me and was working in my life. However, the things I learned from the supposed Christians and leaders made me question my relationship with God. Mainly, the pressure to become baptized in the Holy Spirit evidenced by speaking in tongues proved very troublesome for me.

I had a strong inclination to avoid what I believed at that time to be error, even though I did not have a solid understanding as to why the Holy Spirit was giving such a strong check in my spirit. It was years later that an in-depth understanding from sound doctrine in Scripture proved that I was correct in my adamant objection. However, I did not escape without a detour into this vexing movement, which nearly made shipwreck my faith.

Ministry Case: *Conjuring counterfeit gifts*

December 18, 1974 was my last day in the Marines, and that evening I was on a flight from San Diego to Seattle with plans to begin my biblical studies at Seattle Pacific College. Classes began January 5th—I was starting the new year with a new life in Christ, working to complete four years of undergraduate work and then go on to seminary.

My first quarter in college proved to be somewhat challenging with the shift from military life to college/civilian life. One evening while studying, I asked the Lord how in the world I would be able complete seven years of study under my current circumstances. It was at that moment of desperation that I distinctly heard Christ say to me, "You are not going to go through man's school; you will go through my school!"

The next two years turned into a roller-coaster ride where difficulties caused old feelings and desires to surface. Unfortunately, the false doctrine that states that once you are born again, the sin nature, with its carnal influences is gone for good made my condition worse. The confusing and condemning thought was that having temptations and evil thoughts meant that I might not be born again.

What was my condition? I could not get a straight answer from mainstream evangelical Christianity. I held down a part-time job at a local Christian bookstore while attending Bible college. In addition, I was appointed the assistant pastor in my hometown Free Methodist church with $50.00 per month in compensation. With all this supposed network of support and education, I was still in a dark place with virtually no resources or mentoring to help me understand how to overcome the old nature or become cleansed of past defilements and a wounded spirit.

Reading the older authors such as Andrew Murray, Charles Finney, Watchman Nee and Corrie ten Boom proved to be encouraging and insightful. I received more mentoring from these people of faith from past generations than from the leadership in my denomination or my professors at Bible college. My job at the bookstore allowed me to review and purchase books at a discount and my library grew quickly as I studied intensely, looking for answers.

Within two years, the Free Methodist denomination and I parted company and I was led to strike out on my own and hold a weekly college-age Bible study in my home while I searched for another denomination to become associated with.

Pentecostal friends from high school kept encouraging me to become baptized in the Holy Spirit—in their view this was all that I needed to overcome any issues of faith and to have power to ward off temptations and evil spirits. I finally decided to try this.

The Olsons were the hot local ministry that walked in the supposed anointing. In 1977, their ministry was on the cutting edge of the expanding charismatic movement, where authors like Dennis Bennett led the way in writing about his experience with the gifts of the Spirit in the bestselling book

Nine O'Clock in the Morning. His ministry inspired many Episcopalians and Catholics to become baptized in the Holy Spirit and speak in tongues as well as pursue other gifts of the Spirit.

In spite of doubts and checks in my spirit, I attended one of the Olsons' meetings and succumbed to their invitation to stay after the meeting for ministry and to receive the gifts of the Holy Spirit.

As I look back years later, it was clear how contrived the whole encounter and experience had been. Norm Olson would lay hands on each person and help them move their mouth to "prime the pump" so to speak. This got a candidate to learn how to start speaking in tongues and help each learn how to release themselves to interpret their own unintelligible prayer language, and to prophesy, receive words of knowledge, and discern spirits.

Not long after this encounter, more troubles came, along with more temptations, even more failures such as not finding work. It was if all hell broke loose. In frustration, I focused my energy on obtaining a Bachelors of Science in Business Administration and picking up my old military profession in computers and telecommunications. I was not so much mad at God as I was disgusted with denominational Christianity; however, I did not realize this for some time, thus in my heart God took the brunt for my frustration.

I spent ten years in anger with Christianity and running from the call of God until everything broke down. Now God had my attention again—and I finally found resources to help, as well as godly counsel to set me in the right direction in dealing with my old sin nature, past childhood defilements, and severe wounds to my spirit.

The Lord miraculously turned things around after I received sufficient mentoring, healing, and training, and then I became obedient to the call of fulltime ministry again.

June of 1988 was the start of the ministry God had intended for me all along. I began as the counseling pastor in a Foursquare fellowship in my home town. My counseling schedule skyrocketed by word of mouth and soon a stream of struggling, wounded, and hurting Christians were adding their names to the waiting list.

Yet there was one more thing that the Lord had to set right. About three months into this new ministry, the Lord confronted me about the so-called gifts that I had received years ago in the Olsons' meeting.

Every morning before going to the church to counsel, I would pray from thirty minutes to an hour. I started by speaking in tongues, diligently following Larry Lea's handbook that our senior pastor and many other charismatic pastors widely recommended. Casey Treat (a well-known pastor and leader in the Pacific Northwest) endorsed Larry Lea's method of praying. Casey helped sponsor one of Larry Lea's Prayer Rallies that I attended in the Puget Sound region. Lea's ministry centered on taking down the powers of darkness in regional areas of our nation.

One morning as I was speaking in my prayer language, the voice of the Holy Spirit interrupted me by clearly saying, "Chuck, will you stop that gibberish?"

I said, 'Lord is that you?"

And I heard, "Yes, and you have been speaking in a false tongue to get a high from your own spirit and avoiding the painful issues in your heart that I am trying to get you to deal with."

Somewhat stunned, but knowing the voice of the Lord, I listened for more instruction. The Lord led me to renounce the false gifting I had received at the Olsons' meeting years before and to seek cleansing and healing from the counterfeiting spirits that latched onto me back then in a satanic attack to destroy my faith and cause trouble and confusion.

I did as the Lord commanded and within two weeks, the true gifts of the Holy Spirit began to manifest in the counseling ministry. Here is a Scripture to help clarify this position and the turning away from false gifting is:

"Brothers, do not be children in your thinking. Be infants in evil, but in your thinking be mature. In the Law it is written, 'By people of strange tongues and by the lips of foreigners will I speak to this people, and even then they will not listen to me, says the Lord.' <u>Thus tongues are a sign not for believers but for unbelievers</u>, while <u>prophecy is a sign not for unbelievers but for believers</u>. If, therefore, the whole church comes together and all speak in tongues, and outsiders or unbelievers enter, will they not say that you are out of your minds? <u>But if all prophesy, and an unbeliever or outsider enters, he is convicted by all, he is called to account by all, the secrets of his heart are disclosed</u>, and so, falling on his face, he will worship God and declare that God is really among you" (1 Corinthians 14:20-25).

The true gift of prophecy was bestowed upon the counseling ministry, and the Holy Spirit was able to reveal to me the counselee's past forgotten wounds, defilements, and secrets of the heart in God's timing. The counseling ministry was also structured to provide sound doctrine and support to help many of these wounded Christians in their journey. They began to work on these roots of bitterness, unbelief, and bad attitudes—breaking cycles of generational curses and strongholds.

This is the work of the Holy Spirit which is unfortunately often ignored or subverted by quick-fix magic formulas and false-spirit manifestations. *"Since we have these promises, beloved, let us cleanse ourselves from every defilement of body and spirit, bringing holiness to completion in the fear of God"* (2 Corinthians 7:1). Ω

By ignoring sound doctrine and the Lord's discipline that facilitates true sanctification, we run a great risk of falling into the hands of the living God. Many are exempt for lack of knowledge; however, those Christians who know the right thing to do and do not do it—that is the same as sinning deliberately: *"Whoever knows the right thing to do and fails to do it, for him it is sin"* (James 4:17). To explain further about deliberate disobedience the author of Hebrews warns:

"If we go on sinning deliberately after receiving the knowledge of the truth, <u>there no longer remains a sacrifice for sins, but a fearful expectation of judgment, and a fury of fire that will consume the adversaries</u>. Anyone who has set aside the law of Moses dies without mercy on the evidence of two or three witnesses. How much <u>worse punishment, do you think, will be deserved by the one who has spurned the Son of God, and has profaned the blood of the covenant by which he was sanctified, and has outraged the Spirit of grace</u>? For we know him who said, 'Vengeance is mine; I will repay.' And again, 'The Lord will judge his people.' <u>It is a fearful thing to fall into the hands of the living God</u>" (Hebrews 10:26-31).

We must learn how to cooperate with Christ to work out our own salvation and grow up. The discipline of the Lord cleanses, heals, and transforms our character. Unfortunately, most learn to create a pseudo-Christ-like personality that overshadows the old nature with its deceitful lusts.

Sound doctrinal resources are desperately needed to equip the sincere saint to grow in maturity, walk in holiness, and prepare for the coming troubles. Great darkness has engulfed the body of Christ and few see that the coming evil days are right around the corner.

Religious Rote and Spiritual Ritualism
Magic incantations, superstitious myths, and carnal gimmicks replacing sound doctrine

Worship services in most churches in America consist of hymns sung by rote or entertaining songs sung in the power of one's personal spirit. Back in the late eighties, I witnessed worship in that Foursquare church devolve from genuine praise unto the Lord to carnal manipulation of the human spirit. As the counseling pastor, I had little input in that area of fellowship.

Truth left this fellowship as the senior pastor became charmed with false revival and false worship, lusting after church growth. He decided to replace the members of the congregation who led worship and played their instruments with professional worship leaders and singers.

The worship had not been perfect but it had been genuine, and often the congregation spontaneously broke into true worship. Sometimes deep weeping and repentance would come upon some. It seemed that those leading praise and worship knew exactly the chorus to sing to bring the congregation to a place where the Holy Spirit had freedom to minister to the hurting, release joy to others, and bring comfort and for many a sense of belonging to our Heavenly Father.

Then the senior pastor announced that a team of worship leaders were going take over that portion of Sunday fellowship—that was a shock for many. The idea was to move the congregation towards the current fad where praise and worship was now the appropriate approach to lift the congregation into spiritual blessings.

Each Sunday this team would work up the congregation into a state of "blessing" through selected choruses that were now becoming popular in the larger, fast-growing fellowships.

These select choruses were repeated until the congregation "entered into the presence of God," and it worked—as most in the congregation responded to the worship team's urgings and repetitive mesmerizing songs.

Music is a powerful way of touching the soul and manipulating our emotions. Movie sound-tracks can use background music to prepare the audience for a scene that will be dramatic, violent, humorous, etc. Movies, music videos, and the many genres of the music industry cater to the various entertainment preferences of our culture.

Now, music has become a way of entertaining the worshippers within many congregations where chorus selections are geared to stir and guide the congregation into a common mood. Worship music in a churchianity[21] congregation has digressed into an emotional, soulish[22] genre, where music is sung and performed to change the mood of the congregants, rather than to come before God and worship him. This soulish type of worship is a subtle shift of focus, where the soul is aroused to delve inwardly to influence and awaken the personal spirit of the worshipper. This is an angel of light work, just as the Apostle Paul describe taking place within the very charismatic Corinthian church. In this worked-up soulish state the human spirit becomes aroused by this carnal activity, making an avenue for a demonic counterfeit spirit to boost the pleasurable aspects of activating one's personal spirit.

---

[21] The term churchianity, in this context encompasses the emerging church movement, the purpose-driven church movement, and other mega-church, fast growth fellowships, as well as denominations and independent fellowships that pursue converts to their church organization instead of bringing them to Christ with the intent to grow each convert into a solid servant of Christ.

[22] Soulish is another term that describes a carnal Christian. Soulish Christians function in the soul realm, where emotions and selfish motives drive their worship, ministry, and good works. In this context of worship, music stirs the emotions or the soul and in-turn stirs the person's personal spirit. Mixing the soul and spirit to enter into a supposed "blessing," but usually void of the Holy Spirit.

Participants are led to believe they are entering into the presence of the Holy Spirit by engaging this form of soulish worship genre. Unfortunately, the spirit they enter into is not the Holy Spirit but a strange harmonious synergy of human spirits channeling a conjured up demonic force. These deceived believers fall under the spell of the worship team's mesmerizing showmanship, which uses spiritualism and conjuring techniques similar to superstitious practices in pagan cultures.

The following is an account from a discerning sister who finally saw worship in this fellowship degenerate to a narcissistic form of entertainment and spiritualism that numbed unwanted feelings and troubling thoughts.

Ministry Case: *Hired worship leaders*

One thing I always loved in the church was the music, [she says] I loved to sing praises to the Lord and enter into full-hearted worship. God was beginning to reveal to me the things that were ungodly in the church I attended. One morning in church, the praise and worship began. With eyes closed, I could always shut everything else out and sing directly to the Lord. This particular morning I found I could not enter in at all. No matter how much I closed my eyes or prayed to the Lord, I could not enter into worship. The Lord was opening my eyes for the first time. I heard the music differently. It sounded harsh and deliberately contrived. I looked around at the people. Everyone seemed to be acting, trying to conjure up a devout attitude of worship. At first I thought it was me, so I tried harder to enter in. I could not—it was phony. It was so upsetting to me, that in my spirit, I was weeping. Weeping for the people and yes, for myself not being able to enter in.

At last, I asked God to let me enter in with the rest of the fellowship. He did! Immediately, all that I was discerning lifted. I could praise and worship along with everyone else. However, I knew it was wrong! I had asked God for something to make me feel better, not what was on his heart. Immediately, I repented and asked God to forgive me for being selfish and wanting a buzz from the worship service. I said, "God, your will not mine." I had prayed for discernment many times and now God was granting that request. In my selfishness to feel good, I did not realize the gift of discernment comes with a high cost to the self-life. God in his grace and mercy answered my prayer, took away the false worship, and allowed me to see spiritually what he saw in this congregation concerning praise and worship. Ω

This fellowship, like so many in the end, reaped the whirlwind that resulted in the senior pastor falling from grace. About two years after he instituted these practices although he was warned not to, he succumbed to the issues hidden in his own heart. All these antics and entertaining gimmicks employed in worship and so-called manifestations were the work of a counterfeit spirit to soothe and suppress the quickening of the Holy Spirit and his conviction and warnings.

In 1992, this pastor stood in front of his Foursquare congregation, just like Jimmy Swaggart had done in the mid-eighties, and admitted to having a sexual encounter with a prostitute while attending a denominational conference in California.

Nevertheless, the hired singers and worship team was only one of the issues that destroyed this fellowship which was eventually completely disbanded.

Additional major reasons were that the pastor lacked Christ-like character to stay the course, and to preach and teach sound doctrine that would expose hidden issues amongst the brethren. His leadership rejected the work of the cross and the discipline of the Lord in the believer's life. He allowed a constant stream of false prophets and false evangelists to come and teach short-cut doctrines that covered painful symptoms of carnal living and squelched the Holy Spirit's war against the desires of the flesh (see Galatians 5:13-26). These were the primary reasons for this fellowship to come to its demise.

Many pastors have been taught to lead their congregation into myths, repetitive chanting, and worldly spiritualism that uses mesmerizing rhythms and lyrics as a substitute for the painful hard work of sanctification, which brings death to the passions and desires of the flesh.

These conjured-up false manifestations do not help the sincere Christian draw near to God—rather, they activate the human spirit individually and collectively. In this carnal spiritual state, the human spirit easily becomes a gateway for counterfeit demonic spirits that can now work with the personal spirit to create an inner hypnotic effect—like spiritual Prozac. Being in this state numbs painful symptoms that God allows to get our attention concerning defilements of spirit and impurities of heart.

Spiritual Sensuality, Defiling Passion and Sexual Perversion

When Sodom passed the point of no return, when the only righteous people left were Lot and his family, the defiling passion and sexual perversion in that city had become very vexing. The Apostle Peter wrote about Lot's plight as being, *"greatly distressed by the sensual conduct of the wicked (for as that righteous man lived among them day after day, he was tormenting his righteous soul over their lawless deeds that he saw and heard); then the Lord knows how to rescue the godly from trials, and to keep the unrighteous under punishment until the day of judgment, and especially those who indulge in the lust of defiling passion and despise authority"* (2 Peter 2:7-10).

The culture in America cannot be looked upon in any other way than that of what Christ warned concerning his return—that society would become as vile as it was in the days of Lot.

Can we not see that the wickedness and rampant sexual perversion has passed the point of no return on God's judgment scales? Few Christians see this flash point as a significant sign that the end of the age is upon us—most are spell bound, like Lot hesitating to leave the defiling vexation in Sodom. When the angels came to lead Lot and his family to safety, the account in Scripture states: *"But he lingered. So the men seized him and his wife and his two daughters by the hand"*(see Genesis 19:1-29).

Millions upon millions have responded to the call of salvation over the last forty years. Few in comparison receive the whole counsel of God and learn to become truly sanctified and cleansed. We see that many Christians—from pastors, Catholic priests, and noted evangelists on down to those sitting in the pews—become embroiled in scandal after scandal as immoral failures corresponding to society's slide into wickedness and immorality ever increase.

The body of Christ has become inundated with bedeviled people who are told that they are born again and thus completely cleansed. This could not be further from the truth. Yes, for many there is repentance in their initial experience of being born again; however, the defilements of their soul and spirit are not thoroughly cleansed.

Christians coming out of this sodomite culture are vexed by defiling powers and are still tainted and haunted by the demonic as they live in the midst of depravity. This influx of defiled Christians has influenced doctrine and body life to carry perverse and strange practices, including spiritual sensuality in worship, fellowship and everyday living. Christians throughout congregations and fellowships learn to deny their defiled condition and exchange the presence and power of the Holy Spirit by activating the power of the human spirit.

In his second letter to the Christians at Corinth, the Apostle Paul exhorts them to deal with these latent defilements: *"Since we have these promises, beloved, let us cleanse ourselves from every defilement of body and spirit, bringing holiness to completion in the fear of God"* (2 Corinthians 7:1).

New worship fads keep pushing the limits as we see the addition of sensuous dancing and now flag waving at the front of the sanctuary. Here is the purpose of flags and banners in worship as described on the Waves of Worship Flag Ministry web-site:

> "In a worship service, Flags and Banners are used for God's people as a visual tool on which to focus. They can declare a time of battle in spiritual warfare, God's love, His grace, holiness and power. As the Spirit of God (the watchman) directs, the waving of Flags and Banners will open the "spiritual gates" of heaven allowing the Holy Spirit to flow freely among His people with healing, deliverance and encouragement. Flags and Banners are vital to the body of Christ. They make a statement – a statement of our worship, our praise, our warfare, and a statement that reflects our work with the Lord. They are a form of visual worship and they make a powerful statement to the non-believer. They are a silent witness in ministry but they speak volumes to anyone who looks at them."

This "flagging" is another carnal activity to entertain God's people during worship, alleviating the need for heart felt worship, brokenness, cleansing, prayer, and prophetic ministry to non-believers and outsiders. In reality, it draws attention to the activity and distracts from sincere devotion to Christ and ministry to each other and newcomers.

Each new gimmick increases carnal spiritualism and in the case of dancing, introduces another level of sensuality—in some instances the dancers become entertainers emanating a form of erotica or sensuousness, which becomes obvious to the discerning Christian.

Erotica has also crept into teaching on making marriage fun and exciting sexually. The Apostles Paul's writing that the marriage bed is to be held in dignity and honor is ignored in some of these teachings across Christianity. Christian women are instructed to act like a "vamp" or a "seductress" to keep their lustful husband in check. However, Scripture is explicit on keeping the marriage bed undefiled: *"Let marriage be held in honor among all, and let the marriage bed be undefiled, for God will judge the sexually immoral and adulterous"* (Hebrews 13:4)

Further, Paul instructs men on this matter in his letter to the Christians at Thessalonica: *"For this is the will of God, your sanctification: that you abstain from sexual immorality; that each one of you know how to control his own body,* [or how to take a wife for himself] *in holiness and honor, not in the passion of lust like the Gentiles who do not know God; that no one transgress and wrong his brother in this matter, because the Lord is an avenger in all these things"* (1 Thessalonians 4:3-6).

Ministry Case: *Narcissistic dancers and flaggers*

The World Prayer Center in Colorado Springs is supported by churches across the nation and locally by a mega-church of over 11,000 members. In 2004, I joined in on one of their "concerts of prayer," only to be horrified at what I saw. In 1989, a similar concert of prayer movement came to the Pacific Northwest with the intention of praying and beseeching God for revival and restoration of America. I preached in some of these concerts. I bowed out after it turned into just another church meeting full of entertainment. In this recent visit, some 15 years later, I saw how this carnal activity had evolved into an absolutely warped and nightmarish dance and chant ritual, not unlike voodoo gatherings that I have witnessed in researching the spiritual foundation for these sensuous activities now termed legitimate worship unto God. The comparisons were very similar, where dancing and chanting worked the participants up into a mental and emotional state of numbness.

One meeting had a band blasting away under a giant spinning globe. Young and old alike began to walk around the chairs, praying, which soon turned into speaking in tongues, yelling, and dancing. Mark, an associate in ministry, attended these meetings with me and both of us became disgusted. He commented that he had never seen anything so appalling and erotic, other than when he was unsaved and went to dance clubs to join in sensuous, slam-dancing mosh-pit revelry.

Those involved in these carnal escapades pray in their spirit with no understanding. Many have unclean issues in spirit and heart causing their so-called prayer language to spew out poisonous *human spirit prayer vibes* that do not align with God's will. This prayer center and other movements practicing carnality in prayer have an effect in promoting man's will and Satan's purposes, but not the will of God.

The World Prayer Center in Colorado Springs contained a number of sick, humanistic depictions of the Holy Spirit and Christ. One picture in the main hallway was a picture of a bald, muscular, bare-chested man kneeling behind a giant cup. There was liquid flowing down over his head and naked torso then on down into this cup, with the cup overflowing. As one's eyes followed up the liquid flow, one could see it was coming from a giant tipped vase. Two women on each side, clad in scanty robes with their breasts about 70 % exposed, held this vase. The caption for the picture refers to how the Holy Spirit fills our cup to overflowing.

This revolting depiction of the Holy Spirit, and other pictures and artwork lined the hallways of this prayer center. Instead of a place to meet a holy God in reverence and prayer, this mega-church program pushed carnality into humanism, similar to the way the Greeks and Romans worshipped their gods of human form.

The World Prayer Center is a ministry of New Life Church and Pastor Ted Haggard was in leadership at the time. We prayed that these vile practices be exposed and finally in 2006 the truth came out, stunning the Christian church worldwide. Haggard's moral fall that finally went public proved to be a major flash point of judgment upon the body of Christ's moral influence upon this nation.

About the same time another brother, Andrew Strom, who left the prophetic movement in disgust, started confronting these false teachings and empty manifestations. In one of his newsletters back in 2003, Strom gave the following account of how far this movement had gone pagan:

"The ON-STAGE DANCING throughout this conference was a good example [of paganism]. Now, I myself am a rock musician, but from the beginning these dance items had a rather 'wild' aspect to them that truly made me uncomfortable in my spirit. There was even one that came across like a sensual 'Harem' dance. Much of it really felt off—and almost anyone who sees the videos will tell you so. Even the worship had a very 'tribal' feel to it at times. And by Day Three they were doing dance items with just loud voodoo-style drums only—and leaping around in a frenzied circle making weird cries to the super-amplified beat. The feeling in the room was so oppressive and 'pagan' during this, that I could hardly even bear to stay in there. Then came one of the most shocking statements of the whole conference—from one of the main prophets. He got up and said that people may feel uncomfortable with such obviously 'pagan' type dancing, but that it was originally God's type of dancing and we were just now 'stealing back' what the pagans had stolen from God!"

"I have to admit, this was the last straw for me. What could be more blatant? What kind of 'spirits' do they think are being transmitted to people who open themselves up to that music? There is no discernment in this movement at all." (Andrew Strom November 2004 newsletter). Ω

The sensuousness and attention-drawing and distracting activities in worship continue to exceed previous milestones—as waving flags, dancing, making animalistic sounds such as barking and cackling, uncontrolled laughing, and drunken-like staggering are declared genuine forms of worship.

In the fellowship in which I served as the counseling pastor (where the senior pastor fell into sin with a prostitute), the pastor had invited one prophet and evangelist after another into the pulpit in an attempt to ignite a revival and grow his congregation into a mega-church.

Some of the teachings were outright error, and the congregation received very little sound doctrine that dealt with sin, the works of the flesh and working out one's own salvation in fear and trembling. The most popular evangelists were those that yielded slain-in-the-spirit power.

One guest speaker did receive a thumbs down by the pastor after he taught on how one could astrally project one's own spirit at will anywhere in the world. This false teacher used the Scripture reference in 1 Corinthians 5:3-5 as the foundation for his assertion. If Paul's personal spirit was out of body, as Scripture indicates, then it was in the power of the Holy Spirit according to God's will, not in his willful choice with demonic assistance.

These teachings, dating back in the late eighties and early nineties were not just coming to this four hundred-member Foursquare church, but were sweeping through other charismatic and Pentecostal fellowships worldwide. Now many of these errant teachings have taken root and become ingrained as standard doctrine and practices.

Back then, visitors coming to this fellowship would think it was growing in the love of God and in Christ-like character. However, I had the opportunity to work with the hurting and troubled, and to see the hidden issues revealed in counseling. Through this work, it became apparent to me that this body of believers suffered from a very sick condition. There were schisms, destructive relationships, backbiting, gossip, and infidelity, superficial kindness that hid bitterness and jealousy and carnal spiritualism (*carnal spiritualism* meaning that this fellowship chaotically spoke in unknown tongues and as the Apostle Paul warned the Corinthians that if an outsider walked in while they carried on in that manner), *"Will they not say that you are mad?"* (1 Corinthians 14:23 RSV).

My counseling schedule became almost overwhelming as Christians from the fellowship came, confessing and struggling with all manner of sins and carnal issues. By word of mouth a three-month waiting list was formed. Not only the hurting came for counsel but also the seemingly righteous that had perplexing problems and trials or were stuck in unhealthy relationships.

A small clique of women married to weak men formed a prayer group where they excessively and fervently practiced their prayer languages, the laying on of hands for the baptism of the Holy Spirit and prophecy. They also attempted to employ many of the far-out teachings brought to the congregation by the many guest speakers. The women wanted spiritual power to affect their circumstances and the people around them, and to get their unsupportive husbands saved or changed.

They became bold and willful in enforcing their practices upon other women at retreats, home Bible studies, and other meetings. Other women in the fellowship began to complain of the overbearing approach to ministry these women used, as they developed a reputation at large of being the "spiritual" women of the fellowship.

Ministry Case: *Jesus is my husband?*

One of the ringleaders of this informal movement came to me for counsel. She held an obstinate attitude towards any counsel that challenged her waywardness. The spirit on her exemplified the out-of-control, downward spiral into spiritualism and sexual perversion that eventually destroyed this fellowship.

This woman came to enlist my prayers to win her husband to Christ and to check out my ministry (since the help received by others in counsel was spreading by word of mouth). I soon detected a testing of sorts on her part and sensed she was looking for something to use against me.

In the first and only session, she admitted that she was frustrated with her husband's distance, obsession with work and their lack of intimacy. As our discussion progressed, she proclaimed that Christ was her husband and he would see her through this difficult time. After affirming her confidence in her relationship with Jesus, she then brought up a dream she recently had, asking for my counsel concerning this dream. At the onset she described her thoughts about what took place in the dream as wonderful but at the same time disconcerting—in the dream Jesus came to her and *made love to her!*

When I explained that this was not Jesus but rather a demon posing as Christ, that this kind of demon is called an *incubus*, a male demon who has sex with women, she recoiled.

Her reaction was sullen and defensive. She finally disagreed—in her mind there was no way that she, being a spirit-filled, tongues-speaking believer could have any encounter with any kind of demon. She ended our session and I found out after I left this fellowship that she and others formed an ad-hoc prayer group to pray me out of the fellowship. Ω

Over many years of counseling, ministry, and study, and through the many battles since, I am left with no doubt that most Christians involved in these fellowships are outright deceived. They have no discernment as to the demonic activity hidden in these perverse practices and are unaware that many evil people have become intertwined in their lives and have infiltrated their fellowship.

These deceived saints lack understanding of how their own personal spirit has become awakened and empowered by the counterfeiting spirits that are invited into fellowship through false doctrine, false teachers, and the many encounters with empty manifestations.

The sincere saint must become trained and equipped to properly discern false teachings, false teachers, and the carnal Christian or false brethren whom Satan may use to attack God's true servants.

Chapter Seven

True Leadership, Growth in Christ, and Safe Fellowship

Christ's True Leaders

When the crowds followed Christ, he noted how vulnerable they were, *harassed and helpless, like sheep without a shepherd (Matthew 9:36),* and he commanded his disciples to pray for workers to be sent into the field (the crowds of believers) to bring them into the Kingdom.

Christ did not command that a giant amphitheater be built so the crowds might be comfortable in order to pack in more people. He did not instruct his disciples to form leadership symposiums and conferences using techniques from successful business tycoons to promote church growth methods. He commanded that his disciples pray that God (the Lord of the harvest) would send workers out amongst those interested in knowing the truth of the Gospel.

Crop harvesting occurs in seasons, and so it is with the Holy Spirit drawing those who are ready to hear and receive the Gospel and submit to the lordship of Christ.

When God has true workers who can disciple, mentor, and minister by the leading of the Holy Spirit, then harvesting on a large scale can be wrought in true Pentecostal power.

That was the plan of God in Christ with the first disciples. Jesus personally called, taught and trained leaders who could walk in the true power of God and not abuse their positions of authority, or pervert their anointing. This plan has never changed as we see historically how true movements of God drew people to the true Christ through true servants, servants who taught others to observe all that Christ commanded.

These true leaders made disciples and workers who walked in true Christ-like character. These were and are men and women, husbands and wives, everyday common people, who grew up into salvation. These learned the ropes in leading others to Christ at the right time, discerning game players and wolves; these were workers who led stable lives as examples, who patiently mentored the sincere new convert until they also grew to maturity.

This foundation of true disciples and workers (saints in ministry) must be established in every fellowship so that the Lord of the harvest can draw those ready to give their lives to the lordship of Christ. The Apostle Paul instructs, *"Through him we both have access in one Spirit to the Father. So then you are no longer strangers and aliens, but you are fellow citizens with the saints and members of the household of God, <u>built on the foundation of the apostles and prophets, Christ Jesus himself being the cornerstone, in whom the whole structure, being joined together, grows into a holy temple in the Lord</u>. In him you also are being built together into a dwelling place for God by the Spirit"* (Ephesians 2:18-22).

True church growth is building disciples of those whom the Holy Spirit brings to Christ. God's people becoming sanctified, disciplined and knowledgeable—are made into the temple of the Holy Spirit. The Lord is the one who adds to the body of Christ using true servants who walk in obedience: *"And the Lord added to their number day by day those who were being saved"* (Acts 2:47).

This biblical approach requires leaders trained by the hand of Christ just as the Apostle Paul explains in his letter to the Christians at Ephesus (Ephesians 4:8-16).

It is Christ's plan to call and make true disciples, taken captive by Christ, who exclusively follow him, and train them to become true leaders who will serve in obedience to him and him only. True leaders in Christ will not go out to make a name for themselves, causing saints to follow after them, and become people pleasers.

The Apostle Paul made his position clear on confronting those who preached a perverted Gospel. In his letter to the Christians at Galatia he wrote, *"If anyone is preaching to you a gospel contrary to the one you received, let him be accursed"* (Galatians 1:9). These are strong words that carry consequences in life—that those misleading others concerning the truth about the Gospel of Christ be cursed?

Paul boldly follows up with a very powerful leadership axiom that every leader should be well acquainted with, *"For am I now seeking the approval of man, or of God? Or am I trying to please man? If I were still trying to please man, I would not be a servant of Christ"* (Galatians 1:10). The term *servant of Christ* in this passage means slave or bondservant of Christ.

Many in leadership today focus on popularity with people and do little in developing Christ-like character that steps on the toes of the false and challenges carnal Christians to grow up into Christ.

Leadership: Personality vs. Character
Looking to serve with servant-leaders having Christ-like character and attitude

Jesus was very adamant concerning leadership hype and hypocrisy amongst his disciples. He constantly pointed out to his followers the game that the Pharisees and other Temple leaders played, where the higher-ups lorded over others and made special efforts in self-glorification and recognition, with honor and prominence.

It is important to become fellow workers with true bondservants of Christ who have endured Christ's fiery discipline that transforms character. Many become infatuated with a leader's outer persona, their personality, and their formal education—not looking for Christ-like character qualities that allow leadership by example and shepherding accountability.

Holding saints accountable to grow up into Christ and maturity requires leaders who have grownup themselves, through the hard knocks of everyday living—not from mimicry, mental adaptation, or formal studies.

The body of Christ is bogged down with overeducated leaders who rely on their education and not on God. They push themselves beyond their own ability and away from the Holy Spirits inspiration to preach practical theology for everyday living. Far too many pastors find it hard to relate to the struggling Christian because they value academia and philosophy over knowing Christ intimately and his practical teachings, being trained in Christ's school of living and abiding in him.

W. Phillip Keller wrote a powerfully riveting warning in 1988 titled *Predators in our Pulpits*, and over 25 years later, Keller's insights are still on target. Concerning leadership character, he writes:

> "The person in a position of leadership, no matter how prominent or how obscure, must be one whose very life is grounded in God himself. The energy and vitality and love to reach the lost must come from Christ resident within that individual. Any action taken and any decisions made should be under the clear direction of God's Spirit.
>
> It simply will not do to use one's own charm, talents, or elaborate techniques to try to accomplish God's work in the world. And so laypeople are entitled to see the very life of Christ in their leaders.
>
> Positive proof that one in the pulpit is sent of God lies not only in his humility, compassion, and communion with Christ, but also in the calm courage of his character. The leader must be one who is utterly fearless for God, not in an overbearing or dictatorial manner, but rather in relentless loyalty and love to the Master" (*Predators in Our Pulpits: A Compelling Call to Follow Christ in These Perilous Times*, Eugene, OR: Harvest House, 1988 page 26)

As disciples of Christ, we must learn to discern between a personality leader and a leader who has Christ-like character. The following excerpt by Y. Sankar found online helps solidify the difference.

"Character Not Charisma is the Critical Measure of Leadership Excellence: The leadership crisis in ethics in many organizations partially stems from the crisis in character of our leaders. The character of the leader is grounded on such core values as integrity, trust, truth and human dignity, which influence the leader's vision, ethics and behavior. The moral literacy of the leader and the essentials of an ethical culture are connected to his/her character and not to his/her charismatic personality. The quest for leadership excellence is based more on character than charisma. The leader is also empowered through his/her character to serve as a mentor." (Y. Sankar, "Character Not Charisma is the Critical Measure of Leadership Excellence," *Journal of Leadership and Organizational Studies*. 2003)

The qualities of Christ-like leadership come in many forms but all have a common framework:

Christ-like leaders are personable, approachable, wise, reserved, not over-reaching, and compassionate, but they do not allow self or others to wallow in pity. They build up others and do not build up themselves at the expense of others; they refrain from boasting and do not promote their ministry by touting their work in helping others or promoting the divine gifts bestowed upon them. They will give credit where credit is due, and do not use flattery to gain credence in the eyes of others. They carry the true fear of God, humbly serving others as unto the Lord and they continue to seek the full love of God, towards God, others and self.

A true servant-leader will have unflinching courage to be obedient to Christ and all his teachings, leading to fuller knowledge of Christ; and to obey his voice. He or she will not be afraid to confront evil, if necessary in front of all, and chase out the wicked from the midst of the camp.

The key question to ask is—are you following a leader who brags about his relationship with Christ or are you working with a servant of Christ who leads by example in mentoring others in overcoming the world, the flesh, and the devil? Many love to preach to the crowd, but few learn and take the time to personally mentor and disciple individuals to grow in maturity, and teaching others to do so as well.

The Apostle Peter instructs leaders to, *"shepherd the flock of God that is among you, exercising oversight, not under compulsion, but willingly, as God would have you; not for shameful gain, but eagerly; not domineering over those in your charge, but being examples to the flock. And when the chief Shepherd appears, you will receive the unfading crown of glory. Likewise, you who are younger, be subject to the elders. Clothe yourselves, all of you, with humility toward one another, for 'God opposes the proud but gives grace to the humble.'"* (1 Peter 5:2-5).

A truly Christ-centered leader will demonstrate calm and stability under duress of trial, in the strain of command responsibility, and in the tempered use of power and authority. The personality leader who lacks Christ-like character will bark like a junkyard dog when challenged, be indecisive, and demonstrate narcissistic pettiness in the exercise of authority.

Five-fold Servant-Leaders and the Saint's Work of Ministry
Ministerial triage for newcomers and new converts

Through the centuries, God's plan for growing the body of Christ and maturing believers has been turned upside down. Observing all that Christ taught within leadership, then applying sound doctrine, to include screening and mentoring with firmness and accountability, has become passé. Those in ministry are the leaders, and the rank and file believers (laymen)[23] have become bystanders, or if they attempt to do the work of ministry, most are poorly equipped and cause more harm than good.

Of course, this condition is not universal; however, those fellowships that hold to correct biblical principles in evangelism, disciple building, and mentoring are few.

When Jesus saw the crowds, he explained to his disciples, *"The harvest is plentiful, but the laborers are few; therefore <u>pray earnestly</u> to the Lord of the harvest to send out laborers into his harvest"* (Matthew 9:37-38). Leaders must pray earnestly for God to raise up qualified workers who know how to walk in discernment, know how to minister according to the gifts bestowed upon them, and above all are mature in Christ.

---

[23] Layman: A non-ordained member of a church, a person without professional or specialized knowledge in a particular subject or vocation, a person who does not belong to the clergy.

Part of the answer to the earnest prayer for qualified workers is the willingness of leaders to fulfill Christ's great commission to *"make disciples of all nations, baptizing them in the name of the Father and of the Son and of the Holy Spirit, teaching them to observe all that I have commanded you. And behold, I am with you always, to the end of the age"* (Matthew 28:19-20).

Thus, if leaders are true disciples of Christ first and foremost, then the function they fill as apostle, prophet, evangelist, pastor, or teacher is to help facilitate the growth and maturity of every saint that the Holy Spirit births—who are brought into leadership's care. The five-fold work of servant-leaders established by Christ is to mature, to grow, and to lead by example in making disciples of Christ—saints who obey and follow Christ. They are not to raise up followers of the name of Jesus and manipulate them to follow church leaders, as they go off on their carnally motivated and egotistical ministries campaigns.

When an ample number of saints (qualified workers) are raised up in a local body, then the Holy Spirit has a team of leader-servants and qualified workers (saints) who can handle new converts to Christ as they are birthed in the power of the Spirit—and added to the company of saints as the Holy Spirit directs.

A true body of believers (a local fellowship) should be taught to walk in the gifts of the Spirit as the Holy Spirit wills. True leaders should lead by example in the practicing of the gifts and help each Christian worker receive and minister properly in the gift that the Holy Spirit assigns—in God's timing (usually when a new convert is ready).

True leaders should have the primary goal that all become proficient in the true gift of prophecy, so that when newcomers or outsiders come to fellowship the secrets of their hearts are revealed and thus the newcomer will truly understand, without a doubt that God is there amongst them. (Again, see 1 Corinthians 14:20-24.)

Ministerial Triage

Then there will take place a true and divinely inspired ministerial-triage for newcomers and new converts. Each newcomer or new believer will receive direction, guidance, encouragement and training led by the Holy Spirit and facilitated by qualified workers. They will be treated with dignity and care, not as a herd of cattle on the way to market.

A *triage ministry* is defined as a process of prioritizing and directing the wounded, defiled, sin-laden, demonized, double-minded, or the not so messed up believer towards the right ministry facilitated by qualified worker(s), and ensuring that new believers who are not struggling are afforded proper discipleship training.

Thus, Christ desires to raise up servant-leaders first, then in turn they will be led to minister to the new converts coming to the body of Christ. The saints being added to fellowship should be afforded the opportunity to participate in solid likeminded fellowship and be fed, encouraged, challenged, and protected by true leadership (Ephesians 4:11-16).

Special note: Not only are new believers to receive appropriate ministry and be prepared for discipleship training, but also the wolves, false brethren, and the carnal game players are to be discerned, exposed, confronted, held accountable and—if necessary—chased out.

The Burden of Leadership and Ministry Burnout
Avoiding the Moses syndrome—a double-bind state of mind that leads to leadership idolatry

Every saint in the body of Christ in some manner will experience the burden of leadership—from pastor, evangelist, or apostle to helper, administrator, or as a Christian worker leading someone to Christ. Those called to be a gift of Christ to the body of Christ (apostle, prophet, evangelist, pastor, or teacher) will have a heavier burden of leadership. Leaders of this nature will be required to give an account for the souls in their sphere of influence. (See Hebrews 13:17.) Many in leadership today groan from the burden of leadership because of lack of qualification, training, and support—as well as the ever-increasing fellowship and relationship conflicts and stress.

More than ever, pastors are pressed to perform with perfection in all the associated duties of preaching, teaching, counseling and mentoring—not to mention church organization, risk and legal compliance, administration, finances and facility maintenance and expansion. On top of all that, leaders must be a model husband, wife, father, mother, and community leader.

The pressure from all this can become very demanding, and even more so with the added spiritual oppression sent by hell in opposing the work of leadership; that is, growing saints into maturity and discipleship, fighting to hold sound doctrine before the people, chasing out wolves, and discerning evil lurking within and without.

The study of leadership principles is important for all the saints. Christians must understand the burdens of leadership, learning to take an even strain with true and responsible leaders, pulling their own weight in the work of ministry as they live and work in a fallen world as ambassadors for Christ.

The Scriptures tell of miserable leaders, weak leaders, and strong and successful leaders with Christ the consummate example of leadership, in character, attitude, and principles.

There is one dangerous pitfall that every leader and every saint must comprehend in order to avoid: leadership idolatry.

We should all be familiar with the story of God calling Moses and sending him along with Aaron to Egypt to confront the Pharaoh with the message from God, saying *"Let my people go"* (Exodus 5:1-10:4). The resounding message from God to the ruler of Egypt was "let <u>my people</u> go" — from their cruel bondage of the Egyptians.

Moses and Aaron had their hands full in fulfilling their mission, and found that they were very inadequate in power to force Pharaoh to release Israel from slavery and allow them to leave to serve God. However, these two servants soon found that their responsibility was to hear the commands of God and simply repeat them to the Pharaoh; the rest was up to God and the Pharaoh.

Leaders must come back to the truth that all ministerial work is to be of God and directed towards God's people. Those in leadership are servants of Christ, appointed by God, not hired by God's people. With this in mind, let us look at the outcome of the leadership trap that Moses and Aaron fell into—as many fall prey to in leadership today.

God had to demonstrate great power to convince the Pharaoh to let Israel go. Moses and Aaron learned how to convey God's will and directives in confidence to the Pharaoh and later to God's people in the wilderness. As spokespersons for God, mainly with Moses, having the people like him and befriend him became a problem.

Israel, while in the wilderness angered the Lord, making the burden of leadership fall heavily upon Moses, as described in Psalm 106: *"They angered him [the Lord] at the waters of Meribah, and it went ill with Moses on their account, for they made his spirit bitter, and he spoke rashly with his lips"* (verses 32-33)—here we have one of the first cases of ministry burnout for a leader appointed by God.

Moses experienced ministry burnout because he unknowingly allowed the people to idolize him, making him (Moses) responsible for their welfare and happiness—and he took upon himself undue care for their bad attitudes that caused extra suffering. Many of the people blamed Moses, which was difficult for him to accept and which led to a caretaking approach in leading disgruntled people.

Leaders who are unprepared for the burden of leadership frequently fall headlong into false responsibility for those in their charge, a false responsibility to make sure God's people are convinced to do what is right, embrace sound doctrine, understand it, apply it, and learn to be obedient to the commands of Christ.

In this account of the conversation between God and Moses concerning Israel, we detect a subtle shift in how God refers to his people when he speaks to Moses on Mt. Sinai. *"And the Lord said to Moses, 'Go down, <u>for your people, whom you brought up out of the land of Egypt</u>, have corrupted themselves'"* (Exodus 32:7).

"Your people, whom you brought up out of the land of Egypt" is how the Lord refers to Israel in speaking to Moses, no longer referring to them as his own people. However, Moses responds by saying, *"O Lord, why does your wrath burn hot against your people, whom you have brought out of the land of Egypt with great power and with a mighty hand?"* (Exodus 32:11).

Moses responds to the Lord's reference concerning leadership; however, Moses does not comprehend the significance of the Lord's comments. In this exchange between the Lord and Moses, I believe the Lord is trying to help Moses see how he (Moses) has allowed the burden of leadership to shift from being upon God's shoulders, to be upon his own shoulders.

Moses becomes snared by Israel's bitterness and complaining, as if he was responsible to make the people believe and cooperate. This type of error of false responsibility creates an internal no-win dilemma or double-bind[24] relationship between him (Moses) and the people of

---

[24] Christian leadership double bind: In this setting, I define a leadership double bind as a self-induced paradox or contradiction. It is based on the belief that leadership is responsible for those in their care to successfully become mature in Christ, in which both the leader and the congregation embrace this expectation, usually unconsciously. It is similar to a relationship double-bind, where both parties in the relationship expect the other to make them feel happy and secure within themselves, in spite of the fact that no

God. Moses allowed himself to become more than an intermediary between God and the people. The people began to look to him as a savior, rather than an intercessor, spokesperson and leader. The people began to look to Moses rather than turn to God, blaming Moses for the repercussions (consequences) of their unbelief, murmuring, and faultfinding.

This is a no-win position for any leader called of God, and will eventually bring trouble. For Moses, his inability to see and deal with this subtle shift into a savior role proved to be problematic in his relationship with God and was the reason for the Lord not to allow Moses to cross into the Promised Land with Israel.

This bears out in this passage, *"Because you rebelled against my word in the wilderness of Zin when the congregation quarreled, failing to uphold me as holy at the waters before their eyes"* (Numbers 27:14).

God's people often prefer human saviors, who can be manipulated and controlled by setting the leader on a pedestal to be idolized. The people can pressure the leader with disapproval when they rebel against God's ordinances and so get their own way. This is now the standard for leadership success—can the leader enthrall, inspire, and magnetically attract newcomers while appeasing the congregation to keep the appearance of righteousness.

Moses and Abraham became idols for the religious leaders of Christ's day. I personally believe that if the body of Moses had remained with Israel and was taken into the Promised Land (like Joseph's body leaving Egypt), the people would have erected a monument to hold the body of Moses to be sacredly worshipped, like the pharaohs entombed in the pyramids of Egypt. The following peculiar passage in Jude makes perfect sense in light of the leadership idolatry that God's people repeatedly fall victim to. *"When the archangel Michael, contending with the devil, was disputing about the body of Moses"* (Jude 1:9). It is my contention that this passage in Jude implies that Satan wanted the body of Moses, in order to have it put on display or entombed, as was the bodies of the Pharaohs (placed in the pyramids) to elevate Moses as a historical figure to a position of a god in the hearts of God's people. As it was, when Christ came to Israel as their savior only a remnant received him, partly due to near idol worship of Moses.

True leadership must resist being held as an indispensable mini-savior; if not, a leader in the making will fall into the Moses syndrome and either become burned-out and frustrated, a tyrannical cult leader, or a weak hireling who flees at the first sign of trouble.

People pleasers and heroes are a dime a dozen in this hour. God is looking for men and women who will answer the call of true leadership training who will be able to stand against the gates of hell and chase off the wolves. They must not be afraid to tell God's people what they need to hear, without the fear of rejection. If you are serious about being used of God and desire to walk in true discernment, becoming involved with leadership who demonstrate the fruit of serving Christ above all else is vital.

---

one can make another person feel good about their self, ever. Extreme frustration, often leading to burnout occurs for a leader feeling this type of false responsibility, as was the case with Moses.

True Leadership Won't Compete in Fellowship Popularity Contests
Affable leaders can expect a trouncing as carnal believers and satanic implants run amok

Leaders who have the desire to be liked at the expense of righteousness and truth and worry what the community may think if sin is exposed in the fellowship have no place as shepherds over God's flock. A weak leader will allow jealousy and selfish ambition to surface in fellowship life; disorder and vile practices will spawn and gain a foothold.

This is a serious issue in most fellowships today, where insubordinate people come to fellowship professing to know God but set up divisions and undermine leadership, leading the weak believer astray into false doctrine. These people can be subtle, vicious if crossed, and loud-mouthed gossipers who will not back down or leave without a fight.

An easy-going leader will have a very hard time following Christ's and the Apostle's directives for leaders. Strong leaders must learn to deal swiftly and decisively with the wayward person who habitually sins, such as in this example of the Apostle Paul's instruction to Timothy, *"As for those who persist in sin, rebuke them in the presence of all, so that the rest may stand in fear"* (1 Timothy 5:20).

Leaders who desire to be liked by everyone run the risk of fellowship blackmail; the veiled threat that the congregation will fall out of love with the leader and have them replaced. The insecure leader, who is more affable (good natured, genial, pleasant, easygoing) than firm and tough on sin and carnality in the camp, will in the end come to ruin. Jesus warns every sincere believer, *"Woe to you, when all people speak well of you, for so their fathers did to the false prophets"* (Luke 6:26).

In the book of Titus, the Apostle Paul warned about and instructed on dealing with defiant empty talkers and deceivers who come to fellowship with false teachings for shameful gain. Leaders need to rebuke them harshly to silence them and possibly correct them so that their faith may become sound. These people upset the congregation and whole families with base suspicions, myths and the commands of men. They sneak into a fellowship, cause trouble, and are defiling, having impure minds and a defiled conscience. He finished his discourse on this subject by stating, *"They profess to know God, but they deny him by their works. They are detestable, disobedient, unfit for any good work"* (Titus 1:10-16).

Dealing with one who is repugnant without hesitation, promptly, and decisively is a mark of a true and courageous leader. The milquetoast leader who has not the stomach for open and sometimes public confrontation will see their fellowship eventually be taken over, or be out of a leadership position.

The Apostle Paul warned of the last-days popularity contests for leaders by the following: *"For the time is coming when people will not endure sound teaching, but having itching ears they will accumulate for themselves teachers to suit their own passions, and will turn away from listening to the truth and wander off into myths"* (2 Timothy 4:3-4). Today, leaders are measured on showmanship, knowledge of the teachings of men, social acceptance, appeal, and eloquent speech. This is contrary to this exhortation by the Apostle Paul, *"Do your best to present yourself to God as one approved, a worker who has no need to be ashamed, rightly handling the word of truth. <u>But avoid irreverent babble, for it will lead people into more and more ungodliness, and their talk will spread</u>*

like gangrene. Among them are Hymenaeus and Philetus, who have swerved from the truth, saying that the resurrection has already happened. They are upsetting the faith of some. But God's firm foundation stands, bearing this seal: 'The Lord knows those who are his,' and, 'Let everyone who names the name of the Lord depart from iniquity.'" (2 Timothy 2:15-19).

Troublemakers and implants are everywhere like a disease, corrupting congregation after congregation. Pastoral and elder leadership in the coming days will become very stressful and demanding. As trouble in the world increases and fellowship infighting becomes more acute, each pastor and elder, regardless if trained, under-qualified, or false, will have to demonstrate what kind character they are made of. From the large mega-church down to the small congregation and even in the home church, the marauding wolves will devour the affably weak leader and scatter the sheep.

A true leader in Christ will not be ashamed to stand without wavering upon solid doctrine and the message and work of the cross upon the daily lives of those in his or her care.

Transforming our Carnal Nature—God's Way
Working out our own salvation and growing up into the true Christ

We would be frauds or self-deceived also if we call out the errors of these deceived teachers and do not present sound doctrine to help the sincere Christian become Christ-like in character. God's people more than ever are crying out for help in achieving true Christ-like character transformation. What is missing is proper presentation of the biblical principles that the Holy Spirit works with—sound doctrine that is in accord with the Gospel and all the teachings of Christ.

As already expressed, the harder, confrontational words of Christ and the writings of the disciples are often ignored. However, it is these harder teachings within the Gospel that have an antiseptic affect upon the soul and spirit, clearing the way for the believer to repent, become cleansed, and seek Christ personally and become changed in character by his Spirit in the discipline of the Lord. Again, transformation of character and healing wounds to the spirit and emotions comes from the Lord. (See 2 Corinthians 3:17-18.)

The real nature of false teachings veils the truth of who we truly are, inevitably leaving our carnal motives of heart and disturbing attitudes intact and hidden. These issues come out and become very glaring when carnal Christians become irritated or suffer a severe testing of faith. These false doctrines teach the carnal and undiscerning to ignore, minimize, justify, and rationalize their carnal nature traits.

However, an often-misunderstood ministry of the Holy Spirit within the believer's life is the work in checking and exposing wrong motives, impure issues of heart, flawed character and carnal personalities. In addition, the devil and the trials of life become tools in the hand of the Lord to bring us to a sincere desire to change. Often the Lord will allow pressing circumstances to corner us and break denial—in order to bring understanding of what must be changed if we learn to walk with a humble-contrite heart that desires change.

The work of the cross within the believer is also a very important New Testament principle, which is hard to understand at first and often painful to embrace. Nevertheless, the work of the cross for the believer is the means by which the Holy Spirit facilitates death to the passions and desires of the flesh. Inappropriate feelings, sinful and selfish desires, along with bad thoughts are the very indicators that God calls us to take into account, to pay attention to, to use in examining ourselves, and then when they are acknowledged and contritely owned, death to the root desire of sinfulness can be accomplished.

Another mindset these destructive heresies establish and that grips the faith of so many is how Scripture is twisted away from holding the believer accountable, shifted to judge and point the finger at the wayward lost sinner. The Apostle Paul instructed that we can associate with the sinners of the world (not live like them); however, we are to chase out those in fellowship who claim to be Christian, yet are sexually immoral, greedy, drunks, or swindlers.

In addition, the Apostle Paul points out that the Word of God is for the believer: *"All Scripture is breathed out by God and profitable for teaching, <u>for reproof, for correction, and for training in righteousness</u>, that the man of God may be competent, equipped for every good work"* (2 Timothy 3:16-17).

Therefore, as you study the following biblical principles along with the confirming Scriptures, allow the Holy Spirit to use the Word of God to speak to *you*, instead of reading a passage as so many do as if it were speaking to the wicked. Let the written Word become alive and speak into your own life as a beloved son or daughter, *for reproof, correction, and for training in righteousness!* With that, leadership must exert most of their effort in confronting God's people—not the sinner and an evil wicked culture.

Overcoming an Abridged Gospel
Growing from a newborn Christian to maturity and eternal security

Most Christians are misinformed about the Gospel (good news) of eternal salvation offered by God through his only begotten son Jesus Christ. Multitudes over the last seventy plus years of intense evangelism worldwide have heard only part of God's work in bringing a new believer into eternal salvation. Christians, new and old, suffer from embracing the short version of God's plan and his work in leading a lost sinner all the way to eternal salvation, where they would never fall from grace and lose their eternal life. The born-again experience that many claim to be the completed work of salvation is only a part of the process of knowing Christ, growing up into Christ, and receiving eternal security (completed salvation).

The biblical promise of salvation and eternal security in Scripture is not an instant moment or one-time encounter, but rather a series of works facilitated by God, a process whereby God works upon an individual—where a person experiences various divine encounters with the Holy Spirit and the Word of God, mostly through servants of Jesus Christ.

Each encounter requires a believer to exercise faith, from the initial belief in Christ on up into maturity. Faith, if it is true, is to be acted upon from the time that a person first hears the Gospel of Christ and throughout those divine encounters that lead all the way to maturity and eternal security. Until that process is complete, there is the risk of a new believer or even a believer in process falling away and losing their salvation.

The new believer must become strengthened to complete their faith through obedience and grow up into the fullness of Christ, obtaining the grace of God and eternal security. *"So put away all malice and all deceit and hypocrisy and envy and all slander. Like <u>newborn infants</u>, long for the pure spiritual milk, that by it you may <u>grow up to salvation</u>—if indeed you have tasted that the Lord is good"* (1 Peter 2:1-3).

While a sincere Christian is in the process of growing up and experiencing these encounters with Christ, leading towards maturity and eternal security, they are under an umbrella of God's grace. This is God's guarantee while in process: his grace, mercy, protection, and guidance leads the willing to continue on to maturity. To help this process, God's work calls for mentoring by true disciples who have already become mature and secure.

If at any point in this process a new believer passes away or is called to eternity, they are guaranteed eternal salvation. However, this eternal security while working out one's salvation is based on maintaining faith in God and not falling away.

Unfortunately, true leadership and mature saints working in the ministry to nurture, support, and live as examples for new believers are sorely missing today.

New Christians are at risk of falling away during this process of growing up into Christ and eternal security. False doctrine, poor leadership, and lack of genuine support in fellowship, along with impurities of the heart and defilements in the spirit cause many to fall away, become lukewarm and deceived and become at great risk of losing eternal life.

Eternal security is for those true and good-hearted Christians who have succeeded in growing up into the fullness of Christ, crucified the passions and desires of the flesh and obtained the grace of God. The Apostle Paul warns Christians about allowing the works of the flesh to thrive, instead of being crucified: *"I warn you, as I warned you before, that those who do such things will not inherit the kingdom of God… And those who belong to Christ Jesus have crucified the flesh with its passions and desires"* (Galatians 5:21, 24).

A study of the parable of the sower is a powerful warning to Christians who have received the good news of God's plan of salvation, yet have not dealt with certain serious issues. Many receive the Gospel and are not warned of how the devil can steal one's understanding or how troubles can cause them to turn away, and how the love of money and riches strangle faith in a new believer. (See Luke 8:4-18.)

Christ is speaking to many Christians today in this parable, as the devil continues to take a toll on new and old Christians alike, during the tests of life and when the cares, riches and pleasures of this life deceive and choke out true faith.

Many Christian have never been told of the risk being passive and in love with this world. Christ warns us about indifference and avoidance of working out salvation in his discipline, *"Those whom I love, I reprove and discipline, so be zealous and repent. Behold, I stand at the door and knock. If anyone hears my voice and opens the door, I will come in to him and eat with him, and he with me. The one who conquers, I will grant him to sit with me on my throne, as I also conquered and sat down with my Father on his throne. He who has an ear, let him hear what the Spirit says to the churches."* (Revelation 3:19-22).

General Phases of Maturing that Leads to Full Salvation and Eternal Security

Not everyone comes instantly to the knowledge of the Gospel and responds the same way to the call of salvation in Christ. However, in general terms, God works in phases upon those who have a good heart[25]: 1) Awakening and receiving. 2) Knowledge and understanding. 3) Discipline and maturity. 4) Obtaining grace and eternal security. The following is a brief explanation, for deeper explanations; see one of our forthcoming books on this often-misunderstood topic.

1) *Awaking and receiving*, also referred to as the born again experience comes upon a person by the work of the Holy Spirit in God's timing, and occurs primarily when a person is ready to hear the truth, respond appropriately, apply changes to their life style, and receive mentoring. Often this initial work by the Holy Spirit (helped by other Christians) will take place in a person who does not know God intimately or spiritually (but may know of the Gospel religiously), or when a person is seeking salvation in Christ. The awakening will involve the Holy Spirit bearing witness in the person's heart, resulting in an almost overwhelming need for Christ to be their Savior and submitting to him as their Lord and Savior. Also, if they receive proper instruction when the Holy Spirit awakens them, they should ask and receive the gift of the Holy Spirit. (It should be noted that as soon as possible the new believer should make a public announcement of their belief in Christ and become baptized in water to demonstrate ceremonially and publicly that they now believe in and choose to follow Jesus Christ).

This awakening, *if it is of God*, instills a desire to repent of past sins and give up any and all sinful alliances. In addition, a desire to become a godly person and to love God and receive God's love is deeply sensed within the heart. This phase is an expression of God's grace and mercy extended to each individual who has faith when the Holy Spirit draws that person (usually when the individual hears the Gospel of Christ).

A distinction must be made for new converts concerning repentance. Many seek God's help and come to Christ because of the repercussions of a sinful lifestyle but lack a godly grief over their sinful lifestyle. The pain of being caught doing wrong and being held accountable fills the hearts of many with self-pity and bitter sorrow—not a genuine grief over the evil they brought into the lives of others and against God. They come to meeting seeking a bailout from God and prayers from others to save them from their problems. *"Godly grief produces a repentance that leads to salvation without regret, whereas <u>worldly grief</u>* [self-pity and bitter sorrow] *produces death"* (2 Corinthians 7:10).

---

[25] Jesus explained in the parable of the sower (Mark 8:9-15), that some people had different issues and conditions of heart that in one way or another caused them not to respond to the Word of God and mature into salvation. However, Christ explained that those who had an honest and "good heart" succeeded in growing into salvation and bearing fruit.

Each individual who has faith must act on the invitation of salvation and ask Christ to be their Lord and Savior, and repent of their former manner of life with true contrition of heart. They must also understand that this is a very infantile beginning. Then the next phase of the growing up into salvation and eternal security process will begin.

2) *Knowledge and understanding* must become a vital every day desire and prayer request for a new believer. In that, they must continue to learn more about Christ, the Gospel, salvation, sanctification, and true holiness—along with sound doctrine that is in accord with the Gospel.

They must understand that following Christ will not be easy. They must learn to obey him and allow him to transform their old nature into a Christ-like nature and that they need to model their life after Christ, not by mimicry, but achieving true outward change by being transformed inwardly in heart and character as exemplified by Christ's character, life, and all of his teachings.

Each new born-again believer must understand that they are vulnerable to falling away or sliding back into a sinful life-style if they do not earnestly desire to work out their salvation in its entirety. Therefore, during this time of growing in the knowledge of Christ and the Gospel, a practical understanding must be applied to what is learned. The new believer learns to discern the Holy Spirit's presence, his comfort, the truth in life based on the Word of God, and discern and seek the illuminating power of the Holy Spirit concerning the written Word of God.

Being mentored and hearing the preaching and teaching of sound doctrine expounded from the Scriptures is vital for the new believer. The goal is to build up a sure foundation and a strong faith in preparation for the next phase, when learning to embrace the work of the cross in the new believer's life will become much harder. The new believer at the end of this phase has become proficient in Bible study, prayer, and has a thorough understanding of the basic or elementary doctrines of Christ. (See Hebrews 6:1-12.)

We must grow in understanding the grace of God and its power over the sin nature, the crucifying of our carnal nature[26] with its works of the flesh, and how the Spirit of Christ leads in our transformation process. Becoming transformed into a Christ-like person is enhanced and expedited through the study of Scripture, fellowship with likeminded believers, and our willingness and desire to work this process out and obtain the grace of God, resting in his strength and love.

3) *Discipline and maturity* starts when a believer understands and is prepared to be led by the Holy Spirit into a time of discipline. This is not punishment, but rather a difficult time

---

[26] Our *sin nature* is our fallen state that every person suffers, the natural propensity to sin that does not go away in this life. The deeper work of grace with understanding and true relationship to God in Christ will bring us to receive power to rise above the power of our sin nature. Our sin nature is like gravity always pulling us down and growing in Christ, leading to the fullness of God's grace is the power within us overriding the power of the sin nature. Our *carnal nature* is the derivative of our sin nature that is unique to each individual. The carnal nature is our personality and character traits developed in growing up in a sinful world and still has influence within us as believers. The carnal nature pushes us to do things that are not of God as listed in Galatians 5:16-26 and elsewhere is Scripture. The passions and desires of the flesh (carnal nature) are dealt with in a process whereby we embrace the principle of the cross where the root motives and feelings within our heart, spirit and spirit of the mind are in a death and then newness of life process. This is how we become Christ-like in our nature, putting off the old and learning to allow Christ to instill newness of life in the place of the old beliefs and emotions. More on this subject in a forthcoming publication.

orchestrated by the Lord to bring pressure upon his disciples—pressure through challenging circumstances, at various times requiring suffering and sometimes a fiery ordeal. The main purpose is to bring to the surface[27] hidden impurities within the heart, in the spirit and mind (subconscious) that most new believer is not aware that they have. The other main purpose is training each servant to learn how to rely on God and not his or her own abilities, talents, knowledge and wisdom. (We learn to allow the Lord to lead and empower in applying or using of our abilities, talents knowledge and wisdom). In the book of Hebrews it is taught that the discipline of the Lord is required of every son or daughter, and if not, that Christian runs the risk of becoming an illegitimate child of God and may in the end suffer the loss of their salvation. (See Hebrews 12:1-18.)

In another passage the Apostle Peter explains about why fiery trial will eventually come upon the sincere saint; *"Beloved, do not be surprised at the fiery trial when it comes upon you to test you, as though something strange were happening to you. But rejoice insofar as you share Christ's sufferings, that you may also rejoice and be glad <u>when his glory is revealed</u>"* (1 Peter 4:12-13).

The Lord leads his sincere and more mature disciples into these times of testing to expose those hidden carnal character flaws so he can use us in a much more powerful way. The Apostles were thoroughly tested in those difficult days during our Lord's suffering, and then later on the Day of Pentecost, God bestowed upon them great power, since in their discipline they became trustworthy witnesses to Christ as messengers of the Gospel. (See also James 1:2-4).

One may take longer in this time of discipline and testing, depending on the number of issues of heart and the importance of the call upon the life of the disciple. If the calling is to be very public, one can expect discipline that will ensure the old nature will be thoroughly crucified (dead) so as not to rise up within the disciple and allow for pride and self-glorification.

4) *Obtaining grace and eternal security* will eventually come to mature and disciplined Christians who by faith continued in the process of sanctification and the work of grace. They will come to a place in their relationship with Christ where the Lord becomes their very life and there are no longer hidden issues within the heart or personal spirit that could become a stronghold used by Satan. The devil will attempt to sift the saint in process with confusion and doubt or attempt to destroy their faith (if they were still immature and undisciplined).

A mature disciple will come to a place as described by the Apostle Paul, where their life is no longer their own, *"It is no longer I who live, but Christ who lives in me. And the life I now live in the flesh I live by faith in the Son of God, who loved me and gave himself for me"* (Galatians 2:20).

This is a phase when, as the Apostle put it, Christ is formed within the believer, where eternal security is not based on our righteousness and good works, but based on a changed character resting in God's grace as an obedient servant who is led by the Holy Spirit. (See Galatians 4:19.)

---

[27] The term, bring to the surface, I refer as allowing the Lord to show us during times of trials, issues of the heart and of character that normally stay hidden from the believer's awareness when life is easy. The issues hidden will surface and become bothersome to the point that requires the disciple to address it in prayer, repentance, cleansing and seek change of heart and character in the power of the Holy Spirit.

Maturing in Christ, until He is Formed Within
From plodding along using Christ's name to "Christ in us the hope of glory"

We as believers, both individually and corporately, are to be made into the temple of the Holy Spirit. This is to be accomplished by God working within us and supported by mature saints working with God. If we try to make ourselves into religious Christians in our own ways, following false doctrine, all our work will be in vain. *"Unless the LORD builds the house, those who build it labor in vain"* (Psalm 127:1).

Jesus said, *"If anyone loves me, he will keep my word, and my Father will love him, and we will come to him and make our home with him"* (John 14:23). In order to allow Christ and the Father to build within us a home for the Holy Spirit to dwell, we must love Christ above all else and learn to embrace all that Christ taught—to learn and keep his Word.

Those in ministry must allow Christ to be formed within themselves in order to successfully be used of God to build up the body of Christ. Many today build upon the foundation of Christ within new believers using false teachings that glorify themselves. Many actually compete with each other for followers and new converts. The Apostle Paul confronted this leadership idolatry forming in the body of believers at the church in Corinth by clarifying how we should consider each other and our leaders:

"What then is Apollos? What is Paul? Servants through whom you believed, as the Lord assigned to each. I planted, Apollos watered, but God gave the growth. So neither he who plants nor he who waters is anything, but only God who gives the growth. He who plants and he who waters are one, and each will receive his wages according to his labor. For we are God's fellow workers. You are God's field, God's building" (1 Corinthians 3:5-9).

The growth that we must desire to achieve is moving from using Christ's name in faith, to having the person of Christ infill us, so that he personally directs our prayers, and spiritual warfare, along with leading our daily lives.

Think about when the seventy-two disciples went out two by two with power to heal the sick and cast out demons, they came back saying, *"'Lord, even the demons are subject to us in your name!' And he said to them, 'I saw Satan fall like lightning from heaven. Behold, I have given you authority to tread on serpents and scorpions, and over all the power of the enemy, and nothing shall hurt you. Nevertheless, do not rejoice in this, that the spirits are subject to you, but rejoice that your names are written in heaven'"* (Luke 10:17-20).

These disciples were excited about the spiritual power they exercised in using Christ's name, yet the Lord had tempered their joy by scolding them and instructing them to rejoice in their eternal salvation. These disciples were immature in understanding and at risk of becoming flippant concerning the use of Christ's name. They were developing a relationship with the power of the name of Christ—a dangerous error.

That same level of immaturity of the seventy-two is throughout the body of Christ today. Many of the same seventy-two disciples later could not bear the harder sayings of Christ and turned away from following Christ, and so it is with many now. Many take on prayer and spiritual warfare in the power of using Christ's name without having the maturity and Christ-like character that tempers that power in wisdom and leadership of the Holy Spirit.

These plod along using fancy prayers and commands, yet are completely out-of-sync with the will and timing of the Holy Spirit. Jesus did nothing on his own accord and only did what he saw the Father doing (see John 5:19)—because he had a personal relationship with the Father.

Many today are power mongers, lusting after the power of the name of Christ, who lack a true desire to know Christ and the power of the resurrected life in Christ. Few are willing to suffer the loss of all things so they may intimately know the person of Christ. Study the Apostle Paul's explanation concerning the requirements of knowing the person of Christ in Philippians 3:1-21.

As the disciples grew in maturity, especially after the day of Pentecost, their approach in exercising spiritual authority for healing the sick, raising the dead, and casting out devils was more deliberate in direct correlation to the presence of Christ's Spirit within them.

Notice how Peter proclaims the healing of Aeneas as recorded in the book of Acts, *"Now as Peter went here and there among them all, he came down also to the saints who lived at Lydda. There he found a man named Aeneas, bedridden for eight years, who was paralyzed. And Peter said to him, 'Aeneas, <u>Jesus Christ heals you</u>; rise and make your bed.' And immediately he rose. And all the residents of Lydda and Sharon saw him, and they turned to the Lord"* (Acts 9:32-35).

This account reflects a distinct interaction with the Spirit of Christ dwelling within Peter leading Peter to proclaim what Christ just did and for Aeneas to rise up. Another account in Acts demonstrates how the Holy Spirit directly speaks through the Apostle Paul:

"So, <u>being sent out by the Holy Spirit</u>, they went down to Seleucia, and from there they sailed to Cyprus. When they arrived at Salamis, they proclaimed the Word of God in the synagogues of the Jews. And they had John to assist them. When they had gone through the whole island as far as Paphos, they came upon a certain magician, a Jewish false prophet named Bar-Jesus. He was with the proconsul, Sergius Paulus, a man of intelligence, who summoned Barnabas and Saul and sought to hear the Word of God. But Elymas the magician (for that is the meaning of his name) opposed them, seeking to turn the proconsul away from the faith. <u>But Saul, who was also called Paul, filled with the Holy Spirit</u>, looked intently at him and said, 'You son of the devil, you enemy of all righteousness, full of all deceit and villainy, will you not stop making crooked the straight paths of the Lord? And now, behold, the hand of the Lord is upon you, and you will be blind and unable to see the sun for a time.' <u>Immediately mist and darkness fell upon him</u>, and he went about seeking people to lead him by the hand. Then the proconsul believed, when he saw what had occurred, for he was astonished at the teaching of the Lord" (Acts 13:4-12).

These examples are to inspire us not to learn to use Christ's name in the flesh presumptuously; rather, we must become disciplined by the Lord to walk in the fullness of Christ, where he and the Father abide in us and we, living as one with them, are led and directed as the Holy Spirit commands.

The Apostle Paul wrote to the Galatians how he was in anguish until Christ was formed within them (see Galatians 4:19). The goal of true discipleship is becoming Christ-like in character and abiding in the Spirit where there can be no mistake concerning who is performing the miracles, signs, and wonders that glorify Christ.

Another passage to consider is where the Apostle Paul describes the mystery hidden throughout the ages and revealed within the saints—and that is *Christ in us the hope of glory*. It is his presence in us and his leadership in ministry and for all of life that truly glorifies God and truly accomplishes God's will on earth:

"To them God chose to make known how great among the Gentiles are the riches of the glory of this mystery, which is <u>Christ in you, the hope of glory</u>. Him we proclaim, warning everyone and teaching everyone with all wisdom, <u>that we may present everyone mature in Christ</u>. For this I toil, struggling with <u>all his energy that he powerfully works within me</u>" (Colossians 1:27-29).

Ministry is to be in his energy, in his power, doing his will, in his timing—not in ours! Many presume on God and use Christ's name to do their own thing in ministry, not according to the will of God or in the power of the Holy Spirit.

Many, as mentioned several times in this book, will be rejected by Christ when he judges us all. He will say to those who bragged about using Christ's name in their own willfulness and how they did mighty works in his name, *"I never knew you; depart from me, you workers of lawlessness"* (Matthew 7:23).

One of the most destructive errors among the many false doctrines today is learning to arbitrarily claim or speak forth in prayer a healing, a blessing, or a supposed purpose of God. This teaching has turned many naïve and deceived believers into Harry Potter practitioners, presuming upon God and using sorcery to speak into existence their heart's desires. Many will be damned because they learned to practice sorcery that resulted in the devil using them to do great transgressions.

In a psalm by David we are instructed, *"Who can discern his errors? Declare me innocent from hidden faults. Keep back your servant also <u>from presumptuous sins; let them not have dominion over me!</u> Then I shall be blameless, and <u>innocent of great transgression</u>"* (Psalm 19:12-13).

One must abide in the true Christ and fearfully be led by the Holy Spirit—then in Christ's energy, in his time, and according to God's will—you will be used to speak, pray, or command God's will to be done on earth.

Beatitude Living
No room for sin, carnal motives, religiosity, or legalism

What is the standard attitude of heart that the sincere believer must maintain? Here it is, in Christ's words ringing forth from the Sermon on the Mount!

"And he opened his mouth and taught them, saying: 'Blessed are the poor in spirit, for theirs is the kingdom of heaven. Blessed are those who mourn, for they shall be comforted. Blessed are the meek, for they shall inherit the earth. Blessed are those who hunger and thirst for righteousness, for they shall be satisfied. Blessed are the merciful, for they shall obtain mercy. Blessed are the pure in heart, for they shall see God. Blessed are the peacemakers, for they shall be called sons of God. Blessed are those who are persecuted for righteousness' sake, for theirs is the kingdom of heaven. Blessed are you when men revile you and persecute you and utter all kinds of evil against you falsely on my account'" (Matthew 5:2-11).

Christians cannot mimic these Christ-like character attributes. Church attendance, Bible study, Bible college, seminary or any earthly discipleship program or hyper-faith ministry cannot instill or create this kind of purity. The way to receive heaven's blessing on earth as described by Christ in his famed sermon on the mount can only be obtained by those who belong to Christ and obey all that he teaches. Becoming Christ-like in nature will bring the blessed state of being that so many crave, yet most find so elusive. That desire to be at peace with God and life while living in a sinful and often evil world is the desire for most people of all races, religions, and cultures.

This core desire of living in a constant state of contentment and blessing is what drives so many followers of Christ to the many false teachers, cult leaders, and spiritualistic movements. Yet beatitude living is obtained by anyone who chooses to seriously embrace all that Christ taught. What makes the alternatives and false paths so attractive for the masses of Christianity is how Christ prescribes the way or method in obtaining a heavenly-blessed life on earth:

"Enter by the narrow gate. For the gate is wide and the way is easy that leads to destruction, and those who enter by it are many. For the gate is narrow and the way is hard that leads to life, and those who find it are few" (Matthew 7:13-14).

Few search and enter by the way Christ teaches, while many fall headlong into every new movement or teaching that promises an easier way. If we cling to sin and enjoy any aspect of unrighteous living, beatitude living is unsustainable. If we drive ourselves in our natural abilities and strength, we will be precluded from the blessed life on earth. Returning to strict religious do's and don'ts will just incite the works of the flesh, and sinning will just get worse, or even more damning if we become content in our self-righteous pretense. Deliverance of demonic oppression without the work of the cross upon the desires of the flesh will only give temporal relief.

No superlative apostle or anointed prophet of the hour can lay hands on you and download beatitude living into your heart, spirit, and mind. Jesus said of himself, *"I am the way, and the truth, and the life. No one comes to the Father except through me"* (John 14:6). Thus, it is the person of Christ working with us, working in us, and leading us that causes anyone ever to arrive at beatitude living—however, we must make sure it is the true Christ!

Loving Truth
Overcoming passivity, idolatry and vain imaginings

Jessie Penn-Lewis with Evan Roberts warned of this very hour, when Christians would passively follow lies and deceptions leading to their own destruction. Their co-authored work *War on the Saints* is still a powerful message for the discerning saint and a thorn in the flesh for the purveyors of shortcut fanaticism so widely embraced today. (Look for the unabridged edition.)

> "The primary cause of deception and possession in surrendered believers may be condensed into one word, PASSIVITY; that is, a cessation of the active exercise of the will in control over spirit, soul and body, or either, as may be the case. It is, practically, a counterfeit of 'surrender to God.' The believer who 'surrenders' his 'members'—or faculties—to God, and ceases to use them himself, thereby falls into

'passivity' which enables evil spirits to deceive, and possess any part of his being which has become passive." Jessie Penn-Lewis and Evan Roberts, *War on the Saints: Unabridged Ninth Edition* New York: Thomas E. Lowe, 1994, pages 69)

War on the Saints was written by Penn-Lewis and Roberts as the outcome of the hijacking of the 1904–1905 Welsh Revival in Wales. The authors witnessed the counterfeiting work of deceiving spirit upon susceptible believers led astray by false teachings.

During the later stages of the Welsh revival, an influx of immature teachers began to instruct new believers and revived Christians in using teachings that produced emotional manifestations and spiritual encounters. In their sincere effort to manage the growth in numbers, many of the new teachers and preachers minimized and even avoided sound doctrine on character transformation and the principle of the cross bringing death to the passions and desires of the flesh.

Christians involved in the Welsh revival were deceived into a passive approach in seeking the infilling and baptism of the Holy Spirit, where submission to spiritual sensations and emotions became the sign of maturity (a false sign). This allowed a subtle tincture or mixture of the counterfeit demonic to flow with the work of the Holy Spirit, an insidious plan of the enemy that continues to grow in most subsequent movements. False teachings added in these movements reinforce the widening of the doorways of individual believers for increased infestation with the counterfeiting demons.

Whenever manifestations of the Spirit receive credence over sound doctrine and discernment in the testing of these spiritual experiences, then passivity of mind and spirit make these faculties (mind and spirit) ineffective in discerning the counterfeit. The mind and spirit become programmed to act like a sponge soaking up counterfeit and empty manifestations.

The passivity that plagues so many believers today directly correlates to a culture of "magic thinking" that is now pervasive throughout societies worldwide. Pretending and expanding the human imagination has become a major genre in television, motion pictures, literature and music. Pushing the exotic in imagery, sound, and thought to be as realistic as possible reflects a culture of magic thinking, fantasy, and illusion. Especially in the American culture, escapism and magic thinking become a way of living daily, more than ever, and this sickness of passivity has infected the preaching and teaching of the Gospel of Jesus Christ.

As the end of this age approaches, delusional thinking will continue to increase. Embracing the truth of Christ, and the reality of a trouble-filled world will become harder for the lukewarm and deceived Christian, as well the masses of the lost and the rebellious.

In fact, the Apostle Paul prophesied concerning this end-of-the-age trend of passivity and magic thinking in the following passage:

"The coming of the lawless one is by the activity of Satan with all power and false signs and wonders, and with all wicked deception for those who are perishing, because they refused to love the truth and so be saved. Therefore God sends them a strong delusion, so that they may believe what is false, in order that all may be condemned who did not believe the truth but had pleasure in unrighteousness" (2 Thessalonians 2:9-12).

Christians will not be exempt from exposure to the anti-Christ lies. The sincere saint must all the more press in and gain solid knowledge of our Lord Jesus Christ and become disciplined in obedience and discernment. Another excerpt from *War on the Saints* reinforces how easily Christians become tripped up because they do not exercise their faculties in testing the spirits.

Christians are as open to possession by evil spirits as other men, and become possessed because they have, in most cases, unwittingly fulfilled the conditions upon which evil spirits work, and, apart from the cause of willful sin, given ground to deceiving spirits, through (1) accepting their counterfeits of Divine workings, and (2) cultivating passivity, and non-use of the faculties; and this through misconception of the spiritual laws which govern the Christian life. (*War on the Saints* page 69)

"Beloved, do not believe every spirit, but test the spirits to see whether they are from God, for many false prophets have gone out into the world" (1 John 4:1).

Renounce seeking pleasure in disassociation and escapism. Test everything and do so by loving and seeking the truth! Then the person of Truth will have your cooperation to train and discipline you, guiding you in all truth. (See John 16:13-1.)

True Servants and Christ-like Character
Becoming a saint for the work of the ministry

Choosing to become a true servant of Christ demands commitment and a thorough understanding of the cost required to go all the way with Christ. Over the last forty or so years the term "disciple of Christ" has acquired a somewhat unwholesome connotation. The shepherding movement and other oppressive cult-like movements that required a deep commitment to Christ proved to make naïve Christians vulnerable to tyrannical leadership, and Christians involved in this particular movement became oppressed and were steered in the wrong direction. Most new Christians become easily misled to obey man's programs instead of learning to hear the voice of Christ and obey him.

Often those desiring to become a true saint and Christian worker are misled into becoming obsessed with a self-righteous holiness and an outer perfection that often makes lost sinners feel unredeemable and the struggling believer hopeless. It is a major trap to become so self-conscious in appearing righteous, holy, and heavenly minded that their witness and good works becomes putrid, conflicting, and useless.

A true disciple of Christ is made by the hand of Christ through serious study of the Word, embracing daily challenges and trials, and forming a practical theology that emanates genuine and humble holiness without any pretense. Through life's trials and the discipline of Christ, true holiness is imparted by Christ's presence and it is not contrived or worked-up by becoming mystical or obsessed with being ascetic (living like a monk).

Some fall into the a John-the-Baptist type of faith, living an austere life, beating upon themselves moment by moment in fear of temptation or making a mistake. The Apostle Paul pointed out this type of approach to discipleship as a trap, by explaining,

"If with Christ you died to the elemental spirits of the world, why, as if you were still alive in the world, do you submit to regulations—'Do not handle, Do not taste, Do not touch' (referring to things that all perish as they are used)—according to human precepts and teachings? These have indeed an appearance of wisdom in promoting self-made religion and asceticism and severity to the body, but they are of no value in stopping the indulgence of the flesh" (Colossians 2:20-23).

Many Christians imitate their pastor or favorite leader, assimilating particular mannerisms or conversation style. Even if that leader may be genuine, mimicking Christ in third person is a subtle way of following men. The true saint must know Christ personally and allow his or her faith to be built with firsthand knowledge and experiences guided and directed by Christ. This approach creates genuine saints who have their own unique and godly personality—a personality that is dynamic and in concert with the Holy Spirit's abiding presence and undergirded by true Christ-like character.

Many saints become distracted from following and obeying the true Christ by being a faithful church worker, tirelessly carrying out the goals and dreams of the church elders and leaders. Many follow personality leaders who are glib (slick or superficial) and run a house of entertainment where pleasure-driven worship becomes an idol.

Learn to discern those of likeminded desire in becoming a true servant, walking in Christ-like character.

True Deliverance for the Wounded and Demonized Believer
A process of resisting, working out, and growing up

The following is a basic overview of the processes and required raw elements for an effective support team to help wounded and unstable Christians recover and grow in grace to obtain the fullness of Christ. Detailed explanation of the process of deliverance, healing and recovery for the wounded and demonized Christian will be published in a later volume.

A wounded Christian can suffer from co-habitation of the demonic when that believer has experienced past abuse—abuse in sexual, emotional or mental form (the difficulties vary depending on the severity of the abuses).

There are many dangerous approaches for deliverance by well-meaning ministries. Most lead to temporary relief, only later to end in frustration and blowing-up within the believer's life. Many more learn to construct or fabricate a pseudo-Christian personality that covers an impure heart and defilements of spirit—this state is perhaps the worst, since the demonic backs off, allowing the deceived to feel false peace thinking they are following and know the true Christ.

Attempts at deliverance for those who are severely wounded and suffer from dividedness of soul and spirit in many cases will retain ground for demonic co-habitation to remain. In many cases the demons come back and the last condition becomes worse, penetrating deeper into the fragmented soul and spirit, often brining additional demons.

The net result from false deliverance—where the demons leave temporarily then return—is that when the symptoms return with the demons, many fall away, only to return to Christ when they hit bottom (suffering unnecessary trouble and pain). Worse, many become truly damned and walk away from Christ completely. Then there are the exceptions, where many become immersed in false doctrine and hypocrisy; they make shipwreck their faith religiously and the demons need no longer harass them.

In the latter case, the demonic learned to play possum in many forms and quit the oppressive work in exchange for false doctrine and spiritualism, including false spirit manifestations that work as numbing doses of ecstatic feelings through the personal spirit.

However, there is hope in embracing sound doctrine and receiving proper ministry from those who have succeeded in their own deliverance and recovery.

Various Scripture passages, in particular the book of James prescribe biblical principles for the unstable Christian to embrace that leads to true deliverance. Receiving help from others who have succeeded in the processes of true deliverance and sanctification will be the most difficult aspect, (there are so few). Those basic principles with a brief overview follows— finding temporal help and support will be difficult, but not impossible—for God, all things are possible.

- **Burden Bearing:** The mature saint must learn how to fulfill the law of Christ by bearing the burdens of the wounded and troubled new and old believers, who find themselves struggling in their walk with Christ. Every true fellowship must have a team of intensive facilitators who proficiently walk in gifts of the Holy Spirit and can provide prophetic insight into the hidden issues of heart and defilements of spirit. This work includes walking in a position of authority to bind the demonic from interfering with the revealing of strongholds, gateways and areas of co-habitation. Part of the ministry team must include seasoned prayer warriors who undergird the whole process with intercessory prayer. This prayer team is in addition to the fellowship's prayer life of consistent, fervent and earnest prayer (which should be the practice of the whole fellowship). (See Galatians 6:1-10.)

    There are times that the ministry team must engage the demonic lodged in the person asking for deliverance with intense prayer and fasting. Those trained and experienced in such warfare should be the frontline support and spearhead any deliverance work. Those in training must be prepared to receive oppression and attacks as well.

    Those who are not prepared or are concealing impurities within their heart or spirit, and then try their hand at deliverance, can expect a beating. Satan and the demons will have ground to attack well-meaning saints who are not called to practice deliverance and attempt to walk in prophetic counsel, or who are not sanctified, mature enough, and trained.

- **Resisting the devil:** Each person in process must learn through study and mentoring how to resist the devil and exercise faith in battle towards deliverance and wholeness. Too many come to so-called deliverance meetings and have devils cast out, then walk away partially delivered but never learn to resist the devil when he returns to gain entrance again, thus they never learn to grow in faith. They become passive and lazy, falling back into temptations and overtaken again. Many do not carry their own load because those interceding and working in ministry like the attention of being heroes and famously be known as the "anointed go-to" exorcists.

    In addition, many are taught to practice superstitious acts such as pleading the blood of Christ repeatedly when they are oppressed or harassed by the demons, as if it were some magic incantation to perform. They may get temporal relief in doing these superstitious rituals because the demonic decides to play possum to gain a deeper stronghold through false doctrine.

    The triage-ministry team (see page 243) must ensure each person learns to stand on their own two feet of faith, resist the devil and draw near to God, learning to work with the Holy Spirit who is our master-counselor and Spirit of truth—who we all can access twenty-four hours a day, every day of our life. (See James 4:1-10.)

- **Confession, repentance, prayer, and cleansing—humbly:** Humility is key in working with the Lord and with his appointed servants in working out one's salvation and overcoming demonic strongholds. Sincere repentance from a humble spirit and a contrite heart is also vital in obtaining the Holy Spirit's help in receiving cleansing and forgiveness. Many initially repent of all their sins when they first come to Christ—however, the deeper issues of the heart often carry roots of bitterness and self-righteousness that harden the heart and spirit. These issues allow the demonic to linger, oppress, and find doorways to infest further, especially for the more severely double-minded (divided) where demonic co-habitation can take place. God may sometimes allow demonic oppression and satanic buffeting during trials or in preparations for ministry. These types of trials will run their own course as the Lord dictates, in order to produce steadfastness and Christ-like perfection. (See James 1:1-16).

    However, the cleansing process may also involve fiery trials to break denial of hidden defilements, carnal motives, and spontaneous works of the flesh. A willingness to renounce sinful attitudes, sinful alliances, and sinful motives in contrite, genuine repentance allows the Holy Spirit to cleanse and instill peace with God in forgiveness by the indwelling of his Spirit. (See James 5:13-20.)

- **Intensive care for deeper healing:** The gift of prophecy when working properly within a trained team of burden bearers and intercessors (counselors and mentors) will help facilitate intensive healing. After some initial breakthroughs in broader areas of bitterness and wounds, often a more intensive work will be required, especially if there is severe fragmentation of the personal spirit and the spirit of the mind. (See Proverbs 15:13, 17:14 and Ephesians 4:22-24.)

Often there will be intense spiritual warfare required involving the binding of the demonic from opposing the exposure of deeply rooted defilements, wounds to the spirit and misbeliefs. Inquiring of the demonic when an evil spirits manifest is a trap, where the demonic misleads those ministering to go on a wild goose chase and end up tormenting the inflicted person all the more.

Often, what is thought to be a demon emerging is a personality (a divided part of the person possessed) that has switched out and gained control and exhibits similar attributes of the demonic such as hate, rage, bitterness, jealousy, sexual lust or perversion—in other words, one of the works of the flesh as an agenda. The personality is the home for the demonic, when cohabitation exists. Casting out the demonic and properly leading the divided part to repentance, cleansing, renewal in the Holy Spirit and then eventually integration (fusing) with the core-faith part of the tormented Christian must take place.

Thus, the gift of prophecy, word of knowledge, word of wisdom, and discernment of spirits will pin point the areas that the unclean and evil spirits have gained a right or ground in which to infest and even cohabitate.

- **Recovery and transformation:** There will be a required space of time between each area of deliverance, cleansing and purification of where the demonic had ground to infest, oppress or cohabitate. Recovery and transformation from demonization hinges on understanding why the demonic found ground. With this understanding, a thorough resolution in forgiveness, accountability, and receiving Christ's healing love and truth must be applied about the matter. Bitterness, revenge, animosity and fear are to be expunged from the heart concerning all persons connected to the point of trauma, defilement or abuse. For each fleshly desire with its roots, a Christ-like attitude and understanding comes to replace those deep wounds with associated selfish and evil desires, emotions, and misbeliefs about God, others, and self. This is the recovery and transformation process in summary and must have the necessary time to process, all in God's leading and timing.

- **The daily work of the cross:** Embracing the cross must take place as each issue that gave ground to Satan and his minions emerge. This process must continue until all the pools of anger, bitterness, resentment, hate, fear, insecurity, self-pity, etc., are resolved and die. If not, the fruit of the Holy Spirit and God's healing grace and comfort will be not find place to work in renewing and imparting newness of life in Christ.

- **The process of renewing the spirit of the mind:** We have discussed purifying the heart and the personal spirit. Further, facilitation for renewing of the spirit of the mind must be planned and implemented. It took some time for us to realize that this principle described by the Apostle Paul in the book of Ephesians points to what secular psychology terms the unconscious mind. (See Ephesians 4:17-24.) Many try carnal methods of re-programming the unconscious mind, however, any effort such as mind control, hypnosis, meditation, or positive thinking leads to harmful results where inner issues of the mind can be aggravated when probed in the flesh outside of God's timing, grace, and healing power.

Unclean, evil and selfish thoughts usually originate from either the heart or the spirit of the mind. Of course, the demonic can inject thoughts, but those devilish thoughts, often find resonating or similar defiling issues within. Old-nature structures within the spirit of the mind carry old-nature desires and deceitful lust. Taking these thoughts captive, submitting them to Christ, and asking the Holy Spirit's help to track down the old nature character structures for renewal will often be an ongoing process. This process will require the Holy Spirits counsel and help from the ministry team. Members of the team should be familiar with this process from their own experience in putting off their old nature and putting on the new by the renewal of the spirit of the mind. *"As the truth is in Jesus, to put off your old self, which belongs to your former manner of life and is corrupt through deceitful desires, <u>and to be renewed in the spirit of your minds</u>, and to put on the new self, created after the likeness of God in true righteousness and holiness"* (Ephesians 4:21-24).

Walking in the True Gift of Prophecy

As the end-of-this-age troubles increase, many false Christians will become more obnoxious and even dangerous to the safety and welfare of the fellowship they infiltrate. One of the most important gifts to help clean up a fellowship and chase out the wolves and false believers as well as confront and help the wounded and defiled Christian, is the gift of prophecy. In the Book of Acts we see how the Holy Spirit used Peter and the gift of prophecy to disclose two would-be liars who were trying to sneak into fellowship on pretense in order to glorify themselves.

Peter asked Ananias, *"Why has Satan filled your heart to lie to the Holy Spirit?"* The Holy Spirit had informed Peter that Ananias and his wife Sapphira had contrived to lie concerning the amount they had received for the sale of their property, keeping back some, but telling Peter they were donating the full amount they had received. If you are not familiar with this account in the Scripture, then read Acts 4:32- 5:11.

This husband-and-wife team, in deceit and greed for recognition, were stopped dead in their tracks—literally; they both fell dead at the feet of Peter. First Ananias and then his wife a few hours later dropped dead, because she also lied.

The point requiring explanation is the key outcome of this prophetic word spoken through the Apostle Peter. Obviously, these two implants of Satan were stopped from gaining a foothold within the new church, but the ripple effect of this Holy Spirit-led intervention must be understood as well: *"Great fear came upon the whole church and upon all who heard of these things"* (Acts 5:11).

The healthy fear of God should be amongst the brethren in any solid fellowship, and thus be sensed by newcomers and outsiders. The fear of God is accomplished by the practice of the true gift of prophesy. *"But if all prophesy, and an unbeliever or outsider enters, he is convicted by all, he is called to account by all, the secrets of his heart are disclosed, and so, falling on his face, he will worship God and declare that God is really among you"* (1 Corinthians 14:24-25). Notice Paul describes these new people coming to fellowship, who are called to account of hidden issues of heart (troubling issues as well as secret sins) will fall on their face in a healthy fear and reverence as they realize God is in the midst the congregation. Certainly, not fall on their backs titillated, mesmerized and left to their own issues of heart.

Ministry Case: *Chasing out the wolves*

Every Thursday night from 7 to 9, the ministry's support group worked with Christians who struggled with various issues. Addictions, abuse, and destructive relationships were the primary issues addressed. On occasion, we would find a person attending to be *insincere*. We would confront them appropriately and if they did not repent and stop, they could not attend. One particular man was coming to hit on women. We went through the confrontational process, but he continued his sexual advances, so we barred him from the group and fellowship.

He continued to call one particular woman in the group. As per our counsel, she had a restraining order served. He was not to call her, or me, as her pastor, or use anyone as a go-between to contact her. In spite of the legal restraint, he attempted to get me to pass on a message to her. He telephoned my residence and posed the request and I said "no." He would not listen to reason and he started railing at me. Filled with righteous indignation, the Holy Spirit prompted me to tell him, *"You son of the devil, the next time I see you, I'll see you in handcuffs."* He finally hung up. I reported this to the police and they served him a court appearance. About two months later, the prosecuting attorney requested that I testify at his court appearance.

All the parties concerned had arrived, except the accused. He was late. Finally, we all heard his voice booming in the hallway. He was telling his attorney that this crazy minister was to blame for his court appearance. He continued his loud assessment of me as they walked into the courtroom.

He came in *handcuffed* to another person. Evidently, his imprisonment was for some past felony. It never dawned on him that the prophetic word the Lord spoke through me two months prior had come to pass. The Lord knew he had warrants for his arrest and had a servant of the Lord speak forth his incarceration. Like Elymas the Magician, this man did not repent, even though the Lord executed judgment upon him. Ω

Secrets of the heart not only include any wicked agendas, but also for so many, they can contain unresolved damaged emotions and wounds to the spirit. Those hidden or forgotten wounds should be exposed and brought to the light of Jesus for healing in a true New Testament fellowship ministry.

Ministry Case: *Prenatal wounds*

Often, wounds to the personal spirit are deep and reside within a person for a long time. The following ministry case is a good example.

During a counseling session with a young Christian woman, the Holy Spirit prompted me to inform her of a wound that occurred to her spirit, before she was born, that is, while she was still in her mother's womb.

After prayer, she closed her eyes and began to describe a vision recounting an incident. The gift of knowledge was in operation. The Holy Spirit revealed to her that her father had punched her mother while pregnant with her. *"The spirit of man is the lamp of the LORD, searching all his innermost parts"* (Proverbs 20:27). Her spirit suffered wounds from this incident and the Holy Spirit gave light to her personal spirit to reveal this event.

We prayed over this revelation and prayed for healing of this trauma to her spirit. The healing would take some time, since there could be fragmented parts of her spirit contaminated by such perverse abuse.

I suggested that she also talk to her mother about this revelation for confirmation. Indeed, at the next session this woman described a past incident that totally confirmed what the Holy Spirit was trying to heal within her spirit.

Her mother said, "When I was nine months along with you, your father and I were playing cards and I was winning. He became enraged and punched me in the stomach."

The Holy Spirit revealed many other defiling and cruel abuses for this counselee. Each required cleansing and emotional resolution. This wounded Christian was getting at the truth concerning why she also abused and neglected her own children. Ω

Finding True End-of-the-Age Fellowship
Finding safe fellowship in a time of persecution, betrayal, and trouble

There is nothing wrong with attending fellowship in a church building if it is used to help facilitate true growth in Christ, and other legitimate ministry operations. Today, most church facilities are designed and operated to propagate socialization and entertainment among the attendees. The act of worshiping becomes the focus and little is taught on walking in true Christ-like character and avoiding wolves disguised as fellow believers. The sincere servant of Christ must walk in keen wisdom and divinely inspired discernment when seeking true fellowship.

Most sincere fellowships have few resources and little training to walk in the gift of prophecy as a people. In practice, this would result in the secrets of the heart within newcomers or outsiders being exposed to keep the unsavory reprobate away and help the struggling sinner find salvation, sanctification and maturity.

This is God's way to make sure each part of the body of Christ becomes pure and stays pure. This gift of the Holy Spirit is to be used to screen new comers, new converts and outsiders by exposing secrets of the heart and carnal motives, just as we discussed. The story of Ananias and Sapphira is an example of the Holy Spirit in action, screening and stopping evil from gaining a foothold and spreading amongst the brethren.

As more persecution mounts in the U.S. and around the world, attending a genuine New Testament minded fellowship will become very important. There is global religious tension boiling where the powerful influences of Islam, Judaism, and Israel (as a nation), along with Christianity are meeting head on.

Christians who hold that the coming of Christ is the only way to end the world's troubles and those churches that emphasize evangelism will be seen as anti-world peace agitators. This will be part of the reason for increased persecution escalating into outright hatred. This end-of-the-age persecution will be just as Jesus warned: *"Then they will deliver you up to tribulation and put you to death, and you will be hated by all nations for my name's sake. And then many will fall away and betray one another and hate one another"* (Matthew 24:9-10).

Hatred and betrayal between Christians will become intense and political. Now is the time to seek Christ's leadership in finding solid fellowship, even if it is necessary to hold your own fellowship with others that you definitely know to be likeminded.

Many existing fellowships and congregations will eventually wake up to the truth and begin to clean house while many will stay frozen in false doctrine until it is too late to change. Some end-times ministries will still hang on to the American dream and radically oppose the continuing loss of freedoms and actively (overtly or covertly) oppose the coming new world order and the anti-Christ rule. (Review the following passage reference and keep it in mind if you come upon a fellowship that maintains a radical survival agenda; Revelation 13:5-10.)

There is coming a day in the near future when many non-believers and Christians alike will be imprisoned or slain because they opposed or resisted the coming new world order of the beast. Look to find an end-of-the-age fellowship that understands that the true saint must keep a low profile in the coming dark times: not to fight the coming anti-Christ rule, yet not worship the beast or take its mark. Rather we must be prepared and ready to endure to the end in God's grace, mercy, guidance, and divine protection and provision—and proclaim the good news as directed by the Holy Spirit.

What to Look for in Finding Safe Fellowship
Restoring the true gifts of discernment and prophesy—a matter of fellowship safety and survival

In the late 60s and 70s—and since—the big push in many sectors of the body of Christ was operating in the gifts of the Holy Spirit. Speaking in tongues became an absolute rule for many, a rite of passage and a sign of spiritual elitism. Dr. Rick Walston writes an excellent discourse dealing with speaking in tongues as a perquisite and sign of receiving the baptism of the Spirit. Entitled *The Speaking in Tongues Controversy* this work is thorough and clears up the debate.

Of course, the Apostle Paul's writings give specific instruction on seeking the gifts that, if truly understood and applied, would dissipate much of the confusion, controversy and divisiveness. However, there is an often-overlooked directive that Paul penned concerning the gift of tongues and the gift of prophecy as previously cited. (see 1 Corinthians 14:20-25).

If most fellowships practiced the gift of prophecy correctly; false brethren, game players, wolves, hirelings, charlatans, liars, and the perverse as well as the wicked would be exposed and led to repent or be chased out. Further, outsiders or believers suffering from instability in their walk with Christ would be afforded a prophetic ministry to bring to the light secrets of their heart, exposing hidden defilements, wounds and dividedness for cleansing, healing, and transformation. Many attempt to walk in these gifts without having their powers of discernment increased sufficiently, causing many to wander into false gifts and counterfeit faith activities. Training our powers of discernment establishes a foundation for the gift of discernment or discerning of spirits and the gift of prophecy to operate properly.

Jesus personally taught his disciples by word and example with circumstances and situations that reinforced his teachings. Christ took the disciples through experiences that quickened their faculties (mental powers) to readily distinguish good from evil. Judas was a primary learning and training experience as well as the Pharisees and the other false religious leaders.

Christ's method of training the disciples in discernment by those painful experiences laid the foundation for the gifts of the Holy Spirit to operate effectively after the day of Pentecost. The gifts of discernment and prophecy operated within the original disciples with minimum hindrance since they understood the deceit of evil and did not hesitate or question the Holy Spirit's prompting because of unbelief.

Peter immediately and effectively heard from the Holy Spirit concerning Ananias and his lies. Peter did not hesitate to prophesy God's judgment that took the life of this deceiving believer. Peter did not hinder the gifts of the Spirit because his powers of discernment had been trained by Christ, beforehand. Ananias' death was no fluke, since Peter was used of God to bring down Sapphira, Ananias' wife for lying also—her death occurring in a matter of hours from her husband's passing.

Many Christians are taught to seek the gift of discerning spirits and the gift of prophecy having very little training by practice in life's experiences or by learning from the Lord in his discipline. The deeper, more solid food of the Word of God must be worked into the believer's life for growth and maturity before these profound and powerful gifts can manifest in truth.

Instead, believers seeking these gifts prematurely, run into trouble because they cannot receive what the Holy Spirit would prefer to be pronounced prophetically. Few today can fathom the gift Peter received, let alone have the courage to execute such a deadly prophecy.

In the days to come, safe fellowship must allow the Lord to discipline and restore the true gift of prophecy and the discerning of spirits.

Chapter Eight

Developing Our Powers of Discernment

Start by Breaking the Spell of this Age
Wake up now to the reality of the coming age

Serious students of Scripture should be realizing that the signs Christ spoke of concerning the end of this age are now happening at breakneck speeds. However, the deceptive powers of this age have many sincere Christians spellbound, taking ease and trying to make the best of it here and now.

In being serious about developing our powers of discernment, a major hurdle that will stand in the way is the love of this present world. This will be hard for many due to the popular teachings that put Christians at ease, with hope in material blessings. Jesus warned about letting the cares of this world bog us down lest that day come upon us like a snare.

As one wakes up and turns to the truth in Scripture concerning this hour, realizing that all the indicators and signs are bearing witness—any end-of-the-age gloom and doom should be replaced with great joy *"Now when these things begin to take place, straighten up and raise your heads, because your redemption is drawing near"* (Luke 21:28).

For those yearning for Christ, it is not as difficult to wake up, but nevertheless, there must be a deliberate effort in seeking Christ to help understand, embrace the truth, and discern the increasing darkness and deception. Because of the idea that the end of this age will never happen in our life time, and because so many mock anyone who challenges the mindset that the world will never end, it is hard to shake off the comforting thought that the sun will always come up tomorrow. (The world is not going to end, rather the end of this age about to take place.)

Of the lethargy of this last generation—and how every generation of sincere believers ought to live—Peter writes, *"Where is the promise of his coming? Forever since the fathers fell asleep, <u>all things are continuing as they were from the beginning of creation</u>... Since all these things are thus to be dissolved, what sort of people ought you to be in lives of holiness and godliness, waiting for and hastening the coming of the day of God, because of which the heavens will be set on fire and dissolved, and the heavenly bodies will melt as they burn! But according to his promise <u>we are waiting for new heavens and a new earth in which righteousness dwells</u>"* (2 Peter 3:4-13).

New heavens and a new earth are coming at the end of this age. Do you truly believe this is reality or are you coasting along with the notion that it will not be in your lifetime? As the birth pangs of the coming Kingdom increase in frequency and intensity, many will begin to put the puzzle together and shake off the spell of this age—the lie that everything will continue as it was from the beginning. The reality is, Christ is coming soon and great trouble will precede his appearance.

Indeed, Jesus said it would be like the days of Noah; *"And they were unaware until the flood came and swept them all away, so will be the coming of the Son of Man….Therefore you also must be ready, for the Son of Man is coming at an hour you do not expect."* (Matthew 24:39,44). We will not know the day or hour, but Christ did instruct us to be alert, watching to recognize the season and know, *"that he is near, at the very gates"* (Review Matthew 24:32-33). This will be a major step in developing one's powers of discernment—to shake off the Pollyanna (worldly optimism) spell of churchianity.

Let Us Get Our Theology Right!
Practical theology based on observing all that Christ commanded

Another major reason for the lack of true discernment amongst the saints is that most Christians are in a theological no-man's-land—a place full of uncertainty, ignorance, denial and confusion. While most modern theologians can agree on and explain the elemental doctrines of Christ and the basics of his Gospel, that is the extent of clarity and unity. When it comes to the end-of-this-age events and timing, overcoming the sin nature, the gifts of the Holy Spirit, practical theology that develops true maturity in Christ—here the sincere and hungry Christian suffers great theological confliction, and is pretty much left to his or her own study.

Many popular teachings are based on what I call *junk theology* rooted in man's precepts, where the truth of Scripture is misinterpreted and applied by the will and energy of man. This creates confused and anemic Christians who will soon find themselves in deep trouble when raging end-of-this-age storms reach us. The only theology that is true, practical and approved by God comes from Christ; from all the teachings of Christ, revealed and applied with proper understanding by help from the person of Christ. The great commission that he gave to his disciples, which was and is to be passed on to every generation of disciples, is simple and practical, that is *"to <u>observe all that I have commanded you.</u> And behold, <u>I am with you always, to the end of the age</u>."* (Matthew 28:20).

A true disciple will know the true Christ intimately, understand his harder teachings, and in turn teach new disciples to observe all that Jesus taught and commanded and learn to discern his leading, his presence and his voice. Stop missing out on learning how to embrace sound doctrine under the discipline of Christ and the leadership of the Holy Spirit. When one truly grasps the situation and understands what Christ taught about his second coming, vacillation, confusion and doubts vanish and the false teachings become obvious.

Allow Christ to Be Your Teacher
Give him permission to do whatever it take;, learn to be doers of the word, not just hearers

If you desire to walk in true discernment, then you must submit yourself to the true Christ and give him permission to deal with you on his terms, in every aspect of your life; but first sit down and count the cost of following the true Christ. It will hard at first, as he leads each in training to pick up their cross daily and demands that each of us give up running the show and owning and living for our piece of the earthly pie. (See Luke 14:27-33.)

Be willing to have whatever manmade theology you have embraced be exposed, wrecked, and renounced. Christ will certainly reveal the word of Righteousness (through Scripture made alive) to destroy those doctrines that conceal issues of heart, selfish motives, and carnal works that so many walk in today—works that produce nothing but death. The sincere disciple must move beyond the elementary doctrines of Christ. (See Hebrews 6:1-8.)

I guarantee Christ will be faithful to bring your theology in line with all of his words. At the end of this transforming work personally wrought by Christ, you will understand the full meaning of the following Scripture: *"If you keep my commandments, you will abide in my love, just as I have kept my Father's commandments and abide in his love. These things I have spoken to you, that my joy may be in you, and that your joy may be full"* (John 15:10-11).

Study those who went before you and compare what they teach to what Christ taught. If you are confused by the writings of the apostles, again seek Christ and study what he taught, using his words as a filter to help you reach the right understanding of the more difficult writings in the New Testament and by other teachers, past and present.

Eventually you will discard those authors and teachers that mix truth with the teachings of men; as you mature, a revulsion of the false will develop and you will you dump those works in the trash. You will become quick to discern any hint of carnality in their messages and see through a false teaching, *"hating even the garment stained by the flesh"* (Jude 22).

The New Testament explains how to obtain a proper relationship with God, so exhaust your energy and study in comprehending the truth of the new covenant—the Gospel of Christ. Then, as the Spirit of truth leads you into the Old Testament, confusion will be minimized between the Old and the New. (You must learn to study the Old Testament in light of Christ, and his work for us and in us, as with the writers of the New Testament).

This will be difficult, but it is what Christ calls us to do. *"Ask, and it will be given to you; seek, and you will find; knock, and it will be opened to you. For everyone who asks receives, and the one who seeks finds, and to the one who knocks it will be opened"* (Luke 11:9-10).

Persevere, and he will be faithful to open your heart and mind, making God's Word alive and practical. Resist the temptation of having others do this hard work for you. Even if a teacher is true and he or she brings forth sound doctrine, if you do not allow Christ to make the teaching your own, then you are at risk, just hearing the Word and not working it into your life is folly. You will run the risk of never knowing Christ, but only knowing of him by what others teach. *"But be doers of the word, and not hearers only, deceiving yourselves"* (James 1:22).

Developing a Healthy Fear of God

Because of religious ritualistic behavior and fabricated doctrines of men, the believer's fear of God often becomes false and misguided—causing many to be in awe of leadership instead of being in awe of God. Masses follow their favorite teacher or pastor in blind loyalty and learn to model their favorite leader's version of Christ. If we truly desire Christ and his fullness, then we can expect suffering and through that suffering we will develop a godly fear. *"In the days of his flesh, Jesus offered up prayers and supplications, with loud cries and tears, to him who was able to save him from death, and <u>he was heard for his godly fear</u>. Although he was a Son, <u>he learned obedience through what he suffered</u>; and being made perfect he became the source of eternal salvation to all who obey him, being designated by God a high priest after the order of Melchizedek"* (Hebrews 5:7-10 RSV).

Many believe that the fear of the Lord is a state of mind that sinners reach in the process of becoming born again, but this passage shows us that it is a quality of Christ himself. Resist the spellbinding powers of the prosperity teachings that systematically cause Christians to presume upon God and walk in arrogance; instead develop a healthy fear for his discipline and chastising love. *"Those whom I love, I reprove and discipline, so be zealous and repent"* (Revelation 3:19).

Many deceived Christians believe God will sanction whatever they set their heart and mind to do, as long as it is not immoral or dishonest. If they have any need, they should exercise a word of faith and command fulfillment of that need into existence; this is really Satan's same old approach; if you have true faith then *"<u>command these stones</u> to become loaves of bread"* (Matthew 4:3). Many succumb to this satanic temptation in the guise and justification that working for God gives the green light to command it into existence.

Many Christians panic in the midst of a trial assigned by God that is meant to expose wrong motives and associated defilements. In confusion and panic, these satanically inspired thoughts take hold: *"If you are truly born again you should be able to command rocks to become bread, speak into existence a new car, command money to fall out of the sky and demonstrate with power that you should be in leadership."* Learn how to avoid presumption and fearfully allow the Lord to expose and clear you of any hidden faults. (See Psalm 19:12-13.)

Few understand that obedience includes finding and doing God's perfect will in all of life. Many Christians are unknowingly driven by bitter jealousies and selfish ambition in serving God (James 3:16). Money and material possessions become motivators for many Christians, and this drive is sanctioned by popular doctrines embraced throughout the body of Christ.

Learn to discern the difference between boldness in doing the Lord's will and presumption and arrogance in doing carnal works using Christ's name. God does bless us by providing for our material needs—money, clothing, food, cars, a home, a job—however these blessings should not manage us, but we must learn in obedience to manage them as faithful stewards. We must learn to seek the Kingdom of God first, above all else, and then what we need will be added unto us. We must trust everything in our sphere of influence to a loving heavenly Father, especially our loved ones.

Ministry Case: *The untrusting pastor*

Unfortunately, most Christians do not want to participate in God's true disciple-making program. They want to have God in their lives—but on their terms. Giving God permission to bring trials into their lives in order to produce true Christ-like character becomes too hard to accept and far too many believers *run from this kind of sacrificial life and covenant.*

Once I was associated with a pastor who had personal issues and difficulties and occasionally came to me for counsel and prayer support. Some of these issues were sexual in nature.

Finally, one day I encouraged him to give God permission to do whatever it took to change his inner nature by way of the work of the cross. His countenance turned pale, and I could tell deep fear arose within him.

After a moment of silence he said to me, "I just can't; I am afraid God will take away one of my children!" Through several situations and issues, this precious brother and I parted fellowship. About a year and a half later, he fell into sin, committed adultery and had to step down from ministry, at least for a while. Ω

Resist choosing the easy way in getting our sin nature to be powerless, and allow the work of the cross become the change agent in crucifying the carnal nature and resurrecting the new nature. The choice this man made ended in destruction. He did not understand that a healthy fear of God is the proper starting point to gain insight, understanding and wisdom—*"The fear of the Lord is the beginning of knowledge"* (Proverbs 1:7).

Yes, the trials will be hard—but not too hard. This man's reason for not submitting to God's plan for inner character transformation was the fear that God would take away one of his children! This is not a healthy fear of God, but a perverse fear. *"With the merciful you show yourself merciful; with the blameless man you show yourself blameless; with the purified you show yourself pure; and with the crooked you make yourself seem tortuous"* (Psalm 18:25-26). He projected from his own evil unbelieving heart that God was crooked and perverse. *"Take care, brethren, lest there be in any of you an evil, unbelieving heart, leading you to fall away from the living God'"* (Hebrews 3:12). Many Christians have not learned how to overcome an unbelieving heart, which limits Christ working mightily in their lives. It is written, *"And he did not do many mighty works there, because of their unbelief"* (Matthew 13:58).

Jesus comes to believers and challenges them with the cross and true discipleship, but far too many today will not give up their own lives so Christ will have preeminence in all things. They hang onto life vicariously, clinging to others and making idols out of children, a spouse, ministry, work, material goods and reputation. They refuse to surrender to the "all-owning demands" of Jesus. They mistrust him! Christ demands to transform our nature so that it becomes like his. (Study John 6:60-66.) At first, these demands of Christ seem unreasonable; however, that is not the case, as God has proved his faithfulness to me time and again.

Entering the Narrow Gate and Following the Hard Path
The wilderness journey and dying to human energies and carnal passions

"Since therefore Christ suffered in the flesh, arm yourselves with the same way of thinking, for whoever has suffered in the flesh has ceased from sin, so as to live for the rest of the time in the flesh no longer for human passions but for the will of God" (1 Peter 4:1-2).

Settle it now; following the true Christ and learning true discernment requires a certain amount of suffering. Your call, your own unbelief, the purposes of God, and the number of latent carnal issues that must be worked out and crucified in your life determines the amount of suffering and discipline required. This is the key to increasing our powers of discernment—to live for the will of God and to no longer be hindered by "gung-ho" human energies, carnal passions, and youthful desires as well as unbelief and fear. *"So flee youthful passions and pursue righteousness, faith, love, and peace, along with those who call on the Lord from a pure heart"* (2 Timothy 2:22).

Most teachings today actually portray human-carnal passions as normal and needed to become energized to serve Christ. All manner of schemes have been developed to determine and harness a believer's knack or personality-type energy to be placed and used in the ministry. A car sales representative with an outgoing personality would certainly make an excellent evangelist—winning souls to Christ; this is the current thinking in church staffing and equipping.

Nothing could be farther from the truth. In fact—human or carnal passions of the flesh are what Satan delights in promoting in his angel of light ministries. It is these carnal pools of energy that must be drained so that the true saint in ministry relies on the power of the Holy Spirit, his leadings and his workings.

It is paramount that the old self or old nature with its self-centered motives and intentions of the heart be exposed and crucified—drained of its carnal energy. To do this we must enter the narrow gate (learning to detect and refusing to rely on our natural abilities) and follow the hard path (the daily work of the cross) that brings death to our carnal motives, including some seemingly legitimate passions and desires. *"And those who belong to Christ Jesus have crucified the flesh with its passions and desires"* (Galatians 5:24). Some of our abilities, natural gifting, and knowledge often do come into play in life and ministry; however, we must learn not to rely on such, rather learn to allow the Lord to use them at his leading.

Many equate the passions and desires of the flesh strictly to sexual passions; however, carnal passions and desires include anything that drives us into doing our own thing in work, occupation, how we raise our children, ministry—as many do so driven by passions and desires rooted in bitter jealousy and selfish ambition.

Loving the Truth Revisited
Knowing the truth and being resolute—an oddity in most fellowships

An aspect of loving truth, abiding in Christ, and embracing all that he taught is having all doubts resolved about life and the end-of-the-age events now springing upon us. Jesus said for those who truly follow him, *"If you abide in my word, you are truly my disciples, and you will know the truth, and the truth will set you free"* (John 8:31-32).

After coming to Christ (in 1973), various teachings were in conflict and opposed to each other, and at first these conflicts seemed inconsequential for me: Eternal security, sanctification, grace, trials of life, free choice and the gifts of the Holy Spirit, and exactly how the end of this age would unfold were left alone by those in leadership.

The pat answers from popular Christian teachers and mentors in my early life as a Christian appeared to satisfy my doubts and concerns until the newness of my born-again experience wore off. Not long after my conversion, the three main differing rapture theories began to trouble me.

I was still in the military and relied heavily on our base Navy Chaplain to explain some of the more difficult New Testament principles and on one occasion I queried him about his position on the three popular theological positions on the rapture.

The popular book of the time on this subject was *The Late Great Planet Earth* by Hal Lindsey and Carole C. Carlson (1970), which holds that the rapture will take place prior to the start of the Great Tribulation. The popular abbreviation for the big three versions of the coming millennium and the timing for the rapture was and still is; the pre-tribulation rapture, mid-tribulation rapture, and post-tribulation rapture.

I sat in the chaplain's office presenting my question: which scenario was correct? At the end of my inquiry he stated his position. He emphatically said that he believed in the pan-millennium rapture. Of course, I was dumbfounded and asked, "What? I never heard of that one."

His pat explanation was, "If you believe in Christ, it will all pan-out in the end." His answer gave me temporary peace, however, as the years advanced that quip for a very important question proved very troubling. Sidestepping the question with a patronizing answer did not challenge me to seek to know the truth and understand what Christ taught about this very important biblical teaching.

Getting back to what Christ taught about knowing the truth when we abide in him *you will know the truth, and the truth will set you free,* applies to every aspect of life on earth, the coming age and the Kingdom of Heaven.

The timing of the rapture, the sanctifying work of the Holy Spirit, the work of the cross in the believer's life, the resurrected life for the believer, obtaining the grace God, our free will, judgment and discipline for the believer, demon possession, and so on—these are very important issues to understand and to know the exact truth concerning.

Most Christians, like my chaplain of years ago, avoid debate concerning conflicting theological positions. Some are afraid of ostracism by their denomination or being shunned by close friends or Christians who want to believe the contrary. Most leaders prefer everyone speculate rather take a stand, keeping all sides happy by not determining the truth (especially the rapture timing).

What becomes easy to believe is "consensus theology," where a more pleasant interpretation of difficult biblical teachings allows disassociation from nagging doubts, dulls conviction from the Holy Spirit, and maintains peace with others. In general, our carnal human nature as believers tends to lead us to embrace pleasant beliefs that are often contrary to the truth.

There are factions within Christianity that hotly contend for what they hold to be true concerning these deeper theological positions, and often the contention between the opposing camps of interpretation becomes troubling and even divisive. The ecumenical movement (fostering unity between Christian denominations) pushes for friendship and unity among all sects of Christianity. One main argument used is to "agree to disagree" with the underpinning goal to maintain harmony for the sake of the believers and especially to show solidarity to the world and the lost.

Unity and Harmony at the Expense of Truth—Never!

The Apostle Paul gives sound teaching that helps us understand the importance of heated debate over these very important matters of doctrine—that truth prevail and those who are genuine be recognized in fellowship. However, many of the reasons for divisions were over various favorite leaders, and arguments were spouting up where cliques and schism were forming, even when celebrating the Lord's Supper.

"But in the following instructions I do not commend you, because when you come together it is not for the better but for the worse. For, in the first place, when you come together as a church, I hear that there are divisions among you. And I believe it in part, for there must be factions among you in order that those who are genuine among you may be recognized" (1 Corinthians 11:17-19).

Paul is contending against lack of unity in fellowship; however, in his writing here, he realizes there will be and must be factions amongst the brethren so that those who are genuine will stand apart and the truth be recognized. This is the call to all true leaders, to stand apart holding the truth without fear of reprisal and the label of divisiveness. We have such a cloud of great witnesses from history, those who chose to be burned at the stake, rather than give way to false doctrine. These stood for truth of Scripture without compromise. Many were martyred for bringing the Word of God in print, that the commoners could read the Scriptures in their own language.

The fight concerning the truth on important issues of doctrine within Christianity has been going on since the beginning, and is reaching its peak in these last days. The ecumenical movement to bring Catholics and Protestants together is a major push for Christian unity.

However, this kind of unity is not what Christ has in mind, where unity and harmony comes by relaxing conviction on the truth of Scripture. Ecumenicalism at the expense of truth allows false believers and the disingenuous to romp through fellowships, leaving a trail of trouble and confusion. Many will come in secretly and gain a stronghold causing divisions (Jude 1:17-19).

The fight for true unity in the body of Christ will cause division; however, unity in fellowship of the likeminded is Christ's goal.

This unity in a likeminded fellowship is to be maintained, but if you are in a fellowship that is not aligned with your convictions and the fellowship is set in staying deceived, then come out and find solid fellowship with likeminded believers. There is a gigantic upheaval coming to Christianity concerning sound doctrine. When the dust starts to settle many denominations and fellowships will change positions on these key doctrines and align with each other and work together.

The birth pangs and persecution will shake and wake the genuine, in many denominations and independent fellowships. Judgment and trouble coming to Christians allowed by God will help straighten out theological error and solidify the true body of Christ. Those denominations and fellowships that hold to lies and false doctrines will be seen for what they are (at least by the true body of Christ).

Seek and Find the Truth
Then be willing to defend the truth, and stand faithfully!

Every sincere disciple of Christ, regardless of denominational or fellowship preferences must allow Christ to bring them to the full truth concerning these vital doctrines that deal with full salvation and eternal security, deception by the false, evil people, the end-of-the-age trouble, when the rapture occurs and the daily work of the cross within the believer's life.

Jesus said, *"Ask, and it will be given to you; seek, and you will find; knock, and it will be opened to you."* (Matthew 7:7). Ask, seek, and knock for the truth concerning these all-important doctrines. Once you know the truth first-hand from Scripture, wrought by the Spirit of Truth, doubts and misgivings will vanish and you will stand firm and resolute. You will continue to see others vacillate on these issues and choose to avoid the topics or any discussion. They run from the debate or avoid aggressive contest for the truth mainly because their hearts are not set free in knowing the truth. Underneath, they sense the conviction of the Holy Spirit yet do not recognize that is the case.

Those who are staunch in believing myths, especially concerning the end-of-the-age rapture often reject any sound argument and often become argumentative. They are like those Jude spoke of in the passage quoted in this section, and wisdom dictates to leave them alone, and learn to work where the Holy Spirit is working.

When you settle on a likeminded fellowship, work with leadership to contend for unity of the brethren. Do not let newcomers bring in divisive false doctrines to suit their liking. This is how the Purpose Driven Church hostile takeovers occur, because the saints have their heads buried in the sand, making the pastor do all the heavy lifting. Be alert, and be willing to defend the truth, taking a stand when necessary.

Most of the people coming will be understanding and willing to see the truth as you explain lovingly and firmly. When contention arises to a stalemate, inform leadership and allow wisdom that leadership conveys to prevail. Many a saint has tried to squelch a scoffer or a worldly false Christian, on his or her own only to make things worse and in the end receive a royal beating.

"Whoever corrects a scoffer gets himself abuse, and he who reproves a wicked man incurs injury. Do not reprove a scoffer, or he will hate you; reprove a wise man, and he will love you" (Proverbs 9:7-8).

Jesus warned, *"Do not give dogs what is holy, and do not throw your pearls before pigs, lest they trample them underfoot and turn to attack you"* (Matthew 7:6).

Again, once you become resolute and set free by knowing the truth, make every effort to find likeminded fellowship, otherwise you will be an oddity and possibly become a target.

Beware of Designer Bibles Branded by Personality Leaders

I recommend a quality word-for-word translation such as the American Standard, Revised Standard, or English Standard versions. (I use several translations as well several Bible dictionaries and a concordance.) Stay away from what I term *designer Bibles* written by some of the popular but errant teachers who add their commentary to reinforce their false doctrine. They do not change canon text, but in their notes and study guide they add their slant and false interpretations.[28] This approach is a powerful tool for the devil to elevate wayward teachings and wrong interpretation to an almost equal stature to the Word of God. When a gullible believer reads Scripture using a designer Bible, the subliminal effect upon the impressible reader often equates the author's notes and interpretation to that of Scripture.

Designer Bibles are like designer clothing bearing the name or logo of a recognizable fashion designer; they are customized designs that present flair, prestige, and fashion. Correspondently, a designer Bible is produced by a popular teacher who adds their slant on Scripture, and ensures that their followers stay true to their special interpretation of the Word of God. Here are some examples of designer Bibles:

> <u>The Everyday Life Bible: The Power of God's Word for Everyday Living</u> by Joyce Meyer—Amazon.com describes this edition as follows: "Joyce Meyer's no-nonsense approach to life and dedicated study of Scriptures has endeared her to millions as teacher, mentor and friend. Now, for the first time, her followers can see her notes blended with the biblical text."

> <u>KJV Kenneth Copeland Reference Bible</u> This designer Bible is described with emphasis on Copeland's perspective on the Gospel of Christ: "Prosperity, grace, righteousness, honor, faith, and covenant. You'll find Kenneth Copeland's personal study notes on these topics in the Kenneth Copeland Reverence Edition Bible!"

> <u>Hope for Today Bible by Joel Osteen</u> Another edition described with the following accolades: "Published to coincide with the 50th anniversary of the founding of Lakewood Church, this Bible is designed for everyday use. It will be filled with years' worth of Joel's inspirational and encouraging insights… This Bible will feature a presentation page with the *This Is My Bible* statement, book introductions, reading plans, devotional inserts, purposed Scriptures, and indices. The text is the New Living Translation.

In producing their own branded designer Bibles, these personality leaders reach the pinnacle of arrogance. What heights of presumption to deem God's people so faithless and intellectually impoverished to be unable to understand the Word of God without their interpretive guidance.

Insidiously, these false teachers interpret Scripture instead of expounding on the Word to inspire believers to seek understanding from Christ and the Holy Spirit. Destructively, these false teachers impugn or censor the work of the Holy Spirit, hindering inspired understanding through direct revelation in conjunction with the discipline of Christ. The believer is dumbed down and led away from the personal leadership, training, and discipline by Christ. This is

---

[28] Scofield Reference Bible was the first Bible published to popularize man's interpretation of the Word of God in note form side by side Scripture. Cyrus I. Scofield first published his work in 1909 and systematically interwove his own interpretation of Scripture in his notes. Scofield's work proved to be the source of the false doctrine of the pre-tribulation rapture. Scofield's notes on the Book of Revelation are a major source for the various timetables, judgments, and plagues elaborated by Hal Lindsey and Tim LaHaye, who also promote this same error.

another wide gate and easy path that leads to destruction offered by Satan through false personality leaders of these last days.

When you study, have solid references: at least a concordance, a dictionary of biblical words, and an unabridged dictionary. Spend time looking up the true meaning of key words.

Fight the many distractions and shut off the TV; say no to the temptations to take it easy; fight the good fight, do the work of coming to Christ with your whole heart, and be serious.

We cannot blame our pastor, favorite author, popular teacher, anointed prophet, or evangelist when we stand before Christ and find ourselves hearing the words, *"I never knew you; depart from me, you workers of lawlessness"* (Matthew 7:23).

Many will be rejected and locked out because they walked in false giftings, driven by the flesh, they were foolish and unprepared for that day—or simply because they were lazy and did not study and seek Christ for themselves.

Truth, Righteousness, and the Way of the Cross
Obtaining the grace of God in light of our wretchedness

Jesus said, *"I am the way, and the truth, and the life,"* and he demands that we follow him in the way that is truthful, where guile (cunning and deceitfulness) is vanquished. If we desire to walk in ever-growing discernment, then we must walk in truth; that is, we must choose to see the truth about ourselves as Christ sees us.

When Nathanael approached Christ, our Lord said of him, *"Behold, an Israelite indeed, in whom there is no deceit! Nathanael said to him, 'How do you know me?'"* (John 1:47-48).

Christ knows everything about us and can see through our masks, our lies, our acting, and our denial (self-deception). The problem facing the sincere saint is the leaven of the Pharisees that we have so easily learned to ingest through the guile of churchianity. This leaven is hypocrisy or guile, and it seeps into a new convert's life and grows to become a natural way of looking at ourselves as followers of Christ.

We learn to lie to ourselves and embrace false doctrines that say *we are clean and true in heart* when so often the opposite is true. If you desire to be a true disciple of Christ, then allow him to show you what still lingers hidden in your heart and character. Forget growing in discernment if you are not willing to see the hidden stuff in your own life. *"Why do you see the speck that is in your brother's eye, but do not notice the log that is in your own eye? Or how can you say to your brother, 'Let me take the speck out of your eye,' when there is the log in your own eye? You hypocrite, first take the log out of your own eye, and then you will see clearly to take the speck out of your brother's eye"* (Matthew 7:3-5).

Embracing the truth about ourselves in the light of Christ's piercing discipline is not easy at first. However, when one sees the healing, the insights, and the increased ability to discern the motives within the hearts of others (to help them or to expose evil), all the personal pain of self-disclosure makes life in Christ meaningful.

As believers, we need to realize that the following statement is true about ourselves: *"The heart is deceitful above all things, and desperately sick; who can understand it? 'I the Lord search the heart and test the mind, to give every man according to his ways, according to the fruit of his deeds'"* (Jeremiah 17:9-10).

The gunk in others brings out the gunk in us and it behooves us to deal with our gunk thoroughly. When we succeed in walking in truth, so that our issues are dealt with, then our discernment becomes even keener and our righteousness more genuine.

Many Christians walk in self-righteousness even though they theoretically realize that salvation is by faith in Christ's sacrificial death and God's grace. Many develop a *self-righteous and self-justifying inner stance* so that they never see their true sinfulness and wretchedness.

As the cultural war between the righteous and the wicked grows, self-righteous Christians more than ever are pointing their finger at the lost, the wicked, and the immoral while ignoring their own inner vileness. The parable in Luke 18:9-14 of the self-righteous Pharisee and the tax collector describes this widespread condition throughout Christianity.

A prime example of how the enemy can gain the upper hand in the saint's life is found in the book of Job. We must learn to discern the hidden unclean issues in our own life that give Satan place or ground to deceive and abuse us—any thread of inner self-righteousness becomes a tool in the devil's hand. An inner self-righteous stance has become a major satanic stronghold in many a saint's life.

Job story is a powerful example of how we can learn to rely on our own righteousness, thinking that it is a magic umbrella of protection. Job had true faith but he did not discern that Satan was the one causing his troubles; rather, Job blamed God.

Job believed he should have been exempt from this kind of trouble in light of his true and right standing with God. Finally, the author of the book of Job in describing how his three friends finally stopped their attempt to help Job revealed this self-righteous stance, *"So these three men ceased to answer Job, because he was righteous in his own eyes"* (Job 32:1). Many Christians today are righteous in their own eyes.

The fourth man, Elihu saw Job's issue. *"Then Elihu the son of Barachel the Buzite, of the family of Ram, burned with anger. He burned with anger at Job because he justified himself rather than God. He burned with anger also at Job's three friends because they had found no answer, although they had declared Job to be in the wrong"* (Job 32:2-3). In the end, God rebuked Job's first three counselors, but said nothing concerning Elihu other than reiterating Elihu's counsel to Job.

Elihu had gone through the process of ridding himself of his own inner self-righteousness and self-justification in facing life's challenges and trials. When Elihu finally had the opportunity to speak to Job, he was able to discern exactly why Job was suffering at the hands of Satan. Elihu stated, *"Job has said, 'I am in the right, and God has taken away my right; in spite of my right I am counted a liar; my wound is incurable, though I am without transgression.' What man is like Job, who drinks up scoffing like water, who travels in company with evildoers and walks with wicked men? For he has said, 'It profits a man nothing that he should take delight in God'"* (Job 34:5-9).

Elihu successfully pointed out to Job that his transgression was his reliance on his righteous walk with God, thinking this would allow him to be immune to any real suffering. When Elihu finished his discourse and instruction, God broke forth and finally spoke to Job (Job 38). In the end, because of Elihu's discernment and counsel, Job's eyes were opened to the truth of his predicament and thus Job declared: *"I had heard of you by the hearing of the ear, but now my eye sees you; therefore I despise myself, and repent in dust and ashes"* (Job 42:5-6).

Today, a true saint must allow God bring to death any reliance on self-righteousness which can only come by God showing us our innate wretchedness. This is a process used by God—with the help of Satan—to bring us to true humility. The devil will be allowed to buffet and attack us until we come to a complete understanding of what it means to walk in true humility without a hint of religious, self-righteous pride.

This process is called the work of the cross in the believer's life. Not only are the negative works of the flesh, with their passions and desires to be put to death, but also any vestiges of self-righteousness and carnal good works are to be put to death.

Most unsaved outsiders who are looking for the true Christ can detect a Christian who is a self-righteous hypocrite almost immediately—however, few Christians can say the same concerning their own discernment of the self-righteous.

When we walk in the righteousness that comes by faith in Christ, we will begin to discern the power of the flesh in ministry and in the lives of others. It often smacks of self-righteous living and self-justification. When we die to our self-righteousness, the pure and unhindered living water from Christ will flow through us to satisfy the tired sinner who calls out for help. The Holy Spirit will open up in the true saint rivers of living waters to flow out to a lost and dying world.

It is the work of the cross in the believer's life expounded on in Hebrews, which is the discipline of the Lord. *"For the moment all discipline seems painful rather than pleasant, but later it <u>yields the peaceful fruit of righteousness</u> to those who have been trained by it"* (Hebrews 12:11).

When we see who we truly are in the light of Christ's discipline, then the grace of God becomes our life and humble righteousness becomes a blessing to others, not a finger-pointing and condemning charade. The grace of God has become a theological license for false teachers to baby Christians—to sooth the conscience, to negate the ramifications of deliberate sinning and to cheapen Christ's sacrifice on the cross.

Grace is the cornerstone of the New Covenant, whereby God demonstrates his plan to free his people from the bonds of sin. However, most Christians misunderstand this expression of God's love. Coming back to the book of Hebrews, we are warned about sinning deliberately and taking God's grace lightly. (Review Hebrews 10:26-31.)

In the days to come, this cavalier approach before God's throne of grace will end, as individual Christians and the body of Christ begin to feel the heat of trouble, persecution and silence from heaven. The cry of Job will be heard throughout Christianity very soon. That was Job's main complaint; that God was silent in his darkest hour.

"God has cast me into the mire, and I have become like dust and ashes. I cry to you for help and you do not answer me; I stand, and you only look at me. You have turned cruel to me; with the might of your hand you persecute me" (Job 30:19-20).

However, that was to bring Job to his the realization of his self-righteous peril. As Elihu confronts Job with God's ways of breaking denial, *"For God speaks in one way, and in two, <u>though man does not perceive it</u>. In a dream, in a vision of the night, when deep sleep falls on men, while they slumber on their beds, then he opens the ears of men and terrifies them with warnings, that he may turn man aside from his deed and conceal pride from a man; he keeps back his soul from the pit, his life from perishing by the sword. 'Man is also rebuked with pain on his bed and with continual strife in his bones, so that his life loathes bread, and his appetite the choicest food. His flesh is so wasted away that it cannot be seen, and his bones that were not seen stick out. His soul draws near the pit, and his life to those who bring death. ... Behold, God does all these things, twice, three times, with a man, to bring back his soul from the pit, that he may be lighted with the light of life"* Job 33:14-22; 29-30).

Allow God to speak to you now, that you may learn to walk in his righteousness, in purity and obedience so that you may escape the coming troubles, while enduring to the end.

Holy Spirit-Led Counsel

Jesus encouraged his disciples saying, *"If you love me, you will keep my commandments. And I will ask the Father, and he will give you another Helper,* [Counselor] *to be with you forever, even the Spirit of truth, whom the world cannot receive, because it neither sees him nor knows him. You know him, for he dwells with you and will be in you"* (John 14:15-17). We must accept this promise, provided we are serious about keeping the commands of Christ, being determined to fulfill God's purposes.

Knowing what Christ taught and commanded is one thing; however, understanding and applying his teachings and commandments in everyday living is the challenge. Moreover, when we come to a roadblock in understanding what Christ meant in a particular parable or teaching, the Holy Spirit will counsel and reveal the truth.

All of us at one time or another will need a jump-start from someone who is in tune with the Spirit of Truth. (God sent Elihu to help Job realize what had happened to him and why). We will need someone from time to time who can tell us what we need to hear, someone who will point to Christ and not dictate or make us dependent on their ministry, but rather help for as long as necessary until we are standing on our two feet of faith and receiving Holy Spirit-inspired counsel.

In our mentoring and counsel to others, our goal was to work ourselves out of a job, teaching, mentoring and counseling others to learn how to hear and receive counsel from the Holy Spirit. A key to fulfilling this objective was to discern if the person receiving our help was making an effort to hear and obey on his or her own, without our help.

In this work, those in our care learn to stay humble after our part is complete in their journey to the fullness of Christ—humble and willing to ask for support in case they need a confirming word or sound counsel. We all learn to carry our own load, while learning to bear each other's burdens as we watch out for each other—without controlling, caretaking, or elevating ourselves.

There is a caveat to mentoring and counseling others: Beware of the embittered and narcissist who refuses to do the basic work required to start personally receiving counsel from the Holy Spirit and eventually not need counsel, standing on their own two feet of faith.

We experienced many defiled and wounded Christians who came sobbing for help. They received sound counsel and prayer ministry, only to operate in hope and faith for a season, and then return with another helpless situation—in hysteria. After a season of extensive burden bearing, we began to see a pattern emerge of laziness stemming from an inner stance of self-pity with a subtle agenda to make others responsible for inner wellbeing and happiness.

They walked in a poor-me attitude for years and eventually their self-pity expanded into a core agenda of "others owe me"—a welfare-recipient mentality subtly blaming God for their life situations. This type of bitterness carries a demonic and human spirit vampire dynamic, where counselors and Christian workers experience extreme energy loss and a sense of hopelessness in many cases.

"There are those who are clean in their own eyes but are not washed of their filth. There are those—how lofty are their eyes, how high their eyelids lift! There are those whose teeth are swords, whose fangs are knives, to devour the poor from off the earth, the needy from among mankind. The leech has two daughters; 'Give' and 'Give,' they cry. Three things are never satisfied; four never say, "Enough": Sheol, the barren womb, the land never satisfied with water, and the fire that never says, 'Enough.'" (Proverbs 30:12-16).

These never take ownership for their own wickedness and attack those who hold them accountable to deal with their selfishness and laziness. These wounded Christians never see their intrinsic need for a savior; coming to fellowship leeching energy, time, and resources as they emanate an aura of false guilt and false responsibility on the saints and upon leadership. Their inner agenda is camouflaged with an outer "you are so wonderful" flattery.

"These are blemishes on your love feasts, as they boldly carouse together, <u>looking after themselves</u>; waterless clouds, carried along by winds; fruitless trees in late autumn, twice dead, uprooted; wild waves of the sea, casting up the foam of their own shame; wandering stars for whom the nether gloom of darkness has been reserved for ever. These are <u>grumblers, malcontents, following their own passions</u>, loud-mouthed boasters, <u>flattering people to gain advantage</u>" (Jude 12-16 RSV).

After the patterns appear with confirmation in the Holy Spirit, the only hope is to hold such a person accountable until they see the light—even then most move on to the next fellowship looking for a shoulder to sob upon, as they continue in their malcontent-entitlement stance throughout life.

Led by the Holy Spirit in the Lord's Discipline
Learning to stand firm and not flinch while enduring fiery trials

Many Christians have some experience in self-discipline and self-control—whether in the area of sports, academia, the military, or learning to be a caring and responsible parent, eventually those times of self-discipline become relaxed.

However, the discipline of the Lord is a lifelong work and requires courage to face the divine challenges that originate not from our own election but from his providence. We learn not to be obsessed with difficulties or become a masochistic martyr, but rather take each trial and count it as joy knowing that the Lord knows how much and how long we must endure a certain trail.

James states, *"Count it all joy, my brothers, when you meet trials of various kinds, for you know that the testing of your faith produces steadfastness. And let steadfastness have its full effect, that you may be perfect and complete, lacking in nothing"* (James 1:2-4). Part of the reasoning for the testing of our faith is to produce confidence in God's sustaining powers and expose of our carnal influences that conflict with the leadership of the Holy Spirit within our lives. We must take courage and allow the Holy Spirit to have his way and if necessary give him permission to make it impossible for us to quit prematurely from our time of testing. Far too many want to find some manmade method that will transform our old nature into a Christ-like nature overnight and without pain.

Most would love to readily recognize the desires of the old carnal nature before they appear and cause trouble—and for certain, if our carnal nature is allowed to continue living, we will have difficulty seeing in these dark, evil days and will likely put our faith at risk.

The ability to proactively (at will) find and kill the root desires that drive the works of the flesh is *not* received when we are first born anew; rather, this ability is developed within us through Christ increasing our faith over a period of time.

We must allow Christ himself, and sometimes a fiery trial, to help us see hidden issues; and we need his power to die to the desires of the flesh, and then be changed into his likeness. Through the years of ministry, we reminded ourselves of this principle with the saying, THE FLESH CANNOT CRUCIFY THE FLESH. It is by Christ's glorious presence, as we acknowledge the need to change and become willing to go through the emotional and mental epiphanies that are often painful that facilitates death to our carnal desires. These epiphanies (realizations and revelations) are divinely inspired and are character changing, where our inner motives, unresolved wounds, defilements and bad attitudes find death, healing, cleansing and change respectively.

Overcoming the World, the Flesh, and the Devil
Not shrinking back from the faith walk in the wilderness

If it is your intention to walk in true discernment then there are three distinct wars that you must wage and win. The deeper aspects of discernment hinge on the saint overcoming these arenas of battle in a true walk of faith.

The world has its power to bring successful living, and your flesh (carnal desires) will gravitate to those powers and buck you every step of the way. The devil will attempt to trip you up in these areas of battle. Your fight against the world and the flesh will be fueled by the devil's subtle influences and they will be very hard to detect.

As you succeed in overcoming the world and your own flesh, Satan will see your progress, change his underhanded methods, and take you on directly, in dastardly, outright, frontal assaults.

"Do not love the world or the things in the world. If anyone loves the world, the love of the Father is not in him. For all that is in the world—the desires of the flesh and the desires of the eyes and pride in possessions—is not from the Father but is from the world. And the world is passing away along with its desires, but whoever does the will of God abides forever" (1 John 2:15-17).

The serious disciple of Christ will eventually be led by the Holy Spirit to surrender control of life completely to Christ, then ultimately be led by the Spirit into a wilderness-like journey to be tested in these areas, love of this world, desires of the flesh, the desires of the eyes, and the pride of life.

God will be faithful to point out each stronghold where the powers governing these evils become belligerent, so that the true servant will eagerly embrace the work of the cross. Christ commands, *"Whoever does not take his cross and follow me is not worthy of me. Whoever finds his life will lose it, and whoever loses his life for my sake will find it"* (Matthew 10:38-39). This command is one of the most avoided in Christ's list of harder teachings.

Few understand why Christ demands death to the believer's life in this world. This death is not as his was, a physical death on the cross, but rather we are to pick up our cross and embrace a death like his—a death to the worldly carnal life, that which we draw our energy, sense of fulfillment, and pride of accomplishment from, the things of this age and of this world.

We must die to living for such things as work, hobbies, education, material possessions, ministry, and people. Relationship life is the hardest aspect of dying to the life on earth. Few realize how we derive life from others, especially family and friends. Love and happiness derived from relationships on earth tend to make us live for others, and demands that others live for us. Yes, the love of relationship makes us become prideful and possessive with others, as if we owned them. Jesus said of this selfish relationship bonding *"Therefore, any one of you who does not renounce all that he has cannot be my disciple"* (Luke 14:33).

Most Christians today receive instruction on how to magnify these aspects of life on earth. Pronouncing any success or increase in this world-orientated life is often attributed to being blessed by God—and this assessment is a false reference to what Christ meant about receiving the abundant life he promises.

On the contrary, Christ is speaking to this life on earth as a hindrance. The love of this world—*the desires of the flesh and the desires of the eyes and pride in possessions*—opposes the true love towards God and hinders obtaining the blessed life Christ promises. Once we lose the love for this life on earth, that we have grown to idolize—a life we lust for, a life we draw from and often demand from others—then God will be allowed to live in his fullness within our hearts.

This divine love will flow out to others with no strings attached and appropriately convey a tough love to hold the wayward accountable.

Jesus commands us to pick up our cross and follow him, which implies a journey that must be taken. This journey (which is entered upon through a narrow gate and following the hard path) is not easy and will not end until every aspect of the idolatrous love of this world dies.

Just as the Holy Spirit led Christ into the wilderness, to be tempted and where he succeeded in winning this war—so too will every sincere and willing saint be led by the Spirit, with Christ helping, guiding, and encouraging every step of the way.

This Holy Spirit facilitated wilderness journey is personally tailored to apply pressure upon the saint to work out those areas of the carnal attachments. The key is to keep going and not shrink back: *"Do not throw away your confidence, which has a great reward. For you have need of endurance, so that when you have done the will of God you may receive what is promised. For, 'Yet a little while, and the coming one will come and will not delay; but my righteous one shall live by faith, and if he shrinks back, my soul has no pleasure in him.' But we are not of those who shrink back and are destroyed, but of those who have faith and preserve their souls"* (Hebrews 10:35-39).

The pain that this journey produces is having the very depths of our heart's emotional love and bond to this world crushed and then replaced by the love of God that is shed upon our hearts by the Holy Spirit. This is a process that God ordains at a speed that each individual can handle and based upon their knowledge of the Word of God in these matters.

The most rewarding aspect of the wilderness journey is having the works of flesh dealt with and the carnal pools of emotion, lusts and desires drained. *"Since therefore Christ suffered in the flesh, arm yourselves with the same way of thinking, for whoever has suffered in the flesh has ceased from sin, so as to live for the rest of the time in the flesh no longer for human passions but for the will of God"* (1 Peter 4:1-2).

This process of picking up our cross and dying to this life on earth would seem callous, cruel and senseless if it were not for the replacement life given to us from Christ himself, *"I came that they may have life and have it abundantly"* (John 10:10). This life Christ speaks of is life from God given in its fullest. It is life with the Father that allows our life on earth to carry that divine life and love from God to flow into ourselves and out to the lives of others around us.

Remember, Christ succeeded in defeating Satan's lies and Christ promises never to leave or forsake us. He is well acquainted with our weaknesses and is able to hold us up as we endure to the end of our journey. *"No temptation has overtaken you that is not common to man. God is faithful, and he will not let you be tempted beyond your ability, but with the temptation he will also provide the way of escape, that you may be able to endure it"* (1 Corinthians 10:13).

Satan will come and tempt in every way possible to get you to quit. You will feel that the wilderness suffering will go on and on with no end. At times, you will be convinced that God has forsaken you and all hope will seem to go up in a vapor without a sound. This is a lie. Look to the promises of God and to the scriptural accounts of those who went before you and finished the course.

You must learn what it means to walk by faith not knowing how or when the wilderness journey will end, (see Hebrews 11:8-9). You will learn to hope against hope, just as true servants in Scripture succeeded in walking with unwavering trust in God. *"But if we hope for what we do not see, we wait for it with patience"* (Romans 8:25).

When you can withstand the devils temptations through the world and your own carnal issues—no longer having issues of the heart to snag, then a door that no man or devil can close will open up for you, allowing you to walk out of the wilderness victoriously.

Remember, the devil's and his temptations have their power from within; *"Each person <u>is tempted when he is lured and enticed by his own desire</u>. Then desire when it has conceived gives birth to sin, and sin when it is fully grown brings forth death"* (James 1:14-15).

True and accurate discernment cannot be achieved if your heart is in love with this world, driven by the lust of the flesh, the lust of the eye, and the pride of life.

Receiving the Crown of Life

Another passage that helps us to understand why God allows trials and often a journey of trials to come upon us in found in the book of James.

"Blessed is the man who remains steadfast under trial, for when he has stood the test he will receive the crown of life, which God has promised to those who love him. Let no one say when he is tempted, 'I am being tempted by God,' for God cannot be tempted with evil, and he himself tempts no one. But each person is tempted when he is lured and enticed by his own desire. Then desire when it has conceived gives birth to sin, and sin when it is fully grown brings forth death" (James 1:12-15).

Remaining steadfast is vital during a trial, which often proves not the case. At times, we may enter a trial in the testing of our faith, only to have the pressure draw out issues of heart such as unbelief, bitterness, or an unhealed wound. What I learned in my times of instability during trial, is to keep going, though the trial itself was not completely withstood to the end.

I learned to consider the exposed issue that caused instability as success for the partially passed test. This is where many are overtaken in the trials of life while in the wilderness journey; they berate themselves, and shrink back by not taking to heart what inner issue caused the falter or instability.

If we look to our trials as a journey leading to the promises of the Lord, then each time we make a mistake or miss catching the lesson, we should consider the faltering moment as a bump in the road for the purpose of instruction.

Grace and forgiveness will always be at our side by the Lord's Spirit, provided we humbly acknowledge the truth about the matter and allow the reasons why we failed to find proper recognition in our self-examination. *"If we confess our sins, he is faithful and just to forgive us our sins and to cleanse us from all unrighteousness. If we say we have not sinned, we make him a liar, and his word is not in us"* (1 John 1:9-10).

It is a working out in fear and trembling, yet with determination. (Philippians 2:12-13). Then when bucked off the horse (if you will)—God knows we will fail at times, some of us repeatedly—we then get back on the horse and go again.

The faith that Christ is cultivating in us is that when we fail by sinning, or by laziness or in fear, or any besetting weight, sin, or issue—we confess whatever the case may be, repent and seek the Lord for healing and transformation of the weak character or unbelief, getting to the root cause within. Turn to Christ who is familiar with our weaknesses and who will stand with us, if we honestly and humbly take ownership of our weaknesses and issues of heart.

"Therefore, since we are surrounded by so great a cloud of witnesses, let us also <u>lay aside every weight, and sin which clings so closely</u>, and <u>let us run with endurance the race that is set before us</u>, <u>looking to Jesus</u>, the <u>founder and perfecter of our faith</u>, who for the joy that was set before him endured the cross, despising the shame, and is seated at the right hand of the throne of God. Consider him who endured from sinners such hostility against himself, so that you may <u>not grow weary or fainthearted</u>. In your struggle against sin you have not yet resisted to the point of shedding your blood. And have you forgotten the exhortation that addresses you as sons? 'My son, <u>do not regard lightly the discipline of the Lord</u>, nor be weary when reproved by him. For the <u>Lord disciplines the one he loves</u>, and chastises every son whom he receives'" (Hebrews 12:1-7). In the end of this tough journey, we will receive the crown of life—a transformed Christ-like nature that only Christ can produce within us.

Always Carrying in the Body the Death of Christ
That the life of Christ may manifest in us and through us freely

In the fullness of life in Christ, we will often experience setbacks and hardships. We must learn to discern between these types of trials as opposed to those difficulties associated with reaping the consequences of bad attitudes or hidden issues, as well as judgments for wrongdoing (these we will discuss later in this chapter).

The Apostle Paul explained why the saint, when coming to the place of the fullness of Christ and the abundant life, often incurred difficulties and sometimes unusual and extreme trials. In this passage rests a wealth of insight for the determined disciple of Christ who may wonder why the continued challenges: *"But we have this treasure in jars of clay, to show that the surpassing power belongs to God and not to us. We are afflicted in every way, but not crushed; perplexed, but not driven to despair; persecuted, but not forsaken; struck down, but not destroyed; <u>always carrying in the body the death of Jesus, so that the life of Jesus may also be manifested in our bodies. For we who live are always being given over to death for Jesus' sake, so that the life of Jesus also may be manifested in our mortal flesh</u>. So death is at work in us, but life in you"* (2 Corinthians 4:7-12).

In addition, the Apostle Paul wrote to the Christians at Corinth (and to us) concerning a specific rough time he and his ministry had while on mission in Asia. *"For we were so utterly burdened beyond our strength that we <u>despaired of life itself</u>. Indeed, we felt that <u>we had received the sentence of death</u>. But that was to make us <u>rely not on ourselves but on God who raises the dead</u>. He delivered us from such a deadly peril, and he will deliver us. On him we have set our hope that he will deliver us again"* (2 Corinthians 1:8-10).

Through these many years of ministry, often we were led by the Lord to expose darkness requiring us to wrestle against principalities, or received acute spiritual opposition from other

Christians deceived into believing we were a cult. Depending on your call and the faith given you, afflictions, battles, and oppression that make living miserable will be at your side from time to time. Learn to discern and detect how much affliction is extra due to issues within; learn to deal with them, and be encouraged that the opposition you receive will keep you dependent on God who raises the dead.

Hating and Giving up Family Carnal Bonds
Understanding and applying one of Christ's most difficult teachings

Our family of origin and extended family and often our spouse will make demands on our relationship to Christ for their selfishness and misguided agendas. A mother who smothers in the name of caring can sidetrack and even derail Christ's calling and purpose in her adult son or daughter.

As a father, I learned that my unfulfilled dreams concerning football and the love of sports impinged upon my children's life, especially for my oldest son. The following story will help demonstrate the importance of breaking carnal and unhealthy bonds with family.

Ministry case: *Not dropping our cross*

This nation's love of sports heroes has degenerated into worshipping the human physical body. Like many children of dysfunctional families, a sport becomes an escape with fantasies of heroic accolades that garner attention, and that is what I did with the game of football.

As a youngster, I idolized football and had my own unfulfilled dreams, which became a subtle pressure on my children. Years ago, when the Lord began to challenge me with this carnal issue, the Holy Spirit quickened Christ's teachings on loving others more than him and renouncing all that we own in context with relationships. (See Matthew 10:34-38 and Luke 14:25-33).

This stirring by the Lord and his teachings led me to pray for a release from any invisible spiritual impingement upon my children. Within two days of this prayer, my oldest son decided not to play football during his senior year in high school.

I had some difficulties accepting his decision; he certainly had the build and the attitude to compete at college level: 6' 3", aggressive, and tough as nails. He told me he loved to compete on the high school swim team and chose to make swimming his main sport to help him develop physically.

Immediately I started to argue against his decision and felt feelings of frustration building up. Then the Lord reminded me of my prayer in the midst of imploring my son to reconsider. I toned it down and tried to wholeheartedly encourage him with his choice, however, I was having a hard time reconciling my son's decision to that being God's will for him.

For about three weeks, maybe a month I kept going over my prayer and what it means to pick up one's cross. For a while, I thought God answered that "Abraham-Isaac" sacrificial prayer a little too quickly. Finally, from more of a stern coaxing from the Holy Spirit, I submitted to the will of God, and in my heart, I decided to let my son live his own life.

After he graduated from high school, he joined the Coast Guard. His first duty was aboard the USCGC Vigilant; Cape Canaveral, Florida was homeport. He volunteered and trained to be the ship's rescue swimmer and was involved in the Haitian trouble in the early nineties.

On one of his first rescue missions, the Vigilant was dispatched to help search for a father and son overdue from a scuba diving excursion just off the Florida shores. The search had been frustrating, since there were no flags, boat, or specific location information—just a general vicinity of where they might be.

The cutter was making its planned search pattern as the crew had *eyes on the water*, looking for the lost scuba divers. My son operated the "big eyes," which is a permanently mounted high-powered binocular set on the cutter's flying bridge. Finding two divers bobbing on the ocean waves was an almost impossible chore, and dread soon set in for the crew as dusk was approaching.

My son began to think of what he would do if he were in their place. The thought came quickly: swim to the nearest buoy. He began to scan for the closest buoy and saw two figures clinging for life onto a buoy about a mile from the cutter and quite a distance from the shore. These two men were exhausted, and very thankful when brought aboard.

Tears swelled up as my son told me this account. It was very inspirational, his being so new to the demands of such service for our country; I was very proud. Then the Holy Spirit started to remind me of the prayer, embracing my cross and the sacrifice of heart that the Lord had led me to just a couple of years prior.

Christian parents must die to living out their dreams, fantasies and failures through their children. Relationship idolatry and enthrallment destroys people, drains life from others, and often subverts God's plans. Ω

This story had a powerful ending that has blessed many; however, many cases where others followed Christ's commands in breaking those unhealthy family bonds and it turned into intense battles. *"Whoever loves father or mother more than me is not worthy of me, and whoever loves son or daughter more than me is not worthy of me. And whoever does not take his cross and follow me is not worthy of me. Whoever finds his life will lose it, and whoever loses his life for my sake will find it"* (Matthew 10:37-39).

The mistake I almost made and many do make is picking up our cross, and then dropping it because we did not properly consider the consequences of following Christ completely. When it comes to our life with others, Jesus is serious because he knows when we live for others instead of living and obeying Christ—in the end we destroy the life and plans God has for us and for them.

As for my case, I had begun to look back after making my commitment to Christ in prayer concerning pushing and controlling my children. Fortunately, I responded to Christ's chiding. Many however, make such commitments and when they lose the familiar, yet unhealthy love of others, they look back in regret. Jesus warned not to look back in sentimentality or regret when we give ourselves to him. *"As they were going along the road, someone said to him, 'I will follow you wherever you go.' And Jesus said to him, 'Foxes have holes, and birds of the air have nests, but the Son of Man has nowhere to lay his head. To another he said, 'Follow me. But he said, 'Lord, let me first go and bury my father. And Jesus said to him, 'Leave the dead to bury their own dead. But as for you, go and proclaim the kingdom of God.' Yet another said, 'I will follow you, Lord, but let me first say farewell to those at my home.' Jesus said to him, 'No one who puts his hand to the plow and looks back is fit for the kingdom of God.'"* (Luke 9:57-62).

We must temper these harder teachings of Christ concerning family bonding with the following, *"And he said to them, 'Truly, I say to you, there is no one who has left house or wife or brothers or parents or children, <u>for the sake of the kingdom of God, who will not receive many times more in this time, and in the age to come eternal life'</u>"* (Luke 18:29-30).

The key is giving up ownership and clinging to others within the heart, not at all becoming a derelict to family responsibilities. Some I have personally known, and others I have read about, take these teachings of Christ as a license to walk out on one's children or spouse; however, Christ is calling us to walk away from them as idols of the heart where we live for each other. Many Christians will cling to an unsaved or carnal spouse and miss eternity.

When we successfully live for Christ, unfettered by our relationships, we will gain back those we give up, but it will be on God's terms, in a healthy manner, and the blessings for giving up ownership of things and others will include gaining eternal life in the age to come.

Establishing Relationship Boundaries in Christ
Avoiding the perils of having an open heart to the world and the false

The push for new converts to proselytize their family members has become an obsession with many fellowships and ministries. Few receive mentoring and instruction on how to break the unhealthy ties that still exist between them and their family of origin, extended family, or unsaved friends. New believers desperately need assistance in establishing appropriate boundaries between themselves and those still living in sin; they need help to break the hold that old relationships have on them, that enables backsliding into those sick and selfish influential lifestyles.

Old friends and family already feel awkward and insecure with a newly born-again Christian. Yet most fellowships manipulate new believers to employ their excitement about Christ towards these relationships with little to no understanding concerning relationship boundaries or a solid foundation in Christ.

New believers are thrown back to the world as lambs and often succumb to manipulation by old relationships. Lacking skills and strength to discern and navigate through the relationship traps with old friendships and family members (that are still bad company), many new Christians become trapped again in sick relationships.

There is a natural yet unhealthy desire for new Christians to be carnally excited about Christ and ignorantly, rambunctiously, and foolishly attempt to convert family and friends. Solid leadership will know how to temper this enthusiasm with guidance and instruction warning young converts of the many pitfalls and the perils of not properly relating to old relationships and family members—it is these people who often subtly undermine the fragile faith of a new Christian.

New believers have little opportunity to grow up into Christ and learn to resist those old friends and family members who may be impressed by the change, yet are not at all interested in submitting to Christ and repenting. Most old relations for the new believer intuitively arouse within them old carnal issues yet to be dealt with and cause the new found desire for a godly and sin free life to wane.

Bad company corrupts good morals, and much more: *"Do not be deceived: 'Bad company ruins good morals.' Wake up from your <u>drunken stupor</u>, as is right, and do not go on sinning. For some have no knowledge of God. I say this to your shame"* (1 Corinthians 15:33-34).

What is even more deplorable is how new Christians are subjected to false Christians within most fellowships who inevitably pounce upon a new believer and lead them down the wrong path. Many fellowships have accommodated worldliness by offering entertaining messages, emotionally thrilling worship, and activities to appease the desire to head back into worldly pleasures when the narrow gate and hard path becomes reality. This makes new Christians who are truly touched by the holiness we are called to seek slide right back into unsavory relationships.

New believers and older believers who want to follow Christ all the way often experience an intoxicating influence from the unsavory elements within these carnal fellowships. New Christians often fall into a drunken stupor that brings them back into unhealthy relationships with old friends, family members and false Christians, swimming like sharks in most fellowships. Flattery, worldly activity, emotional ties to old friends, and desires of the flesh yet dealt with act like a drug and numb any warnings that the new believer might receive from the Holy Spirit.

Peter warned in 2 Peter 2 about the perils of bad company for believers and described them as accursed children (false brethren), waterless springs, and likened them to irrational animals and blots and blemishes who, *"Entice by sensual passions of the flesh those who are barely escaping from those who live in error"* (2 Peter 2:18).

It was said of Christ, *"Now when he was in Jerusalem at the Passover feast, many believed in his name when they saw the signs which he did; but Jesus did <u>not trust himself to them</u>, because he knew all men and needed no one to bear witness of man; <u>for he himself knew what was in man</u>"* (John 2:23-25).

Great care must be taken in learning not to be open hearted and vulnerable to these types of people. However, to minimize our vulnerability the sincere disciple of Christ must learn to ascertain these problematic people. To assist in this we must follow Christ's example and not haphazardly trust ourselves to just anybody who calls themselves a Christian—brother or sister or friend—without knowing for sure their character and if they have a true relationship with God.

As you grow in discernment you will begin to pick up on the mannerisms and comments that emanate from an unclean, selfish, and defiling person, such as peculiar body language, out-of-place comments, actions and words that undermine faith and hope, control and manipulation, flattery, selfishness, jealous innuendos, contention, a "party spirit," relationship obsession, and other subtle works of the flesh. Remember, Christ taught: *"Out of the abundance of the heart the mouth speaks"* (Matthew 12:34).

Many waterless springs or accursed children learn to become powerful spiritual bullies, bossing, obsessing, controlling the naïve, weak, or carnal, as they push, and pull victims to fulfill their own agendas. Many put on a religious mask and develop spiritual powers that are demonic in nature. Their carnal prayers (prayers often disguised as Christian concerns, yet are self-centered) do great damage to others and oppose God's will.

Some even host power demons (ignorantly), allowing them to project their own spirit onto a person of concern or an opponent and cause harm or even death. These accursed children live in an internal torrent of bitter jealousy, hatred, and selfish ambition that can project murderous waves of oppression or cast a malignant, long-term set of physical symptoms.

The true saint must learn to fear God and respect the power of the enemy working through evil people. False doctrines, along with laidback and superficial leaders who act like everyone's friend, cause many sincere believers to presume upon God and walk in ignorance, arrogance and pride. They become giant targets for the unsavory, evil, waterless spring.

When taking on these problematic false believers, the fear of God will be restored and humility will become a genuine characteristic for the saint in training. Overcoming the fear of confrontation with people who are bullies is accomplished by fearing God above all.

Saying no and avoiding these people who are accurately characterized as "accursed children" or "waterless springs" are two major challenges for the sincere child of God. After one is burned enough times, it will be much easier to identify and avoid such without causing a blowup.

However, in the beginning, blowups in these relationships will be inevitable. The primary issues for the one trying to become free of an unhealthy relationship are these: lack of insight, false responsibility to sick relationships, fear of what others may think, fear of hurting their feelings when confronting their deceptions and manipulations, and lack of sound doctrine and support from the pulpit.

As stated before, the discerning saint who desires to set proper boundaries will virtually be on their own—however, Christ will always be on the side of the sincere; he will never leave or forsake those who are seriously learning to obey him.

Unresolved issues within the true believer will allow wayward people to frustrate, and make one feel hopeless. In general the wayward will surround the sincere yet naïve and be a consistent source of contention. Sooner than later, a blowup will occur if the sincere Christian stays true to Christ and desires to grow in maturity.

However, no one starting out will be mature enough to wean such troublemakers in calmness, firmness and with all wisdom. Thus, blowups will occur and often the true saint will end up looking like they are off, unloving, or in some kind of a cult or false teaching.

Eventually the discerning saint will learn to avoid unhealthy relationships, learn to detect false teachers and false doctrine, and walk in a strong faith that keeps dubious family members at arm's length.

The grand deception is that at first contact these deceitful people appear to be godly, but when fruit of Christ-like character is expected or required it becomes apparent they have denied Christ's power to change, and their true character emerges. The Apostle Paul points to this kind of person as, *"having the appearance of godliness, but denying its power. Avoid such people"* (2 Timothy 3:5) Paul also says, *"I appeal to you, brothers, to watch out for those who cause divisions and create obstacles contrary to the doctrine that you have been taught; avoid them. For such persons do not serve our Lord Christ, but their own appetites, and by smooth talk and flattery they deceive the hearts of the naïve"* (Romans 16:17-18).

The best policy is doing as the Apostle exhorts—not letting such people get to first base in your life by avoiding them—and this can only be accomplished by not having an open and naïve heart susceptible to deception.

Cult Family Systems Hidden in the Church
Relationship idolatry is actually promoted in much of Christianity

Few Christians are taught correctly about family relations: how they can become idolatrous, controlling, and faith destroying; and few are taught how to be free and become detoxified from the emotional, mental, and spiritual poison that such relationships create.

Through many years of counseling and witnessing the cult-like symptoms of victims of unhealthy families, it became evident to me that the more acutely dysfunctional family systems both Christian and non-Christian, can truly be classified as a *cult family system*. Naming such family systems as cult helps identify the idolatrous and zombie-like allegiance that members develop toward the family leader and the family group-system. The cult family system can yield a subtle, yet insidious power that can cast a spell upon its victims even down to the following generations.

A cult is a group in which a person, philosophy, ideology or activity is regarded with extreme or excessive admiration and allegiance. In the case of a cult family, the family system dynamics and certain idiosyncrasies of personality and behavior become the life of the family system—in most cases with destructive results.

Each member of a cult family system becomes groomed to fill a role in the family to naturally maintain a sense of belonging, a sense of well-being and obtain motivational life-energy. The cult family environmental dynamics form personalities and an internal belief system within each member. These personalities with associated beliefs are abnormal or unhealthy concerning self, others in the family and in society and have a very tainted, even perverted perception of God. In a cult family system, foundational character structures are not formed according to societal norms, and certainly are not based on solid biblical doctrine or on Christ's teachings.

The outcome is what the world calls dysfunctional families and individuals. Prominent characteristics and symptoms include the followings:

Conflicts, misbehavior, hidden abuse, denial of the problematic issues, lack of empathy, relationship boundary problems, jealousy, extreme fears and phobias, paranoid behavior, sexual perversion, parental abandonment, rejection or resentment of children, favoritism, rebellion, arrogance, pride, false loyalty that overlooks sin and abuse, false responsibility, caretaking (doing for others things they can and should do themselves).

The fallen nature of humanity and sinfulness in the world produces differing decrees of dysfunction within all family systems, from mild to extreme. However, within many cult family systems secret sins and secret abuses are appearing to be more common today, creating deep emotional trauma and flawed character structures that often exhibit anti-social behavioral characteristics within cult family members.

Relationship idolatry and works of the flesh are the prime reason for the massive number of cult family systems hiding and prospering within Christian congregations and fellowships.

I have seen many cases where a spouse becomes a Christian and influences other members to become Christian as well and attend a fellowship; however, the existing dysfunctional cult family dynamics are not dealt with properly but painted over with superficial changes and learned Christian public behavior. However, behind the closed doors of the family, symptoms of past abuse and/or active secret abuse continue to thrive.

Idolatry between the parents and/or towards the children is carried into a pseudo-Christian family dynamic. In other words, the cult family system receives a Christian makeover without any true change of the dysfunctional family dynamics. The idolatrous cult family learns to look like a Christian family on the outside and hide deeply imbedded dysfunctional relationships and behavioral issues by smearing on religiosity.

When Christ calls individuals unto himself, he commands the following, *"If anyone comes to me and does not hate his own father and mother and wife and children and brothers and sisters, yes, and even his own life, he cannot be my disciple. Whoever does not bear his own cross and come after me cannot be my disciple... So therefore, any one of you who does not renounce all that he has cannot be my disciple"* (Luke 14:26-33).

Understanding why Christ used the word *hate* and the phrase *renounce all that he has* in the context of family relationships will shed light on this very difficult teaching by Christ. Many fellowship problems stem from the influence of a cult family system disguised as a model Christian family.

Pastors, elders, Christian workers, and the discerning saint must understand and embrace all that Christ taught in order to lead, equip, and maintain Christian maturity and holiness. We must include the harder teachings of Christ such as the above quoted passage. If not, family relationship idolatry will thrive within the congregation due to the lack of sound doctrine. We must apply Christ's teachings to bring us back to loving God above everyone and every other thing.

Owning and controlling loved ones within the family is what Christ is addressing in this teaching. Cult family systems are founded in relationship idolatry, selfishness, and life-sacrificing allegiance to parents, children, and siblings.

Far too many Christian parents fail to crucify the passions and desires of their carnal nature. They live in hidden bitterness, allowing lost dreams and aspirations to impinge upon the lives of their children. Vicarious living replaces the *zōē* life to be received in finding and doing God's will in life—for each family member.

Christian parents carry on their own family-of-origin cultish idiosyncrasies and can ultimately provoke their children to anger as they control, harangue, and push their children into looking good for their parents' own ego. They leave instruction on following Christ and living godly lives to the Sunday school teacher.

Resentment can seep in concerning quality time and financial costs required to rear children in the admonition of the Lord—nurturing, leading by example, and offering loving discipline according to God's instructions and the leadership of the Holy Spirit.

In the name of promoting Christian family bonding, teachings throughout the body of Christ can actually contradict what Christ teaches concerning family relations. For instance, Christian spouses are encouraged to live for each other, sacrificing a pure devotion to Christ. The Apostle Paul enlightens us concerning spousal idolatry within Christian marriage in the following passage:

"I want you to be free from anxieties. The unmarried man is anxious about the things of the Lord, how to please the Lord. But the married man is anxious about worldly things, how to please his wife, and his interests are divided. And the unmarried or betrothed woman is anxious about the things of the Lord, how to be holy in body and spirit. But the married woman is anxious about worldly things, how to please her husband. I say this for your own benefit, not to lay any restraint upon you, but to <u>promote good order and to secure your undivided devotion to the Lord</u>" (1 Corinthians 7:32-35).

Christ calls us to hate the spell of family relationship idolatry where members are programmed to live for each other and fulfill each other's impinging expectations and desires.

As to the darker side of the Christian cult family systems, where abuse, shame, religiosity, hypocrisy, secret sin, emotional extortion, and psychological blackmail are practiced—the sincere Christian will be called to a tough battle in exposing this insidious darkness.

Inevitably, the Christian embracing discernment and desiring to walk in obedience must learn to discern, confront, and even cause division in helping members break free from spellbinding allegiance to the Christian family system that is still living in darkness.

Jesus said, *"Do not think that I have come to bring peace to the earth. I have not come to bring peace, but a sword. For <u>I have come to set a man against his father, and a daughter against her mother, and a daughter-in-law against her mother-in-law.</u> And a person's enemies will be those of his own household. Whoever <u>loves father or mother more than me is not worthy of me</u>, and whoever <u>loves son or daughter more than me is not worthy of me</u>. And whoever does not take his cross and follow me is not worthy of me. Whoever finds his life will lose it, and whoever loses his life for my sake will find it"* (Matthew 10:34-39).

If you find yourself in conflict between obeying Christ or going along with your family's wishes, you must chose Christ at the expense of family togetherness and bonding. Do not shy away from this tough battle and the possibility of becoming estranged from your family.

Christ will demand our utmost allegiance. Take courage in the hope that the process of becoming free from your own sick family system may inspire others in your family to see the light. Often, when a member breaks free of the cult family spell, other members still spellbound might be jolted awake and break loose from the control and oppression of a cult family system.

Dealing with Carnal and Evil Cult Family Systems

One extreme area of caution for leadership is the increasing number of newly born-again Christians dragging their family of origin to church. The initial raw enthusiasm from that new Christian often spreads to other members of their family. In turn, family members follow, one by one, to fellowship and accept Christ, not by the call of God, but by the lure of carnal enthusiasm.

This seemingly wonderful move of God upon a family easily turns into spiritual nepotism. Favoritism or partiality develops as the family members become intertwined in church ministry and various leadership positions. An over focus on family togetherness in worship and the work of ministry often creates strain and difficulty, especially when the family still operates in carnal dynamics such as a domineering mother or a father who subtly promotes or overprotects another family member within the workings of church administration, ministry appointments and other fellowship activities.

Those in fellowship with some discernment will catch the spiritual nepotism and become resentful or even leave, believing the playing field for ministry opportunities is not even. What is worse is that if the family coming together to fellowship suffered extreme dysfunction or secret sins, and the members all disassociate or pretend away the darkness, and then most likely an evil cult family system has subtly infiltrated fellowship and put the whole congregation at great risk.

In the case of confronting sinful behavior or squelching carnal self-powered activities, for the carnal or cult family involved—family blood is thicker than fellowship bonding. I have seen matriarchal and patriarchal cult families in church attack others to protect and guard a family member at the expense of righteousness, fairness, and truth. As an example: a caretaking mother on the missions board covering and manipulating for a daughter-in-law who is full of bitter jealousy and undermining another participant in the Christmas pageant.

A carnal or cult Christian family system, with its members selfishly connected, will tend to cause trouble, even if not attending the same fellowship. We discovered that when one of the family members tries to escape the family abuses and controlling dynamics and receive counsel to stop the intrusiveness, the other family members attending other fellowships will mount an orchestrated and oppressive attack. The abusing person in the family will often enlist their fellow congregates to pray wrongly, gossip, and disparage the character of the supporting leadership of the victim trying to escape.

The following case is about the elderly patriarch of a very sick family system. All the family members professed Christ and all suffered, in one way or another from the secret sins that the grandfather perpetrated against his family. Until the secret sins are disclosed and repented of, each generation will become ensnared by the fountainhead's evil (the sin started by the father or mother). To keep the sins hidden, the perpetrator will exercise cult like control over the family system, and enlist other family members to become loyal to the family's secret sickness. An evil spirit will be assigned to keep the memories suppressed and perpetuate the sinfulness. The following Scripture helps explain how secret sin and un-confessed sins will flow down to each generation, as red dye poured into a mountain stream, polluting and staining its pristine beauty and freshness:

"The Lord, the Lord, a God merciful and gracious, slow to anger, and abounding in steadfast love and faithfulness, keeping steadfast love for thousands, forgiving iniquity and transgression and sin, but who will by no means clear the guilty, <u>visiting the iniquity of the fathers on the children and the children's children, to the third and the fourth generation</u>" (Exodus 34:6-7).

Ministry Case: *Torching the church for mother*

One of our first encounters with a Christian cult family system occurred when counseling a young man in the legal system. He was in the process of divorce and the state required him to receive long-term counseling for molesting his daughter. This was his first offense and the state law allowed first offenders to stay out of prison if they admitted guilt and submitted to the required therapy. However, he could never be around children for the rest of his life.

Someone had recommended that he receive additional Christian counseling from our ministry. He was seeking help to find out why, as a Christian, he struggled with pornography throughout his teens and adulthood, leading him into the evils of pedophilia.

Eventually his mother and grandmother also began attending our fellowship after hearing the progress he was making in our counseling program. Soon, they also entered into counseling and on several occasions, they brought the grandfather to counseling, he was suffering from dementia and living in a nursing home.

The inability to live at home was bothering him and he was becoming very combative and argumentative with his wife and daughter when they visited him. They suggested the he come for counseling.

During counsel, he demonstrated extreme self-pity about his situation and insisted that God could heal him and he wanted my counsel and prayer in the hopes of changing his situation. As a normal approach in dealing with Christians who struggle, we query each counselee if there is any un-confessed and un-repented sin harboring in their heart.

He broke down, wept like a little boy, and then confessed a sin that he had committed years prior when he was an elder at a small church. His family attended this fellowship and his mother was the church bookkeeper. He explained that his mother confided in him that she had stolen several times from the treasury and feared the pastor was about to discover that funds were missing. The stolen funds were spent, and she knew the family could not pay back the money and most likely, she would be charged with embezzlement.

Unfortunately, to save his family from shame and keep their good standing in the church and to prevent his mother from prosecution, he decided to burn down the church building to cover up his mother's crime. This he did, burning up all evidence and successfully keeping the secret locked up for over forty years.

This secret sin was the only bad thing he ever did, at least that was his claim. However, there was a sense that more evil lurked within him. The whole family, his adult daughters and wife all had a strange sexual aura about them—a subtle spiritually defiling impingement that eventually came to the light in counsel.

The grandfather passed away soon after his confession and his daughter who was also receiving our counsel (she was the mother of the man who had molested his daughter, and had initially come to us) started to vaguely remember as a young girl, lying in bed with her father and doing sexual things. Then, separately with no sharing with each other, her son began to remember that his mother fondled him as a young boy.

These revelations took months of counseling, prayer, and courage for these two people to acknowledge these past sins and begin to heal. However, the layers of carnal character structures for both, especially the mother, circumvented total recovery.

Just as the son fell into pornography, his mother was obsessed with Christian romance novels and complained of overwhelming lust and sexual desires.

The grandfather's secret iniquities against his daughter were visited upon the children and the children's children to the third and the fourth generation and caused trouble in fellowship and amongst other family members.

When his daughter realized she had married an abusive man like her father (who also was an elder in the local Assembly of God church) she began to hold him accountable. Then the battle was on, as her extended family attending different churches became involved, attacking our ministry and spreading false accusations that our ministry was a cult. Ω

This is just one of many cases where a struggling Christian came to fellowship and began to become whole and stable, resulting in a flood of family members tagging along unwilling to deal with their secret sins and sick family dynamics. A healthy fellowship must have leadership that understands these issues and employs sound doctrine in dealing with this potentially destructive element within Christian families that are carnal and sinfully bonded.

The New Testament principles of confession of sin and repentance are a vital and are to be a constant activity to be incorporated into the everyday life of fellowship.

"Is anyone among you suffering? Let him pray. Is anyone cheerful? Let him sing praise. Is anyone among you sick? Let him call for the elders of the church, and let them pray over him, anointing him with oil in the name of the Lord. And the prayer of faith will save the one who is sick, and the Lord will raise him up. <u>And if he has committed sins, he will be forgiven. Therefore, confess your sins to one another and pray for one another, that you may be healed</u>" (James 5:13-16)—not only physical healing, also emotional, mental and wounds to the spirit.

Support group work and sound biblical counsel is also vital where confidential confessions help facilitate healthy and godly fellowship. *"If we say we have no sin, we deceive ourselves, and the truth is not in us. If we confess our sins, he is faithful and just to forgive us our sins and to cleanse us from all unrighteousness. If we say we have not sinned, we make him a liar, and his word is not in us"* (1 John 1:8-10). Many Christians are living lies, pretending their sins are all under the blood, yet keep those sins to themselves along with the defiling side effects.

One major reason why so many cult families (carnal as well as evil) thrive in fellowships throughout the body of Christ is due to the unchecked relationship idolatry from leadership on down to the congregants.

Sealing Your Election and Call
Spiritual conditioning in godliness—partaking in the divine nature

Sound doctrine given by those who have endured the wilderness training will encourage you to supplement your faith through *spiritual conditioning* in your relationship with Christ. Years ago, there were men and women of God to lead by example, who taught the deeper things of God. Unfortunately, few resources are available today to help the sincere disciple of Christ work out genuine godliness and help in traveling the hard path that leads to life.

Wilderness training is difficult and lonely, and there may be numerous times of isolation when few are available to offer guidance or help. However, the wilderness is where the true servant becomes bonded to Christ, taught and trained by his hand and sealed in a divine relationship to never ignore or defy the leadership of the Holy Spirit.

The wilderness is not pleasant, and pretending the pain away will not make it easier. You cannot speed up the wilderness journey; however, you can make it longer if you try to avoid its fiery smelting work. Keeping the end in mind will give you courage to endure. *"Count it <u>all joy, my brothers, when you meet trials of various kinds</u>, for you know that the testing of your faith <u>produces steadfastness</u>. And let steadfastness have its full effect, that <u>you may be perfect and complete, lacking in nothing</u>"* (James 1:2-4). This ordained process of God does bring perfection and completion. As to a formal education and training for ministry, this should be considered a supplement to God's discipleship and leadership program—Christ's school of ministry wrought in the wilderness is your true ordination and divine credentials.

As we come to the end of our carnal motives while in the wilderness, we must learn also to supplement our faith with virtue, more knowledge, self-control, steadfastness, and godliness, love of God, and a healthy love of the brethren (see 2 Peter 1:3-11). This divine faith-enhancement work is often contrary to the popular self-help and self-growth books and programs, and opposes many ministry gurus that dominate Christian education and ministry.

We are to embrace God's way of building Christ-like nature in us, so that we manifest all the characteristics of the divine nature. If we follow Christ and his way, we will become effective and fruitful in knowing and demonstrating the true Christ within us. As we make sure we are following the true Christ and diligently working towards our calling (knowing and doing God's will for your life), we will enter the Kingdom of God here on earth and have a secure entrance into eternity. *"Therefore, brothers, be all the more diligent to make your calling and election sure, for if you practice these qualities you will never fall. For in this way there will be richly provided for you an entrance into the eternal kingdom of our Lord and Savior Jesus Christ"* (2 Peter 1:10, 11).

Digest and Absorb Today's Manna before Moving on

Why does God not give us a steady stream of revelation and insight to increase our discernment? Many today want a wide-open fast freeway to knowledge. When we get greedy or impatient in growing our discernment, we wrongly apply what we currently know, thus painting ourselves into a corner and suffering extra. Therefore, God in his faithfulness will slow down our insights and knowledge, and let hell buffet us to shape our knowledge and discernment with wisdom and in the love of God. One of the reasons for this slowdown is due to our inability to handle the increased knowledge without becoming puffed up or overly elated (see 2 Corinthians 12:7).

When the crowd clamored after him—when he fed the multitudes miraculously—Jesus exhorted all to seek the manna from above instead seeking for an abundance of food to eat on earth. Manna is the word used to describe the divinely provided sustenance that God gave the Israelites in the wilderness: a bread-like food that fell from heaven. The Israelites were instructed to gather only what was needed for the meals for that one day. However, some were fearful and greedy and took much more than they needed. Their leftover manna rotted by the next day. (See Exodus 16:13-20).

Christ exhorted the crowd that followed him to seek the manna from above, in heaven. That kind of manna would deepen a believer's relationship with God and increase knowledge, insight and wisdom—coming from God himself to those who seek, ask, and knock.

Believers who desire deeper understanding, insight and discernment directly from God can easily become greedy and try to take in more than they are ready to receive. Many seek more knowledge before what they just received assimilates into their nature. Be patient, humble and wise in applying the manna you receive, learning to wait upon the Lord. Allow his hand of discipline and training to mold that information, revelation or insight from the written Word into Christ-like character founded in the love of God. *"We know that 'all of us possess knowledge.' This 'knowledge' puffs up, but love builds up. If anyone imagines that he knows something, he does not yet know as he ought to know. But if anyone loves God, he is known by God"* (1 Corinthians 8:1-3).

Let Your Yes be Yes, and Your No be No
Learning to mean what you say and say what you mean—in wisdom

A major leap in developing sharper discernment is learning to communicate with others truthfully and in wisdom. Jesus said of Nathanael: *"Behold, an Israelite indeed, in whom there is no deceit!"* (John 1:47).

Deceit comes to us naturally; especially if raised in a shame-based family system, where abuse, dysfunction or poverty created the need to put on a front when we walked out the front door on the way to school, play, or at extended family get-togethers.

We learned to disguise our true feelings, to pretend to be happy when we are sad, and we learned to be manipulative, coy, tell fibs, exaggerate, and portray a false persona through carefully chosen words and body language—thus most walk in guile (cleverness, cunning, and deceit). How much deception a person employs depends on each person and their life experiences and upbringing.

When we come to Christ, our heavenly Father works to bring us to truth—and expects us to learn how to stop pretending and stop putting on a mask (walking in hypocrisy). *"Having purified your souls by your obedience to the truth for a sincere brotherly love, love one another earnestly from a pure heart, since you have been born again, not of perishable seed but of imperishable, through the living and abiding Word of God"* (1 Peter 1:22-23).

So many come to Christ, attend church, and fellowship and learn to lie. When we see this in ourselves, then decide to come clean, many of us make a terrible mistake and tell what we really think and feel to the wrong people at the wrong time. Jesus taught: *"Let what you say be simply 'Yes' or 'No'; anything more than this comes from evil"* (Matthew 5:37). He also taught: *"Do not give dogs what is holy, and do not throw your pearls before pigs, lest they trample them underfoot and turn to attack you"* (Matthew 7:6). Discerning what to say to whom and when is vital. Trial and error with the Holy Spirit's mentoring will guide you along the way towards wisdom (along with knowing Scripture— especially the sermon on the mount and Proverbs).

All this is predicated on giving up our self-deceit. Learn to be honest with yourself and then you will start to be honest with God—he already knows everything about us—our problem is we do not want to know what he knows about us. *"And no creature is hidden from his sight, but all are naked and exposed to the eyes of him to whom we must give account"* (Hebrews 4:13).

One more caution from Christ: *"Behold, I am sending you out as sheep in the midst of wolves, so be wise as serpents and innocent as doves"* (Matthew 10:16). The more we say what we mean when we are supposed to, the less we will find ourselves involved with people who love to walk in deceit.

Physical Conditioning and Eating Healthy

We have exhorted extensively on becoming sanctified and walking in true holiness, which is vital in growing our discernment. If you harbor bad feelings and deeply rooted jealousy and bitterness in pretense, then do not expect to discern these same issues in others.

We have found that spiritual attacks will heighten blood pressure, aggravate old injuries and exhaust one physically. If we let our physical body go to pot, we can expect severe trouble physically, especially in the coming difficult times.

God expects us to take appropriate care of his temple! Do not give the devil extra ground by being lazy, out of basic conditioning, or eating or drinking wrong foods and wrong liquids. One does not have to be a health nut to maintain an appropriate physique. Minimizing such things as caffeine and sugar will go a long way in keeping your body's metabolism shipshape. The physical, emotional, and mental symptoms will be more manageable when wrestling with principalities and dealing with carnal Christians who employ witchcraft prayers if we take care of our body.

The Gall of Bitterness and the Bonds of Iniquity
Millions of believers have never resolved the defilements of their former manner of life

There are impure Christians everywhere. They are angry, jealous, bitter, malice-ridden, controlled by selfish ambition, self-righteous, rebellious, and struggling with an unclean spirit, and are often buffeted in life by bitter expectations. They frequently make an idol of their favorite leader instead of following Christ personally—the list is long and the consequences are troubling and often destructive.

To walk in true discernment one must resolve all past defilements. In Simon the magician's case, Peter says he *discerned* that Simon was in the gall of bitterness and bond or iniquity.

Many Christians stuck in the bonds of iniquity and carrying bitter jealousy easily conceal the associated symptoms and characteristics from others and themselves. This deception (denial) causes widespread carnal and sinful behavior that goes undetected until a crisis, a disappointment, or some form of competition brings out their hidden condition. True discernment requires understanding these hidden issues and the ability to catch the telltale words and behavior of an impure heart.

If we desire to walk in keen discernment and expect to detect the heart, as Peter did, of those who are struggling in bitter jealousy and selfish ambition, then we must be free of those same issues. We will be unable to discern and confront Christians who are still under the influence of their past defilements unless we become cleansed ourselves of all past defilements.

Love, Forgiveness, and Holding Evil Accountable
Reconciling Christ's teachings that appear to contradict

Christians historically struggle with Christ's teachings on confronting evil and loving those who are obviously opponents, or hateful enemies. In studying the lives and writings of the Apostles, we find specific instructions on distinguishing between types of enemies and evils and developing appropriate Christ-like attitudes towards each.

In learning to walk in true discernment, we must reconcile to our satisfaction the seeming conflicts in Scripture on dealing with evil in a loving way. If we are confused in understanding the nature of evil as defined in Scripture, thinking that it is unloving to assess someone as evil, then the Holy Spirit will be hampered in revealing and warning the confused saint. It is the intent of this section to help clear up any doubts and conflict concerning Christ-like attitudes and actions in discernment and holding evil accountable.

Christ instructed his followers to love their enemies and to demonstrate forgiveness and generosity to those who are hateful, mean and abusive. However, our Lord also taught us to deal firmly with believers who are unrepentant when they became hateful, mean, and abusive. Specifically, confront a repugnant Christian with witnesses, and if necessary bring him or her before the church. Then if they are still unrepentant, Christ tells us to have nothing more to do with them.

We have examples where Christ himself demonstrated appropriate attitudes and actions towards certain people who approached him with flattery, manipulation, or disingenuousness. Those who follow Christ are to develop these same Christ-like attitudes and walk in them.

Christ confronted religious hypocrites, describing them as liars having the same nature as that of the devil, characterizing them as whitewashed tombs that appear to be righteous and beautiful but inwardly are full of uncleanness, lawlessness, rapacity (greed), and murder.

In contrast, Christ taught us not to judge others because of race, sinfulness or occupation. He showed compassion to such people as Samaritans, Gentiles, tax collectors, prostitutes and lepers. The caveat here is that the sinners he showed grace towards demonstrated true repentance and a desire to walk in righteousness.

Perhaps the most poignant example of the distinction between the repentant and the unrepentant was how Christ conducted himself while dying on the cross between two sinners. *"One of the criminals who were hanged railed at him, saying, 'Are you not the Christ? Save yourself and us!' But the other rebuked him, saying, 'Do you not fear God, since you are under the same sentence of condemnation? And we indeed justly, for we are receiving the due reward of our deeds; but this man has done nothing wrong.' And he said, 'Jesus, remember me when you come into your kingdom.' And he said to him, 'Truly, I say to you, today you will be with me in Paradise.'"* (Luke 23:39-43).

Jesus did not say one word to the criminal who railed at him, demanding that Jesus should save himself and them as well. The other criminal, who was truly repentant and accepting of his sentence was given a word from the Savior—a word that would numb the pain of dying on the cross and the sting of death: *"Truly, I say to you, today you will be with me in Paradise."*

Another example is when a man called from the crowd demanding Christ take sides in a petty dispute over an inheritance. Christ replied, *"'Man, who made me a judge or arbitrator over you?' And he said to them, 'Take care, and be on your guard against all covetousness, for one's life does not consist in the abundance of his possessions'"* (Luke 12:14-15).

It is vital that a true servant of Christ reconcile any seemingly contradictory teachings of Christ and the Apostles. Avoiding, exposing, confronting and holding the wicked accountable is not to be nullified in the Christian's life. Teachings that condemn such firmness in holding sinfulness, carnality, and evil accountable as unforgiving, unloving or unmerciful are wrong. This terrible misunderstanding has allowed evil to run wild in many fellowships and throughout society. The Apostle Peter wrote, *"The Lord is not slow to fulfill his promise as some count slowness, but is patient toward you, not wishing that any should perish, but that all should reach repentance"* (2 Peter 3:9). However, the freedom of will granted by God requires that we must understand the dark side of humanity as expounded in God's Word and not walk in naiveté. The belief that there is good in everyone and that everyone is redeemable is a very destructive false ideology within Christianity.

Christ confronted evil people without hesitation, especially the religious evil of his day. The following passages demonstrate Christ's attitude and approach in dealing with those who bore evil fruit and Christ identified their very nature to be evil:

"You brood of vipers! How can you speak good, when you are evil?" (Matthew 12:34).

"You serpents, you brood of vipers, how are you to escape being sentenced to hell?" (Matthew 23:33).

"You are of your father the devil, and your will is to do your father's desires" (John 8:44).

Christ warned that anyone who defiled children and caused children to sin—that this evil type of person would be better off if they were summarily executed:

"Whoever causes one of these little ones who believe in me to sin, it would be better for him if a great millstone were hung around his neck and he were thrown into the sea" (Mark 9:42).

The Apostle Paul taught in the book of Romans to *"watch out for those who cause divisions and create obstacles contrary to the doctrine that you have been taught; avoid them. For such persons do not serve our Lord Christ, but their own appetites, and by smooth talk and flattery they deceive the hearts of the naive. For your obedience is known to all, so that I rejoice over you, but I want you to be wise as to what is good and innocent as to what is evil. The God of peace will soon crush Satan under your feet"* (Romans 16:17-20).

Few Christians learn to be on guard and avoid or shun divisive people. These people use flattery to blind those who are naïve to their insidious and devious desires—many a deceived Christian embraces or befriends evil people wholeheartedly, only to learn their lesson after the damage has taken great toll. Many sincere Christians have never received instruction on how to discern the difference between an evil person disguised as good, who *acts* as if they are good, and a person who is genuinely sincere and *does* good. Unfortunately, to the contrary, far too many Christians are taught there is good in everyone and that those who appear to be good and friendly outwardly can be trusted.

We need to understand why Christ did not trust himself to anyone, and we need to walk in discernment and not judge on the outside, but be open to hear from Christ concerning potential evil lurking in the heart of people we encounter, in fellowship, work and even extended family.

Learning the Proper Use of the Four Letter Word: EVIL
Effectively distinguishing good from evil involves naming evil—EVIL

Jesus made a startling statement concerning one of the disciples: *"Did I not choose you, the twelve? and yet one of you is a devil"* (John 6:70). This he said referring to Judas well in advance of the betrayal, *"'But there are some of you who do not believe.' (For Jesus knew from the beginning who those were who did not believe, and who it was who would betray him)"* (John 6:64).

Again, as mentioned in the previous section, Judas was referred to as the son of perdition; however, the rest of the disciples did not realize what Christ was trying to get them to understand until the betrayal took place. From then on, the disciples used the terms *evil* and *devil* distinctly to expose such a person and to teach others the ramifications of doing evil or allowing Satan to fill one's heart with evil intent.

Until we embrace the teachings of Christ and the apostles concerning evil and learn to name it "evil" in full understanding, evil will stay hidden and continue its destructiveness. Evil hides in fellowships everywhere and prospers right under the noses of the naïve, the aloof leader and the dumbed-down saint. The first step in displacing evil is to detect it, name it, and confront it directly. Evil only backs down when it is called for what it is and held accountable in front of all. *"As for those who persist in sin, rebuke them in the presence of all, so that the rest may stand in fear"* (1 Timothy 5:20).

Few understand how powerful and dangerous it is to be involved in any type of sorcery good or bad. Few understand how Satan uses the good side of evil to entice millions of naïve and deceived people into the dark arts. Children are special targets and millions of Christian children become exposed to these evils annually, as each new book or movie is released along these lines.

Introduction to dark powers in the form of comedy or presented as a means to do good has seduced millions over the last four decades. Violence, sexual perversion, horror, sorcery, homosexuality, and other defiling activities have seeped into the mind and heart of society gradually and now saturates most of our culture, institutions and even portions of Christianity.

Movies, video games, literature and so many other venues are now powerful delivery methods of evil defilements that penetrate into the psyche and spirit of all ages in our culture. No one now dare call these defiling activities and the associated debauchery EVIL, for fear of lawsuits, criminal prosecution for hate speech, or outright abuse from those who now openly and arrogantly practice these dark and defiling activities.

The fruit of all the years of mounting evils and immoralities has all but completely removed any sense of right and wrong. Family systems become heavily influenced and held captive by individual family members who have some form of evil hold on the rest of the family members. (Case in point: the recent massacre at Sandy Hook Elementary School on December 14, 2012, where the murderer, a deranged 20 year old, held his mother in terror—she was murdered because she had finally begun seeking a way to have him committed).

In a recent news article published March 18, 2013, on Foxnews.com it was reported that the gunman Adam Lanza produced a spreadsheet 7 feet long and 4 feet wide which comprised results of extensive research on about 500 people. The sheet listed the names of those who had been killed in mass murders (such as the one Adam committed), the types of weapons and the model of weapons that had been used. This obsessive analysis took years to compile and police now label Lanza and others like him "glory killers" who approach mass murdering as a game to amass the most points. (FoxNews.com, "Sandy Hook Gunman Reportedly Compiled Massive Spreadsheet on Previous Killings," March 18, 2013).

There are countless evil family systems strewn throughout Christian fellowships worldwide because the sincere saint and leadership ignore the telltale indicators of evil. In many cases, evil is accommodated or pretended away for the sake of donations, superficial peace or for appearance's sake.

Christians in evil family systems make concessions with evil due to fear of being labeled as divisive. However, evil in Christian families is being exposed all too often: evil parents, an evil spouse, an evil child, or an evil sibling have been brought to justice by the legal system, while the church recoils at the repercussions of evil's exposure within the midst of the congregation.

Jesus desires to have these evils exposed, but few desire training in discernment along with the required discipline to expose the hidden darkness and take courage to call evil "evil."

"So have no fear of them, for nothing is covered that will not be revealed, or hidden that will not be known. What I tell you in the dark, say in the light, and what you hear whispered, proclaim on the housetops. And do not fear those who kill the body but cannot kill the soul. Rather fear him who can destroy both soul and body in hell" (Matthew 10:26-28).

False responsibility in protecting a family member, a church elder, a coworker, or the family reputation and—fear and lack of training in properly determining what is truly good from what is truly evil are the main issues. Many walk in self-righteousness and call a sinner caught doing evil "evil." The recent Penn State University scandal is another powerful example to drive home the reality of evil and how it thrives when not called out and held accountable, especially when those in the position of authority and responsibility look the other way. "The only thing necessary for the triumph of evil is that good men should do nothing," said Edmond Burke.

The Apostle Paul instructs us to walk as children of light and discern the Lord's will and be willing to expose darkness (see Ephesians 5:8-12). Over these many years of ministry we have exposed these kinds of evils within the church, families, in the extended community, and even in our own fellowship as new attendees come bringing with them their own darkness—evils done in secret. These cases continue to grow as this nation and the world races towards the end-of-the-age wickedness predicted in Scripture. All the while, the bulk of God's people are busy playing church and reeling from their own scandals and attempting to continue to pretend that all is okay.

We learned to call evil "evil" boldly yet wisely. This is the challenge for every Christian worker and leader in the coming days. Evil is now at every Christian's door-step—a church member doing evil in secret, an uncle, a teacher, or a neighborhood teen preying on other children—a society wallowing in and glorifying filth, calling evil "good," and good "evil."

Warning: Make sure you understand the power of hell and its influence, learning to be wise as a serpent and innocent as a dove in the midst of darkness and in the company of evil wolves.

We are not to judge and condemn the outsider, but rather drive out those who are phony and evil from the midst of the congregation and from our own personal lives. *"Drive out the wicked person from among you'* (1 Corinthians 5:13 RSV). In order to walk in true discernment we must identify evil, and call it "evil." We must call "evil" what God calls evil and humbly walk before him in the fear of the Lord, being courageous to hold evil accountable.

Discerning and Dealing with Christians Who Are Under Judgment
Reaping what was sown, mortal sins, and sinning against the Holy Spirit

Many Christians wonder why they continue to fall under extreme troubling circumstances as though their reward for following Christ is invalid. Few learn the principles of judgments, bitter expectations, sinning deliberately, and other satanic strongholds rooted in carnal character.

True discernment requires understanding the biblical principles described in the following passages explaining that sincere forgiveness is to be from the heart: *"Judge not, and you will not be judged; condemn not, and you will not be condemned; forgive, and you will be forgiven; give, and it will be given to you. Good measure, pressed down, shaken together, running over, will be put into your lap. For with the measure you use it will be measured back to you"* (Luke 6:37-38). *"And in anger his master delivered him to the jailers, [torturers] until he should pay all his debt. So also my heavenly Father will do to every one of you, if you do not forgive your brother from your heart."* (Matthew 18:34-35).

If we are serious with Christ, he will point out any vestige of unforgiveness lodged within our hearts. Unforgiveness and self-pity are Satan's most common and effective strongholds within God's people.

This is the case because most are convinced that when they became born again and were led to say a blanket prayer of confessing all sins and forgiving everyone that ever sinned against them, through that prayer, Christ magically wiped the slate of their heart clean.

The teaching that everything in the past is under the blood of Christ and should be forgotten is one of the most destructive heresies ever to sweep through the body of Christ. To the contrary, it is those specific incidents where our heart became embittered from hurts that form grudges, vengeful motivation, resentments, bitter expectations, jealous streaks, envy that opens us to Satan's temptations. Many fall into sin because they ignored the promptings of the Holy Spirit concerning these latent heart-embedded disorders.

When we are taught to pretend we have become a completely new creation in Christ instantly—then Satan will have a right to throw one nasty problem after another in our path.

God has put in place the principle of reaping and sowing for the born-again Christian to help the discerning saint deal with those buried and forgotten segments of the heart that contain unforgiveness. The discipline of the Lord is meant to expose these in a manner and pace that we can manage, so as to deal with them thoroughly and individually. Using blanket prayers to forgive boils down to the practice of myths and magic incantations that give false peace.

When these roots of bitterness within the heart spring up it will cause all manner of trouble and defile many in family and fellowship. (See Hebrews 12:7-17). This is very serious and the Lord will not be put to the test concerning hidden unforgiveness and bitter jealousy.

"Do not be deceived: God is not mocked, for whatever one sows, that will he also reap. For the one who sows to his own flesh will from the flesh reap corruption, but the one who sows to the Spirit will from the Spirit reap eternal life" (Galatians 6:7-8).

Many came to our counseling ministry complaining of all manner of calamities and problems. Most suffered from hidden and unresolved hatreds, bitter expectations, resentments and angers—and underneath these issues were unresolved wounds laced with unforgiveness as root causes.

These formed subtle beliefs within the heart such as: "All men are selfish, all women are lazy, and I will never amount to anything."

The list of satanic stronghold lies can be many, and are deeply lodged within the hearts of millions of sincere but struggling Christians. When we as discerning disciples of Christ learn to deal with our own reaping and sowing course that leads to cleansing and forgiveness from the heart, we can see clearly to help our brethren overcome these same strongholds that bind so many.

Remember, God judges his people, and often severely, if they are deliberately, secretly sinning. Christian workers and saints will be increasingly called upon to pray for others who suffer from reaping and sowing, but also from the judgment of the Lord; discerning the difference is vital in counsel and prayer. Counseling and praying wrongly for such a person will just add to the problem.

"In the presence of God and of Christ Jesus and of the elect angels I charge you to keep these rules without prejudging, doing nothing from partiality. Do not be hasty in the laying on of hands, nor take part in the sins of others; keep yourself pure" (1 Timothy 5:21-22).

Praying for deliverance for those reaping what they sowed in the discipline of the Lord or for one who is sinning and under judgment will cause you to become a partaker of someone else's sin and judgment, though ignorantly, but yet accountable due to lack of due diligence in discernment.

Another serious condition that some fall into is the committing of a mortal sin. Ananias and Sapphira together committed a mortal sin by lying to Peter. (See Acts 4:36-5:11). These committed the following as described by the Apostle John, *"If anyone sees his brother committing a sin not leading to death, he shall ask, and God will give him life—to those who commit sins that do not lead to death. There is sin that leads to death; I do not say that one should pray for that. All wrongdoing is sin, but there is sin that does not lead to death"* (1 John 5:16-17).

It was by the Holy Spirit that Peter received knowledge of Ananias lying about the sale of the property he and his wife owned, then saying to Ananias, *"Why is it that you have contrived this deed in your heart? You have not lied to men but to God"* (Acts 5:4). Immediately upon hearing these words from Peter, Ananias fell down and died instantly.

Ananias committed a mortal sin (a sin leading to death) and the Holy Spirit executed that judgment instantly. What is an important fact to note concerning the following judgment that befell Ananias' wife Sapphira, is that Peter knew exactly what would happen if she lied like her husband did. Here we see the importance of not interfering or praying for someone who has committed a sin that leads to premature death.

Mortal sin or a sin that leads to death in the context here is not eternal death (necessarily), but rather a last opportunity for contriteness that leads to repentance. Unfortunately, many of God's people are hardened in heart to the point where lying or other wrongdoing is trivial to them. The Apostle Paul explains that when we sin and then are confronted with it, whether we sin deliberately or carelessly, we should become grieved into repenting; *"For godly grief produces a repentance that leads to salvation without regret, whereas worldly grief produces death"* (2 Corinthians 7:10).

The Apostle John is instructing us to pay attention to the kind of sinning that is being committed amongst the brethren and note the judgment and consequences in life, being careful to hear rightly from the Lord and to ascertain the truth.

Scripture does not lay out specifics on what is a mortal sin—a sin leading to death as judgment—however, Christ speaks of abuse towards children as an offense so despicable that the perpetrator would be better off summarily executed.

The Lord summarily executed both Ananias and Sapphira. He did the same to Herod as described here, *"On an appointed day Herod put on his royal robes, took his seat upon the throne, and delivered an oration to them. And the people were shouting, 'The voice of a god, and not of a man!' Immediately an angel of the Lord struck him down, because he did not give God the glory, and he was eaten by worms and breathed his last"* (Acts 12:21-23).

The Apostle Paul had the authority to turn a believer over to Satan for the destruction of his flesh (physical death) that his spirit might be saved in the day of the Lord. (See 1 Corinthians 5:1-5). These accounts of certain sins causing premature death for believers produced a fear of God. God's people learned to not be arrogant or develop a cavalier attitude toward any kind of wrongdoing.

Understanding the principle of reaping what we sow in order to expose hidden carnal issues; discerning a judgment for wrongdoing and being careful not to enter into another's sin; learning to hear rightly concerning someone who has committed a sin that leads to premature death—all must be part of our discernment course of instruction directed by the Lord.

What constitutes a mortal sin is the Lord's judgment; a lie committed by a believer most likely would not cause instant death as it did for Ananias and Sapphira. We must understand why these two people lied as they did which is hinted at in this passage, *"Thus Joseph, who was also called by the apostles Barnabas (which means son of encouragement), a Levite, a native of Cyprus, sold a field that belonged to him and brought the money and laid it at the apostles' feet"* (Acts 4:36-37).

Joseph must have received some recognition for his generous offering, which spurred Ananias and Sapphira to sell their extra piece of property, also to gain recognition. However, they were insincere about the reason for giving and made their offering a ploy to gain accolades in competition with Joseph. This was the very type of evil that Christ confronted the Pharisees with doing. The Holy Spirit made an example of them and stopped such people from entering into the recognized ranks of the fledgling church.

In the coming days the Holy Spirit will reinstitute this type of judgment upon the false and the game players, where sin leading to death will begin to be recognized. Outright fear of God will once again have its rightful place in the hearts of the true church that Christ will raise up as the end of the age presses on.

Sin against the Holy Spirit

A very import teaching of Christ that we must understand is the sin against the Holy Spirit. Part of discernment is learning what constitutes a sin against the Holy Spirit. Jesus taught, *"Then a demon-oppressed man who was blind and mute was brought to him, and he healed him, so that the man spoke and saw. And all the people were amazed, and said, Can this be the Son of David? But when the Pharisees heard it, they said, 'It is only by Beelzebul, the prince of demons, that this man casts out demons.'*

Knowing their thoughts, he said to them, 'Every kingdom divided against itself is laid waste, and no city or house divided against itself will stand. And if Satan casts out Satan, he is divided against himself. How then will his kingdom stand? And if I cast out demons by Beelzebul, by whom do your sons cast them out? Therefore they will be your judges. <u>But if it is by the Spirit of God that I cast out demons, then the kingdom of God has come upon you.</u> Or how can someone enter a strong man's house and plunder his goods, unless he first binds the strong man? Then indeed he may plunder his house. Whoever is not with me is against me, and whoever does not gather with me scatters. Therefore I tell you, every sin and blasphemy will be forgiven people, <u>but the blasphemy against the Spirit will not be forgiven</u>. And whoever speaks a word against the Son of Man will be forgiven, but whoever <u>speaks against the Holy Spirit will not be forgiven, either in this age or in the age to come'</u>" (Matthew 12:22-32).

In the context of the situation that Christ is warning of "sinning against the Holy Spirit" concerned the Pharisees declaring that Jesus cast out demons by the power of the devil. However, the truth was that Christ cast out evil spirits by the Holy Spirit, not in his own power or the power of Satan.

On the surface it would seem that the failure of Pharisees was that in hearing from the people (not seeing first hand) that blind and mute were healed and delivered of evil spirits, they declared that Christ did it by the power of the devil. However, Jesus said, *"But if it is by the Spirit of God that I cast out demons, then the kingdom of God has come upon you."*

With the signs also came the witness of the Holy Spirit upon the hearts of those who witnessed these events and other who had heard and marveled. When Pharisees heard of the accounts, the Holy Spirit also bore witness in their hearts (*"then the Kingdom of God has come upon you"*).

When a person rejects a sign or wonder (healing or deliverance) and has the witness of the Holy Spirit confirming the event was of God, and that person hardens their heart and declares it is not of God—then, depending on their reaction and sacrilegious accusations, that may very well will put that person at risk of sinning against the Holy Spirit.

An important aspect of the work of the Holy Spirit is to *"Convict the world concerning sin and righteousness and judgment"* (John 16:8). The born again work by the Spirit of God must include the convicting verdict within the heart of the sinner in process of becoming born again.

The recipient of God's work of salvation must have within their heart the compelling knowledge and conviction that they are full sin, that their righteousness amounts to nothing, and that they deserve the wrath of God in full judgment.

This convicting work can only come from the Holy Spirit at God's discretion through his grace. Without truly realizing their terrible and hopeless situation concerning eternity, which is granted by the Holy Spirit in his convicting work, the message of salvation by grace through faith in Christ cannot come to fruition.

When the Pharisees began to attack the work of the Holy Spirit as being of the devil, they were on the path to permanently rejecting the convicting and regenerating work of the Holy Spirit as well.

I have counseled quite a few wounded Christians who were convinced that they had sinned against the Holy Spirit because they struggled with sin and were thoroughly miserable. They believed God had turned his back on them permanently.

This kind of condition plaguing a born-again, immature believer is primarily due to false doctrine that insists that <u>if one is truly born again they will not have a sin problem</u>. I have witnessed struggling Christians run up to an altar call to become born again-again, time after time, thinking that this time they might become truly born again and have eternal life and be free of sin issues.

Once they realized through mentoring and counseling that their issues were typical, that the Holy Spirit had never left them, and that their lack of understanding of grace, sanctification and growing up into salvation were the main issues—their sense of belonging to God was restored.

Many suffer from wounds to the spirit and damaged emotions that easily become inflamed and overshadow their ability to sense God's love and presence. As these trouble believers learn to work out their own salvation in the fear of God, without self-condemning when a mistake is made or if they are overtaken by a trespass, then they make great progress in learning to deal with their hidden wounds and unresolved damaged emotions.

However, in my own studies and study of Scripture, coupled with firsthand experience, the type of Christian or lost soul who denounces the convicting work of the Holy Spirit and ends up rejecting their conscience is the kind of person who is at great risk of sinning against the Holy Spirit.

The Pharisees, in the context of the passage where Christ warns of this eternally damning sin, were jealous of Christ's popularity and looked upon themselves as saved already. Many false Christians have this same condition of heart, in one form or another, where they refuse to see their own sinfulness, deny their conscience, and rebuff the prompting and convicting (not condemning) work of the Holy Spirit.

The Holy Spirit does not condemn; however, he does convict and help convince a lost sinner of their great need of a savior. *"For God did not send his Son into the world to condemn the world, but in order that the world might be saved through him. Whoever believes in him is not condemned, <u>but whoever does not believe is condemned already</u>, because he has not believed in the name of the only Son of God. <u>And this is the judgment: the light has come into the world, and people loved the darkness rather than the light because their deeds were evil.</u> For everyone who does wicked things hates the light and does not come to the light, lest his deeds should be exposed. But whoever does what is true comes to the light, so that it may be clearly seen that his deeds have been carried out in God"* (John 3:17-21).

The Holy Spirit is the only agent in the world that brings one to salvation, and if the work of the third person of the Trinity is rebuffed, his convicting work rejected—then all is lost now, and in age to come since there will be no opportunity to receive forgiveness by faith in heaven.

Spiritual Vibes and Our Personal Spirit
Understanding the function of our spirit in discernment

In the news recently, a Christian woman and beauty queen contestant in the 2012 Miss California pageant, Miss Victoria Kinney, reported that she was most likely the next targeted rape victim by a man now charged with raping another woman he met using the dating website ChristianMingle.com.

In her explanation of encountering Sean Patrick Banks through the dating website, she expressed regrets saying, "I didn't listen to my instincts, in those instances and looking back. He seemed like a good strong, Christian man." Miss Kinney, in her interview on NBC added, "Women need to be aware that even if someone looks safe and nice and Christian and spiritual, they might be a predator" (Christianpost.com, *California Beauty Queen Says ChristianMingle.com Rape Suspect Threatened Her,* March 22, 2013).

"I didn't listen to my instincts" is a common lament of many who have been defrauded, raped, robbed, and abused by a wolf (predator) that appeared as a nice harmless sheep. The very warnings we have been expounding upon are relevant in every aspect of life. Not just predators in the pulpit, but also predators everywhere—the neighbor next-door or a date from a social website—and Christians make good targets.

Most believers are excellent targets due to being naïve, gullible, and taught to ignore his or her instincts, and to give everyone the benefit of doubt. Therefore, when a doubt or a twinge pops up from our spirit (a sense or instinctive warning), many just ignore it and plunge ahead without pause for discernment.

Christ and the disciples are not teaching us to walk as "paranoids" afraid of our own shadow; however, the general state of naiveté of most Christians makes God's people walking targets, sending out spiritual vibes to attract evil.

Our personal spirit has many functions as we have already discussed, where communion with God is facilitated, and a pure and healed spirit will sustain us in sickness, where life vigor and perception, along with revelation from the Holy Spirit flow to us by our spirit.

One other function of our spirit is the ability to sense evil with no other clue than by picking up a vibe or an instinctive warning. Everyone at some time has walked past a mess left by a neighborhood dog, only missing stepping in the pile because of the smell. Just as our physical senses warn of unseen bad in the physical realm, so does our personal spirit warn us of unseen unpleasant evils lurking within people or situations encountered every day.

This function is dormant or hampered until our personal spirit is cleansed, trained, and abiding in the Holy Spirit. However, we must understand that these God-given functions of our personal spirit can be activated wrongly by involvement in new age teachings, and other religious teachings on mysticism.

New age mysticism has swept into Christianity disguised as the gifts of the Holy Spirit, leading people to delve into their own personal spirit as they look to find power to read minds, sense spiritual things, or tune in to spirit guides. Many charismatic and Pentecostal Christians operate in a spirit of divination or sorcery, deceived into believing that they walk in the gifts of discernment and prophecy.

We are made to be like God (*"Let us make man in our image, after our likeness"* Genesis 1:26), in that we are spiritual beings having a personal spirit, though our spirit is temporarily confined and limited within our mortal flesh.

Having a spirit gives us the ability to sense spiritual things and to relate to the Holy Spirit when he manifests his presence. *"The Spirit himself bears witness with our spirit that we are children of God"* (Romans 8:16).

However, the downside of our spirituality is that we can be led into inappropriate spiritual experiences and carnally activate our own spiritual powers—which, though limited, can affect our own internal sense of wellbeing and can be projected onto others around us, affecting their thoughts, feelings, nervous system and sometimes invisibly acting upon the physical world.

Paranormal psychic powers have been debated and studied for years, but are yet to be accepted by science; however, more and more people are beginning to believe in psychic phenomena, spiritual powers, and demonic powers. More and more creditable testimony is accumulating that invisible powers through humans or by other entities such as ghosts, demons or extraterrestrial beings exist that can and do act upon the physical, which cannot be explained by science. Thus, science maintains its skepticism.

Christians who are born again by the Spirit of God become aware of the reality of the spirit world—and aware of their own spirit, and learn that their personal spirit was created by God. Jesus taught, *"God is spirit, and those who worship him must worship in spirit and truth"* (John 4:24).

God desires that his people return to him and allow him to regenerate, cleanse and hold to himself our personal spirit so that we may become a temple of the Holy Spirit. God is serious about having our spirit come into his presence rightly. He desires that we no longer have a spirit held captive by the powers of Satan, our flesh, and the world, but that we become cleansed and transformed by the power of Christ through obedience to his Gospel. *"He yearns jealously over the spirit that he has made to dwell in us'"* (James 4:5).

As we submit to the Lord's sanctifying processes, our personal spirit will become God's connection to our mind and heart, and facilitate sensitivity to spiritual activities upon us and around us.

In this sanctification process, we learn what the Holy Spirit's presence is like and how to receive and be filled with the Holy Spirit. We come to see how he bears witness to our spirit and heart with understanding. In this work, the Holy Spirit will increase our perception of the spiritual conditions of others and the influences of evil spirits in and around us. This is to be accomplished within the parameters of the Word of God and the leadership of the Holy Spirit in Christ's discipline.

Before one comes to Christ, and even afterwards, we can develop avenues into our personal spirit that are not of God. These avenues or doorways must be identified, renounced, cleansed and often healed. Relationship idolatry, spiritualism, mysticism, sorcery, and other sinful activities can penetrate into our personal spirit and allow Satan and the demonic access to our spirit. This causes us to pick up spiritual vibes or premonitions without understanding that these perceptions, premonitions, vibes, or mystical voices are demonic in nature.

Christians leaving the false teachings of Catholicism are very needful of the Spirit's cleansing process, since much of the spiritual experiences within this sect are demonic in nature. Likewise, with much of the charismatic renewal movements and extreme manifestation exhibitions, counterfeit spirits have actually been invited to take up residence within millions of deceived Christians.

Once we renounce unhealthy spiritual ties that we had with others and the demonic, and we become cleansed of the associated spiritual defilements (avenues for the demonic to channel), then our personal spirit and our faculties become keener in discerning accurately.

When we embrace the discipline of the Lord, allowing our motives of heart and thoughts to become pure and of God, our personal spirit becomes united with the Holy Spirit more fully. Our faculties become trained by practice to distinguish good from evil and those doubts, instincts, or vibes concerning a situation, a person or a teaching or a movement are received, examined, and tested, as we look to Scriptures and the Holy Spirit for discernment.

When a true union of purity and holiness is established between our spirit and the Holy Spirit, true perceptions, sensitivities, and keenness of discernment while in the presence of others will increase dramatically. The Holy Spirit will have the freedom to warn us based on our gained understanding.

Religious Dictators and Self-righteous Caretakers
Insecure Christians who rule the roost and destroy true faith

The body of Christ has been invaded by converts who have taken on a self-righteous approach in expressing their faith in Christ. Insecure and eager to demonstrate to others a right relationship with Jesus, many believers today develop and emanate religious control over the lives of others.

I am speaking of converts to Christianity who are not born of the Spirit, rather born of the will of man in the spiritual powers of the flesh. *"Now you, brothers, like Isaac, are children of promise. But just as at that time he who was born according to the flesh persecuted him who was born according to the Spirit, so also it is now"* for complete context see Galatians 4:21-30).

These learn to elevate themselves as mini-leaders who work tirelessly within fellowship and family to make sure other Christians and family members get it right. Like hawks, they observe mannerisms, words, behavior, decisions and even attire—becoming more than ready to correct, guide, chide, and even harshly scold others into being perfect Christians.

In the guise of helping, the self-righteous mini-leader becomes obsessed with pointing out even the smallest flaw and has instant suggestions for others to improve by. Like the Pharisees in Christ's day, they become expert at straining out gnats, and in the process subtly condemn and belittle others. In many cases their insistent perfectionism and perform-to-be-loved attitude destroys true faith in the lives others.

They undermine the work of God's discipline and grace, circumventing an individual's character transformation opportunities wrought by the Holy Spirit and Christ. This type of self-righteous Christian micro manages the lives of those in their influence. They attempt to prevent the undiscerning Christian from making any decisions in life without their approval.

They rob the sincere but immature Christian from learning to hear from Christ on their own through the normal trial and error process, where carnal mistakes become maturing moments in Christ. These self-appointed guides destroy true faith in the lives of young Christians by preventing others to learn how to stand on their own faith and be personally led by the Holy Spirit.

Those in the company or influence of these religious dictators often become shame ridden and even gun-shy, believing that any mistake makes one eligible for terrible retribution from God—or at least a severe reprimand by the self-appointed saint. If one in the supervision of a super-saint (self-righteous dictator) is overtaken by the smallest trespass, the offender is often brow-beaten, shamed or pitied into an even deeper dependency on the religious mother, father, or self-appointed super-religious caretaker.

These religious abusers have learned to maintain their own sense of wellbeing at the expense of other people's problems, mistakes, sins, and dignity.

Christ frequently warned of this type of religious oppression and the Apostle Paul wrote specifically about how to restore others who struggle, make mistakes or are overtaken by a trespass. *"Brothers, if anyone is caught in any transgression, you who are spiritual should restore him in a spirit of gentleness. Keep watch on yourself, lest you too be tempted"* (Galatians 6:1).

Those who are under the power of a super-saint are at great risk of eventual rebellion, regression, falling away, or drifting to the dark side and becoming like their abuser, a self-righteous self-centered religious dictator.

It is vital that the true disciple-in-training become an expert in discerning those who walk in a self-righteous faith, carnal holiness, and learn how to minister to such people. If the super-saint is open to correction and willing to work on changing, a firm approach is required. Most who suffer from elevating their self-worth by pointing out the flaws in others will frequently experience a relapse into the old habit, which will require correction in each relapse; this type of firm help will often be required over a prolonged period before true changes take place within the heart.

Unfortunately, many stuck in the role of the religious dictator or the self-righteous caretaker never see their incessant pressure on the lives of others. They never grasp how they attack and even at times put to death grace and liveliness in Christ.

When a religious destroyer of faith dominates, most often the only relief for their victims is for strong leadership to expunge such from fellowship in concert with sound doctrine. Those in the fellowship must become equipped to discern and head off such people from gaining a foothold in the lives of others.

For the religious self-righteous, this is a very nasty form of evil because their perfectionistic outer persona often covers a very evil heart. Money and recognition are often found to be the root of their need to appear perfect, making others feel condemned in their presence. Jesus said of this type of hypocrite: *"Woe to you, scribes and Pharisees, hypocrites! For you tithe mint and dill and cumin, and have neglected the weightier matters of the law: justice and mercy and faithfulness. These you ought to have done, without neglecting the others. You blind guides, straining out a gnat and swallowing a camel! Woe to you, scribes and Pharisees, hypocrites! For you clean the outside of the cup and the plate, but inside they are full of greed and self-indulgence. You blind Pharisee! First clean the inside of the cup and the plate, that the outside also may be clean.*

Woe to you, scribes and Pharisees, hypocrites! For you are like whitewashed tombs, which outwardly appear beautiful, but within are full of dead people's bones and all uncleanness. So you also outwardly appear righteous to others, but within you are full of hypocrisy and lawlessness" (Matthew 23:23-28).

One of the characteristics of Judas was browbeating someone for what he thought was wrong behavior in front of others, specifically when it a came to money. (See John 12:1-8).

Discerning the Immoral, Irreligious, and Self-indulgent Christian

Unfortunately, many do not know how to obtain the grace of God or they outright refuse his grace by rejecting conscience or live in extreme denial of their own sinfulness and sin nature. This condition and associated with an arrogant attitude will allow embedded bitterness and defilements to turn rotten (like gangrene), causing corruption throughout the fellowship and defile family and friends. The whole world has witnessed a constant stream of scandals, where corruption, sexual immorality, or perversion has become all too common within Christianity.

Even more prolific are the many Christians who turn unholy when the trials of discipline bring a little suffering. They are like Esau, who gave away his birthrights instead of enduring some hunger pains. Such Christians turn their backs on righteousness when the slightest pressure begins during persecution or a trial.

They hide in the pews and even in pulpits disguised as pure and dependable saints. However, when required to suffer they will cop out and throw the true servant under the bus to save their own skin. Detecting the irreligious Christian will become one of the biggest challenges in the days ahead. Jesus warned about this type of believer during times of persecution and trouble, especially at the end of this age.

Akin to the irreligious Christian is the believer who has become self-indulgent, making life's pleasures their objective for living. Many in this condition form obsessive desires to have their inner peace and happiness fulfilled in finding the perfect mate. This drives many Christians into marriage apart from God's will and his timing.

Beware of the Devils Disguised as Christians
Satan's last day betrayal plan via Judas replicas

A particular purpose was put in motion with the betrayal our Lord, by one of the twelve disciples, a purpose often overlooked. Some misguided theologians have made the conjecture that Judas was instructed by our Lord to turn him over to the high priest and be arrested.

Fortunately, most theologians believe Judas was allowed to betray the Lord so the Scriptures would be fulfilled, which is correct. However, there is a very important aspect of

Christ's betrayal that is often overlooked that we must consider. Judas became an invaluable example of how Satan can use people who are evil in nature, yet pretend to be a true believer who can betray the brethren at the most opportune time for the devil—and the most inopportune time for the saints.

The lesson and training that Judas afforded the remaining eleven disciples was to prepare them for future ministry after Christ's ascension. Every true disciple must understand this lesson today! Those who desire to endure the coming end-of-the-age darkness successfully must be trained in discerning those who would betray and cause trouble, especially those disguised as disciples of Christ.

"And the chief priests and the scribes were seeking how to put him to death; for they feared the people. Then Satan entered into Judas called Iscariot, who was of the number of the twelve; he went away and conferred with the chief priests and officers how he might betray him to them. And they were glad, and engaged to give him money. So he agreed, and sought an opportunity to betray him to them in the absence of the multitude" (Luke 22:2-6).

Satan has a multitude of devils implanted throughout society—family, church, business and government. Few are able to discern and hear rightly concerning these imposters. Paul warned of evil men and imposters in these last days, *"Indeed all who desire to live a godly life in Christ Jesus will be persecuted, while evil men and imposters will go on from bad to worse, deceivers and deceived"* (2 Timothy 3:12,13).

Jesus trained the disciples in what I refer to as the Judas training course. Thus, Peter was able to hear rightly concerning evil people attempting to enter into fellowship when the first-century church was most vulnerable—in its beginning.

As you progress in your discernment training, Christ will allow you to suffer trouble by someone who will be a Judas in character. Jesus allowed the disciples to learn firsthand and he did so with the Apostle Paul. If you are serious with Christ in asking to grow in discernment, then prepare yourself for the shock of your life. Christ will guide you through his Judas training program as he did with the disciples, however, you will also experience similar anguish, as did the disciples, in making sure your lesson is learned and retained.

Christ is calling his true leaders and workers to understand and detect the characteristics of a Judas replica—Satan has many of these implanted throughout the body of Christ, in marriages, family and throughout society. These are not maniacs or wicked sinners, rather they act like Judas did, with subtle idiosyncrasies akin to selfishness, pointing out flaws in others, and are often worried about finances or appearances—they are working side by side with true Christians in ministry—even casting out demons and doing many good works.

Effective Spiritual Warfare vs. Fighting Demonic Phantoms
Spirit power of the flesh, casting out the flesh and demonic Feigning

The true saint must understand the deception Satan has cast upon a large portion of the body of Christ concerning spiritual warfare. Through the deceitful wiles of men and their false doctrine, Christians everywhere are put at ease by believing they have authority over the devil and his minions *at will*.

Christians are taught to take on Satan's domain without a thorough understanding and walking in obedience to God's specific will in each encounter or battle. They have learned to exercise warfare in the *spiritual powers of the flesh* apart from God's power.

Servants of Christ must learn to know the difference between their own spiritual power in opposing the demonic and the power of God in Christ's name when conducting ministry and spiritual warfare. The power of Christ's name is not available to just anyone who spouts out Christ's name; even believers in Christ who are carnal in the coming days will have a rude awakening to their inability to use the name of Christ willy-nilly.

The power of God to fight the demonic is exercised through those who know Christ and are known by Christ. Jesus warned, *"On that day many will say to me, 'Lord, Lord, did we not prophesy in your name, and <u>cast out demons</u> in your name, and do many mighty works in your name?' And then will I declare to them, 'I never knew you; depart from me, you workers of lawlessness.'"* (Matthew 7:22-23).

Again, we must heed this warning: many believers in Christ exercise spiritual power, yet Christ does not know them. As explained in chapter six in the sections covering the spiritual powers of the flesh, the power that false and deceived Christians (as well as spiritualists in differing cultures and religions) have learned to develop is rooted in their own spiritual power to withstand and even cast out demons. The human spirit has great potential and is only hampered by limitations imposed by God (mankind being made a little lower than the angels).

Often the demonic feigns being cast out to gain a deeper stronghold. Many suffer from a divided soul and spirit (a double-minded condition) and the demonic burrows deeper into divided parts of the victim's spirit. Others experience a temporary deliverance only to experience the demonic returning later in a stronger and deeper penetration due to the lack of cleansing and character change.

When Christ cast out demons he was accused of using the power of the devil; however, our Lord refuted their claim by pointing out that if this was the case, Satan's kingdom would be divided and fall, saying, *"Every kingdom divided against itself is laid waste, and a divided household falls. And if Satan also is divided against himself, how will his kingdom stand? For you say that I cast out demons by Beelzebul. And if I cast out demons by Beelzebul, by whom do your sons cast them out? Therefore they will be your judges. But if it is by the finger of God that I cast out demons, then the kingdom of God has come upon you."* (Luke 11:17-20).

Jesus did not use his own spirit or the devil's power to chase out the demonic; rather, he explained that his power came from God. This is important to understand.

Today, deceived, immature, and naïve Christians are taught to take on Satan's territory as if the devil and his minions are powerless. Many shadow-box phantom demons because Satan and evil spirits have learned to play possum, hiding deeper within the oppressed individual and in some cases the demons beat up the exorcist as well as the victim.

Accounts of Catholic exorcists taking on hell and the demons living in the possessed are chilling. Priests are brutally accosted and even crippled while performing deliverance rituals using the spiritual powers of the flesh. In my studies and my own battles against the demonic, it became apparent concerning the final and absolute authority over the demonic that: *the finger of God in Christ's name, flowing through a purified saint requires no ritualism, conjuring or other such antics*, though sometime prayer and fasting is required.

The false Christian, those stuck in Catholicism, or shamans in other cultures practicing deliverance must awaken and strengthen their own spirit and spiritual powers through various forms of religious or superstitious rituals to exercise spiritual power against the demonic.

Many immature, carnal, or false Christians attempt to practice deliverance and end up like the sons of Sceva, as told in the book of Acts.

God was doing extraordinary feats through the Apostle Paul: even when others touched Paul's handkerchiefs or aprons diseases were healed and demons left.

Hearing of the authority and the success of Paul's ministry, seven itinerant Jewish exorcists attempted to use Christ's name in performing an exorcism. These imposters received a severe beating from the possessed man. The evil spirit they tried casting out by invoking Christ's name said, *"Jesus I know, and Paul I recognize, but who are you?"* (See Acts 19:11-20.)

Defilements, wounds to the spirit, double-mindedness, and the practice of wickedness in a sin-ridden and pleasure-driven society cause millions of Christians to be infested with demons—but they are ignorant of why they are continually haunted. Unclean Christians have become carriers of demons because of hidden defilements and practicing the works of the flesh, and many are demon possessed (demons often cohabitate with double-minded believers and this causes mental and emotional instability and psychotic symptoms).

Many turn over a new leaf and clean house from a sinful lifestyle when they come to Christ. The demons may leave temporarily, only to return and find that the former host only superficially put things in order, doing little to become Christ-like in nature, thus leaving gaping holes in the soul and spirit.

Christ taught this principle by saying, *"When the unclean spirit has gone out of a person, it passes through waterless places seeking rest, and finding none it says, 'I will return to my house from which I came.' And when it comes, it finds the house swept and put in order. Then it goes and brings seven other spirits more evil than itself, and they enter and dwell there. And the last state of that person is worse than the first."* (Luke 11:24-26).

Demonic elements find avenues to return through hidden defilements, dividedness and impurities of heart and character structures yet to be cleansed and transformed. The demonic comes back even stronger and burrows deeper into the spirit, mind and heart of the deceived believer.

Another tactic is that the demonic will give up harassment and oppression for a deeper hold through false doctrine and false manifestations; they drill deeper and wait for the right time to bring total destruction. While these demonic powers wait, they inspire false doctrine, instigate works of the flesh, and attempt to create defilements in others, allowing more demonic infestation into and throughout deceived and carnal fellowships, marriages, and family systems.

As one learns discernment concerning evil spirits residing within people, a thorough understanding is needed concerning how the human spirit, mind, and heart can have demonic strongholds and inroads due to unresolved wounds, damaged emotions, double mindedness and defilements.

The Apostle Paul instructed all Christians to actively deal with these latent defilements that so many carry today (see 2 Corinthians 7:1). In this passage, Paul refers to the human body, meaning the flesh (soul and the physical body) as well as the human spirit.

Christians receive few instructions, if any, on learning to cooperate with the Holy Spirit's work in cleansing hidden defilements. Due to the lack of doctrine that aids in the Holy Spirit's decontamination process of the spirit and soul, Christians suffer unnecessarily. They suffer from mental, emotional, and spiritual symptoms along with the associated demonic infestations, demonically heightened sinful desires and pleasures, demonic oppression, and in some cases demonic possession.

Far too many believers are taught that these disturbing symptoms are all from the demonic, having nothing to do with the believer's heart. They are blindly led into believing that spiritual deliverance is all that is needed to relieve the symptoms. Wounded, divided, and defiled believers throng to so-called deliverance ministries for relief, thinking that the mixed symptoms of inner issues and demonic harassment will disappear when the demonic is cast out or chased away.

Satan is having a heyday messing with multitudes of Christians who are clamoring for deliverance by way of shortcut doctrines and false "anointing ministries." The worst is yet to come.

As the end of this age presses forward, Satan will be allowed to come and collect his investment in these angel of light ministries; millions who have bought into false manifestations, false deliverances, and false spiritual warfare will not escape from the coming torment. Satan will destroy countless mentally and emotionally disturbed and infested believers when he sets off his demonic time bombs.

Watch out for false Christians who prophesy, cast out demons, and brag about doing mighty works in Christ's name. These boasters are deceitful workmen, who sucker the undiscerning and teach Christians to practice false spiritual warfare, leaving millions of Christians at risk of an end-of-the-age torrent, by the dormant demonic, awakened within their inner beings—when they least expect it.

Effective spiritual warfare requires learning to be led by the Holy Spirit and to operate in the power of the Spirit of God, not in the carnal power of the human spirit.

Masses today, including Christians, have learned to practice sorcery using their own personal spirit to influence the world around them. The true saint must have these issues cleansed from their own life through the sanctifying process led by the Holy Spirit.

Learn to Avoid Using Christ's Name in the Power of the Flesh

Learning to use Christ's name in his power and not in the spiritual powers of the flesh is a process that Christ must be allowed to conduct personally—the goal is learning to rest in his power. His power is made perfect when we allow the Word of God to become living and active by his Spirit, making our motives and intentions of the heart pure and in line with God's perfect will. We must strive to rest from our valiant but futile efforts in doing spiritual warfare in the flesh. (Hebrews 4:11-13).

Not only are we to learn to discern situations, evil lurking, and wolves in our midst, we must learn to discern our own mixed motives for living, for ministry, and in prayer. Be mindful of moving from praying in Christ's name as if to get God's stamp of approval to hearing specifically what God's will is in the matter and then pray as the Holy Spirit leads. Many prayers are not answered because we pray amiss. (See James 4:1-5.)

God sees and knows everything about us, both of faith and of the flesh, but we only like to hear good things about ourselves from God. If we hear anything negative, we tend to condemn ourselves, which is not God's intention, or we decide the negative warning was not from God but of the devil.

To increase discernment we must allow God to show us what we do not want to see within ourselves. When we work through our own errant motives, the ability to discern the motives and hidden agendas in others becomes more natural and easy. Because we worked through our own, we can help others see hidden dangers and prevent problems and even disaster.

Training in Effective Warfare in Christ's Discipline
Wrestling against principalities and exposing darkness

The Apostle Paul learned to embrace intense suffering that allowed him to walk in the true power of God. Christ still trains his servants the same way. When in training, you will not start out walking in the pure power of Christ. Rather, you will find a mixture of self-reliance in the form self-energy, self-confidence and gung-ho faith along with true faith in Christ's leadership. As your training progresses with Christ, battling against the demonic and people the devil may use against you, there will be times of intense suffering where Satan will be allowed to strike back in areas in your walk that you are still self-reliant in.

In this training and discipline you will come to know God's grace experientially, seeing his power made perfect in weakness. There will be times when the suffering will seem relentless; the Apostle Paul described this as if receiving a death sentence, explaining: *"We do not want you to be ignorant, brothers, of the affliction we experienced in Asia. For we were so utterly burdened beyond our strength that we despaired of life itself. Indeed, we felt that we had received the sentence of death. But that was to make us rely not on ourselves but on God who raises the dead. He delivered us from such a deadly peril, and he will deliver us. On him we have set our hope that he will deliver us again."* (2 Corinthians 1:8-10).

Elsewhere Paul describes how he was continually buffeted by a messenger from the devil coming in the form of insults, beatings, various weaknesses, hardships, persecutions and calamities. Paul asked that these harassing attacks be removed, but the Lord told him, *"My grace is sufficient for you, for my power is made perfect in weakness."*

Most today fight a paper-tiger Satan, where there is no suffering or training in the dying to one's own spiritual power. God's grace is nullified by false doctrine allowing spiritual pride, conceit, presumption, and arrogance to prevail in the attitude for many in these so-called deliverance ministries.

The Apostle Paul's explanation on how God maintains humility among leaders is seldom taught, allowing most who are in ministry to remain short on the power of God and to resort to spiritualism and counterfeit spirits feigning the power of the Holy Spirit. God has given the false and the deceived over to their own devices, allowing the devil and his minions to play possum and give the carnal minister a false sense of security.

Deliverance for the sincere Christian has become a quest for a magic incantation or some kind of quick-fix gimmick that requires a special leader anointed with power to cast out devils and relieve symptoms. Learn to discern these carnal spiritual war strategies and avoid them. Be careful not to correct others who are steeped in these misguided methods; most become indignant and turn against anyone who attempts to correct them.

Effective spiritual warfare is founded in our own training and learned ability to deal with the strongholds in our own life. These strongholds and hidden issues allow the devil to oppress, infest, and even cohabitate within one's personal spirit. When we work out these spiritual battles within our own lives, then we become equipped and qualified to discern clearly the demonic strongholds in the lives of others. Then we can effectively help others to resist the devil and the demonic. The following passage became foundational in making sense of some of the nightmarish battles we found ourselves in, feeling hopeless, victory seemingly swallowed up in defeat.

"<u>Humble yourselves</u>, therefore, under the mighty hand of God so that at the <u>proper time he may exalt you</u>, casting all your anxieties on him, because he cares for you. Be <u>sober-minded; be watchful</u>. Your adversary the devil prowls around like a roaring lion, seeking someone to devour. <u>Resist him, firm in your faith, knowing that the same kinds of suffering are being experienced by your brotherhood throughout the world</u>. And after you have suffered a little while, the God of all grace, who has called you to his eternal glory in Christ, will himself restore, confirm, strengthen, and establish you. To him be the dominion forever and ever. Amen" (1 Peter 5:6-11). Our training is progressive and Christ gives us only what we can handle as he continues to prepare each to stand in faith against Satan and the powers of darkness.

We learned that this saying by President Theodore Roosevelt (if I remember correctly) has helped us stay humble, "Every victory just clears the ground for the next battle."

Spiritual Warfare and Discernment
Satan and his human servants, principalities, and mindsets

Satan opposes the saint who decides to grow in maturity and develop powers of discernment. Be prepared to battle Satan, as he will come at you with intense rage and determination to get you to back down, and return to a mediocre walk with Christ. When we desire to increase our power of discernment, one of the first challenges is learning to discern what kind of demonic influences are involved and how to fend off Satan working through evil people or carnal Christians who are in opposition.

In dealing with Christians opposing the truth, our ministry has encountered angry opponents who practice a form of sorcery. They do so by directing hostile prayers towards us and actually cursing or praying judgment upon the ministry, me or other team members. The symptoms can become acute and harmful, physically, spiritually, and psychologically.

In seeking understanding and discernment on how to ward off these attacks, we learned that the demonic component of the attacks hide behind the astrally projected human spirit. Sometimes, several opponents would form prayer groups and enlist others to pray against us, compounding the symptoms.

Fending off the demonic exclusively produced little relief; however, when we realized the human spirit was leading the attack, and the demonic power boosted the human spirit and used the human spirit as a shield, we became more successful.

By employing the gifts of word of knowledge and discerning spirits and prophecy, we learned to identify who the person or persons were in the attack. This led in taking a specific approach in prayer. Once we learned who was practicing sorcery in praying wrongly, we would specify the person's name or identify the person in our own prayers.

For example, if we found from the Holy Spirit that Pastor Smith (fictitious name) was praying wrongly, we would command prayerfully the following: "The Lord rebuke Pastor Smith's spirit and break his curses over us, in Christ's name." Alternatively, "The Lord Jesus rebukes you, Pastor Smith and breaks your curses." This approach is successful if the Holy Spirit is prompting these prayers.

Praying amiss ourselves only aggravated the situation, and praying curses in response brings a swift reprimand from Lord. Praying retaliatory prayers would be something Satan would rejoice in. We learned to ask the Lord for deliverance from the person or persons spiritually attacking us, to command the appropriate demonic to leave us and to pray God's discipline and will be done for those practicing Christian sorcery. We learned to pray for God's will to be done in the matter, and that if possible the deceived praying amiss might come to repentance and a change of heart.

Some of the opponents developed an obsession with derailing or destroying the ministry or me personally. This situation developed into an ongoing battle where the human spirit and the demonic involved would become almost permanently assigned to attack and oppress.

Until we realized that this was the case, we often confused the continued oppression as that of a messenger from Satan to keep us humble. This can be the case temporarily; however, we found that praying for deliverance and hearing rightly how to pray God's will for such a situation proved successful in curtailing the attacks and breaking the assigned demonic and human spirit out-of-body attacks.

In some cases, a prophetic proclamation was given by the Holy Spirit in ending the matter, when the Apostle Paul, filled with the Holy Spirit spoke forth blindness to come upon Elymas the magician as described in Acts 18-20. Another example in Scripture is turning a person over to the devil for judgment as the Apostle Paul gave as an example in the following passage:

"This charge I entrust to you, Timothy, my child, in accordance with the prophecies previously made about you, that by them you may wage the good warfare, holding faith and a good conscience. By rejecting this, some have made shipwreck of their faith, among whom are Hymenaeus and Alexander, whom I have handed over to Satan that they may learn not to blaspheme" (1 Timothy 1:18-20).

The key in successfully surviving these types of demonic/human spirit attacks is discernment, operating in the true gifts of the Holy Spirit and above all, one's own cleanliness of soul and spirit and purity of motives. Most importantly, learn to discern rightly the leading of the Holy Spirit (his voice) and then obeying.

When we have removed our own logs from our eyes, we will hear rightly, see clearly, and be trusted to pronounce judgments upon those practicing Christian sorcery or doing evil amongst the brethren.

Another passage to aid us in standing with spiritual authority (from God) to pray God's will upon those who practice this kind of evil, as the true Holy Spirit commands, is this:

"For though we walk in the flesh, we are not waging war according to the flesh. For the weapons of our warfare are not of the flesh but have divine power to destroy strongholds. We destroy arguments and every lofty opinion raised against the knowledge of God, and take every thought captive to obey Christ, being ready to punish every disobedience, when your obedience is complete" (2 Corinthians 10:3-6).

The Apostle Paul is challenging carnal Christians at Corinth by explaining the difference between advancing the Gospel of Christ in the power of the flesh and the power of God through a true servant. Christians promoting the Gospel in self-power (the flesh) will not be able to destroy opposing arguments, not having the spiritual power and authority backed by God. Nor will the Gospel message resonate in the hearer's spirit when conveyed by carnal self-powered evangelism. This is why so many false conversions take place, where people respond to a carnal call to salvation, responding not to the Spirit of God, by the will and power of man. (See John 1:9-13.)

It is important to understand also that we must work in the power of God to destroy mindsets held in place by the powers of darkness. Until I realized that spiritual warfare prayer and *authority in Christ had to be exercised* when witnessing, counseling, and occasionally when mentoring, those I was working with could not understand—often having a dazed look upon their face.

Even more important was when I experienced the work of the cross in my own life, so that the life of Christ flowed through me to others that those hearing received Holy Spirit confirmation, insight and revelation. As the Apostle Paul declared, *"But we have this treasure in jars of clay, to show that the surpassing power belongs to God and not to us. We are afflicted in every way, but not crushed; perplexed, but not driven to despair; persecuted, but not forsaken; struck down, but not destroyed; always carrying in the body the death of Jesus, so that the life of Jesus may also be manifested in our bodies. For we who live are always being given over to death for Jesus' sake, so that the life of Jesus also may be manifested in our mortal flesh. So death is at work in us, but life in you"* (2 Corinthians 4:7-12).

Even as millions responded to the Gospel message over the last forty years, how many have really experienced the Spirit of God birth new life into them? Watchman Nee, (1903-1972) was a profound author and minister who was imprisoned by the Chinese Communists for faith in Christ and his ministry. His last twenty years were spent in prison, where he died without announcement or funeral, and was cremated before his family arrived at the prison, on June 1, 1972. He wrote many books and publications and inspired many servants of Christ. His work entitled *The Messenger of the Cross* hit the mark, expounding on the centrality of the message and work of the cross as God's life giving and character changing theme of the Gospel.

> "The message which Paul preaches is Jesus Christ and Him crucified. His subject is the cross of Christ or the Christ of the Cross. He knows this one matter—and nothing else. What a tremendous loss it will be to our audience as well as to ourselves if we forget the cross and do not make it and its Christ our one and only theme. I trust we are not among those who do not preach the cross at all.
>
> Hence, in the light of this Scripture passage [1 Corinthians 2:1-5], our message and our theme may indeed be most correct. But do we not have the experience that despite the correctness of our message, we do not impart life to people? Let me tell you, that though it is essential to preach the right message, our labor shall be half in vain if it does not result in people receiving life.
>
> We must underscore the point that the objective of our work is for people to have life. We preach the substitutionary death of the cross in order that God may grant His life to those who believe. What is the use if they are merely excited and moved to repent (even approving of what we preach) but their sympathy is only skin-deep and the life of God does not enter into them. They are still unsaved." (Watchman Nee, *The Messenger of the Cross*, New York: Christian Fellowship Publishers, 2010, pages 11-12)

Nee, in this book originally written in the 1950s, goes on to elaborate how the talents and abilities of man in preaching, teaching, and evangelism are substitutes for the power of God, where the power of the soul affects people, not the power of the Holy Spirit.

In my case, my personal lack of success was due to the principality that held people's minds passive by the mindset and inner beliefs they held within that opposed the knowledge of God. As the Apostle Paul explained, spiritual warfare is required to break the stronghold within the person's mind and heart that we are contending for, in the battle for the revelation of the Gospel so that person may understand and become born again—of the Spirit of God.

For example, the theory of evolution, that humans evolved from animal life, is a demonic mindset or stronghold keeping millions captive. This is an example of archetype or standard thinking commonly accepted in most cultures and set in place over the last 150 years by Charles Darwin. However, the theory of evolution was concocted by Darwin it was inspired by the demonic and through the years, fallen angels (principalities) fostered this theory into a worldwide mindset.

We can classify these satanic activities as the work of principalities or demonic rulers of this present darkness who are in charge of creating universally accepted lies that oppose the truth taught in Scripture.

There are many types of demonically inspired mindsets[29] that work into the thinking of people throughout nations, society and in culture, and which are filtering into the body of Christ. The Apostle Paul wrote in the letter to Titus of a very serious problem concerning Jewish Christians, members of the circumcision party who were going about preaching Christ but also pushing Jewish myths and Jewish rites, especially circumcision. In the following passage the Apostle is highlighting how mindsets work as he explains what the circumcision party was doing. Gentiles who believed in Christ and were being persuaded and even coerced into embracing Jewish myths and pressured to become a Jewish Christian through circumcision. These were false Christians teaching error for shameful gain:

"For there are many who are insubordinate, empty talkers and deceivers, especially those of the circumcision party. They must be silenced, since they are upsetting whole families by teaching for shameful gain what they ought not to teach. One of the Cretans, a prophet of their own, said, 'Cretans are always liars, evil beasts, lazy gluttons.' This testimony is true. Therefore rebuke them sharply, that they may be sound in the faith, not devoting themselves to Jewish myths and the commands of people who turn away from the truth" (Titus 1:10-14).

Paul expresses his concerns and describes the audacity of one of these proselyting Jewish Christians, who was from Crete. This person was spreading a mindset about Cretans,[30] *"Cretans are always liars, evil beasts, lazy gluttons"* (Titus 1: 12).

Mindsets governing the gender war, racism, or idolatry of certain people or leaders are all the work of dark spiritual forces set in place by the devil. Mindsets like "all Cretans are lazy," or like the Polish or Irish defaming statements. "Black people are created inferior to whites," or "women are a second-class creation to be oppressed for their own good and ruled by men." This

---

[29] A Christian can have an unhealthy mindset hidden within the heart, or an impurity of heart. An example would be heart felt thinking by a husband who was raised by a verbally abusive mother, where in the heart he believes all women are unloving. On the other hand, a woman reared by absentee father often creates a deep-seated belief that the man she would marry would be distant, uncaring and a poor communicator. These types of wounds and impurities of heart can easily resonate with sinful archetypal mindsets fostered by the principalities of darkness. We see hidden bitterness and hatred come out between the gender roles and their relationship dynamics. For example, men fostering a hidden mindset that "women are inferior to men" and women fostering a hidden mindset that "all men are irresponsible." These mindsets became apparent in our many years in counseling Christians in destructive relationships and troubled marriages. Of course "gender gap" has become a very hotly debated issues in society as hot an issue as racism.

[30] This passage has stumped many people because of the manner of translation or perhaps because of how the Apostle Paul writes a defense for having these empty talkers rebuked and stopped, that these Jewish-Christians might become sound in faith. Paul writes to Titus that one of them is a Cretan convert and now a prophet amongst them helping spread lies and upsetting people. The Apostle repeats what this former Cretan is now saying about his own native people (other Cretans), *"Cretans are always liars, evil beast, lazy gluttons."* These Jewish-Christians still carried extreme prejudice towards Gentiles, especially Cretans, and they now employed a Cretan proselyte to act insubordinately and defame Cretans to foster others to convert to Judaism. The Apostle Paul, in telling Titus to watch out for and to take action, Paul makes sure Titus understands the validly of his charge. Therefore, Paul adds, *"This testimony is true."* Many misinterpret the Apostle's statement and think Paul is telling Titus that this deplorable and inflammatory statement about Cretans is a truism. No, to the contrary, the Apostle Paul is confirming that this despicable judgment about all Cretans was being spread; that his testimony of the account is a fact—not hearsay.

particular mindset about women still prospers in many Christian sects, denominations and certain fellowships. Look for this tough and often ignored topic in an upcoming publication.

Discernment of the principalities involved in helping another believer to overcome issues of heart must include an understanding of how errant and evil mindsets become strongholds in the life of Christians. Often, only the tip of the ice burg appears in a subtle comment; however, like Peter tracking Simon the magician's comment in wanting to buy the power of God, this comment led Peter to a hidden stronghold in this new believer's heart.

Some of these errant teachings come up with the wildest descriptions of the demonic and of the spiritual powers controlling people, communities, and nations.

The main names of the principalities are the names of the false gods and idols worshipped by the Gentiles in biblical times. Through the years and in different cultures, their names have changed. To give an example, Asherah worship—found in Canaan—is closely similar to Ishtar and Isis worship found in Babylon and Egypt respectively. Later, this female false god appeared in Greek and Roman mythology. In New Testament times, Asherah was "Diana of the Ephesians" and today in the Catholic church is "Mary, mother of God—Queen of Heaven."

You can see this impact in our culture with the resurrection of these principalities in the TV characters of She-Rah, Isis, Wonder Woman, and so forth. The male counterparts traced into our culture are Baal, Hercules, and Superman.

Certain principalities continue to spawn the Middle East crisis. These satanic powers are determined to destroy Israel. In the book of Daniel, it states that the prince of Persia (a demonic governing power over Persia) opposed the archangel Michael and delayed God's answer to Daniel's prayers concerning the release of Israel from their captivity.

Baal and Asherah worship is the biblical counterpart to relationship idolatry. The name Baal means husband, owner of the wife, and Asherah means wife. This kind of idolatry swept into Israel. Soon this idolatry mingled into their worship of God. Here you see Satan's work continued on from Adam and Eve: *you will be like God*.

These relationship issues stem from making each other a god in various aspects of life. This results in each spouse requiring the other to be responsible for inner peace, joy, and happiness, leading to weaknesses and dependencies. This carnal and selfish relationship dynamic becomes destructive, controlling, and manipulative where each learns how to dominate the other. The current legalistic submission teaching concerning husbands and wives within many denominations, which demands that the wife be submissive and treated as a second-class creation, is the work of these principalities.

Moloch is another pagan cult god worshipped in biblical times. This pagan cult god was a more radical form of Baal and Asherah worship where children were made to walk into fire as a sacrifice. Today child abuse, child abductions, child rape, and child pornography are widespread. There is an epidemic of child molestation in different Christian sects. The Roman Catholic heresy of celibacy and other sick doctrines facilitates a safe harbor for the wicked and the pedophile. Of late, certain extremists and offshoot cults from Mormonism are being exposed for their wayward doctrines that facilitate, yet conceal, the practices of polygamy and sexual child abuse.

Paul made it clear that Satan was involved in deceiving Christians by sending evil human agents into the midst of God's people. The demonic powers behind this scheme can be called *angel of light* principalities. Satan attempted to destroy Christ; you and I know that failed. Then, in like manner, he attempted to destroy the first-century Christians through persecution and martyrdom. That did not work either.

Therefore, he began a campaign of infiltration and institutionalization of Christianity. Rome makes Christianity its state religion and we see Roman Catholicism take root and begin to suppress truth and bury the true Gospel in religion. This and other so-called orthodox Christian sects twisted the Gospel to the surrounding pagan culture, making Christianity attractive to pagans by using similar rituals and myths. These *angel of light* principalities inspired all manner of heresy and disguised their work with half-truths. Those in leadership took on these false teachings in order to compete for souls and keep converts from going back to the pagan cults.

Today, this practice is widespread. Even evangelical denominations allow worldly entertainment and false teachings with pretended signs and wonders to sway converts.

The message of instant change and gold dust falling from the air comes from an *angel of light* principality stemming from the ancient practices of alchemy. (See 1 Corinthians 11, Acts 20:29-32, 1 Timothy 4:1-10, 2 Timothy 3:1-9 & 4:1-5 and 2 Thessalonians 2:3-15.)

Ask God to open your eyes to the powerful principalities that control relationships, marriages, church services, and many other activities in the community and in fellowship. Demons run in the works of the flesh as listed in Galatians 5:19-21, blinding Christians to inner carnal passions and desires. For example, a familiar demonic spirit of strife can incite quarrels within relationships and family systems, feasting on hidden bitter jealousies.

Until the work of the cross gains access to the inner roots of bitterness, these familiar spirits within family systems will perpetuate secret sin, abuse and carnality—perpetuating deep hidden ruts of defiling family-of-origin sins. These will be handed down from generation to generation until they are exposed and secret sin is brought to the light. Again, this is the work of the powers of darkness through hidden evil people and deceived Christians.

Be forewarned, you must patiently endure a demanding personal learning curve. This will equip the sincere Christian for spiritual battle with the full armor of God as well as instill Christ-like character. Christian workers, intercessors and those in ministry who graduate from Christ's training course will enable Christ's authority to flow through them as disciplined saints. The sold-out warrior of Christ will break the demonic strongholds in the lives of the people in the community, in families and in the congregation.

However, another important key in standing in the full armor of God is becoming immune to the enemy's work by learning to be strengthened by God in the inner person.

Building up Immunity in the Inner Person
Cleansing of heart, mind and spirit—filled with the fullness of God

"For this reason I bow my knees before the Father, from whom every family in heaven and on earth is named, that according to the riches of his glory <u>he may grant you to be strengthened with power through his Spirit in your inner being</u>, so that Christ may dwell in your hearts through faith—that you, being rooted and grounded in love, may have strength to comprehend with all the saints what is the breadth and length and height and depth, and to know the love of Christ that surpasses knowledge, <u>that you may be filled with all the fullness of God.</u> Now to him who is able to do far more abundantly than all that we ask or think, <u>according to the power at work within us</u>, to him be glory in the church and in Christ Jesus throughout all generations, forever and ever. Amen" (Ephesians 3:14-21).

The saint seeking to walk in true discernment must learn how to build up spiritual immunity to the vicious onslaughts of hell and the out-of-body human spirit attacks. The Lord will strengthen us through his Spirit in our inner being, provided we pay attention and deal with latent issues of heart and defilements that magnify the symptoms of these attacks.

Spiritual immunity is similar and related to our physical body's immune system, where immune system deficiencies can exist, and when they do, common bacteria and other disease causing agents can quickly and acutely cause sickness, illness, and death.

Allowing the love of God to become the washing and healing agent in our inner being builds a proper foundation within our inner being. However, most wounded Christians struggle with allowing the love of God to penetrate to the inward being and replace bitter roots of hate, jealousy, insecurities, spitefulness and self-loathing with God's love. Wounds that carry self-hatred and self-condemnation rooted within the inner being take the form of death wishes or murder. These latent death wishes become a major stronghold for the devil and magnify symptoms in a spiritual attack. When we start to pay attention to our thoughts during crisis or a trial, such thoughts as "I wish that I was never born," or "I wish I was dead," these thoughts directly relate to bitter roots of self-loathing and require the healing grace of God.

There are other root issues similar to death wishes, such as inner vows and expectations and these can be detected in thoughts along the lines of, "I'll never let anyone love me, then I won't have to love them and get hurt," or "I'll never amount to anything," respectively.

To receive God's healing grace, we must take ownership of these thoughts and present them in prayer to Christ and seek the Holy Spirit's leadership in resolving and healing these latent roots of bitterness and receive cleansing of any remaining defilements from our former manner of life.

As to the magnification of the symptoms caused by these latent issues within the battle weary saint, in research we discovered that the world of medicine has categorized a specific set of symptoms as "malignant hypertension."

The following symptoms occur, which directly correlate to a demonic human spirit attack: blurry vision, chest pain, seizures, decreased urine output, weakness or strange tingling/numbness in the arms, legs or face, headaches, weakness of the legs, and shortness of breath.

There are other sets of symptoms from these spiritual attacks such as:

Sleeplessness, oppression, extreme loss of pep energy, hopelessness, abnormal body pains and aches, confusion, evil thoughts that are uncharacteristic of the victim, hypertension, increased tendency to overeat due to extreme loss of energy, the wearing down of the immune system which results in illnesses, terminal illnesses, cancers, heart attacks, strokes, temporary or permanent paralysis and even mental and emotional breakdowns.

We found that certain persons with an unclean, impure and divided condition of heart and spirit cause unique symptoms in their attacks; we call these unique symptoms brought on by an individual opponent, *attack signatures*, which often help determine who might be behind the attack and who is channeling demonic powers.

Another insidious aspect of these attacks is that often other people who were wounded and had issues would somehow become the scapegoat and be blamed, allowing the true perpetrator to stay hidden amongst the brethren. We learned to be patient and become cleansed of our own issues that might be magnifying the symptoms of attack and sought for confirmation in exposing the true culprit.

Through years of battle and research, we learned the hard way how best to deal with exposing, confronting and avoiding such people. Our initial approach was to be lenient and forbearing; however, we soon learned that most of these struggling carnal Christians who still have faith, yet channeled for the demonic took our generous patience as license to continue, and not become serious in working out their inner bitter issues.

We learned that immediate admonishment for a sinful or carnal behavior that fostered channeling for the demonic or projecting their spirit against others was sound scripturally and the best approach. This approach proved very helpful in determining if the person was a struggling believer or a false Christian. Once we realized that a person did not intend to take ownership and develop a desire to change, this person was most likely a false brother and our admonished turned to avoiding them, and in many cases we had to ask them not to attend fellowship.

This approach is explained in the following passage: *"As for a man who is factious, after admonishing him once or twice, have nothing more to do with him, knowing that such a person is perverted and sinful; he is self-condemned"* (Titus 3:10-11).

We also found that direct confrontation, sometimes in front of others at the time of their antics, made the appropriate impact that has led some to repent and work out a change of character. *"As for those who persist in sin, rebuke them in the presence of all, so that the rest may stand in fear"* (1 Timothy 5:20).

Saying no to someone's selfish or rambunctious antics would usually incur wrath, demonstrated through either irrational outbursts or a subtle storm of revengeful actions that often proved destructive or hurtful over time.

In fellowship and in their own family, this type of person can never truly forgive from the heart; instead, they catalog unappreciated or disturbing actions of others in their vengeful and vindictive inner life. This type of wounded Christian can secretly hold a grudge for a lifetime and often unknowingly project their pent-up rage at others who had nothing to do with the original hurt.

Detecting why they lose stability in life's normal afflictions and blame others for their own failings requires paying attention to the truth and sorting out their distortion of facts. They wallow in self-pity and allow hysteria and malicious accusations to make others around them feel responsible for their lack of inner peace and poor sense of well-being.

When we first started tracing individuals in family, fellowship and counseling who might be causing these difficulties, we had to fight the sheer confusion and swirling-overwhelming oppression from the spiritual power of their human spirit mixed with the demonic, which was a powerful camouflage in detecting who was truly responsible.

We had to fight with prayer and learn to operate in the true gifts of the Spirit in order to detect the perpetrator(s) and to prevent hopelessness setting in. Self-control and patience had to be exercised to resist acting irrationally during the episodes that precipitated spiritual attacks.

Finally, we learned to jump straight to the issues by sorting out the truth and to hold the instigators accountable as soon as possible.

Sound doctrine, counsel and teaching on confessing sins to one another and forgiving one another eventually brought relief and helped restore harmony to fellowship, families involved and the individuals in conflict. *"Let all bitterness and wrath and anger and clamor and slander be put away from you, along with all malice. Be kind to one another, tenderhearted, forgiving one another, as God in Christ forgave you"* (Ephesians 4:31-32).

However, not all embrace this work and because we insisted on practicing sound doctrine to get to the root issues, many chose to leave and some we asked to leave. Part of increasing our immunity and minimized the symptoms of attack was to chase out the perverted, self-condemned perpetrators. *"Do not be deceived: "Bad company ruins good morals." Wake up from your drunken stupor, as is right, and do not go on sinning. For some have no knowledge of God. I say this to your shame"* (1 Corinthians 15:33-34).

Ignorant and ill-trained leadership become easily overwhelmed when this type of carnal or false Christian becomes involved in fellowship and allow their roots of bitterness to spring up, cause trouble and defile anyone in proximately to them. It is this type of person coming to fellowship, working tirelessly for the church and gaining recognitions, that Satan plans to use at the right time to bring trouble, subvert true leadership, and in general wreak havoc.

It is vital that we build up our immunity to the symptoms and expose those similar issues in us. If we harbor a certain form of insecurity, bitterness or lust, yet have the issue suppressed (not operating in it) but not having the defilement thoroughly cleansed from within our inner being, then we will not be able to discern one who is operating in such issues in fellowship or family.

Suffering and Sifting by the Hands of the Satan
Christ's measured discipline in using the devil to break denial

Another significant tool that Christ will use to help us develop our powers of discernment is to allow the devil to wreak extra inner turmoil through a trial that ends in failure and humiliation.

My prime biblical account to help explain this principle is found in the Gospel of Luke.

[31]"'Simon, Simon, behold, Satan demanded to have you,[31] that he might sift you like wheat, [32]but I have prayed for you that your faith may not fail. And when you have turned again, strengthen your brothers." [33]Peter said to him, 'Lord, I am ready to go with you both to prison and to death.' [34]Jesus said, 'I tell you, Peter, the rooster will not crow this day, until you deny three times that you know me.' (Luke 22:31-34).

The verse numbers are included in the above passage to help understand the note found for this passage in the English Standard Version translation. In studying this passage in light of the translation footnote, the word *"you"* in verse 31 is plural, literally to be rendered *"both of you"* or *"the two of you."* Then in the next verse (32) all four times the word *"you"* is singular, "one of you."

What we discovered from this passage along with the understanding of the term *double-minded* in the book of James, is that Christ was calling Peter to account for being in denial of a twice a soul condition.

We must understand that Satan prowls around like a lion looking for someone to destroy or emotionally and mentally sift to the point of complete breakdown and a falling away from faith in Christ.

Peter walked, like so many gung-ho Christians today walk in overconfidence in a carnal empowered faith. They have true faith; however, they presume upon God and rely upon self in serving Christ. (Carnal and false leadership exploits this serious condition). This common condition shows up on Satan's radar frequently, as he looks for place or a right to destroy real faith within an immature and carnal Christian.

Notice in this passage, Christ tells Peter of his condition, yet Peter denies having duality of mind and heart. Jesus knew Peter would respond as such, so the Lord cuts to the point by saying that he has interceded for him so that his true faith contained in the genuine part of Peter would not fail.

Satan had a right to sift Peter to a point, similar to Job's experience where Satan demanded to destroy Job completely, but God drew a line that Satan could not cross concerning Job, and likewise, we see Jesus interceding for Peter that his faith not fail.

The point to take very seriously is how the Lord will allow the devil to sift his saints who refuse to see their self-righteous, self-dependence, and presumptuous attitude in life. In developing our powers of discernment, we must be willing to listen and receive what the Lord wants to show us, especially those areas of character that need change.

Learning to be Vigilant and Proactively Expose Darkness
Satanic time bombs, hidden evil, cult family systems—a product of a godless sick culture

International newswires are now frequently telling the world of one horrible tragedy upon another in America, as deranged killers cut loose on the innocent. The frequency and intensity of the unspeakable is now common. Theaters, workplace, high schools, elementary schools,

---

[31] The Greek word for *you* (twice in verse 31) is plural; in verse 32, all four instances are singular.

places of worship all have become shooting galleries for massacres, leaving human carnage and inconsolable grief.

Regardless of explanation for motive or reason from politicians, psychiatrists, pundits, law enforcement, and criminal experts, as well as most church leaders—the answer to *why*, and the reason for so many atrocities that are upon us now can only be found in Scripture.

Satan is on his way down to earth for the final conflict. Not only is he using false Christians, self-righteous evil, and the wicked evil—Satan is increasingly igniting his demon-possessed people who are deranged and mentally ill to fill a perverse, godless and sick culture with terror and chaos.

On September 11, 2001—for the first time in our modern history—this nation was attacked. That terror-filled morning resulted in the creation of the Department of Homeland Security to fight and protect its citizens from terrorist attacks from abroad and from within. Now, like Israel we are under constant siege from the threat of terror from abroad and from within in all forms—and most people and even Christians are passive and aloof.

The spiritual protection that this nation was once blessed with for decades is dissipating rapidly. Symbol after symbol and every vestige of God and Christ are being eradicated from view in every public venue and government-supported institution. Our nation's sense of morality and decency has become undermined with violence, filth, greed, and every kind of sexual perversion, and yet holds a form of religion—and in all this, many have the gall to ask why God allowed these tragedies to occur.

Woe to a people: *"who call evil good and good evil, who put darkness for light and light for darkness"* (Isaiah 5:20). We as a nation and as a lukewarm church are reaping the whirlwind.

Again, looking at the Apostle Paul's warning for the last days—where people will be *"lovers of self, lovers of money, proud, arrogant, abusive, disobedient to their parents, ungrateful, unholy, heartless, unappeasable, slanderous, without self-control, brutal, not loving good, treacherous, reckless, swollen with conceit, lovers of pleasure rather than lovers of God"* (2 Timothy 3:2-4).

Jesus said concerning the coming trouble of the last days, *"For it will come upon all who dwell on the face of the whole earth. But stay awake at all times, praying that you may have strength to escape all these things that are going to take place, and to stand before the Son of Man"* (Luke 21:35-36).

The Apostle states that we are to avoid such people. Really, how can one avoid a heartless and inhuman lunatic driven by demons who starts shooting up the grocery store where you are standing in line with your children to pay for groceries?

You may think this is alarmist and paranoid. To the contrary, as these last-days advance, more than ever *anyone* can become a potential victim of violence and terror just by going to the bank, shopping, attending a movie, or sending one's child to school on Monday morning.

We are vulnerable not just to a mass murder rampage, but to robbery, carjacking, rape, home invasion, identity theft, or any number of other crimes that are now on the rise.

Are you in a relationship with Christ and in tune with the leadership of the Holy Spirit to hear the voice of our Lord telling you, "Keep your children at home today," or to warn you in a dream to avoid a certain section of the road on the way to work?

Part of discernment is hearing the voice of Christ distinct and separate from your own inner self-talk and from any demonic static or interference. Not only to hear correctly, but also to have a prayer life so consecrated that Christ could warn you, since he knows you would obey.

Many cannot receive warnings or specific direction for the Lord because they chose to be lazy and did not pay the price of discipline in learning to seek him, to hear and discern his voice and be willing and trained to obey.

The Lord wants to protect his people in the coming days, but cannot for many. Most Christians are taught to follow their pastor and ignore, or never learn to perceive, the voice of Christ and his guidance and warnings. Do not leave your powers of discernment to decay by following the false and filling your life with false light. *"My sheep hear my voice, and I know them, and they follow me"* (John 10:27).

"If then the light in you is darkness, how great is the darkness!" (Matthew 6:23).

"Walk as children of light (for the fruit of light is found in all that is good and right and true), and try to discern what is pleasing to the Lord. Take no part in the unfruitful works of darkness, but instead expose them. For it is shameful even to speak of the things that they do in secret. But when anything is exposed by the light, it becomes visible, for anything that becomes visible is light. Therefore it says, 'Awake, O sleeper, and arise from the dead, and Christ will shine on you.' Look carefully then how you walk, not as unwise but as wise, making the best use of the time, because the days are evil" (Ephesians 5:8-16).

An aspect of hearing what is done in secret or what may be about to be done in secret carries responsibilities. Not just to take heed, but also to wage war, if led by the Lord. Jesus said, *"So have no fear of them, for nothing is covered that will not be revealed, or hidden that will not be known. What I tell you in the dark, say in the light, and what you hear whispered, proclaim on the housetops. And do not fear those who kill the body but cannot kill the soul. Rather fear him who can destroy both soul and body in hell"* (Matthew 10:26-28).

If the Lord exposes darkness, it is our fiduciary responsibility as disciples of Christ to also hear what God's will is on the matter, and, if so directed, expose by prayer and however else the Holy Spirit would direct in dealing with revealed darkness.

Ministry Case: *Prophetic intervention*

Evil raises its ugly head in many ways and we must be careful how we walk, being awake and alert. Marine Corps training teaches eleven general orders when on duty, and the second basic order is, "To walk my post in a military manner, keeping always on the alert and observing everything that takes place within sight or hearing." A true Christian is a servant of Christ to serve as a soldier of light arrayed against the spiritual host of wickedness of this present darkness. (Ephesians 6:10-20).

I shared how my oldest son, Don, enlisted in the Coast Guard in 1991 and became a rescue swimmer on the USCGC Vigilant stationed at Port Canaveral, Florida. On one of the patrols during operation Support Democracy (1994-1995), the cutter Vigilant conducted seven migrant repatriations, returning over 1,400 migrants to Haiti. Many were saved from drowning, as many migrants attempted to come to America in makeshift and unseaworthy ships.

One night during the time my son was on one of those missions as the ship's rescue swimmer, the Lord gave me a prophetic warning dream. In the dream, a female relative within the family system approached me stating, "Did you hear? Don died!" There was a sense of loss expressed by her; however, she also had a glowing demeanor from the attention she would gain by my son's death. This was her profile, to jealously incite trouble, an accident or harm to a family member to get the family and others to pour upon her sympathy and attention.

She was raised in Catholicism and in an abusive family, where she developed what she thought was a gift to foresee the future in the form of premonitions. We all thought it strange, especially when her premonitions came to pass. Somehow, she developed a spiritual power that would occasionally allow her to foresee trouble or a disaster within the family.

Fortunately, when this warning dream came to me, the Lord had shown me by then that this person was demon possessed with a spirit of divination and an evil spirit. Her demonic possession was similar to that of the slave women that Paul and Silas encountered who had a spirit of divination and earned her owners profit in fortune telling. (See Acts 16:16-24).

In this person's case, many of her premonitions were self-fulfilling through the empowerment of the evil spirit that was also resident within her. This is an example of false gifting, where Satan attempts to carry out his work and will, contrary to God's will. Selfish people who, out of envy, jealousy or revenge inflict spiritual powers onto others are those who become the main channels for this type of satanic work. This power can cause people to become unaware of dangerous situations and cause accidents that harm or even cause death.

I have learned to take these encounters by the Holy Spirit very seriously, making sure I remember them, and even journal them and refer back for insight and confirmation. Many receive warning dreams from the Lord and false dreams, yet pay no attention and do not examine them in light of Scripture and serious intercession.

I interpreted this dream to be from the Lord as a warning to intercede for the safety of my son, and also to break the demonic evil spirit assignment of death that this misguided and selfishly evil family member had imposed upon my son.

It took about two months before my son told me the most amazing account of a situation that almost took his life. Don had contacted us when his last mission was completed, and as he often would, he filled us in on his adventures and duties.

On this last mission, during the time I had the dream, he told me of a situation that came up when about thirty to forty Haitians were intercepted by the Vigilant on the open seas off Haiti. The craft was floundering and the rescue required ferrying these desperate souls from their sinking craft to the cutter Vigilant.

During this intercept-and-rescue mission Don had to enter the water between the two boats and was nearly crushed by the cutter and the smaller rescue boat. He would have been, if it were not for a vigilant crew member getting Don's attention in time.

I believe every discerning saint must learn to discern dreams: if they are from God, what they mean, and what should be done in prayer or otherwise. Many Christians miss God's warnings because they do not believe God speaks to us in dreams, warning, directing, and encouraging. In the coming days, we must utilize everything God has afforded in his Word and by his Holy Spirit and truly be vigilant servants.

The motto of the USGC Vigilant is *Semper Vigilans,* meaning *always vigilant.* Jesus also calls us to do nothing less than, *Semper Vigilans,* as the Apostle Peter expounds:

"Be <u>sober-minded; be watchful</u>. Your adversary the devil prowls around like a roaring lion, seeking someone to devour. Resist him, firm in your faith, knowing that the same kinds of suffering are being experienced by your brotherhood throughout the world. And after you have suffered a little while, the God of all grace, who has called you to his eternal glory in Christ, will himself restore, confirm, strengthen, and establish you. To him be the dominion forever and ever. Amen" (1 Peter 5:8-11). Ω

Presenting Our Lives as a Living Sacrifice

The challenge for every true saint who desires to walk in discernment is not learning all the ins and outs of human nature, memorizing Scripture, or learning set scripts to use in every situation. It boils down to having and maintaining an intimate relationship with the true Christ, in its fullness.

This state of grace cannot be religiously worked up or obtained from academia or any formal Bible college or seminary. Any sincere believer in Christ can come to this wonderful, abiding relationship by simply presenting to Christ one's life with no reservations.

It is the person of Christ whom God has made to be our all and in all. *"He is the source of your life in Christ Jesus, whom God made our wisdom and our righteousness and sanctification and redemption. Therefore, as it is written, 'Let the one who boasts, boast in the Lord'"* (1 Corinthians 1:30-31 RSV).

In 1976 I was led by the Holy Spirit to make the following covenant with Christ in a simple prayer. "Lord Jesus, I give you permission to do whatever it takes to make me the kind of person you called me to be. I know you will allow trouble and challenges to come into my life and I make this covenant with you, that you should not stop your work, even if I ask you to stop."

In a matter of a couple of months of that prayer, it seemed like all hell broke loose in my life. From then on, trials and circumstances guided and often forced me into the direction and training experiences the Lord intended and ordered for me. Most were contrary to what I thought to be of good orthodoxy; however, at the end of each change of course from the doctrines of men, came tremendous insight and an even closer walk with the Master.

If you choose to give all to Christ that he may change you, it will be hard, but you can take comfort in the character-changing examples found in Scripture: Jacob, Joseph, Moses, David and the prophets endured a tailor-made leadership training programs. The disciples went on the same roller coaster ride (blind folded) to be changed and trained.

James brings this type of real-time practical work into focus with the following passage:

"Count it all joy, my brothers, when you meet trials of various kinds, for you know that the testing of your faith <u>produces steadfastness</u>. And let steadfastness have its full effect, that you <u>may be perfect and complete, lacking in nothing</u>" (James 1:2-4). Learn to trust and let the training, testing and trials

produce steadfastness. Resist shrinking back in fear and unbelief; rather let God show himself to be true, that you may receive the promise.

One last passage that leads us to the ultimate giving of ourselves to Christ:

"I appeal to you therefore, brothers, by the mercies of God, <u>to present your bodies as a living sacrifice</u>, holy and acceptable to God, <u>which is your spiritual worship</u>. Do not be conformed to this world, but be transformed by the renewal of your mind, that by <u>testing you may discern what is the will of God, what is good and acceptable and perfect</u>" (Romans 12:1-2).

Crippled by the Lord
Sometimes it seems as though God cheats in the process of changing our carnal nature

Many who are called of God are very strong in the power of their own carnal nature concerning the Christian walk. For those of us who have a hard time seeing how our faith is mixed with self-reliance in fulfilling God's promises, or how we become over-involved in the lives of others, the Lord often tricks or leads us into our own carnal conundrums. Patiently, the Lord will use our carnal-soaked faith to our own disadvantage.

So often, like Peter, we refuse to listen to the Lord when he whispers warnings to our heart, or gives us a warning dream. The Lord will use another gifted servant like Elihu, whom Job finally received counsel from, only after Satan had taken everything from him.

During those terrible times of overwhelming trial and humbling circumstance, after we sensed God was leading in that very direction, the hammer falls with no solution or way out, and what is even more demoralizing, there is no solace from the Lord. We are trapped and helpless!

At that worst moment, at the height of hopelessness, the devil brings temptation upon temptation to take a short cut, to quit the call of ministry, or even deny the Lord. The most frequent vexing thought from Satan is, "Did God really call you, and are you even saved?"

Your own doubts and unbelief scream within your heart and the thoughts and feelings of anguish drive you to the verge of a nervous breakdown. Recall Peter's moment of sifting by the devil:

"Then they seized him and led him away, bringing him into the high priest's house, and Peter was following at a distance. And when they had kindled a fire in the middle of the courtyard and sat down together, Peter sat down among them. Then a servant girl, seeing him as he sat in the light and looking closely at him, said, 'This man also was with him.' But he denied it, saying, 'Woman, I do not know him.' And a little later someone else saw him and said, 'You also are one of them.' But Peter said, 'Man, I am not.' And after an interval of about an hour still another insisted, saying, 'Certainly this man also was with him, for he too is a Galilean.' But Peter said, 'Man, I do not know what you are talking about.' And immediately, while he was still speaking, the rooster crowed. And the Lord turned and looked at Peter. And Peter remembered the saying of the Lord, how he had said to him, 'Before the rooster crows today, you will deny me three times.' <u>And he went out and wept bitterly</u>" (Luke 22:54-62).

Peter's denial was finally broken concerning his inner character flaw and his counterbalancing overconfidence of following Christ to death. No one enjoys being proved wrong, especially when we confidently pride ourselves as able to "do all things through Christ" (see Philippians 4:10-13).

Our carnal nature has a life of its own and most refuse to acknowledge their flesh-driven schemes and efforts, so God gives us over to those pride-centered motives and even leads us into that moment of pure hell: *"'Therefore, behold, I will allure her, and bring her into the wilderness, and speak tenderly to her. And there I will give her her vineyards and <u>make the Valley of Achor a door of hope'"</u>* (Hosea 2:14-15). The meaning of *the Valley of Achor* is—"the Valley of Trouble."

From our perspective, God set us up and tricked us—to be precise, God cheated! However, from God's perspective this was and is often the only way to break denial of our inner carnal outlook on serving God and obeying him, believing we are doing so, in pure motive and unwavering trust.

Many solid believers in Christ will soon enter into a seemingly endless nightmare of circumstances that offer no way out. All opportunities to circumvent the run-and-quit or stand-in-trust showdown will finally be blocked. Like Jacob, the untested servants of Christ will be forced to win the struggle of trusting God in the face of death. The disciples experienced the same ordeal in preparation to receive power from upon high.

They learned to walk in the death and resurrected experience in trust in obedience, as the Apostle said of this walk, *"always carrying in the body the death of Jesus, so that the life of Jesus may also be manifested in our bodies"* (2 Corinthians 4:10).

If you expect to walk in a level of discernment required to navigate in the coming dark and evil days, then settle it now, and allow Christ to become your all in all by presenting your life as a living sacrifice. Though we talk of the difficulties and hardships in following Christ and growing in maturity and discernment, each step of faith in the journey has great reward. We learned to trust God at each unexpected turn, and as we grew in faith, more insights were granted with greater understanding.

While so many Christians struggle to know positively what is happening to the world and where all this turmoil and evil is headed, part of our reward is that we know what is in store, without doubt and know the Lord is preparing us to handle what is coming.

Some of the experiences will be heart-wrenching if and when the Lord calls you to expose and battle against darkness. Expect the Lord to take you through his school of discipline removing any unhealthy issues of heart or any attachment towards this world that Satan can use against you.

We as God's people will make it easier on each other and ourselves if we learn to walk in humility allowing the Lord to point out the old nature and him to transform each of us

"But God has so composed the body, giving greater honor to the part that lacked it, that there may be no division in the body, but that the members may have the same care for one another. If one member suffers, all suffer together; if one member is honored, all rejoice together" (1 Corinthians 12:24-26).

Very soon, as persecution increases, the body of Christ in America and around the world will begin to shape up in unity, purity and power, *"that he might present the church to himself in splendor, without spot or wrinkle or any such thing, that she might be holy and without blemish"* (Ephesians 5:27).

Chapter Nine

The Midnight Cry Final Awakening
The last chapter of this age—the saint's finest hour

The Bible speaks of gloom, doom, and misery concerning the end of this age; many try to teach otherwise, but Scripture is indisputable. The goal of this book was not to present another scenario to read, and then have its message relegated to the back burner of your mind.

All signs point to his coming, not years from now, but very soon. *"When you see all these things, you know that he is near, at the very gates"* (Matthew 24:33). It is time to wake up and become ready, for the true saint's finest hour is also nearing.

Let us not be bogged down with the cares of this life and idols of the heart, for in a short, short time the final awakening will start. Many are lulled to sleep through false doctrine and the signs of his return are misunderstood. God's people faced the same self-imposed problem at Christ's first coming, and the Lord told them, *"You know how to interpret the appearance of the sky, but you cannot interpret the signs of the times. An evil and adulterous generation seeks for a sign, but no sign will be given to it except the sign of Jonah"* (Matthew 16:3-4).

Whom will you believe: Tim LaHaye, and his famous *Left Behind* teachings, or Christ and his words? You have to do the work in growing in maturity and in discernment. You cannot blame your pastor, your favorite author, or your own passivity for missing what is about to happen by not being prepared.

This book on discernment is not to garner followers who like what is written, but to shake awake as many as possible before the midnight cry final awakening. It is not an easy read; it was not designed as such. Rather, with the companion study guide, it is presented as a solid resource conveying sound doctrine to help in maturity and learning to discern the hour.

Many will not accept this warning message; however, many will. If we ignore the truth and the witness of the Holy Spirit because it does not fit our favorite last-days scenario, Scripture warns that we will have no excuse and will be held accountable.

For those who take advantage of this resource, the Holy Spirit will have more freedom to bring personal revelation and understanding to those harder teachings of Christ. Christ is calling his last-days army together for the final awakening and final harvest of precious souls.

The Saint's Finest Hour

This coming hour will not be gloom, doom and misery for the prepared saint. No doubt the coming days leading up to the final awakening will be very tough; therefore, we must not waste a minute on anything that distracts us from God's purpose and his discipline for our life in preparation for our part in the coming work of ministry by the saints. There will be no more one-person shows, where a personality leader will be heralded as the go to anointed leader; rather, individual Christian workers will become the backbone of the body of Christ winning souls and mentoring each into maturity.

There is now a great need for mature Christian workers and laborers who are "in the know", living and working from a solid foundation. Multitudes will soon be waking up in the coming increased birth pangs and persecution.

The midnight cry that is about to be heralded may take months to sweep into and throughout the body of Christ, as individual believers in fellowship after fellowship, congregation after congregation, denomination after denomination are confronted with the midnight cry and are forced to decide what to believe.

The Great Tribulation that will start with the anti-Christ's rule will be the final shout in the midnight cry awakening, thrusting the unprepared into the purifying fires of the Great Tribulation.

Christ will have a pure and holy bride that will glorify him and testify to his soon appearance. Multitudes will come to the Lamb of God while he is still in his saving dispensation, before he rescues his beloved and returns as the Lion of Judah, King of kings, and Lord of lords to rule for a thousand years, to govern the nations with an iron rod.

The final harvest of the earth is coming soon; we must be ready in order to be used of him in this final work: *"Then I looked, and behold, a white cloud, and seated on the cloud one like a son of man, with a golden crown on his head, and a sharp sickle in his hand. And another angel came out of the temple, calling with a loud voice to him who sat on the cloud, 'Put in your sickle, and reap, for the hour to reap has come, for the harvest of the earth is fully ripe.' So he who sat on the cloud swung his sickle across the earth, and the earth was reaped"* (Revelation 14:14-16).

The balance of this final chapter will direct our attention to some of the challenges facing the saint in the coming days as well as drastic changes that are coming to the church. There will be changes to our approach to ministry and leadership priorities. The first shock from the midnight cry awakening will be a separation throughout the body of Christ, as the true wake up and the false recoil from the truth.

Birth Pangs are about to Go Viral
Not a good time for church leadership to be pondering and vacillating about the rapture

Pastors, leaders, and dear saints, now is the time to settle it. Make your mind up by the study of the Scriptures and receive confirmation from the Lord, as to what type of Christian will be raptured and when the rapture will occur. Vacillating concerning which interpretation is correct is as damning as being wrong.

Christ and the Scriptures are explicit in the sequence of key events leading to Christ's coming: birth pangs, then the Great Tribulation, then his appearance in the clouds with the rapture of the purified saint, then the wrath of God upon the earth, then his return when he sets his feet on earth—from where he first ascended.

I wrestled with these questions for years and by study and the Holy Spirit's illumination, I have become convinced as to when the rapture will take place. Indeed, we are not destined for the wrath of God; however, the Great Tribulation is the devil's wrath to create chaos and confusion. We are not exempt from tribulation or death as believers; however, if we are not prepared to endure to the end, we run the risk of selling out to the devil's work and the anti-Christ's lies. For in the coming Great Tribulation Jesus warned, *"For false christs and false prophets will arise and perform great signs and wonders, so as to lead astray, if possible, even the elect"* (Matthew 24:24).

Leaders who keep pondering and stay undecided are not doing a service for God's people. Many shepherds will have blood on their hands because they kept those in their care at ease and worried about life on earth rather than preparing to endure to the end and stand victoriously at Christ's appearance.

"But watch yourselves lest your hearts be weighed down with dissipation and drunkenness and cares of this life, and that day come upon you suddenly like a trap. For it will come upon all who dwell on the face of the whole earth. But stay awake at all times, praying that you may have strength to escape all these things that are going to take place, and to stand before the Son of Man" (Luke 21:34-36).

We must be prepared; if leadership continues to vacillate on what to believe, preparations will be put on the back burner for those in their care. Many will wake up finding that they were foolish and unprepared suffering the terrors of hell unleashed on earth during the Great Tribulation and then the wrath of God. What's more is the high risk of being locked out of eternity.

A World Gone Mad with Chaos, Debauchery, and Persecution
Come out of her, my people, lest you take part in her sins, lest you share in her plagues

Many are beginning to see that the world is spinning out of control. China and Russia are arming themselves and prospering, while Europe and America are on the verge of financial insolvency and economic chaos. Iran and North Korea are determined to destroy America as they both expand their nuclear capabilities.

Egypt and the so-called Arab Spring revolt to install democracy fell into the hands of Muslim extremists whose reason for existence is to destroy America and Israel. The Arab Spring uprising in Syria is still a wait-and-see situation. All of these destabilizing issues are geared towards Satan's global chaos plan to ignite the call for a new world order leading to the anti-Christ rule and the destruction of Israel.

The world and America took a deep sigh of relief when the wall came down in Berlin and the cold war ended; however, in a matter of twenty years the world has become more dangerous than before and on the verge of a major conflict leading to Armageddon.

The surreal aspect about all these rapidly happening events is that most are numb to the madness, and for many it's just like watching another end of the world movie, passively ignoring the signs—desensitized and disassociating. Millions of believers in Christ are in the very condition Christ warned of, *weighed down with dissipation and drunkenness and cares of this life.*

The cost of living is skyrocketing, yet as long as the entertainment industry, fine dining, the fast food industry, and individual mobility is maintained—who cares? Even as the black horse and rider of Revelation 6 carries forth its work of trouble, passivity and indifference keeps the world spellbound: *"A quart of wheat for a denarius, and three quarts of barley for a denarius, and <u>do not harm the oil and wine</u>!"* (Revelation 6:6).

God is judging his people and the world with a stupor, as the birth pangs scream "wake up," the wicked and the lukewarm Christian become even more deceived and asleep. *"Therefore God sends them a strong delusion, so that they may believe what is false, in order that all may be condemned who did not believe the truth but had pleasure in unrighteousness"* (2 Thessalonians 2:11-12).

Many sincere Christians are spellbound due to wrong beliefs in the pre-tribulation rapture or the wrong belief that the body of Christ (Christianity) will tame and change the world. The only thing that will bring many believers to their senses is the coming political chaos and immoral debauchery. If you think it is bad now, it is about to get far worse in wave after wave of increased debauchery and obscene public wickedness.

America is on the brink of final judgment, suffering affliction after affliction. Very soon, we will hear, as part of the midnight cry, a calling out to the multitude of believers to come away morally and spiritually from America, the Great Babylon of Revelation:

"Come out of her, my people, lest you take part in her sins, lest you share in her plagues; for her sins are heaped high as heaven, and God has remembered her iniquities. Pay her back as she herself has paid back others, and repay her double for her deeds; mix a double portion for her in the cup she mixed. As she glorified herself and lived in luxury, so give her a like measure of torment and mourning, since in her heart she says, I sit as a queen, I am no widow, and mourning I shall never see.' <u>For this reason her plagues will come in a single day</u>, death and mourning and famine, and she will be burned up with fire; for mighty is the Lord God who has judged her." (Revelation 18:4-8).

Just a few years ago, few would believe America could be associated with the end-of-the-age Babylon; however, the American culture is fulfilling Christ's warning that society would succumb to the condition in Noah's day; before the deluge and as it was with Lot and his family in Sodom. You may think it is a wrong conclusion to associate America with the wicked Babylon described in the book of Revelation; however, at this rate of increasing depravity, it will not be long until the sincere student of Scripture will see the direct correlation.

The Word Trade Center towers fell in one day—as a warning of the coming final judgment. An international band of thugs succeeded to attack this nation on 9/11; still, few politicians, most of the public, and far too many Christians are discounting the belligerent threats by

North Korea and Iran, or the sly military buildup of China or Russia. *"Since in her heart she says, I sit as a queen, I am no widow, and mourning I shall never see"* (Revelation 18:7).

Now is the time to let go of America—it has gone beyond the point of no return. Learn to become a true citizen of the coming Kingdom:

"The Lord is not slow to fulfill his promise as some count slowness, but is patient toward you, not wishing that any should perish, but that all should reach repentance. But the day of the Lord will come like a thief, and then the heavens will pass away with a roar, and the heavenly bodies will be burned up and dissolved, and the earth and the works that are done on it will be exposed.

Since all these things are thus to be dissolved, what sort of people ought you to be in lives of holiness and godliness, waiting for and hastening the coming of the day of God, because of which the heavens will be set on fire and dissolved, and the heavenly bodies will melt as they burn! But according to his promise we are waiting for new heavens and a new earth in which righteousness dwells" (2 Peter 3:9-13).

America will fall and leave Israel alone to fend for herself. Regardless of how terrible all these biblical predictions sound, seemingly full of gloom and doom, this is God's plan: to allow the world to turn in upon itself and bring on its own destruction.

As Satan, the god of this world, attempts to bring about his world order, the God of all creation is about to destroy the wicked and demonstrate his plan hidden through ages— Christ's rule and the government upon his shoulders and his preeminence in all of creation.

"For to us a child is born, to us a son is given; and the government shall be upon his shoulder, and his name shall be called Wonderful Counselor, Mighty God, Everlasting Father, Prince of Peace. Of the increase of his government and of peace there will be no end, on the throne of David and over his kingdom, to establish it and to uphold it with justice and with righteousness from this time forth and forevermore. The zeal of the Lord of hosts will do this" (Isaiah 9:6-7). Get ready for *new heavens and a new earth in which righteousness dwells!*

Final Move of God at the End-of-this Age Harvest
Restoration of the great commission—no longer saving the world, but saving souls!

Jesus explained that the end would not come all at once, stating, *"And when you hear of wars and tumults, do not be terrified, for these things must first take place, but the end will not be at once"* (Luke 21:9). These birth pang troubles are coming in phases, stages, and spurts in which the frequency and intensity are ever increasing. We are being given ample warning and soon there will be a moment in all this insanity, where God's voice will be heard once more and break through the darkness.

A powerful and well-trained army of true bondservants of Christ will suddenly break forth. They will know the truth and live it by example, and boldly proclaim the message that Christ prophesied, and this message will spread throughout the world just before the end begins.

"And this gospel of the kingdom will be <u>proclaimed throughout the whole world as a testimony to all nations</u>, and <u>then the end will come</u>" (Matthew 24:14).

The final move of God is coming and will be wrought in the true power God and facilitated by Christ's true servants. Truth concerning the end of the age, the coming Kingdom of light and righteousness, and the thousand-year reign of Christ will spread like a wildfire. Millions will hear the truth just in time before the lights go out and the Great Tribulation starts.

The world and its people will hear the truth dramatically, just in time before many find themselves in the valley of decision trying to decide whom to follow. Many will have a hard time choosing between the new world order with the anti-Christ rule, or enduring to the end for the soon appearance of Christ, the rapture of the true believers, and his return with the saints to set up his rule on earth.

The main doctrine preached by these servants of Christ coming in this final move of God, will be the fulfillment of the great commission, making disciples and being used to save souls for eternity. This mighty army of disciples will preach repentance and sanctification, and reject outright the false social gospel that pathetically attempts to save the world through the church and Christianity; (churchianity).

There are ministries already being raised up and used to prepare and equip likeminded believers called to work in the coming final move of God. One such ministry is International House of Prayer, which is doing just that; preparing on-fire believers to work in the coming triumphant church and final harvest. The following excerpt from their statement of faith gives us a glimpse of how other ministries are embracing the truth concerning how the end age will unfold.

> "We believe in the literal second coming of Christ at the end of the age when He will return to earth personally and visibly to consummate His Kingdom. We believe that the church will go through the Great Tribulation in great power and victory. We believe the church will be raptured at the end of the Great Tribulation. We also believe in and are praying for a great end–time harvest of souls and the emergence of a victorious church that will experience an unprecedented unity, purity, and power in the Holy Spirit. (Palms 2:7–9; 22:27–28; John 14:12; 17:20–26; Romans 11:25–32; 1 Corinthians 15:20–28, 50–58; Ephesians 4:11–16; Philippians 3:20–21; 1 Thessalonians 4:13–5:11; 2 Thessalonians 1:3–12; Rev. 7:9–14) (International House of Prayer website: *www.ihopkc.org/about/statement-of-faith*)

The Midnight Cry—Final Awakening—Shock-and-Awe Testimony
The good news of the coming kingdom heralded by a glorious church

In the parable of the ten virgins, Jesus speaks of a sleeping church (the ten virgins) —asleep at the darkest hour; *"At midnight there was a cry, 'Here is the bridegroom! Come out to meet him.' Then all those virgins rose and trimmed their lamps"* (Matthew 24:6-7). The parable explains that there were five wise virgins, and the other five were foolish. The wise had extra oil to trim their lamps in order to keep them bright all through the midnight hour to see in the dark as they went out to meet the bridegroom.

I believe this parable speaks of the condition of God's people today and speaks of a remnant of believers, bondservants of the bridegroom who will shout out the midnight cry to awaken a sleeping church. Their message will be powerful, profound, frightening and glorious.

This midnight cry remnant will consist of ministries and workers who have been in preparation for some time, and their relationship with Christ (the bridegroom) is as true bondservants. They will herald the truth of what is about to happen with unction and boldness that will be spiritually equivalent to a military bombardment before an invasion, a shock and awe testimony that will stun the world and the peoples of all nations for a season of time.

Jesus spoke of this stating, *"And this gospel of the kingdom will be proclaimed throughout the whole world as a testimony to all nations, and then the end will come"* (Matthew 24:14).

These sold-out disciples will stand their ground, warding off slander and rejection from leadership of compromised churches. At first the media will treat this sudden movement of God as a phenomenon, due to the shock-and-awe power of their testimony that includes signs and wonders. However, as persecution and hatred increase the media will begin to attack and undermine the coming final move of God.

The Rapture Will Convert Israel to Christ
They shall see the Lamb upon the throne and call out to their savior whom they pierced

Israel's conversion to Christ has been a theological question for centuries, but with the shaking and waking of the church, the awakened remnant and true believers will focus on lost Gentile souls, leaving Israel's salvation and conversion to Christ to the hand of God.

Israel, as a nation is still dead-set against recognizing the crucified Christ as their messiah. However, this position will change after they (Israel) and the world buys into the anti-Christ promise of peace and then betrayal at the end of the Great Tribulation period, which will be marked by the rapture of all true Christians.

Israel will be alone and surrounded by her enemies and America will not be there at her side. The following passage explains how Israel will finally acknowledge that Jesus was and is their messiah and call out to Christ, *"On that day the Lord will protect the inhabitants of Jerusalem, so that the feeblest among them on that day shall be like David, and the house of David shall be like God, like the angel of the Lord, going before them. And on that day I will seek to destroy all the nations that come against Jerusalem. 'And I will pour out on the house of David and the inhabitants of Jerusalem a spirit of grace and pleas for mercy, so that, when they look on me, on him whom they have pierced, they shall mourn for him, as one mourns for an only child, and weep bitterly over him, as one weeps over a firstborn.'"* (Zechariah 12:8-10).

The people of Israel, the house of David will cry out in pleas of mercy to him who they pierced, as the whole world will witness Christ appearing in the clouds. *"Behold, he is coming with the clouds, and every eye will see him, even those who pierced him, and all tribes of the earth will wail on account of him. Even so. Amen"* (Revelation 1:7).

The world will be terrified when Christ appears—as the whole world simultaneously beholds Christ upon his throne. As the wicked try to hide from the coming wrath of God, Israel as a people collectively will cry out to the Lamb who sits upon the throne, and finally and formally recognize that Jesus Christ is their savior too and their long awaited messiah.

Keep Looking up and Do Not Look Back—the Saints Will Rule with Christ Afterward
Remember Lot's wife; let the wicked have the world—we get it back in the end!

It is difficult to realize our beloved America is in process of being taken over by the wicked. However, we need to step back from the current efforts to regain political control, to bring America back from an immoral and anti-God suicide. In that we must realize America is past the point of no return and concentrate on preparing for the coming Kingdom and the final harvest. We need to pray for more time to become ready to be used in the coming end-of-the-age harvest—becoming a conservative activist will be a waste of time and put an adverse spotlight on you and your family.

Many sincere believers will be pulled into a zealot type of fight to restore America to its founding fathers' vision and the Constitution. This is not the way to go; the fight is for souls to be added to the Kingdom of God, not converting America to Christ and restoring the magic kingdom to family wholesomeness.

Scripture and Christ's teaching are very clear on giving up the love and the cares of this world and making sure all heartstring attachments are severed. Many believers will not accept this and decide to fight to regain control of America, joining a patriotic fight against the takeover of America by the wicked and the coming anti-Christ new world order.

This is a time of preparation, the harvest of souls, and praying for strength to endure, just as the Apostle John was shown in his revelation of the end of this age and how the beast will prevail for a season:

"*<u>Also it was allowed to make war on the saints and to conquer them</u>. Authority was given it over every tribe and people and language and nation, and all who dwell on earth will worship it, everyone whose name has not been written before the foundation of the world in the book of life of the Lamb that was slain. <u>If anyone has an ear, let him hear: If anyone is to be taken captive, to captivity he goes; if anyone is to be slain with the sword, with the sword must he be slain. Here is a call for the endurance and faith of the saints</u>*" (Revelation 13:7-10).

Israel's Zealots, in their fight for freedom, enraged Rome, bringing on the destruction of the Temple and Jerusalem and the dispersing of the Jewish people. Already the elements within the Obama administration are subtly trying to indoctrinate the Department of Defense to classify Catholics and evangelicals as extremists. Now the IRS is embroiled in illegal harassment suit and congressional investigations towards Tea Party and other Christian organizations seeking 501 (c) 3 statuses.

In a Washington Times online article it was reported that the Defense Department came under fire because of a presentation that listed Catholics and evangelical Protestants as "extremist" religious groups alongside al Qaeda and the Ku Klux Klan. ("Defense Department classifies Catholics, evangelicals as extremists," www.washingtontimes.com, April 5, 2012)

Now is the time to relinquish any idols of heart, lest you be given over to the love of this world (including America) and miss the coming final visitation and rapture. The five foolish virgins did not take enough extra oil, and turned to the merchants of this world and found themselves locked out from the wedding feast.

Learn to abide in Christ, be led and sustained by him and become a true citizen of heaven. We must work and live in this world and pray God's will be done and learn to manage the material resources and finances in our care according to God's principles—not allowing the things of this world to manage us and dictate and control our heart.

Jesus reminds us concerning unhealthy attachments to this world in his sayings, particularly: *"And he said to the disciples, 'The days are coming when you will desire to see one of the days of the Son of Man, and you will not see it. And they will say to you, 'Look, there!' or 'Look, here!' Do not go out or follow them. For as the lightning flashes and lights up the sky from one side to the other, so will the Son of Man be in his day.... <u>so will it be on the day when the Son of Man is revealed.</u> On that day, let the one who is on the housetop, with his goods in the house, not come down to take them away, and likewise let the one who is in the field not turn back. <u>Remember Lot's wife. Whoever seeks to preserve his life will lose it, but whoever loses his life will keep it</u>. I tell you, in that night there will be two in one bed. One will be taken and the other left. There will be two women grinding together. One will be taken and the other left'"* (Luke 17:22-36).

Therefore, how should we walk in light of these things that are now coming upon us? Again, Jesus instructs, *"Now when these things begin to take place, straighten up and raise your heads, because your redemption is drawing near"* (Luke 21:28).

More Birth-Pang Perplexities and Distress of the Nations
Religious and political upheaval—no one has the answers as fear grips millions

Notice how earthquakes, tsunamis, droughts, and other natural distress increase with intensity and frequency. Many are wondering what is happening, as old pat answers such as global warming and other explanations begin to be understood for what they are—guessing and political hype to garner votes.

Soon, millions will recognize that the only plausible answer is in the Scriptures and prophecies of Christ and the Apostles. While the masses demand answers, phony pastors, priests and noted religious leaders along with politicians, scientists and elected officials will start to avoid comments and public explanation; they will become stymied in presenting solutions and reasons why so many calamities are happening and, in fear of an enraged public demanding government intervention, they will keep their mouths shut.

Just as Christ declared, people will faint *"with fear and with foreboding of what is coming on the world"* (Luke 21:26). Panic, chaos, hoarding, people withdrawing funds from the banks like Cyprus experienced recently, along with increased lawlessness and thefts will increase in waves as each birth pang ripples through the nations.

Politicians and the false church will find new answers in scapegoating. Unable to develop plausible answers and solutions, Christians and Israel will become the reason for the global mess. The popular political blame strategy will be a widely employed strategy in the coming days, as persecution toward Christianity grows. Logical and rational thinking will be replaced by hatred and emotional irrationalism as the divide between the wicked and righteous widens.

Just as Hitler successfully used the Jews and other ethnic groups to take the rap for Germany's miseries, so too will national and international political leaders succeed in blaming Christians, Israel, and the moral conservative voice.

The coming final message and awakening will force the world to pause for a short time, and then the final wave of delusion allowed by God will come, plunging the wicked into a "hate the truth" and "hate Christians" craze. This is what we can expect as the birth pangs move toward the start of the Great Tribulation and the rise of the anti-Christ. *"The coming of the lawless one is by the activity of Satan with all power and false signs and wonders, and with all wicked deception for those who are perishing, because they refused to love the truth and so be saved. Therefore God sends them a strong delusion, so that they may believe what is false, in order that all may be condemned who did not believe the truth but had pleasure in unrighteousness"* (2 Thessalonians 2:9-12).

The coming blame towards the righteous for the world's woes may seem absurd. However, people hearing of the genocide that was taking place during the first stages of WWII would not believe the initial reports. It was absurd that an educated and civilized society such as Germany would ever allow such horrors to be committed upon other human beings.

To further bolster my assessment and warning that Christians and Israel will be blamed for the unraveling of the world, consider how Revelation describes humanity's reaction to the death of the prophets who were witnesses of God's truth:

"And when they have finished their testimony, the beast that rises from the bottomless pit will make war on them and conquer them and kill them, and their dead bodies will lie in the street of the great city that symbolically is called Sodom and Egypt, where their Lord was crucified. For three and a half days some from the peoples and tribes and languages and nations will gaze at their dead bodies and refuse to let them be placed in a tomb, and those who dwell on the earth will rejoice over them and make merry and exchange presents, because these two prophets had been a torment to those who dwell on the earth" (Revelation 11:7-10).

Multitudes will believe that these two witnesses made the coming plagues occur, completely discounting the power of God and the testimony they proclaim. Therefore, it should be reasonable to believe that most of the world will blame Christians and Israel for the woes that these birth pangs will increasingly produce.

Christians must learn to discern the hour and avoid panic. Many foolish and lukewarm believers will buckle under the pressure of persecution, renounce Christ, and fall away. However, during these final throws of the birth pangs and persecution, those who endure through these frantic and hysterical times, holding their faith and trust in Christ will receive supernatural provision, comfort, and a continuous infilling of the Holy Spirit's presence. Like Daniel in the lion's den and the roaring furnace that could not scorch even a single hair upon Meshach Shadrach and Abednego, not even the smell of smoke was upon them. *"But not a hair of your head will perish. By your endurance you will gain your lives"* (Luke 21:18-19).

The Y2K false alarm and the hysteria it created, as with other premature scares, will be remembered by many as the next wave of birth pangs roll in. This will cause many to hesitate in making any sensible preparations. Take this warning seriously and begin to research reasonable precautions with food supplies, fuel, and other survival necessities.

Trust God, take reasonable precautions, and learn to hear from the Lord as to when and how to extend help to others. Scammers, thieves, and freeloaders will be roaming and marauding, looking to take advantage of the naïve and gullible, especially the arrogant who brags and speaks out of turn.

As the birth pangs and persecution expand, the world will look for a savior, and Satan will soon offer the anti-Christ. No one will have the answers or resources to calm the panic. Settle it now, count the cost of following the true Christ, and seek his face with the confidence that God has everything planned out, and become prepared to endure to the end. *"Then they will deliver you up to tribulation and put you to death, and you will be hated by all nations for my name's sake. And then many will fall away and betray one another and hate one another. And many false prophets will arise and lead many astray. And because lawlessness will be increased, the love of many will grow cold. But the one who endures to the end will be saved. And this gospel of the kingdom will be proclaimed throughout the whole world as a testimony to all nations, and then the end will come"* (Matthew 24:9-14).

Safe Fellowship—Standing Against the Terrors through the Gates of Hell
Brace for satanic sleeper cells betraying the saints and wreaking havoc

Terror and its threat to America and Christians has adversely affected our peaceful, easygoing and prosperous lifestyles. Individual freedoms and liberty are starting to vaporize right before our eyes. This and all the other perplexities, distresses of the nations, the roaring of the waves, and earthquakes will soon cause many to faint in terror.

The increasing upheavals with world politics, revolts, hatreds, wars and Mideast turmoil are plain to many as obvious signs of Christ's soon return. Astounding is the denial that many Christians still maintain about the coming persecution towards Christians. The world is about to turn ugly and demonstrate pure hatred towards Christians.

This coming trouble and persecution of Christian individuals and fellowships everywhere will be the catalyst for the gates of hell to open wide and unleash terror upon the true saint— *even from other so-called Christians.*

Christ warned that many believers in the last days would fall away and betray one another in hatred and distrust. The true body of Christ has become a magnet, attracting satanically groomed implants that are now beginning to explode in hatred, rage, jealousy, and immorality and discharge deadly jolts of spiritual electricity, terrorizing with havoc, discord, betrayal and a malignant sorcery. Jude warned, *"These are grumblers, malcontents, following their own sinful desires; they are loud-mouthed boasters, showing favoritism to gain advantage. But you must remember, beloved, the predictions of the apostles of our Lord Jesus Christ. They said to you, '<u>In the last time there</u>*

will be scoffers, following their own ungodly passions.' It is these who cause divisions, worldly people, devoid of the Spirit" (Jude 16-19).

The main reason why these hordes of malcontents and bitter unbelieving Christians have become so entrenched in the body of Christ is due to their ability to be so convincing—most have learned to live a lie by believing their own lies. Many suffer from a split personality condition, which is key to understanding the insidiousness of the mischievous evil they perpetrate, having severe dividedness of heart and mind, making these false Christians very hard to detect.

They develop an outer persona that mimics Christian mannerisms; however, internally a division exists where hidden within their core character is a toxic and malicious agenda. The inner subtle twice-a-soul condition (double-minded) is real and does exist.

Secular psychology would label the symptoms as split personality, multiple personality, or some form of schizophrenia. These people learn how to gain advantage, hide their issues through a nice fun-loving outer demeanor, and use flattery to manipulate. However, their inner true character is comprised of self-pity, bitter jealousy, entitlement expectations, slothful work ethics, hatred and murderous rage when their narcissistic ambitions are hampered or thwarted; Peter described these as accursed children with hearts trained in greed.

Caution must be exercised in distinguishing an *accursed child* from a wounded and insecure believer operating in the flesh. These wounded Christians are also driven by bitter jealousy and selfish-ambition, which is how James' describes an unstable Christian. However, we must detect the accursed fake Christian from the wounded believer. Here is Peter's description of this type of false brethren, *"They count it pleasure to revel in the daytime. They are blots and blemishes, reveling in their deceptions, while they feast with you. They have eyes full of adultery, insatiable for sin. They entice unsteady souls. They have hearts trained in greed. Accursed children! Forsaking the right way, they have gone astray"* (2 Peter 2:13-15). I recommend reading all of 2 Peter 2 as well as Jude 10-19 to build a deeper understanding of these false Christians who end up leaching the very life out of the fellowship they become involved in.

To help qualify these warnings from Peter and Jude: Jesus also warned of this in his teachings and parables. The parable of the weeds in Matthew 13:24-43 explains how Satan implants evil people amongst the true believers; these Jesus referred to as weeds (noxious plants) that cause trouble reaching its insidious climax at the end of the age.

On the other hand, James describes the unstable Christian who also causes trouble as follows: *"But if you have bitter jealousy and selfish ambition in your hearts, do not boast and be false to the truth. This is not the wisdom that comes down from above, but is earthly, unspiritual, demonic. For where jealousy and selfish ambition exist, there will be disorder and every vile practice"* (James 3:14-16). For further in-depth understanding concerning unstable Christians, the book of James lays out God's recovery program in James 4:1-10.

Getting back to the false Christian who refuses to become cleansed and changed—leadership and the Christian worker must understand that these people come to fellowships and congregations everywhere thinking they are Christian but never were called of God or born-again.

Due to false doctrine and untrained shepherds, satanically planted weeds have infiltrated the church and have fooled everyone. They naturally live and breathe the lie, living as full-blown hypocrites. Millions are now in place ready to be demonically activated. Few pastors realize what is about to be unleashed through the gates of hell within their own flock. Fellowships will be unprepared to handle the coming internal malicious and deadly attacks; however, safe fellowship will provide a steady diet of sound doctrine in dealing with implants and satanic human time bombs.

Wrestling Against Principalities and Human Spirit Channels

The gates of hell are often disguised as people who are righteous, who have learned to subtly carry out Satan's plans. Many of these people do so unwittingly due to false doctrine. The power of hell increases mightily due to its darkness—deceit and craftiness is used to undermine God's people of faith and prevent the saint from doing God's will. When the gates of hell came to arrest Christ (through Judas and the Temple leaders), Jesus said, *"Have you come out as against a robber, with swords and clubs? When I was with you day after day in the temple, you did not lay hands on me. But this is your hour, and the power of darkness"* (Luke 22:52, 53). The gates of hell are evil people and carnal Christians who have learned to walk in darkness (purposely or inadvertently), cloaked in the light of superficial decency and fake goodness.

At some point in your training, perhaps several times, you will experience the power of darkness and the hour of evil, as the gates of hell momentarily prevail against your life and ministry. "Unbelievable" is the most popular word that victims use to describe the hour of evil and the powers of darkness when evil bears its fruit and exacts destruction.

Healthy and safe fellowship understands the suffering involved and courageously stands the test. When Herod arrested Peter and ordered his execution to please the Jews, the church went into action, *"But earnest prayer for him was made to God by the church"* (Acts 12:5).

An angel of the Lord was dispatched to break Peter out of jail. Further, later in the same narrative in the book of Acts, concerning Herod—when the people declared Herod to a god, *"an angel of the Lord struck him down, because he did not give God the glory, and he was eaten by worms and breathed his last"* (Acts 12:23). These acts of the Apostles and the founding church should also be common place within a last-days safe and healthy fellowship.

The disciples were required to endure the discipline in fighting and withstanding the gates of hell, and ingrained in their minds and hearts was the need to ever be alert and observing the fruit of the people around them.

Jesus gave the disciples plenty of hints concerning Judas, even informing them all that a betrayer was in their midst. Even on the night of the betrayal, when Jesus pointed out Judas as the one who would sell him and the others out, the disciples were still confused and entirely misunderstood the warning.

When we taste firsthand the power of darkness under the veil of satanic mist and suffer the consequences, all the key indicators that were overlooked leading to that moment are illuminated and indelibly written in our consciousness. When the hour of evil hits us with the force of darkness, we become shaken free from living in the world haphazardly.

We truly realize how vulnerable we are to the gates of hell. We learn to walk in a manner that allows us to detect beforehand the seeds of evil.

Most, when taught the truth about evil and darkness react as the disciples did. Even as Christ, at different times, confronted Judas before the others for his pilfering, greed, and game playing, and when Christ taught about wolves in sheep's clothing, the disciples were puzzled and were still cognitively removed from the reality of evil within their presence.

One of the first lessons that Christ gives the sincere saint-in-training is a taste of the insidious powers of darkness. After this, the Lord has that saint's undivided attention for the coming lessons in increasing the powers of discernment.

Though we wrestle against the powers of darkness, the gates of hell are the avenues of attack. Therefore, to withstand the onslaught of the dark powers flowing through the gates of hell, we must learn to detect the principalities, demons, ideology, hidden wickedness and secret sin operating in the people whose fruit bears witness to a wolf or viper dressed up as a saint.

Some are obvious channels for hell, while others are subtle: merely a carnal, defiled, or a divided Christian. Peter and Jude refer to the more obvious as waterless springs and accursed children with hearts trained in greed.

You will find that standing against the devil's work becomes a strenuous and painful wrestling match, where prayer, intense study of God's Word, and the gifts of prophesy and discernment brings victory. There will be very few times, especially while in training, that attacks by the enemy are quickly and easily commanded away.

Healthy and likeminded fellowship is vital in withstanding attacks of the enemy through the gates of hell. Everyone in fellowship must understand what it means to seek, ask, knock and practice self-examination in these wrestling matches. You will learn to pray earnestly, sometimes for days and with fasting in resisting the devil.

Magic formulas will be exposed for what they are: a waste of time and energy. You will learn to do battle for God's specific will to be done; sometimes standing alone on an issue you know to be God's perfect will. True fellowship of the saints should be working as a team in supporting each other in these times of private battles, just as the church went to prayer for Peter to spare him certain death.

At times, you will wake up from a night's rest more exhausted than when you retired the night before; spiritual warfare involves wrestling with the powers of darkness and night often becomes a time of intense battle. Most victories are wrought by on-the-job-training, where mistakes become precious nuggets of insight and wisdom and a means of grace.

Seek the true gifts of the Holy Spirit with the understanding that you will receive a gift when needed and when you are ready, walking in wisdom and the love of God; *"All these are empowered by one and the same Spirit, who apportions to each one individually as he wills"* (1 Corinthians 12:11). Teamwork within fellowship is vital in standing against the gates of hell as a congregation and in support of the pastor in his personal battles. Only seasoned saints should be invited or engaged in this kind of warfare—carnal Christians doing deliverance and spiritual warfare are ignorantly begging to be beat up—sooner than later, for the powers of darkness are about to go viral.

Recognizing a Destructive Person

The true end-of-the-age fellowship must walk in perfect discernment, as the powers of hell will rage against God's people. Like Peter hearing from the Holy Spirit concerning Ananias and Sapphira or Simon the magician, or when the Apostle Paul stood up to Elymas the magician in the power of the Holy Spirit—these acts and attributes of true leadership including Christian workers must be restored to maintain the health and spiritual vitality of fellowship life.

When a demonic, destructive type of personality invades a fellowship and opposes true leadership, a major characteristic of that person's presence is subtle. These people carry deceitfully long-term hatred and a vengeful agenda that produces physical, emotional and psychological symptoms within the victim. Victims can be anyone who opposes or becomes a perceived threat or becomes an object of jealousy to the embittered and evil hearted who has power to destroy.

In most cases, the destructive person's spiritual attacks cause mild waves of mental confusion and oppression. We learned that God allowed us to receive a small dose of a destructive person's power (as in the ministry case *The exploding glass of milk* page 213) but later this part of this person's profile was very helpful in understanding the physical destructiveness and malignant power that can emanate from such a person.

Alert Leadership Must Brace for Viral Fellowship Implosions
Satan's Trojan horse strategy to destroy true leadership and discipleship

Jesus and the apostles hammered the importance of discerning the false prophets, wolves, and devils gaining authority and leadership. In addition, Scripture warns of everyday people coming to fellowship, claiming to be born-again believers, but who are inwardly wolves.

In these lasts days a multitude of false believers have been drawn by the devil through use of false leaders, false doctrines and false movements and now have taken up positions within fellowships everywhere.

Like the famed Trojan horse attack on Troy from within, Satan has implanted time-bombs in fellowships through all denominations, from the small congregation to the mega-church fellowship—few fellowships will escape the coming demonic detonation of these evil false believers or at best carnal Christians, when they go amuck.

Just as Jude wrote, *"These are grumblers, malcontents, following their own sinful desires; they are loud-mouthed boasters, showing favoritism to gain advantage. But you must remember, beloved, the predictions of the apostles of our Lord Jesus Christ. They said to you, 'In the last time there will be scoffers, following their own ungodly passions.' It is these who cause divisions, worldly people, devoid of the Spirit"* (Jude 16-19).

If you are in leadership, as a pastor or elder in authority, now is the time to seek the Lord and determine if others in leadership are willing to see the true condition of those in their care.

Time is short to learn how to expose, confront, and chase out, if necessary those who prove to be a satanic Trojan horse implant—to proactively deal with such and not wait to be attacked on the devil's terms and in his timing.

If not, and you are in leadership when Satan lights the fuses, be assured that the carnage from the trouble will be overwhelming. You can expect all manner of discord, attacks upon the true saints in your congregation, attacks on true leadership, and in general disharmony, dissension, base suspicions, gossip, slander, and self-righteous cliques demoralizing new comers and weak yet sincere believers. Meddlers will rise up from hiding and cause all manner of trouble—all this will be demonically inspired to shut down true discipleship and the preaching of sound doctrine and chase off true leadership.

Overreaction and Hysteria when the Gates of Hell are Opened
A warning to prevent a "witch hunt" mêlée

One of the devil's objectives when activating implants within the church is to create emotional hysteria and irrational thinking in a fellowship, thus inducing overreaction to the many symptoms from these spiritual attacks.

Fear of losing other members of the congregation if such wickedness is exposed and properly handled is a main cause for most in leadership to accommodate or cave in to the mannerisms, mischief-making and general troublesome antics of these imposters and implants; many pastors are constantly smoothing over the trouble these people cause.

These people learned how to impose spiritual blackmail, and it will take courageous and deliberate leadership to quell this evil work. Many in leadership are too affable, and for the sake of church growth and the appearance of a happy fellowship most pastors look the other way; unfortunately, many leaders themselves walk in darkness and defile others.

As James pointed out, when bitter jealousy and selfish ambition flourish and establish their agenda, there will be falsehood, lack of wisdom, earthly sensuousness, and unspiritual desires driven by the demonic. All manner of disorder, secret sin and vile practices will thrive within such a fellowship.

When leadership begins to get hints of the source of these maladies, often they will overreact and suspect every unstable Christian within the fellowship of channeling for the devil or being a gate for hell. What often ensues is a "witch-hunt" mêlée, and wisdom and truth vanish as carnal believers and weak and unlearned leaders overreact.

On the other hand, American culture recoils from holding accountable those who practice sorcery. In the not-so-distant past, any kind of white magic or the notion that there were good witches was taboo within the general social norms across America. However, these activities and practices have gained credibility and good standing within much of society.

The progressive change of these social mores or unwritten moral standards concerning sorcery and witchcraft can be accredited in a large part to very powerful cultural influences: The Wizard of Oz movie, the TV sitcom Bewitched, the popular Star Wars movies referring to the good use of the "force" and now the current Harry Potter mania. I could list more devilish influences over the last seventy-five years that have helped make it taboo to shun or shame such practices today—similarly to how social norms changed concerning the practice of homosexuality.

These social norm changes have also affected Christianity, as most fellowships consider it taboo to expose hidden sin within fellowship, or to shun those who live in unrepentant open sin. To confront publically those who continually practice any of the works of the flesh is now a no-no, contrary to sound doctrine. *"As for those who persist in sin, rebuke them in the presence of all, so that the rest may stand in fear"* (1 Timothy 5:20).

Evils such as Christian sorcery (praying not according to God's will), bitter jealousy leading to gossip, meddling, contentions, and other devilish activities as James describes, are ignored, minimized, rationalized and often justified by ignorant leaders.

Leaders, who attempt to expose and confront hidden evils within a fellowship and teach on exposing carnal Christians who deliberately or inadvertently channel for the demonic are often accused of going on a "witch-hunt."

This is one very powerful reason why sincere leaders within the body of Christ are reluctant to restore the sound doctrine widely taught throughout Scripture in chasing out wolves in sheep's clothing and boldly correcting the wayward.

In the coming days true shepherds will be forced to learn and apply sound teachings that will help the true saint call to account those who are disingenuous, mischief-makers and outright satanic implants.

The shepherds and elders must learn how to embrace and apply sound teaching on exposing the false within fellowship and strongly correct the carnal Christian. As this age unfolds this aspect of true leadership will become very important, because Christ will send forth his angels to bring to light those who are false.

"The Son of Man will send his angels, and they will gather out of his kingdom all causes of sin and all law-breakers, and throw them into the fiery furnace. In that place there will be weeping and gnashing of teeth. Then the righteous will shine like the sun in the kingdom of their Father. He who has ears, let him hear" (Matthew 13:41-43).

Christ does not explain in this parable how this separation or purging will come about at the end. However, we do know that Satan will be waging a very intense war against the saints during these last days. This coming clash between the angels sent to expose and separate Satan's evil implants and Satan's push back in this coming conflict within the body of Christ will not be pleasant.

God will have a pure and glorious church during the last battle for millions of souls as persecution increases and as the Great Tribulation begins.

The true saint will be used mightily in the coming final harvest and will witness angelic help sent by the Lord to remove the wicked from the ranks of the body of Christ, making a clear distinction between the false and the true.

The Second Fulfillment of Malachi's prophecies is at hand!
True messengers of Christ are coming and a day of reckoning for the wicked

The prophet Malachi rebuked God's people for their shallow worship practices and confronted the priesthood for despising the name of the Lord. The people of Israel had returned to their land from years of captivity in Babylon. At first, they were zealous about rebuilding Jerusalem and the Temple, but soon they began to doubt God's love.

Their worship became disingenuous; they wandered from the Lord's statutes and ordinances, robbing God of the whole tithe. The priests did not take to heart their solemn position of leadership and their responsibility to convey sound instruction and give full glory to God. For this, God cursed the priests in Malachi's day.

The name Malachi means "my messenger" or "messenger of Jehovah" and this prophet proclaimed the message of God without wavering, focusing on the true issues that plagued God's people.

Part of Malachi's prophecy foretold the coming of the Messiah, when Christ would come to his temple and purify the leadership as a refiner purifies silver and gold. Malachi proclaimed a day when God would act swiftly and be a witness against all sorcerers, adulterers, those who swear falsely and those who oppress the worker's wage and the weak.

During the period between Malachi's day and the first coming of Christ, God's people lost their vision concerning God, his promises and his ways. The leadership did not fear God, stand in awe of God, or give true instruction to turn God's people from their iniquity.

The Word of God taught by the priesthood was so convoluted that it became impossible for the people of God to discern evil from good, or tell the difference between true servants of God and the many who are false.

In his scathing rebuke, Malachi declares that on the day God acts, *"Then once more you shall distinguish the righteous and the wicked, between one who serves God and one who does not serve him."*

This visionless condition grew worse, and when Christ appeared he did not choose his priests from the corrupt Temple worship system; rather, he chose a group of common, uneducated men from the people of Israel.

Christ was the Messenger Malachi spoke of: *"The Lord whom you seek will suddenly come to his temple; the messenger of the covenant in whom you delight, behold, he is coming, says the Lord of Hosts. But who can endure the day of his coming and who can stand when he appears?"* (Malachi 3:1-2).

The word apostle in New Testament means "messenger." Well do we see the fulfillment of Malachi's prophesy in the ministry of Christ and his Apostles, as recorded in the Gospels and the book of Acts.

The people of Israel saw a stark contrast between Christ's ministry and his messengers, and those of the high priest, the priesthood, the scribes, and the Pharisees— *"And when Jesus finished these sayings, the crowds were astonished at his teaching, for he was teaching them as one who had authority, and not as their scribes"* (Matthew 7:28-29).

As the church age ends, the counterfeit will look very much like the real. Jesus warned that at the end of the age many would come in his name and mislead many, causing them to follow the false rather than to grow up into Christ and be led by the Holy Spirit. The deception will be powerful as Christ warned, *"For false christs and false prophets will arise and show great signs and wonders, so as to lead astray, if possible, even the elect"* (Matthew 24:24).

Fortunately, true messengers of Christ for these last days will suddenly appear from nowhere, trained and made ready through years of wilderness living where Jesus has become their master and commander. God's people will see these in a very dramatic manner, as God starts to act through them with astounding miracles, signs, and the message of Christ's soon appearance.

The power that they will walk in will dwarf the counterfeit manifestations that are so popular now. Like Moses and Aaron under the power of God that shut down the Pharaoh's court magicians, the true messengers of Christ will startle, confound and even infuriate the false as the power of God bears witness to the message of these messengers. Many deceived Christians and even some of the false will repent at the coming demonstration of the true power of God—many declaring, *"This is the finger of God"* (Exodus 8:19).

These true messengers of Christ will preach the true Gospel and the good news of the coming Kingdom. They will be easily distinguished having clear authority from God. If you will, the true messengers of Christ will shout or give out a cry at midnight *"Behold, the bridegroom! Come out to meet him"* (Matthew 25:6).

Just as Malachi's prophecy came to pass in the first coming of Christ and with his Apostles (messengers), another fulfillment of Malachi's prediction is about to occur. True and devout servants of Christ will be released shouting the message of Christ's soon return, and as Malachi predicted, *"Then once more you shall see the distinction between the righteous and the wicked, between one who serves God and one who does not serve him"* (Malachi 3:18).

The message will be a season of intense ministry by these true messengers. Their work in the coming days will ignite controversy throughout christendom, creating great confusion and division for all Christians. Multitudes will be forced to choose between the message of these true servants and the false teachers that walk in demonic power and pretended signs and wonders. (See 2 Thessalonians 1:9-12).

Many will awaken to their message, *"Behold the bridegroom! Come out to meet him,"* and find they are unprepared. They will fall prey to the false. Many will buy in to the great end-of-the-age deception and be locked out from the marriage feast.

The coming true messengers will also pronounce judgments upon the wicked, starting with the satanic weed implants within the body of Christ. Some of these messengers will bring forth pronouncements of specific afflictions during the increased birth pangs. Government officials, politicians, and the false church leaders will not like these predictions, even as they happen. Unfortunately, persecution will heighten as the wicked reject these as true predictions and judgment from God, like the Pharaoh hardening his heart against the voice of God given through Moses and Aaron.

This will be part of God raising his voice during the birth pangs with the message of the good news of the coming Kingdom, as a testimony to the nations. These predictions of the coming disasters, as they come to pass, are part of the testimony from the Lord. They will be a precursor to the two witnesses coming during the Great Tribulation as mentioned in Revelation during the Great Tribulation period. (See Revelation 11:3-13.)

Discerning False Christs, False Prophets, and the Anti-Christ
Avoiding hysteria and mass confusion of the masses of unprepared Christian

There is not much time left to prepare and get our priorities in life aligned with God's perfect will. When the false christs and false prophets appear, many Christians will panic and chase after anyone that predicts earthly hope, and an all is well message. The deception in the coming days will become increasingly vexing, drawing foolish and unprepared Christians into all manner of activities and plans to escape the coming troubles and survive to rebuild the world when the madness stops.

These false saviors and false prophets will enlist millions to jump head long into wild schemes and plans to protect self and family from the coming disasters and wars. You must settle it now and make sure you know and follow the true Christ, knowing and obeying his voice. He and he alone will guide the sincere saint in the coming difficult times.

Be careful around slothful Christians, for when the trouble really hits they will plead in hysteria that you help and even sustain them when everything collapses. Yes, give to others as the Lord will lead; however, many who will be crying out as a believer for help are masquerading as Christians looking to rob, betray, and even murder to obtain food, water, and supplies.

As for the foolish Christian begging for help, learn to be wise as a serpent and innocent as a dove (Matthew 10:16), remembering what Christ warned in the parable of the Ten Virgins:

"And the foolish said to the wise, '<u>Give us some of your oil, for our lamps are going out.' But the wise answered, saying, 'Since there will not be enough for us and for you, go rather to the dealers and buy for yourselves.'</u> And while they were going to buy, the bridegroom came, and those who were ready went in with him to the marriage feast, and the door was shut. Afterward the other virgins came also, saying, 'Lord, lord, open to us.' But he answered, 'Truly, I say to you, I do not know you.' Watch therefore, for you know neither the day nor the hour" (Matthew 25:8-13).

Praise and Worship in the Wilderness

Every true fellowship and sincere saint must anticipate persecution that will demand wisdom concerning those invited to worship and how praise services are conducted. Praise and worship will be truly revered as a time to come together as a holy people and enter into the presence of a holy God.

In some cases game-playing believers who want worship to stay in the carnal will fall dead, like Aaron's two sons, *"And Nadab and Abihu died before Jehovah, when they offered strange fire before Jehovah, in the wilderness of Sinai"* (Numbers 3:4 ASV).

Praise and worship in the coming days will become transformed, from carnal spiritualism (strange fire) to true reverence and awe in brokenness and in honest fear of the Lord. The fires of persecution will cleanse the wayward heart and bring about a true joy, knowing that the end of the age is now in process, as the body of Christ is shaken awake.

A holy divine manifestation of Christ's presence will warm each heart. Singing will have a unique angelic harmony that will glorify Christ in purity and without pretense. Weeping before the Lord in repentance and true contrition of heart will accompany times of worship. No more manipulation of the Holy Spirit by way of showmanship, but rather, a solemn attitude of heart will characterize worship leaders, who dare not stand in God's presence and before the congregation to entertain.

The lost and carnal Christian who might come to the praise and worship meeting, not knowing what to expect, will know they are in the presence of the Holy Trinity. The body of Christ will begin to experience just a taste of heavenly worship as described in the Apostle John's revelation.

> *"And I saw what appeared to be a sea of glass mingled with fire—and also those who had conquered the beast and its image and the number of its name, standing beside the sea of glass with harps of God in their hands. And they sing the song of Moses, the servant of God, and the song of the Lamb, saying,*
>
> *"Great and amazing are your deeds, O Lord God the Almighty!*
> *Just and true are your ways, O King of the nations!*
> *Who will not fear, O Lord, and glorify your name?*
> *For you alone are holy. All nations will come and worship you,*
> *for your righteous acts have been revealed"* (Revelation 15:2-4).

Enroll in Christ's School of Ministry Now

It was in the spring of 1975 that I first heard about Christ's school of ministry. I was asking the Lord for grace and strength to finish Bible college and then seminary; the voice of the Lord, plain as day, said, "You are not going to go through man's school, but my school." That thought from the Lord took a long time for me to understand, even after I entered Christ's school of ministry.

For me, the entrance into his training occurred about a year later when I gave him permission to do whatever it would take to make me into the person he desired. In about two months after that prayer, my whole life turned upside down.

Through all the years that followed, Christ's lessons were life changing by way of pressure, allowing me to fail in the flesh, and revelation of glory that transforms. Most importantly, the written Word of God and understanding of the New Covenant became practical and full of life. I have no regrets entering into the Lord's school of discipline; it was and is still difficult, but only by his glorious presence in the fiery challenges that he ordains will change come. This is Christ's way to show us those deeper aspects of our carnal character and prepare the saint to walk in the fullness of Christ.

There is little time left to prepare one's life for the coming dark times, yet Christ is faithful and he will complete that which he has begun, if we allow him and if we learn to cooperate. The journey will be more pleasant and quicker (but not easier) if you take to heart the experiences and lessons shared in this book.

Use this work as a sound resource to help understand those harder teachings of Christ that so many avoid. Our prayer is that you awake in time to get ready, that you never hear those words that many will hear, *"Truly, I say to you, I do not know you."*

Rather, we pray that you hear these words, *"Well done, good and faithful servant. You have been faithful over a little; I will set you over much. Enter into the joy of your master."*

Index

Aimee Semple McPherson, 112
Alert Leadership Must Brace for Viral Fellowship Implosions #9, 355
Allow Christ to Be Your Teacher #8, 270
Always Carrying in the Body the Death of Christ #8, 288
America is on the Brink! #1, 28
America—Past the Point of No Return #1, 14
An Enraged Violent-Filled Culture #1, 18
Andrew Strom: Testimony of leaving the prophetic movement, 235
Another Jesus, a Different Spirit, a Different Gospel, and Cheap Grace #4, 134
Astral projection, 202
Beatitude Living #7, 256
Benny Hinn's Bolts of Supernatural Plasma #3, 93
Beware of Designer Bibles Branded by Personality Leaders #8, 277
Beware of the Devils Disguised as Christians #8, 317
Biblical Diagnosis –versus– Secular Psychology #2, 59
Biblical principles; Double minded "twice a soul", 74; personal revelation, 82; Turning over a new leaf - fatal error, 106; spirit of the mind, 159; Relationship idolatry, 294; Absorb today's manna before seeking more, 301; anxiom, work where God is working, 39
Bill Hybels: Quote; local church hope of the world, 101
bilocation, 203
Birth Pangs are about to Go Viral #9, 342
bitter jealousy, 25, 40, 107, 122, 162, 196, 215, 216, 220, 274, 293, 297, 303, 308, 352, 356, 357
Brace for a Sorcery Mêlée between Carnal Christians and Evil-False Brethren #6, 215
Breaking Denial that Evil Exist and defining its Nature #2, 33
Building up Immunity in the Inner Person #8, 330
Burden of Leadership and Ministry Burnout, The #7, 244
Carnal Deliverance Ministries #3, 102
caveat to mentoring and counseling others, 283
Christ Defines Evil #2, 32
Christ's True Leaders #7, 239
Christian Human Spirits Harnessed by Counterfeit Demonic Activity #6, 208
Christian Judaism: Another Bewitching, Enslaving Lie #4, 145
Christian Marriages Made in the Flesh #2, 50
Church Leadership as a Covering #5, 177
Churchianity is Too Far Gone for Reform #5, 183
Controlled Temperment analysis, 176
Counterfeit Supernatural-Power Brokers #3, 91
Crazy Evil—Walking Time Bombs #2, 61
Criminally Evil—Prisons Overflowing into Society #2, 60
Crippled by the Lord #8, 338
Cult Family Systems Hidden in the Church #8, 294

Dark Human Spiritual Powers Growing—Exponentially #6, 207
David Wilkerson: Solid minister of the Gospel, 28, 29, 48, 94, 142, 165
Dealing with Carnal and Evil Cult Family Systems #8, 297
Defense Department: Catholics and evangelicals listed as extremist, 348
Demonic Fracking of the Human Psyche #2, 42
demonic principalities, 327
Denominationalism #5, 190
Designer Bibles: Examples, 278
Destructive Heresies Reinforces Denial #3, 113
Developing a Healthy Fear of God #8, 271
Devil and the Gates of Hell, The #3, 81
devoid of the Spirit, 52, 78, 150, 151, 352, 355
DID: Dissociative Identity Disorder, 45, 74
Dietrich Bonhoeffer: The Cost of Discipleship - cheap grace, 135
Digest and Absorb Today's Manna before Moving on #8, 301
Discerning and Dealing with Christians Who Are Under Judgment #8, 307
Discerning Between the Wounded and the Demon Possessed-Mentally Ill #2, 64
Discerning False Christs, False Prophets, and the Anti-Christ #9, 360
Discerning the False who Mislead God's People #3, 100
Discerning the Immoral, Irreligious, and Self-indulgent Christian #8, 317
Discerning the Power of the Lord and the Spiritual Power of the Flesh #6, 205
Discernment terms; devoid of the Spirit, 78; Christian sorcery, 81; test the spirits to see whether they are from God, 92; Strange and unholy fire, 96; Designer Bibles, 108; Spiritual shrike, 123
Disclaimer, 9
double-minded: "twice a soul", 45, 56, 57, 73, 74, 87, 104, 105, 158, 160, 162, 211, 262, 319, 333, 352
E. Fuller Torrey: The Insanity Offense, 63
Easy-Going Jesus and Shoo-In Salvation, An #4, 138
Effective Spiritual Warfare vs. Fighting Demonic Phantoms #8, 318
End of the age Vortex of Trouble #1, 27
End-of-the-Age Fear Mongers and the Paranoid #3, 116
End-of-the-Age Maturing of the Wheat and the Weeds #4, 150
End-of-this-Age Darkness #1, 11
Enlisting the "Gung-Ho" Faith of the Naïve #5, 188
Enroll in Christ's School of Ministry Now #9, 361
Entering the Narrow Gate and Following the Hard Path #8, 273
Establishing Relationship Boundaries in Christ #8, 291
Everything Demonic Deliverance Ministries #3, 103

Evil #2, 31
Evil Perpetrated Against Children #2, 41
Evil Political Leaders with an Anti-Christ Agenda #3, 124
Evil World Getting Worse, An #2, 33
Exposing the Works of Darkness—Amongst the Brethren #3, 96
False Gifts #6, 226
False Leaders Demonstrating Great Signs and Wonders #3, 86
False Teachings roducing Gospel Hardened Carnal and False Believers #4, 132
False Will Lead Many Astray, The #5, 186
Family pedophilia: American culture, stats, and symptoms, 221
Fatherhood: the Fatality of the Gender War #2, 47
Final Move of God at the End-of-this Age Harvest #9, 345
Finding True End-of-the-Age Fellowship #7, 266
Five-fold Servant-Leaders and the Saint's Work of Ministry #7, 242
Flagging: Another carnal activity, 233
Flood of Simon the Magician Christian Leaders, A #3, 89
From Swaggart to Haggard—In Between and Since #1, 17
Full Grown Evil Weeds amongst the Wheat #1, 25
Gall of Bitterness and the Bonds of Iniquity, The #8, 303
General Phases of Maturing that Leads to Full Salvation and Eternal Security #7, 251
Given Over to a Debased Mind and an Evil Heart #1, 17
Good evil—the Most Insidious Evil of All #2, 36
Greed and the Abundant Life Syndrome #4, 136
Growing up into Salvation #4, 140
Harbinger of the Harbinger, The #3, 127
Hating and Giving up Family Carnal Bonds #8, 289
Heartbreaking List of Fallen Personality Leaders #3, 112
Hitler, 31, 32, 38, 124, 125, 135, 350
Holy Spirit-Led Counsel #8, 282
homosexuals, 15, 18, 126
Hordes of Malignantly Evil Spirits Cohabitating in the Schizophrenic #2, 60
Hostile church takeovers: The fruit of the Purpose Driven Church scheme by Rick Warren, 174
Hounds of Glory #3, 107
Hour of Evil and the Power of Darkness, The #2, 34
How Satan Hijacks God's Work #3, 118
How Satan's Works to Awaken the Human Spirit for His Purposes #6, 201
Human spirit attacks: Warned of by other; Penn-Lewis, Nee, 209
In the Power of the Lord or by the Power of the Flesh, Boosted by Demons #6, 202
International House of Prayer: Other post-tribulation rapture ministries, 346
Jack Nicholson: Quote - Nicholson's warning Heath Ledger on the Joker role, 19
James Eagan Holmes: Aurora Colorado theatre shooter, 20
James G. Friesen, PH.D.: Uncovering the Mystery of MPD, 44

Jamie Foxx: Quote; Barack Obama "our lord and savior", 125
Jeanette Harder: Let the Children Come, 41
Jessie Penn-Lewis: Quote; Perils of revival, 118; Soul and Spirit, 219
Jessie Penn-Lewis and Evan Roberts, 118
Jessie Penn-Lewis with Evan Roberts: War on the Saints, 257
Jesus movement, 134
Jimmy Swaggart, 17, 112, 231
Josh Reich: Quote; Church should be like a dance club, 101
Joyce Meyer, 109, 112, 146, 157, 160, 162, 278; Critique of her book, Power Thoughts, 157; The power of "I", 161; twelve power thoughts - her self-programing method, 161
Keep Looking up and Do Not Look Back—the Saints Will Rule with Christ Afterward #9, 348
Keirsey Temperament Sorter, 176
Kingdom Now: Dominion theology, reconstructionist, postmillennial, 143
Kingdom Now Theology a Bust #4, 143
Lack of Knowledge and Understanding—Lack of Discipline #1, 25
Last Days Evils Are upon Us, The #1, 13
Lawlessness and Cold Love #1, 20
Leadership: Personality vs. Character #7, 240
Learn to Avoid Using Christ's Name in the Power of the Flesh #8, 321
Learning the Proper Use of the Four Letter Word: EVIL #8, 305
Learning to be Vigilant and Proactively Expose Darkness #8, 333
Learning to Not Trust Yourself to False Christians #2, 54
Led by the Holy Spirit in the Lord's Discipline #8, 283
Let Us Get Our Theology Right! #8, 270
Let Your Yes be Yes, and Your No be No #8, 301
Lethargic and Lukewarm Followers #1, 23
Life's Ultimate Battle is Within #2, 45
Lists; key indicators that produce maturity, 90; Short list of popular teachers who twist Scripture, 109; Faulty premises, 110; Common carnal formulas, 111; Guidelines for confronting leaders over error, 180; Profile of characteristics of an evil person, 219; Symptoms of of humn spirit attack, 223; General phases of maturing and eternal security, 251; Basic biblical principle for true deliverance and healing of wounds, 261; basic indicators of mentally ill evil walking time bombs, 67; characteristics and attributes of "crazy evil" in Scripture, 67; Good Evil fruit or characteristics, 39; reasons for landslide of evils, 62
Love, Forgiveness, and Holding Evil Accountable #8, 303
Loving the Truth Revisited #8, 274
Loving Truth #7, 257
Lure and Deceit of the World and False Christianity #1, The, 12
Lust for Spiritual Power #6, 196

M. Scott Peck: People of the Lie – The Hope for Healing Human Evil, 37

Magdalene laundries asylums: Catholicism's hidden abuse exposed, 112

Making Followers of the Leader, Not Disciples of Christ #3, 109

Malachi Martin: Hostage to the devil, 102

Marketing Churchianity—Managing Instead of Maturing the Saints #5, 171

Maturing in Christ, until He is Formed Within #7, 254

Mega-Crowd Enthrallment and Groupthink #3, 88

Midnight Cry—Final Awakening—Shock-and-Awe Testimony, The #9, 346

militant leaders: Hinn, Copeland and others, 121

mindsets, 323, 325, 327, 328

Ministerial Triage #7, 243

Ministries Capitalizing on Carnal Spiritualism #3, 79

Ministry Cases; A job here, a job there, 26; A beautiful mind, 55; The irrational ninja, 69; Spirit of divination, 80; Drowned Ducks—False Gift of Faith, 84; Satan's bait and switch tactic, 87; Church picnic darkness, 97; Pleading Buckets, 105; Pastor's hidden nukes, 116; Your Jesus can't help you here, 146; Just manage and funnel, 173; Let my people go!, 183; False tongues vacation wrecker, 211; Charismatic church witches, 216; Conjuring counterfeit gifts, 227; Hired worship leaders, 231; Narcissistic dancers and flaggers, 234; Jesus is my husband, 236; Chasing out the wolves, 265; Prenatal wounds, 265; The untrusting pastor, 272; Not dropping our cross, 289; Torching the church for mom, 298; Prophetic intervention, 335; The terrified wife, 208

More Birth-Pang Perplexities and Distress of the Nations #9, 349

Most are Wounded and Weak Men and Women #6, 221

Motivational speakers: Discerning the next generation, 166

Mystery of Lawlessness and the Power of Chaos, The #1, 21

Nazi Germany, 31, 32, 124, 125

New Testament Out-of-Body References #6, 203

Newsweek: Declared Obama, "god of all things", 125

Next Generation of False Motivational Speakers, The #5, 166

Obama's ideology: The Audacity of Hope, Reclaiming the American dream - like Hilter's Mein Kampf, 125

Oblivious to the Coming Judgments #4, 142

Og Mandino: The Greatest Salesman in the World, 165

Overcoming an Abridged Gospel #7, 249

Overcoming the World, the Flesh, and the Devil #8, 284

Overreaction and Hysteria when the Gates of Hell are Opened #9, 356

passivity, 77, 169, 181, 210, 257, 258, 259, 341, 344

pattern of deception: Obama, 126

Payday Is Coming to Absentee and Divorced Parents #2, 48

Peddlers of God's Word with a Twist #3, 100

Personal Testimony (portion): Deceived into practicing false gifts **#6**, 226

Personality Leaders with an "I am the Christ" Message #5, 153

Physical Conditioning and Eating Healthy #8, 302

positive thought preachers: common error, 157

Positive-Power Thoughts do not Change the Carnal Nature #5, 157

Praise and Worship in the Wilderness #9, 360

Prepare for the End-of-the-Age Weed Uprising #4, 149

Presenting Our Lives as a Living Sacrifice #8, 337

Pre-tribulation Rapture Lie, The #4, 144

Principles of Holy Spirit-led Transformation #5, 159

Profile of Evil and the Carnally Wayward in Fellowship and Family #6, 218

Profiling with Discernment #6: Taking note of fruit - not judging outward appearances, 219

prosperity Gospel movement, 112

Psychiatric Drugs—Side Effects, 65

Purposely Driven by the Flesh #5, 174

Rabbi Cahn: The Harbinger, 127

Rapture Will Convert Israel to Christ, The #9, 347

Reality Surveys Point to the Truth #3, 114

Receiving the Crown of Life #8, 287

Recognizing a Destructive Person #9, 355

Relationship idolatry, 290, 294, 295, 314

Religious Dictators and Self-righteous Caretakers #8, 315

Religious Rote and Spiritual Ritualism #6, 229

Remember Lot's wife, 348

Reprogramming the Mind in the Power of the Flesh #5, 155

Reprogramming the Mind Instead of Renewing the Spirit of the Mind #5, 166

Rick Warren's Purpose Driven program, 174

Safe Fellowship—Standing Against the Terrors through the Gates of Hell #9, 351

Saint's Finest Hour, The #9, 342*

Saints Married to Evil Christians #2, 51

Saints Misled to be at War with God #5, 171

Sara Kliff: Washington Post article; Seven facts about America's mental health-care system, 61

Satan's most insidious work: Deceiving Christians with Scripture #3, 108

Satanic harnessing of this 'last-days' bewitched generation, 195

satanic sleeper cells, 351

Sealing Your Election and Call #8, 300

Seek and Find the Truth #8, 277

selfish-ambition, 40, 303, 352

Separating the Spirit from the Soul #6, 199

Shoo-in theology, 140

Sin against the Holy Spirit #8, 310

Sinners who do Evil versus the Wicked who are Evil #2, 35

Small Group Indoctrination #5, 181

Smooth Talkers Who Flatter to Deceive #3, 78

Sodomite Intimidation and Vexation, #1, 15

Solid ministers from the past, 165
spirit of divination, 80, 81, 212, 226, 313, 336
spirit of the mind, 159, 162, 168, 252, 263, 264
Spiritual abuse: other credible resources, 216
Spiritual Sensuality, Defiling Passion and Sexual Perversion #6, 232
Spiritual Shrikes Incognito #3, 122
Spiritual Vibes and Our Personal Spirit #8, 312
Spiritual Warfare and Discernment #8, 323
Stanley Frodsham: Prophesy - 1965 concerning the false and counterfeit gifts, 92
Start by Breaking the Spell of this Age #8, 269
Rodney Howard Browne's Laughaholics, 95
Suffering and Sifting by the Hands of the Satan #8, 332
Surrogate Bonding to the False Leader's Counterfeit Faith #5, 192
Symptoms from a Demon Boosted Human Spirit Attack #6, 223
Systematic Dumbing Down of the Saints #5, 168
TBN: Celebrity Christians - prosperity Gospel, 25
Ted Haggard, 14, 17, 112, 234
The Dark Knight: Batman movie - Joker character a powerful caricature of Satan, 19
The Erosion of Parenthood in America #2, 46
The rise of the Antichrist is just around the Corner! #3, 128
The Second Fulfillment of Malachi's Prophecies is at Hand! #9, 358
The Spiritual Power of the Flesh #6, 204
The Vision: David Wilkerson - 1973 prophesy, 28, 29, 48, 49
Tim LaHaye: Spirit Controlled Temperment - error from ancient history, 175
Training in Effective Warfare in Christ's Discipline #8, 322
Transforming our Carnal Nature—God's Way #7, 248
triage, 182, 242, 243, 262
True Deliverance for the Wounded and Demonized Believer #7, 260
True Leadership Won't Compete in Fellowship Popularity Contests #7, 247
True Servants and Christ-like Character #7, 259
Truth, Righteousness, and the Way of the Cross #8, 279

Typical Dynamics of a Destructive Relationship, The #2, 53
Typical Foundations for Popular False Teachings #3, 110
Ultra Control to Compensate for Lack of Mentoring and Discipleship #3, 119
Understanding the Difference in Christ's Meanings of Life #4, 137
Understanding the Insanity Immunity Mentality #2, 72
Understanding the Latent Supernatural Power of the Human Spirit #6, 197
Unity and Harmony at the Expense of Truth—Never! #8, 276
Ushering in the Millennial Reign of the Church #5, 182
vexed, 16, 233
Voices of the True Prophets Drowned Out, The #1, 28
W. Phillip Keller: Predators in our Pulpits, 241
Walking in the True Gift of Prophecy #7, 264
Walter, ministry associate: Quote - Parents in church with wild children, 49
Watchman Nee: Messenger of the Cross, 326
What Manner of Spirit? #3, 121
What to Look for in Finding Safe Fellowship #7, 267
Win Worley: False deliverance and hexing deceived Christians, 104
witch hunt" mêlée, 356
World Gone Mad with Chaos, Debauchery, and Persecution, A #9, 343
Worldly Motivational Leaders Using Principles that Work! #5, 164
Wounded and Deceived Christians Walking in Dark-Light #6, 224
Wounds, Defilements, and Double-Mindedness #2, 74
Wrestling Against Principalities and Human Spirit Channels #9, 353
Y. Sankar: Character not Charisma in leadership excellence, 241
Y2K false alarm: other premature scares - causing many to hesitate, 351
You Will Be Like God—Relationship Idolatry in the Church #4, 147

About the Author

Charles Pretlow has over twenty-eight years of experience in ministry and pastoral counseling. He completed his basic Bible classes at Seattle Pacific College and finished his undergraduate work at Central Washington University.

He has years of experience and study in practical theology, working in a ministerial capacity with evangelical, Pentecostal and charismatic congregations, as well as independent fellowships. In 1988, he founded a non-denominational ministry, emphasizing pastoral counseling that incorporated sound biblical principles to help Christians cooperate with God in the sanctification and healing process that God gives through Jesus Christ.

It was in 1973, while in the Marines, that he came to know Christ. In the ensuing years, he has seen much trouble, abuse, and confusion within the body of Christ. Since his conversion, he has overcome his own obstacles and challenges that, like so many others, prevent Christians from coming to the full grace of God and a stable life in Christ.

Over these years of ministry, Charles has dealt with a wide spectrum of Christians who complain of a troubled walk with Christ. Many of these were severe cases and this forced him to develop a scriptural understanding concerning the source of these Christians' difficulties.

His ministry is practical—helping others work out their salvation, always leaning on the Lord and sharing from his own healing process and experiences.

The main thrust of ministry is to help the sincere Christian prepare for the coming trouble leading to Christ's appearance.

Workshops, seminars and other ministry training by the author are available to help equip pastors, leaders and Christian workers for the coming final true move of God and the ensuing trouble leading to the rapture of those who are truly Christ's own.

Ministry Information

For information on workshops, ministry engagements, and fellowship:

Mailing Address:	Message of the Cross Chapel Fellowship PO Box 857 Canon City, CO 81215
Physical location:	The Abbey/St. Josephs' Building Suite 102 2951 E. Hwy 50 Canon City, CO 81212
Internet:	Email: contact@mccfcanoncity.com www.mccfcanoncity.com
Telephone:	(888) 575-9626

www.ingramcontent.com/pod-product-compliance
Lightning Source LLC
Chambersburg PA
CBHW081615170426
43195CB00040B/2512